SOCIAL SKINS OF THE HEAD

Social Skins of the Head

Body Beliefs and Ritual in Ancient Mesoamerica and the Andes

EDITED BY

VERA TIESLER AND MARÍA CECILIA LOZADA

UNIVERSITY OF NEW MEXICO PRESS · ALBUQUERQUE

ISBN 978-0-8263-5963-6 (cloth)
ISBN 978-0-8263-5964-3 (electronic)

Library of Congress Cataloging-in-Publication data is on file with the Library of Congress.

The Institute for Field Research and UC MEXUS generously provided funding to support publication of this book.

Cover photograph courtesy Andrea Vazquez de Arthur
Composed in Minion Pro

To the heads of the future,
our children
Fabio Cucina Tiesler
and
Alicia Haydon

Contents

❧

Illustrations

❧

ix

COLOR PLATES

Color plates follow page 142.

TABLES

Preface

VERA TIESLER AND MARÍA CECILIA LOZADA

This collection of essays was initiated by a passion for the study of Native American head treatments, shared among the contributors and the editors of this volume. Both editors look back on decades of active (bio)archaeological work on bodies and body modifications in the Andes and Mesoamerica. It was probably our sheer academic curiosity to learn more about the "other side" that triggered our initial conversations regarding the heads and skulls from the lands south and north of the Panama Canal. This curiosity was certainly tailgated by our dissatisfaction with the many ready-made, simplified, or Westernized explanations of Native "corporeity" to permeate the popular and academic literature alike.[1] Sadly, the scrutiny of Native headworks does not make an exception. A more rigorous and culturally aligned (or emic) reflection of the tantalizingly complex undercurrents that once bolstered Native body practices should go *a la par* with statistical validation and Western social semantization. We believe that these efforts are timely, given the amount of published groundwork on indigenous body models in the Andes and Mesoamerica.

Both cultural spheres stretch over extended territories and are known for the diversity and complexity of their world views and body works, focused on the head. The latter included a myriad of permanent modifications in the past, backed by deeply embedded beliefs about the cosmic makeup and its corporeal models. Once this connection is established, a host of specific inquiries fall into place:

How would Native concepts about life, cosmic vitality, and constructed, body-inscribed values motivate specific forms of embodiment? Which ideas about vitality, protection, and health led mothers to wrap and shape their babies' head over the months and years? What did the first haircut mean to Natives for whom the hair harbored animic energy? Why were earspools important for hearing among ancient Andeans and Mesoamericans? And beyond the threshold of death: what cultural rationales inspired the protracted treatments of heads and skulls?

In 2012, we first shared the discussion table with twenty other invitees who had arrived from near and far in order to engage in dialogues on ancient head-shaping practices during a thematic symposium. This encounter was held in the "white city" of Mérida, Mexico, and was organized by the Autonomous University of Yucatán (fig.I.1). Our series of enlightened talks on heads culminated with a hands-on workshop on cranial taxonomies and an exhibit of artificial cranial vault modifications in the Americas. At the end of the late-autumn symposium, all participants were treated to a visit to a traditional community and its acclaimed celebration of Hanal Pixan ("food for the souls"), or simply Day of the Dead. Blending in with local Maya, we watched folk recover and clean the ancestral bones and skull *calacas* in the local cemetery as they prepared jointly for the long-awaited arrival of their deceased kin. Each year, the dead spirits are expected to stay with their family over the whole month before they leave again

Figure I.1. Participants of the Second Mesoamerican Symposium of Bioarchaeology hosted in 2012 by the Universidad Autónoma de Yucatán, Mérida, Mexico (photo, Laboratory of Bioarchaeology and Histomorphology, UADY).

in late November. As part of this "Maya way of receiving" dead kin, we were offered to eat "bodies" (*pibes*), as they were pulled out of the smoking soil. The delicious cakes are made of corn and red *achiote*. They come wrapped in green leaves and are baked beneath the ground, the earthy domains of the dead.

It was clear to both of us already that the topic of ancient head treatments in truth subscribes to a Pandora's box of meanings, purposes, and culturally sanctioned body techniques, a subject abstrusely complex and varied both south and north of the Panama Canal, yet holding some common undercurrents in terms of both procedures and social values. At this point, both editors started to talk about a second, still more culturally engrained symposium, open to specialists in regional linguistics, art history, and ethnography. A two-part paper session entitled "Cultural Meanings of Head Treatments in Mesoamerican and Andean Societies" followed in 2014. Organized for the annual meeting of the Society for American Archaeology in Austin, Texas, it was this symposium that spurred the preparation of the present volume. A select group of international and local scholars working in Mesoamerica and the Andes engaged in a dialogue on culturally ingrained anthropological research related to the head. Building on the momentum of Native body and embodiment

research in the humanities, this dual-regional approach was intended to encourage out-of-the-box thinking. By bridging two highly specialized academic traditions in the Americas, we wished to find conceptual and analytical commonalities and/or points of disjuncture between Andean and Mesoamerican cephalic practices. Back home, the symposium-guided dialogues continued as the discussants' comments were circulated among the participants to further encourage and enrich the ideas presented during the encounter. In this same spirit, we also invited a number of other scholars to write on the subject.

Each of the contributors was enheartened to align with a number of "cornerstones" from which to interpret and understand the cultural roles and meaning of the head in Native world views. First, we want to conceptualize the head and its physical insignia as a spiritual locus within the Native cosmos, the embodied *anecumene* within the *ecumene* if you will. This complementary notion between the sacred and the profane is an inherent part of Native cosmology on both sides of the Panama isthmus. Its confrontation contributes a new level of understanding of particular Native body treatments and prepares the ground for a renewed discussion of body concepts and physical embodiment in general.

We identify the term "physical embodiment" in this

volume as the physical representation of sociocultural conditions in the human body, enacted in body treatment and the cultural modification of its segments (in life or death). To achieve this, our modus operandi (and that of many contributors) confronts different sets of information with autochthonous body concepts, specifically those of the head and its vital components.

Second, we promote an interdisciplinary, dual approach between the Andes and Mesoamerica, as both spheres held—and still hold—body-anchored and specifically head-anchored world views. Despite the pitfalls in comparing two parallel but separately evolving cultural spheres, we believe that the cross-continental juxtapositions should facilitate a deeper causal understanding of the Native body beyond the region and invite broader questions regarding body concepts and embodiment. Interdisciplinary approximations have been encouraged whenever possible, drawing from discursive media and material data sets. Their joint interpretation and discussion is meant to re-create and contextualize broader meanings at the interstice between the self, the head, and culture, along with their mutual interactions.

Third, we encourage the wide thematic treatment of permanent and not-so-permanent forms of enhancement of the head and its surfaces (both in life and past death). In practice, this does not go as far as we would have wished, given the dominance of scholarship on head shaping and the ancient Maya. However, in addition to these head modifications, this volume does treat other forms of physical enhancement such as haircuts and facial paint, hair arrangements, dental reductions, and ear piercings, all of which have been covered only sparsely in the anthropological literature to date. Past death, the many meanings and mortuary pathways of trophy heads, venerated skulls, and headless bodies in the Andes and Mesoamerica acquire importance.

Our efforts would not have expanded into a thick oeuvre had it not been for the continued support and active engagement by the participants in this project. We wish to extend a heartfelt thank you to each and all of our contributors for sharing efforts and expertise during the different stages of preparation and editing. Needless to say, both of us have enjoyed immensely our exquisite rounds of discussion and the academic exchange with everyone involved. This includes all those who for one reason or another could not be part of this book, namely Rosaura Yépez and Mary Weismantel. Jane Buikstra's discussion at our session at the SAA and her permanent inspiration in general have been instrumental for both of us in our advancement of this project and in conducting bioarchaeology from a human lens in the Andes and Mesoamerica. A thank you also goes to Josefina Mansilla and the late Carmen Pijoan Aguadé, whose rigorous analytical approaches in the human taphonomy of Mexico are well recognized worldwide. We are indebted to Pilar Zabala, our colleague and historian friend, with whom we have the pleasure of sharing also this continued quest for physical embodiment in the eyes of the conquerors.

Last but not least, we extend our thankful recognition to those institutions that have promoted this project through the years, specifically the University of Chicago and the Autonomous University of Yucatán. Thanks go to the editorial team of the University of New Mexico Press, led by John Byram, all of whom have generously supported us throughout. We are indebted to Khali Ashton, Flavius Beca, Catherine Harrison, Raúl López Pérez, and Kristie Sanchez for style correcting, formatting, and unifying the drafts as they came in. The feedback we received by two reviewers have strengthening the volume substantially. Their comments have been instrumental in stringing together the parts and chapters and in providing a more balanced treatment of information and conceptual frames.

NOTE

1. We conceive "corporeity" simply as the quality or state of having or being a body.

Introducing the Social Skins of the Head in Ancient Mesoamerica and the Andes

VERA TIESLER AND MARÍA CECILIA LOZADA

A HEADS-UP ON CULTURAL CONCEPTIONS

Society has long associated symbols, metaphors, and significations with the head and its vital components. Strongly influenced by modern biological sciences, our own Westernized conception usually identifies human evolution as the driving force behind the size, posture, and anatomical location of the human head. When the head became the uppermost part of the body—once hominids acquired an erect posture—it also became increasingly distinct from the trunk. The throat and neck narrowed, gradually separating the head from the body, both in topographic and functional anatomy. In their present anatomical arrangement, most of our sense organs are in the anterior portion of our head. Compared to our evolutionary ancestors, it is our relatively hairless and circumscribed *visage* that acts as the hub for our sensory exchange with the extrinsic world.[1]

Beyond mainstream Western thought, really all cultures, past and present, have imbued the head with a central cultural paramountcy due to its prominent placement atop the body and because it is the physical locus of so many sensory, emotional, and spiritual domains (Arnold and Hastorf 2008). In this panorama of embodiment, the modern Westernized conception constitutes only one of the many ways of understanding our organic capital "hardware" for perception, thinking, feeling, and spiri-

tuality. For some cultures, heads and their components are social personifiers, which can vary epistemologically and ontologically with a tantalizing tandrum of possible acceptations of bodies and what they stand for or not (Harris and Robb 2012). Within this spectrum, a head can represent an individual or metaphorically identify hierarchically organized groups, factions, or institutions (Arnold and Hastorf 2008). A significant number of societies have treated (or indeed still treat) heads as ritual objects, either venerated as the relics of ancestral kin, or as telluric or saintly beings, or collected as trophies from socially distant persons (Grewenig and Rosendahl 2015). One of the practices that has led to intense debate within the anthropological community is human headhunting: the separation and curation of the head after killing a person. This form of processing can be related to a number of social situations, most of which are identified with notions of collective superiority and attributions of soul power, appropriated and controlled by the head takers.

The head, in its natural or culturally adapted presentation, is a central locus not only of spirituality but also of appearance and body display. Put on the social stage, the head turns into a canvas for social discourse and performance—in reality, all human interaction (Turner 1984; Turner 2007). Above and beyond all else, this capital human canvas expresses socioculturally sanctioned ideals, standards, prohibitions, and taboos.[2] It is the organic hardware of what David Le Breton (1984:79–80) and Marcel

Mauss (2007; see also Turner 1984; Turner 2007) describe as "corporal socialities" (*socialités corporelles*), body techniques (*techniques du corps*), and embodied interactions. Equally sanctioned by society, and still more passive, is the notion of human corporeity described by Michel Foucault (1995). A plastic and fundamentally docile matter, the body (and therefore the head) can be trained, managed, disciplined, punished, and sometimes tortured in order to make it socially and economically productive. Thus, not only is the body the recipient of socially mediated action, but it also reflects and represents society as it assimilates self-assigned group identity.

These and other humanistic inquiries about the relationship between the body and society typically touch upon notions of physicality and corporeity, corporeality (i.e., corporeal existence), material interaction, self-reflection and representation, and ontogenetic and cosmological models (Lock and Farquhar 2007; Mauss 2007; Skibo and Schiffer 2009; Sofaer 2006; Turner 1984). Most work on this subject addresses the social "construction" of the body and its embodiment with the goal of inquiring about perceptions of the interstice between the mind, the body, and society. Note that not only is the head the sole part of our body that we cannot see directly, but it is also through it that we see the remainder of our body and our surroundings. In a similar fashion, we hear, smell, taste, and breathe through elements of our face and thereby define "organically" the locale of our personal sensatory experiences.

The embodied layers of sociocultural conditions and norms may relate to gender, social age, or purely social constructs such as power, subordination, or ethnicity. In explaining the complexities involved in the relationships between society, persons, and bodies, modern scholars have been receiving increasing feedback by engaging with phenomenological, structural, and semiotic concepts (Csordas 1994:10–12). The social signification of bodies as readable texts, interwoven with their experienced realities, makes up much of the recent scholarship on the subject. This way of conceptualizing bodies has been taken up as a proxy—together with more objectifiable material information—by a number of the contributors in this volume.

HEADS, BODIES, AND NATIVE AMERICAN COSMOGRAMS

Although separate geographically and culturally, ancient Mesoamericans and Andeans imbued the morphology of the head with deep ideological signification by recognizing it as a spiritual locus (fig. 1.1). Even during the contact period, the Inkas (Classen 1993) and the Aztecs (López Austin 1989, 2009) still clearly identified the head as the locus of human vitality and, at least among the Aztecs, as the abode of the heat-soul, *tonalli*. Additionally, the head (or whole body) could constitute a model for a broader entity, even the cosmos itself. In this role, it would become an anthropomorphic blueprint for the experienced landscape with its natural constituents, as Diego de González Holguín demonstrated semiologically for the Inkas in his dictionary of 1608. In this example, a nose is synonymous with a hilltop, and the term *uma* equates a head with a mountain peak (Classen 1993:110). In a number of other Native contexts, the head equally provides an anthropomorphic model for the spiritual universe and specifically for the appearances of gods and goddesses. This relationship is illustrated by the veneration of the maize god among the Classic-period Maya (250–900 CE). They often represented the tonsured head of this god with a postcoronary sulcus (a secondary morphological attribute found in some forms of head elongation), just as if his head had been artificially shaped during infancy (Tiesler 2014:226–28). Focusing on the same cultural sphere, María Luisa Vázquez de Ágredos Pascual and her colleagues, in this volume, reflect upon the head as the native crown of a Maya body, which could offer points of contact and exchange between humans and their sacred celestial universe.

The head, with all its representative qualities, clearly made a supreme anatomical canvas for body modification and treatment, the motivation for most of which, as several of our contributors conclude, went well beyond embellishment and visible display. Specifically concerning the regions under scrutiny, the illuminating studies by Alfredo López Austin (1989, 2009; Lopez Austin and Millones 2008), Stephen D. Houston and colleagues (2006; Houston and Cummins 2004; Houston and Stuart 1998), Jill McKeever Furst (1995), Constance Classen (1993), Cheryl Classen and Rosemary Joyce (1997; Joyce 2009), and Denise Arnold and Christine Hastorf (2008) have aided the contributors in this volume and have also been helpful in guiding the editors' own past and present inquiries on head enhancement and permanent modifications (Garcia and Tiesler 2011; Lozada 2014; Lozada and Buikstra 2002; Tiesler 2000, 2012, 2014).

The first part of our book title—"Social Skins of the Head"—pays direct tribute to Terence Turner's seminal

Figure 1.1. General map of the two cultural spheres treated in this volume, highlighting major sites, countries, and modern cities mentioned in this book. Countries shaded in gray denote the cultural areas under study (drawing, Laboratory of Bioarchaeology and Histomorphology, Universidad Autónoma de Yucatán, Mérida, adapted by Vera Tiesler and María Cecilia Lozada).

work on the subject (2007; see also Arnold and Hastorf 2008). At the same time, by using this title we hope to draw attention to the multilayered social meanings of head embodiment and its behavioral correlates in Mesoamerican and Andean societies. Here, the head was viewed not as a passive artifact but rather as a crucial anchor of identity and power. Note that both cultural spheres held—and still hold—body-anchored world views that convey particular importance to the head (Arnold and Hastorf 2008; Classen 1993:96–112, 154; Houston and Cummins 2004; López-Austin 2009; Wilkinson 2013). Ancient peoples all over the Americas embraced the head as a metaphor for the person, as a signifier for the individual, for the "self," and for personhood. In doing so, the heads epitomized the constructed identity of a person or ancestor and, beyond that, served as a blueprint and spiritual locus for the indigenous universe (Classen 1993; Houston and Stuart 1998; Houston et al. 2006; López-Austin 1989; Velásquez García 2011; Weismantel 2015).

Crafting Heads, Working Heads, and Forging Identities

The anthropological study of Native body modification not only communicates fads and fashions, and individual and collective looks and styles, but, more to the point, sheds light on the enactment and effects of identity-forging practices. Among many pre-Hispanic communities of Mesoamerica and the Andes, these modifications began immediately after birth. The Inkas, for instance, celebrated the "presentation of the [head compression] crib to divinity" (*huahua, quirau*) (Latcham 1929:542; Purizaga Vega 1991:43–45). While invoking the family *huaca* or totem, close kin would fabricate a child's cradleboard, designed not only to shape the head but also to shelter and to protect the child from harm. Throughout the Inka Empire, this early crib placement, or *ayuscay*, was celebrated only a few days after a baby's delivery and was recognized as crucial during this stage of life (Purizaga Vega 1991:6). Fetuses and infant *wawas* were permitted by this process of modification to transit smoothly through their liminal state of existence before becoming social, gendered persons. The practice of wrapping and molding a child's head, as described by Deborah Blom and Nicole Couture for the Tiwanaku in chapter 13, speaks to the importance of heads in the active crafting of personhood. In the view of these authors, the physical binding of the head contained the "wild or presocial" child before the child could evolve and

reintegrate as a full human being representing his or her social group. This innovative interpretation adds to the conventionally understood significations of Andean head shaping, such as connoting group membership (among the coastal Chiribaya, see Lozada and Buikstra 2002), or connoting emblems of sacred adoration, as for the lunar cult among the Chancay and Ancon people on the central coast of Peru (Yépez 2017).

North of the Panama Canal, infant heads were transformed both physically and spiritually by being wrapped, hidden, sealed, or "ensouled," as William Duncan and Gabrielle Vail note in chapter 2 of this volume (see also Tiesler 2012, 2014). In chapter 4, Andrew Scherer speaks of this same process as a form of "bodywork," the active act of crafting, cultivating, and shaping little "unripe creatures" into humans by swaddling and shaping their heads. The calendrical and semantic connotations of these practices—with all their phrenological baggage—are brought into the open one more time in the discussion chapter by Vail (chapter 10) in this volume.

If we are to conceive of the head-shaping procedures used both north and south of the Panama Canal as a concerted set of body techniques (according to Marcel Mauss), these are not tied to festive occasions but rather to a quotidian routine that could be prolonged over months or sometimes even years. If not their daily enactment, at least their beginnings and ends would often be ritually sanctioned: these were occasions for seminal haircuts, naming ceremonies, and festivities of "rebirth." In this light, head-shaping procedures appear as gradual transformations, concealments, and preparations rather than "ritual steps" in any strict sense. They were perhaps more akin to the concept of the training of the body (and specifically its capital segment), which prepared posterior integration per se, at least in the three-stage ritual frame adopted by Arnold van Gennep (1960; see also Scherer, chapter 4 of this volume). Some Highland Maya traditions still recognize this scheme. In this case, a baptism or *kaput-sihil* (literally, "to be born a second time") sanctions the passage from childhood to puberty (Duncan and Vail, chapter 2 of this volume).

It is of note that the procedures leading to permanent head transformations that were enacted in later stages of childhood tended to be much less prolonged than head shaping (Dembo and Imbelloni 1938). Ear piercings, tooth filings, and facial tattoos, practiced on both sides of the isthmus, were accomplished not over the course of months and years but over a span of seconds, minutes, hours, or days. They were often culminations of ritual preparations, such as among the Aztecs, for whom the piercing of the ears formed part of family celebrations called *pillaoano*, which took place every four years:

> Moctezuma then danced a princely dance before the temple of Xiuhtecutli. The name of the place was Tzonmolco. And at this time all people, everyone, tasted, sipped, the wine; [even] the small children. Thus the [feast day] was called pillaoano. And then they gave uncles, they gave aunts to the small children, a man, a woman whom those with children sought out and gave gifts [to]. These took [the children] upon their backs, and carried them to the temple of Ixcocauhqui. [The parents] perforated their ears, they pierced their ears; thus they placed a sign upon them, while their uncles and aunts looked on. Afterwards food was eaten. (Sahagún 1981:30)

Among the Inka, male youth, at the onset of their fertility, had their ears pierced in a manner that caused them to bleed copiously. This was a symbolic equivalent to the girls' menarche according to Constance Classen (1993:70), who, equating hearing with bleeding (sound and fluidity), associates the control of sexual activity with the degree to which a person obeyed oral traditions and respected cultural taboos. Classen demonstrates this connection through a number of the ritual elements of this transition rite, such as the coupled endowment of the youngster with both ear ornaments (to denote obeying orders) and breechcloths (from this point forward, he would cover his private parts and thus prevent shameful exposure).

In the context of puberty rites, body transformations often turned into trials of physical endurance. Now older, the youth possessed more individual agency. They were active participants and voluntary endurers of measures that could be quite painful (van Gennep 1960). Pain and blood were central elements in a number of these body practices, which took the form of scarifications, tattoos, tooth filings, or piercings of cartilage and mucous tissues. Bishop Diego de Landa (Tozzer 1941:91) remarked that during the sixteenth century, in Yucatecan societies, "this work [tattooing] is done a little at a time on account of the extreme pain, and afterwards, they would get quite sick of it, since the designs festered and matter formed. On account of all this they mocked those who were not tattooed" (see also Thompson 1946:18–19). Painfully engraved, these markings conjured social integration

and adulthood through penance, valor, rites of passage, and sometimes punishment of transgressions. However orchestrated, these rituals were tightly entwined with the concept of physical consumption (the deprivation of physiological needs, particularly sleep, and the endurance of intense pain), which was made visible by the end result inscribed in living tissue and which also left an invisible mark in the process: a challenging life experience as the hallmark of adulthood.

And finally, what distinguished permanent transformations from those that were shorter lasting or transient? Responses to this question are offered in this volume by María Luisa Vázquez de Ágredos Pascual and colleagues (on Native cosmetics), Virginia Miller (on hair color), and Andrea Vazquez de Arthur (on facial enhancement). All three essays relate to specific forms of body enhancement enacted daily or only during specific occasions. Although typically absent from mortuary inquiries, these arrangements do materialize in the imagery of ancient communities and cities. They may signify gender, age, social standing, or personal choice. They also identify festive occasions, subordination versus dominance, and the sacrificer versus the one to be sacrificed, as Miller traces at Chichén Itzá.

Miller's work specifically underscores the malleable quality of hair. Dead outside the body but living and growing from within, hair possesses a dual quality. Unlike tearing hair out by its roots, cutting hair causes no pain. Just like the act of grooming itself, Miller argues that it is the visible arrangement that counts: its color, length, texture. In an additional layer of signification, hair was thought to harbor the vital heat-energy of its human carrier. This person could experience the feeling of death and the loss of personal identity when it was disarrayed, or worse, shorn or torn out by captors and sacrificers, a point that both Miller and other scholars make clear (see, for instance, Houston et al. 2006).

The Social Skins of Heads

Above, we introduced the social construction of heads as a cultural process. But beyond the often symbolically laden procedures for the processing and adjustment of heads, the very results of these treatments were bound to carry a highly symbolic value. Denoted in shape, size, color, or texture, emblematic heads and head garb communicate gender, locale, and social age within groups. Outside the confines of communal areas, they convey ethnicity or foreign status. Some head displays even seem to have acted as boundary-marking mechanisms, as, in this volume, Bruce Mannheim and colleagues argue regarding the Formative Cuzco area and the Colca Valley. Further north, in the Southern Maya lowlands, the confrontation between standardized and diversified cranial shapes, one profile against another, leads Vera Tiesler and Alfonso Lacadena to attest to their roles as collective statements of ethnic pertinence versus otherness. This association finds an astounding confirmation in the spoken isoglosses and artistic conventions of head portraiture among locals. The authors also note that the elongated head profiles were still crafted by mothers even after the collapse of the Classic Southern Mayan kingdoms, and they draw conclusions about the conservative reproduction of head shapes by successions of different generations of females. Just like spoken language, passed on in the domestic spheres of households by mothers and female kin, local head shaping traditions likely outlived more conflict-ridden, androcentrically led activities such as trading, political networking, and warring.

In other contextual situations, community identity was not embodied organically by the human carrier but instead crafted into head portraiture. Such are the paired and multiple Wari ceramic faceneck vessels, which are explored by Vazquez de Arthur in this volume. The author argues that facenecks were produced to represent the identities of individuals in unique ways. Their relationships may have extended beyond purely biological ties, as they likely expressed social connections among individuals and their respective roles within social networks. This approach is similar to the one taken by Laura Filloy Nadal in this book, who analyzes the rendering of individualizing features by elaborating on the concept of visage and the physical likeness among the portraits of the upper echelon of Palenque's Maya kingdom. She notes that ancient viewers identified a paragon by virtue of his or her individual physical traits and idiosyncratic markings, inscribed on the body or displayed in adornments, headdress, and garb. It is quite impressive to see that in the image of one noted local dynast, his visage was still recalled and reproduced faithfully decades after his passing, underscoring his transcendence and the continued use of this apical ancestor in his descendants' political affairs.

The facial skin as a screen for display for the ancient metropolis of Teotihuacan is addressed by Luis Adrián Alvarado-Viñas and Linda Manzanilla in this chapter 5. The authors discern a number of theater-type censers, which display human heads with facial paint and partic-

ular cranial contours. They conclude that within the multiethnic landscapes of urban Teotihuacan, human heads must have functioned as social signifiers of ethnic identity and cultural provenience, whereas facial paint and corporal paint would have been useful media for visual recognition within the urban core of this Early Classic metropolis (Manzanilla et al. 2011). Also, Vázquez de Ágredos Pascual and her colleagues focus their study on the face painting of different social factions rendered in Classic Maya polychrome vase painting. Here, what is important was not only form and symbolism but also the signification of the colors with which faces were covered. Particularly red and black hues, followed by white and occasionally yellow tones, signaled publically the condition of the human carrier as a warrior, ritual participant, or mourner. Unsurprisingly, the neck, cheeks, and forehead were the most frequently colored surfaces, visibly framing the center of the face. The application of facial paint went beyond the realms of aristocracy. Beyond the symbolic and aesthetic meaning, the colorful potions possibly held additional therapeutic value for their users. Most important for us was the conclusion of the authors that the colors radiating from the head and neck re-created the Native cosmos and its cardinal directions, each one representing a particular god or natural force. This last aspect certainly brings home the notion of the head as a blueprint for the Native cosmos and its forces.

Heads as Seeds, Heads as Tokens

Heads held a pivotal role in ceremonial acts of embodiment related not only to life but to death, such as in capital punishment, sacrificial decapitation, postsacrificial processing of severed heads, and veneration. The last aspect of this progression could take heads and skulls on often protracted journeys, materialized in the archaeological record by commingling and otherwise complex mortuary pathways (Chacon and Dye 2007). Cross-culturally, postmortem heads (full-fleshed, skinned, defleshed, artificially mummified, or skeletonized) range in signification from honored ancestors to devastated enemies or simple criminals. Categorically, the severing of the head from the body dissociates the body, denying proper corpse treatment. Whether destroying or curating heads, given that they are potent sources of cosmic and personal vitality, these acts come to empower the living and establish continuity, as Sara Becker and Sonia Alconini point out in chapter 15 of this book.

In the Mesoamerican sphere, the cyclical movement of heads can be understood directly or indirectly from a *hierophagic* religious perspective (i.e., mutual but hierarchically organized consumption among humans and cosmic entities) that embodied life and all cosmic functioning (Monaghan 2000). Especially pre-Hispanic Mesoamericans deemed eating an essential activity not only among people but among their gods. The cosmic food chain started in the divine underworld and traveled to the earth, where food abounded and would be consumed by humans. Humans, in turn, were to feed the gods by donating food staples. These could be real or symbolic food provisions and usually comprised maize or copal. During ritual offerings, these foods became transcendent as fragrance or smoke, in a burned, roasted, boiled, or raw state, or in the form of copal balls or as tamales. In the eyes of the ceremonial congregation, these turned into flesh (specifically human flesh) and vital essences. Likewise, human heads were held to be appropriate "foodstaples" to feed the divine during human sacrifice, turning them into life-renewing seeds (Freidel and Reilly 2010; Stross 2010; Taube 1985).

By detaching the head from the body, the body is made partible (Duncan and Schwarz 2014; Geller 2014). The head then can act as a consecrated offering and be deposited near an altar, as Alvarado-Viñas and Manzanilla state is the case for Teopancazco, Teotihuacan. The authors suggest that decapitations and posthumous head processing in the seats of power of Teotihuacan's central neighborhoods modulated social contradictions and promoted the transformation of roles, just like in other hierarchically organized traditional societies. More ideologically tinted is the conclusion drawn by Ximema Chávez Balderas from the complex chain of head processing at the Great Aztec Temple of Tenochtitlan. Decapitated and worked into skull masks by Mexica priests, or stuck on *tzompantli* racks, heads would experience a metamorphosis in the eyes of the Aztecs and turn into the supernatural beings they had already represented before their sacrificial immolation. Composing the divine mountain tree-paradise, these skulls reenacted mythical passages and created divine models of the cosmos (López Austin and López Lujan 2009; Taube 2004). This practice is an old and extensive tradition. The tzompantli imagery, and even series of perforated skulls, have been dated to as long ago as the close of the first millennium CE. Additionally, some of these early representations and skulls have been documented well beyond the Mexican central highlands,

such as a couple of recently studied crania from the Sacred Cenote of Chichén Itzá (plate 1; fig. 1.2) (see also López Austin and López Luján 2009; Miller 2007, chapter 8 of this volume; Taube 2004).

Also in past Andean societies, the millenary traditions of head taking, head curation, and trophy skulls are powerful testaments to the significance of these body parts, as Vazquez de Arthur notes in chapter 16 of this volume. Similar to the Mesoamerican sphere, not all heads were treated equally. Here, even single heads could change their signification and purposes during different stages of preparation and curation (Arnold and Hastorf 2008). More than those from Mesoamerica, the shrunken or dried heads of the Andes can be instantly recognized as human. These "onlooking" heads or preserved skulls could be stern visual reminders of victory or power (Tung 2012; Tung and Knudson 2008; Verano 1995).

Cephalocentric practices were indeed deeply rooted in most ancient Andean cultural traditions including those of the Paracas, Nasca, Wari, and Moche, as John Verano demonstrates below in chapter 11. While the head is undoubtedly the focus of such corporeal treatments, Verano's key point is that its removal from the body was aligned with much more complex social and cultural meanings such as warfare, human sacrifice, fertility, and other commensurate ritual activities more directly associated with ancestor veneration. Specifically in the Kallawaya area (Bolivia) during the arrival of Tiwanaku, decapitation appeared to provide a way for the new regime to consolidate power, as Becker and Alconini argue in chapter 15. This may suggest that the vital power harbored by severed heads was considered subversive and was therefore eliminated by destroying the heads prior to burial. Conversely, trophy heads were contained and transformed into wawas among the Tiwanaku, signifying both seeds and ungendered offspring, as Blom and Couture posit in chapter 13.

Disembodied heads and headless bodies often experienced dissimilar afterlives—that of the head may have involved protracted curation to preserve the facial features and hair, or processing of the head and skull by defleshing, perforation, sectioning of the cranium, surface decoration, or the attachment of suspensory cords. In chapter 12, Lozada and her colleagues suggest that heads were separated from the body for the rather mundane reason of ease of transport. They hypothesize that the heads of warriors who were killed in combat while away from their communities were removed from the body to be repatriated for proper burial. They also argue that, for La Ramada culture,

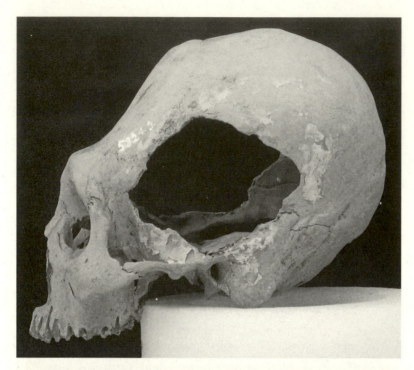

Figure 1.2a. A male skull with perforated sides from skullrack exposure, Sacred Cenote, Chichén Itzá. Note the significant head elongation, typical for the Maya during the Classic period (photo by Vera Tiesler; no. 07-7-20/58242), Peabody Museum of Archaeology and Ethnography, Harvard Museum, © 2018, President and Fellows of Harvard College.

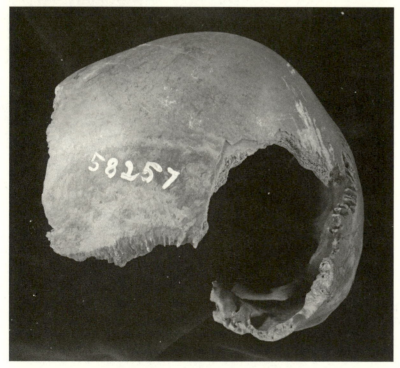

Figure 1.2b. A tabular erect neurocranium with perforated sides from skullrack exposure, Sacred Cenote, Chichén Itzá (photo by Vera Tiesler; no. 07-7-20/58248 and 58257.0), Peabody Museum of Archaeology and Ethnography, Harvard Museum, © 2018, President and Fellows of Harvard College.

the head, as opposed to other body parts, was particularly important as a receptacle of personhood. This belief was and is also observed in other past Andean cultures.

It goes without saying that the impressive range of motivations for head processing suggests a considerable variety of meanings for the heads of naturally deceased

kin, either in ancestor worship or in fertility rituals and concealed power troves (Arnold and Hastorf 2008). Not dissimilar to trophy heads, these cult objects connected the human world and the otherworld. Beyond heads, the role of exchange is highlighted by the almost ubiquitous inclusion of food preparation and/or consumption vessels (usually bowls and jars) in burial contexts. These forms of ancient manipulation could be instrumental for individual or group protection and spiritual strengthening. As these traditions show, the heads of the dead express multiple social situations, offering powerful venues for exploring social interaction and discourse, integration versus distinction, ancestor veneration versus profanation and sacrifice, and power display versus humiliation.

HEAD PRACTICES AFTER EUROPEAN CONTACT

After the arrival of the Spaniards, centuries of collective humiliation and devastation altered modern Native lifeways and distanced us, the observers, from the ancient cultural repertoires and belief systems, including those of physical embodiment. Different from other colonial powers such as the Portuguese, French, and Anglo-Saxon invaders (who were more interested in the economic exploitation of local resources), the Hispanic colonizers of New Spain and Peru not only claimed political and economic domination (fig. 1.3), they also bolstered their reigns with absolutist claims of cultural and religious superiority. The stated goal was the complete assimilation of all segments of Novohispanic society into the service of God and the Catholic kings (Tiesler and Zabala 2017). As part of these efforts, the Spanish Crown remained acutely alert to Native beliefs, dress, and customs.

All but the most strict European mentalities, and specifically Catholic attitudes toward the body, were used as arguments to discredit the "sacrilegious" modification of the natural form of the head, which had "been created by God to mirror his own image" (Cieza de León 1984:227; see also Lozada 2011; Tiesler 2014; Tiesler and Zabala 2011; Zabala 2014). By these standards, visible alterations of appearance seemed corrupt in the eyes of the conquerors. The effects of the European suppression efforts were severe in the Andes and Mesoamerica. Native forms of resilience and assimilation were diverse and depended significantly on the amount of control that the urban strongholds had on the indigenous communities, and most probably on the visibility of the bodyworks in the public sphere. Whether hidden and so continued, substituted, transformed, or abandoned altogether, the perpetuation of Native head treatments did not progress uniformly within the broader sphere of Hispanic America.

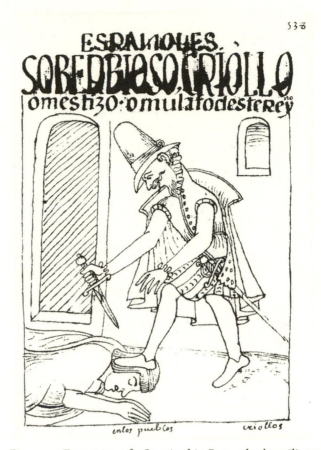

Figure 1.3. Engraving of a Spaniard in Peru who humiliates a Native by stepping on his head (adapted by Vera Tiesler and María Cecilia Lozada from Guaman Poma de Ayala 1944:552).

From Sacrilege to (Bio)Cultural Approximations

In the aftermath of Novohispanic oppression and faced with modernity and religious syncretism, most precontact Native forms of head enhancement had either been shifted, substituted, abolished, or forgotten altogether (Dingwall 1931). In today's world, the bulk of information on head modifications is, therefore, transmitted by ethnohistorical accounts and the archaeological record, including epigraphic inscriptions, portraiture, and, more directly, mummified or skeletonized remnants of the dead. Using physical remains to anchor our understandings of the Native world allows us to "zoom" in and out on mortuary assemblages. Without changing data sets, we may focus on individuals or move up the scale to encompass residential populations, village folk, urban neighborhoods, and areas beyond the local and regional cultural landscapes. In this manner, bioarchaeological research of culturally modified tissues has provided us with multifaceted insights into the everyday lives and spiritual beliefs of communities long since vanished. With its interdisciplinary quality, this research interacts with other disciplinary approximations and, still more importantly, with the conceptual foundations of corporeity, corporeality, and the embodiment we have laid out in the paragraphs above.

In fact, most of the chapters in this book have benefited directly from advances in the field of bioarchaeology, a recently consolidated line of anthropological research that examines archaeologically retrieved human remains from a biocultural perspective. Because it focuses on the scientific analysis of human remains, bioarchaeology is uniquely positioned at the interstice between the humanities and material research and is therefore well suited to offer integrated explanations of humanity's past experiences (Buikstra and Beck 2006; Larsen 2015). The objects of study used in bioarchaeological analysis are the remnants of individuals, those who have shaped past societies and who, when alive, engaged actively in ancient interaction and belief systems (Sofaer 2006). The importance of bioarchaeology in developing a more nuanced understanding of the past is therefore more than apparent. It provides insights into important life issues ranging from health and diet to occupational stress and migration, from body enhancement to posthumous treatments of corpses and skeletons. As opposed to epigraphy or ethnohistory, bioarchaeological approximations typically encompass large time frames and can inform not only about the upper echelon of society but also about those members (non-elites, women, and children) whose voices tend to remain elusive, or altogether silent, in past discursive media. Thus, unsurprisingly, bioarchaeology has had an increasing impact in the research agendas of Mesoamericanists and Andeanists (Bonogofsky 2011; Chacon and Dye 2007; Tiesler 2014; Tiesler and Cucina 2014; Tung 2012; Verano 1995).

In the Mesoamerican sphere, physical anthropologists Eusebio Dávalos Hurtado (1909–1968), Javier Romero Molina (1910–1986), and Arturo Romano Pacheco (1921–2015) once spearheaded the skeletal research of pre-Hispanic head treatments in Mexico (see Romero Molina 1958; Romano Pacheco 1965). They addressed in detail the ancient techniques and outcomes of trephining, head shaping, and dental reductions. Juan Comas (1900–1979) also addressed pre-Hispanic head modifications in different parts of Mexico and engaged, beyond the Mesoamer-

ican sphere, in the research of traditional head flattening in contemporary Amazonian communities (Comas 1958). Likewise, nonlocal scholarship has made important contributions to the study of Mesoamerican physical embodiment. For example, the pan-continental works of T. Dale Stewart (1950, 1974) include discussions of trephination, dental decoration, and head form. Although most studies conducted during the twentieth century are methodological and descriptive, they have succeeded in reaching culturally tenable conclusions thanks to their incursions into nonosteological sources of data such as portraiture and ethnographic testimonials. By incorporating multiple fields of scholarship and different types of cultural artifacts, these researchers have been able to draw their conclusions from a larger breadth of indigenous heritage.

More recent Mesoamerican inquiries on the relationship between head practices and the head's sociocultural roles have more explicitly bridged the separate aspects of the head's physicality, its spiritual embodiment, its role in personal identity, and its ability to act as a model for the Native cosmos (Duncan and Hoflin 2011; Tiesler 2000, 2014). In addition to progress in bioarchaeology, this advancement has been supported directly by new frames of scholarly reference and a massive surge of scholarship on ancient Mesoamerican art. The breathtaking pace of epigraphic decipherment of Maya and Aztec scripts also has promoted religiously interwoven insights on head manipulation, especially due to the dominant place that the body and its animic components occupy in Native thought and religious action (McKeever Furst 1995; Houston et al. 2006; López Austin 1989; Velásquez García 2011).

Like in Mesoamerica, the head has long been a favorite study object in the Peruvian Andes. Since the early 1900s, mummified heads and skulls from archaeological contexts have been addressed by prominent physical anthropologists such as Aleš Hrdlička and Pedro Weiss. For Hrdlička and his contemporaries, skulls and heads already appear to have represented a basic research unit and were regularly called upon to answer questions regarding human variation, populational filiations, genealogies, migration, and evolution. During this period, not only were heads used to answer questions about indigenous history and ancestry, but they also anchored direct examinations of cultural practices such as cranial modification, head taking, and surgical trephinations. It is within this context that cranial modification was first described and identified as an intentional act of body alteration. Julio C. Tello and Pedro Weiss were perhaps the first researchers to situate their osteological studies within an archaeological context in an effort to understand the meaning of such practices (Lozada 2014). Weiss, for instance, proposed that head shapes were culturally specific. To him, heads could be used to identify a particular ethnic group, just like ceramic types can. Trophy heads also became a focus of study during this period, generating debates about their significance and cultural meaning that continue even today: are they mementos of war, or are they revered ancestors?

During the early twentieth century, the head still served as the basis for many studies in the Andes, and it was not until much later that researchers began to depart from purely typological analysis. For example, Jane E. Buikstra and collaborators (Hoshower et al. 1995) conducted a study of head molding among the Tiwanaku people buried outside the Andean highlands. They incorporated ethnohistorical accounts and osteological data (sex and age), along with other contextual archaeological information, in an effort to understand the meaning of head modification practices in pre-Hispanic Peru. From this data, they determined that cranial modification was used to codify group membership in ayllus, a basic social unit in the Andes. John Verano conducted a seminal study of the indigenous body in 1995 in which he initiated bioarchaeological discussions regarding human sacrifice, warfare, decapitation, and the collection, curation, and burial of body parts. Today, his rigorous osteological analysis of the head, along with his archaeological and iconographic studies, serve as the basis for the study of disembodied heads in the Andes and beyond.

Another important and even more culturally aligned supplement to the study of the Andean head has materialized recently in the influential book by Denise Arnold and Christine Hastorf, *Heads of State: Icons, Power, and Politics in the Ancient and Modern Andes* (2008). Although not necessarily anchoring their work in bioarchaeology, these authors provide an exemplary account of the head from multiple viewpoints and time periods. They point out key arguments regarding the special and often complex significance of the head in relation to other parts of the body, and the many manifestations and variations that exist in cephalic practices. Within their work, they use both archaeological data and rich ethnographic data to provide detailed accounts not only about the symbolism of the head and the meanings and belief systems attached

to it but also about how the head once was procured, processed, and curated.

Likewise, a recent study by Mary Weismantel (2015) has provided a new perspective on the interpretation of the indigenous body in the Andes. Her study is based on Moche ceramic iconography, mortuary patterns, and, to a lesser degree, direct evidence from human remains. She proposes that the Moche understood the head as a repository of multiple energies that accumulated over a lifetime. Once an individual died, the vital powers contained in the head could be dispersed among the surviving population. According to Weismantel's interpretations, the body in the Moche perspective was a partible and permeable organism from which energies could escape and be recycled to contribute to the vitality of the community. The head in this context transcended from the individual to the collective, ensuring group cohesiveness and a long-standing permanency.

Similarly, Darryl Wilkinson (2013) has redefined how we comprehend the roles of the Inka body by moving away from Western standards of interpretation and attempting to understand the body through a detailed ethnohistorical analysis from the indigenous perspective. In his view, the Inka person was conceived as a biological (flesh and blood) and nonbiological categorical statute or *wawqi*, which was involved in a variety of affairs at the same time and in multiple spaces, and each was treated as if it were the Inka himself. Along the same vein, recent archaeological and ethnohistorical research is reconsidering relationships between the living and dead in the Andes, highlighting the often complex and unique perspectives of such indigenous categories (Shimada and Fitzsimmons 2015).

Although these provocative works are not necessarily based on physical remains, they contribute significantly to our understanding of indigenous anatomies and invite researchers to conceptualize the body in different dimensions. These novel propositions, in part generated by a philosophical current known as the "ontological turn," propose, among other things, that some Western perspectives do not apply to pre-Hispanic indigenous world views, especially those that include fluid perceptions of the body and personhood (Alberti et al. 2011; Viveiros de Castro 1998). Taken together, these (bio)cultural studies have provided a wealth of knowledge regarding cephalic practices in the Andes. They have been based on a combination of resources: ethnography, skeletal studies, art history in textiles and ceramics, and historical research. It is our intention that this volume contribute to this rich dialogue by offering new insights, methodological approaches, and conceptual guides to the study of the head in both the Andes and Mesoamerica.

THE AGENDAS FOR THIS BOOK

Following in the spirit laid out in the previous paragraphs, this volume goes to great lengths to illuminate ancient Native head treatments and their multilayered meanings and purposes as observed in the Andean and Mesoamerican landscapes past and present. As is clear to us, the body, and specifically the head, can only be understood within the broader frames of cultural belief systems and daily practice. Society often defines an individual based on the inner and outer characteristics of the head. On a collective scale, therefore, cultural practices involving the head, whether heads of the living or of the dead, can be seen as promoting overall group cohesion and providing continuity for social and religious life. In this volume, we intend to explore the diverse ways in which cultural modifications of the head both reflect Native beliefs and fit within the context of daily life in Mesoamerica and the Andes. By balancing the reconstruction of the material and discursive records with emic (i.e., through the lens of Native mentalities) body inquiries, we seek to better understand the roles of a number of different head techniques and their linkages with past Native social processes, cultures, and identities. Although this is necessarily a *pars pro toto* approach to broader subject matter, there is no doubt that the head is a useful agent to explore central concepts of embodied ideology, culturally constructed (versus inner) beauty, personhood, aesthetics and portraiture, ideologically driven emulation of the divine, social distinction, and group identity in general.

The goals of this volume provide a roadmap for the chapters that follow. The volume is divided into two main parts: Mesoamerica and the Andes. Each of the two sections contains works written by scholars from a wide range of backgrounds and fields, including skeletal biology, archaeology, aesthetics, forensics, taphonomy, and art history. Each chapter offers textured interpretations of the indigenous body at the intersections of (bio)archaeology, osteology, ethnohistory, linguistics, and imagery. Jointly, these contributions are meant to promote state-of-the-art studies of specific Native body modifications, points

of departures for future scholarship, and new analytical agendas for studying past human expressions from the material record. These include a wide array of indigenous head treatments, including facial cosmetics and hair arrangements, permanent cranial vault and facial modifications, dental decorations, posthumous head processing, and headhunting (see also Bonogofsky 2011; Chacon and Dye 2007; Romero Molina 1958; Tiesler 2014; Tung 2012).

The combined explorations that constitute this volume not only re-create ritual enactment and quotidian routines but also are united by their quest to grasp broader Native emic concepts, namely those concerning representation, beauty, visage, and even the more general concept of desirability. From here, they unfold novel examinations of power, social age, gender, identity, and ethnicity. These often lead the authors to generate vibrant ideas, and in addition to new answers, original questions. As this volume shows, given the tantalizing complexity of these subjects, there will not be a comprehensive resource book on head practices or a titanic work that captures everything. Rather, we privilege much wider concoctions of long-standing indigenous customs, inextricably entwined with their subtle, obvious, or profound meanings, which recognize that body practices are inseparable from our corporeity, our lives, and our condition as humans.

NOTES

1. Our eyes, ears, nose, and mouth provide the organic hardware for sight, sound, smell, and taste. It is through the mouth in particular that we interact actively with the outer world, by uttering sounds and words, by processing food, and by communicating emotions through verbal or mimic expressions. And of course it is through the mouth (and nose) that we exhale and inhale enlivening air. Behind the face is the highly evolved brain, which coordinates the nervous system and mental activity and also oversees more ethereal dynamics related to our conscience, spirituality, and sensory experiences. Encapsulated by the cranial vault, the brain is the organic anchor of such areas of study as neurology, psychology, and even theology.

2. Although it is likewise mediated by individual choice, biology, and, of course, dynamics of a more circumstantial nature.

REFERENCES CITED

Alberti, Benjamin, Severin Fowles, Martin Holbraad, Yvonne Marshall, and Christopher Witmore
2011 Worlds Otherwise: Archaeology, Anthropology, and Ontological Difference. *Current Anthropology* 52:896–912.

Arnold, Denise, and Christine A. Hastorf
2008 *Heads of State: Icons, Power, and Politics in the Ancient and Modern Andes.* Left Coast Press, Walnut Creek, California.

Bonogofsky, Michelle (editor)
2011 *The Bioarchaeology of the Human Head: Decapitation, Decoration, and Deformation.* University Press of Florida, Gainesville.

Buikstra, Jane E., and Lane A. Beck (editors)
2006 *Bioarchaeology: The Contextual Analysis of Human Remains.* Academic Press, Burlington, Massachusetts.

Chacon, Richard J., and David H. Dye (editors)
2007 *The Taking and Displaying of Human Body Parts as Trophies by Amerindians.* Springer, New York.

Cieza de León, Pedro de
1984 *La crónica del Perú: edición de Manuel Ballesteros.* Historia 16, Madrid.

Classen, Cheryl, and Rosemary A. Joyce (editors)
1997 *Women in Prehistory: North America and Mesoamerica.* University of Pennsylvania Press, Philadelphia.

Classen, Constance
1993 *Inca Cosmology and the Human Body.* University of Utah Press, Salt Lake City.

Comas, Juan
1958 La deformación cefálica intencional en la región del Ucayali, Perú. *Miscelánea Paul Rivet* 2:109–19. Universidad Nacional Autónoma de México, Mexico City.

Csordas, Thomas J. (editor)
2003 *Embodiment and Experience: The Existential Ground of Culture and Self.* Cambridge University Press, Cambridge.

Dembo, Adolfo, and José Imbelloni
1938 *Deformaciones intencionales del cuerpo humano de carácter étnico.* Biblioteca Humanior, Buenos Aires.

Dingwall, Eric J.
1931 *Artificial Cranial Deformation: A Contribution to the Study of Ethnic Mutilations.* Bale, Sons, and Danielsson, London.

Duncan, William, and Charles Andrew Hofling
2011 Why the Head? Cranial Modification as Protection and Ensoulment among the Maya. *Ancient Mesoamerica* 22:199–210.

Duncan, William, and Kevin Schwarz
2014 Partible, Permeable, and Relational Bodies in a Maya Mass Grave. In *Commingled and Disarticulated Human Remains: Working toward Improved Theory, Method, and Data,* edited by Anna Osterholtz, Kathryn Baustian, and Debra Martin, pp. 149–70. Springer, New York.

Foucault, Michel
1995 *Discipline and Punish: The Birth of the Prison.* Vintage Books, New York.

Freidel, David, and F. Kent Reilly III
2010 The Flesh of God: Cosmology, Food, and the Origins of Political Power in Ancient Southeastern Mesoamerica. In *Pre-Columbian Foodways: Interdisciplinary Approaches to Food, Culture, and Markets in Ancient Mesoamerica,* edited by John Edward Staller and Michael Carrasco, pp. 635–80. Springer, New York.

García Barrios, Ana, and Tiesler, Vera
2011 El aspecto físico de los dioses mayas. *Arqueología Mexicana* 112:59–63.

Geller, Pamela
2014 Sedimenting Social Identity: The Practice of Pre-Columbian Maya Body Partibility. In *The Bioarchaeology of Space and Place: Ideology, Power, and Meaning in Maya Mortuary Contexts,* edited by Gabriel D. Wrobel, pp. 15–38. Springer, New York.

González Holguín, Diego de
1952 [1608] *Vocabulario de la lengua general de todo el Perú.* Imprenta Santa Maria, Lima.

Grewenig, Meinrad, and Wilfried Rosendahl
2015 *Schaedel: Ikone, Mythos, Kult.* Verlag Wunderhorn, Frankfurt.

Guaman Poma de Ayala, Felipe
1944 [1616] *Primer nueva coronica y buen gobierno (1580–1613).* Instituto Tiahuanacu de Antropología, Etnografía e Prehistoria, La Paz.

Harris, Oliver J. T., and John Robb
2012 Multiple Ontologies and the Problem of the Body in History. *American Anthropologist* 114(4):668–79.

Hoshower, Lisa M., Jane Buikstra, Paul Goldstein, and Ann Webster
1995 Artificial Cranial Deformation at the OMO M10 Site: A Tiwanaku Complex from the Moquegua Valley, Peru. *Latin American Antiquity* 6:145–64.

Houston, Stephen D., and Tom Cummins
2004 Body, Presence, and Space in Andean and Mesoamerican Rulership. In *Palaces of the Ancient New*

World, edited by Susan T. Evans and Joanne Pillsbury, pp. 359–98. Dumbarton Oaks, Washington, DC.

Houston, Stephen D., and David Stuart

1998   The Ancient Maya Self: Personhood and Portraiture in the Classic Period. *RES: Anthropology and Aesthetics* 33:73–101.

Houston, Stephen D., David Stuart, and Karl A. Taube

2006   *The Memory of Bones: Body, Being, and Experience among the Classic Maya*. University of Texas Press, Austin.

Joyce, Rosemary A.

2009   *Ancient Bodies, Ancient Lives: Sex, Gender, and Archaeology*. Thames and Hudson, New York.

Larsen, Clark Spencer

2015   *Bioarchaeology: Interpreting Behavior from the Human Skeleton*. 2nd ed. Cambridge University Press, New York.

Latcham, Ricardo E.

1929   *Las creencias religiosas de los antiguos peruanos*. Balcells, Santiago.

Le Breton, David

1994   *Corps et sociétés: essai de sociologie et d'anthropologie du corps*. Méridiens Klincksieck, Paris.

Lock, Margaret, and Judith Farquhar (editors)

2007   *Beyond the Body Proper: Reading the Anthropology of Material Life*. Duke University Press, Durham, North Carolina.

López Austin, Alfredo

1989   *Cuerpo humano e ideología: las concepciones de los antiguos nahuas*. Universidad Nacional Autónoma de México, Mexico City.

2009   El dios en el cuerpo. *Dimensión Antropológica* 46:1–34.

López Austin, Alfredo, and Leonardo López Luján

2009   *Monte Sagrado: Templo Mayor*. Instituto Nacional de Antropología e Historia, Universidad Nacional Autónoma de México, Mexico City.

López Austin, Alfredo, and Luis Millones

2008   *Dioses del norte, dioses del sur*. Ediciones ERA, Mexico City.

Lozada, María Cecilia

2011   Marking Ethnicity through Premortem Cranial Modification among the Pre-Inca Chiribaya, Perú. In *The Bioarchaeology of the Human Head: Decapitation, Decoration, and Deformation*, edited by Michelle Bonogofsky, pp.228–40. University Press of Florida, Gainesville.

2014   The Emergence of Bioarchaeology in Peru: Origins and Modern Approaches. In *Archaeological Human Remains: Global Perspectives*, edited by Barra O'Donnabhain and María Cecilia Lozada, pp. 177–88. Springer, New York.

Lozada, María Cecilia, and Jane E. Buikstra

2002   *El Señorío de Chiribaya en la costa sur del Perú*. Instituto de Estudios Peruanos, Lima.

Manzanilla, Linda, Raúl Valadez, Bernardo Rodríguez-Galicia, Gilberto Pérez Roldán, Johanná Padró, Adrián Velázquez, Belem Zúñiga, and Norma Valentín

2011   Producción de atavíos y tocados en un centro de barrio de Teotihuacan: el caso de Teopancazco. In *Producción artesanal y especializada en Mesoamérica: areas de actividad y procesos productivos*, edited by Linda Manzanilla and Kenneth Hirth, pp. 59–85. Instituto Nacional de Antropología e Historia, Mexico City.

Mauss, Marcel

2007 [1934]   Les techniques du corps. *Journal de Psychologie* 32:3–4.

McKeever Furst, Jill Leslie

1995   *The Natural History of the Soul in Ancient Mexico*. Yale University Press, New Haven, Connecticut.

Miller, Virginia

2007   Skeletons, Skulls, and Bones in the Art of Chichén Itzá. In *New Perspectives on Human Sacrifice and Ritual Body Treatments in Ancient Maya Society*, edited by Vera Tiesler and Andrea Cucina, pp. 165–89. Springer, New York.

Monaghan, John D.

2000   Theology and History in the Study of Mesoamerican Religion. In *Handbook of Middle American Indians*. Supplement 6, *Ethnology*, edited by John D. Monaghan, pp. 24–49. University of Texas Press, Austin.

Purizaga Vega, Medardo

1991   *El rito del nacimiento entre los incas*. Universidad de San Martín de Porres, Lima.

Romano Pacheco, Arturo

1965   *Estudio morfológico de la deformación craneana en Tamuín, S.L.P., y en la Isla del Idolo, Veracruz*. Instituto Nacional de Antropología e Historia, Mexico City.

Romero Molina, Javier

1958   *Mutilaciones dentarias prehispánicas de México y América en general*. Instituto Nacional de Antropología e Historia, Mexico City.

Sahagún, Fray Bernardino de

1981   *Florentine Codex: General History of the Things of New Spain*. Book 1, *The Gods*. Translated and with commentary by Arthur Anderson and Charles Dibble. University of Utah Press, Salt Lake City.

Shimada, Izumi, and James L. Fitzsimmons
2015 Introduction to *Living with the Dead in the Andes*, edited by Izumi Shimada and James L. Fitzsimmons, pp. 3–49. University of Arizona Press, Tucson.

Skibo, James M., and Michael B. Schiffer
2009 *People and Things*. Springer, New York.

Sofaer, Joanna R.
2006 *The Body as Material Culture*. Cambridge University Press, Cambridge.

Stewart, T. Dale
1950 Deformity, Trephining, and Mutilation in South American Indian Skeletal Remains. In *Handbook of South American Indians*. Vol. 6, *Physical Anthropology, Linguistics, and Cultural Geography of South American Indians*, edited by Julian H. Steward, pp. 43–52. Smithsonian Institution, Bureau of American Ethnology, Bulletin 143, Washington, DC.
1974 Human Skeletal Remains from Dzibilchaltun, Yucatan, Mexico, with a Review of Cranial Deformity Types in the Maya Region. In *Archaeological Investigations on the Yucatan Peninsula*, edited by E. Wyllys Andrews, pp. 199–225. Middle American Research Institute, Tulane University, New Orleans.

Stross, Brian
2010 This World and Beyond: Food Practices and the Social Order in Maya Religion. In *Pre-Columbian Foodways: Interdisciplinary Approaches to Food, Culture, and Markets in Ancient Mesoamerica*, edited by John Edward Staller and Michael Carrasco, pp. 553–76. Springer, New York.

Taube, Karl A.
1985 The Classic Maya Maize God: A Reappraisal. In *Fifth Palenque Round Table,1983*, edited by Merle Greene Robertson and Virginia M. Fields, pp. 171–81. Pre-Columbian Art Research Institute, San Francisco.
2004 Flower Mountain: Concepts of Life, Beauty, and Paradise among the Classic Maya. *Anthropology and Aesthetics* 45:69–98.

Thompson, Eric
1946 Tattooing and Scarification among the Maya. *Notes on Middle American Archaeology and Ethnology* (Carnegie Institution) 3(63):18–25.

Tiesler, Vera
2000 *Decoraciones dentales entre los antiguos mayas*. Instituto Nacional de Antropología e Historia, Mexico City.
2012 *Transformarse en maya: el modelado cefálico entre los mayas prehispánicos y coloniales*. Universidad Nacional Autónoma de México; Universidad Autónoma de Yucatán, Mexico City.

2014 *The Bioarchaeology of Artificial Cranial Modifications*. Springer, New York.

Tiesler, Vera, and Andrea Cucina
2014 Past, Present, and Future Perspectives in Maya Bioarchaeology: A View from Yucatan, Mexico. In *Archaeological Human Remains: Global Perspectives*, edited by Barra O'Donnabhain and María Cecilia Lozada, pp. 165–76. Springer, New York.

Tiesler, Vera, and Pilar Zabala
2011 El modelado artificial de la cabeza durante la Colonia: una tradición maya en el espejo de las fuentes históricas. *Estudios de Cultura Maya* 38:75–96.
2017 Survival and Abandonment of Indigenous Head-Shaping Practices in Iberian America after European Contact. In *Colonized Bodies, Worlds Transformed: Toward a Global Bioarchaeology of Contact and Colonialism*, edited by Melissa S. Murphy and Haagen D. Klaus. University Press of Florida, Gainesville.

Tozzer, Alfred M.
1941 *Landa's "Relación de las cosas de Yucatan."* Peabody Museum, Harvard University, Cambridge, Massachusetts.

Tung, Tiffiny A.
2012 *Violence, Ritual, and the Wari Empire: A Social Bioarchaeology of Imperialism in the Ancient Andes*. University Press of Florida, Gainesville.

Tung, Tiffiny A., and Kelly J. Knudson
2008 Social Identities and Geographical Origins of Wari Trophy Heads from Conchopata, Peru. *Current Anthropology* 49:915–25.

Turner, Terence S.
2007 The Social Skin. In *Beyond the Body Proper: Reading the Anthropology of Material Life*, edited by Margaret Lock and Judith Farquhar, pp. 83–105. Duke University Press, Durham, North Carolina.

Turner, Victor
1984 *The Body and Society: Explorations in Social Theory*. Basil Blackwell, Oxford.

Van Gennep, Arnold
1960 *The Rites of Passage*. University of Chicago Press, Chicago.

Velásquez García, Erik
2011 Las entidades y fuerzas anímicas en la cosmovisión maya clásica. In *Los mayas: voces de piedra*, edited by Alejandra Martínez de Velasco Cortina and María Elena Vega Villalobos, pp. 235–54. Editorial Ámbar, Universidad Nacional Autónoma de México, Mexico City.

Verano, John

1995   Where Do They Rest? The Treatment of Human
        Offerings and Trophies in Ancient Peru. In *Tombs for
        the Living: Andean Mortuary Practices*, edited by Tom D.
        Dillehay, pp. 189–227. Dumbarton Oaks, Washington DC.

Viveiros de Castro, Eduardo

1998   Cosmological Deixis and Amerindian Perspectivism.
        Journal of the Royal Anthropological Institute 4(3):469–88.

Weismantel, Mary

2015   Many Heads Are Better Than One: Mortuary Practice
        and Ceramic Art in Moche Society. In *Living with
        the Dead in the Andes*, edited by Izumi Shimada and
        James L. Fitzsimmons, pp. 76–100. University of
        Arizona Press, Tucson.

Wilkinson, Darryl

2013   The Emperor's New Body: Personhood, Ontology and
        the Inka Sovereign. *Cambridge Archaeological Journal*
        23:417–32.

Yépez, Rosaura

2017   La modificación cultural de la cabeza y sus formas
        simbólicas como procesos de comunicación y signifi-
        cacieon social en las culturas del área central andina:
        una aproximación semiótica. In *Modificaciones
        cefálicas culturales en Mesoamérica: una perspectiva
        continental*, edited by Vera Tiesler and Carlos Serrano
        Sánchez. Universidad Nacional Autónoma de México,
        Mexico City; Universidad Autónoma de Yucatán,
        Mérida.

Zabala, Pilar

2014   Source Compilation on Head-Shaping Practices in
        Hispanic America. In *The Bioarchaeology of Artificial
        Cranial Modifications: New Approaches to Head Shap-
        ing and Its Meanings in Pre-Columbian and Colonial
        Mesoamerica*, authored by Vera Tiesler, pp. 99–129.
        Springer, New York.

PART ONE

Mesoamerica

❧

2

What Was Being Sealed?

Cranial Modification and Ritual Binding among the Maya

WILLIAM N. DUNCAN AND GABRIELLE VAIL

INTRODUCTION

In the Maya area, head shaping and cranial modification were practiced as early as seven thousand years ago and continued through the time of contact with Europeans (Tiesler and Oliva Arias 2010; Tiesler and Zabala 2011). Researchers have demonstrated that the practice was widespread within Mesoamerican populations (Tiesler 2012a, 2012b, 2014) and was associated with a variety of meanings and motivations that varied considerably over time and space, including following aesthetic preferences, shaping heads to look like the imagined heads of gods, and defining group membership and/or gender roles (García Barrios and Tiesler 2011; Scherer, chapter 4 of this volume; Tiesler 2012a, 2012b). Over the past ten years, researchers have increasingly come to agree that cranial modification was a normal part of growing up in Maya society (Duncan 2009; Duncan and Hofling 2011; Tiesler 2012a, 2012b). Research has further shown that Meso-american bodies were highly fluid, dynamic, and parti-ble, composed of multiple animating entities, animating forces, and coessences.[1] This was true prior to contact with Europeans (Houston et al. 2006) and continues to be true today (Pitarch 2010). Previously, researchers argued that head shaping stemmed in part from a desire to fix souls within infants' bodies and protect them from harm (McKeever Furst 1995; Duncan 2009; Duncan and Hof-ling 2011). Although we know that this was accomplished

in part by ritually wrapping and sealing their heads, the relationship between ritual sealing, cranial modification, and head shaping remains poorly defined across Meso-america. In this chapter, we review research on cranial modification in the Maya area, in particular the notion that the practice reflects a ritualized sealing of the head, and consider evidence from ethnohistorical sources and the Madrid Codex to bolster this work. We further build on previous research by reviewing components of Classic-period Maya bodies to explore which animating essences and forces may have been targeted for such sealing among the pre-Columbian Maya.[2]

MAYA CRANIAL MODIFICATION

Cranial modification in Mesoamerica has been a topic of fascination and comment since the 1830s (Romano Pacheco 1974). Much early work focused on classifying and describing types of cranial modification (see Duncan and Hofling 2011; Tiesler 2014 for a review) or calculat-ing frequencies of different types of cranial modification within various assemblages (Dávalos Hurtado 1944, 1946, 1965). Other documentary efforts attempted to track spa-tial, temporal, or demographic trends in the use of cranial modification (Alva R. et al. 1987; Peña Gomez and Lopez Wario 1989; Romano Pacheco 1972, 1973a, 1973b). This work continues today (Scherer, chapter 4 of this volume;

Tiesler and Lacadena, chapter 3 of this volume). Andrew Scherer, for example, documents that cranial modification found during the Classic period in the Usumacinta River region, constituting the border between southwestern Mexico and southeastern Guatemala, seems to have been dominated by the tabular oblique style. Many researchers coming from a purely biological background have focused on assessing the morphological or health impacts of cranial modification (Duncan and Hofling 2011). Juan Comas (1966, 1969) considered how cranial modification impacted shape in Mesoamerica in particular. No study has demonstrated any pathological impact of cranial modification to date, though one author once speculated that it may have contributed to the Maya collapse (Feindel 1988).

More recent work on cranial modification has focused on aspects of embodiment, processes through which culture is manifest in and on bodies. Ana García Barrios and Vera Tiesler (2011) have cogently argued that head shaping in the Classic period reflected an attempt to make heads look like those of deities, as the Maya conceptualized them. Scherer, in chapter 4 of this volume, argues that the tabular oblique cranial modification found in the Usumacinta River region was designed to make the head look like an ear of corn, the shape taken by the maize god's head. He notes that the tonsured hairstyles seen in Maya iconography suggest that the hair might have resembled the tassels on corn. In the largest survey to date, Tiesler (1998, 2014) found that over 90 percent of skulls excavated from the Maya area were modified in some manner. This is consistent with colonial-era accounts from the Maya and Aztec region that indicated that cranial modification was an expected aspect of citizenship in Mesoamerican societies (Tiesler 2014; Tiesler and Lacadena, chapter 3 of this volume). In part due to this work, over the past ten years researchers have increasingly come to agree that head shaping and cranial modification were integral processes in the growth and development of pre-Columbian Mesoamerican children (Tiesler 1998:202).

SEALING, WRAPPING, AND BINDING

Bodies in Mesoamerica were particularly dynamic with regard to animacy and personhood (see below). Many essences needed to be actively tended to ensure the proper development of the individual, and this, in part, reflected

the cyclical nature of time in the Mesoamerican cosmos. The entire Mesoamerican landscape underwent cycles of birth, death, and rebirth (Rice 2007:35–38). Everything that was born would die, and everything that died would be reborn in some fashion. Humans, animals, houses, ceramic vessels, caves, jade, and other media were all part of these cycles, and thus the entire landscape was spiritually potent and dynamic. These cycles were not simply automated units of time; they required action. Sealing, wrapping, or otherwise binding various materials arises from the need to frame time and space through ritual in Mesoamerica (Christenson 2006; Houston et al. 2006:83–85; Klein 1982; Megged 2010:136–39). This worldview has roots stemming back to the Middle Preclassic period (Reilly 2006) and is still seen today. The Mesoamerican cosmos was perceived as inherently tenuous, and there was an obligation to engage the passage of time. Specifically, rituals helped Mesoamericans exercise control over the aforementioned cycles of birth and death, and sealing and unsealing were important parts of that process. For example, the beginning of k'atuns (cycles of approximately twenty years in the Maya area) were marked archaeologically by unwrapping stelae (Stuart 1996:154), and Cecelia Klein (1982:25) and others (Houston et al. 2006:83–85; Stuart 1996:154) have shown that k'atun completions were marked by k'altuun (stone binding) rituals (plate 2). Sacred bundles and ritualized wrapping were also particularly important in founding myths (Boone 2000a, 200b:58, 145, 152; Duncan and Schwarz 2014; Megged 2010:96), of which the best-known example is the use of Huitzilopochtli's sacred bundle during the founding of Tenochtitlan by the Aztecs, or Mexica (Megged 2010). The bundle was placed in the newly built Templo Mayor after it was dedicated (Boone 2000a:551–65). The use of sacred bundles in founding myths and accession rites is common throughout Mesoamerica (Pohl 1994:82) and is particularly evident in the iconography at Yaxchilan (Reents-Budet 2006:115), Palenque, and Bonampak (Benson 1976), Classic-period sites in the Maya area. Analogous practices were documented in colonial highland Guatemala and still occur in that region today (Christenson 2006). Allen Christenson (2006:226–28) notes that the founding ancestors of all the major K'iche' lineages left bundles for their descendants, along with explicit instructions for veneration by subsequent generations. These bundles are typically kept out of sight, stored in wooden boxes in cofradía houses, only to be brought out on special occasions such as New Year's Day and Easter week. Although the practices in which these bundles are involved reflect considerable syncretism, their use for framing time reflects deep, continuous roots in the region.

Space as well as time needed to be ritually framed in pre-Hispanic Mesoamerica. Tz'utujil Maya speakers today, from the Lake Atitlán region of highland Guatemala, view the fabric in looms as a model of the cosmos (Looper 2006:80). In colonial texts, the heavens were sometimes perceived as a well-organized weaving, while the underworld was viewed as a tangled mess of threads (Klein 1982). Ropes as an organizing framework are also prominent in pre-Hispanic sources, where they may be seen painted on polychrome vessels from Classic-period contexts and in codices and murals from the Postclassic period (Looper 2006; Miller 1982). Rulers were particularly responsible for this framing of time and space and were thus shown bearing the burden of time. One sign of authority and rulership, for example, was the mat sign, a woven icon. Other iconography reflecting ritualized wrapping and sealing included knotted bands (Reilly 2006), twisted cords (Miller 1982), and symbols reflecting weaving such as oblique interlacing (Looper 2006) or piles of cloth (Reents-Budet 2006). Weaving was (and is) primarily done by women in Mesoamerica, and, as such, it is worth noting that women were explicitly in charge of manufacturing this extremely important item of the ritual economy (Reents-Budet 2006; Christenson 2006). This highlights the fact that, although framing time and space was a duty of the ruler, it was a responsibility that permeated society, and the execution and symbolism of that framing may have reflected a gendered binary dualism, as is the case with the cofradía rituals in highland Guatemala today (see, e.g., Christenson 2001; Prechtel and Carlsen 1988).

Sacred bundles and ritualized wrapping were explicitly associated with whiteness throughout Mesoamerica. Amos Megged (2010) notes, for instance, that Aztec ancestor bundles were depicted as white in the Aztec codices. The word *sak* refers to white in multiple Maya languages, and it is frequently associated with coverings and animacy (see Wagner 2006 for review). For example, Elisabeth Wagner (2006:63–64) notes that *sak hunal* can refer to the white leaves that cover young corncobs, the white film covering newborns (*vernix caseosa*), and the white cloth covering sacred bundles.

PRE-COLUMBIAN MAYA BODIES

Mesoamerican bodies were not inherently unified entities but contained many essences that were corporeally manifest in varying degrees. This was true for Maya bodies prior to contact with Europeans (Houston et al. 2006) and is still true for contemporary Maya societies (e.g., Boremanse 1998; Groark 2005; Pitarch 2010; Vogt 1992; Watanabe 1992). In addition, Mesoamerican bodies were thought to be crafted rather than born in a completed state (Boremanse 1998; Groark 2005; Scherer, chapter 4 of this volume). Infants in Mesoamerica are (and were) particularly raw and vulnerable, and consequently their bodies needed to be actively shaped and protected (Joyce 2000:474–75; Scherer, chapter 4 of this volume). Infants needed to have their souls anchored within their bodies (specifically within their heads) and prevented from leaving, and (at least among contemporary societies) to receive protection from evil winds (Boremanse 1998; Duncan 2009; Duncan and Hofling 2011; McKeever Furst 1995; López Austin 1988). Contemporary Tzeltal Maya speakers believe that swaddling newborns for fifteen days and avoiding contact with outsiders would protect them from soul loss and evil winds (Cosminsky 1982:244, 2001:196; Pitarch 2010). Tzotzil Maya children are regarded to have "unripe heads" (Groark 2005:183). Similarly, Tz'utujil Maya speakers bathe infants for eight days after birth to protect them from similar dangers (Cosminsky 2001; Paul 1974:284).

Cranial modification and head shaping were clearly part of a series of rites explicitly concerned with protecting and developing pre-Columbian and colonial Mesoamerican infants' bodies during the first six months of life. These rites included washing babies after birth, molding their head shape, fixing their souls in their bodies, naming them, and assigning gender and occupational roles to the infants (Duncan and Hofling 2011). Comparing the order and timing of rituals as described for colonial Yucatec and modern Yucatec and Tzotzil Maya speakers suggests that cranial modification occurred at the same time or shortly before the time that souls were being fixed in infants' bodies and gender roles were assigned (Duncan and Hofling 2011). Specifically, in colonial accounts head molding (Tozzer 1941:129) occurred a few days after birth and before the priest would determine the child's destiny and profession. This description of head shaping in colonial accounts is paralleled in modern Yucatec and Tzotzil communities when baptism occurs, a ritual that is also thought to help fix the soul of the infant in his or her body. These rituals resulted in a socially integrated person within Mesoamerican society (Tiesler 2012a). Head shaping and cranial modification in Mesoamerica were part of this embodiment because they helped wrap and seal infants' heads to protect them.[3]

Before turning to the Postclassic and colonial-period data sets, it is helpful to consider what we know about the souls that these ritual practices seek to fix in infants' bodies among contemporary Maya speakers. It is important to recognize that conceptions regarding souls vary greatly across both time and space, but it is clear that there is a general belief in multiple souls inhabiting a person. As Andrew Scherer discusses in greater detail in chapter 4 of this volume, a number of contemporary Maya groups distinguish between a soul that is said to inhabit the heart and form part of the blood and circulatory system (known as ch'ulel among the Tzeltal Maya of highland Chiapas), and a second type of soul (the "spirit soul") of which there may be up to thirteen manifestations in the form of animals or celestial beings (also see Pitarch 2010). With respect to the ch'ulel and conceptions of the soul as a person's essence, it is interesting to note that it is believed to leave the body during illness, drunkenness, and sometimes also when sleeping (McGee 1990; Pitarch 2010). Several recent studies have suggested Classic-period counterparts to these ideas (discussed in further detail below), but little work has been done previously to explore these ideas in Postclassic and colonial Maya sources, a topic to which we now turn.

POSTCLASSIC AND COLONIAL DATA

Puberty Ceremonies to Increase the Life Force

Data from the Maya codices and ethnohistorical sources suggest that ensoulment practices and binding rituals among the Yucatec Maya during the Postclassic and colonial periods explicitly targeted animating essences. Connections between a ritual "baptism" depicted in the Madrid Codex and Diego de Landa's description of this ceremony have long been recognized (Gates 1978; Vail 2005). What we find especially interesting about this particular ceremony is that it is called kaput-sihil, meaning "to be born a second time," and it appears to represent the passage from childhood to puberty (Gates 1978:42). Like the rituals associated with a child's birth, when he or

she is bathed shortly after entering the world, kaput-sihil involves anointing an older child with sacred water (Gates 1978:44–45). Although there is no explicit connection to bathing in Landa's description, the almanacs depicting this ceremony in the codices make specific use of the term ichkil, "to bathe."

The ritual described by Landa is complex and involves a number of different stages (outlined in table 2.1). Those that are most relevant to our discussion include steps 10 through 18 (Gates 1978:43–45). It is significant that all of the children of the relevant age (i.e., approaching puberty) were gathered together "with an aged woman as matron for the girls, and a man in charge of the boys" (Gates 1978:43). The ceremony celebrating puberty—an important change in life status—was a public one that involved many of the same preparations as those undertaken for other community rituals, such as fasting, a ritual purification of the area, and the burning of incense. In this sense, therefore, it can be related to rituals such as that pictured on page 19b of the Madrid Codex, which shows the purification of a temple courtyard by a series of deities (Landa's "chacs") and the priest (represented by the creator Itzamna, who appears in the central panel) dressed in his vestments. As part of the "rebirth" ceremony, the priest covers the children's heads with a white cloth, which is reminiscent of the sacred bundles described previously. He also begins "to bless the children, with long prayers, and to sanctify them with the hyssop, all with great serenity" (Gates 1978:44). A similar hyssop, in the form of a rattlesnake, is depicted on several occasions in the Madrid Codex, twice in conjunction with Itzamna wearing the garments of a priest (a cape and high cap, or what Landa terms a "miter"; see Gates 1978:44). Both take place within shelters—one involving the sanctification or animation of deity effigies represented by the glyph k'uh (see discussion below) and the other the blessing of stingless bees after their hives have been established in their new home within a thatched structure. These examples are of particular interest in that they represent the use of the priest's hyssop not only for the purposes of sanctification and blessing but also as part of the process of animating beings and structures.

The next part of the ritual is undertaken not by the priest but by the sponsor of the rebirth ceremony, who uses a bone given to him by the priest to "menace" each child by tapping him or her on the forehead nine times. After this, he dips the bone in a jar of sacred water (made from water collected from the forest, mixed with a

TABLE 2.1. COMPONENTS OF THE "BAPTISM" CEREMONY DESCRIBED IN LANDA'S *RELACIÓN*

STEP	DESCRIPTION	NOTES
1	Selection of *chacs*, or ritual specialists, by festival officials.	
2	Fasting for three days prior to the ceremony by parents of children and officials.	
3	Scattering of fresh *sihom* leaves on the patio of the house of the ritual sponsor.	
4	Girls and boys arranged in lines on the house patio.	
5	Cord stretched between the four *chacs* around the perimeter of the patio.	Landa describes this as a means of purifying, or sanctifying, ritual space.
6	Scattering of ground maize and incense into a lit brazier by the children.	
7	The cord and brazier taken outside of the village to be deposited.	This leads, according to Landa, to the "exorcising of the demon."
8	Original leaves taken away; new ones (from a *kopó* tree) laid down.	
9	Priest changes into another outfit consisting of a tunic of red feathers with strips of cotton hanging below and with a miter of the same feathers. He carries a hyssop made of a decorated stick and rattlesnake tails.	The term "priest" is used by Landa to refer to a ritual specialist such as an *ah k'in* (day keeper) or *chilan* (prophet). Many of the functions undertaken by scribes during the Classic period are also attributed to priests in Landa's *Relación*.
10	White cloth placed on the heads of the children. Those children who had "done any bad thing" are separated from the others.	
11	Children seated. Prayer by the priest, who sanctifies children with his hyssop.	
12	Sponsor of the ceremony (the one whose house is the venue) given a bone by the priest, used to "menace" each of the children on the forehead nine times.	
13	Sponsor wets the bone in a jar of water and uses it to anoint the children on their forehead, face, between the fingers of their hands, and between the bones of their feet.	The water is collected from the forest (*suhuy ha'*) and mixed with certain flowers and ground cacao.
14	Priest collects the white cloths from the heads of the children. *Chacs* collect the offerings they wear suspended from their shoulders (including feathers and cacao).	
15	Symbols of childhood/purity removed from the boys, who are given a bouquet of flowers to smell and a pipe to smoke.	Flowers are a symbol of sexual maturity and are one of the offerings given during marriage negotiations (Reents-Budet 1994).
16	Children given gifts to eat; wine offered to gods by the *kayom* (singer), who empties the chalice in a single draught.	
17	Girls take their leave; their mothers cut off the cord and shell worn by prepubescent girls as a sign of their chastity.	
18	Boys depart. Their fathers bring gifts to the officials (a heap of mantles).	
19	Festival continues with general feasting and imbibing for another nine days.	This is referred to as *em-k'u(h)*, "the descent of the god(s)."

particular type of flower and ground cacao) and anoints the children "on the forehead, the face, and between the fingers of their hands and the bones of their feet" (Gates 1978:44). The "menacing" of the children has parallels to a ceremony Landa described as taking place in the Maya month of Yaxk'in, which, at the time he was writing, coincided with mid- to late November. Much as occurred during the rebirth ceremony, in Yaxk'in the children were assembled and each given "nine little blows on the knuckles of their hands" so that they might grow up to be expert craftspeople in their parents' occupations. It appears that the children were separated by gender and that an old woman called Ixmol was responsible for the girls (Gates 1978:75).[4]

The two ceremonies described above, which undoubtedly merged into each other, are represented by two

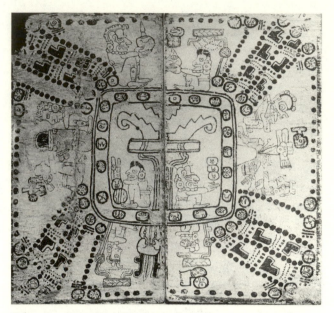

Figure 2.1. Creation of humans from maize seeds in the Madrid Codex, 75–76. Note the *ik'* glyphs above Itzamna's outstretched hand (right side of central panel) (Gates 1933).

almanacs in the Madrid Codex, found on pages 63a and 92c–93c (plate 3). The latter fits more closely with Landa's description, so it will form the focus of our discussion. The four frames of this almanac show the elderly version of the earth goddess pouring water over the head of a second, smaller figure (likely representing a child). The four captions follow a ritual circuit, beginning with the east and moving in the standard counterclockwise direction. What is of particular interest is that, in each case but one, the figure who is being ritually "bathed" (*ichki[1]*) is given the title of the wind and flower god Nik.

As Karl Taube (1992:59) has pointed out, this figure also serves as the god of the number three, who is associated with *ik'*, "wind, breath, and life." Through the act of bathing—which centers on ritually anointing the head—the life force of the figure pictured (believed to be a child) is reinforced. That such a ceremony would take place at puberty makes a great deal of sense, in that this is a time when the body undergoes significant physical changes—in other words, a time when the spiritual essence or animating forces would require extra care and protection.

In the almanac on Madrid 92c–93c, the Maya creator god Itzamna is named in place of Nik in reference to the western direction. It may be the case, as suggested by Gabrielle Vail (1996, 2000), that Itzamna is the aged variant of the god Nik (i.e., of the life force); this would

fit well with the association of Itzamna with the western direction, which corresponds to the place where the sun sets as an old man before entering the underworld and being reborn (Prechtel and Carlsen 1988). Additional support for this interpretation comes from the second frame, associated with the north, where the sun god's title (K'inich Ajaw) is given, possibly a reference to the *k'ihn* essence (discussed below in relation to the Classic-period material). Indeed, the sequence as a whole might refer to the birth of the soul in the east, its maturity (like that of the sun) in the north, its old age in the west, and its rebirth in the south/underworld region.

A similar set of associations is suggested by the other almanac that depicts ritual bathing in the Madrid Codex (63a), although here the figures are shown bathing themselves, and they are in the form of mature deities (rather than children) representing different natural forces. Although the sun god is mentioned in the first frame (rather than the second, which pictures Nik), the same general associations are suggested—birth and maturity in the first two frames, followed by death in the western sector (represented by the death god) and rebirth in the south (represented by the god of lightning and sustenance, K'awiil).

A previous study of deity-naming patterns (Vail 1996, 2000) revealed that Nik's portrait glyph (T1059) appears with a number of other deities having associations with fertility and the life force (including Itzamna, the maize god, and an earth/fertility goddess). Moreover, the day glyph *ik'* appears in various iconographic contexts, where it is used to represent "seed" or "maize seed" in the Madrid Codex (see, e.g., Madrid 75–76, 97c–98c). On Madrid 75–76 (fig. 2.1), for example, the depiction of the creator couple seated in the central panel of the almanac signifies the time of creation (which is also expressed by the stylized world tree beneath which they sit). The creation of humans from maize seeds is made manifest through the three ik' glyphs that appear above Itzamna's outstretched hand (Vail 2004). It may therefore be the case that ik' serves as one of the key animating essences among the Late Postclassic Yucatec Maya.

Of additional relevance to the discussion is the fact that both of the "rebirth" almanacs begin on the same date in the *tzolk'in*, or 260-day ritual calendar, corresponding to 4 Ajaw. As studies have previously shown (Vail 2005; Vail and Hernández 2013), a series of almanacs in the Madrid Codex incorporate this date in relation to rituals of renewal and renovation. The association of 4 Ajaw with renovation and renewal likely stems, at least in part, from the fact that the calendrical era in which the pre-Hispanic Maya were living was initiated on the date 4 Ajaw 8 Kumk'u (August 3114 BCE). Another and perhaps more relevant association of the 4 Ajaw almanacs to the Maya who used and composed the Madrid Codex involves the series of renewal rituals (discussed below) taking place in Yaxk'in or Mol—during the same months as the ceremony in which children were prepared for their adult lives and professional roles through the offices of Ixmol.

Landa's *Relación* describes the renewal rituals associated with Yaxk'in or Mol as involving anointing with a blue pitch "all the instruments of all the various occupations, from that of the priest to the spindles of the women, and even the posts of their houses" (Gates 1978:75). It is interesting that this ritual anointing is described as taking place in conjunction with the Yaxk'in ceremony described previously—that in which the children receive nine blows on their knuckles to ensure that they will become proficient in the crafts of their parents, which in turn has a number of parallels to the rebirth ritual.

The close calendrical connection between ceremonies of both types is highlighted in the Madrid Codex by almanacs that have initial dates of 4 Ajaw (twenty-nine, or over 10 percent of the total number of almanacs in the codex). Many of these can be related directly to the ceremonies Landa describes involving the use of a blue pitch or bitumen. For example, Madrid 60b shows three deities holding forked sticks (likely house posts) that are painted blue, whereas other almanacs (Madrid 14a–16a, 19b) show blue-painted structures. Additionally, several of the almanacs that show deity bundling or animation rituals (e.g., Madrid 60b–61b, 100d), as discussed below, are also associated with 4 Ajaw dates.

Animation Rituals Involving Deity Effigies

A series of almanacs depicting the making, animating, wrapping, and deanimating of deity effigies is also relevant to the themes being explored in this chapter. These almanacs occur in two distinct groupings: the first (on Madrid 60b–61b, 62b) in the same general region of the codex as the first of the "bathing" almanacs on Madrid 63a, and the second (on pages 96–100) following just after the second almanac referring to the *ichkil* ceremony on Madrid 92c–93c.

In the discussion that follows, we refer to only some of the relevant almanacs. They depict the following activities:

- Madrid 97b–98b: carving of deity images (note that the effigies are represented by the *k'uh* glyph to signify their sacred status or identification as supernaturals)[5]

- Madrid 100d: animating of images (takes place on 4 Ajaw)

- Madrid 60b–61b: wrapping/bundling of images (takes place on 4 Ajaw, with a second example on 13 Ajaw)

- Madrid 96c: presentation of wrapped images or their installation in ceramic vessels

- Madrid 99b–100b, 109c–110c: deposition/deanimation of deity effigies during the harvest ceremony

We suggest that this series of almanacs parallels, in a number of respects, the rituals attending the birth of a child. Of interest here is the emphasis on the head, which is the only portion of the effigy that is shown in the scenes that depict the carving of the wooden deity images, the ceremony portraying their animation (Madrid 100d; fig. 2.2), and those that show the bundling or wrapping of the effigies (Madrid 61b; plate 4).

Landa's discussion of the making of wooden deity figures emphasizes important aspects of this ceremonial endeavor, including the necessity for fasting and seclusion and the fact that this act was undertaken during the month of Mol (Gates 1978:76–77). In this way, his discussion serves to link this endeavor both with childbirth and the rituals surrounding the mother and newborn, as well as with the rebirth ceremony practiced at a later point in the child's life. These parallels strongly suggest that themes associated with the ritualized sealing of the head run through each ceremony.

CLASSIC-PERIOD MAYA CORPOREAL BODIES

Among the colonial Aztecs, Alfredo López Austin (1988) has argued that head shaping and cranial modification were practiced explicitly to seal *tonalli*, an animating essence associated with heat and destiny, in the head. However, while we have remarkably detailed insight into pre-Columbian and colonial-period Aztec bodies, our understanding of Maya bodies is less extensive (although that is beginning to change; see Houston et al. 2006).

Figure 2.2. Examples of wooden deity effigies being wrapped in the Madrid Codex, 61b (Gates 1933; Brasseur de Bourbourg 1869–1870:plate 13).

Here, we draw on the previous review of Postclassic and ethnohistorical life cycle rituals in light of what we know about select specific bodily concepts from the Classic period to explore whether there is evidence to suggest that certain animating essences and entities were targeted for ritual sealing or binding among the pre-Columbian Maya.

B'aah

Classic-period Maya bodies contained and reflected several key corporeal concepts whose relationship to cranial modification deserves exploration. *B'aah,* a reflexive noun that means "self" among contemporary Yucatec speakers (Bricker et al. 1998:24), referred not just to a soul but was a conceptual conflation of the body, the head, and a person's identity and personhood (Houston et al. 2006:60–76). B'aah could be extended metaphorically to refer to the top of something (Houston et al. 2006:60–76). It could also be extended beyond the body; images of individuals' heads contained their b'aah (Houston et al. 2006:60–76). This was one reason that heads were so important in Maya ritual and iconography—images offered an opportunity to interact with the individual (Houston et al. 2006:60–76).

Thus, images of rulers' heads on stelae and in other media presented an opportunity for people to engage the ruler long after his death (Houston and Stuart 1998; see also Vázquez de Ágredos et al., chapter 6 of this volume). This is also the reason heads and images of heads were targeted for violence (Duncan 2011; Duncan et al. 2009). Taking someone's head was tantamount to taking, manipulating, and controlling the individual's personhood, which allowed the extension of humiliation across generations (Houston and Stuart 1998; Houston et al. 2006; Stuart 1996).

B'aah, then, shared some characteristics with the Nahuatl conception of tonalli: it was associated directly with the head, and with individual identity and personhood. However, our understanding of b'aah is meager relative to that of tonalli (Houston et al. 2006:81), and they do not seem to have had the exact same relationship with the head. Tonalli was *in* the head whereas b'aah *was* the head. By virtue of this, there is less evidence that b'aah had the same fluidity that tonalli did, that b'aah could flow from the head in whole or part. Tonalli was clearly not permanently fixed within the head and could be lost through a variety of means. These differences may imply that cranial modification either permanently sealed b'aah when the fontanels closed, or that perhaps b'aah per se was not being sealed.

Although b'aah may not have been fluid, Erik Velásquez García (2011:244) has recently argued that there was an animating force that came from the sun, reflected heat, and was accumulated through age. Velásquez García (2011:244) argues that maintaining the appropriate balance of this heat was an important aspect of good health. *K'ihn* and related words found in modern Itzá, colonial and modern Yucatec, and colonial Tzeltal refer to the sun but are associated with strength, bravery, and ferocity as well as with vigor, life, and venerable things (see below). Velásquez García (2011:244) argues that in the Classic period, older members of society were specifically called *k'inich* in part because they had accrued social status due to their increased heat (cf. Martínez González 2006a:120; Chávez Guzmán 2006:122, 136; Gossen 1975: 449–50 for discussion in other Maya ethnographic contexts). Rulers in Classic Maya society would have had a particularly important warmth from the sun (Houston and Cummins 2004:365). Velásquez García (2011:244) suggests a relationship between b'aah and k'ihn, noting that, in contemporary Ch'orti' Maya, *b'ahn* means heat.[6] If they are indeed related, this may imply that there was a fluid animating force that was a counterpart to b'aah and that cranial modification may have been an attempt to seal it in the same way tonalli was for colonial Nahuatl speakers (Houston and Cummins 2004:169–70).

Ik'

Ik' was explicitly associated with both breath and wind among the pre-Columbian Maya (Taube 2004). It was considered to be a manifestation of gods' and ancestors' essences (Taube 2004) and as such was associated with memory (Houston et al. 2006:33). Ik' appears to have been particularly fluid and could pass through the mouth, nose, and ears (fig. 2.3a) (Taube 2004, 2005). Additionally, it was explicitly associated with jade (Taube 2005). Taube (2005) has argued, for example, that the jade stones placed in the mouth of the deceased were manifestations of ik' and that jade earspools were portals through which ik' passed. Ik' in these contexts is sometimes represented as a serpent, but many iconographic representations of earspools were actually shown breathing (Taube 2005). This last point is interesting because it demonstrates that ik' could pass through holes that were created in the body, much like tonalli for the Aztecs.

Taube (2004) has shown that ik' was associated with the verb *ochb'ih*, which means "enter the road," an expression related to a person's death. This was likely a reference to the association of ik' with the passage to a flowery mountain paradise characterized by sweet smells (Taube 2004), and this point is important for two reasons. The first is that all members of Maya society were not likely to have had access to this paradisiacal afterlife. It would have been reserved for rulers, nobility, and brave warriors who died in battle (Taube 2004). This is consistent with the notion that breath and the words of rulers, or *ajaw*, were particularly precious.

Figure 2.3. (a) Representation of the *ik'* glyph at the ear of the Classic-period wind god, shown here in the glyph for the month Mak (redrawn from Taube 2005:fig. 8a); (b) the ik' glyph on a jade pectoral from Structure 10L-11, Copán; note how the ik' glyph is bound by knotted serpents (redrawn from Taube 2005:fig. 9b); and (c) an image of breath emerging from the maize god's forehead (redrawn from Taube 2005:fig. 9g).

a

b

c

Ajaw refers to "lord" or "he who shouts or proclaims," for example (Rice 2004; Stuart 1995:190–91). Thus, although most members of society probably had some breath soul, this may suggest that there were different breath souls, or one type of breath soul with a range of manifestations throughout society. The second point is that the Classic-period association of ik' with a flowery mountain paradise is somewhat at odds with the notion of evil winds that is so commonplace in contemporary Mesoamerican cultures. Christophe Helmke and Jesper Neilsen (2009:59) have argued that this concept reflects syncretism with European cultures, however, so it is likely not relevant to Classic-period contexts.

Both of these factors confound our ability to assess the relevance of ik' to cranial modification. With that said, however, the Classic Maya frequently depicted ik' as being wrapped or sealed (fig. 2.3b). As noted above, Taube (2005) has demonstrated that many iconographic representations of earspools show them breathing. Some of these earspools are found on ceremonial bars that are covered in flowers and have spool-like flares on the ends. These ceremonial bars are frequently shown as being wrapped in mat symbols (e.g., the ceremonial bar on Tikal Stela 2; Taube 2005:fig. 15), which were associated with rit-ualized sealing as well as authority. Some jade pectorals were drawn in the form of these ceremonial bars as well (fig. 2.3b). Finally, some representations of gods showed breath emerging from the top of their heads, or the ik' symbol on the forehead or headband (fig. 2.3c). Thus, there are explicit associations of ik' with the forehead or crown of the head, as well as examples in which it was wrapped. This does not sufficiently demonstrate that ik' was being bound in cases of cranial modification, but it justifies future exploration of the point, especially in light of the Postclassic data discussed previously in which ik' figures prominently in rebirth (i.e., puberty) ceremonies that target the head.

Ch'ulel

Ch'ulel is described by contemporary Tzotzil Maya speak-ers as an "eternal and indestructible" soul (Houston et al. 2006; Vogt 1969:370). Ethnographically, it is explicitly associated with the blood and the essence of an individ-ual, but it is somewhat ethereal (Taube 2004:70). Two distinct senses of ch'ulel are found in contemporary Maya communities. Pedro Pitarch (2010) describes it as being in the heart for Tzeltal speakers but also as a "shadowy double" that is found in a nearby mountain, where the ch'ulel of other lineage members reside. In this regard, ethnographic descriptions of ch'ulel suggest that the con-cept encompassed aspects of both the Aztec *yolia*, or heart soul, and tonalli, respectively. López Austin (1988:1:228) suggests that this dual meaning may reflect central Mex-ican origins.[7]

Ch'ulel and related contemporary words incorporate the same root as the word k'uh, which means "god" and in general refers to sacrality (Houston et al. 2006:228).[8] Taube (2004:70, 92–93) notes that it was explicitly linked to sweet-smelling flowers and a flowery paradise. Although it was associated with blood and the heart, it could come from royal hands; moreover, Stephen Houston and col-leagues (2006:34) suggest that not everyone in society would have had ch'ulel. Currently, we find no explicit rea-son from the archaeological evidence to think that cranial modification would have sealed ch'ulel in infants' heads. However, the potential associations with tonalli and ik' raise the possibility, and data from the Madrid Codex and ethnohistorical sources suggests that it may be beneficial to reexamine the Classic-period material.

O'hlis and Sak b'ook(?)

O'hlis is an animating entity associated with the heart during the Classic period. Linguistically, o'hlis (and related words such as o'hl, ohl, and ool) are associated with the soul, appetite, character, conscience, confidence, dedi-cation, doubt, and energy in various contemporary Mayan languages (Velásquez García 2011:239; also Bourdin 2007; Martínez González 2007). It appears to have been the basis for cognition, rationality, will, and memory. On the basis of epigraphic evidence, Erik Velásquez García (2011:239) argues that o'hlis was explicitly associated with the maize god and that after death it continued on the road of maize.[9]

Velásquez García (2011:240) argues that o'hlis was asso-ciated with an animating force called *sak b'ook(?)*, although he notes that this is a somewhat tenuous association at the present time and does not yet reflect a consensus among epigraphers. He argues that the word b'ook means "vapor or smell" and that generally it was an impersonal animat-ing force of divine origin that was manifest in the chest, was transmitted by blood, and could exit through the crown of the head during sleep. He further argues, fol-lowing Christian Prager (cited in Velásquez García 2011), that the word was represented in Classic-period texts by

Figure 2.4. An Early Classic jade figure in which the maize god is portrayed as the foliated jester god. Note the *ajaw* sign on top of his head (redrawn from Taube 2005:fig. 6e).

a variant of the *ajaw* glyph (T533), which was depicted with scrolls of breath and shown in association with the top of the head or in the headdress of lords (fig. 2.4) (Proskouriakoff 1963:158–60).[10] These scenes, according to Velásquez García (2011), show actors who are possessed by gods or ancestors. Velásquez García (2011) further notes that some variants of this use of T533 are associated with the word *k'uh*, which may indicate a connection between k'uh, o'hlis, and sak b'ook(?). The connection between this animating force and the top of the head raises the possibility that cranial modification is an attempt to seal it within the head, although this idea requires additional testing before it can be given more serious consideration.

Wahy

Wahy were animal companion spirits (Grube and Nahm 1994; Helmke and Nielsen 2009). They were impersonal but had masculine characteristics, may have been hereditary (Helmke and Nielsen 2009), and shared bonds with the body until death (Houston et al. 2006:35, 61, 79). Additionally, wahy were thought to be wild and had clear associations with the forest and underworld. During sleep, the wahy would leave the body and were subject to attack by sorcerers. Diseases were manifestations of such attacks. Unfortunately, the complexity of the wahy and their murky corporeal manifestations make assessing their potential relevance to cranial modification difficult, but present evidence does not make a connection seem likely.

DISCUSSION AND CONCLUSIONS

Our review of animating essences that may have played a role in cranial modification (i.e., by being ritually sealed in infants' heads) suggests that some of those identified epigraphically by scholars in recent years were more likely to have been the focus of cranial modification than others. For the Classic period, we believe that b'aah probably was relevant to modifications made to crania, but its relationship to the practice requires further exploration. Additionally, there is some evidence for the importance of k'ihn as a force that expanded or contracted over an individual's lifetime, but this remains to be explored more fully, as does the relationship between b'aah and k'ihn and their correspondences with the head. Our research indicates that k'ihn appears to have been important as an animating force associated with the sun in Postclassic data sets, especially in almanacs pertaining to rituals focusing on the life cycle. Studies of incantations from the colonial Yucatec Ritual of the Bacabs, currently being undertaken by Timothy Knowlton, offer a potential source of information to help illuminate these concepts in postconquest contexts.

The fluidity of a breath soul (ik') among the pre-Hispanic Maya, the fact that it is presented as wrapped in iconography, and its explicit association with the head all support the notion that it was targeted for ritualized sealing. Analyses of Postclassic puberty rites depicted in the Maya codices are especially suggestive in this regard, as the deity personifying ik' substitutes for the children (or adolescents) who would have been participating in the ceremony. Moreover, evidence from the Madrid Codex suggests a relationship between ik' and the maize from which humans were formed. Similarly, the concepts of o'hl and o'hlis, related linguistically to the heart, have been linked to the maize god. Previous studies suggest that o'hlis, along with sak b'ook(?), may well have been associated with the top of the head, as suggested by iconographic representations from both Classic and Post-classic contexts. These essences and their relationship to the head and to each other merit consideration in future research. Finally, although we found no definitive association between ch'ulel or k'uh and cranial modification, these concepts were explicitly associated with Postclassic animation ceremonies in which the effigy heads of deities were emphasized in bundling rites. This offers a productive avenue for future research pertaining to Maya embodiment and personhood and for tracing changes over time in how they were conceptualized. While these studies are still in their infancy, future research along these lines offers the opportunity to assess how these practices relate to cranial modification and head shaping in the past.

While only an initial foray into these questions, this chapter highlights the utility of an approach that combines archaeological, epigraphic, and iconographic data sets to explore emic perspectives of embodiment, personhood, and ensoulment among both Classic and Postclassic Maya peoples. Using this methodology, we have attained greater clarity relating to these matters for Classic-period populations, building on William Duncan's earlier studies, and have made important strides in understanding how Yucatec Maya speakers in the Late Postclassic and early colonial periods embodied these concepts as part of life-cycle rituals and those involving the animacy of deity effigies. These findings are of value in a number of respects—in particular, in allowing more detailed comparisons with central Mexican data from the same time period, as discussed in several of the chapters in this volume (see, e.g., Chávez Balderas, chapter 9), and to help fill in some of the gaps stemming from colonial Yucatán's less voluminous documentary record, as compared to that from highland Mexico. We anticipate a fruitful series of future collaborations building from the ideas and discussions generated initially for the session organized by Vera Tiesler and María Cecilia Lozada for the Society for American Archaeology meetings in Austin and later for this interdisciplinary project.

ACKNOWLEDGMENTS

We would like to thank Vera Tiesler and María Cecilia Lozada for organizing this volume and inviting our participation. Additionally, seeds of this paper were planted during the time in which both authors were studying at Dumbarton Oaks; we are grateful for that institution's support. All remaining errors are our own.

NOTES

1. A similar observation about the necessity of swaddling to form proper children's bodies has been made in Mesoamerica, in highland Chiapas, by Patricia Marks Greenfield (2004:29–31) in observing the socialization of girls. There, mothers build on their newborn daughters' upper body stillness and visual attention by swaddling them. This is said to prepare the infant for practices in later life, such as cooking tortillas and, most importantly, weaving with a backstrap loom.

2. In his 1612 Spanish-Aymara dictionary, Ludovico Bertonio (1984) includes terms and phrases referring to three different head shapes, each produced via a different technique. A number of terms refer to tapered or conical heads (*cabeza ahusada*), but there are a few that refer to round heads (*cabeza redonda*) and flattened heads (*cabeza aplastada*). Apparently, tapered was the most common head shape in the western basin, where Bertonio resided.

3. It should be noted that some of the tenon heads present today were carved and added during excavation and reconstruction of the temple between 1961 and 1963 (John Janusek, personal communication from Marcelino Quispe, July 2011).

4. The preparations for this ceremony were said to have taken place in Yaxk'in, but it appears likely that it was actually performed during the following month, Mol. This would fit well with the name given to the elderly woman performing the ritual (Ixmol). *Ix* is a female title; *ix mol* is defined as "one who provides or supplies" or "a woman who gathers others who are weaving or spinning together" (Barrera Vásquez et al. 1980:528).

5. Although colonial-period and contemporary dictionaries translate *k'uh* as "god, sacred, or holy" (Barrera Vásquez et al. 1980:416), these definitions have clear Christian overtones. An exploration of the concept of k'uh is beyond the scope of this chapter, but interested readers should refer to Ringle 1988; Taube 1992; Vail 1996, 2000, 2018. We suggest that, rather than embodying the concept of deity specifically, in this context the k'uh glyph (T1016c) may instead have had the reading of *k'ulel* (paralleling the Ch'olan term *ch'ulel*). In that case, the almanacs showing the

T1016c glyph are emphasizing not only the carving of deity effigies but also the association of these figures with an essence that flowed through the blood, or was perhaps concentrated in the head.

6. This has not been explicitly established, however, and further linguistic analysis is required to determine whether the two (*b'aah* and *b'ahn*) have the same underlying root.

7. *Yolia* is "heart soul" among the Aztecs and was associated with vitality, energy, and action (McKeever Furst 1995; Martínez González 2006b).

8. See the previous discussion regarding the translation of k'uh. Note also that the /k'/ in Yucatecan languages is cognate with /ch'/ in the Ch'olan language family.

9. It is worth noting that there is a reference to o'hl in the Dresden Venus table, 47b. It specifies a prognostication for a primordial time in which "the hearts of the gods were buried" (i.e., relegated to the underworld) when the Venus deity Lahun Chan shot his dart at the underworld sun in the form of the great jaguar, or Chak B'alam.

10. Epigraphers continue to debate the reading of this variant of the T533 glyph, and *b'ook* is only one of several possibilities that have been suggested.

REFERENCES CITED

Alva R., Gabriel, Josefina Bautista M., Mario Ceja M., Luis García N., Emma Limón, Miguel Angel Murillo M., José Luis del Olmo C., Carmen Maria Pijoan A., and Dolores Saavedra O.

1987 Malformaciones cráneo-faciales. *Avances en Antropología Física* 2(3):59–64.

Anders, Ferdinand

1967 *Codex Tro-Cortesianus (Codex Madrid)*. Akademische Druck- und Verlagsanstalt, Graz.

Barrera Vásquez, Alfredo, Juan Ramón Bastarrachea Manzano, William Brito Sansores, Refugio Vermont Salas, David Dzul Góngora, and Domingo Dzul Poot (editors)

1980 *Diccionario maya cordemex: maya-español, español-maya*. Ediciones Cordemex, Mérida.

Benson, Elizabeth P.

1976 Ritual Cloth and Palenque Kings. In *The Art, Iconography, and Dynastic History of Palenque*, edited by Merle Greene Robertson, pp. 45–58. Pre-Columbian Art Research Institute, Pebble Beach, California.

Bertonio, Ludovico

1984 *Vocabulario de la lengua Aymara*. Centro de Estudios de la Realidad Economica y Social; Instituto Francés de Estudios Andinos; Museo Nacional de Etnografía y Folklore, Cochabamba, Bolivia.

Boone, Elizabeth Hill

2000a Bringing Polity to Place: Aztec and Mixtec Foundation Rituals. In *Códices y documentos sobre México: Tercer Simposio Internacional*, edited by Constanza Vega Sosa, pp. 547–73. Instituto Nacional de Antropología e Historia, Mexico City.

2000b *Stories in Red and Black: Pictorial Histories of the Aztecs and Mixtecs*. University of Texas Press, Austin.

Boremanse, Didier

1998 *Hach Winik: The Lacandon Maya of Chiapas, Southern Mexico*. Institute for Mesoamerican Studies, State University of New York at Albany.

Bourdin, Gabriel

2007 *El cuerpo humano entre los mayas: una aproximación lingüística*. Universidad Autónoma de Yucatán, Mérida.

Brasseur de Bourbourg, Charles E.

1869–1870 *Manuscrit Troano: études sur le système graphique et la langue des Mayas*. Imprimerie Impériale, Paris.

Bricker, Victoria R., Eleuterio Po'ot Yah, and Ofelia Dzul de Po'ot

1998 *A Dictionary of the Maya Language as Spoken in Hocabá, Yucatán*. University of Utah Press, Salt Lake City.

Chávez Guzmán, Mónica

2006 El sol como fundamento curativo de las terapias Mayas Yucatecas en el período colonial. In *Estudios de cultura Maya*, vol. 28, edited by Maricela Ayala Falcón and Roberto Romero Sandoval, pp. 121–40. Centro de Estudios Mayas e Instituto de Investigaciones Filológicas, Universidad Nacional Autónoma de México, Mexico City.

Christenson, Allen J.

2001 *Art and Society in a Highland Maya Community: The Altarpiece of Santiago Atitlán*. University of Texas Press, Austin.

2006 Sacred Bundle Cults in Highland Guatemala. In *Sacred Bundles: Ritual Acts of Wrapping and Binding in Mesoamerica*, edited by Julia Guernsey and F. Kent Reilly III, pp. 226–46. Boundary End Archaeology Research Center, Barnardsville, North Carolina.

Comas, Juan

1966 *Manual de antropología física*. Instituto de Investigaciones Históricas, Universidad Nacional Autónoma de México, Mexico City.

1969 Algunos cráneos de la región maya. *Anales de Antropología* 6:233–48.

Cosminsky, Sheila

1982   Knowledge and Body Concepts of Guatemalan
       Midwives. In *Anthropology of Human Birth*, edited by
       Margarita Artschwager Kay, pp. 233–52. F. A. Davis,
       Philadelphia.

2001   Maya Midwives of Southern Mexico and Guatemala.
       In *Mesoamerican Healers*, edited by Brad R. Huber and
       Alan R. Sandstrom, pp. 179–210. University of Texas
       Press, Austin.

Dávalos Hurtado, Eusebio

1944   Tlatelolco a través de los tiempos: la deformación
       craneana entre los Tlatelolca. *Memorias de la Academia
       Mexicana de la Historia Correspondiente de la Real de
       Madrid* 4:111–30.

1946   Las deformaciones craneanas. In *México prehispánico:
       culturas, deidades, monumentos*, edited by Jorge A.
       Vivó, pp. 831–40. Editorial E. Hurtado, Mexico City.

1965   *Temas de antropología física*. Instituto Nacional de
       Antropología e Historia, Mexico City.

Duncan, William. N.

2009   Cranial Modification among the Maya: Absence of Ev-
       idence or Evidence of Absence? In *Bioarchaeology and
       Identity in the Americas*, edited by Kelly J. Knudson
       and Christopher M. Stojanowski, pp. 177–93. Univer-
       sity Press of Florida, Gainesville.

2011   Bioarchaeological Analysis of Sacrificial Victims from
       a Postclassic Maya Temple from Ixlú, El Petén, Guate-
       mala. *Latin American Antiquity* 22:549–72.

**Duncan, William N., Christina Elson, Charles Spencer, and
Elsa Redmond**

2009   A Human Maxilla Trophy from Oaxaca, Mexico.
       Mexicon 31:108–13.

Duncan, William N., and Charles Andrew Hofling

2011   Why the Head? Cranial Modificiation as Protection
       and Ensoulment among the Maya. *Ancient Mesoamer-
       ica* 22:190–210.

Duncan, William N., and Kevin R. Schwarz

2014   Partible, Permeable, and Relational Bodies in a Maya
       Mass Grave. In *Commingled and Disarticulated
       Human Remains: Working toward Improved Theory,
       Method, and Data*, edited by Anna Osterholtz, Kathryn
       Baustian, and Debra Martin, pp. 149–72. Springer, New
       York.

Feindel, William

1988   Cranial Clues to the Mysterious Decline of the Maya
       Civilization: The Hippocampal Hypothesis. *América
       Indígena* 48:215–19.

Fink, Ann E.

1987   Shadow and Substance: A Mopan Maya View of
       Human Existence. *Canadian Journal of Native Studies*
       7(2):399–414.

FitzSimmons, Ellen, Jack H. Proust, and Sharon Peniston

1998   Infant Head Molding: A Cultural Practice. *Archives of
       Family Medicine* 7:88–90.

Förstemann, Ernst

1880   *Die Maya Handschrift der Königlichen öffentlichen
       Bibliothek zu Dresden*. Verlag der A. Naumannschen
       Lichtdruckeret, Leipzig.

García Barrios, Ana, and Vera Tiesler

2011   El aspecto físico de los dioses mayas. *Arqueología
       Mexicana* 112:59–63.

Gates, William

1933   *The Madrid Maya Codex*. Maya Society, Baltimore.

1978   *Yucatan before and after the Conquest*, by Diego de
       Landa. Translated with notes by William Gates. Dover,
       New York.

Geller, Pamela

2012   Parting (with) the Dead: Body Partibility as Evidence
       of Commoner Ancestor Veneration. *Ancient Meso-
       america* 23:115–30.

Gossen, Gary H.

1975   Animal Souls and Human Destiny in Chamula. *Man*
       10(1):448–61.

1986   Mesoamerican Ideas as a Foundation for Regional
       Synthesis. In *Symbol and Meaning beyond the Closed
       Community: Essays in Mesoamerican Ideas*, edited
       by Gary Gossen, pp. 1–8. Institute for Mesoamerican
       Studies, State University of New York at Albany.

Greenfield, Patricia Marks

2004   *Weaving Generations Together: Evolving Creativity in
       the Maya of Chiapas*. School of American Research
       Press, Santa Fe.

Groark, Kevin Patrick

2005   Pathogenic Emotions: Sentiment, Sociality, and
       Sickness among the Tzotzil Maya of San Juan Cham-
       ula, Chiapas, Mexico. Unpublished PhD dissertation,
       Department of Anthropology, University of California,
       Los Angeles.

Grube, Nikolai, and Werner Nahm

1994   A Census of Xibalba: A Complete Inventory of *Way*
       Characters on Maya Ceramics. In *The Maya Vase
       Book: A Corpus of Rollout Photographs of Maya Vases*,
       vol. 4, edited by Justin Kerr, pp. 686–715. Kerr Associ-
       ates, New York.

Guiteras Holmes, Calixta
1961 *Perils of the Soul: The World View of a Tzotzil Indian.* Free Press of Glencoe, New York.

Helmke, Christophe, and Jesper Nielsen
2009 Hidden Identity and Power in Ancient Mesoamerica: Supernatural Alter Egos as Personified Diseases. *Acta Americana* 17(2):49–98.

Houston, Stephen, and Tom Cummins
2004 Body, Presence, and Space in Andean and Mesoamerican Rulership. In *Palaces of the Ancient New World*, edited by Susan T. Evans and Joanne Pillsbury, pp. 359–98. Dumbarton Oaks, Washington, DC.

Houston, Stephen, and David Stuart
1998 The Ancient Maya Self: Personhood and Portraiture in the Classic Period. *RES: Anthropology and Aesthetics* 33:73–101.

Houston, Stephen, David Stuart, and Karl Taube
2006 *The Memory of Bones: Body, Being, and Experience among the Classic Maya.* University of Texas Press, Austin.

Joyce, Rosemary A.
2000 Heirlooms and Houses: Materiality and Social Memory. In *Beyond Kinship: Social and Material Reproduction in House Societies*, edited by Rosemary A. Joyce and Susan D. Gillespie, pp. 145–50. University of Pennsylvania Press, Philadelphia.

Klein, Cecelia
1982 Woven Heaven, Tangled Earth: A Weaver's Paradigm of the Mesoamerican Cosmos; Ethnoastronomy and Archaeoastronomy in the American Tropics. *Annals of the New York Academy of Science* 385:1–35.

Laughlin, Robert M.
1975 *The Great Tzotil Dictionary of San Lorenzo Zinacantán.* Smithsonian Institution Press, Washington, DC.

Looper, Matthew G.
2006 Fabric Structures in Classic Maya Art and Ritual. In *Sacred Bundles: Ritual Acts of Wrapping and Binding in Mesoamerica*, edited by Julia Guernsey and F. Kent Reilly III, pp. 80–104. Boundary End Archaeology Research Center, Barnardsville, North Carolina.

López Austin, Alfredo
1988 *The Human Body and Ideology: Concepts of the Ancient Nahuas.* 2 vols. Translated by Thelma Ortiz de Montellano and Bernard Ortiz de Montellano. University of Utah Press, Salt Lake City.

Martínez González, Roberto
2006a El tonalli y el calor vital entre los nahuas: algunas precisiones. *Anales de Antropología* 40(2):117–52.

2006b El ihiyotl, la sombra y las almas-aliento en Mesoamérica. *Cuicuilco* 13(38):177–99.

2007 Las entidades anímicas en el pensamiento Maya. *Estudios de Cultura Maya* 30:153–74.

2011 *El nahualismo.* Universidad Nacional Autónoma de México, Mexico City.

McGee, R. Jon
1990 *Life, Ritual, and Religion among the Lacandó Maya.* Wadsworth, Belmont, California.

McKeever Furst, Jill Leslie
1995 *The Natural History of the Soul in Ancient Mexico.* Yale University Press, New Haven, Connecticut.

Megged, Amos
2010 *Social Memory in Ancient and Colonial Mesoamerica.* Cambridge University Press, New York.

Miller, Arthur G.
1982 Cycles of Cult: An Iconology of the Tulum Mural Tradition. In *On the Edge of the Sea: Mural Painting at Tancah-Tulum, Quintana Roo, Mexico*, pp. 86–98. Dumbarton Oaks, Washington, DC.

Paul, Lois
1974 The Mastery of Work and the Mystery of Sex in a Guatemalan Village. In *Woman, Culture, and Society: A Theoretical Overview*, edited by Michelle Zimbalist Rosaldo and Louise Lamphere, pp. 281–300. Stanford University Press, Stanford, California.

Peña Gomez, Rosa M., and Luis A. Lopez Wario
1989 Un cráneo deformado del preclásico de Ecatepec, Estado de Mexico. *Estudios de Antropología Biológica* 4:609–16.

Pitarch, Pedro
2010 *The Jaguar and the Priest: An Ethnography of Tzeltal Souls.* University of Texas Press, Austin.

Pohl, John M.
1994 *The Politics of Symbolism in the Mixtec Codices.* Vanderbilt University Publications in Anthropology, Nashville.

Prechtel, Martin, and Robert S. Carlsen
1988 Weaving and Cosmos amongst the Tzutujil Maya of Guatemala. *RES: Anthropology and Aesthetics* 15:122–32.

Proskouriakoff, Tatiana
1963 Historical Data in the Inscriptions of Yaxchilan Part I. *Estudios de Cultura Maya* 3:149–67.

Reents-Budet, Dorie
1994 *Painting the Maya Universe: Royal Ceramics of the Classic Period.* Duke University Press, Durham, North Carolina.

2006 Material in Ancient Mesoamerica: The Roles of Cloth

among the Classic Maya. In *Sacred Bundles: Ritual Acts of Wrapping and Binding in Mesoamerica*, edited by Julia Guernsey and F. Kent Reilly III, pp. 105–26. Boundary End Archaeology Research Center, Barnardsville, North Carolina.

Reilly, F. Kent, III

2006   Middle Formative Origins of the Mesoamerican Ritual Act of Bundling. In *Sacred Bundles: Ritual Acts of Wrapping and Binding in Mesoamerica*, edited by Julia Guernsey and F. Kent Reilly III, pp. 1–21. Boundary End Archaeology Research Center, Barnardsville, North Carolina.

Rice, Prudence M.

2004   *Maya Political Science: Time, Astronomy, and the Cosmos*. University of Texas Press, Austin.

2007   *Maya Calendar Origins: Monuments, Mythistory, and the Materialization of Time*. University of Texas Press, Austin.

Ringle, William

1988   Of Mice and Monkeys: The Value and Meaning of T1016c, the God C Hieroglyph. Research Reports on Ancient Maya Writing, no. 18. Center for Maya Research, Washington, DC.

Romano Pacheco, Arturo

1972   Deformación craneana en Tlatilco, México. In *Religión en Mesoamérica*, edited by Jaime Litvak and Noemí Castillo, pp. 415–19. 12 Mesa Redonda de la Sociedad Mexicana de Antropología, Mexico City.

1973a   Deformación cefálica intencional en la población prehispánica de Cholula, Puebla. *Comunicaciones Proyecto Puebla-Tlaxcala* 8:49–50.

1973b   Los cráneos deformados de Zapotal I, Veracruz. In *Balance y Perspectivas de la Antropología de Mesoamérica y Norte de México*, pp. 57–64. 13 Mesa Redonda de la Sociedad Mexicana de Antropología, Mexico City.

1974   Deformación cefálica intencional. In *Antropología física: época prehispánica 3*, edited by Javier Romero Molina, pp. 195–227. Colección México, Panorama Histórico y Cultural, Instituto Nacional de Antropología e Historia, Mexico City.

Stross, Brian

1998   Seven Ingredients in Mesoamerican Ensoulment: Dedication and Termination in Tenejapa. In *The Sowing and the Dawning: Termination, Dedication, and Transformation in the Archaeological and Ethnographic Record of Mesoamerica*, edited by Shirley B. Mock, pp. 31–40. University of New Mexico Press, Albuquerque.

Stuart, David

1995   *A Study of Maya Inscriptions*. PhD dissertation, Department of Anthropology, Vanderbilt University, Nashville.

1996   A Consideration of Stelae in Ancient Maya Ritual and Representation. *RES: Anthropology and Aesthetics* 29–30:148–71.

Taube, Karl A.

1992   *The Major Gods of Ancient Yucatan*. Studies in Pre-Columbian Art and Archaeology, no. 32. Dumbarton Oaks, Washington, DC.

2004   Flower Mountain: Concepts of Life, Beauty, and Paradise among the Classic Maya. *RES: Anthropology and Aesthetics* 45:69–98.

2005   The Symbolism of Jade in Classic Maya Religion. *Ancient Mesoamerica* 16(1):23–50.

Tiesler, Vera

1998   *La costumbre de la deformación cefálica entre los antiguos mayas: aspectos morfológicos y culturales*. Instituto Nacional de Antropología e Historia, Mexico City.

2012a   Studying Cranial Vault Modifications in Ancient Mesoamerica. *Journal of Anthropological Sciences* 90:1–26.

2012b   *Transformarse en maya: el modelado cefálico entre los maya prehispánicos y coloniales*. Universidad Autónoma de Yucatán, Mérida; Universidad Nacional Autónoma de México, Mexico City.

2014   *The Bioarchaeology of Artificial Cranial Modifications: New Approaches to Head Shaping and Its Meanings in Pre-Columbian Mesoamerica and Beyond*. Springer, New York.

Tiesler, Vera, and Iván Oliva Arias

2010   Identity, Alienation, and Integration: Body Modifications in the Early Colonial Population from Campeche. In *Natives, Europeans, and Africans in Colonial Campeche: History and Archaeology*, edited by Vera Tiesler, Pilar Zabala, and Andrea Cucina, pp. 130–51. University Press of Florida, Gainesville.

Tiesler, Vera, and Pilar Zabala

2011   El modelado artificial de la cabeza durante la colonia: una tradición maya en el espejo de las fuentes históricas. *Estudios de Cultura Maya* 37:77–96.

Tozzer, Alfred M.

1941   *Landa's "Relación de las Cosas de Yucatán."* Peabody Museum, Harvard University, Cambridge, Massachusetts.

Vail, Gabrielle

1996 *The Gods in the Madrid Codex: An Iconographic and Glyphic Analysis.* PhD dissertation, Department of Anthropology, Tulane University, New Orleans.

2000 Pre-Hispanic Maya Religion: Conceptions of Divinity in the Postclassic Maya Codices. *Ancient Mesoamerica* 11:123–47.

2005 Renewal Ceremonies in the Madrid Codex. In *Painted Books and Indigenous Knowledge in Mesoamerica: Manuscript Studies in Honor of Mary Elizabeth Smith,* edited by Elizabeth Hill Boone, pp. 179–209. Middle American Research Institute, Tulane University, New Orleans.

2018 Transformations of Indigenous Yucatec Conceptions of k'uh. In *Restructuring the Universe: How the Conquest Changed Mesoamerican Cosmology,* edited by Ana Guadalupe Díaz and Jesper Nielsen. University Press of Colorado, Boulder.

Vail, Gabrielle, and Christine Hernández

2013 *Re-Creating Primordial Time: Foundation Rituals and Mythology in the Postclassic Maya Codices.* University Press of Colorado, Boulder.

Velásquez García, Erik

2011 Las entidades y las fuerzas anímicas en la cosmovisión maya clásica. In *Los mayas: voces de piedra,* edited by Alejandra Martínez de Velasco Cortina and María Elena Vega Villalobos, pp. 235–54. Editorial Ámbar, Universidad Nacional Autónoma de México, Mexico City.

Vogt, Evan Z.

1969 *Zinacantan: A Maya Community in the Highlands of Chiapas.* Belknap Press of Harvard University Press, Cambridge, Massachusetts.

1992 *Tortillas for the Gods: A Symbolic Analysis of Zinacanteco Rituals.* University of Oklahoma Press, Norman.

Wagner, Elisabeth

2006 White Earth Bundles: The Symbolic Sealing and Burial of Buildings among the Ancient Maya. In *Acta Mesoamericana.* Vol. 16, *Jaws of the Underworld: Life, Death, and Rebirth among the Ancient Maya,* edited by Pierre R. Colas, Geneviève Le Fort, and Bodil Liljefors Persson, pp. 55–70. Verlag Anton Saurwein, Markt Schwaben, Germany.

Watanabe, John

1992 *Maya Saints and Souls in a Changing World.* University of Texas Press, Austin.

Wisdom, Charles

1940 *The Chorti Indians of Guatemala.* University of Chicago Press, Chicago.

3

Head Shapes and Group Identity on the Fringes of the Maya Lowlands

VERA TIESLER AND ALFONSO LACADENA

INTRODUCTION

One of the central themes of this volume speaks to the ostensive display of artificially produced head forms. The highly visible nature of culturally formed heads renders this subject particularly suitable for exploring social interaction and the display of identity within or among groups. Head forms may publicly signal gender and personhood, sociopolitical inferiority or superiority, or group adherence or contrariety. This is especially true for Mesoamerica, with its head-anchored weltanschauung (see Dembo and Imbelloni 1938 or Dingwall 1931 for a review across traditional and past world cultures). Beyond the backdrop of the undeniable diversity in practice and its surrounding local lore, several body concepts and treatments—such as precisely cranial modification (Tiesler 2014)—appear to have been shared among the majority of the natives who lived across its landscapes.[1]

Such were the Maya who settled the lowland kingdoms during the first millennium CE. They are known for the personal cult afforded by and to their aristocratic upper crust and that went hand in hand with physical enhancement. Exhibited in public, noble bodies usually appeared exquisitely adorned, garbed in jewels and laden with individualized symbols of personhood, distinction, and divine epitomes (Houston and Cummins 2004; Houston and Stuart 1998; Houston et al. 2006; Houston and Taube 2000; Velásquez García 2015). Beneath the upper crust, how-

ever, most forms of permanent body enhancement were performed across the social and cultural spheres. Some forms of physical embodiment were hidden or displayed discreetly, others were more obvious, and still others seem to our eyes blunt and gaudy (McCafferty and McCafferty 2011). Among the Classic-period Maya, common forms of body enhancement range from headgear to facial paints, from tattoos to scarifications and dental works, as well as diverse head shaping procedures in infants (see also Miller [chapter 8], Scherer [chapter 4], and Vázquez de Ágredos et al. [chapter 6] of this volume). The latter led to varied head forms within and across the cultural landscapes that subscribe linguistically to the Maya sphere (Tiesler 2014). While head broadening and shortening was predominantly displayed among Maya highlanders and the trader communities that lined the eastern shores of the Yucatecan peninsula, the wide corridors toward the low and middle watershed of the Usumacinta River staged a clear predilection for elongated and reclined head morphologies (see also Scherer, chapter 4 of this volume).

This chapter focuses on head display and correlated cultural dynamics across the Maya lowlands and its surrounding territories during the Classic period. This data-rich study arena is privileged because it allows the researcher to confront a host of different academic approximations, namely (bio)archaeological research (as reconstructed from the cranial record of settlement populations) and studies of different discursive media. The ancient portraits stand out in particular for their detailed, realistic rendering of the physical attributes of people. In this regard, ancient Maya artistic conventions stand leagues apart from those of most other parts of Native America, including most of Mesoamerica itself, where the absence or scarcity of pre-Hispanic written sources and the idiosyncrasies of iconographic conventions limit any further comparative explorations.

Our present incursions into the subject are precisely fostered by the confrontation between cranial and discursive information and still other, more conventional venues such as (ethno)history and archaeology. The combination of these approaches is designed to enrich the current debate regarding the roles of head forms among the Classic-period Maya in forging identity and ethnicity. For our purposes, the term "ethnicity" denotes specific forms of group cohesion and population affiliations, which usually go along with self-identification in opposition to "others." An ethnic group's members identify with each other, usually on the foundations of a common genealogy and ancestry, which may be presumed or real. Other historical ties are founded on a common language, religion, or myth (Barth 1969; see also Díaz-Andreu et al. 2005; Jones 1997). Members of groups that hold an affinity of this type tend to identify with each other and express their adherence through common cultural practices, glosses, and ideological beliefs, sometimes in confrontation with others. Albeit under debate and spurious in its grasp, this definition of "ethnicity" resonates well with discursive inquiries on physical embodiment and lends itself to further explorations of long-standing cultural tradition and change in a state-level society with scripts and imagery, such as the Classic-period Maya kingdoms.

ANCIENT MAYA CRANIAL MODIFICATIONS

Just like most other Native American peoples, ancient Maya families treated the heads of their newborns, babies, and toddlers in a host of temporary or permanent ways. Here, cranial vault modifications describe a deeply embedded Native tradition that harks back to thousands of years of practice. The archaeological record of cranial remains gives testimony to its antiquity, with the earliest modified skulls dated to the Early to Middle Preclassic periods (Saul 1972). Throughout the different eras, ancient Maya head practices appear to have subscribed to and

reflected a unified yet evolving system of beliefs about the cosmos, the individual, and the body. These ideas were materialized in different contexts of cultural display, straddling both public and private domains (Tiesler 2010, 2011, 2012; Tiesler and Zabala 2011; see also Duncan and Vail [chapter 2] and Scherer [chapter 4] of this volume). Far from the more ephemeral fads of dress, hair arrangements, or body paint (see Miller [chapter 8] and Vázquez de Ágredos et al. [chapter 6] of this volume), infant head shaping is more permanent and therefore carries a more conservative quality. Its enactment (although not necessarily its display) subscribed in all likelihood to the world of women and female cultural reproduction, especially if we believe in the ethnohistorical accounts of Native head practices and in pre-Hispanic portraiture with copious examples of paired mother-child figurines representing compression devices in place (Tiesler 2014; Zabala 2014).

Cranial manipulation was generally begun following birth. These procedures were initiated within the domestic confines of households and usually lasted for weeks, months, and sometimes years. The molding of the little one was thought of as an effective protective measure against harm and thus prepared the baby or toddler for later social integration and for becoming properly a "person." In the course of the procedure's daily enactment, female kin took recourse to compression, swaddling, bandaging, or head massaging until the change had become permanent and the fontanels had "dried" (Duncan and Hofling 2011; Tiesler 2014; Duncan and Vail, chapter 2 of this volume) (fig. 3.1). Postcontact Yucatecans still referred to this process as *up' k'abtah*, which translates as "straightening out the head of the newborn in order to mend or to adapt it" (Barrera Vásquez 1980:901).

Head Forms as Visible Adscription

The long-term behavioral motives for head compression are apparent in the continuity of this practice over the millennia in the Maya lowlands and beyond. However, these motivations do not account by themselves for the variability among those head forms that both iconography and craniology materialize across their cultural cartographies, especially those seen before the Maya collapse. A systematic survey of other works by Vera Tiesler (2012, 2014) reveals a kaleidoscope of elongated, inclined, heightened, shortened, and broadened cranial profiles for these territories.

This chapter is focused on the Classic-period lowland

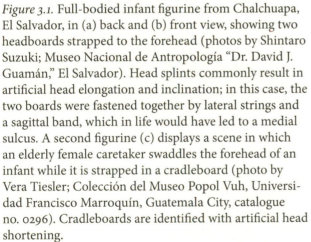

Figure 3.1. Full-bodied infant figurine from Chalchuapa, El Salvador, in (a) back and (b) front view, showing two headboards strapped to the forehead (photos by Shintaro Suzuki; Museo Nacional de Antropología "Dr. David J. Guamán," El Salvador). Head splints commonly result in artificial head elongation and inclination; in this case, the two boards were fastened together by lateral strings and a sagittal band, which in life would have led to a medial sulcus. A second figurine (c) displays a scene in which an elderly female caretaker swaddles the forehead of an infant while it is strapped in a cradleboard (photo by Vera Tiesler; Colección del Museo Popol Vuh, Universidad Francisco Marroquín, Guatemala City, catalogue no. 0296). Cradleboards are identified with artificial head shortening.

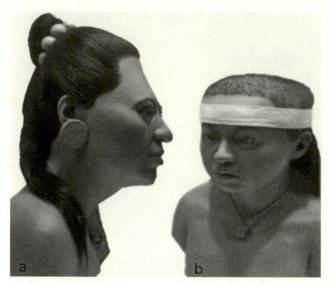

Figure 3.2. Three-dimensional facial reconstructions of (a) a Maya female with an elongated, reclined, and artificially narrowed neurocranium; and (b) a child from Chichén Itzá with a tabular erect head shape from cradling during infancy. Note the top-flattened aspect in this case (photos by Shintaro Suzuki, Gran Museo de la Cultura Maya, Mérida).

Maya, for whom we propose that the regional variation in head shapes must have expressed differences in individual identity and, more so, deeper gaps in group affiliation (fig. 3.2). The pantheon of divine entities themselves may have provided divine blueprints for the variation in head silhouettes across large segments of Mesoamerica, including the Maya (García Barrios and Tiesler 2011; Houston et al. 2006; Taube 2003; Tiesler 2010, 2012, 2014, 2015a; see also Scherer, chapter 4 of this volume). Classic-period anthropomorphic portraits tend to represent young deities, like the maize god, with a receding forehead and an elongated skull (Taube 2003). Some authors have also proposed that the reclined head resembles a jaguar's head (Sotelo and Valverde 1992). Conversely, the old deities, like Chaahk and God L, are depicted with shortened heads. Underworld creatures such as God A and God N are among the few to be depicted occasionally with a rounded, unflattened occiput (García Barrios and Tiesler 2011). Some of the variation we see in cranial modifications may originate from familial or other identification with a particular deity by the practitioners. This connection has been specifically proposed for the Maya maize god (Houston et al. 2006; Taube 2003). When in anthropomorphic guise, this deity is shown with an inclined, strongly elongated head profile, whereas the old Merchand deities are

often rendered with a top-flattened *capitum* (García Barrios and Tiesler 2011).

Despite the patent sacred emulations, studies of large local and regional cranial series have not been able to demonstrate any differences according to biological sex or social status, even among those populations that have exhibited varied head forms (Tiesler 2012). In other words, despite the diversity in looks, male and female babies were most likely granted equivalent artificial morphologies, and nobles showed similar head styles to those that were common within their given town or region. There are two potential explanations for this apparently egalitarian distribution of head shapes. First, head forms were conferred by second- or third-generation female caretakers on all newborns regardless of biological sex. This means that, regardless of the sex of the person whose head has been modified, in all likelihood the modification was done by women. Second, cranial modification was initiated when the individual was still viewed as "ungendered," a "non-person" that had to be prepared for social integration. It occurred before proper social identity had been formed and therefore could not reflect differences in social status or gender, which would only be delineated when the infant grew into childhood (Cervera 2007; Tiesler 2011). In fact, head shaping was only one of several preparatory steps that allowed a child to be transformed into a social being. Communal integration usually was consecrated with specific rites at later stages of childhood, such as name-giving ceremonies, haircuts, and initiation rituals (as described by Scherer in chapter 4 of this volume).

But if not motivated by gender or social status, what were the distinct roles of head display among the Classic-period Maya? The relationship between head shaping and collective group identity—sometimes permeated with ethnic undercurrents—becomes evident once we incorporate data from verified multicultural settlement populations outside the Classic-period heartlands. One example is the ancient borderland capital of Copán, Honduras (with N = 478 scored individuals; Tiesler 2014:215–19), for example. Its urban core population sported predominantly reclined foreheads and an elongated vault. This look distinguished them visibly from the broadened, artificially shortened head features that predominated on the peripheries of the Copán pocket. In an analogous fashion, the coastal settlers of Xcambó (N = 371) demonstrated an ever increasing diversity in head forms and shaping practices toward the Late Classic (Tiesler 2014:219–24). This was a trading port and salt production center with growing trade networks along the Yucatecan coastline and beyond the Maya area itself. In this context, the diversification in head morphologies could be explained by an influx of people from other areas, as has been demonstrated isotopically (Price et al. 2014; Sierra Sosa et al. 2014; Tiesler and Cucina 2010).

Maya Head Shapes and Constructed Beauty

A convenient proxy for exploring culturally modified skulls is the taxonomy of cranial vault forms, which has been previously adjusted to fit Mesoamerican skeletal populations. Note that all of the specific shapes presented in figure 3.3 bear flattened areas from using different hard compression devices. Cradleboard use would result in a short and broad head morphology in the adult (when not combined with tight horizontal wraps), a form coined "tabular erect" by José Imbelloni (Dembo and Imbelloni 1938; see also Romano Pacheco 1965 and Tiesler 2012, 2014 regarding Mesoamerican visual typologies; see compression devices and outcomes in figs. 3.1c, 3.2b, and 3.3b). Conversely, head splinting with free boards (see

compression devices and outcomes in figs. 3.1a, 3.1b, 3.2a, and 3.3a) would eventually lead to an elongated cranial shape with a characteristic backward inclination (tabular oblique type). These compression kits were also either combined or complemented with head massages or tight wraps. When combined with circular wraps, the splinted head would have acquired an almost tubular form that would pull back dramatically the hairline of the flattened and narrow forehead.

Apart from adapting neurocranial morphology, severe head wrapping and splinting caused the face to grow forward and outward (Tiesler 2014:46–48) (fig. 3.2a). Facial features that are secondary to prolonged compression include mid-face prognathism, manifested by a prominent nose, lips, and cheekbones. Sometimes the positioning of the tablets or the outward push of the splinting process would obliterate the notch of the nasal root beneath the eyebrows. Thus the nose would appear visibly emerging directly from beneath the forehead. Apart from the shifts in head morphology, comfortable head posture also shifted. The redistribution of cranial and cephalic weight along with an increased (tendentially pithecoid) inclination of

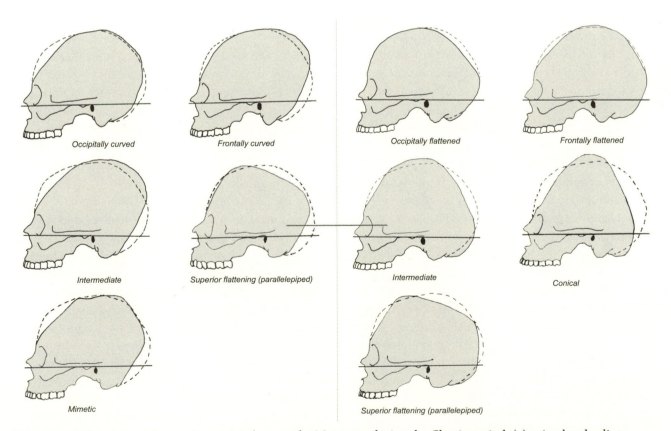

Figure 3.3. Different head shapes documented across the Maya area during the Classic period, (a) using head splints (tabular oblique shapes) and (b) using cradle devices (tabular erect shapes) (adapted from Tiesler 2012, 2014).

the basicranium would result in a manner of walking with the head "held high," causing head-elongated individuals to look down under half-closed eyelids. These capital features, namely head reclination and an outthrusting face with half-closed eyelids, provided blueprints for Native portraiture in turn. They probably signaled desirable traits as visible markers of culturally constructed beauty (Sánchez 2008; Tiesler 2014:48).

Head Forms on the Periphery of the Maya Territories

On a regional scale, the cultural fringes fronting non-Maya Mixe Zoque territories to the west and Highlands K'iche' settlements to the south exhibit geographic shifts in head modeling during the first millennium CE in this sphere's skeletal record, although this relationship is not entirely straightforward, as most of the burial series are heavily biased toward the Late and Terminal Classic with the majority of individuals dating to the second half of the first millennium CE. One other limitation in using "heads-as-pots" from the mortuary record to determine local identity involves the high degree of population mobility during the Classic period, as has been confirmed by isotopic research (Price et al. 2014; Sierra Sosa et al. 2014). This is especially relevant for assigning local signatures to culturally conferred head forms. As the locally shaped infant grew up, he or she would often move to another location near or far, thereby importing "foreign" head traditions into the receiving community.

Despite its shortfalls, a regional survey of lowland heads-turned-skulls confirms the diversity in head shaping practices and their morphological results across the central and eastern Maya lowlands (plate 5). This variety stands in contrast to the more uniform head looks among the western Maya settlers who were to occupy the lands along and across the banks of the Usumacinta River (fig. 3.4) (see also Scherer, chapter 4 of this volume). The great majority of western Maya folk treated the heads of their offspring with head splints and tight circular wraps and worked them into narrow, tubular, strongly reclined shapes. This look characterizes the cranial morphology of adults and infants alike, as the burial populations from Palenque, Piedras Negras, and Chinikihá demonstrate (Montes de Paz 2000; Nuñez 2009, 2010; Scherer 2006, 2007, 2008, 2015; Scherer et al. 1999; Scherer and Wright 2001; Tiesler 2014; Wright 1997; Wright and Witte 1998) (fig. 3.5a). Note that the idea that "cultural separation

meets distinctions in head form" also finds support in less obvious cultural expressions such as the conventions of nasal rendering in portraiture, the geographic distribution of which follows roughly the same patterns as cranial modification (Kettunen 2005:182–86).

Upstream, the Usumacinta River receives the waters of the Río de la Pasión. The watershed of this tributary once provided fertile grounds for a number of Preclassic and Classic Maya settlements, like Altar de Sacrificios and Seibal, with Cancuén as a direct economic gateway to the Maya Highlands further south and up into the mountains (Forné et al. 2009; Sharer and Traxler 2006b). The people who lived in the Río de la Pasión basin also sported prominently narrow, inclined, and elongated heads, although the morphological change appears less pronounced overall than among the populations who lived downstream (Quintanilla 2013; Saul 1972; Tiesler 2014) (fig. 3.5b).

The reclined head shapes along the lowland southern fringes, once again, visibly stand out against the collective head looks in the highland mountains further west and south. The Guatemaltecan highlanders were already predominantly short headed through the Classic period (fig. 3.5c). This trend is evident, for example, in the Classic-era population of Kaminaljuyú, or Nebaj in today's El Quiché department (Tiesler 2014; see also Gervais 1989). Individuals from the adjacent highland town of Acul display tabular erect forms in their intermediate variants or show a predominant lambdoid plane. T. Dale Stewart (1953:296–97) similarly notes the strong predominance of erect forms among skulls from Classic-period Zaculeu in the Maya mountain area (dated to the Atzan and Chinaq phases).

As previously highlighted for different areas outside the expanding, then contracting, lowland networks, Maya bearers of reclined and pseudo-circular cephalic shapes must have stood out among their peers along the borderlands. The strongly reclined and tubular head profiles of Palenque's locals (and the similarly elongated heads of their neighboring settlers along the Usumacinta River) must have been an especially conspicuous sight for bearers of short, broad heads, settlers coming from the rugged and mountainous terrain toward the Grijalva River basin outside the familiar territory of the lowland Maya, starting with sites like Toniná and extending to others further west such as Chiapa de Corzo. Here, only purely tabular erect head morphologies have been documented in Classic-period series (Tiesler 2010) (fig. 3.5d).

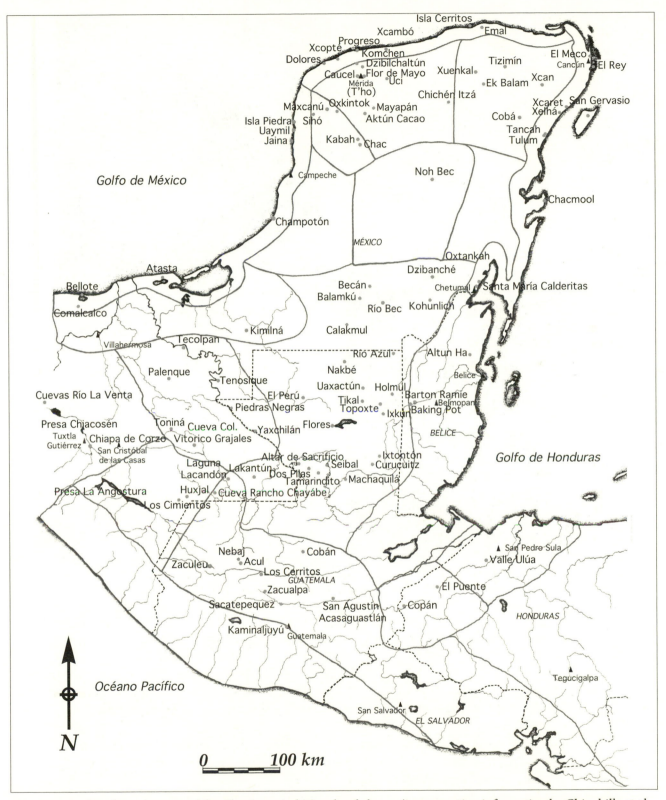

Figure 3.4. Archaeology sites scored for Classic-period Maya head shapes (incorporating information by Chinchilla et al. 2015; Coe 1959; Gómez 1999; Haviland and Moholy-Nagy 1992; Juan Pedro Laporte, personal communication, 2008; Laporte 2005; Nuñez 2009, 2010; Quintanilla 2013; Scherer 2015; Scherer and Wright 2001; Scherer et al. 1999; Stewart 1953; Tiesler 1999, 2012, 2014, 2015b; Tovalín et al. 1998; Wright 1997; Wright and Witte 1998; see also a regional synopsis in Tiesler 2012:129–31).

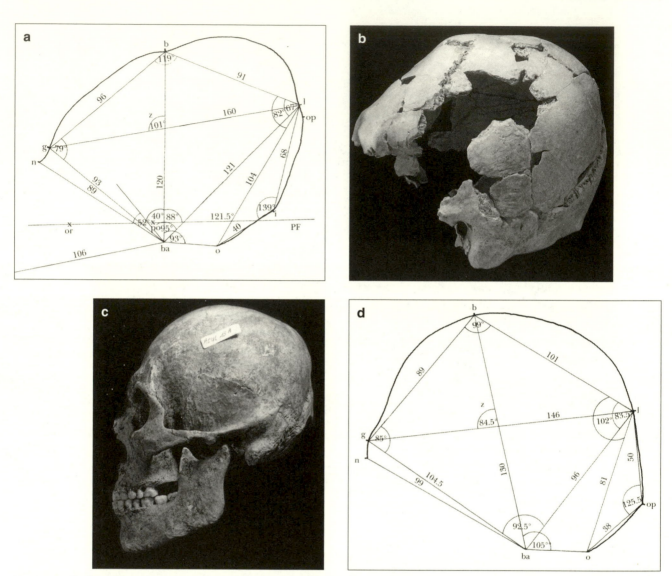

Figure 3.5. Skull profiles of (a) Burial 5(14)-IV from the Cross Group of Palenque, Mexico (Dirección de Antropología Física, Instituto Nacional de Antropología e Historia); (b) reclined burial profile of Burial 4-8 of Seibal, Guatemala (photo by Vera Tiesler, 968-38-20/N9876.2), Peabody Museum of Archaeology and Ethnography, Harvard Museum, © 2018 President and Fellows of Harvard College; (c) Burial 27 of Acul/Nebaj, Guatemala (Centro de Estudios Mexicanos y Centroamericanos, Instituto de Antropología e Historia); and (d) Burial 6(3) of Toniná, Mexico (photos and tracings by Vera Tiesler).

HEAD SILHOUETTES AND ETHNICITY IN DISCURSIVE MEDIA

Considering the shifts and frictions that persisted during the second half of the first millennium CE, a survey of the cranial records invites questions on possibly deeper cultural divergences beyond the head looks around the fringes of the lowland Maya territories. To this end, we will compare the regional distributions of head shapes in the portraiture and vernacular language divides, an approach that seems feasible considering the diversity

and extent of the shifting cultural geography found in the Maya lowlands during the Classic period.

Head Silhouettes and Spoken-Language Divides during the Classic Era

One of the hallmarks of cultural identity is a group's spoken language, which we will explore here among the lowland Southern Maya, comparing the distribution of vernaculars with the geographic divides of collectively reproduced head shapes. Now that the Maya hieroglyphic language has been substantially deciphered (Coe 1992; Houston 2000; Stuart 1987) and subsequent studies have unraveled the grammar of Native texts, it appears likely that the great majority of hieroglyphic inscriptions were written in a language affiliated to Eastern Ch'olan (Houston et al. 2000). This language functioned as a prestigious language for inscriptions, similar to the Akkadian used in the ancient Near East, the Latin written down by medieval scribes, or the French habitually used by the European aristocracy. Despite the apparent linguistic uniformity of the written corpus, however, other tongues coexisted in the Maya lowlands that were quite different from the prestigious Eastern Ch'olan language. Especially relevant for this study is the fact that some of these spoken languages have been documented in the Classic-period inscriptions themselves. They either appear as distinct languages in those inscriptions intended for local use, or permeate, in the form of vernacular inflections, other local inscriptions drafted in the prestigious official language. Although subliminal, these linguistic inflections lay bare the true tongue of their author and therefore the scribe's ethnic heritage. Note that each of these regionally spoken languages is related glottochronologically to Mayan languages that are still in use today. When spoken during the first millennium CE, these tongues diverged openly from the official language not only in phonology but in morphology and syntax (Lacadena 2000; Lacadena and Wichmann 2002, 2005; see also Gronemeyer 2014a, 2014b).

As we map the dialectal isoglosses inscribed on monuments across the Maya area, a coherently dialectal geography emerges that discerns the spoken language distribution across the Maya lowlands during the Classic period (plate 6). This linguistic cartography identifies the territories where Eastern Ch'olan (a precursor to modern Choltí and Ch'orti') was not only written but spoken collectively. This area corresponds to the immense corridor in the eastern half of the Maya lowlands, including large parts of the Petén basin and the basins of the Pasión and Motagua Rivers, and northward into the southern part of the Mexican state of Quintana Roo. Its regional extension skirts a second dialectal area identified with Western Ch'olan (a precursor to modern Chontal and Ch'ol), which was spoken in the Western Petén and along all of the Usumacinta basin. To the west, these Western Ch'olan speakers fronted a third dialectic zone, identified with the Tzeltalan language (affiliated with modern Tzeltal and Tzotzil). Tzeltalan was in use among the settlers in and around Toniná and was also heard in the Chiapenec

Highlands of Mexico toward Comitán. Finally, a fourth dialectal zone, identified with Yucatecan (a forerunner of Yucatec, Lacandon, Itzaj, and modern Mopan), was spoken by the settlers of the northern part of Yucatán.[2]

Noteworthy although perhaps unsurprising are the emerging patterns we detect when we compare the geographic distribution of head shapes and their carriers' language. These overlap and match to a certain degree. As a comparison of the maps shown in plates 5 and 6 show, differences in spoken language and collective preference in cranial form demarcate a geographic boundary along the Chiapas foothills. This was the cultural divide between the isthmian Mixe Zoque language groups and the Ch'olan (Usumacinta) and Chontal dialects that were heard in the coastal plains toward Tabasco and Veracruz (plate 6) (Justeson et al. 1985:68–70; Lacadena and Wichmann 2002, 2005; Mora Marín et al. 2009; Pallán 2009). This Mesoamerican corridor has always been an important intersection of different peoples with different cultural backgrounds, of different political domains and trade networks, a melting pot that we know gained prominence during the second half of the Classic period (Vargas 2001; Wyllie 2002).

Interestingly, the linguistic demarcation between Maya and non-Maya language territories roughly follows the regionally distinct preferences in head shapes, adding an important "ethnic" statement to cephalic modification and a potential for tracing population and sociocultural dynamics that at one time grounded the split in head looks. For instance, while narrow, inclined, and elongated heads are prominently displayed among the Western Ch'olan Maya of the Usumacinta basin, most of the bordering Tzeltalan Maya and Zoquean non-Maya populations on and beyond the western fringes of the Maya region sported visibly broader and shortened heads, some of them even bilobular (by dividing the two parietal lobes with a sagittal strap right in the middle of the head). Likewise, the Southern Maya highlanders of Nebaj and Acul were probably speakers of a K'iche'an language at that time. Also, these settlers exhibited broad and shortened heads, as outlined above (and in table 3.1).

Tracing Western Head Styles in Portraiture and Political Display

Differences in cranial morphology among the speakers of different Maya and non-Maya tongues must have been most obvious in and beyond the Usumacinta corridor. In

TABLE 3.1. FREQUENCY OF ARTIFICIAL CRANIAL VAULT MODIFICATIONS IN DIFFERENT AREAS OF THE CLASSIC-PERIOD CENTRAL LOWLANDS (ALL RESULTS BELOW N=10 WERE SCORED AS "NO DATA")

	EARLY CLASSIC [%]	LATE CLASSIC [%]	TERMINAL CLASSIC [%]	CLASSIC (GENERAL) [%]
Middle and Lower Usumacinta Basin				
Frequency [%]	Not identified [N=1]	93.0 [N=43]	Not identified [N=0]	95.1 [N=74]
Frequency of circular wrap	Not identified [N=0]	70.4 [N=27]	Not identified [N=0]	67.9 [N=28]
Frequency of sagittal groove	Not identified [N=0]	13.6 [N=22]	Not identified [N=0]	13.0 [N=23]
Tabular oblique/erect	Not identified [N=0]	84.8 [N=33]	Not identified [N=0]	85.3 [N=262]
Average degree of modification [0–4]*	Not identified [N=0]	2.43 [N=26]	Not identified [N=0]	2.37 [N=27]
Northern Lowlands				
Frequency [%]	Not identified [N=8]	89.5 [N=38]	100 [N=26]	94.5 [N=91]
Frequency of circular wrap	Not identified [N=2]	28.6 [N=14]	41.7 [N=12]	30.6 [N=36]
Frequency of sagittal groove	Not identified [N=2]	31.3 [N=16]	27.3 [N=11]	25.6 [N=39]
Tabular oblique/erect	Not identified [N=5]	73.9 [N=23]	45 [N=20]	61.3 [N=62]
Average degree of modification [0–4]*	Not identified [N=5]	1.9 [N=18]	1.67 [N=13]	1.85 [N=41]
Southern Lowlands				
Frequency [%]	Not identified [N=4]	75.9 [N=29]	89.3 [N=28]	82.0 [N=61]
Frequency of circular wrap	Not identified [N=3]	N.A. [N=9]	56.3 [N=16]	37.0 [N=27]
Frequency of sagittal groove	Not identified [N=3]	16.7 [N=12]	21.4 [N=14]	17.9 [N=28]
Tabular oblique/erect	Not identified [N=2]	70.6 [N=17]	66.7 [N=21]	65.0 [N=40]
Average degree of modification [0–4]*	Not identified [N=2]	2.35 [N=12]	2.00 [N=15]	2.11 [N=29]
Eastern Lowlands				
Frequency [%]	Not identified [N=5]	63.3 [N=49]	86.1 [N=36]	71.1 [N=97]
Frequency of circular wrap	Not identified [N=1]	37.5 [N=16]	N.A. [N=6]	40.9 [N=22]
Frequency of sagittal groove	Not identified [N=1]	7.7 [N=13]	20.0 [N=10]	12.5 [N=24]
Tabular oblique/erect	Not identified [N=0]	63.6 [N=23]	82.4 [N=17]	70.7 [N=41]
Average degree of modification [0–4]*	Not identified [N=0]	1.84 [N=15]	N.A. [N=8]	1.98 [N=24]

these multiethnic territories of contact and exchange, most of the Western Ch'olan–speaking folk from places such as Palenque, Jonuta, Pomona, Piedras Negras, Yaxchilán, and Bonampak would have been readily recognized as such by their extremely reclined and tubular head form (plate 7, figs. 3.6a, 3.6b). Their western neighbors from Toniná and Chiapa de Corzo would not have shared this appearance collectively. This antagonistic embodiment is showcased by the folk of Toniná, just a few miles uphill from Palenque and once a fierce political opponent. Some scholars argue that Toniná was settled by non–Western Ch'olan and probably other non-Maya speakers (Ayala 2002).

The skeletal remains of a number of residents of Toniná and its satellite villages were explored by the French Mission (Centro de Estudios Mexicanos y Centroamericanos in Guatemala City) in the 1970s and first analyzed by Arturo Romano Pacheco and María Teresa Jaén (1990; see also Tiesler 1998, 1999). In contrast to Palenque, broad and short heads predominate in and around the Toniná region. Many infant heads were visibly divided into two lateral lobes by using tight sagittal straps. This broad, flat

cranial modification style would have been immediately recognized as non–Western Ch'olan by the Usumacinta Maya, a sort of public statement denying any Western Ch'olan Maya roots.

This impression is also echoed, and occasionally even exaggerated, through Native imagery. Although Classic Maya iconography followed its own artistic conventions, it is fortunate for academic scrutiny that its depictions of human physical appearance are more realistic and more detailed than other American iconographic traditions, including most other Mesoamerican artistic conventions. In regard to head form, the sculptors of the panels and stelae of Toniná, who we suppose were Tzeltalan Maya speakers, depict their local dynasts with both high and short cranial profiles (figs. 3.7a, 3.7b). By contrast, their humiliated Western Ch'olan Maya captives from Palenque and other Usumacinta polities are traced with severely inclined foreheads (figs. 3.8a, 3.8b), precisely the head forms found in the cranial records of these sites (Scherer 2006, 2007, 2008, 2015; Tiesler 2012; Tovalín et al. 1998). Captives from other conquered kingdoms like Calakmul,

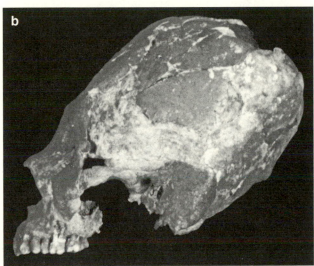

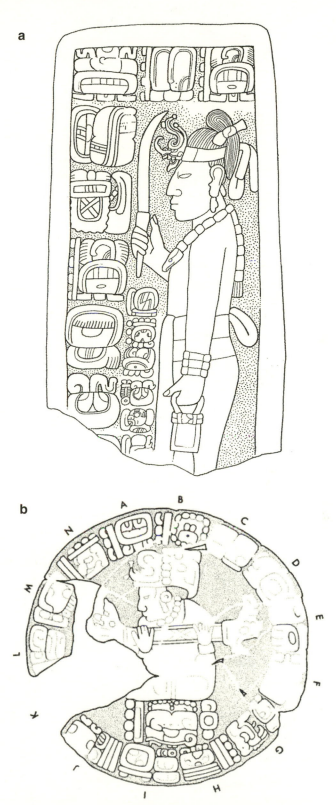

Figure 3.6. (a) Facial features of Lady Tz'ak B'u Ahaw from the Palace Tablet, Palenque, Chiapas (tracing by Mirna Beatríz Sánchez). The head of ruler Janaab' Pakal's wife is shown with a strong backward inclination. Her forehead displays a concavity, and her face is displayed more prominently than anatomically feasible. The woman's facial midportion appears outthrusting, while her chin is receding. The rendering of these physiognomic facial features is exaggerated when compared to (b) the skull profile of the female dignitary buried in Temple XIII-sub, presumed to be that of Lady Tz'ak B'u Ahaw (photo by Arturo Romano, Claustro de Sor Juana, Instituto Nacional de Antropología e Historia). Also note the omission of the occipital portion in (a), which is not as evident in the real head of this noblewoman (b).

Figure 3.7. Paramounts of Tzeltalan-speaking Toniná locals, showing high, shortened head silhouettes: (a) Toniná, Mon. 173, depicting a local Toniná *ajk'uhu'n* priest (drawing by Simon Martin); and (b) Toniná, Mon. 114, depicting Ruler 8 K'inich Chapaht (drawing by Ian Graham).

Figure 3.8. Foreign captives from Palenque depicted at Toniná, showing sunken foreheads and backward-oriented, elongated skullcaps: (a) Toniná Mmt. 122, showing K'an Joy Chitam, ruler of Palenque, as a captive (drawing by Linda Schele); and (b) Toniná panel, depicting K'awiil Mo', a nobleman from Palenque, as a bound captive (drawing by Simon Martin).

with a more diversified repertory of artificial head morphologies, are depicted with diverse head silhouettes. The distinctions in head forms depicted by Toniná's artists apparently echo the local (Tzeltalan) versus the antagonistic foreign (normally Western Ch'olan) provenience of their human motifs. This demarcation by itself would seem to indicate that head form was a distinct cultural element, which, readily visible, was imbued with differentiated, identitarian, and ethnic significance.

On a more regional scale, it also follows that the choice in head shape corresponded with linguistic affiliation to some degree, just as we have outlined above. During the Late Classic, proper dialectal forms of Western Ch'olan, some of them originating in the very area around Palenque, were beginning to be used in the texts of those areas where Eastern Ch'olan was traditionally spoken. These language shifts gradually spread out from the Usumacinta River basin across the Pasión River basin and toward the distant Motagua River on the southeastern edge of the Maya lowlands (Hruby and Child 2004; Lacadena and Wichmann 2002). Possibly, the adoption of these linguistic forms followed the prestige and political power that emanated from the western entities within the region.

In Toniná itself, local scribes drafted their texts in their own peculiar dialect, clinging to the Eastern Ch'olan written conventions and never accepting, indeed resisting, the dialectal introductions of Western Ch'olan. Quite conceivably, the resistance among Toniná's courtiers to adopt the new language *en vogue* was encouraged by their identification of Western Ch'olan with the tongue of Palenque, Toniná's ancestral enemy. It is apparent, therefore, that the antagonism between Palenque and Toniná played out not only in the political struggle between two competing Maya kingdoms. Beyond the political arena, this was indeed a clash between two ethnic groups in which the visibly distinct appearance of heads and the dissonant tones of different tongues played a substantial role.

Head Display in Ethnic Identification among Political Networks toward and beyond the Collapse

The close of the Classic period in the Maya lowlands was marked by an increasingly divisive political landscape. Conflict, war, and the taking of captives became more prevalent in the eighth and ninth centuries, both in imagery and in the (bio)archaeological record of the central

and southern sectors of the lowland territories (Barrett and Scherer 2005; Martin and Grube 2008; Tiesler 2015a; Tiesler and Cucina 2010, 2012; Webster 2002). In this hostile political climate, the shaping of alliances and antagonisms in political exchanges warrants further consideration. For this study, we have documented shifts in both the distribution and form of head shapes and language dialects. As a visual aid, we matched the linguistic and cranial distribution from plates 5 and 6 with the scheme of regional contacts and political networks among Classic Maya kingdoms, elaborated by Simon Martin and Nikolai Grube (2008 and shown in figs. 3.9a and 3.9b).

In this language-divided model, both Eastern and Western Ch'olan networks appear to foster more plentiful exchanges within their own respective language domains, although these networks themselves were not exempt from internal conflict and war. The Snake Kingdom of Calakmul in the northern Petén presents an interesting example; it appears to have adopted Western Ch'olan, according to the shift in inflections in local inscriptions. Somewhere between the Eastern and Western Petén languages lies the tongue spoken in El Perú Waka', clearly affiliated at that time with the realm of Calakmul but not with other Western Ch'olan kingdoms. Conflict and frequent battles appear to define the later relations between the Western Ch'olan polities and Calakmul, and still more acutely between Western Ch'olan and Tzeltalan Toniná.

Less secure than the linguistic attributions of different cities within the political landscape of the Classic Maya lowlands are the preferences in artificial head morphology of those settlers who lived and died in the centers documented by epigraphers. But even if research is incomplete, it does uncover trends in head shaping, which, once again, follow the linguistic tendencies among Classic Maya kingdoms, as illustrated schematically by Martin and Grube (2008:21). Their geographic diagram of hegemonic interaction sets the kingdoms in which we suppose Western Ch'olan was spoken somewhat apart from the networks of the central Petén speakers of Eastern Ch'olan (fig. 3.9a). Mentions in the inscriptions of hierarchy, diplomatic contacts, conflicts, family ties, and other relationships between the two spheres are less frequent than within each language sphere.

Let us put the political networks in context with the geography of head looks (fig. 3.9b). As we have outlined, diversity prevails among the head looks of the central and eastern kingdoms, while head elongation predominates among the western kingdoms. The latter display a different head morphology than that of the Tzeltalan population of Toniná (colored differently in plate 6 and fig. 3.9b). A second trend in this scheme involves the head shapes of the Eastern Ch'olan communities that face the Maya Highlands to their south, such as Cancuén (most of whose residents had elongated heads; Quintanilla 2013) and Copán, on the southeastern fringes of the dynastic networks and surrounded by non-Maya populations of Central American descent (Tiesler and Cucina 2010). Apparently not only language affiliation per se but also the location relative to other populations must have influenced the collective tradition of head shape, supporting the idea that in this context cranial modifications followed ethnic and other cultural undercurrents.

Considered jointly, the distribution of vernacular language and the distribution in type of preferred cranial modifications find rough parallels in the degree and orientations of political networking during the Classic period, although the latter appear much more unstable and divisive toward the bitter end of the Classic period. Constant battles were fought even among groups who had previously cooperated in Western Ch'olan networks. This means that sharing the same spoken language or, for that matter, the same head form did not lead to permanent political bonding or lasting alliances between the aristocracies and settlement populations of Yaxchilán, Palenque, or Piedras Negras (see also Golden and Scherer 2006). The same can be said of course for Copán and Quirigua, or for Naranjo and Caracol, to the east, whom we presume to be speakers of Eastern Ch'olan.

As we move toward the close of the first millennium CE, this climate of political unrest raises questions regarding cultural persistence during and after the Maya collapse. The combined scenario that emerges from language, head shaping, and political networking—as delineated and elucidated above—traces mechanisms of cultural replacement and permanence by identifying those cultural elements and dynamics that were either retained or replaced following the breakdown of Maya social and political institutions. While the epigraphy remains silent on the last discourses of the Classic Maya lowland elite before the destruction and abandonment of their quarters nestled deep within the city cores, the cranial record does support continuity in head form preferences among commoners, underscoring, once again, the equitable and conservative nature of head shaping practices in their gendered and generation-bridging quality. Long after their royals had died or left for good with their families and political and religious staff, Maya remnant popula-

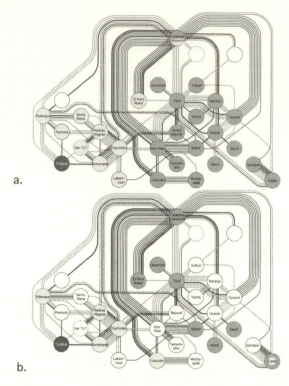

a.

b.

Figure 3.9. Schemes of Classic-period political networks (adapted from Martin and Grube 2008:21) in the central and southern Maya lowlands. Grey lines denote conflict, black ones statements of hierarchy, diplomatic and family ties, along with other communications of a more indefinite nature; a. The distribution of Maya vernacular languages is highlighted in grey hues (see Plate 6): dark grey: Tzeltalan speaking populations; light grey: Western Ch'olan speaking communities; medium grey: Eastern Ch'olan speaking communities; b. The distribution of selected Maya urban cranial series with sufficient sample sizes (see Plate 5; Tiesler 2012:129–31). Strong preferences for head elongation appear in light grey, whereas more equal distributions of head shortening and elongation are shown in medium grey. Local populations noted for predominantly shortened head morphologies are identified with dark grey. Note that Copán's core population sports mostly elongated head shapes, while its urban peripheries and hinterland show a much higher proportion of shortened head shapes.

tions still kept with their ancestral ways of shaping their infants' heads. Indeed, there appears to be continuity in shaping procedures up to the very end, as noted in other work for the last generations of settlers at Seibal and Altar de Sacrificios in the Río de la Pasión area (Tiesler 2015a). This surprising permanence of modeling practices is paralleled once again by continuity in spoken language in the southwestern corner of the Maya lowlands. This area was still inhabited by Ch'olan speakers up to the sixteenth century according to ethnohistorical sources (Mora Marín et al. 2009). In a changed, postcollapse Native world, we are certain that these anachronistic head shapes were to acquire new meanings for their human carriers.

DISCUSSION AND CONCLUSION

Over the course of this chapter, we have explored the relationship between the visible outcomes of cranial modification, language, and political affiliation along the fringes of the Classic-period Maya lowlands. By examining these relationships, we can see how cranial modification played a public role in forging the cultural and social identity of individuals and groups. Taking up our statements in the introduction to this chapter, cultural affinities that delineate ethnicity tend to be expressed by shared quotidian practices including but not limited to language, ideology, and group alignment in confrontation with outsiders and foreigners. From the information at hand it is clear that, at least among Classic-period Maya lowlanders, head-shaping traditions must have counted among those identity-forging cultural measures in both the private and public spheres. From the "inside," this practice was inclusive by all accounts: performed by females on babies and toddlers, its techniques and outcomes—as displayed by the ratio between head elongation and head shortening—did not lead to distinct morphological results in male and female offspring, most of whom would grow to be Maya men and women. Neither did specific head shapes appear to have been ascribed to any specific social sector or any of the lowland kingdoms. These reflections bring home the points made by William Duncan (2009:187–88), who speaks of head shaping as a protective and "incorporating" measure. Our idea also concurs with the judgment of Andrew Scherer in chapter 4 of this volume; he concludes that collective self-adscription to specific Maya kingdoms, indeed to the modern-impregnated notion of being "Maya," must have been "vague" at best.

Head-shaping practices were not only inclusive as practices but held deeper, religious meanings. Revealing are a number of representations on Classic Maya ceramics in which we can recognize characters who are shaping and modeling with their fingertips or with palette knives certain objects that they hold in their hands, as Scherer discusses in chapter 4. Because of their context and the iconographic attributes that they wear, the shaping characters are gods. The modeled objects are human heads. The accompanying hieroglyphic texts, although brief, are clear in their content: "[they] shaped the six first men" or "the first six men were shaped." The key is the verb pak', meaning "to shape something with the hands," like bricks or clay (Beliaev and Davletshin 2014). Very probably, these representations are Classic references to the creation of one of the two humankinds that were modeled, as mentioned in the Popol Vuh: the mud people or the maize people. But which of the two?

In one of the representations, as the primary god sitting to the right of the scene, we can identify Itzam Kokaaj, one of the supreme gods of Classic Maya pantheon (fig. 3.10). In front of him, one of the two artisan gods (with a simian face), Hun Chwen or Hun Batz', is depicted. Behind him, the maize god can be easily recognized, with the maize foliation coming out from his head. The presence of the maize god in the shaping of these six first men allows us to relate this scene with the last (i.e., successful) creation of humanity. In the scene shown in figure 3.10, success precisely rested on maize being used as constituent of the men's bodies. In fact, the modeled human heads in the scene can be clearly identified as Classic Maya. Looking closely, the shape of the heads exhibits different forms of head flattening, clearly noticeable in more than 70 percent of the lowland Maya population by Classic times (Tiesler 2012, 2014). When a Classic Maya individual envisioned the creation of the definitive human, he must have imagined an image of himself.

The idea that the godly craft of human head forming involved more than one deity raises a number of questions about the diversity in head looks, including the roles of short, unshaped, or what the Maya called "rounded" heads. If head shaping was identity forging, then what led a few mothers to leave the heads of their infants unchanged? This issue is compelling, given that in the Classic-period Maya area, a small portion of the systematically surveyed skeletal series does not exhibit the visible effects of cranial modification (table 3.1). Given the lack of any contingent social adscriptions (as inferred from the burial contexts) of unmodified versus modified individuals and the multifold connotations of head flattening and head treatments in general, Vera Tiesler has posited in other work (2014) that maternal carelessness or health issues secondary to the compression process could have led mothers to omit or terminate the head procedures. Another explanation for the absence of head modeling in some infants could

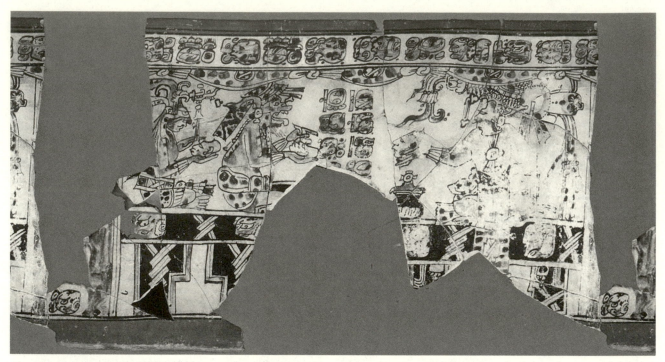

Figure 3.10. Supernatural scene in which Itzam Kokaaj, a supreme god of the Classic Maya pantheon, sits on the right, facing Hun Chwen or Hun Batz', rendered with a simian face. To the left, the maize god participates with the other deities in the shaping of human heads, a scene related to the last successful creation of humanity. Maize dough is used as a constituent of their bodies. The text reads, u-pa-k'a-wa WAK-YAX-WINIK UH-ti-ya HO'-B'AL-NAL (upak'a'w Wak Yax Winik uhtiiy Ho' B'a'l Nal): "they shaped the Six First Persons; it happened at the Five-Flower-place" (photo © J. Kerr, K1080).

relate to the emblematic emulation of specific sacred forces who in the imagery are displayed with rounded, physiological head conformations. Death God A of the Classic-period Maya pantheon and God N are depicted in such fashion (García Barrios and Tiesler 2011). It is noteworthy in this regard that the percentage of unmodified skulls is noticeably lower in the western hemisphere of the Maya lowlands than in the Maya heartlands east and deep within the Petén basin.

Beyond presence versus absence, the distribution of culturally conferred head shapes also displays geographically distinct trends, as we have shown. This is most apparent when we consider head form along the confines of spoken-language areas, specifically in the border territories between the Highland Maya and some of the non-Maya groups. Our data appears to indicate more unified cranial modification practices along the borderlands to the west, south, and southeast of the Maya lowlands, which exhibit proportionately more severely shaped heads. This trend is showcased by the combined distribution patterns of cranial remnants, iconography, and language in the Western Maya hemisphere. Some of the

Western Maya territories on and beyond the Usumacinta River were settled relatively late by Maya who were in direct contact with other, culturally diverse peoples, some of whom were clearly non-Maya.

We conclude, therefore, that head display within and among the different Maya language groups must have held visual meaning for their human carriers, contributing to the long-term construction of identity and driven, among other factors, by the use of spoken language. Passed on over generations of mothers and families, in the midst of changing economic networks, political alliances, and turmoil, these practices must have moved with the slowly shifting frontiers between Maya and non-Maya communities as well as within Maya networks. Some of these publicly constructed identities were clearly antagonistic, in step with the increasingly hostile political environment leading to the collective collapse of the Maya hegemonies. In this dynamic, the conservative, cohesive, *centripetal* quality of head practices in all probability allowed them to outlast other, more *centrifugal* (divisive) cultural dynamics.[3] The latter are beholden to economic and political networks as expressed by access to exotic goods, trade, and the androcentric official record itself. On a broader anthropological and analytic scale, these reflections put artificial head forms in a category similar to other, more resilient, conservative forms of cultural reproduction that were conferred predominantly by women, namely spoken language. Their permanence over generations, passed on by female caretakers to their babies and toddlers, provides a unique window on the gendered structure of long-term forms of reproduction and the active preservation of long-term group identity.

Apart from the generation-bridging female "head techniques" enacted in quotidian life (sensu Mauss 2007), our essay has elaborated on the public aspect of head display. This aspect complements the notion of the head as a social canvas, exposed and inscribed with collectively sanctioned (indeed ethnic) meanings, as outlined in chapter 1 of this volume (Turner 1984; Turner 2007). In its role as screen and mirror of socially mediated (and gender-conferred) norms and ideals, some thought to derive directly from the gods, the head and its artificially assigned morphology provide new lenses and points of departure for academics, especially those of us interested in subliminal but typically conservative, long-term group identity as conferred by females. Besides public emblematic display, it is this last conjecture that we wish to pursue and demonstrate through the combined lens of spoken language and collective head modeling among the Classic-period lowland Maya.

ACKNOWLEDGMENTS

A number of productive project collaborations, personal communications, and studies at research facilities have been instrumental to this work, whose support and access is thankfully appreciated here. We gratefully acknowledge the support received by Simon Martin, Mary Miller, Claudia Brittenham, Heather Hurst, and Leonard Ashby. We are likewise indebted to the late Professor Arturo Romano Pacheco, whose experience and insights in the Western Maya modalities of head shaping practices were crucial for this study. Thanks go also to the Peabody Museum (Harvard University); the Centro de Estudios Mexicanos y Centroamericanos in Guatemala City; the Dirección de Antropología Física (Instituto Nacional de Antropología e Historia); the Claustro de Sor Juana; the Proyecto Restos Humanos del Templo de Inscripciones, Palenque (Secretaría Técnica del INAH); the Proyecto Restos Humanos del Templo XIII-sub, Palenque (Arturo Romano Pacheco, INAH); the Proyecto Arqueológico Palenque (Arnoldo González, INAH); the Proyecto Restos Humanos del Templo de las Inscripciones, Palenque (Vera Tiesler, INAH); and the Proyecto Arqueológico El Perú Waka' (David Freidel et al., Instituto de Antropología e Historia, Guatemala City). Part of the funding has been provided by the CONACYT Proyectos de Investigación Básica (37743-H; 49982, 152105) and the Wenner Gren Collaborative Project (2008–2013). The editorial check by Raúl López and the style corrections by Kristie Sanchez, Nené Lozada, Gaby Vail, Catherine Harrison, and Khali Ashton on subsequent versions of this chapter have worked wonders to enhance flow of reading. All errors in the content are of course ours.

NOTES

1. At the hard core of Mesoamerican thought (or "núcleo duro" in the words of Alfredo López Austin [2001]) stood shared beliefs regarding the body, its light and heavy components, and their loads of sacred entities contained within (McKeever Furst 1995; Houston and Cummins 2004; López Austin 1989, 2009; Velásquez García 2015).

2. In their unpublished communication, Albert Davletshin and Dmitri Beliaev have recently gathered evidence supporting the existence of what could have been a fifth linguistic area. They have identified an ancient tongue, potentially affiliated with K'iche'an, which has been perpetuated in the ceramic inscriptions of Chama and Nebaj of the Guatemaltecan Highlands, just to the south of the Lowland Ch'olan speakers.

3. This scheme builds on the conceptual framework laid out for the Maya area's pre-Hispanic trajectory by Patricia McAnany (1995).

REFERENCES CITED

Ayala, Maricela
2002 Acerca de los sistemas sociales, políticos y religiosos de Toniná. In *La organización social entre los mayas prehispánicos, coloniales y modernos: memoria de la Tercera Mesa Redonda de Palenque*, edited by Vera Tiesler, Rafael Cobos, and Merle Greene Robertson, pp. 147–62. Instituto Nacional de Antropología e Historia, Universidad Autónoma de Yucatán, Mexico City.

Barrera Vásquez, Alfredo
1980 *Diccionario maya cordemex: maya-español, español-maya.* Ediciones Cordemex, Mérida.

Barrett, Jason, and Andrew Scherer
2005 Stones, Bones, and Crowded Plazas: Evidence for Terminal Classic Maya Warfare at Colha, Belize. *Ancient Mesoamerica* 16:101–18.

Barth, Fredrik
1969 Introduction to *Ethnic Groups and Boundaries: The Social Organization of Culture Difference*, edited by Fredrik Barth, pp. 9–38. Little, Brown, Boston.

Beliaev, Dmitri, and Albert Davletshin
2014 "It Was Then That That Which Had Been Clay Turned into a Man": Reconstructing Maya Anthropogonic Myths. *Axis Mundi* 1(9):1–12.

Cervera, María Dolores
2007 El hetsmek' como experiencia simbólica de la construcción de los niños mayas yucatecos como personas. *Revista Pueblos y Fronteras Digital* 4:1–31.

Chinchilla Mazariegos, Oswaldo, Vera Tiesler,
Oswaldo Gómez, and T. Douglas Price
2015 Myth, Ritual and Human Sacrifice in Early Classic Mesoamerica: Interpreting a Cremated Double Burial from Tikal, Guatemala. *Cambridge Archaeological Journal* 25:187–210.

Coe, Michael
1992 *Breaking the Maya Code.* Thames and Hudson, New York.

Coe, William R.
1959 *Piedras Negras Archaeology: Artifacts, Caches, and Burials.* Museum Monograph 4. University Museum, University of Pennsylvania, Philadelphia.

Dembo, Adolfo, and José Imbelloni
1938 *Deformaciones intencionales del cuerpo humano de carácter étnico.* Biblioteca Humanior, Buenos Aires.

Díaz-Andreu, Margarita, Sam Lucy, Staša Babiác,
and David N. Edwards
2005 *The Archaeology of Identity: Approaches to Gender, Age, Status, Ethnicity, and Religion.* Routledge, New York.

Dingwall, Eric J.
1931 *Artificial Cranial Deformation: A Contribution to the Study of Ethnic Mutilations.* Bale, Sons, and Danielsson, London.

Douglas, Mary
1973 *Natural Symbols: Explorations in Cosmology.* Vintage Books, New York.

Duncan, William
2009 Cranial Modification among the Maya: Absence of Evidence or Evidence of Absence? In *Bioarchaeology and Identity in the Americas*, edited by Kelly Knudson and Christopher M. Stojanowski, pp. 177–93. University Press of Florida, Gainesville.

Duncan, William, and Charles Andrew Hofling
2011 Why the Head? Cranial Modification as Protection and Ensoulment among the Maya. *Ancient Mesoamerica* 22:199–210.

Forné, Mélanie, Arthur Demarest, Horacio Martínez,
Paola Torres, Silvia Alvarado, and Claudia Arriaza
2009 Intercambio y afiliación cultural en Cancuen: la complejidad cultural en las vísperas del Colapso. In *XXII Simposio de Investigaciones Arqueológicas en Guatemala 2008*, edited by Juan Pedro Laporte, Bárbara Arroyo, and Héctor Mejía, pp. 1017–36. Ministerio de Cultura y Deportes, Instituto de Antropología e Historia, Asociación Tikal, Guatemala City.

García Barrios, Ana, and Vera Tiesler
2011 El aspecto físico de los dioses mayas. *Arqueología Mexicana* 112:59–63.

Gervais, Veronique
1989 *Déformations artificielles de crânes préhispaniques au Guatemala et au Mexique.* PhD dissertation, University of Caen.

Golden, Charles, and Andrew Scherer
2006 Border Problems: Recent Archaeological Research along the Usumacinta River. *PARI Journal* 7(2): 1–16.

Gómez, Oswaldo
1999 Excavaciones en el interior del Templo V, Tikal. In *XII Simposio de Investigaciones Arqueológicas en Guatemala 1998*, edited by Juan Pedro Laporte and Héctor L. Escobedo, pp. 174–82. Museo Nacional de Arqueología y Etnología, Guatemala City.

Gronemeyer, Sven
2014a The Orthographic Conventions of Maya Hieroglyphic Writing. Unpublished PhD dissertation, La Trobe University, Bundoora, Australia.
2014b E Pluribus Unum: Embracing Vernacular Influences in a Classic Mayan Scribal Tradition. In *Acta Mesoamericana.* Vol. 27, *A Celebration of the Life and Work of Pierre Robert Colas*, edited by Christophe Helmke and Frauke Sachse, pp.147–62. Verlag Anton Saurwein, Markt Schwaben, Germany.

Haviland, William, and Hattula Moholy-Nagy
1992 Distinguishing the High from the Mighty from the Hoi Polloi at Tikal, Guatemala. In *Mesoamerican Elites: An Archaeological Assessment*, edited by Arlen Chase

and Diane Chase, pp. 50–60. University of Oklahoma Press, Norman.

Hicks, Frederic

2001 Ethnicity. In *The Oxford Encyclopedia of Mesoamerican Cultures: The Civilizations of Mexico and Central America*, vol. 1, edited by Davíd Carrasco, pp. 388–92. Oxford University Press, New York.

Houston, Stephen D.

2000 Into the Minds of Ancients: Advances in Maya Glyph Studies. *Journal of World Prehistory* 14(2): 121–201.

Houston, Stephen D., and Tom Cummins

2004 Body, Presence, and Space in Andean and Meso-american Rulership. In *Palaces of the Ancient New World*, edited by Susan T. Evans and Joanne Pillsbury, pp.359–98. Dumbarton Oaks, Washington, DC.

Houston, Stephen D., and David Stuart

1998 The Ancient Maya Self: Personhood and Portraiture in the Classic Period. *RES: Anthropology and Aesthetics* 33:73–101.

Houston, Stephen, and Karl A. Taube

2000 An Archaeology of the Senses: Perception and Cultural Expression in Ancient Mesoamerica. *Cambridge Archaeological Journal* 10:261–94.

Houston, Stephen, John Robertson, and David Stuart

2000 The Language of Classic Maya Inscriptions. *Current Anthropology* 41(3):321–56.

Houston, Stephen, David Stuart, and Karl A. Taube

2006 *The Memory of Bones: Body, Being, and Experience among the Classic Maya.* University of Texas Press, Austin.

Hruby, Zachary, and Mark Child

2004 Chontal Linguistic Influence in Ancient Maya Writing: Intransitive Positional Verbal Affixation. In *The Linguistics of Maya Writing*, edited by Søren Wichmann, pp. 13–26. University of Utah Press, Salt Lake City.

Jones, Siân

1997 *The Archaeology of Ethnicity: Constructing Identities in the Past and Present.* Routledge, New York.

Justeson, John S., William M. Norman, Lyle Campbell, and Terrence Kaufman

1985 *The Foreign Impact on Lowland Mayan Language and Script.* Middle American Research Institute, Tulane University, New Orleans.

Kettunen, Harri

2005 *Nasal Motifs in Maya Iconography.* PhD dissertation, University of Helsinki.

Lacadena, Alfonso

2000 Nominal Syntax and the Linguistic Affiliation of Classic Maya Texts. In *Acta Mesoamericana*. Vol. 10, *The Sacred and the Profane: Architecture and Identity in the Maya Lowlands*, edited by Pierre R. Colas, Kai Delvendahl, Markus Kuhnert, and Annette Schubart, pp. 111–28. Verlag Anton Saurwein, Markt Schwaben, Germany.

Lacadena, Alfonso, and Søren Wichmann

2002 The Distribution of Lowland Maya Languages in the Classic Period. In *La organización entre los Mayas: memoria de la Tercera Mesa Redonda de Palenque*, vol. 2, edited by Vera Tiesler, Rafael Cobos, and Merle Greene Robertson, pp. 275–314. Instituto Nacional de Antropología e Historia, Universidad Autónoma de Yucatán, Mexico City.

2005 The Dynamics of Language in the Western Lowland Maya Region. In *Art for Archaeological Sake: Material Culture and Style across the Disciplines.* Proceedings of the Thirty-Third Annual Chacmool Conference, edited by Andrea Waters-Rist, Christine Cluney, Calla McNamee, and Larry Steinbrenner, pp. 32–48. Chacmool Archaeological Association, University of Calgary, Calgary.

Laporte, Juan Pedro

1999 Exploración y restauración en el Conjunto de Palacios de Mundo Perdido, Tikal (Estructura 5C-45/47). In *XII Simposio de Investigaciones Arqueológicas en Guatemala 1998*, edited by Juan Pedro Laporte and Héctor L. Escobedo, pp. 183–214. Museo Nacional de Arqueología y Etnología, Guatemala City.

2005 Exploración y restauración en la Plataforma Este de Mundo Perdido, Tikal (Estructuras 5D-83 a 5D-89). In *XVIII Simposio de Investigaciones Arqueológicas en Guatemala 2004*, edited by Juan Pedro Laporte, Bárbara Arroyo, and Héctor Mejía, pp. 147–93. Museo Nacional de Arqueología y Etnología, Guatemala City.

Le Breton, David

1994 *Corps et societés: essai de sociologie et d'anthropologie du corps.* Méridiens Klincksieck, Paris.

López Austin, Alfredo

1989 *Cuerpo humano e ideología: las concepciones de los antiguos nahuas.* Universidad Nacional Autónoma de México, Mexico City.

2001 El núcleo duro, la cosmovisión y la tradición meso-americana. In *Cosmovisión, ritual e identidad de los pueblos indígenas de México*, edited by Johanna Broda and Félix Báez-Jorge, pp. 47–65. Ediciones Conaculta, Fondo de Cultura Económica, Mexico City.

2009 El dios en el cuerpo. *Dimensión Antropológica* 46:1–34.

Martin, Simon, and Nikolai Grube

2008 *Chronicle of the Maya Kings and Queens: Deciphering the Dynasties of the Ancient Maya.* 2nd ed. Thames and Hudson, New York.

Mauss, Marcel

2007 Techniques of the Body. In *Beyond the Body Proper: Reading the Anthropology of Material Life*, edited by Margaret Lock and Judith Farquhar, pp. 50–68. Duke University Press, Durham, North Carolina.

McAnany, Patricia

1995 *Living with the Ancestors: Kinship and Kingship in Ancient Maya Society.* University of Texas Press, Austin.

McCafferty, Geoffrey G., and Sharisse D. McCafferty

2011 Bling Things: Ornamentation and Identity in Pacific Nicaragua. In *Identity Crisis: Archaeological Perspectives on Social Identity*, edited by Lindsey Amundsen-Meyer, Nicole Engel, and Sean Pickotas, pp. 234–52. Chacmool Archaeology Association, University of Calgary, Calgary.

McKeever Furst, Jill Leslie

1995 *The Natural History of the Soul in Ancient Mexico.* Yale University Press, New Haven, Connecticut.

Montes de Paz, Javier

2000 La práctica de la deformación cefálica intencional entre los pobladores prehispánicos de Palenque, Chiapas. Bachelor's thesis, Escuela Nacional de Antropología e Historia, Mexico City.

Mora Marín, David, Nicholas Hopkins, and Kathryn Josserand

2009 The Linguistic Affiliation of Classic Lowland Mayan Writing and the Historical Sociolinguistic Geography of the Mayan Lowlands. In *The Ch'orti' Maya Area: Past and Present*, edited by Brent E. Metz, Cameron L. McNeil, and Kerry M. Hull, pp. 15–28. University Press of Florida, Gainesville.

Nuñez, Luis Fernando

2009 Temporada 2008: informe de actividades; conjunto habitacional norte, Operaciones 111, 112, 113. In *Segundo informe parcial Proyecto Arqueológico Chinikihá temporada 2008*, edited by Rodrigo Liendo, pp. 159–221. Universidad Nacional Autónoma de México, Mexico City.

2010 Actividades realizadas en el conjunto F. In *Segundo informe parcial Proyecto Arqueológico Chinikihá temporada 2008*, edited by Rodrigo Liendo, pp. 89–136. Universidad Nacional Autónoma de México, Mexico City.

Pallán, Carlos

2009 Secuencia dinástica, glifos-emblema y topónimos en las inscripciones jeroglíficas de Edzná, Campeche (600–900 d.C.): implicaciones históricas. Master's thesis, Universidad Nacional Autónoma de México, Mexico City.

Price, T. Douglas, Seiichi Nakamura, Shintaro Suzuki, James H. Burton, and Vera Tiesler

2014 New Isotope Data on Maya Mobility and Enclaves at Classic Copan, Honduras. *Journal of Anthropological Archaeology* 36:32–47.

Quintanilla, Claudia

2013 Estudio y análisis de los enterramientos humanos del sitio arqueológico Cancuén. Bachelor's thesis, Universidad de San Carlos de Guatemala, Guatemala City.

Ringle, William, Tomás Gallareta, and George J. Bey

1998 The Return of Quetzalcoatl: Evidence of the Spread of a World Religion during the Epiclassic Period. *Ancient Mesoamerica* 9:183–232.

Romano Pacheco, Arturo

1965 *Estudio morfológico de la deformación craneana en Tamuín, S.L.P., y en la Isla del Idolo, Veracruz.* Instituto Nacional de Antropología e Historia, Universidad Nacional Autónoma de México, Mexico City.

Romano Pacheco, Arturo, and María Teresa Jaén

1990 El material óseo humano procedente de diversos sitios arqueológicos del valle de Ocosingo, Estado de Chiapas. In *Toniná, une cité Maya du Chiapas (Mexique)*, vol. 4, edited by Pierre Becquelin and Eric Taladoire, pp.1661–87. Études Mésoaméricaines 6. Centro de Estudios Mexicanos y Centroamericanos, Mexico City.

Sánchez, Mirna Beatríz

2008 Emblema visual de identidad y distinción: reconstrucción de rostros mayas (fisionomía y rasgos bioculturales). Master's thesis, Facultad de Ciencias Antropológicas, Universidad Autónoma de Yucatán, Mérida.

Saul, Frank P.

1972 *The Human Skeletal Remains of Altar de Sacrificios: An Osteobiographic Analysis.* Papers of the Peabody Museum of Archaeology and Ethnology, vol. 63, no. 2. Harvard University, Cambridge, Massachusetts.

Scherer, Andrew K.

2006 Bioarqueología de El Kinel, La Técnica y Zancudero. In *Proyecto Regional Arqueológico Sierra del Lacandón: informe preliminar no. 4*, edited by Charles Golden, Andrew K. Scherer, and Rosaura Vásquez, pp. 83–94. Dirección General del Patrimonio Cultural y Natural de Guatemala, Guatemala City.

2007 Bioarqueología de El Kinel, temporada de campo 2007. In *Proyecto Regional Arqueológico Sierra del Lacandón, 2007: informe de la quinta temporada de campo*, edited by Andrew K. Scherer, Charles Golden, and Rosaura Vásquez, pp. 186–201. Dirección General del Patrimonio Cultural y Natural de Guatemala, Guatemala City.

2008 Bioarqueología de Tecolote, temporada de campo 2004 y 2008. In *Proyecto Regional Arqueológico Sierra del Lacandón, 2008: informe no. 6*, edited by Charles Golden, Andrew K. Scherer, and Rosaura Vásquez, pp. 160–81. Dirección General del Patrimonio Cultural y Natural de Guatemala, Guatemala City.

2015 *Mortuary Landscapes of the Classic Maya: Rituals of Body and Soul.* University of Texas Press, Austin.

Scherer, Andrew, and Lori Wright

2001 Los esqueletos de Piedras Negras: reporte preliminar no. 4. In *Proyecto Arqueológico Piedras Negras: informe preliminar no. 4, cuarta temporada, 2000*, edited by Héctor L. Escobedo and Stephen D. Houston, pp. 553–57. Instituto de Antropología e Historia, Guatemala City.

Scherer, Andrew, Cassady Yoder, and Lori Wright.

1999 Los esqueletos de Piedras Negras: reporte preliminar no. 3. In *Proyecto Arqueológico Piedras Negras: informe preliminar no. 3, tercera temporada, 1999*, edited by Héctor L. Escobedo and Stephen D. Houston, pp. 387–99. Instituto de Antropología e Historia, Guatemala City.

Sharer, Robert J., and Loa P. Traxler

2006a The Foundations of Ethnic Diversity in the Southwestern Maya Area. In *Maya Ethnicity: The Construction of Ethnic Identity from Preclassic to Modern Times*, edited by Frauke Sachse, pp. 31–43. Verlag Anton Saurwein, Markt Schwaben, Germany.

2006b *The Ancient Maya.* 6th ed. Stanford University Press, Stanford, California.

Sierra Sosa, Thelma, Andrea Cucina, T. Douglas Price, James H. Burton, and Vera Tiesler

2014 Maya Coastal Production, Exchange, Life Style, and Population Mobility: A View from the Port of Xcambó, Yucatán. *Ancient Mesoamerica* 25:221–38.

Sotelo, Laura, and Carmen Valverde

1992 Los señores de Yaxchilán: un ejemplo de felinización de los gobernantes mayas. *Estudios de Cultura Maya* 19:187–214.

Stewart, T. Dale

1953 Skeletal Remains from Zaculeu, Guatemala. In *The Ruins of Zaculeu, Guatemala*, vol. 1, edited by Richard B. Woodbury and Aubrey S. Trik, pp. 295–311. William Byrd, Richmond, Virginia.

Stuart, David

1987 Ten Phonetic Syllables. Research Reports on Ancient Maya Writing, no. 14. Center for Maya Research, Washington, DC.

Taube, Karl A.

2003 Tetitla and the Maya Presence at Teotihuacan. In *The Maya and Teotihuacan: Reinterpreting Early Classic Interaction*, edited by Geoffrey Braswell, pp. 273–314. University of Texas Press, Austin.

Tiesler, Vera

1998 *La costumbre de la deformación cefálica entre los antiguos mayas: aspectos morfológicos y culturales.* Colección Científica. Instituto Nacional de Antropología e Historia, Mexico City.

1999 Rasgos bioculturales entre los antiguos mayas: aspectos arqueológicos y sociales. Unpublished PhD dissertation, Facultad de Filosofía y Letras, Universidad Nacional Autónoma de México, Mexico City.

2010 "Olmec" Head Shapes among the Preclassic Period Maya and Cultural Meanings. *Latin American Antiquity* 21:290–311.

2011 Becoming Maya: Infancy and Upbringing through the Lens of Pre-Hispanic Head Shaping. *Childhood in the Past* 4:117–32.

2012 *Transformarse en maya: el modelado cefálico entre los mayas prehispánicos y coloniales.* Universidad Nacional Autónoma de México, Mexico City; Universidad Autónoma de Yucatán, Mérida.

2014 *The Bioarchaeology of Artificial Cranial Modifications: New Approaches to Head Shaping and Its Meanings in Pre-Columbian Mesoamerica and Beyond.* Springer, New York.

2015a Shifts in Artificial Head Forms, Population Movements, and Ethnicity among the Postclassic Maya. In *Archaeology and Bioarchaeology of Population Move-*

ment among the Prehispanic Maya, edited by Andrea Cucina, pp. 143–45. Springer, New York.

2015b Reporte de los restos humanos, explorados por el proyecto Arqueológico La Blanca, Petén, Guatemala. Unpublished report on file, Universitat de València, Valencia, Spain.

Tiesler, Vera, and Andrea Cucina

2010 La deformación craneana como emblema de identidad, etnicidad y reproducción cultural entre los mayas del Clásico. In *Identidades y cultura material en la región maya*, edited by Héctor Hernández Álvarez and Marcos Noé Pool Cab, pp. 111–34. Universidad Autónoma de Yucatán, Mérida.

2012 Where Are the Warriors? Cranial Trauma Patterns and Conflict among the Ancient Maya. In *The Bioarchaeology of Violence*, edited by Debra L. Martin, Ryan P. Harrod, and Ventura R. Pérez, pp. 160–79. University Press of Florida, Gainesville.

Tiesler, Vera, and Pilar Zabala

2011 El modelado artificial de la cabeza durante la Colonia: una tradición maya en el espejo de las fuentes históricas. *Estudios de Cultura Maya* 38:75–96.

Tovalín, Alejandro, Javier Montes de Paz, and Juan Antonio Velázquez de León

1998 Costumbres funerarias en Bonampak, Chiapas. In *XI Simposio de Investigaciones Arqueológicas en Guatemala 1997*, edited by Juan Pedro Laporte, Héctor L. Escobedo, and Sandra Villagrán, pp. 249–60, Ministerio de Cultura y Deportes, Instituto de Antropología e Historia, Asociación Tikal, Guatemala City.

Turner, Terence S.

2007 The Social Skin. In *Beyond the Body Proper: Reading the Anthropology of Material Life*, edited by Margaret Lock and Judith Farquhar, pp. 83–105. Duke University Press, Durham, North Carolina.

Turner, Victor

1984 *The Body and Society: Explorations in Social Theory.* Basil Blackwell, Oxford.

Vargas, Ernesto

2001 *Itzamkanac y Acalan: tiempos de crisis anticipando el futuro.* Instituto de Investigaciones Antropológicas, Universidad Nacional Autónoma de México, Mexico City.

Velásquez García, Erik

2015 Las entidades y las fuerzas anímicas en la cosmovisión maya clásica. In *Los mayas: voces de piedra*, edited by Alejandra Martínez de Velasco Cortina and María Elena Vega Villalobos, pp. 177–95. 2nd ed. Editorial Ámbar, Universidad Nacional Autónoma de México, Mexico City.

Webster, David

2002 *The Fall of the Ancient Maya: Solving the Mystery of the Maya Collapse.* Thames and Hudson, New York.

Wright, Lori E.

1997 Los restos óseos humanos de Piedras Negras: un reporte preliminar. In *Proyecto Arqueológico Piedras Negras: informe preliminar no. 1, primera temporada, 1997*, edited by Héctor L. Escobedo and Stephen D. Houston, pp. 213–18. Instituto de Antropología e Historia, Guatemala City.

Wright, Lori E., and Amy M. Witte

1998 Observaciones sobre la osteología humana de Piedras Negras: reporte preliminar no 2. In *Proyecto Arqueológico Piedras Negras: informe preliminar no. 2, segunda temporada, 1998*, ed. Héctor L. Escobedo and Stephen D. Houston, pp. 393–97. Instituto de Antropología e Historia, Guatemala City.

Wyllie, Cherra E.

2002 *Signs, Symbols, and Hieroglyphs of Ancient Veracruz: Classic to Postclassic Transition.* PhD dissertation, Yale University, New Haven, Connecticut.

Zabala, Pilar

2014 Source Compilation on Head-Shaping Practices in Hispanic America. In *The Bioarchaeology of Artificial Cranial Modifications: New Approaches to Head Shaping and Its Meanings in Pre-Columbian and Colonial Mesoamerica*, authored by Vera Tiesler, pp. 99–129. Springer, New York.

4

Head Shaping and Tooth Modification among the Classic Maya of the Usumacinta River Kingdoms

ANDREW K. SCHERER

Merely framed,
Merely shaped they are called.

Then they looked like people therefore;
People they became.

—Popol Vuh, K'iche' Maya, translated by
  Allen Christenson

INTRODUCTION

Osteological investigations of cranial and dental modification have traditionally focused on descriptive typology,
status, and geographic variability. This edited volume, organized by Vera Tiesler and María Cecilia Lozada, seeks to
move our understanding of pre-Columbian treatments of
the head beyond these narrow topics and to instead engage
more deeply with issues of identity, power, and embodiment
as they relate to adornments and modifications of the human
head. In this chapter I consider whether these matters are
evident in head shaping and tooth modification among the
Maya of the Usumacinta River region, an area that today
comprises the modern border between Mexico and Guatemala. During the Classic period (350–900 CE), this area was
home to the competing Classic-period kingdoms of Piedras
Negras and Yaxchilán and was a focal region for travel, trade,
and conflict among the Western Maya more broadly (fig. 4.1).

As Tiesler and Lozada make clear in their introduc-
tory chapter, of all human body parts the head is, cross-
culturally, ascribed paramount importance because it is
the primary locus of the sensory apparatuses by which we
engage our external world. Moreover, of all parts of the
human body it is the head that most clearly establishes
humans as distinct from other beings. Yet how different
societies understand and interpret the human head varies
significantly. For bioarchaeologists studying modifications
of the body preserved in tooth and bone, it is imperative
that we at least attempt to tease out emic understandings
of the body. Here, I situate my study of cranial shaping
and dental modification among the Classic Maya of the
Usumacinta River region within broader Maya concepts
of body, self, and the soul. The relevant threads of evidence are many and they require sifting through the epigraphic, iconographic, ethnohistorical, and ethnographic
records. Yet caution is warranted in spinning disparate
threads to construct a single narrative, particularly when
such evidence is gathered among Maya peoples disconnected in time and space. It is incorrect and unjust to
suggest that contemporary Maya peoples have a universal
and monolithic belief system and worldview. It is even
more wrongheaded to assume that Maya beliefs have not
evolved over time. Nevertheless, it is equally suspect to
deny the Maya peoples living in different communities or
periods of time any commonality in tradition or practice.
A balanced approach, therefore, must consider a robust

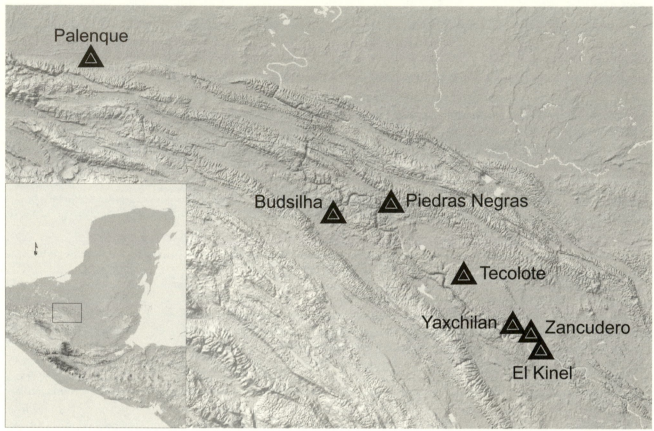

Figure 4.1. Map of the Maya area showing detail of the Usumacinta River region (map by Andrew Scherer and Charles Golden).

body of evidence in order to disentangle deeply shared aspects of Maya world view from the social and temporal particulars of belief and practice.

HEART AND SOUL, HEAD AND SELF

Among the Maya, past and present, there is a common understanding that the body is something that is crafted or cultivated over the course of infancy, childhood, and adolescence (Houston 2009; Houston et al. 2006; Scherer 2015; Tiesler 2011). The quotation that introduced this chapter comes from a passage in the sixteenth-century K'iche' Popol Vuh and pertains to the creation of humans. For the Maya, creation is not something that happened instantaneously; rather, it was a process of construction through trial and error, an act that involved building with preexisting materials and revising those attempts at creation that were inadequate or displeasing to the creators. It was through such efforts that people were given the vital

attributes that distinguish them from other beings and mark them as human:

> Their framing, their shaping,
> By the Framer, Shaper,
> She Who Has Borne Children, He Who Has Begotten Sons,
> Sovereign [the name of the Framer], Quetzal Serpent [the name of the Shaper].
> *Then they looked like people therefore;*
> *People they became.*
> They spoke,
> They talked as well.
> They looked,
> They listened as well.
> They walked,
> They grasped.
> Excellent people, chosen ones.
> Manly faces
> Their countenances.

There was their breath,
　They became. (Christenson 2007a:156–57, emphasis
　　added)

Thus humans are not so much *created* as they are *crafted*. The act is described using the verbs to frame (*tz'aq*) and to shape (*b'it*). As Allen Christenson (2007b:60) clarifies, *Tz'aqol* (Framer) refers to someone who puts things together, an assembler, as in constructing from stone or adobe, preparing a meal from various ingredients, or weaving a piece of cloth from individual threads. *B'itol* (Shaper) then is a modeler, such as a potter or sculptor, someone who gives shape to amorphous substances. Through this process of assembly and shaping, humans gain the ability to speak, see, listen, walk, and manipulate things by hand. That is, to perceive and have mobility are fundamental to being human. The power of perception is rooted in attributes of the head, the aspect of anatomy most closely linked to Maya concepts of self and identity (Houston and Stuart 1998; Houston et al. 2006:58–72).

Whereas the act of making humans (including sexual reproduction) is often likened to craftsmanship, childhood development is generally understood through agricultural tropes. Heads are likened to fruit in Maya thought, and metaphors of development rely heavily on notions of ripening. As Kevin Groark (2005:183) describes for the Tzotzil, "young children have 'unripe heads' (*uninsjol*), and don't feel ashamed when they act badly. As the child ages, his head 'matures' or 'ripens' (*-yijub*), reason and a knowledge of right and wrong enter (*-ochrasonal*), and the ability to feel shame and embarrassment develops . . . a good person, one who is thoroughly socialized, 'knows how to feel shame/embarrassment (*ta sna' xk'exav*)." The convention is similar in Tzeltal thought: "[T]he head is not formed at the moment of birth, and children learn slowly because their brains (*chinam*) are still tender. Only with time, by means of learning and experience, is the brain gradually toughened up, filled out, and given shape, a process that is enabled by the working of the senses— sight, hearing, smell, and taste—that also answer to the head" (Pitarch 2010:89).

According to the K'iche' Popol Vuh, to appear as human is to be human: "Then they looked like people therefore; people they became" (Christenson 2007a:156). Observations from contemporary Maya ethnography echo this sentiment and highlight the importance not only of perception but of being perceived, particularly

for understandings of intersubjectivity. As Pedro Pitarch (2010:5) observes for the Tzeltal:

> From the Indian viewpoint, appearance is the locus of personal identity and morality. One is what one shows to others. The birth of the body is what initiates the process of differentiation, that is, humanization and, ultimately, Indianization. The body gradually takes its shape through nurture and the development of bodily *gestus*. If the Christian moral imperative is the cultivation of the soul, then the indigenous imperative is the cultivation of the body.

Pitarch (2012:93) further highlights the complexity of indigenous notions of the body and how they diverge from Western thought:

> On the one hand, there is a "flesh-body," the union of flesh and bodily fluids making up a whole that is divisible into parts, an object that is sentient, though lacking the capacity to relate socially to other beings, and that represents the substantial homogeneity between humans and animals. On the other hand, there is a "presence body," an active subject capable of perception, feeling and cognition, committed to an inter-subjective relationship with bodies of the same species.

The distinction is that the "flesh-body" (*bak'etal*) comprises all parts of the body except the bones, hair, and nails, anatomical elements that are perceived as divorced from the circulatory-respiratory system and thus disconnected from sentient, animate life. The "presence-body" (*winkilel*) is the complete body, the flesh-body plus all those other elements. As Pitarch (2012:98) explains, "the 'presence-body' is the figure, the body shape, the face, the way of speaking, of walking, of dressing." It is the "presence-body" that is perceived by others and engages in interpersonal action. Both of these aspects of the body are "fabricated" over the course of life:

> On the one hand, the flesh-body is the direct result of nourishment (food is literally incorporated as flesh and blood) and environmental conditions (temperature in particular); on the other, the presence-body is the fruit of social habits of the species/culture (social etiquette, language, gestures, clothing, and so on).

Both processes—food and social code—are required to achieve single bio-moral development. (Pitarch 2012:100)

Owing to the pioneering work of Alfredo López Austin (1980), ethnographers have long recognized a complex relationship between body and soul among indigenous people of Mesoamerica, one that allows the coexistence of many types of souls within a single person. In the Tzeltal worldview, the body is inhabited by a variable number of spirit essences or souls. One type has the shape of a human body and others resemble animals or celestial phenomena (lighting, rainbows, winds, or even ghosts). The former is the *ch'ulel*, a type of soul that exists within the heart but is also capable of traveling external to the body, especially during sleep or drunkenness (Pitarch 2010:24–39). Similar concepts exist throughout the Maya world; such essences are understood to be closely linked to the circulatory system, including the heart and blood, and also the lungs, which signal vitality through breathing (Boremanse 1998:91; Vogt 1992:62; Watanabe 1992:88; Wilson 1995:147).

Among the Tzeltal, the second type of soul is the *lab*, an essence that Pitarch (2012:105) describes as the "spirit-soul." People can have variable numbers of these spirit-souls (to a maximum of thirteen), and the number and type of these animal or celestial souls directly relate to a person's character and power. Again, similar concepts abound among the contemporary Maya and are similar to Nahua notions of the *nagual*, although the correlation is imperfect (Gossen 1975; Fabrega and Silver 1973; Vogt 1970; Vogt and Stuart 2005).

Among the contemporary Western Maya, souls are generally understood as "others" while the "self" is fashioned through the body and performed through one's actions, as described earlier (Groark 2012; Haviland and Haviland 1982, 1983; Pitarch 2010). Since what is in other people's hearts is unknowable, people are therefore judged by public action, relating again to Pitarch's notion of the "presence-body" as that which interacts and is perceived by others. Echoing the passage from the Popol Vuh quoted above, the head is understood as the mechanism of perception, and it serves as the intermediary between the souls of the heart and the external world. As Pitarch observes for the Tzeltal, "the interior of the heart of someone is . . . his *talel*, 'that which comes to you as given,' your nature conferred since before birth and therefore formed a priori. For its part, the head depends on discernment, reason" (Pitarch 1996:123–24).[1] Or, as one Tzotzil informant explained to Kevin Groark (2005:137), "first we think in our heart, second we think in our head."

Obviously Tzeltal, Tzotzil, and other contemporary Maya understandings of the body and soul are not precisely the same as those held by the Maya of the Classic period. However, Classic-period texts and images do suggest that aspects of contemporary Maya understandings of the self are paralleled in earlier philosophies regarding the body and soul. For example, persons are described as *winik* in Classic-period texts, a term that Stephen Houston and colleagues (2006:11) suggest carries the nuanced significance of "animate, sentient being" similar to Pitarch's description of the Tzeltal "presence-body" (*winkilel*). Body parts populate Maya texts and images, and a full discussion is beyond the scope of this chapter (for a thorough exegesis of Maya body parts, see Houston et al. 2006). Nevertheless, two key observations are worth noting here: body parts were frequently used as metonyms for the body whole, and the head especially was used to reference a complete person (Houston et al. 2006:11–12).

There is good evidence that the Classic Maya also had roughly similar understandings of the relationship between self, soul, and vitality as described for the contemporary Maya. Animate life force, wind, and breath are idealized in the Classic-period concept of *ik'* (Houston and Taube 2000:267). *K'uhul* is a linguistic cognate for the Tzeltal *ch'ulel*, although the meanings are subtly but importantly different. In Classic-period script, k'uhul is an adjective derived from the noun *k'uh*, an entity generally glossed as a god, deity, or otherworld being in Mayanist literature. K'uhul is linked specifically to royal beings as part of their courtly titles, the so-called emblem glyphs. In that regard, k'uhul is restricted to particular individuals and the lineages or courts they represent, as, for example, in the Piedras Negras emblem glyph *k'uhul yokib' ajaw* (sacred Piedras Negras lord) (Houston and Stuart 1996). What is less clear is whether k'uhul is the state of *yokib'* (the name of the lineage or the lineage's place of origin), the lord himself, or in some sense both (for more on the nature of emblem glyphs, see Stuart and Houston 1994; Tokovinine 2013).

Stephen Houston and David Stuart (1989) identified spiritual "co-essences" in Classic-period texts as *way*. Although the relationship between *way* and the individual remains a matter of debate, it is evident that these essences relate in some manner to power, witchcraft, and illness (Calvin 1997; Grube and Nahm 1994; Helmke and Nielsen 2009; Stuart 2012). In both pre-Columbian and contemporary contexts there is a sense that on one hand these co-essences are linked to particular individuals but yet also exist external to the person and can be found in the wild, underground, in caves, and in other dark places. In their volatility, dangerousness, and animalistic nature, the Classic-period *way* resemble the Tzeltal *lab*.

For the Classic Maya, Houston and Stuart (1998) demonstrate epigraphically that the head was explicitly linked to concepts of self and identity through the use of *baah* (head, face, body, self) and the *u-baah* expression (himself, herself, itself) (fig. 4.2). The convention of the head as a unique signifier is at the essence of Maya writing systems. A significant portion of logographs were drawn as the heads of various entities. The logic extended to Classic Maya portraiture whereby isolated heads could represent ancestors (as on belt ornaments) and to Postclassic-period ancestor veneration whereby the Cocom lords (the rulers of Mayapan) reconstructed the heads of their ancestors from their skulls, which were "kept in oratories of their houses with their idols, holding them in very great reverence and respect" (Tozzer 1941:131). The practice of representing people by disembodied heads has deep antiquity, as testified by the Olmec colossal heads. Naming conven-

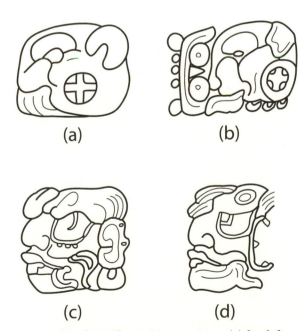

(a)   **(b)**

(c)   **(d)**

Figure 4.2. Heads in Classic Maya writing: (a) *baah* from the Palenque Tablet of the Slaves; (b) *u-baah* from the Yaxchilán Lintel 26; (c) the Palenque Supernatural Patron GI written as his head on the Tablet of the Foliated Cross; and (d) the head of the sun god as the number four on the Palenque Tablet of the Cross (drawings by Andrew Scherer).

tions in Maya art also underscore the head as locus of identity. In order to identify people in painted and sculptural scenes, the Maya invariably placed a person's name next to his or her head, ideally in front of his gaze. Often, Maya kings were depicted wearing their names in their headdress (see Martin and Grube 2008:77). In contrast, names are rarely shown associated with other body parts. The important exception to this rule is the identification of captives, whose names are usually not given near their heads but are instead written across various body parts, a convention that not only marks them as captives but, along with their portrayal as frightened and nearly naked, was perhaps intended to suggest their inhumanity.

Individuation by head is all the more evident in Classic-period depictions of otherworld beings. From the neck down, most Classic-period deities are anthropomorphic and relatively indistinguishable from one another; exceptions include K'awiil's distinctive snake foot. Distinctive skin markings hint at the otherworld nature of such beings but are of little help in their individuation (Coe 1973:54; Houston et al. 2006:16–17), and eyes can be used to sort them into bright/celestial and dark/underworld types (Houston and Taube 2000:283). The Maya convention of identifying otherworld beings by their heads is an interesting contrast to that of other societies where gods and other supernatural beings are distinguished not by their heads but by their associated material culture, as in the classical Greek or Christian traditions. An emphasis on otherworld heads and especially their faces is evident in the Maya tradition of dancing with masks: by appearing as gods, Maya lords and ladies became gods (Grube 1992; Looper 2009).

MAYA HEADS AND THE SHAPING OF SELF

Beyond inscriptions and imagery, the physical remains of the Maya provide another window into how notions of body, soul, and self were materialized through the crafting of the person. Since the late 1990s I have conducted bioarchaeology within the greater Classic Maya kingdoms of Piedras Negras and Yaxchilán. These analyses have included documentation of head shaping and tooth modification. Although my methods have become more refined in recent years, my general approach to cranial shaping has been descriptive and includes recording the absence or presence of cranial modification and the general type observed. Originally I classified using the schema developed by Adolfo Dembo and José Imbelloni (1938) as adopted in the Chicago Standards (Buikstra and Ubelaker 1994). More recently I have followed Vera Tiesler's revised descriptive standards (Tiesler 1998, 2014:table 4.2, fig. 4.5). In addition to assigning modified crania to types, I record detailed observations of the overall shape and take note of any distinctive features that may result from head shaping, including the postcoronal sulcus (a shallow depression that runs over the top of the cranium, more or less from ear to ear), the sagittal sulcus (a shallow depression that runs over the top of the cranium from front to back), and premature synostosis (early fusion of the cranial sutures). I supplement descriptive and typological work with photography and illustration. For dental modifications, I use Javier Romero Molina's (1970, 1986) typology coupled with detailed notes, drawings, and photography. I estimate age and sex using standard osteological criteria (Buikstra and Ubelaker 1994; White et al. 2011).

The largest skeletal sample from the Usumacinta River region comes from the 122 burials excavated at Piedras Negras in the 1930s (Coe 1959; Weeks et al. 2005) and in the late 1990s and early 2000s (Escobedo and Houston 1997, 1998, 1999, 2001, 2005). Since that time, my colleagues and I have excavated burials throughout the kingdoms of Piedras Negras and Yaxchilán on both the Guatemalan and Mexican sides of the river, with the largest series coming from El Kinel (n=12; Yaxchilán-affiliated), Tecolote (n=7; Yaxchilán-affiliated), and Budsilha (n=8; Piedras Negras–affiliated) (Golden and Scherer 2011; Golden, Scherer, and Vásquez 2006, 2008; Scherer et al. 2012, 2013; Scherer, Golden, and Vásquez 2007).

Within the combined Usumacinta skeletal series, there are fifty-five skeletons observable for cranial modification. Of these, forty-seven skulls (85.5 percent) were modified. Following criteria for distinguishing elites from non-elites described in Scherer, Wright, and Yoder (2007), all of the elite crania were modified (8/8; 100 percent) and most of the non-elite crania were as well (39/47; 83.0 percent).

As a result of the notoriously poor skeletal preservation in the Maya lowlands, sex cannot be reliably determined for the majority of the Usumacinta crania, particularly for skeletons where the cranium was incomplete and the os coxae was not preserved (for the limitations of sex estimation from the crania alone, see Rogers 2005; Spradley and Jantz 2011; Williams and Rogers 2006). In the Usumacinta sample, there is a slight bias by sex with more females (11/12; 91.7 percent) demonstrating cranial modification

than males (8/12; 75.0 percent). However, this difference is not statistically significant (χ^2= 2.27; p = 0.132). The greater number of cases of unmodified skulls among the males may have more to do with temporal bias between the two sex samples. As described in the following paragraph, cranial modification is slightly less prevalent in the Early Classic period sample (350–600 CE) than for the Late Classic period sample (600–810 CE). The female sample (for all time periods) includes only one Early Classic skull, whereas the male sample includes four individuals from the Early Classic period.

Combining the crania of known and unknown sex, one skull from the Late Preclassic period is modified (1/1; 100 percent), 69.2 percent (9/13) of the Early Classic skulls are artificially shaped, and 90.9 percent (40/44) of the Late/Terminal Classic-period skulls are modified (fig. 4.3). Although the prevalence of cranial modification along the Usumacinta River is similar to that reported for the entire Maya area by Tiesler (2012:107), the proportion of Early Classic–period modified skulls is low while the Late Classic–period figure is high. This temporal difference may reflect the evolution of regionally specific notions of body aesthetics and beliefs about the development of the human body. Although we have few Early Classic–period depictions of the human head from the Usumacinta region, Late Classic–period art within the kingdoms of Piedras Negras and Yaxchilán is unambiguous with regard to the predominance of the tabular oblique form for kings, queens, and nobility (fig. 4.3a) (Clancy 2009; Graham 1979, 1982; Graham and von Euw 1977; O'Neil 2012; Tate 1992).

Cranial modification does not correlate to social or political affiliation along the Usumacinta River. At Late Classic–period Piedras Negras and its secondary political center of Budsilha, thirty out of thirty-four observable skulls (88.2 percent) are modified. Although data is still forthcoming from the burials at Yaxchilán itself, all seven (100 percent) of the observable skulls from its secondary centers of Tecolote and El Kinel are modified. Within the Piedras Negras kingdom, form can be determined for eighteen of the crania. Seventeen (94.4 percent) of the Classic-period crania are tabular oblique, and one is in the tabular erect form (5.6 percent). Within the Yaxchilán kingdom, form could be determined for three of the Classic-period modified crania; all of them (100 percent) demonstrate tabular oblique shaping. To the northwest, Javier Montes de Paz (2000) reports that at Palenque 90 percent of the skeletal population demonstrates some

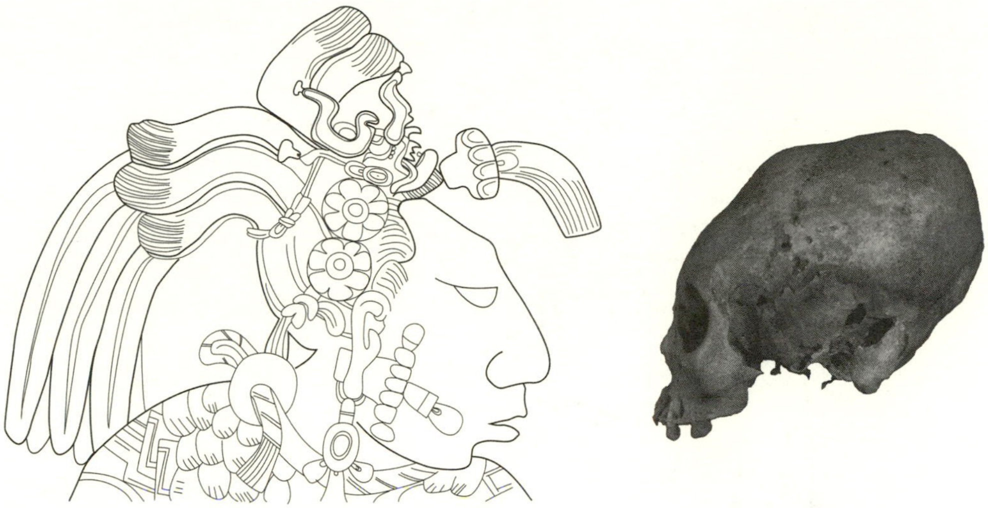

Figure 4.3. Tabular oblique cranial modification along the Usumacinta River: (a) Itzamnaaj Bahlam III from Yaxchilán Lintel 26 (drawing by Andrew Scherer); and (b) left lateral view of the cranium from Piedras Negras Burial 32 (photo by Lori Wright).

(a)

(b)

variant of tabular oblique modification (cited in Tiesler 2012:130). Although variants in tabular oblique forms were not scored at Piedras Negras, all observable tabular oblique skulls at its subordinate center of Budsilha as well as all of the tabular oblique skulls at the Yaxchilán subordinate centers correspond to the tabular oblique mimetic form. The one observable Late Preclassic skull from the region, from the site of Zancudero, is in the tabular erect form.

What is missing from my analysis of cranial modification among the Usumacinta River kingdoms is an assessment of medio-lateral compression (or the absence thereof) with obliquely modified crania. Typically, compression of the cranium with boards led to lateral expansion of the cranium unless an effort was made to limit lateral growth. As Tiesler (2014:88) notes, imagery depicting head binding at Bonampak and Palenque suggests that boards were bound into place with wraps that would indeed inhibit lateral expansion of the cranium. Dembo and Imbelloni (1938) described crania that were modified in such a manner as *pseudocircular* as opposed to true *annular* modification, the latter involving shaping the skull with constrictive wraps alone. My impression is that among the tabular oblique crania of the Usumacinta River region, medio-lateral compression was more common than not. Nevertheless, in my more recent analyses I have noted the presence of tabular oblique crania with lateral expansion at Rancho Búfalo, Mexico (Burial 4), a small community that during the Classic period lay somewhere on the frontier between Piedras Negras and Palenque.

In light of the lack of variability in cranial morphology

among Western Maya from different kingdoms or social standing, the tabular oblique form favored in the West seems to have embodied a general Western Maya belief whereby remodeled heads emulated the shape of maize (Schellhas 1904:24). Tonsuring and binding the hair further accentuated this head form and replicated the tassels of silk found on top of a ripe maize cob. The similarity is part of a broader mythic trope by which humans are like-in-kind to the maize god; as beings of maize, they appear as maize (Fitzsimmons 2009; Scherer 2015; Taube 1985, 2009). Moreover, they have life cycles that mimic this paramount crop and the agricultural cycle more broadly, recalling the agricultural metaphors for growth noted earlier for the contemporary Maya.

Similarly, there is good evidence that the metaphoric link between craftsmanship and human creation, growth, and development has deep antiquity. A series of vessels from the Classic period seem to depict that act of human creation (fig. 4.4) (see also K1185, K5348, K5373, K5597, K6061, K8820, K8940, K9096, K9115 in the Maya Vase Database[2]). Although the details of the scene vary by vase, the common theme is an otherworld being (usually a pair of such entities) seated and shaping what is clearly a human head. In almost all instances, the head is distinctly rendered with the tabular oblique form. In all of the images, there is a sense that creation is still in process as the heads lack hair, jewelry, or other details expected of animate human life. Associated texts provide the verb for the act as either *pak'aj* (it is/was shaped) or *upak'aw* (he shapes/shaped) and the subject or object of the action as *wakil yax winik* (six green/first person) (Boot 2006). Here,

Figure 4.4. Supernatural being crafting a human head from an unprovenienced vessel (drawing by Andrew Scherer after K8457 in the Maya Vase Database).

as to the child's destiny and future occupation (Tozzer 1941:129). What is clear from Landa's *Relación* is that the Yucatec Maya understood a close connection between the head, personal development, and fundamental humanness. Indeed, Classic-period representations of anthropomorphic nonhumans show them with vertical foreheads and apparently lacking cranial modification (the maize god and associated beings are the notable exception). Most Maya otherworld entities were not beings of maize: their bodies were not made of the stuff, nor did they eat it. Thus, unlike humans and mythic maize beings, they lacked the distinctive head shape that marked individuals as entities of maize. Moreover, the very act of binding may have had significance for a child's development, as suggested by William Duncan and Gabrielle Vail (chapter 2 of this volume).

FINISHED HEADS

Just as the binding of the head began the crafting of the Maya self, the modification of the teeth was another important milestone if not the final rite in the process. Within the Usumacinta River sample, there are sixty-four individuals with permanent anterior dentitions that are sufficiently intact to examine for dental modification. The development of the anterior teeth is complete by about the age of twelve or thirteen. The central maxillary incisors, the focal teeth for Maya dental modification, are in place a few years earlier. Thus, the anterior teeth could have been modified any time after about the tenth year of life (deciduous teeth were never modified). Yet, the youngest people to have modified teeth in the Usumacinta skeletal sample are a male and a female from Piedras Negras and a male from El Kinel, all of whom were aged osteologically between eighteen and twenty years old at time of death. Of the six adolescents (twelve to eighteen years old) who are observable in the sample (all from Piedras Negras), none demonstrate dental modification.

One of these Piedras Negras juveniles was buried with a stingray spine that identifies him as a *ch'ok k'in ajaw*, a young or, more literally, *unripe* sun lord. The Classic Maya used *ch'ok* as an adjective to denote young males (and, rarely, females) who were considered still developing or unready (Houston 2009). Most glyphic references to ch'ok indicate young males who have yet to have passed their first *k'atun* (roughly twenty years). Although the connection is

we are almost certainly looking at the creation of the first people by a variety of agents who, depending on the vase, include elderly deities, the maize god, and the Howler Monkey scribe. Both the text and the imagery relate the task of creation to the work of artisans, resonating with the passage from the Popol Vuh noted earlier and placing the singular focus on the head as the embodiment of humanity.

In this sense, supernatural crafting of humans was not unlike the modeling of infants' heads, one of the earliest tasks charged to Maya parents following childbirth. As is widely cited in any discussion of Maya head shaping, Diego de Landa's *Relación de las Cosas* gives us a possible time frame for head shaping, initiated four or five days after birth and lasting for "several days" (Tozzer 1941:125). Presumably a duration of weeks or even months may have been more accurate. Whatever the case, only after head shaping was complete was the infant brought to an indigenous priest to receive a name and the parents instructed not firm, it is possible that the loss of ch'ok status, dental modification, and the passage of the first k'atun were all linked, at least for some individuals.

Judging by a monument from Dos Pilas, one's first bloodletting was another important and painful rite of passage for the Classic Maya, celebrated sometime around the onset of puberty (Houston 2009:163–65). Although certainly not an unbiased perspective, Landa's *Relación* describes head shaping as painful and potentially life threatening (Tozzer 1941:125). Thus, cranial shaping, bloodletting, and dental filing formed a sequence of painful rites of endurance whereby the Maya shaped and marked the body from infancy to adulthood (for more on the value of pain, see Geller 2006; Houston and Scherer 2010). Although such painful acts are no longer practiced today, the Maya still mark their childhood rites of passage with payments to otherworld beings to ensure safe passage from infancy into adulthood (Boremanse 1998:81–88; Love 1989).

Of the sixty-four adult individuals with intact anterior dentition from the Usumacinta River sample, thirty-seven (57.8 percent) demonstrate dental modification (including nine women and eight men). Of the observable maxillary dentitions with incisors (n=32), the most common pattern in the Usumacinta sample is some variant whereby the central incisors are notched, corresponding to Romero's type B4 (12/32; 37.5 percent) (fig. 4.5a; plate 8). The portion of the sample that displays this type of modification includes five men and three women. As Frans Blom (1933:10) noted, this tooth shape corresponds to the Maya sign for *ik'*, denoting wind or breath. Typically, the height of the lateral incisors was filed down (Romero type A4) to accentuate the prominence of the central incisors. The ik'-shaped teeth connote not only the breath that emanates from the mouth but more specifically the body's vital essence as noted earlier. Recall that the contemporary Maya conceive of spiritual essences as embodied by both winds and human breath.

In depictions of humans in Maya art, teeth are rarely seen and modified teeth even less so, although the murals at Calakmul offer a notable exception (Martin 2012). However, teeth are an important attribute of otherworld beings. Although it is the maize god, Hero Twins, and female maize beings that humans most resemble, they share their ik'-shaped teeth with the sun god (figs. 4.2d, 4.5a). The ik' symbolism may indicate not only his vital essence but more generally that he is the source of healthy winds or spiritual essences vital for human life. Although the maize god's teeth are rarely seen in Late Classic–period art, Late Preclassic and Early Classic renderings of this deity do show him to have pronounced central incisors, shown either as a projecting fanglike tooth in profile (especially in the Preclassic period) or "bucktoothed" when viewed frontally (for examples, see Taube 1992:fig. 20).

The ik' incisors of the sun god are part of a broader iconographic program whereby supernatural beings possess prominent central teeth that denote either the essence of their being or the substances upon which they feed (fig. 4.5). The convention can be traced back to Preclassic times when not only the maize god but other gods and otherworld beings were depicted with a fanglike, projecting central tooth. The center fang persists into the Classic period with depictions of a group of related solar and underworld beings who include the jaguar god of the underworld, the Baby Jaguar, and a solar-aquatic being commonly referred to as GI from the Palenque triad (fig. 4.5b). This latter being's projecting central tooth is shown to be either a shark's tooth or a stingray spine, denoting his aquatic nature and linking him to acts of bloodletting. It may be that these projecting central fangs relate to bloodletting and perhaps indicate that beings with such teeth are blood drinkers. In addition to the solar beings, K'awiil and Chaak also have projecting central fangs, although in their mouths these teeth are shown to be even more elongated, especially in Chaak, and may have other significances. Elderly gods are generally depicted edentulous or with only a pair of stunted canines. The one group of supernatural beings who consistently lack a single projecting central tooth are the so-called death gods. With skulls for heads, they are consistently shown as having unmodified, normal-sized, anatomically correct human incisors. That the death gods have unmodified human teeth may simply be a convention to reinforce their skeletal visage, or it may instead be a comment on the nature of their being—that they lack a vital essence found in other beings who are shown with distinct tooth forms. Considering the importance of teeth as indicators of both identity and substance for Maya otherworld entities, it is quite likely that human tooth modification was intended not merely to complete a person but to underscore his or her essence. Unsurprisingly, many Maya likened themselves to the hot, fiery nature of the sun god, a being of power and vitality. At Piedras Negras, the kings frequently took his name, K'inich Ajaw, as part of their regnal titles.

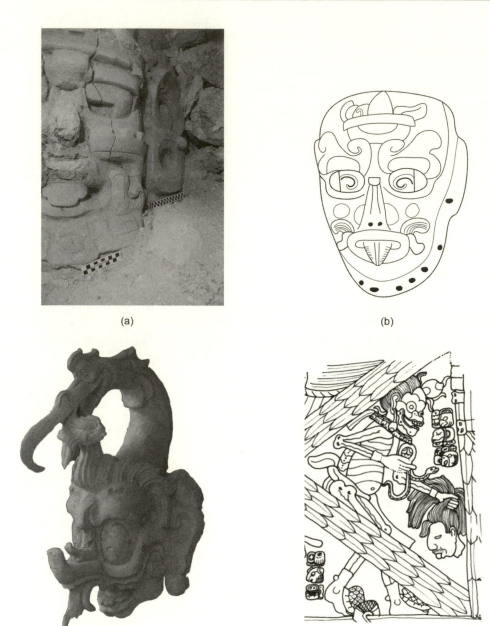

(a)

(b)

(c)

(d)

Figure 4.5. Projecting central tooth of Classic Maya supernaturals: (a) sun god stucco facade from El Diablo, Zotz (photo by Stephen Houston); (b) unprovenienced GI mask, likely from Río Azul (drawing by Andrew Scherer); (c) Chahk architectural ornament from Copán (photo by Andrew Scherer); and (d) death god stucco facade from the fifth terrace of the Toniná Acropolis (drawing by Linda Schele, © David Schele, courtesy of the Foundation for the Advancement of Mesoamerican Studies).

Aside from the common ik' form, other interesting variants of modified teeth are evident in the Usumacinta skeletal assemblage. Three individuals from Piedras Negras have a variant of the ik' incisor pattern: instead of the typical ik'-style right-angled notch, a small triangular wedge was filed into the distal surface of each central incisor (fig. 4.7b). One of these individuals was Ruler 4 of Piedras Negras. This shape is rare among the teeth of the Maya lowlands and includes a Late to Terminal Classic burial at Yaxha (Burial 4; fig. 4.6a), a set of teeth from the tomb of Early Classic Tikal king Yax Nuun Ayiin I (Wright 2005), and a set of teeth attributed to the Early

Classic founder of the Copán dynasty, K'inich Yax Kuk Mo' (Buikstra et al. 2004:fig. 10.1). Epigraphy, iconography, and material culture indicate that the Early Classic–period kings of Tikal and Copán had strong personal connections to the great central Mexican city of Teotihuacan (Stuart 2000, 2004). The kings of Piedras Negras employed Teotihuacan imagery throughout the Classic period, particularly the war serpent headdress, and in general the Maya borrowed heavily from central Mexico for symbolic claims to foreignness and power (Stone 1989).

At Teotihuacan, souls—particularly those of warriors—

Figure 4.6. Modified teeth and Teotihuacan butterfly souls: (a) anterior maxillary teeth from Yaxha Burial 4 (photo by Andrew Scherer); (b) maxillary left incisor from Piedras Negras Burial 13 (photo by Andrew Scherer); (c) butterfly in the Tepantitla murals of Teotihuacan (photo by Andrew Scherer); (d) Teotihuacan *incensario* with stylized butterfly nose ornament (photo by Andrew Scherer); and (e) butterfly (black) conflated with a stylized nose ornament that is suspended in front of a floral element from a Teotihuacan ceramic fragment (drawing by Andrew Scherer after Winning 1987:fig. X-3b).

are represented as butterflies (Berlo 1982). Butterfly souls are shown on the Tepantitla murals, and stylized butterflies are depicted as nose ornaments not only at Teotihuacan but throughout Classic-period Mesoamerica (figs. 4.6c, 4.6d). The connection between the nose ornaments and butterflies is established on a vase from Teotihuacan that conflates the nose ornament and the butterfly (fig. 4.6e). Bodies excavated from the Temple of the Feathered Serpent at Teotihuacan were interred with nose ornaments that resemble the form of butterflies (Sugiyama 2005: fig. 65). Hanging from the nose and in front of the mouth, the butterfly ornament illustrates how the concepts of breath and soul were conflated at Teotihuacan. Thus, the Maya ik' sign and the central Mexican butterfly nose ornament may be considered as complementary concepts. The triangular side-notched incisors recovered at Piedras Negras, Tikal, Copán, and Yaxha recall the stylized shape of the butterfly nose ornament. Importantly, this pattern of

dental modification appears at Teotihuacan with some frequency (Cid Beziez and Torres Sanders 2012:fig. 3; Serrano Sánchez et al. 1993:fig. 4; Spence 1994:fig. 2). In the Maya lowlands, modifying teeth in this distinctive shape may have been another example of the Maya wielding foreign symbols to convey notions of power and legitimacy. More speculatively, such modified forms may have been made as part of specific claims to the possession of foreign souls, much as Tzeltal people can have co-essences who are Castilians and other nonindigenous peoples, entities associated with both otherness and strength (Pitarch 2010:6).

The discussion thus far has focused on modification of the central incisors. However, 32.4 percent (11/34) of the individuals with modified teeth have notches on the distal aspect of the canines, including four men and seven women. Nine of these individuals possessed modified canines with triangular wedges removed from their distal aspects (Romero type B5), similar to the butterfly style

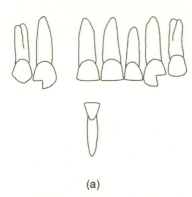

(a)

(b)

Figure 4.7. Teeth shaped to accentuate the canines: (a) Burial 55 from Piedras Negras (drawing by Andrew Scherer); and (b) central Mexican storm god from the Tepantitla Murals of Teotihuacan (photo by Andrew Scherer).

of the incisors. The other two individuals have notched canines similar to the ik' incisors (Romero type B4). Of these eleven individuals, eight have no apparent modification of the incisors. It is possible that dental wear obscured earlier modifications. However, at least in the case of one eighteen- to twenty-one-year-old individual (Piedras Negras Burial 55), the height of the incisors was clearly reduced by filing (Romero type A4) as a means to accentuate the notched canines (fig. 4.7). It is possible that the notching of the canines was intended to suggest a single ik' or butterfly sign. Alternatively, this modification may have been meant to replicate the long, curved fangs associated with various animals (especially jaguars) and some supernatural beings, such as the central Mexican storm god.

The only other style of dental modification observed among the Usumacinta River skeletal sample was found in two individuals who exhibit maxillary teeth with serrated incisal edges (Romero type A3), one from a peripheral house group at Piedras Negras and the other from a peripheral group at the Yaxchilán subsidiary center of Tecolote. The sex of both of these individuals is indeterminate. The pattern is rare in the Maya area and may indicate something particular about these individuals. The meaning behind this pattern is not known, although it could be an attempt to replicate the tiny bumps (mamelons) that are present on erupting incisors in juveniles. Alternatively, Nawa Sugiyama (personal communication, 2015) points out that the style also occurs at Teotihuacan, where it might be meant to replicate the tiny incisors of wolves or other canids.

Aside from shaping the anterior teeth, the Maya also drilled into their surfaces and inset rare stones, including jade, pyrite, and hematite. Altogether, 26.4 percent (8/34) of the individuals with modified dentition in the Usumacinta River sample have inlays in their teeth, all of whom are from Piedras Negras. Two of these individuals have pyrite (or possibly hematite) inlays, one has jade inlays, one has a combination of jade and pyrite, and all of the inlays were missing for the remaining four skeletons. In some sense, dental inlays were a display of wealth and a means to achieve a beauty inaccessible to most other people. However, the substances that were inset also had significance. Jade was a durable symbol of fertility and vitality, and dental encrustations were thus another means for the Maya to embody those virtues. As Karl Taube (2005) shows, jade is closely affiliated with wind and breath, and jade-encrusted teeth reinforce the same principal as ik'-modified teeth. Metaphorically, teeth are conflated with seeds in modern Maya thought, and in the K'iche' myth, Seven Macaw's jeweled teeth were replaced by maize grains (Christenson 2007a:46). Conceptualizing the modified head as a whole, the tabular oblique head embodied the cob of maize, while jade-encrusted teeth may have implied the individual grains of maize.

IDENTITY, POWER, AND EMBODIMENT

As the prior two sections show, head shaping and tooth modification embodied a range of concepts pertaining to growth, development, and beliefs about the nature of body and soul. More challenging is the question of whether such bodywork can be used to understand aspects of identity and notions of power among the Classic Maya of the Usumacinta River kingdoms. Identity is, of course, a slippery concept. It is challenging to articulate what constitutes the "identity" of contemporary peoples today, and it is doubly difficult for archaeologists to tease out identities of ancient peoples (see, for example, Buikstra and Scott 2009; Insoll 2007; Knudson and Stojanowski 2009; Sökefeld 1999). Classic-period Maya texts and imagery allow us to glimpse emic understandings of some dimensions of identity: gender, age, noble titles and occupations, and affiliation with royal courts/elite lineages (i.e., kingdoms) as evidenced by the use of the so-called emblem glyphs (Houston 2009; Miller and Martin 2004; Tokovinine 2013).

Other people and their identities are generally more elusive but no less important, such as non-elites and the lineages to which they were attached or the occupations they engaged in. Only occasional discoveries like the murals at Calakmul offer us a window into the lives and occupations of such individuals (Carrasco Vargas et al. 2009; Martin 2012). The opaqueness of some social actors is itself evidence of the existence of inequality in Classic Maya society; the visibility of members of the royal courts and those proximate to those individuals hints at the greater wealth they possessed and their ability to exercise their authority over others.

From the evidence for cranial shaping in the kingdoms of Piedras Negras and Yaxchilán, there is no indication that different head shapes or tooth styles were related to sex. Body modification clearly was, however, associated with age: head shaping was the first step in the long and often painful process of crafting the Maya person. Modifying the teeth seems to have marked an important milestone if not the completion of the process. Although some aspects of body adornment express inequality in wealth and power, head shaping was not related to status among Usumacinta River Maya. The matter of tooth modification is, however, more complex. In the Usumacinta sample, 62.5 percent of elites (5/8) and 57.2 percent of non-elites (32/56) exhibit some form of tooth modification. Thus, contrary to popular conception, dental modification was not limited to the elites; all members of Maya society seem to have had the right to modify their teeth once they achieved adulthood.

Nevertheless, there is quite a bit of variability in the degree of skill involved in different types of tooth modifi-

cation, and dental inlays in particular would have required both refined talent and access to rare, imported materials. The drilling of teeth and inlaying with rare stone was only evident in skeletons at Piedras Negras, although a possible aborted inlay attempt was observed in a young adult skeleton from El Kinel (Scherer et al. 2014:fig. 8.10). Within the Piedras Negras sample, however, individuals of all apparent statuses had dental inlays, although jade was only observed among elite and especially royal individuals. Yet inlaying itself was relatively rare, suggesting some degree of exclusivity even among people who were otherwise not obviously elite based on their burial context or associated grave goods. The K'iche' Popol Vuh certainly hints at the value of dental encrustations as a sign of beauty, prestige, and even vanity. Seven Macaw boasts that "its seeds my face merely sparkle with glittering green/blue jewels, as well my teeth green/blue brilliant with stones, like its face sky" (Christenson 2007a:38). As a mythic admonition against vanity and pride, two elderly supernatural curers removed Seven Macaw's bejeweled teeth so that "not lord now he appeared" (Christenson 2007a:46).

The rarity of inlaying is likely not a reflection of some formal prohibition of the act. Rather, the careful craftwork involved and especially the preciousness of the materials introduced likely limited such dental work to people who had access to both the rare materials to be inserted into the teeth and the craftspeople with the talent to achieve the desired effect. The drill work necessary to inlay the teeth would have required a degree of skill, and perhaps the craftspeople responsible for placing the inlays were lapidaries, which may in part explain the lack of inlay work outside the polity capital in the Piedras Negras kingdom. The possibly aborted attempt in the individual from El Kinel provides anecdotal evidence as to the risks of inlaying. This young adult's right maxillary central incisor exhibits a carious lesion on the labial surface, an area unlikely to be affected by pathology unless an opening was intentionally made on the surface of the tooth (Scherer et al. 2014: fig. 8.10).

Among the people with inlays in the Usumacinta River sample, there is definite variability in the quality and elaborateness of the dental work that was performed. Ruler 3 of Piedras Negras has the most extensive inlays, with large, finely crafted jade and pyrite encrustations set across his maxillary teeth (incisors to premolars) and mandibular teeth (incisors to canines) (plate 8). The large yet shallow perforations necessary to set such encrustations would not have been easily made using the drills available to the Maya. In contrast, an Early Classic–period elite (or perhaps royal) man who possessed an extra set of supernumerary incisors chose to have five tiny jade encrustations set into a single tooth, dental work that is evidence of not only the skill but also the creativity involved in such a technique (plate 9).

And what of the matter of head shaping, tooth modification, and ethnicity? As with identity in general, the concept of ethnicity is fraught with problems, particularly as we attempt to apply modern notions of ethnicity to ancient societies (Emberling 1997). In Mesoamerica, there is little doubt that ideas of belonging and group identity were constructed along lines that resemble contemporary notions of ethnicity. For example, the sixteenth-century Florentine Codex distinguishes various peoples (e.g., Tolteca, Chichimeca, Otomí, Quaquata, Matlatzinca, Toloque, Totanaque, Huaxteca, Olmeca, Mixteca, and Mexica) based on where they lived, what language they spoke, what foods they preferred, what clothes they wore, what crafts they specialized in, and even what their behavioral inclinations were (Sahagún 1961:165–89). What is less clear, however, is whether the peoples we label today "the ancient Maya" had any notion of what we would identify as ethnic distinctions among themselves. The very concept of "Maya" is, of course, an imposed construct, one that is strategically employed today by academics, outsiders, and, in some instances, the Maya themselves (Fischer 2001; Restall 2004). In speaking of the contemporary Maya, scholars frequently divide and categorize the Maya using language, distinguishing Tzeltal from Tzotzil, K'iche' from Kaqchiquel, and so on. Language does not seem to be, however, the most important unit of group identity among contemporary Mayan speakers. Rather, it is the community and the lineage that are given primacy, much as they were at the time of the conquest (Restall 2004:73). If we assume similar constructions of affiliation in the Classic period, there is little evidence that the data on head shaping and tooth modification among the communities of Piedras Negras and Yaxchilán were in any way used to mark oneself as a member of a particular lineage, town, or even the kingdom at large. As my colleagues and I have explored elsewhere, other aspects of lived experience certainly did, however, distinguish members of these competing and often warring kingdoms (Golden and Scherer 2013; Golden, Scherer, Muñoz, and Vásquez 2008; Scherer 2015; Scherer et al. 2014). For example, funerary rites, ritual orientations, pottery production, and archi-

tecture united peoples of one kingdom and distinguished them from residents of the neighboring kingdom.

This is not to say that non-Maya peoples did not perceive the Classic-period Maya as a common collective, or even that the Maya did not perceive commonalities among themselves that set them apart from other Mesoamerican peoples. The murals at the central Mexican site of Cacaxtla offer a compelling (albeit frustrating) glimpse of the relationship between identity, ethnicity, and head shaping among Classic-period Mesoamerican peoples. These murals date to sometime in the eighth or ninth century (Brittenham 2015:52), coeval with the apogee of the Piedras Negras and Yaxchilán kingdoms and the period of time in which the majority of the people discussed in this study lived and died. The style and symbolism employed in the murals leave little doubt that if they were not made by Maya artisans, then their makers were at least strongly influenced by Maya artistic vision. In a masterful analysis of these murals, Claudia Brittenham (2015) argues that the content of the murals is, however, quite particular to the central Mexican community of Cacaxtla, presumably reflecting the motivations and interests of the lords who commissioned these great works. One particular scene, the Battle Mural, is relevant to the discussion of head shaping and ethnicity. In this scene, jaguar-clad warriors with unmodified (or minimally shaped) crania do battle against eagle-clad warriors with heads shaped in the characteristic tabular oblique style of the Maya (particularly the Western Maya) (fig. 4.8). For some, this distinction in costuming and head shaping suggests that the murals show central Mexican warriors (those without modified heads) defeating a Maya war band (those with shaped crania) (Carlson 1991:14–15; McVicker 1985:86). Sharisse McCafferty and Geoffrey McCafferty (1994:159) go as far as to suggest that the combatants are depicted as "racially distinct factions." In a break from most Maya painterly traditions, many of the warriors from both sides of the conflict are shown openmouthed, with unmodified teeth clearly displayed. The jaguar warriors are led by a man named "3 Deer" (or perhaps "3 Deer Antler"), presumably an important warrior or ruler at Cacaxtla. He is depicted twice in this particular mural, in both cases with an unmodified head and unmodified teeth (figs. 4.8a, 4.8b). His compatriots are also shown with unmodified heads (fig. 4.8d). The central eagle protagonist in the Battle Mural is distinctly clad in women's clothes (for the ambiguity of the gender in these depictions, see

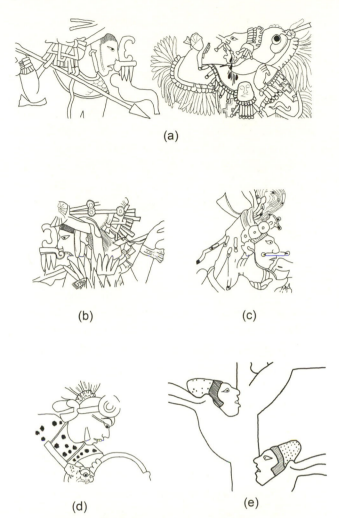

(a)

(b)   (c)

(d)   (e)

Figure. 4.8. Head shaping in the murals of Cacaxtla:
(a) unmodified head of "3 Deer" (left) and his opponent
with a tabular oblique head shape from the Battle Mural
(right); (b) second depiction of 3 Deer Antler in the Battle
Mural; (c) 3 Deer Antler with tabular oblique modification from the south jamb of the Structure A mural;
(d) unmodified crania of the jaguar warrior from the
Battle Mural; and (e) tabular oblique shape of maize beings from the Red Temple (drawings by Andrew Scherer).

Brittenham 2015:122–25; McCafferty and McCafferty
1994). He is depicted twice (or perhaps two different
individuals who are similarly dressed are shown) and is
rendered with tabular oblique modification and unmodified teeth (fig. 4.8a, right-side figure). The sense is that the
artists perceived head shape as a marker of identity (perhaps even ethnicity) in the Battle Mural, whereas tooth
modification was not relevant to such a discourse.

However, the association between head shaping and
identity in the Cacaxtla murals is complicated by a likely

third depiction of 3 Deer in a separate mural on Structure
A (fig. 4.8c). Here, he is rendered with a flattened frontal
bone consistent with a tabular oblique head shape. Is this
simply an artistic error? Is this not the same person? Or,
as some have noted, perhaps the mutability of depictions
of head form suggests plasticity in notions of ethnicity
at Cacaxtla (Piña Chan 1998:99). However, Brittenham
(2015:139) makes a compelling case that the depiction of
head shape and other aspects of the face at Cacaxtla may
have had nothing to do with the portrayal of individual
or group identity. Brittenham points to another mural
painted in the nearby Red Temple that shows anthropomorphic maize with the tabular oblique head shape
and tonsured hair characteristic of the Maya maize god
(fig. 4.8e). Curiously, the maize beings are also shown with
what are undeniably projecting incisors that are characteristic of their depiction in the Preclassic and Early Classic periods. Thus, the elongated head form in the artistic
program at Cacaxtla may pertain less to matters of identity and point instead to perceptions of embodiment and
the nature of beings. In the context of the Battle Mural,
the exaggerated shape may have been intended to explicitly underscore the defeated as like-in-kind to maize. As
Brittenham notes, such a trope is by no means unique
to Cacaxtla and is widely evident in Classic Maya art, in
which captive heads are grabbed like cobs of maize and
harvested as crop by victorious captors. In this context,
the apparently unmodified heads of the jaguar warriors
may not have been intended to clarify their ethnicity but
merely to distinguish them from the defeated.

I introduce the case of the Cacaxtla murals to highlight
what is fundamental about Maya head shaping and tooth
modification: through these acts, humans crafted themselves into idealized beings, entities that embodied maize,
vitality, life, and fertility. This is not to say that modification of the body may not provide clues to understandings of identity. Rather, we must be careful in assuming
that ancient peoples perceived particular head shapes or
tooth modifications as projections of belonging and group
identity. The tabular oblique head form was not a procla-
mation of "Western Mayaness" but was instead the manifestation of a shared practice relating to the permanent
embodiment of common belief. Nevertheless, as Tiesler
and Lacadena demonstrate in chapter 3 of this volume,
when pre-Columbian Mesoamerican people encountered
individuals from other societies where practices such as
head shaping differed from their own, such traditions may

have been ascribed significance in terms of highlighting these foreign individuals as "other."

What, if anything, was signified by unmodified head shapes at Cacaxtla or in the Usumacinta skeletal sample? Two Early Classic–period men in the sample considered in this study (Piedras Negras Burials 26A, 119) demonstrate neither cranial shaping nor tooth modification, perhaps hinting at something fundamentally distinct about these men, rooted in their infancy as evidenced by the lack of head shaping. Moreover, Burial 26 is one of only a handful of flexed or bundled burials at Piedras Negras, a practice that could indicate that this man was a foreigner. A nearby woman (Burial 26B) was also bundled in a flexed position, and her cranium was not modified (unfortunately, her anterior teeth were missing and could not be examined for modification). A Late Classic–period skeleton without cranial modification (Burial 111) had serrated maxillary incisors (Romero's types A1 and A2), a rare form of dental modification as noted earlier. Yet other Early Classic (Burial 34) and Late Classic–period (Burial 41) men with unmodified crania did have filed anterior teeth, shaped in the relatively common ik' motif. If I were to hazard a guess, in some instances the absence of modification should be taken as evidence of something particular or distinct about the identities of the dead (e.g., Burials 26A, 26B, 111). In other cases, however, unmodified crania could speculatively be explained by a variety of scenarios, such as a child born to a mother without the knowledge (or familial support) as to how to properly head shape, or perhaps a child who suffered from a severe illness, making head binding untenable, as also suggested by Tiesler and Lacadena in chapter 3 of this volume. Future work on Maya body modification should consider the cranial and dental data in concert with mortuary practices and migratory isotope data to better tease out the significance of rare modification types or instances in which there are no modifications.

CONCLUSIONS

The Maya head was the seat of the self and the locus of identity. It was the primary means by which the individual experienced the world. In contemporary Maya thought, the head is contrasted to the heart, the seat of one's (plural) souls. The cultural shaping of the head was a metaphor for the social development of the individual. That process began with the modeling of the head in infancy and ended with the modification of the teeth at the transition to adulthood. Among the Maya of the Western Classic–period kingdoms, the tabular oblique form was the dominant head shape and ik'-shaped incisors were the most common dental modification. Both demonstrate the Western Maya's perceived affinity to maize and solar supernatural beings. Although neither head shaping nor tooth modification seems intended as a projection of group identity, both reflect commonalities of shared belief and practice among the Classic-period Maya peoples of the Usumacinta River kingdoms.

ACKNOWLEDGMENTS

I thank Vera Tiesler and Nené Lozada for the opportunity to contribute this chapter. Excavation and laboratory analysis of human skeletons along the Usumacinta River was supported by the Piedras Negras Archaeology Project (directed by Stephen Houston and Héctor Escobedo), the Sierra del Lacandón Regional Archaeology Project (directed by Andrew Scherer and Charles Golden), and the Proyecto Regional Arqueológico Busilja-Chocolja (directed by Andrew Scherer, Charles Golden, Rosaura Vásquez, Ana Lucía Arroyave Prera, and Luz Midilia Marroquín). Permissions and support at Piedras Negras was provided by the Instituto de Antropología e Historia de Guatemala, generous donations by Ken Woolley and Spence Kirk of Salt Lake City, the National Geographic Society, the Ahau Foundation, the Heinz Foundation, Brigham Young University, and the Foundation for the Advancement of Mesoamerican Studies. Permissions and support for the latter two projects were provided by the Instituto de Antropología e Historia de Guatemala, the Instituto Nacional de Antropología e Historia de México, the Foundation for the Advancement of Mesoamerican Studies (Grants #2020, 05027, and 07043), the National Geographic Society (Grants #7575–04 and 7636–04), the National Science Foundation (SBE-BCS Archaeology Grants #0406472 and 075463), a Waitt Foundation–National Geographic Society grant (W90-10, awarded to Kingsley), Dumbarton Oaks Research Library, H. John Heinz III Charitable Trust Grants for Latin American Archeology, the Kaplan Fund through the World Monuments Fund, Baylor University, the Norman Fund and the Jane's Fund at Brandeis University, and Brown University through the professorial funds of Stephen Houston.

NOTES

1. My translation from: "el interior del corazón de alguien es . . . su *talel*, 'aquello que le viene dado,' su naturaleza conferida desde antes del nacimiento y por consiguiente formada *a priori*. Por su parte, de la cabeza depende el discernimiento, la razón."

2. See the Maya Vase Database, created by Justin Kerr, at http://research.mayavase.com/kerrmaya.html.

REFERENCES CITED

Berlo, Janet Catherine

1982 Artistic Specialization at Teotihuacan: The Ceramic Incense Burner. In *Pre-Columbian Art History: Selected Readings*, edited by Alana Cordy-Collins, pp. 83–100. Peek Publications, Palo Alto, California.

Blom, Frans

1933 Historical Background. In *A Maya Skull from the Uloa Valley, Republic of Honduras*, by Frans Blom, S. S. Grosjean, and Harold Cummins, pp. 7–14. Middle American Research Institute, Tulane University, New Orleans.

Boot, Erik

2006 What Happened on the Date 7 Manik' 5 Woh? An Analysis of Text and Image on Kerr nos. 0717, 7447, and 8457. *Wayeb Notes* 20:1–21.

Boremanse, Didier

1998 *Hach Winik: The Lacandon Maya of Chiapas, Southern Mexico*. Institute for Mesoamerican Studies, State University of New York at Albany.

Brittenham, Claudia

2015 *The Murals of Cacaxtla: The Power of Painting in Ancient Central Mexico*. University of Texas Press, Austin.

Buikstra, Jane Ellen, T. Douglas Price, Lori E. Wright, and James Hutson Burton

2004 Tombs and Burials in the Early Classic Acropolis at Copan. In *Understanding Early Classic Copan*, edited by Ellen E. Bell, Marcello A. Canuto, and Robert J. Sharer, pp. 191–212. University of Pennsylvania Museum of Archaeology and Anthropology, Philadelphia.

Buikstra, Jane Ellen, and Rachel E. Scott

2009 Key Concepts in Identity Studies. In *Bioarchaeology and Identity in the Americas*, edited by Kelly J. Knudson and Christopher M. Stojanowski, pp. 24–58. University Press of Florida, Gainesville.

Buikstra, Jane Ellen, and Douglas H. Ubelaker

1994 *Standards for Data Collection from Human Skeletal Remains*. Arkansas Archeological Survey Research Series no. 44. Arkansas Archeological Survey, Fayetteville.

Calvin, Inga

1997 Where the Wayob Live: A Further Examination of Classic Maya Supernaturals. In *Maya Vase Book: A Corpus of Rollout Photographs of Maya Vases*, vol. 5, edited by Justin Kerr, pp. 868–83. Kerr Associates, New York.

Carlson, John B.

1991 *Venus-Regulated Warfare and Ritual Sacrifice in Mesoamerica: Teotihuacan and the Cacaxtla "Star Wars" Connection*. University of Maryland Center for Archaeoastronomy, College Park.

Carrasco Vargas, Ramón, Verónica A. Vázquez López, and Simon Martin

2009 Daily Life of the Ancient Maya Recorded on Murals at Calakmul, Mexico. *Proceedings of the National Academy of Sciences* 106(46):19245–49.

Christenson, Allen J.

2007a *Popol Vuh: Literal Poetic Version; Transcription and Translation*. University of Oklahoma Press, Norman.

2007b *Popol Vuh: The Sacred Book of the Maya; The Great Classic of Central American Spirituality, Translated from the Original Maya Text*. University of Oklahoma Press, Norman.

Cid Beziez, José Rodolfo, and Liliana Torres Sanders

2012 Patrones de mutilación dental en el sector oeste de Teotihuacan. *Estudios de Antropología Biológica* 9:281–94.

Clancy, Flora Simmons

2009 *The Monuments of Piedras Negras, an Ancient Maya City*. University of New Mexico Press, Albuquerque.

Coe, Michael D.

1973 *The Maya Scribe and His World*. Grolier Club, New York.

Coe, William R.

1959 *Piedras Negras Archaeology: Artifacts, Caches, and Burials*. Museum Monograph 4, University Museum, University of Pennsylvania, Philadelphia.

Dembo, Adolfo, and José Imbelloni

1938 Deformaciones intencionales del cuerpo humano de carácter étnico. Biblioteca Humanior, Buenos Aires.

Emberling, Geoffrey

1997 Ethnicity in Complex Societies: Archaeological Perspectives. *Journal of Archaeological Research* 5(4):295–344.

Escobedo, Héctor L., and Stephen D. Houston (editors)

1997   *Proyecto Arqueológico Piedras Negras: informe prelimi-
       nar no. 1, tercera temporada, 1997.* Instituto de Antro-
       pología e Historia, Guatemala City.

1998   *Proyecto Arqueológico Piedras Negras: informe pre-
       liminar no. 2, tercera temporada, 1998.* Instituto de
       Antropología e Historia, Guatemala City.

1999   *Proyecto Arqueológico Piedras Negras: informe pre-
       liminar no. 3, tercera temporada, 1999.* Instituto de
       Antropología e Historia, Guatemala City.

2001   *Proyecto Arqueológico Piedras Negras: informe pre-
       liminar no. 4, cuarta temporada, 2000.* Instituto de
       Antropología e Historia, Guatemala City.

2005   *Informe de las intevenciones en la estructura K-5 de Pie-
       dras Negras.* Report presented to the Dirección General
       del Patrimonio Cultural y Natural de Guatemala.

Fabrega, Horacio, Jr., and Daniel B. Silver

1973   *Illness and Shamanistic Curing in Zinacantan: An
       Ethnomedical Analysis.* Stanford University Press,
       Stanford, California.

Fischer, Edward F.

2001   *Cultural Logics and Global Economics: Maya Identity in
       Thought and Practice.* University of Texas Press, Austin.

Fitzsimmons, James L.

2009   *Death and the Classic Maya Kings.* University of Texas
       Press, Austin.

Geller, Pamela L.

2006   Altering Identities: Body Modification and the Pre-
       Columbian Maya. In *Social Archaeology of Funerary
       Remains*, edited by Rebecca Gowland and Christo-
       pher J. Knüsel, pp. 279–91. Oxbow Books, Oxford.

Golden, Charles, and Andrew K. Scherer

2011   (editors) *Proyecto Arqueológico Busilja-Chocolja:
       informe de la segunda temporada de investigación.*
       Consejo de Arqueología, Instituto Nacional de Antro-
       pología e Historia, Mexico City.

2013   Territory, Trust, Growth, and Collapse in Classic Period
       Maya Kingdoms. *Current Anthropology* 54(4):397–417.

**Golden, Charles, Andrew K. Scherer, A. René Muñoz,
and Rosaura Vásquez**

2008   Piedras Negras and Yaxchilan: Divergent Political
       Trajectories in Adjacent Maya Polities. *Latin American
       Antiquity* 19(3):249–74.

**Golden, Charles, Andrew K. Scherer, and Rosaura Vásquez
(editors)**

2006   *Proyecto Regional Arqueológico Sierra Lacandon:
       informe preliminar no. 4.* Instituto de Antropología e
       Historia, Guatemala City.

2008   *Proyecto Regional Arqueológico Sierra Lacandon:
       informe preliminar no. 6.* Instituto de Antropología e
       Historia, Guatemala City.

Gossen, Gary H.

1975   Animal Souls and Human Destiny in Chamula. *Man*
       10(3):448–61.

Graham, Ian

1979   *Corpus of Maya Hieroglyphic Inscriptions.* Vol. 3, part
       2, *Yaxchilan*. Peabody Museum, Harvard University,
       Cambridge, Massachusetts.

1982   *Corpus of Maya Hieroglyphic Inscriptions.* Vol. 3, part
       3, *Yaxchilan*. Peabody Museum, Harvard University,
       Cambridge, Massachusetts.

Graham, Ian, and Eric von Euw

1977   *Corpus of Maya Hieroglyphic Inscriptions.* Vol. 3, part
       1, *Yaxchilan*. Peabody Museum, Harvard University,
       Cambridge, Massachusetts.

Groark, Kevin Patrick

2005   Pathogenic Emotions: Sentiment, Sociality, and
       Sickness among the Tzotzil Maya of San Juan Cham-
       ula, Chiapas, Mexico. Unpublished PhD dissertation,
       Department of Anthropology, University of California,
       Los Angeles.

2012   Toward a Cultural Phenomenology of Intersubjectiv-
       ity: The Extended Relational Field of the Tzotzil Maya
       of Highland Chiapas, Mexico. *Language and Commu-
       nication* 33(3):278–91.

Grube, Nikolai

1992   Classic Maya Dance: Evidence from Hieroglyphs and
       Iconography. *Ancient Mesoamerica* 3:201–18.

Grube, Nikolai, and Werner Nahm

1994   A Census of Xibalba: A Complete Inventory of *Way*
       Characters on Maya Ceramics. In *The Maya Vase
       Book: A Corpus of Rollout Photographs of Maya Vases*,
       vol. 4, edited by Justin Kerr, pp. 688–715. Kerr Associ-
       ates, New York.

Haviland, Leslie K., and John B. Haviland

1982   Inside the Fence: The Social Basis of Privacy in
       Nabenchauk. *Estudios de Cultura Maya* 14:
       323–51.

1983   Privacy in a Mexican Indian Village. In *Public and
       Private in Social Life*, edited by Stanley I. Benn and
       Gerald F. Gaus, pp. 341–61. St. Martin's Press, New
       York; Croom Helm, London.

Helmke, Christophe, and Jesper Nielsen

2009   Hidden Identity and Power in Ancient Mesoamerica:
       Supernatural Alter Egos as Personified Diseases. *Acta
       Americana* 17(2):49–98.

Houston, Stephen D.

2009 A Splendid Predicament: Young Men in Classic Maya Society. *Cambridge Archaeological Journal* 19(2): 149–78.

Houston, Stephen D., and Andrew K. Scherer

2010 La ofrenda máxima: el sacrificio humano en la parte central del área Maya. In *Nuevas perspectivas sobre el sacrificio humano entre los Mexicas*, edited by Leonardo López Luján and Guilhem Olivier, pp. 167–91. Instituto Nacional de Antropología e Historia, Mexico City.

Houston, Stephen D., and David Stuart

1989 The *Way* Glyph: Evidence for "Co-essences" among the Classic Maya. *Research Reports on Ancient Maya Writing* 30:1–16.

1996 Of Gods, Glyphs, and Kings: Divinity and Rulership among the Classic Maya. *Antiquity* 70:289–312.

1998 The Ancient Maya Self: Personhood and Portraiture in the Classic Period. *RES: Anthropology and Aesthetics* 33:73–101.

Houston, Stephen D., David Stuart, and Karl Taube

2006 *The Memory of Bones: Body, Being, and Experience among the Classic Maya*. University of Texas Press, Austin.

Houston, Stephen D., and Karl Taube

2000 An Archaeology of the Senses: Perceptions and Cultural Expression in Ancient Mesoamerica. *Cambridge Archaeological Journal* 10(2):261–94.

Insoll, Timothy

2007 Introduction: Configuring Identities in Archaeology. In *The Archaeology of Identities: A Reader*, edited by Timothy Insoll, pp. 1–18. Routledge, New York.

Knudson, Kelly J., and Christopher M. Stojanowski

2009 The Bioarchaeology of Identity. In *Bioarchaeology and Identity in the Americas*, edited by Kelly J. Knudson and Christopher M. Stojanowski, pp. 1–23. University Press of Florida, Gainesville.

Looper, Matthew G.

2009 *To Be Like Gods: Dance in Ancient Maya Civilization*. University of Texas Press, Austin.

López Austin, Alfredo

1980 *Cuerpo humano e ideologia: las concepciones de los antiguos Nahuas*. Universidad Nacional Autónoma de México, Mexico City.

Love, Bruce

1989 Yucatec Sacred Breads through Time. In *Word and Image in Maya Culture: Explorations in Language, Writing, and Representations*, edited by William F.

Hanks and Don S. Rice, pp. 336–50. University of Utah Press, Salt Lake City.

Martin, Simon

2012 Hieroglyphs from the Painted Pyramid: The Epigraphy of Chiik Nahb Structure Sub 1-4, Calakmul, Mexico. In *Maya Archaeology 2: Featuring the Ancient Maya Murals of Calakmul, Mexico*, edited by Charles Golden, Stephen Houston, and Joel Skidmore, pp. 60–81. Precolumbia Mesoweb Press, San Francisco.

Martin, Simon, and Nikolai Grube

2008 *Chronicle of the Maya Kings and Queens: Deciphering the Dynasties of the Ancient Maya*. 2nd ed. Thames and Hudson, New York.

McCafferty, Sharisse D., and Geoffrey G. McCafferty

1994 The Conquered Women of Cacaxtla. *Ancient Mesoamerica* 5(2):159–72.

McVicker, Donald

1985 The "Mayanized" Mexicans. *American Antiquity* 50:82–101.

Miller, Mary, and Simon Martin

2004 *Courtly Art of the Ancient Maya*. Thames and Hudson, New York.

Montes de Paz, Javier

2000 La práctica de la deformación cefálica intencional entre los pobladores prehispánicos de Palenque, Chiapas. Master's thesis, Escuela Nacional de Antropología e Historia, Instituto Nacional de Antropología e Historia, Mexico City.

O'Neil, Megan E.

2012 *Engaging Ancient Maya Sculpture at Piedras Negras, Guatemala*. University of Oklahoma Press, Norman.

Piña Chan, Román

1998 *Cacaxtla: fuentes históricas y pinturas*. Fondode Cultura Económica, Mexico City.

Pitarch, Pedro

1996 *Ch'ulel: una etnografía de las almas Tzeltales*. Fondo de Cultura Económica, Mexico City.

2010 *The Jaguar and the Priest: An Ethnography of Tzeltal Souls*. University of Texas Press, Austin.

2012 The Two Maya Bodies: An Elementary Model of Tzeltal Personhood. *Ethnos* 77(1):93–114.

Restall, Matthew

2004 Maya Ethnogenesis. *Journal of Latin American Anthropology* 9(1):64–89.

Rogers, Tracy L.

2005 Determining the Sex of Human Remains through Cranial Morphology. *Journal of Forensic Sciences* 50(3):493–500.

Romero Molina, Javier

1970 Dental Mutilation, Trephination, and Cranial Defor-
      mation. In *Handbook of Middle American Indians*,
      edited by T. Dale Stewart and Robert Wauchope, vol. 9,
      pp. 50–67. University of Texas Press, Austin.

1986 *Catálogo de la colección de dientes mutilados prehis-
      pánicos iv parte*. Instituto Nacional de Antropología e
      Historia, Mexico City.

Sahagún, Bernardino de

1961 *General History of the Things of New Spain: Florentine
      Codex*. Book 10, *The People*. Translated by Arthur J. O.
      Anderson and Charles E. Dibble. University of Utah
      Press, Salt Lake City.

Schellhas, Paul

1904 *Representations of Deities of the Maya Manuscripts*.
      Vol. 4, no. 1. Peabody Museum, Harvard University,
      Cambridge, Massachusetts.

Scherer, Andrew K.

2015 *Classic Maya Mortuary Landscape: Rituals of Body and
      Soul*. University of Texas Press, Austin.

Scherer, Andrew K., Charles Golden, Ana Lucía Arroyave
Prera, and Griselda Pérez Robles

2014 Danse Macabre: Death, Community, and Kingdom at
      El Kinel, Guatemala. In *The Bioarchaeology of Space
      and Place: Ideology, Power, and Meaning in Maya
      Mortuary Contexts*, edited by Gabriel D. Wrobel,
      pp. 193–224. Springer, New York.

Scherer, Andrew K., Charles Golden, and Jeffrey
Dobereiner

2012 *Proyecto Arqueológico Busilja-Chocolja: informe de la
      tercera temporada de investigación*. Consejo de Arque-
      ología, Instituto Nacional de Antropología e Historia,
      Mexico City.

2013 *Proyecto Arqueológico Busilja-Chocolja: informe de la
      cuarta temporada de investigación*. Consejo de Arque-
      ología, Instituto Nacional de Antropología e Historia,
      Mexico City.

Scherer, Andrew K., Charles Golden, and Rosaura Vásquez
(editors)

2007 *Proyecto Regional Arqueológico Sierra Lacandon:
      informe preliminar number 5*. Instituto de Antropología
      e Historia, Guatemala City.

Scherer, Andrew K., Lori E. Wright, and Cassady J. Yoder

2007 Bioarchaeological Evidence for Social and Temporal
      Differences in Subsistence at Piedras Negras, Guate-
      mala. *Latin American Antiquity* 18(1):85–104.

Serrano Sánchez, Carlos, Martha Pimienta Merlin, and
Alfonso Gallardo Velázquez

1993 Mutilación dentaria y filiación étnica en los entierro
      del Templo de Quetzalcóatl, Teotihuacan. In *II coloquio
      Pedro Bosch-Gimpera*, edited by María Teresa Cabrero,
      pp. 263–76. Universidad Nacional Autónoma de
      Mexico, Mexico City.

Sökefeld, Martin

1999 Debating Self, Identity, and Culture in Anthropology.
      Current Anthropology 40(4):417–48.

Spence, Michael W.

1994 Human Skeletal Material from Teotihuacan. In *Mortu-
      ary Practices and Skeletal Remains from Teotihuacan*,
      edited by Martha Lou Sempowski and Michael W.
      Spence, pp. 315–427. University of Utah Press, Salt Lake
      City.

Spradley, M. Katherine, and Richard L. Jantz

2011 Sex Estimation in Forensic Anthropology: Skull versus
      Postcranial Elements. *Journal of Forensic Sciences*
      56(2):289–96.

Stone, Andrea

1989 Disconnection, Foreign Insignia, and Political Expan-
      sion: Teotihuacan and the Warrior Stelae of Piedras
      Negras. In *Mesoamerica after the Decline of Teotihua-
      can*, edited by Richard A. Diehl and Janet C. Berlo,
      pp. 153–72. Dumbarton Oaks, Washington, DC.

Stuart, David

2000 The Arrival of Strangers: Teotihuacan and Tollan
      in Classic Maya History. In *Mesoamerica's Classic
      Heritage: From Teotihuacan to the Aztecs*, edited by
      David Carrasco, Lindsay Jones, and Scott Sessions,
      pp. 465–513. University Press of Colorado, Boulder.

2004 The Beginnings of the Copan Dynasty: A Review of
      the Hieroglyphic and Historical Evidence. In *Under-
      standing Early Classic Copan*, edited by Ellen E. Bell,
      Marcello A. Canuto, and Robert J. Sharer, pp. 215–48.
      University of Pennsylvania Museum of Archaeology
      and Anthropology, Philadelphia.

2012 Maya Spooks. Maya Decipherment: A Weblog on the
      Ancient Maya Script, electronic document, https://
      decipherment.wordpress.com/2012/10/26/maya
      -spooks/, accessed April 24, 2012.

Stuart, David, and Stephen D. Houston

1994 *Classic Maya Place Names*. Studies in Pre-Columbian
      Art and Archaeology 33. Dumbarton Oaks, Washing-
      ton, DC.

Sugiyama, Saburo

2005 *Human Sacrifice, Militarism, and Rulership: Mate-rialization of State Ideology at the Feathered Serpent Pyramid, Teotihuacan.* Cambridge University Press, Cambridge.

Tate, Carolyn E.

1992 *Yaxchilan: The Design of a Maya Ceremonial City.* University of Texas Press, Austin.

Taube, Karl A.

1985 The Classic Maya Maize God: A Reappraisal. In *Fifth Palenque Round Table, 1983*, edited by Merle Greene Robertson and Virginia M. Fields, pp. 171–81. Pre-Columbian Art Research Institute, San Francisco.

1992 *The Major Gods of Ancient Yucatan.* Dumbarton Oaks, Washington, DC.

2005 The Symbolism of Jade in Classic Maya Religion. *Ancient Mesoamerica* 16:23–50.

2009 The Maya Maize God and the Mythic Origins of Dance. In *Acta Mesoamericana.* Vol. 20, *The Maya and Their Sacred Narratives: Text and Context in Maya Mythologies*, edited by Geneviève Le Fort, Raphael Gardiol, Sebastian Matteo, and Christophe Helmke, pp. 41–52. Verlag Anton Saurwein, Markt Schwaben, Germany.

Tiesler, Vera

1998 *La costumbre de la deformación cefálica entre los anti-guos Mayas: aspectos morfológicos y culturales.* Instituto Nacional de Antropología e Historia, Mexico City.

2011 Becoming Maya: Infancy and Upbringing through the Lens of Pre-Hispanic Head Shaping. *Childhood in the Past* 4:117–32.

2012 *Tranformarse en Maya: el modelado cefálico entre los Mayas prehispánicos y coloniales.* Universidad Nacional Autónoma de México, Mexico City.

2014 *The Bioarchaeology of Artificial Cranial Modifications: New Approaches to Head Shaping and Its Meanings in Pre-Columbian Mesoamerica and Beyond.* Springer, New York.

Tokovinine, Alexandre

2013 *Place and Identity in Classic Maya Narratives.* Dumbar-ton Oaks, Washington, DC.

Tozzer, Alfred M.

1941 *Landa's "Relación de las Cosas de Yucatan."* Peabody Museum, Harvard University, Cambridge, Massachu-setts.

Vogt, Evon Z.

1970 Human Souls and Animal Spirits in Zinacantan. In *Echanges et communications: mélanges offerts à Claude Lévi-Strauss à l'occasion de son 60ème anniversaire*, edited by Jean Pouillon and Pierre Maranda, pp. 1148–67. Mouton, The Hague.

1992 *Tortillas for the Gods: A Symbolic Analysis of Zinacan-teco Rituals.* University of Oklahoma Press, Norman.

Vogt, Evon Z., and David Stuart

2005 Some Notes on Ritual Caves among the Ancient and Modern Maya. In *In the Maw of the Earth Monster: Mesoamerican Ritual Cave Use*, edited by James E. Brady and Keith M. Prufer, pp. 155–85. University of Texas Press, Austin.

Watanabe, John

1992 *Maya Saints and Souls in a Changing World.* University of Texas Press, Austin.

Weeks, John M., Jane A. Hill, and Charles W. Golden (editors)

2005 *Piedras Negras Archaeology: 1931–1939.* University of Pennsylvania Museum Press, Philadelphia.

White, Tim D., Michael T. Black, and Pieter A. Folkens

2011 *Human Osteology.* 3rd ed. Elsevier Academic Press, Burlington, Massachusetts.

Williams, Brenda A., and Tracy L. Rogers

2006 Evaluating the Accuracy and Precision of Cranial Morphological Traits for Sex Determination. *Journal of Forensic Sciences* 51(4):729–35.

Wilson, Richard

1995 *Maya Resurgence in Guatemala: Q'eqchi' Experiences.* University of Oklahoma Press, Norman.

Winning, Hasso von

1987 La iconografía de Teotihuacan: los dioses y los signos. Vol. 2. Universidad Autónoma de México, Mexico City.

Wright, Lori E.

2005 In Search of Yax Nuun Ayiin I: Revisiting the Tikal Project's Burial 10. *Ancient Mesoamerica* 16:89–100.

5

Cultural Modification of the Head

The Case of Teopancazco in Teotihuacan

LUIS ADRIÁN ALVARADO-VIÑAS AND LINDA R. MANZANILLA

INTRODUCTION

One of the emblematic cases of urban planned settlements of Mesoamerica is Teotihuacan, in Classic central Mexico. During the first six centuries CE, this twenty-square-kilometer site housed a multiethnic population with a corporate organization (Manzanilla 2015). The inhabitants of the metropolis were involved in craft production, construction projects, ritual practices, military endeavors, and the large-scale movement of sumptuary goods, raw materials, and specialized artisans from allied sites aligned along several corridors (Manzanilla 2011a, 2011b, 2015).

In the roughly twenty-two neighborhood centers in the city (Froese et al. 2014; Manzanilla 2012d), a very competitive intermediate elite managed the neighborhoods and established alliances with people from different regions of Mesoamerica to ensure the provisioning of the most lavish and rare sumptuary goods for elite consumption (Manzanilla 2012d, 2015). During thirteen field seasons of extensive excavations (1997–2005), Linda Manzanilla and her team excavated one of these neighborhood centers: Teopancazco (Manzanilla 2006, 2009, 2012a, 2012b). Teopancazco is a multiethnic neighborhood center located in the southeastern sector of Teotihuacan (Manzanilla 2012a, 2015) and has been studied in the framework of the interdisciplinary project Teotihuacan: Elite and Government, directed by Manzanilla.

Different activity areas and functional sectors were defined in the neighborhood center of Teopancazco (Manzanilla 2009, 2012b, 2012d). Distribution maps of the different archaeological materials and ecofacts, and their analyses, have identified a large variety and quantity of items from the Gulf Coast of Mexico (Rodríguez-Galicia 2010), particularly remains of marine fauna and other species that provided feathers, skin, and plaques for the manufacture of garments and headdresses. According to the remains, the instruments found used by the garment makers (standardized bone needles for embroidery, sewing, and joining fabrics, and awls and punchers to make holes; Manzanilla et al. 2011), and the activity markers in the bodies of many of the individuals buried at the site, it is certain that the shells, bones, and plaques of the coastal animals were used in the production of garments and headdresses for priests and soldiers (Rodríguez-Galicia 2010), but the animals were also consumed in feasting (Manzanilla 2006, 2012b; Mejía-Appel 2011). Such evidence points to the existence of a skilled craft group whose occupational activity in daily life was making fine garments. Other crafts manufactured at Teopancazco include baskets, nets, lacquered and painted pottery, and lapidary pieces, but most important were garments and headdresses.

At Teopancazco, among other remains and archaeological materials, the bones of 129 human individuals in formal burials were found. The purpose of this chapter is to analyze the most salient features of these burials, specifically the cranial modifications found there.

FEATURES OF BONES AND HEADS

Through strontium and oxygen isotope analyses (Morales-Puente et al. 2012; Schaaf et al. 2012), trace elements (Mejía-Appel 2011, 2012), ancient DNA (Álvarez-Sandoval et al. 2015), activity markers and paleopathology, cultural modifications, and standard osteological analysis (Alvarado-Viñas 2013), a very heterogeneous population was defined for Teopancazco (Manzanilla 2015).

Among the young adults, six had evidence of having been directly exposed to fire, sixteen had been indirectly exposed to fire, nine had cut marks, and ten had intentional fractures for bone instrument manufacture. Three individuals evidenced dental filing and one, dental incrustation. Thirty-eight individuals had been decapitated, twenty of whom were covered with cinnabar; of these last, fifteen were buried in room C162F in a series of pits under a floor, of which the largest pit (AA144) housed seventeen individuals; other pits had one or two skulls. In general, each head was set inside a San Martín Orange crater and covered with a cover or bowl (Manzanilla 2006:32, 2012b:35, figs. 17, 19).

Among the decapitated individuals, seven had undergone cultural modifications of their heads. This chapter will focus on them.

THE TEOPANCAZCO ARCHAEOLOGICAL SITE

In this neighborhood center, thirty-eight beheaded individuals were discovered, of whom twenty were male and four were female; because of the poor preservation, the gender of the remainder could not be determined. Twenty-eight individuals were between twenty-one and thirty-five years old at death, which, according to Earnest Hooton's classification, ranks them as young adults; the next-biggest group is that of adolescents between twelve and twenty years, of whom we recorded seven burials. We also have two middle-aged adults between thirty-six and fifty years at death, and, finally, a female of advanced age. Accordingly, most individuals in the group were in their productive age.

The decapitation of these individuals was part of

a termination ritual, dated to late Tlamimilolpa/early Xolalpan times (ca. 350 CE), which indicated a change of organization perhaps related to a general change in Teotihuacan society (Manzanilla 2006, 2012b). In different sectors of the city we see a Tlamimilolpa construction level covered by later constructions belonging to the Xolalpan phase; also during this time, one of the main pyramids of Teotihuacan, the Feathered Serpent Pyramid, was destroyed. Simultaneous to these changes around 350 CE, different termination rituals were performed, one of which involved the decapitation of twenty-nine individuals and the placement of their heads in vessels covered with bowls or covers. Other than Teotihuacan, this practice has only been found in Cerro de las Mesas, Veracruz (Drucker 1943), and thus may be seen as a foreign funerary practice in the metropolis. It is likely that among the beheaded are the masters and leaders of the craft production of Teopancazco, as well as some specialized artisans responsible for the manufacture of garments, some of them having migrated to the city from smaller villages and centers along the corridor toward the Gulf Coast.

Their activity, related to the manufacture of clothing and headgear for the elite, may have provided them with important political and economic status within the city; in La Ventilla 92–94 Glyph Plaza, the only two craft groups represented by glyphs are the garment makers and lapidary workers, which emphasizes their status in Teotihuacan. It is also possible that over time there may have been a reaction against these foreign people by locals whose own interests had been compromised to such an extent that the newcomers were beheaded.

However, in the funerary ritual dedicated to these victims, the inhabitants of Teotihuacan recognized their social status. This can be stated with some degree of certainty because residue of cinnabar (mercury sulfide) was found on top of the skulls of twenty of these decapitated individuals (Manzanilla 2012b). The ancient use of this red mineral has been observed elsewhere in Teotihuacan, especially in very particular mortuary contexts. The application of this mineral on bodies, or parts of bodies of dismembered individuals, has been interpreted as an indicator of social status or preferential access to foreign resources. Cinnabar had great symbolic value because it could be obtained only at great expense due to the physical distance to the deposits and the effort needed to extract the mineral. Therefore, its use was limited primarily to the elite (Gazzola 2004).

In room C162F and activity area 144 (a large pit), fifteen

of the twenty skulls with cinnabar were recovered. Manzanilla (2006, 2012b:34–35) describes that several of these skulls had been placed in individual San Martín Orange craters topped with a cover or bowl, indicating that an elaborate mortuary ritual had taken place. In the classification system proposed by Arturo Romano Pacheco (1974), these are considered secondary burials, because they result from intentional manipulation, and indirect, due to the fact that pits and containers were made for the purpose of depositing the skulls inside.

This particular room and activity area were located northeast of the main ceremonial courtyard, in a former ritual sector of this neighborhood center, and thus were in a place that is symbolically important. This suggests that the decapitated persons were neighborhood leaders or elite persons who perhaps were involved in craft production at this place and possibly monopolized access to items that came from sites along the corridor toward the Gulf Coast region.

DECAPITATION IN ITS CULTURAL CONTEXT

By beheading, we refer to the action of cutting and detaching the head from the body. It is one of the modes of human sacrifice, whose aim was to use an anatomical body part as a sign of power exercised by a dominant group. In Teopancazco, as part of a mortuary ritual, human remains were modified and consecrated as part of an offering to be deposited near an altar. A question that arises is, what determines the choice of the victim? It is very likely that activities and status played a significant role, but other possible causes include the manner in which the sacrificial rite was to be performed. Here, we propose that the decapitation rite served to express and modulate social contradictions, to assign new roles, and to dictate behavior. We suggest that this occurs in a context in which a hierarchical reorganization of the social tissue begins (González 2003).

In the context of Teopancazco, human sacrifice was an act that was performed within a religious framework by means of consecrating the victim when that victim's status changed. The first part of the sacrifice aimed to grant such representation, so that the act could establish a communication between the sacred and profane worlds, earning the consecration with the immolation of the victim in the course of the ceremony (Mauss and Hubert 2010). The

premise is that the selection of these beheaded people was not random. The decapitation of these individuals was in response to a social process, possibly during a time of crisis (see Manzanilla 2012b:36). The decapitation act may have been intended to break the power of a particular group at the onset of a transition of economic and political power. Decapitation is an example of a sacrificial rite of social reorganization; it breaks old social relations and ensures the consolidation of new ones. Human sacrifice thus becomes an instrument of legitimacy by the state.

In order to validate our hypothesis, it is important to establish the context in which these burials were found. The seven individuals with cephalic modification (Burials 26, 46, 47, 48, 50, 75, and 92) especially attracted our attention because, in the context in which they were deposited, such modifications are not common, and the specific types of modifications that these skulls exhibited are unusual for this time period and location.

CULTURAL MODIFICATION OF THE HEAD: THE LOOK MATTERS

All societies assign symbolic content and meaning to the body; sometimes, provisional or permanent modifications are applied to the body to project group associations, intended as identity symbols related to a group or community, to establish differences or similarities. As such, the body is a physical and individual creation, and at the same time a collective and cultural one. As Rosaura Yépez and Ramón Arzápalo (2007) suggest, all modifications to the body have a symbolic purpose; they act as a corporal writing system that contains nonverbal signs shaped into the body of an individual, which have meaning within the group to which the individual belongs.

In traditional societies, there is no distinction between body and person; the raw materials that form a human being are the same that form his or her body. The body is the possession of an individual, and it may be modified or transformed. David Le Breton (1995, 2002) mentions that the body is a social construct, in what is involved both in the collective scenario and in the theories that explain its performance or in the relationship that it maintains with the being it embodies. For Le Breton, the body is the effect of a social and cultural elaboration; it constructs itself and resignifies itself constantly. Human beings are judged by their appearance. One watches over one's own body so that it can become an advantageous representative of oneself (Le Breton 2007:34).

Considering the ethnic diversity of Teotihuacan (Price et al. 2000; Manzanilla 2015), each group tried to keep, manifest, and integrate its identity characteristics within the social dynamics of the metropolis by projecting its corporal image: garments, headdresses, and decorative items for the body such as face paint, earrings, necklaces, labrets, bracelets, and the like, as well as corporal modifications born of the body's plasticity that altered the image of a person permanently (like embedding beads or incrustations in the teeth, filing the teeth, and implementing cephalic modifications, the topic on which we are focused).

With respect to the population that inhabited the city of Teotihuacan during the Classic period, only some individuals' heads were modified or transformed. One can observe that, in this society, appearance mattered; it was a way to present oneself in a multiethnic environment. Such modeling resignified the individual in accordance with cultural traditions, as Le Breton notes.

The cultural modification of the head has been observed in some skeletal remains in Teotihuacan, as noted in the work of Manuel Gamio as well as reports from different archaeological sites such as Oztoyahualco 15B: N6W3, La Ventilla, Zacuala, Yayahuala, and the Oaxaca Barrio (Civera 1993).

In studies of Teotihuacan mural paintings (Fuente 1996), the expression of body modifications in the Tetitla divers (porch 26, mural 3) has been noted; their heads are elongated with cranial deformations. In the mural painting *The Tlalocan of Tepantitla*, one can observe several human figures with intentional cephalic deformation.

In various theater-type censers, we may see human heads with modeled skulls and facial paint; this is another artistic manifestation that captures information concerning the ideology and religion of the Teotihuacan metropolis (Sugiyama 2002) and, at the same time, the representation of the human body.

THE TEOPANCAZCO CASE:
FACTS AND ANALYSIS

At Teopancazco (Manzanilla 2012b, 2015), tangible evidence of permanent corporal modifications made to the head and, in some cases, to the teeth have been found. As stated above, we are here attempting to understand the

presence of these particular individuals in the neighborhood center of Teopancazco as well as the reason for their corporal modification. The modifications may have had an aesthetic motive; or they may have served as markers for ethnicity, gender, or social status; or they may even have served to imitate or represent a deity or force of nature. Whatever the specific reason, as Christina Torres-Rouff (2007) puts it, the modifications may have served to establish a social frontier within a group.

Of the Teopancazco sample, seven individuals (Burials 26, 46, 47, 48, 50, 75, and 92) had intentional modifications of the head. Five of the skulls had tabular erect cranial modifications; two of them—individual 46 (from room C162F, activity area 144, sexed as male by DNA and with an A haplogroup [Álvarez-Sandoval et al. 2015], coming from the Basin of Mexico and neighboring regions), and individual 92 (from room C154A, activity area 172, male, displaying a C haplogroup [Álvarez-Sandoval et al. 2015], coming from altitudes higher than Teotihuacan [Morales-Puente et al. 2012])—had a fronto-occipital tabular oblique cranial modification, in two varieties. This finding is of significant interest because of the scarcity of this type of cranial modification in bone samples from other Teotihuacan compounds.

The practice of modeling the skull to generate a significant morphological change, which may have represented social status, leaves an indelible trace in ancient remains that can be elucidated by osteological analysis. It involves a permanent alteration of the head by different techniques aimed at modifying the head form during the first stages of life by applying two compression planes, one in the front and another in the back.

In his classification system, José Imbelloni has established a basic typology: tabular oblique cranial deformation, tabular erect, and ring-shaped or circular. The first two types were attained by affixing rigid objects such as planks or boards to an infant's head, supported with cords and occasionally with compression bands; in the tabular erect, the compression is applied over the lambda, whereas in the tabular oblique, the compression is applied under the lambda parallel to the frontal plane. Ring-shaped forms are attained with bands that compress the head in a circular way (Tiesler 1999:202, 2012:73).

Both variants, erect and oblique, are defined by the morphoscopic traits of the skull (its form); with respect to the tabular erect, the obliquity axis has an angle of less than 120 degrees with respect to Frankfort's horizontal plane (figs. 5.1a, 5.1b; Burials 48 and 75, respectively).

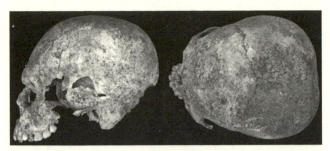

Figure 5.1a. Burial 48: skull with tabular erect modification in the left lateral norm and upper norm.

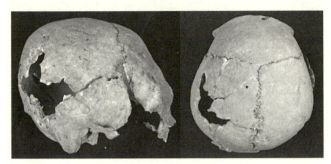

Figure 5.1b. Burial 75: skull in the right lateral norm and upper lateral norm.

The flattening direction is a rear compression plane that forms a very small angle with the basion-bregma line; one can assume that they are practically parallel to one another. The pressure is applied to the entire lambdoid region (parietal and occipital bones), the three bones that form the lambda, by applying a decubit plane in the cradle (Comas 1966:377).

With respect to tabular oblique cranial deformation, the obliquity axis with Frankfort's horizontal plane is an angle of 120 degrees. The compression direction is tangential to the external protuberance of the occipital, and the anatomic pressure only affects the occipital; this type of cranial deformation is attained with free tablets (Comas 1966:378).

During our review of the bone remains in the laboratory, we registered and classified the skulls with intentional modifications (perhaps made as identity or status symbols) when the preservation condition allowed it, for the purpose of identifying particular cultural practices related to groups who worked in the neighborhood.

At a morphological level, the head of individual 46 has a curvo-occipital tabular oblique modeling, whereby the instrument used to achieve the modification exercised pressure on the frontal bone, generating a straight surface and a direction toward the back of the head. Individual 92 has an intermediate tabular oblique cranial modification

with a parallel fronto-occipital compression. It presents a slight sinking mark, perhaps due to a compression band behind the bregma (figs. 5.1c, 5.1d).

A cult dedicated to human heads existed in Mesoamerica from early times. Cult members represented the modeling or modification of the head in figurines, sculptures, mural paintings, and codices. In some cases, trophy heads and *tzompantli* (skullracks) were also collected. For each individual, the head is an external representation of the personality (Romano Pacheco 1987:26). On the other hand, Alfredo López Austin (1996:183–85) maintains that the head is the part of the body that hosts the most varied attributions, such as reasoning power and communications capabilities; the head is the center of an individual's relations with society and the cosmos and the wellspring from which internal life emerges. The head and face of a person mirror the virtues of that individual; there is a connection between a person's head and his or her capacity for honesty. The head worships, it is humble; its face glows, dignifies itself, gives and shows prestige.

Thus, in these ancient societies the intentional modification of the head represents first a differentiation of social status. In research done in the Maya area, it was determined that, in general, the population modified the heads of their children in tabular erect form. However, rulers, chiefs, priests, and warriors, who from their infancy were

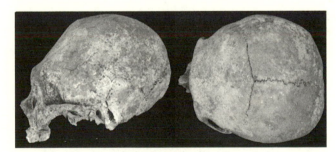

Figure 5.1c. Burial 46: skull with tabular oblique modification in the left lateral norm and upper norm.

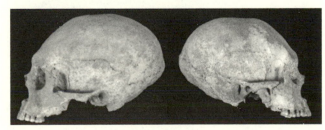

Figure 5.1d. Burial 92: skull with tabular oblique modification in the left lateral and right norm (excavation by Linda R. Manzanilla; photos by Rafael Reyes, Proyecto Arqueológico Teopancazco).

destined to have a high status in their group, had their heads modified in tabular oblique form (Romano Pacheco 1987).

In the Maya area, the oblique modification during the Classic period is considered an emulation of the jaguar, which was a sacred animal and a symbol of authority. In this sense, Vera Tiesler notes that in the coastal zone of Veracruz a parallelepiped modification associated with magical and religious power, venerated by merchants, appeared precisely at the time when long-distance trade was beginning to facilitate the transmission of emergent dominant ideologies, constituting a "new international order." For Tiesler, this order comprised a new class of merchant elite (Tiesler et al. 2009:86–88).

Thus, the following questions about the group of decapitated individuals at Teopancazco can broadly be answered. Are they local or foreign? Most are foreign, coming from different parts of the corridor of allied villages stretching toward the Gulf Coast (Manzanilla 2011b, 2012b, 2015). Do those who display intentional modification of their heads belong to any particular lineage or ethnic group? They come from different altitudes and display different genetic haplogroups. Were those who have oblique modifications group leaders? There is no data to support this claim, although they might have been.

THE APPLICATION OF ANALYTICAL PRINCIPLES TO THE CASE

Following the methodology proposed by Tiesler (1994) for a social interpretation of cephalic modification, the osteological data together with the archaeological information associated with the funerary context should be taken into consideration, keeping in mind four principles:

The Principle of Effort and Energy

This principle indicates that the value of a burial and its meaning for society reflects the social status of the individual being buried. The group of decapitated individuals were treated with a particular funerary ritual: each head was placed in a San Martín Orange crater topped with a bowl or cover, and most of them were laid in pits (of which AA144 was the largest) or on the ruins of a destroyed temple (Manzanilla 2012b:34ff., figs. 17, 19). This type of funerary ritual has not been found elsewhere in Teoti-

huacan, but it has been detected at Cerro de las Mesas, Veracruz, by Philip Drucker (1943), and orange lacquer pottery also came to Teopancazco from the Mixtequilla region where Cerro de las Mesas is located (Manzanilla 2012b:fig. 16).

Fifteen skulls had cinnabar on them; Julie Gazzola (2004) mentions that this was a material with highly symbolic value, generally associated with elites. The largest pit, where seventeen decapitated individuals were buried, was made *ex profeso* for them; no doubt they had performed a particular function in society, and their status was recognized by their heads being covered with cinnabar. Many of them have dental activity markers indicating that they used their teeth to work with fibers (Alvarado-Viñas 2013). Their possible role as part of a select group of artisans earned them a privileged social position with respect to the rest of the group. Another explanation may be that these individuals were sacrificed as part of a termination ritual, victims of the transition from the Tlamimilolpa to the Xolalpan period (ca. 350 CE) (Manzanilla 2002, 2003, 2012b).

The Principle of Spatial Grouping

The skulls of the decapitated group were found in the northeastern sector of the Xolalpan-period main ritual courtyard of Teopancazco, in a former ritual sector (Tlamimilolpa period), distributed in two primary groups and a few smaller groups. The first and largest, in room C162F, includes twenty burials; nine others are located atop the ruins of a destroyed temple; three more are in room C154; and the rest are scattered in different parts of the neighborhood center (plates 10, 11).

This principle states that the formal designation of an area as a place of mortuary ceremonies is indicative of a social organization structured by familial lineages. Nevertheless, Teopancazco is not a domestic compound but a neighborhood center where social actors (priests, bureaucrats, military personnel, specialized artisans) interacted. Thus, it is possible that the decapitated individuals date to the end of Tlamimilolpa times (200–350 CE) and that they were specialized artisans who produced the intermediate elite's garments and headdresses as well as baskets and nets for general use (Manzanilla 2012b, 2015; Manzanilla et al. 2011). With respect to the women buried in Teopancazco (who represent only 15 percent of the sexed adults), they could have been the spouses of the city's leaders, women who performed specific functions in the *chaînes opératoires* of garment making for the elite, or sacrificed women deposited as companions. In fact, the remains of many of these women show evidence that they were multispecialized artisans (Manzanilla 2015).

The Principle of Differentiation According to Social Status

This principle states that mortuary treatment varies according to the social role of the individual, or, in hierarchical societies, the set of social roles that the individual played, which were predetermined from birth. With respect to head modification, the fact that cranial plasticity allows for change in form only during early infancy reveals a particular social pattern (Tiesler 1994:39).

The human remains of Teopancazco can be grouped into three categories of cranial modification:

(a) Individuals who did not undergo cranial modification, who were not among the decapitated group found in other sectors of the neighborhood, and whose mortuary treatment was different from that of the decapitated individuals;

(b) Among the decapitated group, those who did not undergo intentional modification of the head (thirty-one cases); and

(c) The seven individuals who experienced cranial modification, five of which were the tabular erect type and two of which were the tabular oblique type. These last seven may have belonged to a particular set of leaders of the "house group." The modification of their heads may have been symbolic of their identity and authority within the group.

The Principle of Social Complexity

This variability in funerary behavior reveals a degree of social complexity; in a society such as Teotihuacan, one can observe more diversity in mortuary treatments and offerings than one finds in rural settings. This principle cannot be applied to the different forms of burial practices found in Teopancazco: the decapitated individuals, the formal burials of intact individuals, the infants, the secondary burials, plus the dispersed bone material lacking

any mortuary treatment. Other sectors should be investigated in the future to learn more about their inhumation practices and variations in such practices that may be dependent on ethnicity or different social classifications.

The head modifications undergone by the individuals discussed above had to be visible to the rest of Teotihuacan society; it is possible that the diffusion of this cultural practice inside the city was related to a new elite arriving from towns along the corridor leading toward the Gulf Coast. These persons probably maintained relations, or had kin ties, with different groups from their hometowns outside the capital, and they consolidated a specialized group of artisans who manufactured garments using foreign raw materials that were imported to Teopancazco. One can also point to the import of volcanic glass from Altotonga, Veracruz, to manufacture the floors of the Teopancazco compound (Barca et al. 2013).

The tabular oblique modification that was identified in two individuals is a sign of authority; it expresses a greater social status than those bearing the tabular erect type of modification.

Through stable isotope analyses (Morales-Puente et al. 2012) and $^{87/86}$strontium isotope analysis (Schaaf et al. 2012), we know that the group of decapitated individuals came from different altitudes and sites outside Teotihuacan, mainly located along the corridor toward the Nautla region of Veracruz (particularly Puebla, Tlaxcala, Hidalgo, and Veracruz), emphasizing the heterogeneous character of the population of this neighborhood center (Manzanilla 2015). One of the individuals with tabular oblique deformation came from an altitude similar to that of Teotihuacan, but the other came from a higher altitude, perhaps the Cofre de Perote or Pico de Orizaba region of Veracruz.

One final point that we can make is the possibility of facial and corporal paint as an identity marker. The main mural paintings found at Teopancazco (see McVicker 2005:figs. 5a, 5b) depict priestly and military figures who may have painted their faces. In fact, some theater-type censer masks found with the decapitated individuals in AA144 had facial paint (Manzanilla 2012c:508). Different cosmetics made from galena, cinnabar, hematite, jarosite, and other minerals (Doménech-Carbó et al. 2012) were found in miniature vessels associated with important burials in Teopancazco (Manzanilla 2012b:35).

We may conclude that facial and corporal paint would have been another means of visual recognition of different groups in multiethnic Teotihuacan, together with the diversity of attire and headdresses (Manzanilla et al. 2011), personal adornment (Manzanilla 2007), and head modifications.

FINAL CONSIDERATIONS

As we can see in this work, the human body is culturally symbolized due to social processes. Thanks to a precise archaeological record, we were able to determine that the individuals decapitated in Teopancazco were subjects of a specific funeral ritual. After their death, these people were deposited in pits or atop the ruins of a destroyed temple and were covered with cinnabar.

The mortuary space and minerals used as makeup for the dead bodies are indeed symbols of the hierarchical status these people had gained during their lives. Within the beheaded group, as stated before, seven individuals had undergone intentional modification of their head, five undergoing tabular erect modification and the two others fronto-occipital tabular oblique modification. Their bodies had been altered or modified at an early age in order to distinguish them from other members of the greater society. Thus, the modification was in actuality a sign of ethnic identity and status, because their origin was foreign. We presume that they belonged to an elite group of artisans coming from places along the corridor toward the Gulf Coast and that they maintained control over certain trade routes, creating bonds between people from their hometowns and people in Teotihuacan. In a cosmopolitan society, body modification was a privileged tool for the display of ethnic and social differences.

The sorts of cranial modifications we see in Teotihuacan are a development of the predominance of tabular erect types and exceptional tabular oblique types found in the Formative Basin of Mexico (Tiesler 2014:167); tabular oblique types are also common in the Formative sites of Michoacán (Tiesler 2014:167).

In Classic Teotihuacan, where tabular erect types predominate, there are also multiethnic neighborhoods such as La Ventilla, the Merchants' Barrio (Tiesler 2014:186), and Teopancazco, where tabular oblique examples and other variants have been detected. Thus, we may assume that the few tabular oblique examples are related to foreign traditions. One of the examples from Teopancazco (Burial 46) has an A genetic haplogroup, whereas the other (Burial 92) has a C haplogroup. Both are decapitated males.

During the Epiclassic and Postclassic periods of central Mexico, Tiesler (2014:245) cites a predominance of the tabular erect type.

ACKNOWLEDGMENTS

The thirteen field seasons at Teopancazco (1997–2005) were financed by the Mexican National Council for Science and Technology (25563H, G36050H) and the National Autonomous University of Mexico (DGAPA IN307398, IN406199, as well as the Institute for Anthropological Research). The federal permit for each season was granted by the Archaeological Council of the National Institute of Anthropology and History.

REFERENCES CITED

Alvarado-Viñas, Luis Adrián
2013   Tejedores de grandezas: un análisis de la población de Teopancazco, Teotihuacan, a través de sus actividades ocupacionales. Master's thesis, Universidad Nacional Autónoma de México, Mexico City.

Álvarez-Sandoval, Brenda A., Linda R. Manzanilla, Mercedes González-Ruiz, Assumpció Malgosa, and Rafael Montiel
2015   Genetic Evidence Supports the Multiethnic Character of Teopancazco, a Neighborhood Center of Teotihuacan, Mexico (AD 200–600). *Plos One*, doi:10.1371/journal.pone.0132371, July 22.

Barca, Donatella, Domenico Miriello, Alessandra Pecci, Luis Barba, Agustín Ortiz, Linda R. Manzanilla, Jorge Blancas, and Gino Mirocle Crisci
2013   Provenance of Glass Shards in Archaeological Lime Plasters by LA-ICP-MS: Implications for the Ancient Routes from the Gulf Coast of Mexico to Teotihuacan in Central Mexico. *Journal of Archaeological Science* 40:3999–4008.

Civera, Magali
1993   Análisis osteológico de los entierros de Oztoyahualco. In *Anatomía de un conjunto residencial teotihuacano en Oztoyahualco*. Vol. 2, *Los estudios específicos*, edited by Linda R. Manzanilla, pp. 832–59. Instituto de

Investigaciones Antropológicas, Universidad Nacional Autónoma de México, Mexico City.

Comas, Juan

1966   *Manual de antropología física.* Instituto de Investigaciones Históricas, Universidad Nacional Autónoma de México, Mexico City.

Doménech-Carbó, María Teresa, María Luisa Vázquez de Ágredos Pascual, Laura Osete-Cortina, Antonio Doménech-Carbó, Núria Guasch-Ferré, Linda R. Manzanilla, and Cristina Vidal Lorenzo

2012   Characterization of Pre-Hispanic Cosmetics Found in a Burial of the Ancient City of Teotihuacan (Mexico). *Journal of Archaeological Science* 39(4): 1043–62.

Drucker, Philip

1943   Ceramic Stratigraphy at Cerro de las Mesas, Veracruz, Mexico. Smithsonian Institution, Bulletin 141, Washington, DC.

Froese, Tom, Carlos Gershenson, and Linda R. Manzanilla

2014   Can Government Be Self-Organized? A Mathematical Model of the Collective Social Organization of Ancient Teotihuacan, Central Mexico. *Plos One*, doi:10.1371/journal.pone.0109966, October 10.

Fuente, Beatriz de la (editor)

1996   *La pintura mural prehispánica en México.* Vol. 1, *Teotihuacan.* Instituto de Investigaciones Estéticas, Universidad Nacional Autónoma de México, Mexico City.

Gazzola, Julie

2004   Uso y significado del cinabrio en Teotihuacan. In *La costa del Golfo en tiempos teotihuacanos: propuestas y perspectivas; memoria de la Segunda Mesa Redonda de Teotihuacan,* edited by María E. Ruiz-Gallut and Arturo Pascual-Soto, pp. 541–69. Instituto Nacional de Antropología e Historia, Mexico City.

González, Blanca Zoila

2003   Víctimas en el Templo de Quetzalcóatl, Teotihuacan: una perspectiva biocultural. In *Contextos arqueológicos y osteología del barrio de la Ventilla, Teotihuacan (1992–1994),* edited by Carlos Serrano Sánchez. Instituto de Investigaciones Antropológicas, Universidad Nacional Autónoma de México, Mexico City.

Le Breton, David

1995   *Antropología del cuerpo y modernidad.* Editorial Nueva Visión, Buenos Aires.

2002   *Sociología del cuerpo.* Editorial Nueva Visión, Buenos Aires.

2007   *Adiós al cuerpo: una teoría del cuerpo en el extremo contemporáneo.* La Cifra Editorial, Mexico City.

López Austin, Alfredo

1996   *Cuerpo humano e ideología: las concepciones de los antiguos Nahuas.* 2 vols. Instituto de Investigaciones Antropológicas, Universidad Nacional Autónoma de México, Mexico City.

Manzanilla, Linda R.

2002   Living with the Ancestors and Offering to the Gods: Domestic Ritual at Teotihuacan. In *Domestic Ritual in Ancient Mesoamerica,* edited by Patricia Plunket, pp. 43–52. Monograph 46. Cotsen Institute of Archaeology, University of California, Los Angeles.

2003   The Abandonment of Teotihuacan. In *The Archaeology of Settlement Abandonment in Middle America,* edited by Takeshi Inomata and Ronald W. Webb, pp. 91–101. University of Utah Press, Salt Lake City.

2006   Estados corporativos arcaicos: organizaciones de excepción en escenarios excluyentes. *Cuicuilco* 1(36):13–45.

2007   La unidad doméstica y las unidades de producción: propuesta interdisciplinaria de estudio. In *Memoria 2007 de El Colegio Nacional,* pp. 415–51. Colegio Nacional, Mexico City.

2009   Corporate Life in Apartment and *Barrio* Compounds at Teotihuacan, Central Mexico: Craft Specialization, Hierarchy, and Ethnicity. In *Domestic Life in Prehispanic Capitals: A Study of Specialization, Hierarchy, and Ethnicity,* edited by Linda R. Manzanilla and Claude Chapdelaine, pp. 21–42. University of Michigan Museum of Anthropology, Ann Arbor.

2011a   Metrópolis prehispánicas e impacto ambiental: el caso de Teotihuacan a través del tiempo. In *Escenarios de cambio climático: registros del Cuaternario en América Latina 1,* edited by Margarita Caballero and Beatriz Ortega Guerrero, pp. 287–319. Fomento Editorial, Universidad Nacional Autónoma de México, Mexico City.

2011b   Sistemas de control de mano de obra y del intercambio de bienes suntuarios en el corredor teotihuacano hacia la costa del Golfo en el Clásico. *Anales de Antropología* 45:9–32.

2012a   (editor) *Estudios arqueométricos del centro de barrio de Teopancazco en Teotihuacan.* Coordinación de Humanidades–Coordinación de la Investigación Científica, Universidad Nacional Autónoma de México, Mexico City.

2012b Introducción: Teopancazco, un centro de barrio multiétnico de Teotihuacan. In *Estudios arqueométricos del centro de barrio de Teopancazco en Teotihuacan*, edited by Linda R. Manzanilla, pp. 17–66. Coordinación de Humanidades–Coordinación de la Investigación Científica, Universidad Nacional Autónoma de México, Mexico City.

2012c Banco de datos del sitio Teopancazco: Proyecto "Teotihuacan: elite y gobierno" 1997–2005. In *Estudios arqueométricos del centro de barrio de Teopancazco en Teotihuacan*, edited by Linda R. Manzanilla, pp. 467–550. Coordinación de Humanidades–Coordinación de la Investigación Científica, Universidad Nacional Autónoma de México, Mexico City.

2012d Neighborhoods and Elite "Houses" at Teotihuacan, Central Mexico. In *The Neighborhood as a Social and Spatial Unit in Mesoamerican Cities*, edited by M. Charlotte Arnauld, Linda R. Manzanilla, and Michael E. Smith, pp. 55–73. University of Arizona Press, Tucson.

2015 Cooperation and Tensions in Multiethnic Corporate Societies Using Teotihuacan, Central Mexico, as a Case Study. *Proceedings of the National Academy of Sciences* 112(30):9210–15.

Manzanilla, Linda R., Raúl Valadez, Bernardo Rodríguez-Galicia, Gilberto Pérez Roldán, Johanná Padró, Adrián Velázquez, Belem Zúñiga, and Norma Valentín

2011 Producción de atavíos y tocados en un centro de barrio de Teotihuacan: el caso de Teopancazco. In *La producción artesanal y especializada en Mesoamérica: áreas de actividad y procesos productivos*, edited by Linda R. Manzanilla and Kenneth Hirth, pp. 59–85. Instituto Nacional de Antropología e Historia, Mexico City.

Mauss, Marcel, and Henri Hubert

2010 *El sacrificio: magia, mito y razón*. Editorial Las Cuarenta, Buenos Aires.

McVicker, Mary F.

2005 *Adela Breton: A Victorian Artist amid Mexico's Ruins*. University of New Mexico Press, Albuquerque.

Mejía-Appel, Gabriela I.

2011 De pescado los tamales: patrones de consumo alimenticio en un centro de barrio de Teotihuacan. *Estudios de Antropología Biológica* 15:13–27.

2012 Elementos traza aplicados al análisis de la paleodieta en Teopancazco. In *Estudios arqueométricos del centro de barrio de Teopancazco en Teotihuacan*, edited by Linda R. Manzanilla, pp. 325–45. Coordinación de Humanidades–Coordinación de la Investigación Científica, Universidad Nacional Autónoma de México, Mexico City.

Morales-Puente, Pedro, Edith Cienfuego, Linda R. Manzanilla, and Francisco Javier Otero

2012 Estudio de la paleodieta empleando isótopos estables de los elementos carbono, oxígeno y nitrógeno en restos humanos y de fauna encontrados en el barrio teotihuacano de Teopancazco. In *Estudios arqueométricos del centro de barrio de Teopancazco en Teotihuacan*, edited by Linda R. Manzanilla, pp. 347–423. Coordinación de Humanidades–Coordinación de la Investigación Científica, Universidad Nacional Autónoma de México, Mexico City.

Price, T. Douglas, Linda R. Manzanilla, and William H. Middleton

2000 Immigration and the Ancient City of Teotihuacan in Mexico: A Study Using Strontium Isotope Ratios in Human Bone and Teeth. *Journal of Archaeological Science* 27:903–13.

Rodríguez-Galicia, Bernardo

2010 *Captura, preparación y uso diferencial de la ictiofauna encontrada en el sitio arqueológico de Teopancazco, Teotihuacan*. PhD dissertation, Universidad Nacional Autónoma de México, Mexico City.

Romano Pacheco, Arturo

1974 Sistema de enterramientos. In *Antropología física: época prehispánica*, edited by Javier Romero, pp. 83–112. Instituto Nacional de Antropología e Historia, Mexico City.

1987 Iconografía cefálica maya. In *Memorias del Primer Coloquio Internacional de Mayistas*, pp. 25–41. Universidad Nacional Autónoma de México, Mexico City.

Schaaf, Peter, Gabriela Solís, Linda R. Manzanilla, Teodoro Hernández, Becket Lailson, and Peter Horn

2012 Isótopos de estroncio aplicados a estudios de migración humana en el centro de barrio de Teopancazco, Teotihuacan. In *Estudios arqueométricos del centro de barrio de Teopancazco en Teotihuacan*, edited by Linda R. Manzanilla, pp. 425–48. Coordinación de Humanidades–Coordinación de la Investigación Científica, Universidad Nacional Autónoma de México, Mexico City.

Sugiyama, Saburo

2002 Militarismo plasmado en Teotihuacan. In *Ideología política a través de materiales, imágenes y símbolos: memoria de la Primera Mesa Redonda de Teotihuacan*, edited by María Elena Ruiz-Gallut, pp. 185–209. Consejo Nacional para la Cultura y las Artes, Instituto

Nacional de Antropología e Historia, Universidad
Nacional Autónoma de México, Mexico City.

Tiesler, Vera

1994   La deformación cefálica entre los mayas prehispánicos:
       una propuesta metodológica para su interpretación
       social. *TRACE* 24:34–41.

1999   *Rasgos bioculturales entre los antiguos mayas: aspectos
       arqueológicos y sociales*. PhD dissertation, Universidad
       Nacional Autónoma de México, Mexico City.

2012   *Transformarse en Maya: el modelado cefálico entre los
       mayas prehispánicos y coloniales*. Instituto de Inves-
       tigaciones Antropológicas, Universidad Nacional
       Autónoma de México, Mexico City; Universidad
       Autónoma de Yucatán, Mérida.

2014   *The Bioarchaeology of Artificial Cranial Modifications*.
       Springer, New York.

Tiesler, Vera, Arturo Romano Pacheco, and Carlos Pallán

2009   Las formas cefálicas en las vísperas del Periodo

Posclásico: implicaciones para el cambio social en el
Área Maya. In *Memorias: XVIII Encuentro Internacional; los investigadores de la cultura Maya 18, 2009*,
vol. 1, pp. 85–96. Universidad Autónoma de Campeche,
Campeche.

Torres-Rouff, Christina

2007   La deformación craneana en San Pedro de Atacama.
       Estudios Atacameños 33:25–38.

Yépez, Rosaura, and Ramón Arzápalo

2007   La práctica cultural de modificar el cuerpo como
       un texto de información e interpretación social para
       la Antropología Física: una perspectiva semiótica.
       Working papers, no. 15, pp. 75–108. Centro de Estudios
       Interdisciplinarios en Etnolingüística y Antropología
       Socio-Cultural, Rosario, Argentina.

6

Face Painting among the Classic Maya Elites
An Iconographic Study

MARÍA LUISA VÁZQUEZ DE ÁGREDOS PASCUAL, CRISTINA VIDAL LORENZO,
AND PATRICIA HORCAJADA CAMPOS

INTRODUCTION: BODY PAINTING IN MESOAMERICA

Body painting was very common among the pre-Hispanic populations. In fact, the very first descriptions of the inhabitants of the American continent to reach the Old World noted how the natives painted their bodies in different colors. In his journal, Christopher Columbus recorded his first encounter with the inhabitants of the Indies in the following words:

> Ellos andan todos desnudos como su madre los parió, y tambien las mugeres, aunque no vide más de una, farto moza, y todos los que yo vi eran todos mancebos, que ninguno vide de edad de más de treinta años, muy bien hechos, de muy fermosos cuerpos y muy buenas caras; los cabellos gruesos cuasi como sedas de cola de caballos, é cortos; los cabellos traen por encima de las cejas, salvo unos pocos detrás, que traen largos, que jamás cortan, dellos se pintan de prieto, y ellos son de la color de los canarios, ni negros ni blancos, y dellos se pintan de blanco, y dellos de colorado, y dellos de lo que fallan, y dellos se pintan las caras, y dellos todo el cuerpo, y dellos solos los ojos, y de ellos solo la nariz. (Fernández de Navarrete 1999:19–20).

Henceforward, chroniclers and colonial writers made numerous references to this practice of body adornment.

These included, in the specific case of Mesoamerica, those by Fray Diego de Landa in his *Relación de cosas de Yucatan* or Bernardino de Sahagún in his *Historia general de las cosas de Nueva España*, regarding the significance of the colors and their qualities, sources, and preparations.

The information from these ethnohistorical sources has been supplemented by both ethnographic and archaeological investigations. Among the former, we could refer to those related to the Huichol living in the Sierra Madre Occidental range in Mexico (Faba 2003; Lumholtz 1986) or to the Seris (Conca'ac), the inhabitants of the coastal region of Sinaloa (Xavier 1946). While it is possible to discern certain similarities between the designs of these body paints and designs that appear on archaeological ceramics from the same regions, we should not ignore the difficulty, as already highlighted in an earlier work (Vázquez de Ágredos Pascual et al. 2012:227), in demonstrating a continuity between pre-Hispanic traditions and those of other later cultures, which could tempt us to make comparisons that may result in unfounded conclusions.

In this respect, the archaeological remains may, at first and despite their limitations, provide more information regarding this practice among the ancient Mesoamerican cultures. Among these remains, we note the large number of ceramic figurines found in archaeological contexts displaying elaborate designs of body painting and tattoos, as well as other illustrations on ceramic vases, codices, and walls where we find characters with painted

Figure 6.1. Cholchá-style vase showing one individual applying face paint to another (probably deities), detail. Image © Justin Kerr, Kerr Database: K4022.

bodies, or in the process of being painted, as with vases K3009, K764, and K4022 (fig. 6.1) and with the famous scene of a dressing ceremony painted on the North Wall of Room 1 in Structure 1 at Bonampak. Other relevant archaeological finds are the seals or stamps presumably employed to press different motifs onto the skin (Field 1967), the miniature vessels used to hold pigments, and the small stone mortars that were presumably used for grinding the pigments (fig. 6.2).[1]

Recent archaeometric studies have unearthed new information about the origin of the pigments used to color the skin and of certain aromatic substances bound to them, at least in funerary contexts (Doménech-Carbó et al. 2012:1043–62; Vázquez de Ágredos Pascual 2009:61–73; Vázquez de Ágredos Pascual et al. 2012:227, 2015).

However, body painting is an ephemeral process that leaves no trace on the individual, as opposed to other forms of body alteration such as cranial modeling and dental mutilation. Therefore, any study in this area continues to raise awkward questions and hypotheses that are difficult to verify. While fully aware of these problems, we have considered it opportune to contribute to this mono-

graph dedicated to social skins of the head among the ancient cultures of Mesoamerica and the Andean regions, with a chapter dedicated to face painting among the Maya of the Classic period, based on a detailed iconographic study of a selection of representative works. This, therefore, represents a new contribution within the framework of recent proposals regarding the highly expressive and communicative potential of clothing and physical adornments among the ancient Maya, in permanent as well as temporal form (Vela 2010:34–45). As noted by Stephen Houston et al. (2006:134), the ancient Maya converted the body into an active subject through clothing and adornment. Both resources were used to beautify the body and give it movement and sensations—auditory (sounds), tactile (touch), olfactory (smell) (Houston and Taube 2000; Tremain 2011:73–75), and of course visual (color). In previous works, we explored the close relationship between aroma, color, and the body in the Classic Maya courts (Vázquez de Ágredos Pascual and Vidal Lorenzo 2017; Vázquez de Ágredos Pascual et al. 2016), combining, for the first time, precise archaeometric data for which those fragrances and colors could have been used. Here, we offer a work that explores face painting, from iconography, among the elite of the Classic period, without limiting ourselves to royalty and without omitting the necessary data from ethnohistory, ethnolinguistics, archaeology, and archaeometry. However, again, the base discipline is iconography, a challenging approach for the subject matter discussed here.

Our study examines a large number of painted Maya faces for our ensuing iconographic analysis. Prior to proceeding to a description of our analysis and the objective of this study, we wish to give a brief introduction to the Maya concept of the head.

Figure 6.2. Small mortar from La Blanca (Petén, Guatemala), presumably used to grind pigments (photo by Patricia Horcajada Campos).

THE IMPORTANCE OF THE HEAD
AMONG THE ANCIENT MAYA

The vital importance of the head within the context of the human body was common among all the inhabitants of pre-Hispanic Mesoamerica. Its position at the upper end of the body explained the cosmic correspondence that was established between the head and the heavens in these ancient cultures (López Austin 2012:182). As an integral part of this sacred "celestial" region, from ancient times the Maya had conceived of the face as the catalyst for a person's psyche (Tiesler 2012:38), and hence the practice among the Maya of conserving some part of the head during their funeral rites.

The Maya term for the area of the face that was more frequently painted was *ich* (Barrera Vásquez 1980:262), referring to the front of the face and extending from the chin to the forehead, incorporating the lips, cheeks, nose, and eyes. Ich refers to the whole of this area, and the same term is also used to refer only to the eyes (Tiesler 2012:37). In fact, it was precisely this part of the head that Fray Diego de Landa referred to when describing the funeral practices of the Cocom lords:

A los antiguos señores *Cocom*, habían cortado las cabezas cuando murieron, y cocidas las limpiaron de la carne y después aserraron la mitad de la coronilla para atrás, dejando lo de delante con las quijadas y dientes. A estas medias calaveras suplieron lo que de carne les faltaba con cierto betún y les dieron la perfección muy al propio de cuyas eran, y las tenías con las estatuas de las cenizas, todo lo cual tenían en los oratorios de las casas, con sus ídolos, en gran reverencia y acatamiento, y todos los días de sus fiestas y regocijos les hacían ofrendas de sus comidas para que no les faltase en la otra vida donde pensaban (que) sus almas descansaban y les aprovechaban sus dones. (Landa 1985:101–2)

However, the most common practice among the upper classes would have been to preserve the part corresponding to the back of the skull and nape, as similarly related by Landa:

Las demás gente principal hacía a sus padres estatuas de madera a las cuales dejaban hueco el colodrillo, y quemaban alguna parte de su cuerpo y echaban allí las cenizas y tapábanlo; y después desollaban al difunto el cuero del colodrillo y pegábanselo allí, enterrando los residuos como tenían de costumbre; guardaban estas estatuas con mucha reverencia entre sus ídolos. (Landa 1985:101)

The skin from the occiput was removed and affixed to wooden statues representing the deceased, which were kept as offerings and held in reverence by the living, as reported by the chronicler, presumably to preserve the psychic entity of the deceased. This part of the skull would have been considered vital by the pre-Hispanic Maya, which is possibly why it was so commonly painted, as we shall examine further on.

In addition to the back of the skull, Landa also mentions the mouth as an important element in the funerary rituals of the ancient Maya; ground maize would be placed in the deceased's mouth along with "algunas piedras de las que tienen como moneda, para que en la otra vida no les faltase de comer" (Landa 1985:101).[2] The act alludes to the rebirth of the deceased following his or her physical death.

Also, the Maya and other Mesoamerican peoples believed that bodies were composed of different animating essences, animating entities, and companion spirits with varying levels of corporeal manifestation; they considered the head to be one of the most important centers of these supernatural essences and forces in the human body (see Duncan and Vail, chapter 2 of this volume). The rear and lower regions of the skull, the occiput and nape, together with the mouth, were considered the most relevant parts of the head, as this was where the animating essences and forces flowing through them would adhere. The Maya would therefore remove these areas of skin from the deceased in an effort to preserve their animating essences, which were also thought to flow throughout the face in a more diluted form.

According to the Mesoamerican world view, the human body was equivalent to a sacred tree, which was the ceiba tree for the ancient Maya. People's feet are anchored to the ground in the manner of the roots of a tree, whose trunk (body) rises and extends out through branches (arms and hands) until reaching the treetop (the head). Under the human's skin are veins and arteries that carry our lifeblood or *itz*, just as sap (also *itz*) courses through the tree under its "skin" or bark (Freidel et al. 1993:208–11).[3] The head of a person crowns the human body in the manner of a treetop and similarly forms the point of contact between that person and the universe. This explains not only the explicit relation between Maya feather headdresses and divinity but also the striking ornamentation of the head in the form of grave goods prepared from raw materials; the highly significant iconographic representations; and deep-rooted cultural practices and rites such as head shaping and dental insets of precious materials in previously filed and perforated teeth (Miller 2009:38–39).

All of this served to communicate cultural identity from the head and primarily from the forehead and its upper extremity (Houston et al. 2006:60; Nehammer Knub 2014:85–86). However, iconographic analysis of Maya art shows that many of the different forms of head decoration, ranging from headdresses and temporary cranial-facial adornments to permanent head shapings and tattoos, all contributed to defining the identity of the individual (see Miller, chapter 8, and Tiesler and Lacadena, chapter 3, of this volume).

METHODOLOGY

As indicated above, this initial consideration of face painting among the ancient Maya has been based on iconographic sources, specifically the anthropomorphic figures depicted on the beautiful polychrome vases and on limited, but exceptional, pictorial murals of the Classic period. In this study we have followed the methodology employed for several years now within the framework of La Blanca Project for the classification, analysis, and interpretation of artistic images and used as our start-off point the iconographic-iconological method systematized by Erwin Panofsky (Vidal Lorenzo and Muñoz Cosme 2009; Horcajada Campos 2011).

The first part of the work consisted of gathering representative examples of head and face painting. These were stored in a database that had been created to systematically and uniformly record the characteristics of the paintings and organize all the related information. Each record incorporates details that identify the work in which the figure appears and indicate the iconographic category to which the figure belongs, following a set of specific fields created to document the figure's characteristics. We divided the head into the neck, forehead, eyes, nose, cheeks, mouth, and chin, providing the color and design of the markings alongside each of these categories. A graphic section, including images of the work and details of the figure, completes the documentation.

Once we concluded the documentation stage, it was then possible to process and analyze all the information.

First, we devised a general classification of individuals in Maya society, distinguishing between male and female. This presented our first challenge, due to the similarity between these images and the anthropomorphic images of gods and supernatural beings, which in turn presented a second question: which of the scenes analyzed are peopled by human beings and which by gods or supernatural beings? The difference occasionally is clear, but certainly not always. Accordingly, we have attempted to select works that don't raise too many questions in these respects.

The total number of figures with facial paint that we analyzed came to 225: 147 males and 78 females. The first includes 47 governors, 19 musicians, 33 ballplayers, and 48 warriors. The visual sources used were mostly polychrome ceramics from the Justin Kerr Database, together with some samples from painted murals. Other iconographic sources such as sculptures and figurines don't provide sufficient information in this regard.

In view of the greater abundance of males in the illustrations we examined, we chose to subdivide these into categories of governors, warriors, ballplayers, and musicians, as we were in possession of a suitably representative sampling of each, in order to investigate potential patterns of face painting according to status, gender, and type of activity performed by these individuals. In order to do so, we established the types of face painting observed in each of these categories in accordance with the areas of the head that were painted, the color and design of the painting, and the markings that appeared with some frequency.

We then proceeded to analyze the type of each face painting within the context of the overall illustration, examining the complete figure of the characters, their clothing and adornments together with their posture, attitude, alignment within the composition, and other details, before moving on to analyze the scene in its entirety, considering the other individuals and their characteristics, the scene represented, and, when there were elements with spatial references, their scope and nature.

ICONOGRAPHIC ANALYSIS OF FACE PAINTING AMONG THE CLASSIC MAYA

The selected individuals incorporated in our database were all part of hierarchical Maya society and are generally portrayed in palatial scenes or engaged in activities related to war, ball playing, music, or dance.

After embarking on our analysis, we immediately became aware of the difficulty of using the term "face painting," as it was not always easy to distinguish between tattoos and painting—between the permanent coloring of the skin and more temporary or ephemeral facial colorings. It was also problematic to refer solely to the face, as in many cases, as we shall see later, these illustrations showed individuals with other parts of their heads painted in addition to their faces. However, we consider that the terms "face" and "painting" are both sufficiently clear for the purposes of this study.

Female Personalities

The figurative illustrations of female personalities in Maya art, who are generally clearly identified as women by their clothing and their female attributes (especially breasts), reveal different types and designs of face painting, which range from the uniform coloring of the entire face and other parts of the head to more delicate and original designs.

Among the numerous examples of women with completely painted heads, we may refer to the crouching woman supporting an enormous vase on her head, shown in the mural of Substructure 1-4 of the North Acropolis of Calakmul (fig. 6.3); the group of noblewomen depicted in an act of self-sacrifice in the mural of Room 3 of Structure 1 at Bonampak; and the two women with very dark red-painted faces sitting in profile opposite a man, on vase K2707 (plate 12a). As these women have their hair tied up with bands

in the form of a ponytail or braid, one sees how the paint extends all over the face down to the bottom of the neck. In this vase (K2707), the male character in the scene also has a painted face of the same color.

A further variation in face painting occurs for most of the women depicted in our database, in which dark red paint extends up from the shoulders to cover all of the neck and part of the face (mainly the ears), although also extending in some cases to the hair. An example of this may be seen in the two dancing women shown in vase K554. They are facing a number of men who, as in vase K2707, all have their faces painted in the same manner (plate 12e). The women's hair is fastened at the top of the head by simple headdresses in the form of headbands from which long, slender plumes of feathers emerge. Interestingly, this style was common not only among living women but also among depictions of female deities, and a further example of this form of head painting, noted by the strongly contrasting red paint and white skin, is depicted in the goddess shown in vase K5113, known as the Birth Vase. This four-sided vase shows a series of women with shoulders, neck, and part of the face all painted in this manner. On account of their aged faces, dress, headdresses, and feline attributes, these were all interpreted as depictions of Goddess O carrying out the role of a midwife (Taube 1994:657–58).

White paint was commonly applied to the cheeks and around the mouth in female face painting. This is the case with the courtesan shown holding a mask in vase K764 (plate 12b), while the male character holding a mirror

Figure 6.3. Mural at Substructure 1-4 of the North Acropolis of Calakmul, detail (photo by María Luisa Vázquez de Ágredos Pascual).

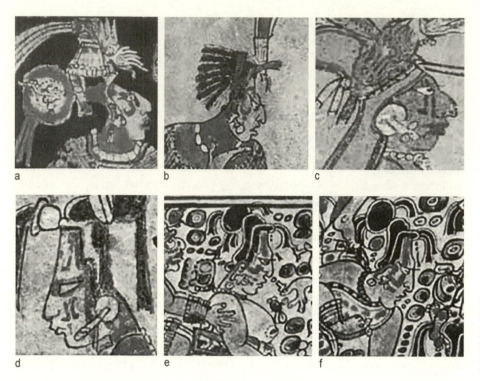

Figure 6.4. Details of different female faces with face paint. Images © Justin Kerr, Kerr Database: (a) K2695, (b) K2573, (c) K764, (d) K559, and (e–f) K1485.

on the opposite side of the vase also shows white paint. On other occasions, this white color is spread over the nose, as shown on the main character wearing a transparent huipil in the mural of Substructure 1-4 of the North Acropolis of Calakmul (fig. 6.3), or alternatively limited to the eyes and nose, leaving the rest of the face red, as seen on the woman seated facing a dwarf in vase K9300 (plate 12c), or the moon goddess depicted in vase K796. Finally, an additional and perhaps more sophisticated variation includes a red line horizontally crossing the center of the face, leaving the upper and lower halves white and the rest in red, as shown in the faces of the ladies wearing hats in vase K5847 (plate 12d).

However, in most examples the face is painted entirely in white with the rest of the head generally painted red. A very clear example of this type of face painting may be seen in vase K5451 (plate 12f), where a group of disconsolate women painted in this manner face the aftermath of war and the collection of bounty. As in the other examples, the male characters who are not warriors also bear the same type of face painting. A further example of this type, but with the lips very much highlighted in red, is shown on vase K956.

Finally, among the most beautiful examples of female face painting are those formed by delicate motifs generally drawn on faces that have previously been painted white (fig. 6.4). These motifs include black circles, such as those

shown on both the male and female characters participating in the sacrificial scene depicted on vase K1377, as well as more elaborate designs around the eyes as worn by the elegant Tikal women in vases K2695 and K2573 (figs. 6.4a, 6.4b) and the central female character of the already mentioned vase K764 (fig. 6.4c). These designs, composed of two geometric shapes, recall the characteristic sign of the young moon goddess (K559) (fig. 6.4d), or those shown on the "descending women" in vase K1485 (figs. 6.4e, 6.4f) who are also participating in an event related to this goddess. These facial markings, which echo the *ix* (lady) logograph, may then be taken to allude to the category of female figures.

From our iconographic analysis of depictions of females in Maya art, there is a diverse range of face decorations that appear in different combinations, both in color (mainly red and white) and form or design. When elite men and women appear together in the same scene, they tend to have their faces painted the same way, which might indicate that face painting, like clothing and other attributes, served the specific role of establishing the social identity of an individual, as previously suggested. Furthermore, there does not appear to be any difference between the face decoration worn by Maya women and that exhibited in depictions of the moon goddess, and hence the difficulty on some occasions of establishing whether a scene takes place in the world of the living or in that of the supernatural.

Male Rulers and Courtiers

Similar to the women, male rulers and members of the court during Classic times tended to paint their necks red, or at least this is what may be discerned from our iconographic study of works from this period, from which we were able to identify two very clear variations of this practice. One of these refers to the type of red used to cover this area, which varies from ocher red, through a range of intermediate reds, to orange red, as may be seen on several vases, such as K1453 (plate 13c). The second of these variations refers to the greater or lesser extension of the paint applied to this area. In this latter respect, it is rare to find examples in which the painting of the neck is restricted to this suboccipital area. On the contrary, as with the female characters, the pigment is seen to continuously extend to other areas such as the sides of the face (K2573, K2695) (plates 13b, 13e), and from there over the cheeks to the lower half of the face (K680) or to the upper half of the face (K1453, K8008) (plates 13c, 13d). The end result leaves the front part of the face totally or partially clear of any facial pigment (K554, K680, K764, K1454) or painted with another color, generally white (K558, K2573, K2695) (plates 13b, 13e). Finally, there are depictions of rulers and noblemen that show the application of just one facial pigment, generally ocher red, that covers the entire face from the forehead down to the neck, extending down to cover the lips under one uniform layer of color (K533).

Red and white are the predominant facial pigments applied to these male characters, extending over a large part of the face and head but primarily the neck, jaw, cheeks, and forehead.

The eyes and lips of these dignitaries and courtiers were also subject to special treatment. While such treatment usually occurred in conjunction with other types of facial adornment, there are some examples of characters exclusively with eye or lip decoration. This is the case with vase K625 (plate 13a), in which the characters are shown smoking tobacco with no sign of any face paint other than thick black lines around the eyes. This same pattern around the eyes, but in a more subtle variation and restricted to a thin black line, can be seen with some frequency on the faces of the privileged classes of the Classic Maya period on other polychrome vases, although not quite as explicitly as on vase K625. It is difficult to establish whether the markings are indeed face paint or simply the outlines of the subjects' natural features. Further depictions suggest the use of black eyelash mascara, due to the intentional and sometimes excessive length of the eyelashes, which in certain cases extend beyond the contours of the face (K764).

As for the lips, the most common practice was to leave these unpainted or painted in warm colors ranging from dark ocher to bright reds and on to orange ocher in many different hues (for example, K594, K764, K787). Color was applied to both lips or just one lip, causing the lips to stand out from the rest of the face, as opposed to those cases where they were hidden under a layer of color that totally or partially covered the face, whether white (plate 13b) or ocher red (plate 13e).

For technical reasons, it is difficult to identify blue and yellow colors in face painting, especially in Maya pottery. These vessels are cooked to eight hundred degrees Celsius, a level of heat that breaks the rings of the indigo. The result is a gray color, not blue. The same temperature darkens the colors of iron, such as yellow, which adopts ocher hues. On the other hand, on Maya figurines the blue color is part of the facial skin but was also applied on other parts of the body and on ornaments. For this reason, is impossible to know if this color refers to the face painting or if it was merely used to decorate the figurine.

Finally, these same iconographic depictions show an effort to combine, on a chromatic level, face pigment with the precious materials used on earspools and flares, this being one of the parts of the face most frequently subject to painting and incorporated over an area extending from the neck to the sides of the face. In this way, the four-lobed earrings that hang from the ears of the main character on vase K558 are as white as the majority of his face but are set in strong contrast to the dark red paint of the neck and nape, thereby establishing a radical chromatic contrast that is similarly found, for example, on the main character of vase K594.

Ballplayers

The ballplayers depicted on polychrome vases and certain codex-style ceramics are frequently seen to wear face paint.[4] This is the case with vase K2912, where the characters appear with faces painted with markings or designs around their eyes and cheeks. The ballplayers are painted with many different forms of pictorial decoration, and it is very rare to find two characters painted the same way on any two different vases. The use of red pigment predominates. This may appear on its own and cover the entire face except for a central area, or it may be restricted to certain parts of the face, particularly the mouth and neck, or it may appear purely in the form of lines or other geometric motifs. On other occasions, the red is combined with black and white pigment, with each of these colors being applied to a particular area of the face. It is also common to find black pigment on the faces of the ballplayers. In some instances, this is spread over the entire face like a mask, whereas in others it appears as vertical or horizontal stripes, and on yet other occasions as simple lines or geometric motifs.

These very diverse forms of face painting lead us to presume that there was no fixed pattern of face painting among the ballplayers. However, on examining the scenes as a whole, we believe that probably—along with body painting, the designs or decorations on clothing, and the type of headdress—this face painting served in some cases to differentiate between players of opposing teams or, alternatively, to distinguish the position or role taken by the players within the same team. This may be observed in the scene shown on vase K1209 (plates 13f, 13g) showing a ball game and two players.

The first of these ballplayers, wearing a deer headdress, has a red-painted neck and nape, with the upper part of his face and entire body painted light (smoked) black, the lower part of the face painted white, and the mouth red. The second ballplayer, positioned opposite the first and separated by a ball, wears a heron headdress and has a red-painted body and nape, white paint around the mouth, and red lips. The positioning of the ballplayers, their headdresses, and their clothing all suggest that these are opposing players.[5] In this scene, the body paint emphasizes the differences between the rivals, as the Maya considered red to represent life and black to symbolize death (Rivera Dorado 2001:21). The assignment of the colors red and black to differentiate between opposing players could well be related to a mythological tale such as that represented on vase K1288, which in turn recalls the ball game narrated in the Popol Vuh that took place in Xibalbá between the Hero Twins and the Lords of the Underworld (plates 13h, 13i). In this vase, we observe a scene from a ball game held in the underworld in which the main characters are two players with grotesque facial features. These supernatural beings are distinguished by their headdresses, one wearing a wide-brimmed hat and the other a deer head, as well as by the color of their bodies and face paint, the first character painted entirely black and the other entirely in red.

A further example of the potential use of face paint to differentiate between players may be seen in vase K1871, which shows five players. Four of these are standing and wearing deer-type headdresses (plate 13j). The skirts of the four standing players, while of different design, all bear a polylobed motif that resembles a flower. They also share the same type of face painting, with the sides of the face and neck all painted in red. These standing players all look down on a fifth player, who is kneeling. The headdress, the symbol on his skirt, and the face paint of this player all differ from those of his standing counterparts (plate 13k). The headdress has the image of the head of a supernatural person or deity, and the central motif on his skirt is in the form of a circle with various concentric inner lines. The player's eyes are outlined in red and black, two thin vertical lines run down from his forehead to his chin, and the sides of his face and the back of his neck are covered in a darker red pigment than that of the other players. Ramzy Barrois and Alexandre Tokovinine suggest that the five players in this scene all belong to the same team and that it could well illustrate a practice session (2005:30). If this were the case, the face paint, together with the headdress and the design on the robes, could serve to distinguish one player on a team who perhaps took on the role of captain.

Warriors

Warriors were frequently shown with some type of face decoration, whether permanent, in the form of tattoos and scars, or temporary, in the form of face paint.[6] These warriors painted their faces in many different ways, ranging from black designs or isolated geometric patterns, red-painted faces and other parts of the body in red, and white-painted faces with red markings (plates 13l, 13m, 13n), to faces completely covered in layers of red or black or combinations of white and black.

Warriors with painted faces appear in battle scenes, in scenes before or after battle, marching in triumphant processions with their prisoners, or in audiences with rulers.

Linda Schele considered that the painted skin of warriors "may have called upon their protector or signaled rank and duty" (1997:95), while Stephen Houston, David Stuart, and Karl Taube confer an exclusively formal nature to face painting, arguing that it served as "a form of camouflage for those desiring stealth. The human body could thereby not be easily distinguished from the mottled light and color under the jungle canopy" (2006:22–23). Given the many different types of face painting observed during our analysis of warrior images, we consider that the hypotheses presented by all these researchers could well hold true and that the use of face paint by this group could have had different functions and meanings according to context or occasion. The face paint could have been used on occasion to show the rank or role of the warriors, as in the case of vase K0638, which includes a procession of four warriors with a captive. The three warriors behind the captive all bear the same type of face paint, formed by a horizontal black line extending from the bottom of the nose to the side of the cheek, set above a series of wavy, vertical, parallel lines (plate 13o). The warrior leading the captive is not wearing any face paint and is dressed in long robes that appear to be made of feathers. The central section of the leading warrior's spear is noticeably different from that of the other three warriors. The lead warrior's position, clothing, and weapons all seem to suggest distinction, and it is therefore very probable that the role of this warrior was different from that of the other three warriors with painted faces.

On other occasions, face paint could have been used symbolically to call on the favor or protection of certain forces, as may be the case of the warriors appearing in vase K6987 (plate 13p). This vase represents another type of battle scene, perhaps the outcome of a battle, as it shows four warriors holding long spears set to either side of dismembered bodies and other elements that seem to allude to a sacrifice. The four warriors are shown with the upper half of their faces and necks painted in red, their mouths outlined in red, and their eyes circled in white. Both the shape of their eyes and their crested headdresses with bases bearing circular motifs appear to make reference to Tláloc, the deity associated by the ancient Maya with war.

Face painting could also serve as camouflage or as a means of hiding the facial characteristics that would identify an individual, in this way dehumanizing the face and endowing it with supernatural characteristics that would undoubtedly cause fear and trepidation among enemies. An example of this use of face painting is shown in vase K4680 (plate 13q), depicting a procession of three warriors all bearing face paint in the form of a mask, with the upper part of the face painted entirely in black, the lower part in white with black spots, and the mouth outlined in black.

Musicians

Musicians are also represented on numerous occasions with painted faces, predominantly in black, often in the form of abstract shapes on the cheeks (K3092, K4412,

K5435) (plate 13r), or randomly applied to certain parts of the face, such as the eyes, in a horizontal stripe resembling a mask (K1549) (plate 13s) or in a vertical stripe in the center, covering all of the nose and part of the eyes (K3247) (plate 13t). There are also examples where the subjects' faces are painted entirely in black, except for the area around the eyes and mouth (K1563) (plate 13u).

Another type of face paint observed among musicians consists of the application of white pigment in the center of the face, covering the nose and part of the forehead, while the neck and cheeks are painted in red. In some cases, as in vase K5233 (plate 13v), the characters appear with black or red geometric designs painted on their cheeks. On other occasions, the musicians' necks and foreheads are painted red, as in vase K6317. It is also common to find musicians with parts of their faces painted red, particularly the neck and forehead. One final form of face painting recorded among the musicians is with the face painted entirely white, with a thin red outlining of the eyes and mouth, as seen in K4824.

It may be noted that musicians with painted faces appear in all manner of representations, whether in courtly scenes, in battle scenes, or in ritual scenes, especially funeral processions and ball games. In all these scenes, the musicians very rarely wear the same face paint as the other characters and are frequently shown wearing different face paint from each other, which seems to suggest that there was no single type of face paint to identify these musicians. An interesting example of this may be seen in vase K5534, which shows a funeral procession in which the deceased is carried on a palanquin. Two musicians form part of this funeral procession, the first holding a large trumpet under his left arm and the other carrying a conch trumpet on his back. Curiously, the latter musician and the deceased are the only ones in the scene to wear black face paint. Both of these figures have the upper part of their faces painted in black, covering the nose and forehead. However, while the face paint of the musician covers half the lips and does not extend below the lower lip, the paint on the deceased comes down to the chin but leaves the lips unpainted.

CULTURAL MEANINGS AND USES OF FACE PAINT AMONG THE CLASSIC MAYA

The head and face painting identified during the course of this analysis is dominated by red and black colors, followed by white and occasionally yellow. These four colors are of great importance in the Maya world view, as each represents a particular god, natural force, element, and cardinal point: north (white), south (yellow), east (red), and west (black), which are in turn bound to concepts of life (red and white) and death or sterility (black and yellow). This association of colors with the four cardinal points and their meanings was registered in the Ritual de los Bacabes (Garza 1998:63). There is a fifth cardinal point that in Maya philosophy represented the quintessence: the center, associated with the sacred color green or blue (Rivera Dorado 2001:21), whose scarce use in facial painting by the elite of the Classic Maya, according to iconography, is discussed further in this work.

A study of dictionaries of the Maya language written in colonial times provides interesting information about the different names used to describe each of these colors in the pre-Hispanic era and their close relation to two key aspects of body painting: the source raw material and the medium on which this was applied. In this regard, with respect to the color red, *kan kuxub* and *u na mukay* refer to achiote and cochineal, respectively (Álvarez 1984:262), while the term *chak tahal* or *ix tahate* refers to the "skin red" that was prepared with hematite (Magaloni 1998:104). Hematite was very probably one of the most widely used red pigments employed by the ancient Maya to paint their skin, particularly the face, as its iron-based physical-chemical composition rendered this pigment harmless to the skin and also provided additional therapeutic benefits. In this regard, a study of the heads depicted in iconographic representations from the Classic period reveals a fairly standardized pattern in which both the female and male members of Maya courts tended to gather their hair in a high ponytail or bun, leaving a totally clear neck, which was painted in brightly hued and saturated-texture red, orange, and dark ocher colors, coinciding with the characteristics of hematite and other iron-based red pigments commonly found in the soils of the Maya area, such as goethite. An example of this practice is illustrated by a number of the figures shown in the present study.

The use of these earths as body pigments was very common in the ancient world due to their abundance, ease of processing, and numerous medicinal properties (Rovesti 1975), including protecting against the sun and offsetting the harmful effects of other red pigments such as cinnabar and mercury sulfide. It is therefore very probable that the illustrations of necks painted in warm-hued, earthy textured colors, so common in Maya art of the Classic period, allude to a common practice during pre-Hispanic times and one that was not exclusive to rulers or the nobility, nor purely founded on aestheticism.

It is also possible that the therapeutic and cosmetic qualities of the iron-based reds led to their extended application from the neck to other parts of the face and even to cover the entire face, as shown by various individuals in the scene shown on vase K680, or indeed to extend below the neck down to the shoulders and the upper part of the back, as illustrated by the main character on vase K764. Both these patterns commonly appear in the Maya art of the Classic period and must have been due in part to the important symbolic value of the color red in Maya culture, representing no less than life itself.

It is also very common in Maya art to observe the color red used to paint the back of the neck, extending upward from the nape over the back of the head and covering the hair gathered in a tie or emerging from this area, as shown by the main character and some of his acolytes on vase K558. This paint served to highlight the area of the head held to be of great significance to the ancient Maya, as previously explained.

This same hematite, when diluted in vegetable-type organic solutions (resins and oils), may also have been used to paint the red lips exhibited by a number of characters in these representations. This could similarly have been the case of the iron-based pigments, such as goethite or even specular hematite, whose luminous and iridescent finish, together with its nontoxic nature, would have made this pigment very much in demand for lip, facial, and bodily application. Any of these reds could have been used, as they are today, to embellish the lips, one of the most sensual parts of the face and, in turn, the opening for the taking in of sacred substances in solid (food) and liquid (drink) form, and for the outpouring of others, such as the blood spilled by bloodletting through the piercing of the tongue, or spoken language, representing the power of communication between humans and their fellow humans or with the gods.

In addition to the reds and the warm colors directly derived from the same iron minerals, particularly orange and dark ocher, the other color frequently applied to the faces of these characters was white, or *sak* in the Maya language. In several scenes, characters appear with their faces painted entirely white, from the chin to the forehead, a magnificent example of this being the distinguished couple shown on vase K2573 (fig. 6.4b, plate 13b).

Whether white paint was used to cover the entire face or just half, our study of these representations reveals the great importance that this color had in the face painting of the Classic period, not only in its frequency of use but also in its chromatic finality, set in sharp contrast to the reddish hues and the blacks, very much in the manner of a full or half mask. These images reveal saturated finishes that would have been based on calcium carbonate and the white clays so widely used in the preparation of the whites in Maya painting (Vázquez de Ágredos Pascual 2010:83–87). Their composition made them both suitable for contact with the skin, and subsequently as face paint, and ideal for the preparation of face masks, as revealed by archaeological and archaeometric evidence from other ancient cultures, such as the Egyptian (Martinetto 2000:43–45). This compatibility with the skin and fully saturated texture made it possible to cover the front of the face or just half the face, as witnessed by the white face painting of many characters represented in Maya art of the Classic period.

The most frequent use of black face paint was to outline the shape of the eyes by very thick, medium, or very faint lines, as may be seen on vase K625. In battle scenes, however, the kings and warriors often appeared with their faces painted completely black, except for the area around the eyes and lips. This pigment has also been observed on ballplayers and on the faces of musicians. When returning to the eye markings, these outlines could have been made in carbon black, widely known and prepared by the Maya for application on all manner of artistic mediums, and even with lead sulfide or galena, whose primary use in ancient times was precisely as a cosmetic eyeliner. While it is true that there are no indications to date of the use of galena in the Maya area, we know that from Early Classic times this was one of the possible body pigments included among the grave goods of the ruling classes who lived in the multiethnic district of Teopancazco, in Teotihuacan (Doménech-Carbó et al. 2012; Vázquez de Ágredos Pascual et al. 2012), which might suggest its same "cosmetic" use among other Mesoamerican cultures, including the Maya. This similarly applies to jarosite, an iron-based yellow color that had an important role as a body pigment in antiquity (Rovesti 1975), and which we have also identified by archaeometric analysis in these same contexts at Teotihuacan and more recently as one of the pigments associated with the masks held at the Museo de la Cultura Maya at Campeche (Edgar Casanova, personal communication, 2014). The recent characterization of this pigment on these Maya works of art as one used to cover the face of rulers, and its presence in other cultural and funerary contexts in Mesoamerica such as at Teotihuacan, suggest the generalized use of jarosite as a face pigment.

Finally, there is no evidence of the use of blue or green in the face painting of the Classic Maya individuals reviewed in the present study. However, the importance of these colors in Maya belief, being associated with the center of the cardinal points connecting the human plane to the supernatural world, was not foreign to the craniofacial decoration of the elites and deities. This is indeed borne out by the blue-green stones that formed part of their headdresses, ear flares, nose plugs, diadems, and many other ornaments arranged to illustrate and emphasize the head as the part of the human body connecting people to the gods and the cosmos. In this way, by means of ornaments and face painting, the heads and faces of the Maya elite incorporated the most important colors of their world view: red, white, black, and blue-green, in multiple combinations that rarely followed a specific pattern and that would have, instead, been a response to aesthetic, therapeutic, and symbolic factors.

EPILOGUE

Our iconographic study of a large collection of work shows that head painting was widespread in the Maya courts of the Classic period, not just among the royalty but also among other members of society who held different roles, functions, and possibly statuses as well. Kings, queens, courtiers, dancers, ballplayers, warriors, and musicians, together with other iconographic types that have not been considered in this initial approach to the subject, all wore body paint over a large part of their heads and necks. Through the use of color, they highlighted certain areas that for aesthetic, symbolic, or possibly therapeutic reasons were considered worthy of the application of body paint. The back of the head, nape of the neck, cheeks, and forehead were the most commonly painted craniofacial areas, followed by the lips and eyes. Both historical sources and the present Mayan languages provide sufficient information to establish these as particularly relevant areas of the head, due to their vital importance for all people in terms of communication, sociocultural identity (see Filloy Nadal, chapter 7, and Tiesler and Lacadena, chapter 3, of this volume), and of the role of the animating essences in connecting a person to the cosmos and the sacred.

The craniofacial pigment in almost all instances is shown as a uniform application of color and only on rare occasions as a design created through stamps or brushstrokes, as appeared among some of the female characters we examined. When these applications of color are extended from the cheeks, along the sides of the face and up to the forehead, they create the impression of a mask that camouflages and protects the face under layers of uniform and consistent pigment, similar to that applied to the back of the head and neck of many of the individuals we observed in this analysis.

One of the conclusions we reached from this iconographic analysis is that the different forms of face painting are not always exclusive to individuals of the same status; rather, the same type of adornment may be employed by both men and women from different sectors of society (dignitaries, musicians, ballplayers, courtiers, etc.). However, more commonly, in any one scene those characters performing similar functions do tend to be painted in the same manner, except for musicians, who, as we mentioned earlier, are usually represented with different types of face paint. On the negative side, our collection of works includes pieces from diverse origins, making it difficult to make comparisons between similar scenes from any one particular place and thus verify whether different types of face paint correspond to tendencies within the same court or not. One of the few available examples of a direct correspondence is the type of face decoration worn by two elite women from Tikal, one shown on vase K2573, who, although coming from the political entity Ik, represents a lady from Tikal, and the other appearing in an important scene with her husband, the king of Tikal, Yax Nuun Ayiin II, on vase K2695. The faces of both women are decorated with delicate geometric designs, which, while dissimilar, are both of the same pattern (figs. 6.4a, 6.4b).

While it is difficult to determine the body pigments employed by the ancient Maya to color their craniofacial regions purely from iconographic study, the choice of pigment was probably determined by its local availability, its nontoxic properties when in contact with the skin, and the cultural meaning attached by the Maya to each particular color since early times. Visual and written sources both refer to the abundant use of body coloring in pre-Hispanic times, which would have required accessible local sources in response to the high demand. And while nontoxic pigments would have been used customarily, some pigments harmful to the skin may have been used on occasion if certain rituals demanded it, such as marking the presence of animating essences within the human body or as an indication of communication and identity, as mentioned earlier. The combination of these three requirements led to the use of very specific pigments in the Maya area: iron oxides and earth reds (reds, ochers, and yellows), lime and clay whites (white), and carbon black, while also incorporating, if warm colors were called for, vegetable- or animal-based dyes that were widely known and employed by the ancient Maya, such as achiote (*Bixa orellana L.*). However, while there are no archaeological remains of the organic colors that may have been employed in the craniofacial painting of the Classic Maya, the written sources refer to colors such as indigo (*Indigofera suffruticosa mill, Indigofera mucrolata, Indigofera jamaicensis*) as body colors. Any of these organic pigments, or indeed the inorganic pigments that were supposedly employed more commonly for the reasons we have mentioned, would have been available to the elite as head decoration for the wide range of activities depicted in Classic-period painting: receptions, dances, preparation for battle, and everyday scenes both public and private, both exterior and interior, without the decorations apparently corresponding to any specific pattern.

This practice would extend to the funerary context, particularly on account of the importance given to color in the posthumous treatment of the corpses of rulers from Preclassic times on. Ritual requirements in this regard must have limited innovation in the use of body pigments that held symbolic meaning as part of burial rites and practices, especially for this "cusp" of sacred connection as represented by the head among the ancient Maya. Archaeometric studies of funerary contexts currently in progress elsewhere in Mesoamerica confirm the use of body paints that have not yet been identified in other contexts, suggesting that the material association of color with a cultural meaning and funeral rite was broadly observed in the postmortem rituals of different Mesoamerican cultures. Burials of the elite from the multiethnic district of Teopancazco, for example, offer dozens of examples of a grayish pigment and the intense brilliance known as lead sulfate, independent of other types of contexts and ritual practices (Doménech-Carbó et al. 2012; Vázquez de Ágredos Pascual et al. 2012). In fact, in ancient times it was not unusual to associate pigments and odors with specific, predetermined parts of the human body, based on their respective cultural significance and depending on their posthumous treatment. Egypt is one of the most significant and best-studied examples of this practice (Janot 2008:178–214). Considering the importance of the concept of *partinomia* (all and part) when interpreting the head as a part of the *b'aah* (the body) (Houston et al. 2006:6, 58–61; Tiesler 2012:36), and within this the relevance of the face, or *wach*, as the K'iche' Maya continue to call it (Houston et al. 2006:58), the material nature and meaning of the adornments that were used on these parts, from pigments to precious stones, must have affected their choice.

It is very possible that this head painting was performed for reasons other than aesthetics and that it could have been employed with a specific purpose or significance in each context. We believe that, in some cases, face painting, together with clothing and adornment, could have served to differentiate individuals within a group, as we have already indicated with respect to ballplayers and warriors. On other occasions, it may have had a more symbolic purpose, as in the case of the painting of designs related to deities. These could possibly have been made to establish a tie between the human and the sacred, such as the signs on the cheeks of a number of women that are similar to those exhibited on depictions of the moon goddess, or the warriors with the semblance of Tláloc. A final possible purpose could have been to hide the features of individuals in order to dehumanize them and give them an otherworldly appearance, as in the case of the warriors shown on vase K4680 (plate 13q).

A further aspect of our study that should be taken into account is that almost all of the images we examined were figures painted on ceramic vases. In this respect, the colors most widely used on these ceramics are red, black, white, and, to a far lesser extent, yellow, green, and blue. The reason for the scarcity of the latter three colors is the difficulty of maintaining their original tone when the ceramics were fired. The fact that these colors were not recorded in images, however, should not be taken to imply that they were not employed by the Maya as face or body paint; Diego de Landa himself refers to the blue paint covering people who were about to be sacrificed (Landa 1985:90). We maintain, therefore, that the high symbolism of these three colors, and particularly green and blue, should have given them far greater prevalence in facial painting of the ancient Maya royalty and aristocracy than that suggested by the ceramics from the Classic period.

ACKNOWLEDGMENTS

This research would not have been possible without the support of the Spanish Ministry of Economy and Competitiveness, through the funding of various coordinated research programs, reference number BIA2014-53887-C2-2-P, "Arte y arquitectura maya: nuevas tecnologías para su estudio y conservación"; and the support of the Spanish Ministry of Education, Culture, and Sport, through the funding of La Blanca Project (2004–2016).

NOTES

1. A selection of these motifs may be seen in the illustrated catalogue of pre-Hispanic body decoration published in special edition no. 37 of *Arqueología Mexicana* (50–53).

2. The practice of placing jade beads in the mouths of the dead has been documented in many burials in the Maya area over the Preclassic, Classic, and Postclassic periods (Ruz Lhuillier 1989:169).

3. This association was very common among many ancient cultures, not only pre-Hispanic societies. In his famous work *The Golden Bough*, published at the end of the nineteenth century, James G. Frazer offered an extensive and illustrative account of this association (1992).

4. There is one known representation of ballplayers on murals, namely the Ballplayers Mural at Group 6C-XVI-Sub.39 of the Tikal "Lost World" complex (Petén, Guatemala) dating to the Early Classic period. Despite the fact that all reproductions have been done in black and white, the characters appearing in the mural are seen to have face paint around their eyes and lips. There are also several scenes showing ball games on the walls of the Naj Tunich cave (Petén); however, the small markings shown on the cheeks of one of the characters cannot be considered face paint but rather an attribute, in the form of face markings, of the god Hunahpú (Coe 1989:171).

5. According to the researchers Ramzy Barrois and Alexandre Tokovinine, in all the representations of ball games, these two headdresses are always worn by opposing players (Barrois and Tokovinine 2005:28).

6. Stephen Houston, David Stuart, and Karl Taube indicate that the people most likely to have tattoos and scars were warriors, who were a "component of society 'marginalized' or distinguished by their ability to kill, maim, and 'hunt' in the wilds" (Houston et al. 2006:19).

REFERENCES CITED

Álvarez, Cristina
1984 *Diccionario etnolingüístico del idioma maya yucateco colonial.* Vol. 2, *Mundo físico.* Universidad Nacional Autónoma de México, Mexico City.

Barrera Vásquez, Alfredo (editor)
1980 *Diccionario Maya Cordemex.* Ediciones Cordemex, Mérida.

Barrois, Ramzy R., and Alexandre Tokovinine
2005 El inframundo y el mundo celestial en el Juego de Pelota Maya. In *XVIII Simposio de Investigaciones Arqueológicas en Guatemala, 2004,* edited by Juan P. Laporte, Bárbara Arroyo, and Héctor Mejía, pp. 27–38. Museo Nacional de Arqueología y Etnología, Guatemala City.

Coe, Michael D.
1989 The Hero Twins: Myth and Image. In *The Maya Vase Book: A Corpus of Rollout Photographs of Maya Vases,* vol. 1, edited by Justin Kerr, pp. 161–84. Kerr Associates, New York.

Doménech-Carbó, María Teresa, María Luisa Vázquez de Ágredos Pascual, Laura Osete-Cortina, Antonio Doménech-Carbó, Núria Guasch-Ferré, Linda R. Manzanilla, and Cristina Vidal Lorenzo
2012 Characterization of Pre-Hispanic Cosmetics Found in a Burial of the Ancient City of Teotihuacan (Mexico). *Journal of Archaeological Science* 39:1043–69.

Faba, Paulina
2003 Los rostros de nuestros antepasados: las pinturas faciales de los Jicareros (*Xucurikate*) huicholes de Tateikita. *Anales del Instituto de Investigaciones Estéticas* 25(82):73–92.

Fernández de Navarrete, Martín
1999 *Viajes de Cristóbal Colón.* Espasa Calpe, Madrid.
Field, Frederick V.
1967 *Thoughts on the Meaning and Use of Pre-Hispanic Mexican Sellos.* Dumbarton Oaks, Washington, DC.
Frazer, James G.
1992 *La rama dorada.* Fondo de Cultura Económica, Mexico City.

Freidel, David, Linda Schele, and Joy Parker
1993 *El cosmos maya.* Fondo de Cultura Económica, Mexico City.

Garza, Mercedes de la
1998 *Rostros de lo sagrado en el mundo maya.* Paidós, Mexico City.

Horcajada Campos, Patricia
2011 Aproximación al análisis iconográfico de las figurillas cerámicas de la ciudad maya de La Blanca (Petén, Guatemala). *Estrat Crític: Revista d'Arqueologia* 5(1):369–78.

Houston, Stephen, and Karl Taube
2000 An Archaeology of the Senses: Perception and Cultural Expression in Ancient Mesoamerica. *Cambridge Archaeological Journal* 10:261–94.

Houston, Stephen, Claudia Brittenham, Cassandra Mesick, Alexandre Tokovinine, and Christina Warinner
2009 *Veiled Brightness: A History of Ancient Maya Color.* University of Texas Press, Austin.

Houston, Stephen, David Stuart, and Karl Taube
2006 *The Memory of Bones: Body, Being, and Experience among the Classic Maya.* University of Texas Press, Austin.

Janot, Francis
2008 *Momies: rituels d´inmortalité dans 1'Egypte Ancienne.* Editions White Star, Paris.

Landa, Fray Diego de
1985 *Relación de cosas de Yucatan,* edited by Miguel Rivera Dorado. Historia 16, Madrid.

López Austin, Alfredo
2012 *Cuerpo humano e ideología.* Universidad Nacional Autónoma de México, Mexico City.

Lumholtz, Carl
1986 *El arte simbólico y decorativo de los huicholes.* Instituto Nacional Indigenista, Mexico City.

Magaloni, Diana
1998 El arte en el hacer: técnicas de pintura mural. In *Fragmentos del pasado: murales prehispánicos,* edited by María Teresa Uriarte, pp. 88–109. Consejo Nacional para la Cultura y las Artes; Instituto Nacional de Antropología e Historia; and Universidad Nacional Autónoma de México, Mexico City.

Martinetto, Pauline
2000 Étude cristallographique des préparations cosmétiques de l'Égypte ancienne: apports du Rayonnement Synchrotron a l'analyse quantitative et microstructurale des matériaux archéologiques. Unpublished

PhD dissertation, Université Joseph Fourier, Grenoble.

Miller, Mary

2009 Extreme Makeover: How Painted Bodies, Flattened Foreheads, and Filed Teeth Made the Maya Beautiful. *Archaeology* 62(1):36–42

Nehammer Knub, Julie

2014 How the Other Half Lives: The Role and Function of Body Paint at Maya Courts. In *Palaces and Courtly Culture in Ancient Mesoamerica*, edited by Julie Nehammer Knub, Christophe Helmke, and Jesper Nielsen, pp. 77–89. Pre-Columbian Archaeology 4. Archaeopress, Oxford.

Rivera Dorado, Miguel

2001 Algunas consideraciones sobre el arte maya. *Revista Española de Antropología Americana* 31:11–30.

Rovesti, Paolo

1975 *Alla ricerca dei cosmetici perduti.* Blow-Up di Marsilio Editori, Venice.

Ruz Lhuillier, Alberto

1989 *Costumbres funerarias de los antiguos mayas.* Fondo de Cultura Económica, Mexico City.

Schele, Linda

1997 *Hidden Faces of the Maya.* Ímpetus Comunicación, Mexico City.

Taube, Karl A.

1994 The Birth Vase: Natal Imagery in Ancient Maya Myth and Ritual. In *The Maya Vase Book: A Corpus of Roll-out Photographs of Maya Vases*, vol. 4, edited by Justin Kerr, pp. 652–85. Kerr Associates, New York.

Tiesler, Vera

2012 *Transformarse en maya: el modelo cefálico entre los mayas prehispánicos y coloniales.* Universidad Autónoma de Yucatán, Mérida.

Tremain, Cara G.

2011 A Multidisciplinary Approach to Ancient Maya Adornment and Costume: Mobilizing the Body and the Senses. *Totem: University of Western Ontario Journal of Anthropology* 19(1):67–80.

Vázquez de Ágredos Pascual, María Luisa

2009 El color y lo funerario entre los mayas de ayer y hoy: ritual, magia y cotidianidad. *Península* 4:61–73.

2010 *La pintura mural maya: materiales y técnicas artísticas.* Centro Peninsular en Humanidades y en Ciencias Sociales, Mérida.

Vázquez de Ágredos Pascual, María Luisa, Linda R. Manzanilla, and Cristina Vidal Lorenzo

2012 Antiguas esencias aromáticas y cosméticos funerarios del barrio multiétnico de Teopancazco. In *Estudios arqueométricos del centro de barrio de Teopancazco en Teotihuacan*, edited by Linda R. Manzanilla, pp. 211–32. Coordinación de Humanidades–Coordinación de la Investigación Científica, Universidad Nacional Autónoma de México, Mexico City.

Vázquez de Ágredos Pascual, María Luisa, Vera Tiesler, and Arturo Romano Pacheco

2015 Perfumando al difunto: fragancias y tratamientos póstumos entre la antigua aristocracia maya. *Arqueología Mexicana* 23(135):30–35.

Vázquez de Ágredos Pascual, María Luisa, and Cristina Vidal Lorenzo

2017 Fragrances and Body Paint in the Courtly life of the Maya. In *Constructing Power and Place in Mesoamerica: Pre-Hispanic Paintings from Three Regions*, edited by Meredith Paxton and Leticia Staines Cicero. University of New Mexico Press, Albuquerque.

Vázquez de Ágredos Pascual, María Luisa, Cristina Vidal Lorenzo, and Patricia Horcajada Campos

2016 Las fragancias rituales del Preclásico en Tak'alik Ab'aj. In *The Dimensions of Rituality 2000 Years Ago and Today*, edited by Christa Schieber de Lavarreda and Miguel Orrego, pp. 30–35. Ministerio de Cultura y Deportes, Guatemala City.

Vela, Enrique

2010 Pintura facial: decoración corporal prehispánica. *Arqueología Mexicana* 37:34–45.

Vidal Lorenzo, Cristina, and Gaspar Muñoz Cosme

2009 Los grafitos de La Blanca: metodología para su estudio y análisis iconográfico. In *Los grafitos mayas: cuadernos de arquitectura y arqueología maya 2*, edited by Cristina Vidal Lorenzo and Gaspar Muñoz Cosme, pp. 99–118. Editorial de la Universitat Politècnica de València, Valencia.

Xavier, Gwyneth H.

1946 Seri Face Painting. *Kiva* 11(2):15–20.

7

The Importance of Visage, Facial Treatment, and Idiosyncratic Traits in Maya Royal Portraiture during the Reign of K'inich Janaab' Pakal of Palenque, 615–683 CE

LAURA FILLOY NADAL

INTRODUCTION

For Maya artists, the human visage and body were preferred means of representation, which they expressed in stone, stucco, mural painting, and clay. Predominant within the vast Maya corpus of human depictions are anonymous individuals distinguished from one another by differences in attire, headdress, and insignia. In a smaller set of images, however, these differences were also conveyed through physical characteristics and facial or corporeal expressions that provided a sense of individualism and singularity to the men and women depicted on the architectural monuments of the Classic period.

In her celebrated book, *La conciencia histórica de los antiguos mayas* (The Historical Consciousness of the Ancient Maya, 1975), Mercedes de la Garza proposed that around 650 CE, Maya art underwent a major transformation characterized by a greater mastery of execution technique and a significant change in the Maya's "consciousness of the human" (Garza 1975:87). The distinguished author hypothesized that "the human," which Maya artists previously had depicted "as a hieratic symbol of the power conferred by the gods, liberated itself from them just enough to be situated with its own dignity in the universe, as something distinct from it and somehow capable of comprehending its meaning"; that is, "the human does not nullify itself before the divine, it creates a space of its own" (Garza 1975:87).[1] Elaborating further

on the matter, she added that the Maya recognized and admired the human as such without ceasing their veneration of the gods (Garza 1975:93), and clearly demonstrated an intent to depict the concrete individuality of every human being (Garza 1978:115).

The renowned art historian Beatriz de la Fuente (1966:11, 1970:7, 1993, 2003a, 2003b:148, 2003c:235), in turn, has written extensively on Maya compositions of the Late Classic period, in which "gods and humans seem to work together to preserve a sacred yet human universe" (Fuente 1966:11).[2] She observed that Maya images reveal a historical consciousness in which human actions are tied to the passage of time, and that Usumacinta River–region art (fig. 4.1), in particular, exhibits a humanistic orientation with an increasing tendency toward naturalism (Fuente 1966:11). She also detected a strong preference in this cultural area for distinguishing the visage and bodies of different protagonists (Fuente 1966). The reflections of both Fuente and Garza are seemingly relevant to the discussion that follows, as many art historians agree that portraiture usually flourishes in the art of cultures that privilege the individual over the collective (see, for example, West 2004:14).

Along with these and many other authors, I believe that a certain body of Maya art is distinguished by the desire to depict the human figure in a more realistic manner, adhering more closely to visual data, although always in accordance with prevailing social conventions.[3] Thus, for a particular pattern of representation, as in other cultures, we may think that individuality predominates. We see that Maya artists depicted their fellow humans by emulating their individual physical reality, that is, following the conventional norms of the "model human" or "canon of beauty" then in vogue, which included a long forehead exhibiting cranial deformation, almond-shaped eyes with an epicanthic fold, straight and beautifully arranged hair, an aquiline nose artificially projected forward and upward, and modified teeth, among other features.[4] A good example of this is evident in the large corpus of figurines from the island of Jaina in Campeche, where we find men and women engaged in various activities wearing outfits, insignias, and objects emblematic of their status or occupation. The body is always treated freely, the face is realistic and expressive, and in all of these cases it is possible to discern a physical type that is characteristic of the group. But instead of finding clear signs of individualization, we see only conventional faces and the use of various attributes to differentiate them.[5]

In addition to the plastic efforts of Classic-period Maya artists to differentiate individuals, an image sometimes may be complemented with glyphs that contribute to its identification. The urban public spaces of Palenque, for example, were dominated by vivid images of its rulers situated in complex scenes depicting births, conquests, enthronements, and other ceremonies accompanied by extensive hieroglyphic texts. In fact, during the long reign (615–683CE) of K'inich Janaab' Pakal (fig. 7.1), or Pakal the Great, when the city began its period of great splendor, this famous ruler ordered many new architectural works that were adorned with stucco representations dominated by full-body anthropomorphic figures. In some instances, the depicted personages are accompanied by patronymic glyphs that indicate their names and facilitate their identification and differentiation within a scene. Thus we know that K'inich Janaab' Pakal, on various monuments, appears alone or in the company of his mother, his wife, one of his sons, and even his grandson.

These hieroglyphic texts, of course, have led us to realize that these visages, carved in stone, modeled in stucco, or painted on walls, represent actual individuals who performed specific acts that played an important role in society and in the governance of the city (Schele and Miller 1986:63). This particular feature clearly distinguishes Maya art from other Mesoamerican examples, as these inscriptions are a source of privileged information concerning the life and appearance of various actors. We

Figure 7.1. The Oval Tablet, House E, palace, Palenque (redrawn by Mirna Beatríz Sánchez from Robertson 1985: fig. 91, courtesy of Vera Tiesler).

must not forget, however, that these narratives were not intended to be a historical record of the city, for the Maya believed that mythic time and the time of the *k'uhul ahau*, or sacred rulers, were continuously intertwined. Even though these texts refer to acts carried out by personages of the Classic period, their lives were interwoven with the actions of gods and, especially, with the Long Count of days in the Maya calendar. The inscriptions highlight dedications or commemorative dates linked to objects, events, and individuals interacting in sacred time. In this manner, within the eternal dance of the days, the actions of humans and gods in the various levels of the cosmos were recorded.

Many other images, however, lack patronymics, either because of deterioration suffered over time or because they never had them to begin with, and this leads me to pose two related questions in terms of the general discussion developed thus far: Would it be possible to identify the portrait of a personage among the city's anthropomorphic images without a patronymic? Could we recognize an individual even without the ability to interpret the inscriptions or those that have disappeared? This chapter will try to address these and other issues concerning portraiture in general and Maya portraits in particular, including the broader question of whether physical likeness between model and image is all that is needed to create a portrait of a particular person, before concluding with a more specific analysis of several images depicting Pakal the Great of Palenque during his reign and even after his death.

THE IMPORTANCE OF CHARACTERIZING THE INDIVIDUAL AND INDIVIDUALIZING IDIOSYNCRATIC TRAITS

The artists of Palenque had as models the individuals of their time. Within the vast corpus of extant human representations in the ancient city, the modern observer at first glance can easily notice differences between such figures based on their attire, headdress, or insignia. A closer, more informed examination, however, reveals diverse physical characteristics, distinguishing marks, and even facial expressions that give these personages a sense of individualism and singularity. From a Western perspective, capturing the likeness of a subject's physical features would seem to be one of the essential requisites for positing the existence of *portraiture* at Palenque, although it has been noted that much of the relevant scholarly literature lacks a definition for the term that is applicable to ancient Mesoamerican art (see, for example, Fuente 1970; Benson 2004). In fact, in 1969, Galienne and Pierre Francastel published their revolutionary *Le portrait: 50 siècles d'humanisme en peinture* (The Portrait: Fifty Centuries of Humanism in Painting), which shattered classicist conceptions of the genre by recognizing many examples of portraiture in preliterate societies and suggesting that "the ideal condition for the existence of the portrait seems to reside in the meeting of . . . two elements: . . . individualizing features and the possibility of identifying the model" (Francastel and Francastel 1969:12). In my view, the present study of sculptural examples from Palenque requires a definition that also takes into account the artistic conception of the visage/head as both a fundamental marker of identity and a reflection of sociocultural phenomena in the creative moment. Because the word *portrait* derives from the Latin *protraho* (to "bring out" or "bring to light"), I would define it in the context of this study as "bringing out" or "bringing to light" an image that depicts

an individual by invoking certain aspects or features of the model, which, on the one hand, allows the recognition and differentiation of the subject within a group, and, on the other, prevents the subject from being confused with someone else (Brilliant 1990:12).

Although an image employing physical particularization to depict an individual may be a *portrait* in the loosest sense of the word, we must keep in mind that not all artistic manifestations that realistically reproduce the essential physical characteristics of an individual are considered *true* portraits. Specialists who study portraits, in fact, have recognized and even advocated the use of various elements beyond the realm of mere physical likeness to ensure the identification of the model and avoid any confusion with other individuals. For example, Oxford art historian Shearer West, in her book entitled *Portraiture* (2004), notes that even though an image may exhibit a certain resemblance to an individual, a portrait should also include features of the individual's identity: aspects such as personality, social relationships, occupation, age, and so on. Obviously, these qualities are not fixed and reflect the circumstances that led to the work's production, the period in which it was made, the culture in which it was created, and the purpose for which it was commissioned (West 2004:11). Similarly, Columbia University art historian Richard Brilliant, in his likewise entitled book (*Portraiture*, 1991), has emphasized that one's social role and the social conventions in one's culture profoundly affect one's appearance and behavior, and therefore elements that derive from these two social aspects help identify a particular individual and thus his or her portrait (see also Brilliant 1987, 1990, 1994).

Building upon these ideas of Brilliant and West, I propose that complementing one's physical likeness with a series of individualizing features that situate a person within his or her context pointedly qualifies the subject of a portrait, heightens viewer recognition, and facilitates the discovery of the model's identity. A portrait, then, is the visual representation of a subject's most important *physical characteristics*, along with certain associated symbols, which I am calling *idiosyncratic traits* (see table 7.1). Together, these two sets of parameters enable the identification of the person (his or her identity) not only by individuals who know the subject personally but also by a wider sector of society who only know the subject from his or her image (Brilliant 1994:5). These idiosyncratic traits may include one's name, gestures, pose, age, grooming, body decoration, attire, accessories, occupation, status, and certain iconographic elements,

TABLE 7.1. PHYSICAL CHARACTERISTICS AND IDIOSYNCRATIC TRAITS IN PORTRAITURE

An individual's portrait is the sum of the subject's *physical characteristics* and *idiosyncratic traits*, which together enable the recognition of the individual by members of the person's cultural group without being confused with someone else.

PHYSICAL CHARACTERISTICS	IDIOSYNCRATIC TRAITS
1. Proportions	1. Patronymic (name)
2. Asymmetries	2. Gestures
3. Shape of head	3. Pose
4. Shape of face	4. Age
5. Type of forehead	5. Grooming (hair, makeup)
6. Size, shape, and color of eyes	6. Body decoration (ritual piercings, tattoos, scarifications, dental mutilation, intentional deformation of any part of the body for individual or group differentiation)
7. Type and size of nose	7. Accessories (jewelry, adornments)
8. Type and size of mouth	8. Attire (dress)
9. Type and size of teeth	9. Occupation
10. Type of chin	10. Status (rank/position)
11. Type and size of ears	11. Iconographic elements
12. Physical complexion	
13. Characteristic marks (moles, blemishes, scars, abnormalities, pathological deformation/disfigurement, etc.)	
14. Skin color	
15. Color and type of hair	

although it is important to note that a true portrait need not incorporate all of these qualifying attributes, as merely a few may suffice to characterize a particular individual. These various attributes, moreover, should not be studied in isolation, for the individualizing plan is reflected in the full context of the image (see also Tiesler and Lacadena, chapter 3 of this volume). By integrating into a single image the social conventions commonly used in a certain cultural and temporal context to both portray the appearance of an individual and convey the social relationships that the individual had with peers, the portrait of a *well-defined person* can be achieved.[6] Thus a portrait is both *body* and *essence*, which together identify the historical person as a distinct entity in society.

In the case of pre-Hispanic Mesoamerican art, however, we must take into account additional elements that involve complex notions about the *human* and *person-hood*. According to Mesoamerican thought, all human beings consist of two basic elements: a perceptible heavy substance with a hard covering, namely the *body*; and an imperceptible light substance of heterogeneous *essences* that reside inside the body in multiple animistic entities or "souls" and produce movement, sensation, and con-sciousness (López Austin 1980, 1988). Both of these basic elements give each being a set of identitary, collective attributes as well as a set of individualizing, personal

attributes, while each of these animistic souls has specific anatomical, physiological, and psychological functions that contribute to the composition of humans. Some of these souls are of an identitary nature—they provide people with attributes, which they share with the rest of the members of the group, including certain names, temperament, similar physical characteristics, and inten-tional biocultural modifications such as deliberate cranial deformation or decorative dental mutilation (for deeper discussions about ethnicity, see Tiesler and Lacadena, chapter 3, and Miller, chapter 8, of this volume). More-over, each human group has a soul that is shared by all of its members because part of its essence—the "seed" or "heart"—is a fragment of the soul of the group's patron deity. Each member, however, also has other souls that are of an individualizing nature which provide various personal attributes that differentiate the individual within his or her group, such as some of the members' names, physical characteristics, destiny, temperament, character, and so on (López Austin 1997). These individualizing at-tributes also include certain elements acquired over the course of one's life through accidents, rituals, meritorious acts, or one's social or political status, as well as their indi-vidual rights and privileges and, of course, their social and religious obligations (Houston et al. 2006; López Austin 1980, 1988, 2004). Such personal attributes apply to the individual alone, as they are not shared with other members of the group (for other cultures, see Mauss 1938; Saghy 1973). In addition, as we shall see, the "lightness" of a person is also important, as some of one's individualizing animistic components can escape the confines of the skin, migrate long distances, and be shared with other beings. These "free souls" that extricate themselves from the heavy substances of the body sometimes enable certain individuals to travel between the *ecumene* and *anecumene* realms of the universe (López Austin 2001, 2006).[7] Together, these heavy and light substances link individuals to their respective groups while simultaneously individualizing them, and they comprise both the personal and the collective elements, whether innate or acquired, divine or worldly (table 7.2). Thus we can say that, in Mesoamerican thought, a *person* is the sum of these various collective and personal attributes that intersect within a particular human or divinity and thus distinguish one from the rest of the group.

Maya artists also had various epigraphic resources for individualizing the personages they depicted. For example, there was a specific term for the material complement of a person, an identificatory phrase that began with the glyph *u-baah*, which means "one's face," "one's head," "one's image," "one's individual essence," or even "one's person" (Houston and Stuart 1998). In Maya artistic manifestations, the u-baah glyph might precede the name of the person being represented. On some occasions, it came before the person's patronymic, indicating, for example, that this is the "*body* of X" or the "*face* of X," where X is the name of the person depicted in the image (Houston and Stuart 1998). One could say, then, that u-baah referred to the qualities and individuality of the depicted personage. On the other hand, the u-baah glyph also was used to accompany the plastic representation of a particular individual without specifically referring to the name itself, in which case it meant the "*representation* itself of X," the "*image* itself of X," or the

TABLE 7.2. PERSONAL (INDIVIDUALIZING) AND COLLECTIVE (IDENTITARY) ATTRIBUTES IN MESOAMERICAN ART

PERSONAL (INDIVIDUALIZING) ATTRIBUTES	COLLECTIVE (IDENTITARY) ATTRIBUTES
Innate	1. Physical characteristics shared with other family members
1. Particular physical characteristics	2. Pathological deformation/disfigurement
2. Temperament	3. Lineage
3. Character	4. Names
4. Destiny	5. Ritual piercings, tattoos, scarifications, dental mutilation, intentional deformation of any part of the body (e.g., the head), ritual painting
5. Pathological deformation/disfigurement	6. Grooming (hair, makeup)
6. Lineage	7. Attire (dress), headdresses
	8. Accessories (jewelry, adornments)
Acquired	9. Insignias, emblems, heraldic devices
1. Name	10. Tools, artifacts
2. Ritual piercings, tattoos, scarifications, dental mutilation, intentional deformation of any part of the body (e.g., the head), ritual painting	11. Occupation
3. Occupational injuries or marks	12. Status, rank, position
4. Grooming (hair, makeup)	13. Pose (position of body and various parts)
5. Attire (dress)	14. Domicile, furnishings
6. Accessories (jewelry, adornments)	15. Environment, surroundings
7. Insignias, emblems, heraldic devices	16. Spatial location within the composition
8. Tools, artifacts	
9. Occupation	
10. Status, rank, position	
11. Pose (position of body and various parts)	
12. Divine revelations/marks	
13. Domicile, furnishings	
14. Environment, surroundings	
15. Spatial location within the composition	

"*essence* itself of X," with X being the person depicted in the image (Houston and Stuart 1998). In this example, u-baah complements the descriptive property of the image. In addition, the glyph also could be used to relate the individual to action that was taking place in the scene. Thus, one could say that u-baah also referred to the inherent property of the image as an extension of one's *body-essence*, so that the representation of a person was much more than a mere image. On the one hand, images maintain a resemblance to the model, and, on the other, they contain the substance and part of the essence and identity of the depicted personage; that is to say, we are dealing with coessential entities. As David Stuart (1996) has noted, such images are a *representation* of the individual, but they are also the *actual person*, and I would add that they are the individual's *portrait* as well (Filloy Nadal 2014).

Similarly, Erik Velásquez García (2015) has pointed out that the ruler's name was sometimes situated on the head of the model (or sitter), implying, perhaps, that symbols of the depicted person's identity were concentrated in this area of the body. For example, the *sak-hu'nal* or *sak H'un* diadem (a white band with three peaks depicting the jester god, a supernatural entity representing the ears and leaves of maize) is found on the forehead (*baahis* or *b'aahal*) (fig. 3.8a). Thus the visage both reveals the model's identity as its locus and functions as a marker of social individuality that allows his or her recognition by viewers. Perhaps as Stephen Houston, David Stuart, and Karl Taube (2006:101) have suggested, among the Maya, "personal identity was embodied, as the Central Mexican *tonalli*, in the face or top or forehead of the cranium, a key location that also was silent in references to peoples of different rank. It was the head and the face that received royal diadems as marks of accession."

The importance of the head and face in pre-Hispanic cultures is well documented, both from a symbolic perspective and in terms of its social importance (see also Tiesler and Lacadena, chapter 3 of this volume). For sixteenth-century Nahuas, the *tonalli*—one of the body's three animistic entities or "souls"—was located in the head. Linking them to the gods and the cosmos, the tonalli was of "hot," solar origin and gave individuals vigor and the ability to grow in every sense (McKeever Furst 1995:155; López Austin 1980). It not only animated the individual during life; it was also able to leave the body when he or she died and still maintain the host's identity. Thus, the head and tonalli retained the essence of the sub-

ject even after death. Among various Maya groups today, it is thought that "hot" elements provide strength, vigor, valor, courage, and authority to the individual (Pitarch Ramón 1996, 2006; Ruz Sosa 1992). Apparently the more "heat" one accumulates, the greater one's economic, political, and social power (Martínez González 2006:137, 2007), and this sociocultural identity is significantly concentrated in the head (Martínez González 2006; Pitarch Ramón 1996; Ruz Sosa 2003). The Maya of the Classic period also believed that this vital heat came from the sun (*k'ihn*) and accumulated with age and public offices.[8]

According to Mesoamerican thought, when creating an effigy of a divine person or the image of a god, a fraction of the archetype's light substance coexists with its depiction.[9] Thus, in order to impersonate their gods, Mesoamerican nobles bore the attributes that enabled them to assume the identity of a particular god. In this case, the resemblance between god and image not only involved a transfer of light substance from the former to the latter; the "object" charged with this supernatural power was considered to be the god itself (López Austin 1973:118–20, 1990:159–80, 1993:112–39).

The Mexica concept of *ixiptla* (representation) refers to the material manifestations of a god, whether in its "impersonator" or in its "image" (Hvidtfeldt 1958:81; López Austin 1973:119). Consequently, the image not only represents the deity; it becomes an extension of that same deity, a kind of container or covering, when acquiring and manifesting the deity's invisible essence (Gruzinski 1990:86–88, 2001:50–52; Klein 2001:175; López Austin 1973:118–27, 1990:137–38, 1993:104–5). Serge Gruzinski (1990:86, 2001:51) has summarized the complexity of the concept in this manner: "The *ixiptla* was the container for a power; the localizable, epiphanic presence; the actualization of the power infused into an object; a 'being here.'" In itself, the relationship between the divine being and its *ixiptla* was not one of a simple representation; rather, there was also a coessence among both, and therefore the two shared the same light substance or essence.

The Maya case is similar. In Late Classic inscriptions, the term *u-baah-il-a-nu* was used to denote the impersonators of a god. Although the phrases are complex, they generally contain the following elements: (1) the *u-baah* ("its essence itself") glyph; (2) the *-il* suffix; (3) *a-nu*, a title yet to be translated; (4) the name of the deity; and (5) the name and titles of the ruler or noble (Houston and Stuart 1996, 1998; Houston et al. 2006:270). Through impersonation rituals, a king or noble shared the qualities and attributes of a god and became a container of that deity and thus a manifestation or incarnation of that god. Therefore, reproducing the image of a king or god involved, on the one hand, a likeness between the subject and its representation and, on the other, the incarnation of the sculpted person or deity. This extrasomatic property of animistic entities—the permanent presence of being represented—conferred infinite power to images and thus to the model as well.

INDIVIDUAL CHARACTERISTICS AND IDIOSYNCRATIC TRAITS THAT DEFINE PLASTIC DEPICTIONS OF K'INICH JANAAB' PAKAL: VISAGE AND HEAD AS A SIGNIFIER OF IDENTITY

As previously mentioned, it was common in Palenque for glyphic inscriptions to complement an image; the human figure was linked to the personage's name, along with a relevant date and the text itself. These inscriptions mention the kin relationships existing between the various personages or the nature of relations they maintained with specific deities, and even the activities each of them performed. Thus we know that they refer to specific men or women and not to anonymous personages. But when images have lost their accompanying text, is it still possible to identify the depicted personage? In order to address this question, it is necessary to examine the physical characteristics employed to portray Pakal, an individual whose name we know from inscriptions, and then determine whether his visage could be confused with anyone else's in the city. But how does one go about verifying whether a naturalistic image really looks like an individual depicted more than thirteen centuries ago? Unlike many cases in European art, we have no contemporaneous documents describing Pakal's physiognomy, although various techniques developed by physical anthropologists and art historians could potentially help us identify anthropometric features that might distinguish him from other male images or individuals in Palenque. In what follows, I will analyze some sculpted images that have been associated with Pakal to see if it is possible to discern some physical characteristics that would allow us to identify this important personage within the corpus of males depicted at Palenque. Included in this group are two stucco heads found under the sarcophagus in the Temple of the Inscriptions, a jade mask from inside that sarcophagus, and five bas-relief sculptures from various locations in Palenque

that are accompanied with glyphs directly referring to K'inich Janaab' Pakal (table 7.3).

The Portraits of K'inich Janaab' Pakal

Although the poor state of conservation of Pakal's facial remains recovered from the sarcophagus ruled out forensic portraiture techniques, fortunately another type of craniometric analysis was possible. In 2002, as part of the restoration work on Pakal's jade funerary mask from the Temple of the Inscriptions (Filloy Nadal 2010) (plates 14a, 14b), physical anthropologists Arturo Romano Pacheco and Josefina Bautista Martínez of Mexico's Instituto Nacional de Antropología e Historia (INAH) conducted a craniometric study of the two stucco heads (see Robertson 1983–1991:1:figs. 232a–f, 233a–f) that were discovered beneath the sarcophagus at the Temple of the Inscriptions in 1952 (figs. 7.2, 7.3). Romano Pacheco and Bautista Martínez (2002, 2010) made several measurements of the two sculptures with a Martin marking gauge following the protocol established by Juan Comas (1966) to ascertain the general structure of the face, the location of the compression plane on each head, the shape of the nose, and the prominence of the cheekbones, among other aspects. They also measured both sculptures in terms of face width and length, maximum head length or height, minimum and maximum frontal width, internal and external interorbital distance, eye height and width, nasal height and width, total and upper face height, and bizygomatic width in order to detect any facial asymmetry in each sculpture (Romano Pacheco and Bautista Martínez 2002, 2010). A register of nasogenian or expression lines useful for estimating an individual's age was created as well. An unaided visual examination of the two stucco sculptures revealed that both images depict a male with fine bone structure, high forehead, intentional pseudo-annular oblique tabular cranial deformation, high cheekbones, straight nasal root and bridge extending forward from a shallow base, square jaw and prominent chin with some protrusion, internal strabismus, and asymmetric facial proportions. This asymmetry is also apparent in the bas-relief images of Pakal, where the top of the left ear exceeds, by more than one-third of its total length, the epicanthic fold of the eye, while the top of the right ear exceeds the fold by nearly one-half the total length of the aural appendage (Martínez del Campo Lanz and Filloy Nadal 2010). In addition, the stucco head with its mouth open has incisors modified in the shape of the *ik'* glyph similar to the capital letter *T*.

TABLE 7.3. DEPICTIONS OF K'INICH JANAAB' PAKAL (603–683 CE)
EXHIBITING HIS IDIOSYNCRATIC TRAITS

OBJECT AND LOCATION	IMAGE*	ROTATED/FLIPPED	PATRONYMIC
1. Stucco head, under the sarcophagus, Temple of the Inscriptions		No/No	No
2. Stucco head, under the sarcophagus, Temple of the Inscriptions		No/No	No
3. Jade mask, 683–684, sarcophagus, Temple of the Inscriptions		No/No	No
4. Oval Tablet (detail), ca.652, House E, Palace		No/No	Yes
5. Sarcophagus lid (detail), ca. 684, Temple of the Inscriptions		Yes/No	Yes
6. Palace tablet (detail), ca. 721, House A-D, Palace.		No/Yes	Yes
7. Dumbarton Oaks panel (detail), 722		No/No	Yes
8. Throne (detail), 736, Temple XXI		No/No	Yes

*1–3, courtesy of the Instituto Nacional de Antropología e Historia, Mexico City; 4–8, redrawn by the author.

Figure 7.2. Stucco head depicting a preadolescent male, discovered below the sarcophagus at the Temple of the Inscriptions, Palenque, in 1952 (photo by Luis Martín Martínez, courtesy of the Laboratorio de Conservación, Museo Nacional de Antropología, Instituto Nacional de Antropología e Historia, Mexico City.)

Figure 7.3. Stucco head depicting an individual of around thirty years of age, discovered below the sarcophagus at the Temple of the Inscriptions, Palenque, in 1952 (photo by Luis Martín Martínez, courtesy of the Laboratorio de Conservación, Museo Nacional de Antropología, Instituto Nacional de Antropología e Historia, Mexico City).

The data obtained by Romano Pacheco and Bautista Martínez (2002, 2010) confirmed that both faces had essentially the same proportions. The differences between the faces are minimal and merely reflect the respective age of the subject depicted in the images: one belongs to a prepubescent male, whereas the other, with elaborately styled hair, is a man around thirty years old. All of this suggests that the two stucco heads are quite likely images of the same individual. Encouraged by the results obtained from the analysis of the stucco heads, Romano and Bautista compared this data with morphoscopic measurements made in 1952 by Eusebio Dávalos Hurtado and Arturo Romano Pacheco (1955, 1973) of the skeleton found inside the sarcophagus at the Temple of the Inscriptions (plate 15). In spite of the skull's poor state of conservation, Dávalos and Romano were able to determine that it had

marked oblique tabular deformation and that its incisors were slightly modified in the shape of the *ik'* glyph. One of the consequences of oblique tabular deformation is internal or convergent strabismus caused by pressure from the orbital walls on the eyeballs (Bautista Martínez et al. 2000), which is characteristically evident in images of Pakal (see table 7.3).

We now believe that both sculptures represent Pakal at different stages in his life, because they share a series of physical characteristics that match the skeletal remains recovered from the Temple of the Inscriptions (for a more detailed discussion, see Filloy Nadal 2010). It seems that the Maya artists paid special attention to reproducing these characteristics when crafting these sculptures. Thus, although they were not depicted identically, these salient physical features were re-created with great precision, especially Pakal's facial structure and asymmetry. Romano Pacheco and Bautista Martínez (2010:103) have even proposed that the Maya artists may have made casts or direct molds from the model's face to produce these stone effigies.

Upon completion of the jade mask's restoration at the Museo Nacional de Antropología in Mexico City (Filloy Nadal 2010), the physical anthropologists took the same measurements of the mask that they had done with the two stucco heads. The results were amazing: all of the images had the same facial proportions (Romano Pacheco and Bautista Martínez 2010). With respect to the morphoscopic qualities of the mask, we discovered that it shares the same physical characteristics as the skeleton and the two stucco heads from the Temple of the Inscriptions, including fine bone structure, oblique tabular cranial deformation, distinct prognathism, an ik'-shaped tooth, and internal strabismus. Most surprising was the presence of facial asymmetry on the same side—shorter on the right, as with the stucco heads and the bas-relief sculptures (Martínez del Campo Lanz and Filloy Nadal 2010).[10] The mask, however, also exhibited certain differences from the other images, including more pronounced nasogenian lines, square chin, and jowls characteristic of an older adult male, which suggests that this piece was made shortly before or soon after the sovereign's death (Filloy Nadal 2014).[11]

When we turn to the sculpted bas-relief depictions of K'inich Janaab' Pakal, we see that they exhibit additional

individualizing idiosyncratic traits of the great lord of Palenque (figs. 7.4, 7.5).[12] In all of the images, for example, Pakal wears different variations of the same hairstyle, including a tonsured section in front between two sets of bangs ending just above the ears, and then a longer set of bangs on each side terminating in a straight cut where the upper ends of the jawbone begin.[13] This elaborate hairstyle facilitated the placement of a diadem that usually had a central motif, the sak-hu'nal (Grube 2000:96; Houston and Inomata 2009:142–43). In the stucco heads and the bas-reliefs, this ruler also wears a small tubular bead that helped suspend a dressed forelock above the forehead to allow viewing, in all its splendor, the central jewel of the diadem. Although the modified ik'-shaped incisors are not always discernible, all of the images have pierced earlobes and thin lips along with a nosepiece that enlarges and extends forward the nasal bridge and the forehead. Thus we can say, in general, that the various portraits of K'inich Janaab' Pakal are characterized by their beauty, deformed skull, tonsured forehead, step-cut bangs, elevated forelock, and jade jewels—especially the sak-hu'nal diadem—that together emphasized the visage and head as a signifier of identity (personhood). Although all of these attributes enabled his contemporaries to distinguish him from his peers, more can be said about the type of entity that Pakal embodied in the stucco figure bearing the elaborate headdress and in the funerary greenstone mask.

The most evident features of these portraits are the king's youth, beauty, deformed cranium, tonsure, raised

Figure 7.4. Portrait of K'inich Janaab' Pakal (middle personage) on the Palace Tablet (redrawn by Mirna Beatríz Sánchez from Robertson 1983–1991, courtesy of Vera Tiesler).

Figure 7.5. Portrait of K'inich Janaab' Pakal on the sarcophagus lid (detail), Temple of the Inscriptions, Palenque (redrawn by Karla Gabriela Palacios from Robertson 1983–1991:1:fig. 123).

tuft, jade diadem, and flowers, all of which are attributes of the tonsured maize god, who emulates a mature ear of corn. The principal traits of the Maya maize god began to be identified early in the twentieth century and have been further refined since that time (Seler 1995; Spinden 1975; Taube 1985; Reents-Budet 1991). Karl Taube (1985, 2001) has distinguished two aspects of the maize god based primarily on the shape of his head. The one that interests us here is the tonsured maize god, the mature maize, with the aforementioned characteristics. On the other hand, the name glyph of the tonsured maize god is composed of the T86 *nal* glyph, sometimes accompanied by the *hun* ("one") prefix, as his complete name is Hu'unal (Houston et al. 1992:449–50).

The principal features of the jade visage/head from the Temple of the Inscriptions include oblique tabular cranial deformation, internal strabismus, straight nasal root and bridge, an artificial nosepiece projecting forward and upward, high cheekbones, thin open lips, and teeth retouched in the shape of the ik' glyph. As we have seen, all of these traits are characteristic of the sovereign K'inich Janaab' Pakal. Although the Maya chose different kinds of minerals for the tesserae of their masks, all of the ones they used had tones ranging from dark green to a lumi-

nescent light green. *Ya'x* is the Maya word for the colors green and blue. Green and blue chromatically represented the center and point of convergence of the cosmos. Green was associated with vegetation, vital liquid, maize, fertility, centrality, breath, and vital essence; thus it was synonymous with status, wealth, immortality, preciousness, and the continuity of life, and its use was restricted to elites who held power (Taube 1998, 2015). Also unique is the presence of ik' symbols on the back of some of the tesserae as well as on the retouched teeth of the mask, which perhaps reinforces an association with breath (*sak iik'aal*), soul, or vital essence (Bourdin 2007:110–14). It could also have the same meaning as placing a greenstone bead in the mouth of the dead (see, for example, Taube 1998:32), which facilitated the passage of the soul of the deceased to the afterlife (Mendoza 2001:65). Even today, some Maya communities, for example, among the Lacandon, Tzotzil, and Chamula (Ruz Lhuillier 1968:19, 22, 23), put maize dough or kernels in the mouths of the dead or on their bodies, as its meaning is equivalent to that of jade in antiquity (Ruz Lhuillier 1968:30–32).

If the mask, as previously mentioned, is an animate object that contains the cognitive essence and powers of the being it represents, when placed on the face of the buried subject it transforms the visage of the deceased into the image that he or she symbolizes (Klein 2001:175; Mack 1994:16; Markman and Markman 1989:88). Thus it could be said that, when reproducing an image of the sovereign in jade, his essence achieves a permanence that the physical body could never have (Houston and Stuart 1998:90; Nunley 1999:83). Furthermore, through the mask, the ruler is transformed into an impersonator of the deity whose attributes he shares, and the mask-visage will play a fundamental role in the sovereign's rites of passage to his new state.[14] Impersonating the maize god, the buried sovereign must likewise germinate, regenerate, and maintain the grain deposited in the earth until the end of time. Pakal the Great is thus equivalent to the maize god, who is constantly renewed inside the sacred mountain at the center of the universe (Taube 2000a, 2000b, 2001).

Let us examine another portrait of the sovereign with other associations on the lid of the sarcophagus. Here, Pakal is depicted in an uncomfortable pose, with his legs flexed forward and his head reclined backward. As elsewhere, he bears an elaborate hairstyle that is step-cut with tufts and on this occasion topped with a singular motif: on his forehead we see a rectangular element framed by a mirror glyph with an emerging, undulating scroll, which is a smoking torch or shining celt. On the tip of the lord's nose is a small "seed" or "flower" (*ahau*), which represents either a breath or an exhalation. In this case, the smoking torch or polished stone celt on top of his hair is characteristic of K'awiil (GII or God K), an entity that is associated with lineage, dynasty, and, especially, live-giving forces, including lightning, rain, and maize (Bassie 2002:37; Martin 2006:172; Robicsek 1975:59–107; Taube 1992:79; Velásquez García 2015). Thus in Janaab' Pakal we see the divine aspects maize and lightning/sustenance.

I should also briefly mention the significant placement of K'inich Janaab' Pakal, the jade mask, and the sarcophagus deep in the Temple of the Inscriptions, the heart of the Sacred Mountain. In fact, the temple's pyramidal base emulates the Sacred Mountain, where the most precious offerings and goods were kept and where the life-generating forces originated. In the sarcophagus—a large stone container—was stored the ruler's body, the "seed/heart" from which the new ruler emerged with greenstone accoutrements that held moisture, generating forces, and vital breath. If the jade mask and accessories, indeed, are the locus of the deity they embody (Freedberg 1989:31–33), then their bearer, Janaab' Pakal, is inseparable from the entity he represents. Therefore, just like the maize god, the sovereign was able to overcome the trials of the underworld—and death itself—to emerge from the depths transformed into a divine being (Houston and Stuart 1996) and a powerful ancestor (Filloy Nadal 2014). And, fulfilling his destiny, Janaab' Pakal will follow the

path of Itzamna to the celestial firmament as K'inich Ajaw, the sun, where he will reign for eternity.

The Last Portrait of the Sovereign

My final example comes from a relief sculpted on a throne inside Temple XXI of the Southern Acropolis at Palenque that depicts a complex scene in which five personages appear in a ceremony that took place in the year 736. In the center of the relief, presiding over the scene, we see Pakal seated on a jaguar-skin throne (fig. 7.6). According to the inscriptions, the famous ruler had died in 683, and by the time the relief was carved his body had lain inside the Temple of the Inscriptions for more than half a century. Pakal offers an autosacrificial instrument—a stingray spine—to his grandson Ahkal Mo' Nahb' III, the ruler at the time. On the opposite side of the scene, to the left of Pakal, is depicted another grandson of his who will subsequently govern Palenque during the second half of the eighth century.

Guillermo Bernal Romero (2006) and David Stuart (2007:228) agree that this scene indicates that K'inich Janaab' Pakal continued to have considerable influence on the governing of Palenque, even several decades after his death. The reign of Ahkal Mo' Nahb' III had been preceded by a period of great instability in the kingdom, caused by the wars against Toniná and the capture of the lord of Palenque, K'an Joy Chitam. Depicting the reigning king, Ahkal Mo' Nahb' III, accompanied by his heir to

Figure 7.6. Relief sculpted on a throne inside Temple XXI of the Southern Acropolis at Palenque (detail, Pakal seated on a jaguar skin throne) (photo by Michel Zabé; courtesy of Estudio Zabé).

the throne, U Pakal K'inich, and by K'inich Janaab' Pakal, as the incarnation of the illustrious ancestors, linked the current ruling generations with virtuous past kings—historical as well as mythical—who were emblematic entities of Palenque royal power, succession, and dynastic origin (Bernal Romero 2004, 2006; Stuart 2007). Thanks to the ability possessed by divinities, the king, and a few others (heirs and ancestors, for example) to travel from the ecumene to the anecumene, where past, present, and future intertwined, the action depicted in the scene lay outside the temporality of the world of humans, and thus the personages in the scene remained eternally engaged in reproducing the activity being performed.

In this last case, it is significant to note that Pakal the Great not only was mentioned in the texts but was also depicted with the same physical characteristics that appear in the images made during this emblematic king's reign, such as the Oval Tablet in House E of the palace exhibiting his patronymic, and the two stucco heads found inside the crypt of the Temple of the Inscriptions without any identifying glyphs. Indeed, the similarities between the Temple XXI portrait and the others made during his lifetime or after his passing are astonishing. The images of Pakal over time exhibit great consistency, both in terms of his physical characteristics and his idiosyncratic traits. In all of these cases, we see a man with fine bone structure, high forehead, intentional pseudo-annular oblique tabular cranial deformation, high cheekbones, straight nasal root and bridge projected forward from a shallow base, square jaw and prominent chin with some protrusion, internal strabismus, and asymmetric facial proportions (Filloy Nadal 2014; Romano Pacheco and Bautista Martínez 2010). I believe that such representations were anatomically conceived before their execution, at different stages (adolescence, adulthood, old age) during his lifetime, and then produced with extraordinary realism, with strict attention to the smallest details, taking into account the essential idiosyncratic traits—individualizing and identitary—that characterized Pakal within the Palenque collectivity. Therefore, I believe that we are dealing with true portraits of Palenque's most famous king, K'inich Janaab' Pakal (see also Filloy Nadal 2011, 2014).

Along these same lines, various authors (Benson 2004:48; Griffin 1976:138; Miller and Martin 2004:205; Robertson 1975) have suggested that perhaps a single sculptor carved all of the images in Palenque that exhibit a greater degree of realism and explore the physiognomy of individuals (which I have called portraits). They propose that during the reign of K'inich Janaab' Pakal—and probably that of his son and successor, K'inich Kan B'ahlam II—there was a sculptor in Palenque who had the technical expertise to achieve the maximum likeness of the image to its model, K'inich Janaab' Pakal.[15] But regardless of whether these portraits are the work of one or more sculptors, we may conclude that the artists who worked in Palenque after the famous ruler's death faithfully depicted the most important physical attributes of the king, the essential characteristics of his face, and the other idiosyncratic traits that distinguished him, thus enabling the identification, even several centuries later, of the depicted person without being confused with anyone else. We may say, then, that in great measure the crux of Pakal the Great's identity, if not Late Classic Maya royal portraiture in general, resided in the ruler's visage and head.

ACKNOWLEDGMENTS

Some of the ideas expressed in this essay were previously presented at the Homage to Alfredo López Austin organized by Mexico's Instituto Nacional de Antropología e Historia and the Universidad Nacional Autónoma de México in 2013, and at the Cultural Meanings of Head Treatments in Mesoamerican and Andean Societies symposium at the seventy-ninth annual meeting of the Society for American Archaeology held in Austin, Texas, April 23–27, 2014. I would like to express my appreciation to Vera Tiesler for inviting me to the symposium and to Scott Sessions for translating my essay from Spanish into English.

NOTES

1. The original Spanish text reads: "[E]l hombre, el mismo que había sido representado . . . como símbolo hierático del poder conferido por los dioses, se emancipaba un poco de ellos para situarse con su dignidad propia dentro del universo, como algo distinto a él y, de algún modo, capaz de comprender su sentido. . . . El hombre . . . no se anula ante lo divino, se crea su propio sitio" (Garza 1975:87).

2. The original Spanish text reads: "[L]os dioses y los hombres parecen colaborar juntos en la conservación del universo sacralizado pero humano" (Fuente 1966:11).

3. For example, Benson (2004), Fuente (1966, 1970, 2003c), Garza (1975:85), Griffin (1976), Kubler (1969), Miller (1999),

Proskouriakoff (1961, 1963, 1964), Schele and Miller (1986), Séjourné (1952), Spinden (1916), and Taladoire (2003).

4. See the interesting articles by María Villanueva Sagredo (2004), Villanueva Sagredo et al. (2003), and Vera Tiesler et al. (2004a, 2004b) on the facial reconstruction of pre-Hispanic skulls.

5. Apparently, this type of modeled or mold-cast figurine would have been produced specifically to serve as a burial accompaniment for elite individuals from Edzná or the nearby Chenes region (Ball 2001:438). Another interesting example of this in Mesoamerican art occurs in the Zapotec urns from Oaxaca studied by Adam Sellen (2007).

6. One can say that the visual representation of a person is a historical-cultural expression through which a human group realizes, according to its conceptions and conventions, the image of a particular individual. This individualizing visual configuration can be divided into two categories. In the first, collective idiosyncratic traits dominate and therefore produce generic images. The second category is the portrait.

7. Alfredo López Austin (2006:95) has defined *ecumene* as the "ámbito del cosmos ocupado por las criaturas, pero también poblado por los entes sobrenaturales" (realm of the cosmos occupied by creatures, but also populated by supernatural entities), while conversely the term *anecumene* refers to the part of the cosmos "reservada a los sobrenaturales" (reserved for supernatural beings).

8. K'inich Jannab' Pakal's name itself makes reference to the heat of the sun (*k'inich ajaw*). In this particular case, k'inich functions as an epithet or prefix of the name (Pakal, or "shield") and therefore as a semantic modifier that equates the bearer with the "heat" or "light" of the star (Stuart 1995, cited in Martin 2010:72). Stephen Houston has suggested that the term *k'inich* may be interpreted as "the essence of the sun" (cited in Martin 2010:72), conceiving the king as the guardian of the sun's qualities while also maintaining a human core distinct from the deity (Houston and Stuart 1996:290).

9. In Mesoamerican thought, the attire, mask, or image not only represented the deity but also became an extension of the divinity when acquiring its essence (Klein 2001; López Austin 1990:137–38). Therefore, the Mexica used the word *xayacatl* to designate both the mask and the face as a metaphor for the being and for the personality of an individual, while the Maya term *k'oh* had the combined meaning of mask, image, and representation (Klein 2001:175). Of course, this is not exclusive to Mesoamerican cultures. In religions that have representations of divinities, the great power of the images consists in their capacity to embody the power and identity of the being they represent (Freedberg 1989:28); signified and signifier—"the *represented thing* and *that which represents it*" (Gruzinski 1990:80, 2001:47, emphasis in orig-

inal)—become one. The power of images resides, then, according to David Freedberg (1989:30), "in the perception that what is represented on an image is actually present, or present in it, . . . because of the fusion of image and prototype."

10. When we have two profiles, as in the case of the Temple of the Inscriptions stucco heads, the asymmetries are even more pronounced. For example, in the representation that characterizes the individual in the prime of life, we see that the top of the left ear exceeds the epicanthic fold by 35 percent, while the right ear exceeds the total length of the appendage by 42 percent (Filloy Nadal and Martínez del Campo Lanz 2004; Martínez del Campo Lanz and Filloy Nadal 2010).

11. The individual buried in the Temple of the Inscriptions is an adult male of advanced age, average height and build, well proportioned, and without apparent pathologies (Dávalos Hurtado and Romano Pacheco 1973; Romano Pacheco and Bautista Martínez 2010; Tiesler 2004).

12. These sculpted bas-relief depictions of Pakal include: (1) the Oval Tablet from House E of the palace (Robertson 1983–1991:2:28–32, figs. 90–91; Schele and Miller 1986:114, fig. II.5); (2) the sarcophagus lid from the Temple of the Inscriptions (Robertson 1983–1991:1:56–62, figs. 123, 139; Schele and Miller 1986:282, plates 111, 111d); (3) the Palace Tablet from House A-D of the palace (Robertson 1983–1991:3:58, figs. 274–75); (4) the Dumbarton Oaks Panel (Schele and Miller 1986:275, fig. VII.3); and (5) the throne from Temple XXI (Stuart 2007:fig. 11.16; Stuart and Stuart 2008:fig. 77).

13. Merle Green Robertson (1985:36–37) labeled this variety "SS-3" in her analysis of Palenque hairstyles.

14. These concepts have been discussed at length by Claude Lévi-Strauss (1982), Pietro Scarduelli (1983), and Arnold van Gennep (1960), among others.

15. Here I should also mention some possible portraits of Pakal's son, K'inich Kan B'ahlam II, who acceded to the throne in 684. Several researchers have noted that he seems to be depicted in three of the buildings in the Group of the Cross and on a tablet in Temple XIV (Miller 1999; Miller and Martin 2004; Schele and Miller 1986), based on these images' apparent similarity and the fact that all of them are identified with a name glyph. Although plastic art was strictly circumscribed by the aesthetic conventions of the time, we still can detect the artist's clear intention to capture the physical characteristics of this particular individual, including strong bone structure, a long face with a high forehead and very marked intentional oblique tabular cranial deformation, eyes with an epicanthic fold, and a prominent nose without an artificial nasal application. The images are relatively simple and have only a few idiosyncratic traits, namely pierced earlobes for wearing large earspools, a necklace with round beads, a royal diadem (in the

Temple XIV example), and step-cut tufts of hair. These attributes, however, are shared with many other Palenque dignitaries (for example, Pakal himself); thus they would be identitary or collective rather than individualizing idiosyncratic traits. His massive tuft and lower lip projecting forward and upward, on the other hand, are characteristic morphoscopic features that distinguish him from others in Palenque. Similarly, the rubble of Temple XIV has also yielded a fine stucco head whose deteriorated condition exhibits only two of the identitary idiosyncratic traits (pierced earlobes and step-cut hair), although it shares one of the aforementioned morphoscopic features (a thick forward and upward projecting lower lip) identified with K'an B'ahlam II and thus may depict the same personage. In contrast, another seventh-century stucco head from Palenque, now at the Museo Nacional de Antropología, depicts a male who shares the strong bone structure of K'an B'ahlam II, but his face is much wider and his continence quite different, thus preventing any confusion between the two. Although we do not know who this sculpted personage was, his circumspect look reveals a small aspect of his personality, while other features, such as well-defined nasogenian lines running from his nose to the corners of his mouth, along with sagging cheeks, jowls, and lower chin, suggest advanced age (Filloy Nadal 2014:167–68).

REFERENCES CITED

Ball, Joseph W.

2001   Maya Lowlands: North. In *Archaeology of Ancient Mexico and Central America: An Encyclopedia*, edited by Susan Toby Evans and David L. Webster, pp. 433–41. Garland, New York.

Bassie, Karen

2002   Maya Creator Gods. Mesoweb, electronic document, www.mesoweb.com/features/bassie/CreatorGods /CreatorGods.pdf.

Bautista Martínez, Josefina, Emma Limón, and Alberto Brown

2000   La deformación craneana intencional y algunas alteraciones oculares. In *Investigaciones en biodiversidad humana*, edited by Tito A. Varela, pp. 183–89. Universidad de Santiago de Compostela, Santiago de Compostela, Spain.

Benson, Elizabeth P.

2004   Varieties of Precolumbian Portraiture. In *Retratos: 2,000 Years of Latin American Portraits*, by Elizabeth P. Benson et al., pp. 46–55. San Antonio Museum of Art, San Antonio; National Portrait Gallery, Smithsonian Institution, Washington, DC; Museo del Barrio, New York; Yale University Press, New Haven, Connecticut.

Bernal Romero, Guillermo

2004   El eterno retorno: Pakal, figura de culto en el señorío de Palenque. Paper presented at the XVIII Coloquio Internacional de Historia del Arte: La imagen sagrada y sacralizada, Campeche, October 24–29, 2004. Manuscript on file, Instituto de Investigaciones Estéticas, Universidad Nacional Autónoma de México, Mexico.

2006   El trono de K'inich Ahkal Mo' Nahb': una inscripción glífica del Templo XIX de Palenque. Master's thesis, Facultad de Filosofía, Universidad Nacional Autónoma de México, Mexico City.

Bourdin, Gabriel

2007   *El cuerpo humano entre los mayas: una aproximación lingüística.* Universidad Autónoma de Yucatán, Mérida.

Brilliant, Richard

1987   Portraits: The Limitations of Likeness. *Art Journal* 47(3):171–72.

1990   Portraits: A Recurrent Genre in World Art. In *Likeness and Beyond: Portraits from Africa and the World*, edited by Jean M. Borgatti and Richard Brilliant, pp. 11–27. Center for African Art, New York.

1991   *Portraiture.* Harvard University Press, Cambridge, Massachusetts.

1994   On Portraits. In *Commentaries on Roman Art: Selected Studies*, edited by Richard Brilliant, pp. 1–17. Pindar, London.

Comas, Juan

1966   *Manual de antropología física.* 2nd ed. Antropológica, 10. Universidad Nacional Autónoma de México, Mexico City.

Dávalos Hurtado, Eusebio, and Arturo Romano Pacheco

1955   Estudio preliminar de los restos osteológicos encontrados en la tumba del Templo de las Inscripciones, Palenque. *Anales del Instituto Nacional de Antropología e Historia* 6:107–10.

1973   Estudio preliminar de los restos osteológicos encontrados en la tumba del Templo de la Inscripciones, Palenque. In *El Templo de las Inscripciones, Palenque*, by Alberto Ruz Lhuillier, pp. 253–54. Colección Científica, Arqueología, 7. Instituto Nacional de Antropología Historia, Mexico City.

Filloy Nadal, Laura

2010   (editor) *Misterios de un rostro maya: la máscara de K'inich Janaab' Pakal de Palenque.* Instituto Nacional de Antropología e Historia, Mexico City.

2011   Imágenes convencionales o retratos: los rostros de

Pakal II, soberano de Palenque, Chiapas. In *Las imá-genes precolombinas, reflejo de saberes*, edited by María del Carmen Valverde Valdés and Victoria Solanilla Demestres, pp. 161–92. Centro de Estudios Mayas, Instituto de Investigaciones Filológicas, Universidad Nacional Autónoma de México, Mexico City.

2014   *Costume et insignes d'un gouvernant maya: K'inich Janaab' Pakal de Palenque.* Paris Monographs in American Archaeology, 34. BAR International Series, 2590. British Archaeological Reports, Oxford.

Filloy Nadal, Laura, and Sofía Martínez del Campo Lanz

2004   La restauración de la máscara funeraria de Pacal: esencia e imagen del soberano. In *Culto funerario en la sociedad maya: memoria de la Cuarta Mesa Redonda de Palenque*, edited by Rafael Cobos, pp. 81–98. Instituto Nacional de Antropología e Historia, Mexico City.

Francastel, Galienne, and Pierre Francastel

1969   *Le portrait: 50 siècles d'humanisme en peinture.* Hachette, Paris.

Freedberg, David

1989   *The Power of Images: Studies in the History and Theory of Response.* University of Chicago Press, Chicago.

Fuente, Beatriz de la

1966   La conciencia histórica entre los antiguos mayas a través de su escultura. *Anales del Instituto de Investigaciones Estéticas* 11(35):5–13.

1970   El arte del retrato entre los mayas. In *Reseña del retrato mexicano*, edited by Gonzalo Obregón, pp. 7–21. Artes de México, no. 132. Artes de México, Mexico City.

1993   *La escultura de Palenque.* Colegio Nacional, Mexico City.

2003a *La escultura del México antiguo.* Edited by Verónica Hernández Díaz. Colegio Nacional, Mexico City.

2003b Peldaños en la conciencia: rostros en la plástica prehispánica. In *El arte, la historia y el hombre: arte prehispánico de México; estudios y ensayos*, edited by Verónica Hernández Díaz, pp. 191–359. Obras de Beatriz de la Fuente, 1. Colegio Nacional, Mexico City.

2003c Rostros: expresión de vida en la plástica. In *La escultura del México antiguo*, edited by Verónica Hernández Díaz, pp. 205–20. Obras de Beatriz de la Fuente, 2. Colegio Nacional, Mexico City.

Garza, Mercedes de la

1975   *La conciencia histórica de los antiguos mayas.* Cuaderno 11. Centro de Estudios Mayas, Instituto de Investigaciones Filológicas, Universidad Nacional Autónoma de México, Mexico City.

1978   *El hombre en el pensamiento religioso náhuatl y maya.* Cuaderno 14. Centro de Estudios Mayas, Instituto

de Investigaciones Filológicas, Universidad Nacional Autónoma de México, Mexico City.

Gennep, Arnold van

1960   *The Rites of Passage.* University of Chicago Press, Chicago.

Griffin, Gillett G.

1976   Portraiture in Palenque. In *The Art, Iconography, and Dynastic History of Palenque: Proceedings of the Segunda Mesa Redonda de Palenque, December 14–21, 1974.* Part 3, *Palenque*, edited by Merle Greene Robertson, pp. 137–48. Pre-Columbian Art Research Institute, San Francisco.

Grube, Nikolai

2000   Los distintivos del poder. In *Los mayas: una civilización milenaria*, edited by Nikolai Grube, pp. 96–97. Könemann, Cologne.

Gruzinski, Serge

1990   *La guerre des images: de Christophe Colomb à "Blade Runner," 1492–2019.* Fayard, Paris.

2001   *Images at War: Mexico from Columbus to "Blade Runner," 1492–2019.* Translated by Heather MacLean. Duke University Press, Durham, North Carolina.

Houston, Stephen, and Takeshi Inomata

2009   *The Classic Maya.* Cambridge University Press, New York.

Houston, Stephen, and David Stuart

1996   Of Gods, Glyphs, and Kings: Divinity and Rulership among the Classic Maya. *Antiquity* 70(268):289–313.

1998   The Ancient Maya Self: Personhood and Portraiture in the Classic Period. *RES: Anthropology and Aesthetics* 33:73–101.

Houston, Stephen, David Stuart, and Karl Taube

1992   Image and Text on the "Juancy Vase." In *The Maya Vase Book: A Corpus of Rollout Photographs of Maya Vases*, vol. 3, edited by Justin Kerr, pp. 499–512. Kerr Associates, New York.

2006   *The Memory of Bones: Body, Being, and Experience among the Classic Maya.* University of Texas Press, Austin.

Hvidtfeldt, Arild

1958   *Teotl and Ixiptlatli: Some Central Conceptions in Ancient Mexican Religion, with a General Introduction on Cult and Myth.* Munksgaard, Copenhagen.

Klein, Cecelia F.

2001   Masks. In *The Oxford Encyclopedia of Mesoamerican Cultures*, vol. 2, edited by Davíd Carrasco, pp. 175–77. Oxford University Press, New York.

Kubler, George

1969   *Studies in Classic Maya Iconography*. Memoirs, 18. Connecticut Academy of Arts and Sciences, New Haven.

Lévi-Strauss, Claude

1982   *The Way of the Masks*. Translated by Sylvia Modelski. University of Washington Press, Seattle.

López Austin, Alfredo

1973   *Hombre-dios: religión y política en el mundo náhuatl*. Instituto de Investigaciones Antropológicas, Universidad Nacional Autónoma de México, Mexico City.

1980   *Cuerpo humano e ideología: las concepciones de los antiguos nahuas*. Instituto de Investigaciones Antropológicas, Universidad Nacional Autónoma de México, Mexico City.

1988   *The Human Body and Ideology: Concepts of the Ancient Nahuas*. Translated by Thelma Ortiz de Montellano and Bernard Ortiz de Montellano. University of Utah Press, Salt Lake City.

1990   *Los mitos del tlacuache: caminos de la mitología mesoamericana*. Alianza, Mexico City.

1993   *The Myths of the Opossum: Pathways of Mesoamerican Mythology*. Translated by Bernard Ortiz de Montellano and Thelma Ortiz de Montellano. University of New Mexico Press, Albuquerque.

1997   De la racionalidad, de la vida y de la muerte. In *El cuerpo humano y su tratamiento mortuorio*, edited by Elsa Malvido, Grégory Pereira, and Vera Tiesler, pp. 13–16. Centro Francés de Estudios Mexicanos y Centroamericanos; Instituto Nacional de Antropología e Historia, Mexico City.

2001   Los mexicas ante el cosmos. *Arqueología Mexicana* 16(91):24–35.

2004   La composición de la persona en la tradición mesoamericana. *Arqueología Mexicana* 11(65):30–35.

2006   Mitos e íconos de la ruptura del eje cósmico: un glifo toponímico de las piedras de Tízoc y del Ex-Arzobispado. *Anales del Instituto de Investigaciones Estéticas* 89:93–134.

Mack, John.

1994   Introduction: About Face. In *Masks: The Art of Expression*, edited by John Mack, pp. 9–31. British Museum, London.

Markman, Peter T., and Roberta H. Markman

1989   *Masks of the Spirit: Image and Metaphor in Mesoamerica*. University of California Press, Berkeley.

Martin, Simon

2006   Cacao in Ancient Maya Religion: First Fruit from the Maize Tree and Other Tales from the Underworld. In *Chocolate in Mesoamerica: A Cultural History of Cacao*, edited by Cameron McNeil, pp. 154–83. University Press of Florida, Gainesville.

2010   Biografía de K'inich Janaab Pakal. In *Misterios de un rostro maya: la máscara de K'inich Janaab' Pakal de Palenque*, edited by Laura Filloy Nadal, pp. 71–90. Instituto Nacional de Antropología e Historia, Mexico City.

Martínez del Campo Lanz, Sofía, and Laura Filloy Nadal

2010   El último retrato de Pakal II: la restauración de su máscara funeraria. In *Misterios de un rostro maya: la máscara de K'inich Janaab' Pakal de Palenque*, edited by Laura Filloy Nadal, pp. 173–96. Instituto Nacional de Antropología e Historia, Mexico City.

Martínez González, Roberto

2006   El *Tonalli* y el calor vital: algunas precisiones. *Anales de Antropología* 40(2):117–51.

2007   El alma de Mesoamérica: unidad y especificidad en las concepciones anímicas de sus indígenas. *Journal de la Société des Américanistes* 93(2):7–49.

Mauss, Marcel

1938   Une catégorie de l'esprit humain: la notion de personne celle de "moi." *Journal of the Anthropological Institute of Great Britain and Ireland* 68:263–81.

McKeever Furst, Jill Leslie

1995   *The Natural History of the Soul in Ancient Mexico*. Yale University Press, New Haven, Connecticut.

Mendoza, Rubén G.

2001   Jade and Greenstone. In *The Oxford Encyclopedia of Mesoamerican Cultures*, vol. 2, edited by Davíd Carrasco, pp. 65–66. Oxford University Press, New York.

Miller, Mary Ellen

1999   *Maya Art and Architecture*. Thames and Hudson, New York.

Miller, Mary Ellen, and Simon Martin

2004   *Courtly Art of the Ancient Maya*. Thames and Hudson, New York.

Nunley, John W.

1999   Rites of Passage. In *Masks: Faces of Culture*, edited by John W. Nunley and Cara McCarty, pp. 40–83. Saint Louis Art Museum, Saint Louis; Abrams, New York.

Pitarch Ramón, Pedro

1996   *Ch'ulel: una etnografía de las almas tzeltales*. Fondo de Cultura Económica, Mexico City.

2006   Conjeturas sobre la identidad de los santos tzeltales. In *De la mano de lo sacro: santos y demonios en el mundo maya*, edited by Mario Humberto Ruz Sosa, pp. 67–90. Centro de Estudios Mayas, Instituto de Investigaciones

Filológicas, Universidad Nacional Autónoma de México, Mexico City.

Proskouriakoff, Tatiana

1961 Portraits of Woman in Maya Art. In *Essays in Pre-Columbian Art and Archaeology*, edited by Samuel K. Lothrop et al., pp. 81–99. Harvard University Press, Cambridge, Massachusetts.

1963 Historical Data in the Inscriptions of Yaxchilán, part 1. *Estudios de Cultura Maya* 3:149–67.

1964 Historical Data in the Inscriptions of Yaxchilán, part 2. *Estudios de Cultura Maya* 4:177–201.

Reents-Budet, Dorie

1991 The "Holmul Dancer" Theme in Maya Art. In *Sixth Palenque Round Table in 1986*, edited by Virginia M. Fields, pp. 217–22. University of Oklahoma Press, Norman.

Robertson, Merle Greene

1975 Stucco Techniques Employed by Ancient Sculptors of Palenque. In *Actas del XLI Congreso Internacional de Americanistas, México, 2 al 7 de septiembre de 1974*, vol. 1, pp. 449–72. Instituto Nacional de Antropología e Historia, Mexico City.

1983–1991 *The Sculpture of Palenque*. 4 vols. Princeton University Press, Princeton, New Jersey.

1985 "57 Varieties": The Palenque Beauty Salon. In *Fourth Palenque Round Table, 1980*, edited by Elizabeth P. Benson, pp. 29–44. Pre-Columbian Art Research Institute, San Francisco.

Robicsek, Francis

1975 *A Study in Maya Art and History: The Mat Symbol*. Museum of the American Indian Heye Foundation, New York.

Romano Pacheco, Arturo, and Josefina Bautista Martínez

2002 Estudios comparativos de las imágenes de Pakal II. Manuscript on file, Archivo del Laboratorio de Conservación, Museo Nacional de Antropología, Instituto Nacional de Antropología e Historia, Mexico City.

2010 Estudios antropométricos de los restos esqueléticos de K'inich Janaab' Pakal y de sus imágenes en estuco. In *Misterios de un rostro maya: la máscara funeraria de K'inich Janaab' Pakal de Palenque*, edited by Laura Filloy Nadal, pp. 99–108. Instituto Nacional de Antropología e Historia, Mexico City.

Ruz Lhuillier, Alberto

1968 *Costumbres funerarias de los antiguos mayas*. Seminario de Cultura Maya, Facultad de Filosofía y Letras, Universidad Nacional Autónoma de México, Mexico City.

1973 *El Templo de las Inscripciones, Palenque*. Colección Científica, Arqueología, 7. Instituto Nacional de Antropología e Historia, Mexico City.

Ruz Sosa, Mario Humberto

1992 Los mayas de hoy: pueblos en lucha. In *Del katún al siglo: tiempos de colonialismo y resistencia entre los mayas*, edited by María del Carmen León Cázares, Mario Humberto Ruz Sosa, and José Alejos García, pp. 191–267. Consejo Nacional para la Cultura y las Artes, Mexico City.

2003 La restitución del ser: identidades mayas de muerte. In *Cuarto Congreso Internacional de Mayistas: memoria, 2 al 8 agosto de 1998*, edited by Mario Humberto Ruz Sosa et al., pp. 155–78. Centro de Estudios Mayas, Instituto de Investigaciones Filológicas, Universidad Nacional Autónoma de México, Mexico City.

Saghy, Lajos

1973 Quelques aspects de la notion de personne. In *La notion de personne en Afrique Noire, Paris, 11–17 octobre 1971*, edited by Germaine Dieterlen, pp. 573–84. Colloques Internationaux, 544. Centre National de la Recherche Scientifique, Paris.

Scarduelli, Pietro

1983 *Dioses, espíritus, ancestros: elementos para la comprensión de sistemas rituales*. Fondo de Cultura Económica, Mexico City.

Schele, Linda, and Mary Ellen Miller

1986 *The Blood of Kings: Dynasty and Ritual in Maya Art*. Kimbell Art Museum, Forth Worth; George Braziller, New York.

Séjourné, Laurette

1952 *Palenque, una ciudad maya*. Fondo de Cultura Económica, Mexico City.

Seler, Eduard

1995 Observaciones y estudios en las ruinas de Palenque, 1915, traducido por Heinrich Berlin (Ruinas de Palenque, mayo de 1940). Unpublished manuscript, Archivo Técnico del Consejo de Arqueología, TXVI, no. 207.2. Instituto Nacional de Antropología e Historia, Mexico City.

Sellen, Adam T.

2007 *El cielo compartido: deidades y ancestros en las vasijas efigie zapotecas*. Monografías, 4. Centro Peninsular en Humanidades y Ciencias Sociales, Universidad Nacional Autónoma de México, Mérida.

Spinden, Herbert J.

1916 Portraiture in Central American Art. In *Holmes Anniversary Volume: Anthropological Essays Presented to William Henry Holmes in Honor of His Seventieth Birthday, December 1, 1916*, edited by Frederick W. Hodge, pp. 434–50. J. W. Bryan Press, Washington, DC.

1975 *A Study of Maya Art: Its Subject Matter and Historical Development*. Dover, New York.

Stuart, David

1995 *A Study of Maya Inscriptions*. PhD dissertation, Department of Anthropology, Vanderbilt University, Nashville.

1996 Kings of Stone: A Consideration of Stelae in Ancient Maya Ritual and Representation. *RES: Anthropology and Aesthetics* 29–30:149–71.

2005 *The Inscriptions from Temple XIX at Palenque: A Commentary*. Pre-Columbian Art Research Institute, San Francisco.

2007 Gods and Histories: Mythology and Dynastic Succession at Temples XIX and XXI at Palenque. In *Palenque: Recent Investigations at the Classic Maya Center*, edited by Damien B. Marken, pp. 207–32. AltaMira Press, Lanham, Maryland.

Stuart, David, and George E. Stuart

2008 *Palenque: Eternal City of the Maya*. Thames and Hudson, London.

Taladoire, Eric

2003 *Les Mayas*. Éditions du Chêne, Paris.

Taube, Karl A.

1985 The Classic Maya Maize God: A Reappraisal. In *Fifth Palenque Round Table, 1983*, vol. 7, edited by Virginia M. Fields, pp. 171–81. Pre-Columbian Art Research Institute, San Francisco.

1992 *The Major Gods of Ancient Yucatan*. Studies in Pre-Columbian Art and Archaeology, 32. Dumbarton Oaks, Washington, DC.

1998 The Jade Hearth: Centrality, Rulership, and the Classic Maya Temple. In *Function and Meaning in Classic Maya Architecture: A Symposium at Dumbarton Oaks, 7th and 8th October 1994*, edited by Stephen Houston, pp. 427–78. Dumbarton Oaks, Washington, DC.

2000a Lightning Celts and Corn Fetishes: The Formative Olmec and the Development of Maize Symbolism in Mesoamerica and the American Southwest. In *Olmec Art and Archaeology in Mesoamerica*, edited by John E. Clark and Mary E. Pye, pp. 297–337. Studies in the History of Art, 58. National Gallery of Art, Washington, DC; Yale University Press, New Haven, Connecticut.

2000b Los dioses de los mayas clásicos. In *Los mayas: una civilización milenaria*, edited by Nikolai Grube, pp. 263–77. Könemann, Cologne.

2001 Maize: Iconography and Cosmological Significance. In *The Oxford Encyclopedia of Mesoamerican Cultures*, vol. 2, edited by Davíd Carrasco, pp. 150–52. Oxford University Press, New York.

2015 "Los significados del jade." *Arqueología Mexicana* 133 (23):49–55.

Tiesler, Vera

2004 Vida y muerte de Janaab' Pakal de Palenque: hallazgos bioarqueológicos recientes. In *Janaab' Pakal de Palenque: vida y muerte de un gobernante maya*, edited by Vera Tiesler and Andrea Cucina, pp. 37–67. Universidad Autónoma de Yucatán, Mérida; Universidad Nacional Autónoma de México, Mexico City.

Tiesler, Vera, Andrea Cucina, and Arturo Romano Pacheco

2004a Vida y muerte del personaje del Templo XIII-sub, Palenque, Chiapas: una mirada bioarqueológica. In *Culto funerario en la sociedad maya: memoria de la Cuarta Mesa Redonda de Palenque*, edited by Rafael Cobos, pp. 455–82. Instituto Nacional de Antropología e Historia, Mexico City.

2004b Who Was the Red Queen? Identity of the Female Dignitary from the Sarcophagus Tomb of Temple XIII, Palenque, Mexico. *Homo: Journal of Comparative Human Biology* 55(1–2):65–76.

Velásquez García, Erik

2015 Las entidades y las fuerzas anímicas en la cosmovisión maya. In *Los mayas: voces de piedra*, edited by Alejandra Martínez de Velazco Cortina and María Elena Vega Villalobos, pp. 177–96. 2nd ed. Editorial Ámbar, Universidad Nacional Autónoma de México, Mexico City.

Villanueva Sagredo, María

2004 Reconstrucción facial escultórica de cráneos prehispánicos. *Arqueología Mexicana* 11(65):48–53.

Villanueva Sagredo, María, Carlos Serrano Sánchez, Jesús Luy, and Karl F. Link

2003 La antropología física y la identificación personal por rasgos faciales. In *Antropología física: disciplina plural*, edited by Josefina Mansilla Lory and Xabier Lizarraga Cruchaga, pp. 331–51. Instituto Nacional de Antropología e Historia, Mexico City.

West, Shearer

2004 *Portraiture*. Oxford University Press, New York.

8

The Representation of Hair in the Art of Chichén Itzá

VIRGINIA E. MILLER

INTRODUCTION

Of all Mesoamerican cultures, the ancient Maya have left the most complete record of the representation of the human form, often rendered quite naturalistically. During the Classic period (ca. 250–900 CE), at sites like Palenque, Tikal, and Yaxchilán, named individuals, usually noble, are portrayed on stone stelae and other monuments as well as in murals and on painted ceramics. These portraits are for the most part stylized—the subjects are rarely shown in old age, with any distinctive physical traits, or displaying emotion—because the Maya aesthetic called for a particular kind of beauty that may have been based on their conception of the slender, youthful, androgynous maize deity. During the Terminal Classic period (ca. 800–1000), however, particularly in the northern Maya lowlands, which continued to flourish after the collapse of the Classic cities to the south, there is a shift away from individual portraits and the sensitive rendering of the human body so characteristic of the Classic era. The human figure is now shown in a repetitive and standardized way, often in stiff and awkward poses and sometimes roughly executed. At Chichén Itzá, the great city that dominated the Yucatán peninsula during this time period, stelae with hieroglyphic texts identifying individuals disappear, to be replaced with processions and group scenes carved and painted on walls, piers, and stone benches.

The art of Chichén Itzá, crowded with multiple human figures, provides a particularly rich environment for the study of costume, adornment, and body decoration, including the treatment of hair. While in Maya monumental art such figures are rarely seen without elaborate headdresses, there are some exceptions, which allow a glimpse at the way the ancient Maya dressed their hair.[1] Furthermore, attendant figures, captives, sacrificial victims, and the dead—all of whom appear in the murals, reliefs, three-dimensional sculptures, and other media at Chichén Itzá—may appear with more modest head coverings or bare headed. Given the relative lack of women in Chichén's artistic record, the examples discussed will be of male coiffures. A wide variety of male hairstyles are seen here. These include ear- or chin-length hair (fig. 8.1)

Figure 8.1. Chichén Itzá, back of head, *chacmool* from the South Building, Great Ballcourt (photo by Virginia E. Miller).

129

Figure 8.2. Chichén Itzá, detail of a figure on a jamb from the Temple of the Tables (photo by Virginia E. Miller).

as well as shoulder-length hair divided into two or three sections (fig. 8.2). Bangs may be present in either style. (The earplug is shown frontally and not hidden by the hair, as it would naturally be seen, for maximum visibility.) While long hair is usually pulled back or sometimes wrapped around the head, very long hair reaching below the buttocks is also occasionally represented. The hairline is often shaved, and crests or tufts may be cut at the crown of the head (fig. 8.3).

HAIR IN MESOAMERICA

Building on the pioneering work of Nancy Scheper-Hughes and Margaret M. Lock (1987), Stephen Houston et al. (2006:4–6) note that the body has four principal properties: it is an organism, it is experienced by the individual, it is social, and, finally, it is subject to control. Human remains, of course, are routinely discovered archaeologically and subsequently preserved and analyzed by bioarchaeologists through a myriad of techniques. But our current understanding of pre-Hispanic Mesoamerican phenomenological experience is naturally quite limited. Fortunately, for the Maya there are countless images extant of the social being, particularly of the elite. The regulation of the human body is revealed not only by the costumes and accoutrements (or lack thereof) of individuals represented, but also through interactions between participants in multifigural scenes. Inferiority may be demonstrated by scale, position within the image, pose and gesture, and clear physical control over subordinate figures. These lesser figures may sit, kneel, or crouch at the feet of their superiors, at times even serving to physically support an important personage. Significantly for this study, the most common trope for taking a prisoner throughout Mesoamerica was to show the victor grasping his opponent's long hair.

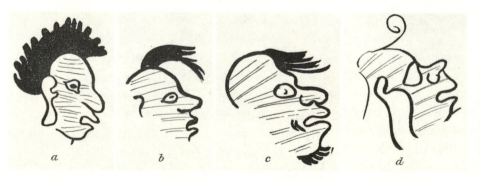

Figures 8.3a, b, c, d. Chichén Itzá, drawings of captives' heads from the murals in the Temple of the Warriors (A. Morris 1931:fig. 300a–d), with permission of the Carnegie Institution of Washington.

Terence S. Turner (1993:18), among others, has commented on the dual nature of human hair, dead outside the body but living and growing within. It therefore has the quality of a frontier between unsocialized biological forces within the body and external social relationships beyond it. Unlike other parts of the body, it is malleable—it can be detached without physical discomfort, preserved after removal, added to (through extensions of real or false hair), colored (temporarily or permanently), braided, curled, matted, stiffened, and straightened. It is a "manipulable representation of the entire person" and, as such, a highly charged personal and social symbol (Firth 1973:296). While the symbolism of hair has for decades been hotly debated by psychologists, anthropologists, sociologists, and historians of religion, no universally accepted meaning for any hair practice has been determined.[2]

In Mesoamerica, human hair was perceived as a receptacle for power, its treatment a marker of gender and social roles. For the Nahua, hair was protective covering, preventing the departure of the *tonalli* (López Austin 1988:1:221). Cutting the hair was a severe form of punishment, and not surprisingly hair was sometimes sheared off the heads of the defeated to give power to their captors (McKeever Furst 1995:126–27; López Austin 1988:1:221; Sahagún 1951–1982:9:63). The captive's hair was placed next to a fire in a temple in order to fortify its tonalli, followed by the victim's sacrificial death when his tonalli-laden blood was drained from his body (McKeever Furst 1995:137). According to colonial accounts, the Mexica dead were cremated and their remains placed in a clay vessel or a stone or wooden box, along with locks of hair taken at birth and then at death, presumably marking the lifetime of the deceased's tonalli. Placed in the family home or within the calpulli temple, the container and its contents linked ancestors to the living, strengthening and revitalizing the family (López Austin 1988:1:322). Among the living, priests and merchants kept their hair long and unwashed in order to provide them with energy and power (López Austin 1988:1:221). Hair and nails were carefully studied by traditional healers (as they are by modern doctors) because changes could signify soul loss (McKeever Furst 1995:127). Hair was even recommended as a cure for various ailments including epilepsy (López Austin 1988:1:221).

Descriptions of the great variety of hairstyles worn by men, women, and children among not only the Nahuas but also their neighbors are provided by various colonial sources: these include long and short hairstyles (the

hair sometimes cut asymmetrically), partly shaved and completely shaved heads, colored hair and bound tresses (Sahagún 1951–1982:8:47–48, 75, 11:177, 178, 179, 185, 188; Schroeder et al. 2010:463, 464, 465). For the sixteenth-century Maya, Bishop Diego de Landa discusses in some detail male and female dress, body painting, and hair treatments. In Yucatán, for example, women wore their hair long and braided, arranging the hair of little girls in two to four "horns" until they reached a certain age, presumably adolescence (Tozzer 1941:126). Men's hairstyles, so different from those of the Spanish, are described in more detail. Maya adult males burned off the hair at the top of the head while leaving the rest of the hair long, braiding it and then wrapping it around the head, leaving a pigtail behind (Tozzer 1941:88). In a variation on this particular style, the ends of the wrapped braids emerged at the sides of the head, giving the wearer the appearance of having calf's horns, at least to Spanish observers (Santillana 1938:199). Upon hearing of the existence of bearded foreigners living in Yucatán, Hernán Cortés, based on Cozumel, persuaded a reluctant native messenger to carry a letter to these men, hidden from prying eyes in his abundant, bound hair (Schroeder et al. 2010:74; Tozzer 1941:15).

Colonial chroniclers, however, reveal little about metaphorical dimensions of hair among the Maya (Bourdin 2007:217). Later ethnographies of highland Guatemala offer some insights, including the prohibition of premature haircutting of small children, thought to affect reason and speech (Duncan and Hofling 2011:203). The Tzotzil believe that those parts of the body that grow and require trimming contain parts of the soul, and as a result Zinacantecos believe that at death the soul (*ch'ulel*) gathers up pieces of flesh, nail, and hair to keep its potential dangers away from the house in which the wake is held (Fitzsimmons 2009:39–40; Vogt 1998:28–29). The Tzotzil place hair combings in the cracks of the walls when a family occupies a new house, while in Yucatán parts of the house are compared to the body, with the thatched roof the equivalent of human hair (Máas Collí 1997:24; Vogt 1998:25). For the ancient Maya, the concept *b'aah*, a very common hieroglyph, relates to self, person, or head, in the literal sense, to a social or political "head" person, and to a physical image of a person (Houston et al. 2006:72). While not directly related to hair, b'aah occurs in phrases about the wrapping of something around the head, a reference to a kind of diadem that Maya lords wore on their forehead (Houston et al. 2006:62). The term overlaps to some extent with the central Mexican tonalli (centered on the

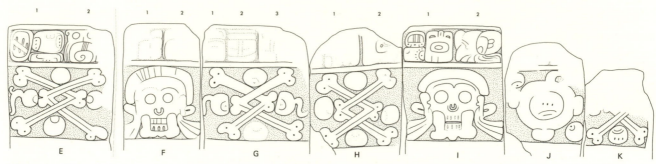

Figure 8.4. Uxmal, Monument 1, panels E–K, in the Cementerio Group (drawing by Ian Graham). Peabody Museum of Archaeology and Ethnology, PM #2004.15.6.9.22 (digital file #99310129), © 2018 President and Fellows of Harvard College.

head) and the modern Tzotzil ch'ulel (found in the heart), but it does not appear to be quite the equivalent of the Western "soul" (Fitzsimmons 2009:41–42, 131).

Classic Maya men's hair, not surprisingly given the time gap, was styled quite differently from the descriptions by the Spanish in the sixteenth century. While treatments vary, for elite males it was usually tightly bound in a ponytail or bun or cut in pageboy style and often covered by an elaborate headdress. Typically, aristocrats are shown with hair pulled back and a highly reclined profile, although in reality everyone's head was shaped in infancy, without class or gender distinction (Tiesler 2014:154, 210, 229). This distinctive profile was most likely enhanced by head shaving, but the hairline may also have been pushed back with advancing age as a physiological consequence of the flattening of infants' heads (Vera Tiesler, personal communication, 2015). Distinctive head shapes and hairstyles have long been cited as signaling ethnic difference as well as indicating long-distance interactions, as perhaps demonstrated by the coiffures shared by the elite of Seibal and Chichén Itzá (Schele and Mathews 1998:figs. 5.8, 5.10, 5.14, 5.17, 6.10, 6.30, 6.40; Tiesler 2014:202, 224ff.; Tozzer 1930:161, 1957:155).

HAIR AT CHICHÉN ITZÁ

But I will begin with the dead at Chichén Itzá. Among the various conventions for representing skeletal figures in Classic Maya art is the skull with a crest of hair running front to back, the hair often adorned with "death eyes." Such skeletal figures, with some exceptions, tend to be confined to painted pottery. Later, in the northern Maya area, skeletons and especially skulls become prominent motifs in monumental art also. The exterior of the Temple of the Warriors at Chichén Itzá, for example, once displayed a

mural depicting a death deity with the "mohawk"-and-eyeball hairstyle (Morris et al. 1931:2:plate 164). In the Puuc area as well, low platforms depict sculpted crania with the crest of hair running from the forehead back or, in the case of frontal skulls, from ear to ear (fig. 8.4). The skulls appearing on the Uxmal reliefs still have hair, recalling the Aztec practice of displaying sacrificial victims' heads defleshed but retaining their hair. These skulls also wear the cloth earpieces typical of those who have let blood (Baudez and Mathews 1979). The eroded text refers to a "star war" event (Grube 2003:fig. 26), making explicit the connection between warfare and beheading in a way not evident at Chichén Itzá, where decapitation, skulls, and ball playing are closely intertwined. While there are many representations of skulls there, none have associated texts to elucidate context. The best-known examples, the profile reliefs from the *tzompantli*, are without their hair, while those with the "mohawk," from the Great Ballcourt, seem

Figure 8.5. Chichén Itzá, detail of a skull from the southwest panel, Great Ballcourt (rubbing © Merle Greene Robertson, 1995).

Figure 8.6. Chichén Itzá, detail of a relief from the Mercado Ballcourt (rubbing by Merle Greene Robertson; Robertson 1994:fig. 14).

to still be "alive," even speaking (fig. 8.5). Like the severed heads carried by participants in Maya ritual dances and processions, such skulls may have embodied the essence of the *way*, or companion spirit (Houston et al. 2006:72).

Captives' Hair

In contrast to the carefully controlled coiffures of nobles, for the Maya loose and tangled hair signaled loss of self-control, whether through emotional release, intoxication, or death (Houston 2001). Captives are frequently shown in twisted, uncomfortable postures, with distressed facial expressions and disheveled or cropped hair, indicating their suffering and lack of agency (Burdick 2016:35; Houston 2001:210–11; Houston et al. 2006:25, 49, 204, 206; Miller and Brittenham 2013:109–12). Compared to Late Classic monumental art, images of individual captive-taking are relatively rare at Chichén—the focus is on active battle scenes and postwar sacrificial acts. There is also a shift from Late Classic representations and statements of individual victories over named enemies to anonymous and repetitive narratives, a reflection of ideological change during the Terminal Classic. Like most Maya captives, Chichén's are distinguished by the following features: they are nude or nearly so, are bound, have distinctive body or hair color or markings, and take submissive positions or are under the physical control of their captors (fig. 8.6). As noted above, a captor grasps the hair of his victim, presumably in order to subdue and control his vital life force (Mendoza 2007:414). After a captive was taken, hair may have been forcibly removed, either before or after death—some male adult skulls deposited in the Sacred Cenote at Chichén Itzá, for

example, show signs of posthumous defleshing (Tiesler and Cucina 2012:170).

The least ambiguous example of captive imagery at Chichén Itzá is from the mural of a waterside village under attack, from the Temple of the Warriors (plate 16). The location cannot be clearly identified, although it may be on the east coast of Yucatán, where there are flat-roofed temples, some set near lagoons (Lombardo de Ruiz 2001:132; Miller 1982:69–70). Below the town in the image, and possibly taking place after the battle, armed warriors lead captives along a road. Landa tells us that captives were taken from town to town before sacrifice, that dances were an integral part of the event, and that those undergoing heart sacrifice were led to their deaths "with a great show and company of people" (Tozzer 1941:117–18). The vanquished are shown naked and bound, with horizontal red-and-white stripes on their bodies. Hair appears to have been shaved, or ripped off, leaving only a shock of long hair at the top (cf. fig. 8.3). In contrast, the captors have darker bodies, almost black. An adjacent mural also shows two contrasting body colors, with dark-skinned warriors ferried by lighter-skinned paddlers, the former possibly traders or hostile visitors, perhaps from Chichén Itzá (Morris et al. 1931:2:plate 159).

A mural fragment from the area next to these scenes shows the torso of a striped figure with chest cut open, indicating the final fate of the walking men depicted in the adjacent mural (Morris et al. 1931:2:fig. 144c). In addition to the distorted facial features typical of many Maya captives, some of the striped figures also appear to have undergone oblique head shaping, in contrast to the victors, whose heads display erect modeling (Vera Tiesler, personal communication, 2013). One has facial hair, occasionally seen on captives in Late Classic art, and the rest appear to have partly shaved heads. Two have shocks of short hair bristling along the tops of their skulls. According to colonial dictionaries, the term *k'os* referred to a certain type of domestic servant with a shaved head, and *k'ostal* to the act of becoming a servant (Bourdin 2007:186). Wealthy Mexica merchants would purchase slaves to be sacrificed as part of the lavish rituals surrounding the feast of Panquetzaliztli, treating them as if they were captives taken in battle. The victims' hair would be pulled out and cast into an eagle vessel before they were killed. The hair was kept in a sacred reed box with the clothing of the slave until the merchant's death, at which point the contents were burned, the same act that occurred at the end of a warrior's life (Clendinnen1991:138–40). While sometimes described as merchants or travelers, the striped figures with tumplines in this scene could also be interpreted as carrying loads for the victors (Morris et al. 1931:2:plate 140b; Tokovinine and Beliaev 2013:184). The men shown in plate 16 are probably being led to their deaths rather than into servitude, but in either case, removing the hair, like leaving it untended, signals loss of control.

Beaded and Blond Hair

At the other extreme, long hair, often studded with beads, is also associated with prisoners and sacrificial victims. Beaded hair appears in earlier contexts, particularly on ruler portraits from Bonampak and related sites (Miller and Brittenham 2013:fig. 283; Krempel et al. 2014:fig. 5). But other rare Late Classic examples, including on an incised bone from Tikal and an unprovenienced polychrome vessel, are clearly prisoners (Trik 1963:14; K638). Beaded hair occurs in a variety of settings at Chichén Itzá and may be worn by mortals and supernaturals, and by the living and the dead. Several examples are associated with the Great Ballcourt complex. Luxuriant beaded hair is worn by the androgynous supine earth (and possibly maize) deities represented at the base of the west column in the doorway of the North Temple as well as in murals of the Upper Temple of the Jaguars (Coggins 1984:figs. 17, 19; Schele and Mathews 1998:fig. 6.49). At least one of the processional figures appearing in the reliefs of the Lower Temple of the Jaguars has long, beaded hair as well (fig. 8.7); he may also be depicted in one of the murals of the Upper Temple of the Jaguars (plate 17). Some of the participants in the complex carved reliefs of the North Temple may also have beaded hair, although wrapped

Figure 8.7. Chichén Itzá, drawing of a figure with beaded hair on the west wall, register B, Lower Temple of the Jaguars (Maudslay 1889–1902:3:plate 39).

around the head rather than hanging loose (Schele and Mathews 1998:fig. 6.51.F4, top register left).[3]

Both the reliefs on the sides of the Great Ballcourt and the related Great Ballcourt Stone show heads, including decapitated ones, sporting the distinctive beaded hair, worn either tied up in a bun at the crown of the head or long and loose down the back (fig. 8.8). The central scene may represent the final treatment of the corpse of the heart-sacrifice victim from the mural—the removal and display of the head, with its possible deposition on the tzompantli. The monument is crucial to the site's chronology, because it bears a date—variously read as 864, 968, or 1020 CE—that might help anchor the chronological placement of the Great Ballcourt itself (Braswell and Peniche May 2012:237). That structure and the Temple of the Warriors may be dated later than previously thought, to the early to mid-eleventh century (Braswell and Peniche May 2012:255).

Figure 8.8. Chichén Itzá, rollout drawing of the Great Ballcourt Stone (drawing by Peggy Diggs and Ruth Krochock, after Wren 1989:fig. 5, by permission of Ruth Krochock and Linnea Wren).

Some of the numerous Atlanteans found at the site also appear to have beaded hair (cf. Schele and Mathews 1998:figs. 6.39.B8, 13, 14). An example from the Temple of the Tables has long reddish hair dotted with green disks (fig. 8.9). While no convincing explanation has been established for the identity or meaning of these figures, because of their different headdresses and costumes, I suspect that they are emblematic of different lineages, allies, or subject groups, serving to support royal authority as they hold up flat stone thrones. Many of the beaded-hair figures are represented in murals, where color remains. What is startling is the fact that they all have yellow hair. Mural fragments in the Temple of the Warriors show a marine battle in which the blonds are the losers (plate 18). Because the painting is so fragmentary, the confrontation's location is even more elusive than the coastal raid scene, although a coastline or a wall appears at the bottom of the image. An adjacent section of the mural shows the sacrifice of one of the blond participants with beaded hair, in a scene similar to the one in the Upper Temple of the Jaguars and on a gold disk from the Cenote (Morris et al. 1931:2:plate 145).

What does the light-colored hair mean? According to Maya informants today, the term *ch'el* refers to someone with light skin, and possibly (but not necessarily) light-colored hair (Laura de los Santos, personal communication, 2013). The term is used for any fair person, whether Maya or not. It is also applied to coastal peoples whose hair is bleached by exposure to sun and sea (Delio Madera Tsab, personal communication, 2007). Mesoamerican peoples are also known to have dyed their hair: among the Huaxtecs, for example, yellow and red were

favored colors (Sahagún 1951–1982:11:185). The hair color represented here may have been used to exaggerate the difference between victors and vanquished, the latter presumably from a coastal region. Notably, although the head shapes shown here are difficult to classify, toward the end of the Late Classic, merchant coastal populations began to practice superior head flattening and to move

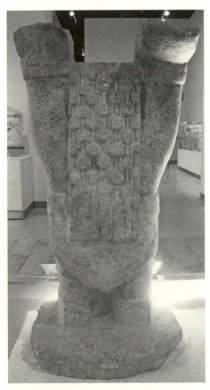

Figure 8.9. Chichén Itzá, back view of an Atlantean from the Temple of the Tables (photo by Virginia E. Miller).

across the peninsula bringing with them new goods and new ideas (Tiesler 2014:240, 259). Almost one-third of the skulls from the Sacred Cenote display this type of head modification, suggesting that sacrificial victims may have come from conquered coastal towns (Tiesler 2014:234). At the time of the Spanish conquest, coastal peoples considered themselves to be more refined than their inland neighbors, presumably reflecting their broader Mesoamerican contacts as traders (Scholes and Roys 1968:60). Circumpeninsular trade is documented beginning in the Late Preclassic and intensifying during the Late Classic, with salt being exchanged for ceramics and lithic materials from distant highland sources (Andrews and Mock 2002; Sierra Sosa et al. 2014:226). This traffic began to increase during the Terminal Classic, when Chichén Itzá rose to power and established coastal ports (Glover et al. 2011:198). These scenes of seaside settlements, in conflict or not, may also have served to remind their viewers of the extent of Chichén's realm, to exotic lands far from the inland city (Hutson 2005:231).

There may be an alternative explanation for the hair color, not incompatible with the idea of foreignness. It has often been noted that the head was reshaped to imitate a corncob, and hair was fashioned to suggest corn silk—in some Mesoamerican languages, the same term is used for both (Brittenham 2015:164; Houston 2014:11; Taube 1992:46). While this particular profile was the preferred look for Classic Maya rulers, it is also associated with human sacrifice, the decapitated head representing the harvesting of maize and the death and renewal of the plant (Taube 1992:44; Mendoza 2007:421–22; Houston et al. 2006:45). This metaphor is made explicit at Cacaxtla, where the "melding of man and maize" is suggested by red-headed figures whose hair also mimics corn silk (Brittenham 2015:133, 138, 139, 170, 201, figs. 288, 291, 236n8, 242n26). In the site's famous battle mural, some of the defeated are depicted with red hair (Brittenham 2015:fig. 194). While no sources mention coloring captives' hair, it is well known that painting the body (often with stripes) and even tattooing were employed in Mesoamerica to identify the victims of battles and those destined to be sacrificed (Vázquez de Ágredos Pascual, Vidal Lorenzo, and Horcajada Campos, chapter 6 of this volume; Miller 2018).

There are blond figures who do not fit the victim profile described above, and if there were more remaining pigments on relief sculpture, others would undoubtedly be identified. Some are part of a complex mural cycle of battle scenes in the Upper Temple of the Jaguars that has been subject to many interpretations (plate 17). Given that the beaded-hair figure is paired with another surrounded by a feathered serpent, he could be the individual nicknamed "Captain Sun Disk," except for the lack of a sun disk behind him. Alternatively, he and perhaps his partner, who is surrounded by rays, might embody the sun (Coggins 1984:159–60; Ringle 2009:35). There is a long tradition of equating Mesoamerican rulers with the sun's vital force, and by extension with agricultural fertility and wealth (McAnany 2013:235; Houston and Cummins 2004:368). Fire, described metaphorically as "yellow-haired," was also invoked in Nahua healing rituals (Ruiz de Alarcón 1984:176, 188, 194, 241). The connection between the divine and yellow hair may have a deep history in Mesoamerica: at Teotihuacan, the principle deity—sometimes called the Great Goddess, although the figure's gender remains ambiguous—is represented with yellow hair in mural paintings in the apartment complexes of Tetitla and Tepantitla (Pasztory 1997:125, 126). In the latter mural program, the deity's acolytes may also have blond hair.

To return to Chichén Itzá and the figure with blond and beaded hair represented in the Upper Temple of the Jaguars, it remains unclear if he is a sun deity, a ruler, or both (plate 17). Perhaps he is a leader of a coastal region, one allied with or under the rule of Chichén Itzá rather than in opposition to the city. If, however, there is any connection between this mural cycle and the one from the Temple of the Warriors showing the defeat of blond/beaded-hair warriors, the paintings might illustrate different moments in the history of relationships between the coastal traders and the expanding Itzá state. The jade beads shown in the Chichén hairstyles could refer to either the preciousness of maize or to an exotic commodity that might have been brought up the coast of Yucatán from its distant source along the Motagua River, and perhaps worn by the new merchant class.

CONCLUSION

As this overview has demonstrated, hair in Mesoamerica was multivalent, marking age and gender, signaling status and occupation, and possessing magical qualities, both while attached and detached from the head. The enormous corpus of Maya art, in which the human form is the central motif, provides a rich source for the study of hair and its treatment over several centuries. At Chichén Itzá, the elite display hairstyles typical of both the Late and the Terminal Classic, just as the site's artists simultaneously engaged two different iconographic and stylistic systems, demonstrating its far-reaching political and economic relationships. Decapitated heads and skulls, while long-standing minor motifs in Maya iconography, become important and repeated elements in monumental art, sometimes imbued with life through the presence of hair and speech scrolls. Captives are shown with hair grasped by their captors, or with hair shaved or ripped off and a disordered lock left at the top, symbols of helplessness and submission carried over from Late Classic traditions. New to the repertoire of Maya hairstyles is the long, beaded, and often light-colored hair undoubtedly used to express otherness and even divinity. More specifically, this hairstyle may identify prosperous coastal areas coming under the control of Chichén Itzá. With the decline of the Maya city and the rise of different types of polities in the Postclassic, the focus shifts from the representation of historical human figures and events to supernaturals and mythical narratives, with the result that costume and accoutrements become more standardized and less reflective of regional fashions and social status. Chichén Itzá, then, remains a pivotal place and time for the study of body ornamentation and modification, and particularly of the treatment of hair.

NOTES

1. In scenes in which rulers are presented with headdresses, such as the west wall of the San Bartolo murals or the Oval Palace Tablet at Palenque, the recipient often already wears a diadem or other ornamentation, but the dressed hair is at least visible. Maya polychrome vases occasionally depict more intimate moments in which an attendant holds a large headdress in anticipation of placing it on the relatively bare head of the noble, sometimes wrapped in paper or cloth. See K1454 and K5738 for examples.

2. Patrick Olivelle's 1998 essay provides a good introduction to both hair treatments and different approaches to the study of hair.

3. It is possible that, rather than beaded hair, the "spangled turban" typically worn by scribes on Maya polychrome ceramics is represented here (Coe and Kerr 1997:105, plates 32, 34, figs. 72, 73).

REFERENCES CITED

Andrews, Anthony P., and Shirley B. Mock
2002   New Perspectives on the Prehispanic Salt Trade. In *Ancient Maya Political Economies*, edited by Marilyn A. Masson and David P. Freidel, pp. 307–34. AltaMira Press, Walnut Creek, California.

Baudez, Claude, and Peter Mathews
1979   Capture and Sacrifice at Palenque. In *Tercera Mesa Redonda de Palenque*, vol. 4, edited by Merle Greene Robertson and Donnan Call Jeffers, pp. 31–40. Pre-Columbian Art Research Center, Monterey, California.

Bourdin, Gabriel L.
2007   *El cuerpo humano entre los mayas: una aproximación lingüística.* Universidad Autónoma de Yucatán, Mérida.

Braswell, Geoffrey, and Nancy Peniche May
2012   In the Shadow of the Pyramid: Excavations of the Great Platform of Chichen Itza. In *The Ancient Maya of Mexico: Reinterpreting the Past of the Northern Maya Lowlands*, edited by Geoffrey Braswell, pp. 229–63. Equinox, Sheffield, England.

Brittenham, Claudia L.
2015   *The Murals of Cacaxtla: The Power of Painting in Ancient Central Mexico.* University of Texas Press, Austin.

Burdick, Catherine
2016   Held Captive by Script: Interpreting "Tagged" Prisoners in Late Classic Maya Sculpture. *Ancient Mesoamerica* 27(1):31–48.

Clendinnen, Inga
1991   *Aztecs: An Interpretation.* Cambridge University Press, Cambridge.

Coe, Michael D., and Justin Kerr
1997   *The Art of the Maya Scribe.* Abrams, New York.

Coggins, Clemency C.
1984   Murals in the Upper Temple of the Jaguars, Chichén Itzá. In *Cenote of Sacrifice: Maya Treasures from the Sacred Well at Chichén Itzá*, edited by Clemency C. Coggins and Orrin C. Shane III, pp. 156–65. University of Texas Press, Austin.

Duncan, William N., and Charles Andrew Hofling
2011   Why the Head? Cranial Modification as Protection and Ensoulment among the Maya. *Ancient Mesoamerica* 22:199–210.

Firth, Raymond
1973   *Symbols Public and Private.* George Allen and Unwin, London.

Fitzsimmons, James L.

2009　*Death and the Classic Maya Kings.* University of Texas Press, Austin.

Glover, Jeffrey B., Dominique Rissolo, and Jennifer P. Mathews

2011　The Hidden World of the Maritime Maya: Lost Landscapes along the North Coast of Quintana Roo, Mexico. In *The Archaeology of Maritime Landscapes,* edited by Ben Ford, pp. 195–216. Springer, New York.

Grube, Nikolai

2003　Hieroglyphic Inscriptions from Northwest Yucatan: An Update of Recent Research. In *Escondida en la selva,* edited by Hanns J. Prem, pp. 339–70. Segundo Simposio Teoberto Maler, Bonn 2000. University of Bonn, Bonn; Instituto Nacional de Antropología e Historia, Mexico City.

Houston, Stephen.

2001　Decorous Bodies and Disordered Passions: Representations of Emotion among the Classic Maya. *World Archaeology* 33(2):206–19.

2014　*The Life Within: Classic Maya and the Matter of Permanence.* Yale University Press, New Haven, Connecticut.

Houston, Stephen, and Tom Cummins

2004　Body, Presence, and Space in Andean and Mesoamerican Rulership. In *Palaces of the Ancient New World,* edited by Susan Toby Evans and Joanne Pillsbury, pp. 359–98. Dumbarton Oaks, Washington, DC.

Houston, Stephen, David Stuart, and Karl A. Taube

2006　*The Memory of Bones: Body, Being, and Experience among the Classic Maya.* University of Texas Press, Austin.

Hutson, Scott

2005　Ways of Seeing: Chichen Itza Landscape Portraiture and Maya Archaeologists. In *Art for Archaeology's Sake: Material Culture and Style across the Disciplines.* Proceedings of the Thirty-Third Annual Chacmool Conference, edited by Andrea Waters-Rist, Christine Cluney, Calla McNamee, and Larry Steinbrenner, pp. 228–38. Chacmool Archaeological Association, University of Calgary, Calgary.

Kerr, Justin

Maya Vase Database, electronic document, www.mayavase.com.

Krempel, Guido, Sebastian Matteo, and Erik Boot

2014　An Unpublished Panel Fragment in the Collection of the Fundación La Ruta Maya, Guatemala City. *Mexicon* 36:2–6.

Lombardo de Ruiz, Sonia

2001　Los estilos en la pintura mural Maya. In *La pintura mural prehispánico en México II, Área Maya.* Vol. 3, *Estudios,* edited by Beatriz de la Fuente and Leticia Staines Cicero, pp. 85–154. Universidad Nacional Autónoma de México; Instituto de Investigaciones Estéticas, Mexico City.

López Austin, Alfredo

1988　*The Human Body and Ideology: Concepts of the Ancient Nahuas.* 2 vols. University of Utah Press, Salt Lake City.

Máas Collí, Hilaria

1997　*Curso de lengua maya para investigadores, nivel 2.* Universidad Autónoma de Yucatán, Mérida.

Maudslay, Alfred P.

1889–1902　*Biologia Centrali-Americana: Archaeology.* 6 vols. R. H. Porter and Dulau, London.

McAnany, Patricia A.

2013　Artisans, *Ikatz,* and Statecraft: Provisioning Classic Maya Courts. In *Merchants, Markets, and Exchange in the Pre-Columbian World,* edited by Kenneth G. Hirth and Joanne Pillsbury, pp. 229–54. Dumbarton Oaks, Washington, DC.

McKeever Furst, Jill Leslie

1995　*The Natural History of the Soul in Ancient Mexico.* Yale University Press, New Haven, Connecticut.

Mendoza, Rubén

2007　The Divine Gourd Tree: Tzompantli Skull Racks, Decapitation Rituals, and Human Trophies in Ancient Mesoamerica. In *The Taking and Displaying of Human Body Parts as Trophies by Amerindians,* edited by Richard J. Chacon and David H. Dye, pp. 400–443. Springer, New York.

Miller, Arthur

1982　*On the Edge of the Sea: Mural Painting at Tancah-Tulum, Quintana Roo, Mexico.* Dumbarton Oaks, Washington, DC.

Miller, Mary E., and Claudia Brittenham

2013　*The Spectacle of the Late Maya Court: Reflections on the Murals of Bonampak.* University of Texas Press, Austin.

Miller, Virginia E.

2018　Body Color and Body Adornment at Chichén Itzá. In *Colors on the Skin: Studies on the Pigments Applied on Bodies and Codices in Pre-Columbian Mesoamerica,* edited by Elodie Dupey and María Luisa Vázquez de Ágredos Pascual. University of Arizona Press, Tucson.

Morris, Ann A.

1931　Murals from the Temple of the Warriors and Adjacent Structures. In *The Temple of the Warriors at Chichén*

Itzá, Yucatan, vol. 1, edited by Earl H. Morris, Jean Charlot, and Ann A. Morris, pp. 347–484. Carnegie Institution of Washington, Washington, DC.

Morris, Earl H., Jean Charlot, and Ann A. Morris

1931 *The Temple of the Warriors at Chichén Itzá, Yucatan.* 2 vols. Carnegie Institution of Washington, Washington, DC.

Olivelle, Patrick

1998 Hair and Society: Social Significance of Hair in South Asian Traditions. In *Hair: Its Power and Meaning in Asian Cultures*, edited by Alf Hiltebeitel and Barbara D. Miller, pp. 11–49. State University of New York Press, Albany.

Pasztory, Esther

1997 *Teotihuacan: An Experiment in Living.* University of Oklahoma Press, Norman.

Ringle, William M.

2009 The Art of War: Imagery of the Upper Temple of the Jaguars, Chichen Itza. *Ancient Mesoamerica* 20:15–44.

Robertson, Merle Greene

1994 The Iconography of "Isolated Art Styles" That Are "Group Supported" and "Individual Supported" Occurring at Chichen Itza and Uxmal. In *Acta Mesoamericana.* Vol. 7, *Hidden among the Hills: Maya Archaeology of the Northwest Yucatan Peninsula; First Maler Symposium, Bonn 1989*, edited by Hanns J. Prem, pp. 197–211. Verlag von Flemming, Möckmühl, Germany.

Ruiz de Alarcón, Hernando

1984 *Treatise on the Heathen Superstitions and Customs That Today Live among the Indians Native to This New Spain.* Translated and edited by J. Richard Andrews and Ross Hassig. University of Oklahoma Press, Norman.

Sahagún, Bernardino de

1951–1982 *Florentine Codex: General History of the Things of New Spain.* Translated and edited by Arthur J. O. Anderson and Charles E. Dibble. 13 vols. School of American Research Press, Santa Fe.

Santillana, Pedro de

1938 Relación de Quinacama o Moxopipe. In *Relación de las cosas de Yucatán, Fray Diego de Landa*, edited by Alfredo Barrera Vásquez, pp. 195–203. E. G. Triay e Hijos, Mérida.

Schele, Linda, and Peter Mathews

1998 *The Code of Kings: The Language of Seven Sacred Maya Temples and Tombs.* Scribner, New York.

Scheper-Hughes, Nancy, and Margaret M. Lock

1987 The Mindful Body: A Prolegomenon to Future Work in Medical Anthropology. *Medical Anthropology Quarterly* 1(1):1–36.

Scholes, France V., and Ralph L. Roys

1968 *The Maya Chontal Indians of Acalan-Tixchel: A Contribution to the History and Ethnography of the Yucatan Peninsula.* University of Oklahoma Press, Norman.

Schroeder, Susan, Anne J. Cruz, Cristián Roa-de-la-Carrera, and David E. Tavárez (editors and translators)

2010 *Chimalpahin's Conquest: A Nahua Historian's Rewriting of Francisco López de Gómara's "La Conquista de México."* Stanford University Press, Stanford, California.

Sierra Sosa, Thelma, Andrea Cucina, T. Douglas Price, James H. Burton, and Vera Tiesler

2014 Maya Coastal Production, Exchange, Life Style, and Population Mobility: A View from the Port of Xcambo, Yucatan, Mexico. *Ancient Mesoamerica* 25:221–38.

Taube, Karl A.

1992 *The Major Gods of Ancient Yucatán.* Studies in Pre-Columbian Art and Archaeology, no. 32. Dumbarton Oaks, Washington, DC.

Tiesler, Vera

2014 *The Bioarchaeology of Artificial Cranial Modifications: New Approaches to Head Shaping and Its Meanings in Pre-Columbian America and Beyond.* Springer, New York.

Tiesler, Vera, and Andrea Cucina

2012 Where Are the Warriors? Cranial Trauma Patterns and Conflict among the Ancient Maya. In *The Bioarchaeology of Violence*, edited by Debra L. Martin, Ryan P. Harrod, and Ventura R. Pérez, pp. 160–79. University Press of Florida, Gainesville.

Tokovinine, Alexandre, and Dmitri Beliaev

2013 People of the Road: Traders and Travelers in Ancient Maya Words and Images. In *Merchants, Markets, and Exchange in the Pre-Columbian World*, edited by Kenneth G. Hirth and Joanne Pillsbury, pp. 169–200. Dumbarton Oaks, Washington, DC.

Tozzer, Alfred M.

1930 Maya and Toltec Figures at Chichen Itza. In *Proceedings of the Twenty-Third International Congress of Americanists*, pp. 155–64. New York.

1941 (translator) *Landa's "Relación de las cosas de Yucatan."* Peabody Museum, Harvard University, Cambridge, Massachusetts.

1957 *Chichen Itza and Its Cenote of Sacrifice: A Comparative Study of Contemporaneous Maya and Toltec.* Peabody

Museum, Harvard University, Cambridge, Massachusetts.

Trik, Aubrey S.

1963 The Splendid Tomb of Temple I, Tikal, Guatemala. *Expedition.* Fall:2–19.

Turner, Terence S.

1993 The Social Skin. In *Reading the Social Body*, edited by Catherine B. Burroughs and Jeffrey David Ehrenreich, pp. 15–39. University of Iowa Press, Iowa City.

Vogt, Evon Z.

1998 Zinacanteco Dedication and Termination Rituals. In *The Sowing and the Dawning: Termination, Dedication, and Transformation in the Archaeological and Ethno-graphic Record of Mesoamerica*, edited by Shirley B. Mock, pp. 21–30. University of New Mexico Press, Albuquerque.

Wren, Linnea H.

1989 Composition and Content in Maya Sculpture: A Study of Ballgame Scenes at Chichén Itzá, Yucatán, México. In *Ethnographic Encounters in Southern Mesoamerica: Essays in Honor of Evon Zartman Vogt Jr.*, edited by Victoria R. Bricker and Gary H. Gossen, pp. 287–301. Studies on Culture and Society, vol. 3. Institute for Mesoamerican Studies, State University of New York at Albany.

9

Effigies of Death

Representation, Use, and Reuse of Human Skulls at the Templo Mayor of Tenochtitlan

XIMENA CHÁVEZ BALDERAS

INTRODUCTION

The Mexica (popularly known as the Aztecs) founded Tenochtitlan in 1325 CE on a small island in Lake Texcoco. An expansionist period started around 1428 with a rebellion against the Azcapotzalco ruler. The Mexica Empire conquered distant regions using warfare as a means to establish tributary obligations as opposed to acquiring territory. The Sacred Precinct of Tenochtitlan was composed of seventy-eight ritual buildings (Sahagún 1997). Among these, the Templo Mayor was the most sacred space. For this reason, important rituals were celebrated in this building, including those connected with human and animal sacrifice.

From 1948 to 2012, the bones of 153 individuals were recovered from excavations of the Templo Mayor of Tenochtitlan. These human remains were deposited on multiple occasions and for different purposes. Some individuals were buried during funerary rituals and others in nonfunerary rituals (Nagao 1985; Tiesler 2007). Funerals were conducted to socialize the death of a person, to dispose of the body, and to help the soul reach its final destination (Thomas 1983). These individuals were not sacrifices, and their deaths required socialization and mourning by the social group.

For the Mexica, the final destination of the soul was determined by the cause of death. The underworld, or Mictlan, corresponded to those who died as a result of

disease and age. Tlalocan, the region equated with paradise by Friar Bernardino de Sahagún (1997), was the final destination for individuals who died under circumstances related to water (like drowning), lightning strike, or specific diseases. In contrast, the House of the Sun (Ilhuícatl Tonatiuh) belonged to defeated warriors, sacrificial victims, and women who died giving birth. Finally, Chichihuauhcuauhco was the region in which infants who died in childbirth or at a very young age were nursed by a tree, waiting for a new opportunity in the human world (Alvarado Tezozómoc 1944; Benavente o Motolinía 1971; López Austin 1996, López de Gómara 1941; Sahagún 1997).[1] A total of seven burials have been found in the Templo Mayor, corresponding to five individuals (Chávez Balderas 2007).[2]

Human remains were also buried inside the Templo Mayor offerings during nonfunerary rituals. In fact, human and animal sacrifices were the most precious gift for the gods. For Debra Nagao (1985:1–2), human remains in a funerary context must be considered as *persons*, while their presence in offerings should be regarded as equivalent to *objects*. We must bear in mind that the two categories may overlap (Becker 1988; Coe 1975).

The practice of sacrifice is well documented in the Templo Mayor. Thousands of flint knives, sacrificial stones, traces of blood, and human remains have been recovered in archaeological excavations (Chávez Balderas 2010, 2012a, 2014; López Luján 1993; López Luján and Mercado 1996; Román 1990). Victims were found in the temple and the main plaza inside Stages IV to VI: the expansionist period (1440–1502 CE) corresponding to the reigns of Motecuhzoma I, Axayácatl, Tízoc, and Ahuítzotl.[3] Evidence from the government of Motecuhzoma II was destroyed after the conquest.

The skulls from only 109 of the victims have been found in the building. According to Friar Diego de Durán (1995:1:97), most of the bodies were thrown into Lake Texcoco. In addition, some body parts were destined for cannibalism (Sahagún 1997:105). In any event, bodies were left behind, and the heads of the victims had different fates: some were buried immediately in the offerings while others were used in diverse rituals before their final deposit. The absence of headless bodies in the archaeological record from the Andes is discussed by John Verano (chapter 11 in this volume). According to Verano, this absence denies normative mortuary treatment of the body.

In this chapter, I shall explore the ritual use of the head at the Templo Mayor of Tenochtitlan in connection with human sacrifice. Transformation of the head will be evaluated in two dimensions: the decapitation and manufacturing processes conducted by Mexica priests, and the reuse and resemantization of the skulls, transforming them from sacrificial victims into effigies of the gods. The symbolism of the human body is key to understanding why the head was the only body part buried inside the ritual deposits representing supernatural beings. By combining osteological evidence, iconography, and written sources, it is possible to explore the use, reuse, and representation of human skulls at the Templo Mayor of Tenochtitlan.

RITUAL DECAPITATION AND POSTSACRIFICIAL TREATMENTS OF THE HEAD

Decapitation and the ritual deposit of heads was a widespread phenomenon in Mesoamerica. Early archaeological evidence has been found in Coxcatlán (5750 BCE), Kaminaljuyú (800–600 BCE), Tlatecomila (600–400 BCE), and Cuicatlán (200 BCE–200 CE) (in Puebla, Guatemala City, Mexico City, and Oaxaca, respectively). Recent discoveries link this practice with domestic and religious contexts from Teotihuacan, such as Teopancazco and the Pyramid of the Moon. Examples dating to 600–900 CE have been reported at La Quemada, Altavista, and Cerro de Moctezuma (Zacatecas), as well as at Xaltocan

(state of Mexico) and Xochicalco (Morelos). During the Postclassic period, ritual decapitation spread into the central highlands. Important findings from Cholula, Teotenango, Teopanzolco, Tlatelolco, and Tenochtitlan support this idea (Alvarado-Viñas and Manzanilla, chapter 5 of this volume; Botella et al. 2000; Chávez Balderas 2012a, 2014; Hernández Pons and Navarrete 1997; Kanjou 2001; Lagunas Rodríguez and Serrano Sánchez 1972; Morehart et al. 2012; Moser 1972; Nájera 1987, Pereira and Chávez Balderas 2006; Pijoan Aguadé 1997; Pijoan Aguadé et al. 1989, 2001; Ruz Lhuillier 1989; Sugiyama and López Luján 2006; Xochipiltécatl 2004).

The heads may have been selected and deposited for several reasons. For Alfredo López Austin (1996), this body part reflected personhood and facilitated the counting of the dead. Nahua populations believed that one of the three body souls—the *tonalli*—was housed in the head. This entity was considered a force related to heat, energy, vitality, and courage. The other two souls were the *teyolía* and the *ihíyotl*. The first, which was related to knowledge and personality, inhabited the heart and was the soul that traveled to the underworld at the time of death. The second, in contrast, was contained inside the liver and was connected to passion, desire, anger, and envy.

According to López Austin (1996), a weak tonalli insufflated into the individual during intrauterine life. The rest of the tonalli traveled to the human world on the day of the ritual bath using cosmic trees until it reached the infant's head. This soul was capable of abandoning the body, causing disease, and failure to recover the tonalli was considered a possible cause of death. This force was not exclusive to humans; in fact, the sun had the greatest tonalli. After death, the tonalli could disperse, and specific rituals were conducted to attract this fragmentary soul (López Austin 1996: 223–51). Rulers had a greater amount of tonalli than regular people (Ortiz de Montellano 1993:77).

Considering the historical sources and archaeological evidence, decapitation and subsequent treatments of the head were performed near the Templo Mayor. Due to the absence of metal tools, decapitation was a slow process. Victims were most likely sacrificed by extracting the heart or slitting the throat. Osteological evidence suggests that decapitation was done by disarticulating the cervical vertebrae, cutting the intervertebral disks in an anterior-posterior direction (Chávez Balderas 2010, 2012a, 2014).[4]

Contrary to what might be supposed, decapitation victims were not just defeated warriors; the biological profiles of the individuals are diverse. Adult females,

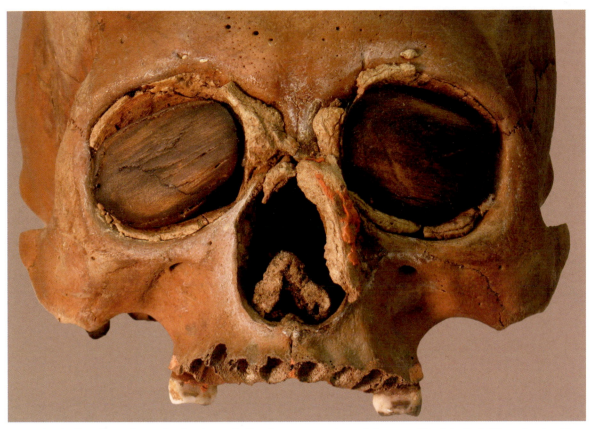

Plate 1. A male skull with perforated sides from skullrack exposure, Sacred Cenote, Chichén Itzá. Note the significant head elongation, typical for the Maya during the Classic period (photo by Vera Tiesler, N31194, Peabody Museum of Archaeology and Ethnography, Harvard Museum, © 2018 President and Fellows of Harvard College).

Plate 2. *K'altuun* (stone-binding) ritual from the Madrid Codex, p. 101c, possibly commemorating a *k'atun* completion (see chapter 2, Brasseur de Bourbourg 1869–1870:plate 12).

Plate 3. Landa's "baptism" ceremony from the Madrid Codex, 92c–93c (see chapter 2, Brasseur de Bourbourg 1869–1870:plates 20–21).

Plate 4. Examples of wooden deity effigies being animated from the Madrid Codex, 100d (see chapter 2, Brasseur de Bourbourg 1869–1870:plate 13).

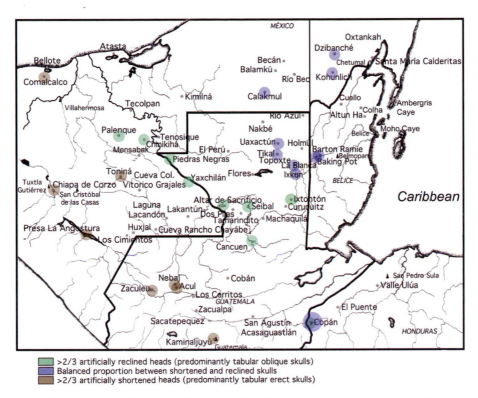

>2/3 artificially reclined heads (predominantly tabular oblique skulls)
Balanced proportion between shortened and reclined skulls
>2/3 artificially shortened heads (predominantly tabular erect skulls)

Plate 5. Distribution of selected Maya urban cranial series with sufficient sample sizes to express local preferences in artificially produced head forms during the Classic period (incorporating information from the following sources from chapter 3: Chinchilla et al. 2015; Coe 1959; Gómez 1999; Haviland and Moholy-Nagy 1992; Juan Pedro Laporte, personal communication, 2008; Laporte 2005; Nuñez 2009, 2010; Quintanilla 2013; Scherer 2015; Scherer and Wright 2001; Scherer et al. 1999; Stewart 1953; Tiesler 1999, 2012, 2014, 2015b; Tovalín et al. 1998; Wright 1997; Wright and Witte 1998; see also a regional synopsis in Tiesler 2012:129–31). Strong preferences for head elongation appear in green, whereas site collections with a more equal distribution of head shortening and elongation are shown in blue. Local populations noted for predominantly shortened head morphologies are highlighted in brown.

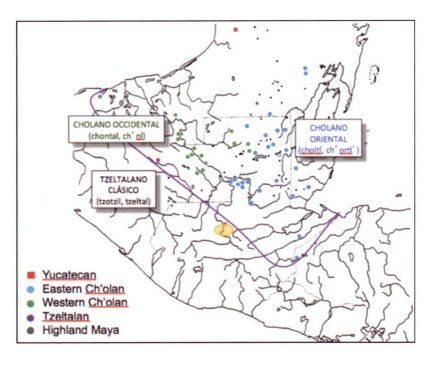

Plate 6. Classic-period distribution of Maya vernacular languages in the southern Maya lowlands (see chapter 3; updated from Lacadena and Wichman 2002).

Plate 7. Classic Maya court scene from Bonampak, displaying strong head reclination in female participants in a penance ritual (National Geographic Society).

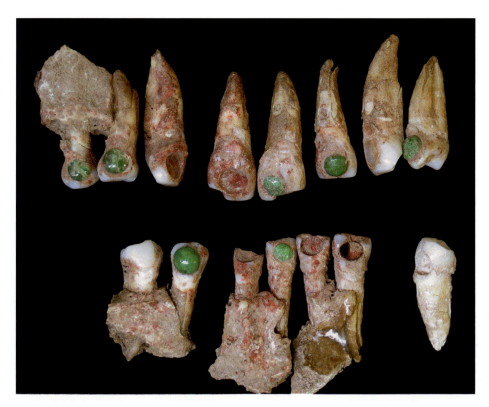

Plate 8. The anterior teeth of Ruler 3 (Burial 5) of Piedras Negras, with jade and pyrite inlays. Note that some of the inlays are missing (photo by Andrew Scherer).

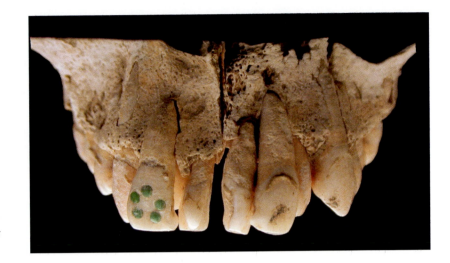

Plate 9. Jade inlays and supernumerary incisors of a young adult male from Piedras Negras Burial 45 (photo by Andrew Scherer).

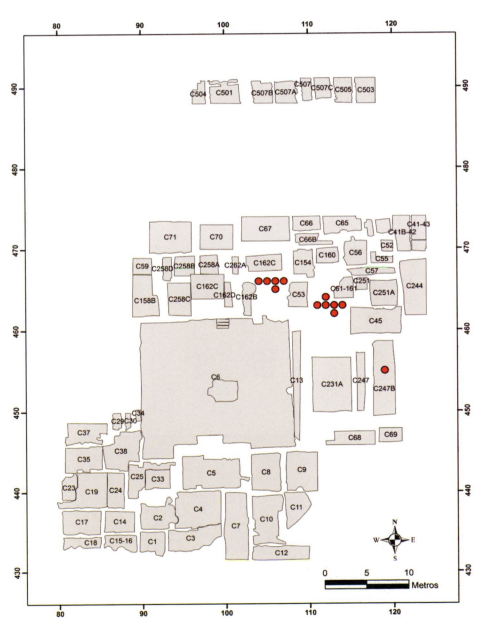

Plate 10. Distribution of decapitated individuals, with the highest concentration in rooms C162F and C161 (map by Linda R. Manzanilla and Luis Adrián Alvarado-Viñas, Proyecto Arqueológico Teopancazco).

Plate 11. On-site construction distribution during excavation (photo by Linda R. Manzanilla, Proyecto Arqueológico Teopancazco).

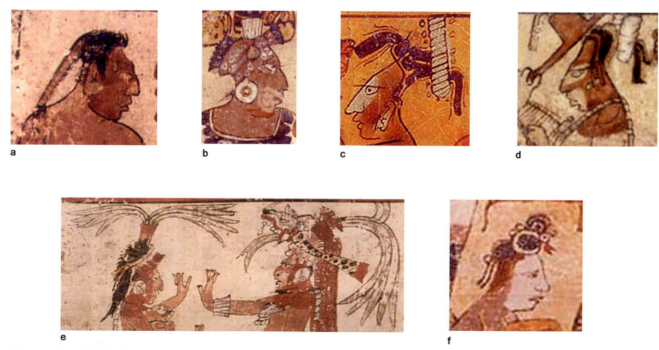

Plate 12. Details of different female faces with face paint. Images © Justin Kerr, Kerr Database: (a) K2707, (b) K767, (c) K9300, (d) K5847, (e) K554, and (f) K5451.

Plate 13. Details of different male faces with face paint. Images © Justin Kerr, Kerr Database: (a) K625, (b) K2573, (c) K1453, (d) K8008, (e) K2695, (f–g) K1209, (h–i) K1288, (j–k) K1871, (l–n) K2206, (o) K0638, (p) K6987, (q) K4680, (r) K3092, (s) K1549, (t) K3247, (u) K1563, and (v) K5233.

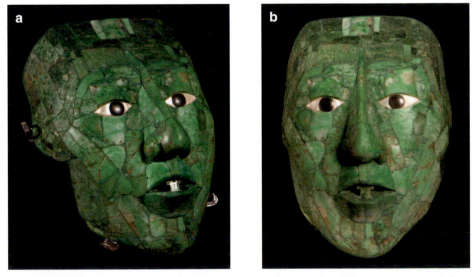

Plates 14a, b. K'inich Janaab' Pakal's funerary mask (10-1300), from the Temple of the Inscriptions, Palenque. Museo Nacional de Antropología, Mexico City (photo from the Proyecto de Digitalización de las Colecciones del Museo Nacional de Antropología, sponsored by the Consejo Nacional para la Cultura y las Artes, the Instituto Nacional de Antropología e Historia, and the Canon Corporation; courtesy of the Museo Nacional de Antropología).

Plate 15. Skeletal remains of K'inich Janaab' Pakal, in situ, Temple of the Inscriptions, Palenque (photo by Arturo Romano Pacheco, © 1952, courtesy of the Laboratorio de Conservación, Museo Nacional de Antropología, Instituto Nacional de Antropología e Historia, Mexico City).

Plate 16. Chichén Itzá, raid on a coastal village, reconstruction painting of a mural in the Temple of the Warriors (see chapter 8, Morris et al. 1931:2:plate 139), by permission of the Carnegie Institution of Washington.

Plate 17. Chichén Itzá, central panel of the east wall mural of the Upper Temple of the Jaguars (watercolor reproduction by Adela Breton), by permission of the Bristol Museum and Art Gallery, Bristol, England.

Plate 18. Chichén Itzá, detail of a marine battle, reconstruction painting of a fragmentary mural from the Temple of the Warriors (see chapter 8, Morris et al. 1931:2:plate 146), by permission of the Carnegie Institution of Washington.

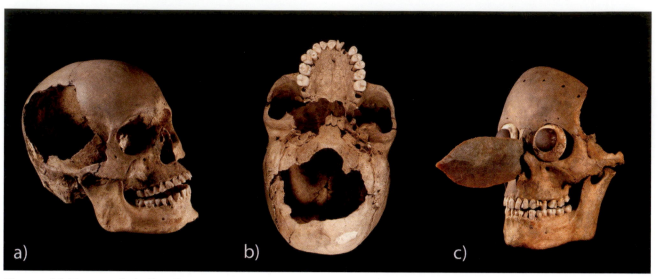

Plate 19. (a) *Tzompantli* skull, Offering 11; (b) skull with basal perforation, Offering 23; and (c) skull mask, Offering 11 (photos by Jesús López, courtesy of the Templo Mayor Museum).

Plate 20. (a) Skull with basal perforation, Offering 141 (polichromy reconstruction; drawing by Erika Robles Cortés and Michelle de Anda, courtesy of the Templo Mayor Project); and (b) the goddess Cihuacóatl (folio 45r, Codex Magliabechiano [see chapter 9, Anders et al. 1996]).

Plate 21. A Jívaro tsantsa (Ecuador, historic), NMNH 39500 (photo by John Verano, courtesy of the National Museum of Natural History, Smithsonian Institution).

Plate 22. Severed head and feet of a captive sacrificed by the Moche. Pyramids of Moche, Huaca de la Luna, Plaza 3C, H33 (photo by John Verano).

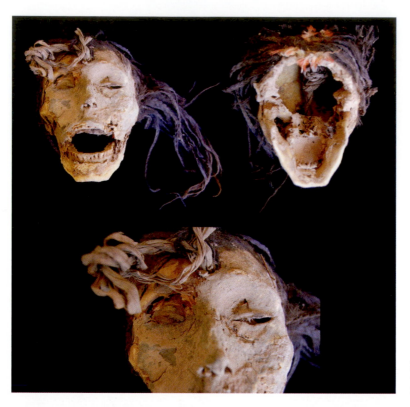

Plate 23. Anterior and basilar views of isolated head #12112. Bottom center: detail of mummified face.

Plate 24. Detail of decorated textile that was used to wrap head #12112.

Plate 25. Tiwanaku monoliths. Left: Ponce monolith; right: Fraile monolith (photos © Jeff Clarke).

Plate 26. Stone, framed human heads. Collections of Centro de Investigaciones Arqueológicas, Antropológicas y Administración de Tiwanaku and the Museo del Sitio de Tiwanaku (photo by Deborah E. Blom).

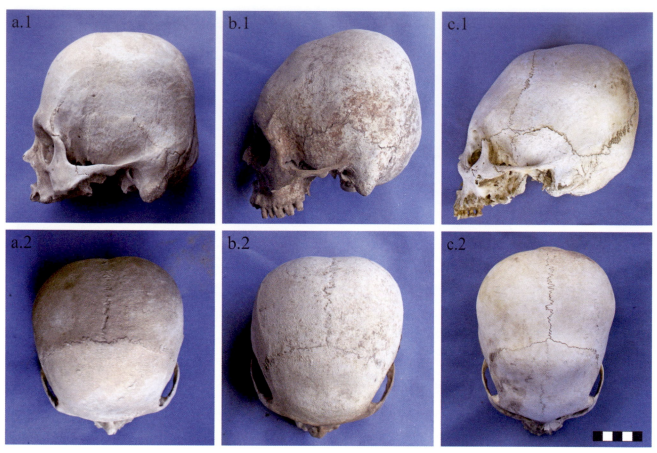

Plate 27. Top row: lateral view of modified crania from Kallimarka (a.1, b.1), located in Cabanaconde, and Yuraq Qaqa (c.1) in the upper valley; bottom row: superior view of the same specimens. Crania do not exhibit marked asymmetry.

Plate 28. Cranial shapes at Yuthu (bilobed, asymmetrical, and not uniform) (photos by Allison Davis).

Plate 29. Multiple cut marks on the neck bone of Individual 1.

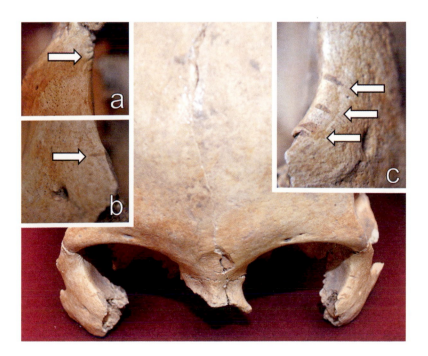

Plate 30. Additional anterior view of Individual 3 with insets noting the cut and scrape marks around both eye orbits.

Plate 31. A pair of identical Wari faceneck vessels. Museo Nacional de Arqueología, Antropología e Historia del Perú, Lima. C-59735: ceramic, 17.5 cm tall × 35.2 cm in circumference. C-59744: ceramic, 18.8 cm tall × 36.2 cm in circumference (photo by Andrea Vazquez de Arthur).

Plate 32. Wari faceneck vessels excavated at Pacheco in 1927. Museo Nacional de Arqueología, Antropología e Historia del Perú, Lima (photos by Andrea Vazquez de Arthur).

males, adolescents, and children were found among the offerings. Considering their physical characteristics and referring to historical sources, the victims were obtained through war, tribute, and trade (Chávez Balderas 2014). DNA and stable isotope analysis has revealed a low genetic diversity but different provenience. Despite the fact that most of the sacrificial victims analyzed were from nonlocal origins, they spent their last years in Tenochtitlan. This profile is more consistent with slaves than with enemies sacrificed after a battle (Barrera Huerta 2014; Bustos 2012). Interestingly, Luis Adrián Alvarado-Viñas and Linda Manzanilla (chapter 5 of this volume) also documented diversity in the biological profiles of decapitated victims from Teopancazco, Teotihuacan. Males and females, most of them of productive age, were decapitated and buried at this site.

In Tenochtitlan, victims were sacrificed and decapitated as part of the consecration of the temple, during festivities marked in the ritual calendar, or as part of exceptional ceremonies (Chávez Balderas 2012a, 2014). The heads were used in different rituals, receiving diverse treatments. Some were deposited in offerings immediately following death, while others were taken to the skullrack or *tzompantli*. It is possible that others were exhibited in ritual spaces or worn as the garments of priests before their final deposition, as I will discuss further.

Sacrificial victims were buried in the temple as *severed heads* or as *god effigies*, two separate categories with different symbolism. By "severed heads" I refer to all skulls found with articulated cervical vertebrae that present disarticulation marks and lack evidence of defleshing. Soon after their sacrifice, the individuals were decapitated and their heads were deposited immediately in the offerings with no further modifications. These were most likely buried at the Templo Mayor for the purpose of consecrating the building (Chávez Balderas 2012a, 2014; López Luján 1993). According to Martha Ilia Nájera (1987), these sacrifices served to consecrate and protect the temples.[5] I prefer the term "severed head" over "trophy head," because these individuals are neither mementos of war nor revered ancestors (Tiesler and Lozada, chapter 1 of this volume). They cannot be linked to war memorabilia or souvenirs (Lozada et al., chapter 12 of this volume), because they were obtained from different sources in addition to warfare. In addition, these victims are not connected to hunting behavior, and they were not meant to "demonstrate and symbolize an extraordinary accomplishment of personal and spiritual significance" (Mensforth 2007:222).

In contrast, god effigies correspond to reused tzompantli skulls, skulls with basal perforation, and so-called skull masks (plate 19). After decapitation, some of the heads were defleshed, and two lateral perforations were made by percussion using a stone tool. These skeletonized heads were taken to the tzompantli. Most of them were adult males; however, females were also exhibited (Chávez Balderas 2014). As we can infer from the research of Michel Graulich (2005), Rubén Mendoza (2007), Mary Miller and Karl Taube (1993), and Sandra Xochipiltécatl (2004), the tzompantli was polysemous. It was related to calendar festivities and ball games and at the same time served as a source of expansionist intimidation through the exhibition of victims. In addition, the tzompantli probably represented a gourd tree. According to Eduardo Matos Moctezuma (1986), these individuals were obtained in honor of Mixcóatl, Xipe Tótec, Huitzilopochtli, Yacatecuhtli, and Tezcatlipoca. In fact, some god impersonators—*ixiptla*—were decapitated and their skulls exhibited in the tzompantli. This was the case of an impersonator of Tezcatlipoca: over the course of one year, this individual was treated like a god, and then was sacrificed with his heart extracted and his head placed in the skullrack (Sahagún 1997:81, 107–9).

Contrary to the proposal of Christian Duverger (1993), the tzompantli was a dynamic structure, as confirmed by Durán (1995:2:31) and by the osteological evidence. According to Durán, these racks were renovated periodically, and some of the skulls were broken as they were removed from the rack. Archaeological evidence supports this idea: tzompantli skulls were constantly renewed and reused. The final destination of some of these individuals was the Templo Mayor of Tenochtitlan. Some were decorated with flint knives in the oral cavity and occasionally with eyes made of shell and pyrite (Chávez Balderas 2014). Some underwent further modification to make the skull masks, as discovered first by Carmen Pijoan Aguadé and colleagues (1989, 2001). These ritual objects correspond to the facial portion of the skull and were not meant to be worn as masks by the priests, since the orbits were covered. Skulls with basal perforations were also transformed into effigies by decorating them with appliqués and by placing flint knives in the nasal and oral cavities. The basal perforation was likely done to extract the brain; however, it may also have been used for display purposes (Chávez Balderas 2012a, 2014).

In the case of Tlatelolco, considered the twin city of Tenochtitlan, 170 tzompantli skulls have been found

(Pijoan Aguadé 1997; Pijoan Aguadé and Mansilla Lory 2010; Pijoan Aguadé et al. 1989, 2001). However, none of them were modified into effigies. This ritual pathway seems to be exclusive to Tenochtitlan.

How do we know that the original function of these skulls was different? How can we tell that they were not manufactured *ex professo* as effigies? Numerous osteological indicators support the idea that most were reutilized. First, the lateral perforations linking the skulls with the tzompantli are the most obvious evidence. As mentioned earlier, most of the skull masks present evidence of lateral perforations. Also, numerous individuals have small perforations in the zygomatic arch and the mandible. These were made to keep the mandible attached to the cranium, meaning that it was disarticulated as a result of the natural decomposition process, which is also confirmed by the absence of cut marks in the articulations. The presence of these perforations suggests that some skulls were suspended. In addition, the existence of effigies composed of the cranium and the mandible of different individuals, lacking disarticulation marks, proves the postmortem manipulation of human bones. Finally, weathering indicators such as longitudinal fractures in the teeth suggest that the skulls were exhibited or exposed.[6] In any case, their original meaning was transformed, as it underwent a process of resemantization.

THE ORIGINAL FUNCTION OF THE EFFIGY SKULLS

If these decapitations were not done to provide effigies for the offerings, what was their original function? Four sources of information give us potential answers to this question: codices, written sources, other skull masks, and Aztec sculptures.

The use of skulls as part of the architecture and garments of supernatural beings is well documented in the codices. Seven skulls were depicted in folio 80r of the Codex Magliabechiano. All were represented with eyes and tongues, possibly corresponding to flint knives. Three of them, located in the center of the ball-game courtyard, were adorned with locks of hair and earplugs, similar to the skull masks found in the offerings. Folio 45v of the Codex Borgia shows a small platform decorated with skulls. Circles in the temporal and parietal regions are common in some depictions, but it is not clear if these represented perforations made to exhibit the skulls in the tzompantli. If this was the case, then these pictographs also represent the reuse of these elements (fig. 9.1).

In some codices, human skulls are part of the garments of supernatural beings and elites. In folio 79v of the Codex Vaticanus B, a female, identified by Patrick Johansson (2006) as a Tepitoton Cihuateteo, is wearing

a)

b)

Figure 9.1. (a) Decorated skulls at the ball-game courtyard (folio 80r, Codex Magliabechiano [Anders et al. 1996]); and (b) platform decorated with human skulls (folio 45v, Codex Borgia [Jansen et al. 1993]).

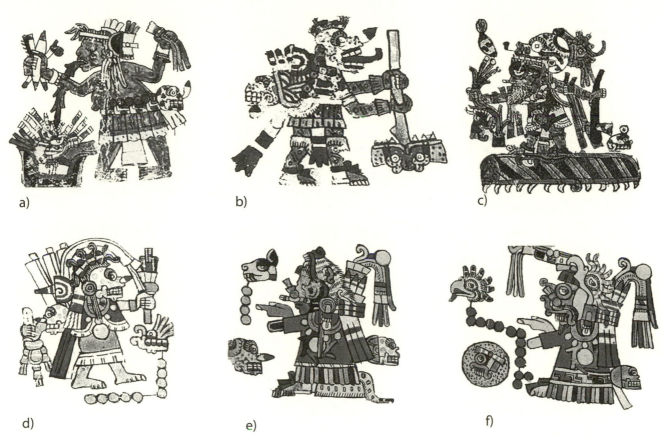

Figure 9.2. (a) Tepitoton Cihuateteo wearing a skull in her belt (folio 79v, Codex Vaticanus B [Anders et al. 1993]); (b) Mictlantecuhtli carrying a skull on his back (folio 12r, Codex Vaticanus B [Anders et al. 1993]); (c) Mictlampa region (a deity with Tláloc attributes wearing a cranium as a headdress) (folio 69v, Codex Vaticanus B [Anders et al. 1993]); (d) Lady 9 Grass of Chalcatongo with a flint knife in the nasal cavity and a human skull on her back (page 18, Codex Zouche-Nuttall [Anders et al. 1992]); (e) Lord Four Dog carrying a skull on his back (page 28, Codex Zouche-Nuttall [Anders et al. 1992]); and (f) Lord Thirteen Eagle carrying a skull on his back (page 28, Codex Zouche-Nuttall [Anders et al. 1992]).

a skull in her belt with eyes and a flint knife in the nasal cavity (fig. 9.2a).[7] She is feeding blood to a skeletonized child. In folio 12r of this document, Mictlantecuhtli carries a skull on his back (fig. 9.2b) with a cranium depicted as a headdress. In folio 69v, the North or Mictlampa is represented by a deity with attributes of Tláloc (Seler 1903). Symbolizing the region of death, the god wears a headdress adorned with eyes and a flint knife, but with no mandible (fig. 9.2c).

In the Codex Zouche-Nuttall, human skulls are part of the garments of different nobles: Lady Nine Grass of Chalcatongo (fig.9.2d), Lord Four Dog of Teozacoalco (fig.9.2e), and Lord Thirteen Eagle of Teozacoalco, son of Lord Seven Water and Lady Eleven Water (Williams 2009) (fig.9.2f). It is interesting to note that in the last two images the skulls are embedded in a semicircular element not depicted in Aztec sculptures.

The illustration on folio 13 of the Codex Tlaxcala is very informative: some skulls were decorated as effigies. The burning of cult images conducted by the Spanish friars included defleshed skulls with headdresses of the god Xipe Tótec (fig. 9.3). These are strikingly similar to the effigies found at the Templo Mayor. Although one of the skulls from Offering 141 included the remains of a headdress made of fibers, its poor preservation prevents us from associating it with any particular deity.

Written sources are less informative. The description of the funerals of Tízoc given by Durán (1995:1:370–71) mention that a priest, representing the lord of the underworld, wore "faces with mirror eyes" at the shoulders, elbows, knees, and waist. Unfortunately, Durán did not state if these faces corresponded to human bones, although the description is consistent with skull masks. However we must bear in mind that in Aztec sculpture, telluric faces

Figure 9.3. Burning of cult images, including
defleshed skulls (folio 13, Codex Tlaxcala
[Muñoz Camargo 1981]).

were also worn by the gods in these anatomical regions, and Durán could be describing this attribute.

Other sources of information correspond to archaeological objects—for example, the skull mask from the British Museum collection. The leather straps suggest that this element was probably worn by a member of the elite, similar to depictions found in the Mixtec Codex Zouche-Nuttall. However, we note that none of the effigies in our collection have marks caused by leather straps or perforations similar to the ones found here. Stylistically and technologically speaking, the British Museum skull is quite different from those from the Templo Mayor, possibly reflecting a Mixtec provenience. Further isotopic analysis of the bones and leather could help resolve the controversy.

The most informative source is Aztec sculpture. Numerous deities connected with the earth, death, and fertility have human skulls as part of their garments. These deities include Coatlicue, Yolotlicue, Cihuapipiltin, Tlaltecuhtli, and Coyolxauhqui (Boone 1999), all of whom are symbolically interconnected. Human skulls were worn by these supernatural beings as belts, pectorals, and headdresses and to cover the joints as elbow and knee protectors. In general, two types of ornaments are represented: pectorals

and headdresses resemble skull masks with the posterior part suppressed, while skulls presented in belts show a perforation similar to those found in the tzompantli.

According to the Mexica, Coatlicue, "Snakes Her Skirt," was the mother of Huitzilopochtli. She was impregnated with a ball of down while sweeping Coatepec Mountain. Because of her pregnancy, her daughter, Coyolxauhqui, and her sons, the Centzon Huiznahua, tried to kill her. Huitzilopochtli was born armed and killed his siblings. This myth was reenacted during the Panquetzaliztli Veintena (Miller and Taube 1993; Sahagún 1997:142–47). The emblematic monolith that represented Coatlicue was found in 1790. This colossal sculpture of outstanding quality was not unique: four fragments corresponding to at least two similar sculptures are stored in the National Museum of Anthropology in Mexico City and in the Templo Mayor Museum. The goddess is dismembered, blood spouting, represented as snakes at the neck and wrists. Coatlicue is wearing a skirt made of woven snakes and a necklace made of hands and hearts and one skull, and another skull on her back (Boone 1999). Interestingly, both skulls seem to be flat or incomplete (lacking the posterior part), and both have circular perforations in the temporal-parietal region. The orbits are represented as two circles. These representations are strikingly similar to the skull masks without flint knives found in the offerings (fig. 9.4a).

In 1933, a monolith of a goddess was found near the Templo Mayor. It is almost identical to Coatlicue, but her skirt represents hearts. For this reason, it was identified as Yolotlicue, "Hearts Her Skirt," or Nochpalliicue, "Red Her Skirt," probably alluding to the parallelism of hearts and tunas, the fruit of the nopal cactus (Boone 1999; Klein 2000, 2008). Although the sculpture is badly damaged, the goddess has a necklace made of severed hands, hearts, and a skull. Yolotlicue has a set of hands in the anterior part, while Coatlicue has two sets: one in the front and one in the back (fig. 9.4b).

Coyolxauhqui, the defeated sister of Huitzilopochtli, was represented decapitated and dismembered, alluding to the myth of the birth of this god. The monolith, found at Stage IVb (1469–1481 CE) of the Templo Mayor, was not unique. The fragments of two identical sculptures were found during the archaeological excavations; it is more likely that these monoliths correspond to later stages. The goddess wears a skull with lateral perforations on her back, which is tied to her waist by a rope made of snakes. This element resembles a tzompantli skull (fig. 9.4c).

Cihuateteo, Cihuapipiltin, and Mocihuaquetzque were supernatural females, corresponding to women who died during childbirth. They were considered warriors, receiving the sun at noon every day. The sun was led by these brave women to the west, where it was devoured by the earth, bringing the night. They were also feared; according to the Nahua cosmovision, these women, depicted as skeletonized and kneeling, descended to earth during the night as *tzitzimime* to cause damage, especially to children (Klein 2000; Sahagún, 1997:25, 34, 35, 380, 381). One sculpture from the National Museum of Anthropology collection includes a necklace composed of hands and a flat skull. The headdress is also composed of skulls (fig. 9.4d). The shape and size of these elements resemble children's skull masks found in offerings 22 and 24, explored in 1978.

Cihuateteo, along with Coatlicue and Yolotlicue, wear severed human hands as part of their necklaces, while Mictlantecuhtli and Mictecacíhuatl wear them as earplugs. Recent archaeological findings documented the use of children's severed hands and feet. Offering 149 was excavated by archaeologists Julia Pérez Pérez and José María García from January to March 2012. Hundreds of objects were deposited in a box made of stone slabs, placed in the construction fill of a circular temple: the Cuauhxicalco. Inside this box, numerous small human and animal bones were found, all commingled due to rodent disturbance. A

Figure 9.4. (a) Detail of the frontal skull, Coatlicue monolith (photo by Boris de Swan, courtesy of Editorial Raíces/Museo Nacional de Antropología); (b) detail of a necklace with hands, heart, and skulls, Yolotlicue monolith (photo by Marco Antonio Pacheco, courtesy of Editorial Raíces/Museo Nacional de Antropología); (c) detail of the skull with lateral perforations in the belt of the goddess Coyolxauhqui (photo by Marco Antonio Pacheco, courtesy of the Templo Mayor Museum); and (d) Cihuateteo wearing skulls in the necklace and headdress (photo by Marco Antonio Pacheco, courtesy of Editorial Raíces/Museo Nacional de Antropología).

a)

b)

c)

d)

taphonomic analysis determined that the body parts of two children were deposited soon after dismemberment. Their faces were positioned to the north, the region associated with death. The severed feet and hands of both children were placed south of the heads; these were deposited articulated and also facing north. The first individual was placed in the eastern half of the offering, while the second was in the western half. This duality was also evident in the distribution of bird pelts and the presence of two incense burners (Chávez Balderas 2012b). Although it is possible that severed hands were used as garments, as suggested by the sculptures, we must bear in mind that no feet are depicted in association with these goddesses.

Most of the skulls in Aztec sculptures are without doubt depicted as part of the garments of Tlaltecuhtli, numen of the earth. This deity was represented as a male, a female, and an animal. It was related to fertility and death; even as the earth gives life to crops, it devours the corpses in a continuous cycle. Matos Moctezuma (1997) classified the representation of these deities in four general groups: (a) male representations; (b) female representations; (c) zoomorphic representations; and (d) depictions with attributes of Tláloc. Despite the overlaps between these groups and the differences between each category, this classification system functions as a heuristic device for organizing this complex corpus. Almost all the sculptures in the first three groups were depicted with skulls as part of their garments. Male representations have attributes of Tláloc (goggle eyes and fangs), a quincunx in the center, and pointed sandals. This deity has two skulls at the elbows, two at the knees, and two at the hands. Those located at articular sites are tied with ropes, apparently from the zygomatic arch but not from lateral perforations (fig. 9.5a). In the female group, the skulls are tied with a belt to the posterior part of the waist. Almost all are

depicted from a lateral view, showing a perforation similar to the tzompantli skulls. In some cases, the eyes are represented as two concentric circles, which are connected to the appliqués found on the effigies from the Templo Mayor offerings (fig. 9.5b). Some of the sculptures from this group also have skulls at the articulations and hands. Finally, some of the zoomorphic depictions with feminine clothing also carry skulls on the back, with the same characteristics as those in the female group (fig. 9.5c).

In sum, some of the supernatural beings in Aztec sculpture as well as deities and elites in the Mixtec and Aztec codices wear skulls as part of their garments. All these divinities have a certain symbolism in common—a symbolism related to earth, death, war, creation, and destruction, as I will explore. After the skulls were used in different ritual activities, they underwent further modification to be deposited inside the offerings.

SKULL EFFIGIES IN THE TEMPLO MAYOR OFFERINGS

The skulls deposited in the offerings represented deities. This idea was first proposed by Leonardo López Luján (1993), who compared the skull masks with representations of the lord of the underworld, Mictlantecuhtli, depicted in the codices of the Borgia Group (fig. 9.6). However, these effigies probably represented other deities, as I will discuss in this section.

Mictlantecuhtli and Mictecacíhuatl

The gods of the underworld, Mictlantecuhtli and his feminine counterpart, Mictecacíhuatl, welcomed the dead to Mictlan, a broad, dark place with no windows and no

a)

b)

c)

Figure 9.5. (a) Detail of skulls in sculptures from Group A (male Tlaltecuhtli) (Templo Mayor Museum); (b) detail of skulls in sculptures from Group B (female Tlaltecuhtli) (National Museum of Anthropology, Mexico City); and (c) detail of skull in sculptures from group C (zoomorphic Tlaltecuhtli), Hackmack Box (drawings by Israel Elizalde).

of hair. Similar perforations were found in the sculptures of the god Mictlantecuhtli discovered at the House of the Eagles, located north of the Templo Mayor (López Luján and Mercado 1996).

In most of the offerings, these effigies were paired; only one individual had flint knives, while the other had *Oliva* snail beads.[8] In most of the codices from the Borgia Group, Mictlantecuhtli is represented with flint knives, while his female counterpart, Mictecacíhuatl, tends to be depicted without knives. However, there are some exceptions that prevent us from confirming this duality. In the codices of this group, Mictlantecuhtli is occasionally represented without knives. Furthermore, in the Codex Zouche-Nuttall, Lady Nine Grass of Chalcatongo (Williams 2009), a skeletonized female, is depicted with a knife in the nasal cavity. It is possible that the pairing of the skull masks reflected a gender distinction, but unfortunately there is no correlation with the biological profile of the victims. After all the postmortem manipulation, the sex of some of the victims was unknown to the priests when the individuals were buried. Despite this fact, in most cases a gracile skull was paired with a robust one, possibly expressing the male-female duality.

Pairing of effigies also included children: effigies corresponding to nine individuals were deposited in Offerings B1, B2, 11, 15, 20, 22, 24, and 64. In some cases, skull masks were composed of two individuals: one adult and one child (Offerings 11 and 15) and two different children (Offering 24). Skull masks of children were regularly deposited without flint knives; however, in Offering B1, found in 1948, one child was adorned with flint knives and appliqués. Also in 2012, two severed heads of children were found in Offering 149, with flint knives in the oral cavities (Chávez Balderas 2012a, 2012b). Unfortunately, we lack evidence to determine why Mictlantecuhtli was represented as a child.

Ehécatl-Quetzalcóatl and Xólotl

Quetzalcóatl, the feathered serpent, was one of the gods of creation and played a major role in Mesoamerican myths. He inhabited the sky, the earth, and the underworld. During the Late Postclassic, he was also identified as Ehécatl, the god of wind, characterized by a buccal mask in the shape of a bird beak. Quetzalcóatl is strongly connected to Mictlantecuhtli: he traveled to the underworld to steal precious bones, thereby creating humanity. While the god was running away with the bones, quails

Figure 9.6. Mictlantecuhtli with eyes, hair, and flint knives in the nose cavity (folio 23, Codex Borgia [Jansen et al. 1993]).

exits. The dead offered cotton cloths, paper, perfumes, and torches, among other goods, to both divinities (Sahagún 1997). These gods were custodians of the precious bones with which humanity was created by Quetzalcóatl. Both deities are represented defleshed, with locks of hair, claws, and flint knives in the nasal and oral cavities. They are also depicted with symbols of night and death, such as paper flags and folded headdresses (*ixcuatechmalli*), a pectoral (*amaixcuatechimalli*), and earplugs in the shape of a femur (*ominacochtli*), among other things (López Luján and Mercado 1996; Mateos Higuera 1993). In addition, Mictlantecuhtli is represented in the Codex Telleriano-Remensis (Quiñones Keber 1995:176) with a royal diadem and a nose plug made of turquoise, along with the symbols of death and night. Mictlantecuhtli was also known as Nextepehua (the one who scatters the ashes) and Tzontémoc (the one who descends head downward) (López Austin 1996; López Luján and Mercado 1996).

Most of the skull masks were decorated with eyes made of shell and pyrite, with flint knives in the oral and nasal cavities. These knives were neither painted nor dressed with miniature garments, as was the case with other examples found in the offerings (Chávez Balderas et al. 2010). Most likely, these elements alluded to the god's desire for sacrificial blood. Some have small circular perforations in the frontal bone, possibly used to place locks sent by Mictlantecuhtli made him fall. The bones were broken, which, according to the myth, explains human diversity. Once on the earth's surface, these remains were "fertilized" with the blood that Quetzalcóatl offered by pricking his penis (Velázquez 1945). According to Johansson (1996), this myth proves that existence emerged from death. These gods are depicted together in the codices of the Borgia Group on several occasions. In one case, they are standing on the earth's surface represented as a skeletonized being with putrefaction stains and teeth in the form of flint knives, demanding blood (folio 56, Codex Borgia [Jansen et al. 1993]).

Xólotl, Quetzalcóatl's twin brother, was represented as a dog with an anthropomorphic body. He was the god of twins, the ball game, duality, and deformities. According to the *Leyenda de los Soles*, Xólotl accompanied Quetzalcóatl to the underworld. In contrast, according to Friar Jerónimo de Mendieta (2002), Xólotl was the one who made this expedition, repeating the journey every night to take the sun into the underworld and then back to the sky the next morning, creating night and day. Consequently, dogs were considered the companions for the deceased traveling to this region. This deity is also related to Venus as the Evening Star (González López 2011).

Life-death duality was expressed through god effigies. In Offerings CA, 6, 11, and 98, one of the skull masks with attributes of Mictlantecuhtli was directly associated with representations of Ehécatl-Quetzalcóatl, god of wind, connected to life and creation (Chávez Balderas 2012a; Olmo 1999; Velázquez 2000). This deity was identified by the presence of his attributes: curved earplugs (*epcololli*) made of shell, necklaces made of *Oliva* sp. snails, *ehecacózcatl* pectorals manufactured with *Turbinella* sp. marine snails, and obsidian *ehecatopilli* scepters (Velázquez 2000). In some cases, Ehécatl-Quetzalcóatl was represented by green stone masks adorned with the attributes mentioned above (Offerings CA, 98, and 11). In two cases, these attributes decorated skulls (Offerings 6 and 11). It is interesting to note that two effigies of this god were buried in Offering 11: one skull mask and one green stone mask. The latter was deposited on top of a skull mask with attributes of the god of the underworld, Mictlantecuhtli.

Despite the fact that these effigies clearly displayed attributes of Quetzalcóatl, representations of this god as a skeleton cannot be satisfactorily explained. However, we must remember that he shares the same iconographic attributes with his twin brother, Xólotl. A skeletonized form made of green stone, part of the Württemberg State

Museum collection in Stuttgart, was identified by Eduard Seler as a representation of Xólotl (González López 2011). The god's face is strikingly similar to the skull masks, based on the presence of epcololli earplugs and concentric circles that resemble the appliqués that form the eyes of some of these objects.

Cihuacóatl

According to Johansson (1998), Cihuacóatl, the "serpent woman," was connected to fertility, motherhood, femininity, war, sacrifice, and death. Her temple, Tillan, symbolized the underworld and the womb. Cihuacóatl has a complex symbolism: she is one of the mother and earth goddesses that overlap with Teteoinnan, Toci, Tlazoltéotl, Ilamatecuhtli, and Xochiquetzal (Miller and Taube 1993:61). According to Elizabeth Boone (1999), Cihuacóatl also merged with the tzitzimime group and was a female warrior also known as Quilaztli, Quauhcíhuatl, Yaocíhuatl, and Tzitzimitl. For Johansson (1998), this deity also overlaps with Coatlicue, Coyolxauhqui, and Malinaxóchitl, and she was also known as Tonantzin, "our mother." She is represented partially defleshed and hungry for human hearts.

The goddess is related to women who died during childbirth and who died as a sacrifice; numerous victims were sacrificed in her honor (Klein 2001). She was considered a warrior goddess with masculine characteristics. She embodied both masculine (war) and feminine (fertility) principles (Sigal 2010). By stretching the argument, this goddess can be considered sinister and sacred, related to the moon and sky and one of the avatars of the earth, Tlaoltéotl (Aguilera 2003; Graulich 2000; Johansson 1998).

Offering 141 was discovered during the seventh field season of the Templo Mayor Project, under the direction of Leonardo López Luján. This ritual deposit is key to understanding new aspects concerning the symbolism, use, and reuse of human heads. Offering 141 contained more than eighteen thousand elements, deposited in a stone box during the reign of Ahuítzotl (1486–1502 CE). Seven effigies were found inside this deposit: after decapitation, three individuals were transformed into tzompantli skulls, and the rest display basal perforations. After their primary use, they were reused and deposited inside the offering. For this purpose, they were painted and decorated with diverse ornaments, such as *anáhuatl* shell rings and a headdress made of fibers. Five effigies were placed on top of bones made of *tezontle* stone, while two were placed on top of brain coral covered with animal pelts (puma and ibis). Six corresponded to males and one to a female. With the exception of one individual who was over thirty years old, all were sacrificed between the ages of twenty and thirty (Aguirre Molina and Robles Cortés 2014; Chávez Balderas et al. 2015).

Without doubt, the most relevant information concerning health conditions is the presence of periosteal reaction and the abnormal morphology of the upper lateral incisors. Four individuals presented unspecific lesions localized on the frontal and parietal bones (*bregma*), which modified the texture of the skull. Fred Longstaffe and colleagues from the University of Western Ontario are performing oxygen isotope analysis to test if these individuals were related geographically. The presence of four cases in the same offering might be a coincidence; however, it is more likely that this was a cultural intervention or a deliberate selection of victims. Three individuals present an anomalous morphology of the upper lateral incisors, and one has severe dental wear, modifying the shape of both upper lateral incisors. Considering the location of these teeth, these features were noticed by the priests. It is important to mention that in the Templo Mayor collection (ninety-nine individuals), we documented morphological variations of the incisors and superimposed incisors, congenital absence, and supernumerary teeth (Chávez Balderas et al. 2015). This data will be part of a new research project to test the hypothesis of a selection pattern based on dental morphology.

Archaeologist Erika Robles Cortés (Aguirre Molina and Robles Cortés 2014) analyzed the polychromy by using DStrech software (commonly utilized for documenting cave paintings), conducting hypothetical reconstructions of the original decoration. She classified the individuals into three different groups: (1) with blue and black pigment; (2) painted in black; and (3) with red painting. Groups 1 and 2 were related to Mictlantecuhtli, while group 3 was related to Cihuacóatl.

The third category is composed of one skull with basal perforation, painted red and decorated with two gray circles on the cheeks. The skull was found with a wooden ring associated with the parietals. A femur carved in wood was discovered to the west. This individual was placed on top of a brain coral covered with the pelt of an ibis. Mictlantecuhtli (folio 52r, Codex Tudela [Robertson and Jiménez Moreno 1980]) was also represented with red paint; however, the circles on the cheeks allowed Robles

Cortés to relate this effigy to the goddess Cihuacóatl (Aguirre Molina and Robles Cortés 2014; folio 27r, Codex Tudela [Robertson and Jiménez Moreno 1980]) (plates 20a, 20b). Therefore, the skull belongs to an adult female. It is important to bear in mind that the mandibles of this individual and of an individual from group 2 were exchanged by the Mexica priests. This fact is relevant because it demonstrates that the skulls were painted *ex professo* for this ritual, when the mandibles had already been disarticulated by natural means; this reveals the reuse and postmortem manipulation (Chávez Balderas et al. 2015).

Tezcatlipoca

The lord of the smoking mirror is a complex god, identified by the absence of one foot and with a mirror as a substitute. He was omnipresent, supreme, capricious, and simultaneously negative and positive (Heyden 1989). He was a fundamental part of the creation myths. Because of his importance, he was mentioned in numerous codices and written sources. He was related to the night, caves, and jaguars through his double, Tepeyólotl, "heart of the mountain" (Olivier 2004).

Tezcatlipoca was connected to death in different ways. His sudden presence in a road in the middle of the night was taken to presage that death was close. Prayers were directed to this god to ask for the death of a bad ruler and also to request a safe journey for dead warriors' souls (Torquemada 1977; Sahagún 1997).

The skull decorated with turquoise mosaics that is part of the British Museum collection, mentioned above, has been interpreted as a representation of Tezcatlipoca due to its black facial bands (McEwan et al. 2006), and the pyrite eyes of this effigy have been interpreted as mirrors. However, this type of eye is not exclusive to this deity. Numerous effigies connected with Mictlantecuhtli have the same appliqués. Flint knives representing Quetzalcóatl, Xochipilli, and other supernatural beings found in Offering 125 likewise have eyes made of this material, preserving its original gold-like aspect.

Despite the fact that some of the effigy skulls found in Offering 141 presented the colors blue and black, these were not arranged as alternating bands. These colors are also present in numerous representations of Mictlantecuhtli (Aguirre Molina and Robles Cortés 2014; Chávez Balderas et al. 2015). The identification of the skull mask from the British Museum as Tezcatlipoca remains controversial: images of the god in the codices combine bands of ocher and black, but not blue and black. For this reason, and considering the available contextual information, the presence of Tezcatlipoca as an effigy skull at the Templo Mayor offerings can be ruled out.

DISCUSSION: GODS WEARING SKULLS AND SKULLS REPRESENTING GODS

Osteological evidence and contextual information confirmed the complex chain of preparation, use, and reuse of human skulls at the Templo Mayor of Tenochtitlan (fig. 9.7). After sacrifice, certain victims were decapitated; some were immediately buried inside the offerings, and the rest underwent further modifications. Some skulls were transformed into skull masks, others were taken to the tzompantli, while skulls with basal perforation may have been exhibited.

Before their final deposition, skull masks may have been used as part of the garments of priests and sculptures or exhibited in ritual spaces. Evidence of postmortem manipulation, such as loss of the mandible due to natural decomposition, proves that it took a long time for these to be buried.

Tzompantli skulls were exhibited, and some were taken from the rack. These were decorated with appliqués and flint knives and deposited as part of the offerings. Others were reused for manufacturing skull masks and possibly used in other rituals, before their final deposition. How long were the tzompantli skulls exhibited before being transformed into skull masks? Most likely from weeks to months. An analysis of these elements suggests that the skulls had enough moisture and collagen content to react

as "fresh bone" when they were transformed into skull masks. Experimental research conducted by Danielle Wieberg and Daniel Wescott (2008) showed that bones start losing their moisture content 28 days after death, and that some preserve it for almost five months (141 days). However, these results reflect local conditions and weathering in Missouri, where Wieberg and Wescott conducted their research. Future experiments in central Mexico will help us to better elucidate this information.

Skull masks and tzompantli skulls were represented in Aztec sculptures as part of the garments of supernatural beings. These elements were most likely real garments. We must bear in mind that the earplugs, headdresses, nose plugs, lip plugs, necklaces, and pectorals, among other ornaments, represented in the iconography were real objects worn by individuals, animals, sculptures, masks, and flint knives, as we can confirm through the archaeological evidence. Based on this logic, skull masks could have been used as the garments of priests, impersonators, or cult images.

The basal perforation found in some of the skulls primarily functioned as a means of discarding the brain; however, it may have been used to insert a wooden pole in order to exhibit the skulls. According to Xochipiltécatl (2004), exhibiting heads using perforations located at the base of the skull was an ancient practice, documented in different cultural areas of Mesoamerica. The exhibition hypothesis is supported by the finding of a wooden scepter found at the staircase of the Templo Mayor: it represents a cylinder with a skull on top.

Who were the victims? Males, females, and children from different places in the empire. Possibly some were defeated warriors, but, judging by stable isotope analysis (Barrera Huerta 2014), numerous slaves were among the

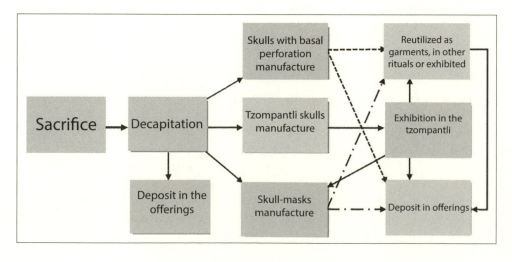

Figure 9.7. Ritual pathways of heads and skulls at the Templo Mayor of Tenochtitlan.

victims. They were sacrificed to consecrate buildings; some of them could have been god impersonators, but not necessarily of the deities that they represented in the offerings. It is more likely that the different posthumous treatments of individuals depended on the ceremony. No clear selection patterns based on age or gender were related to the manufacture of these elements. I can only mention the trend of depositing more males in the tzompantli, although this structure also included females (Botella and Alemán 2004; Chávez Balderas 2012a, 2014).

Manipulation of bones suggests the existence of storage spaces for human and faunal remains (Chávez Balderas 2012a; Chávez Balderas et al. 2011). I have documented instances that show that priests had different bones available, so that they could choose the best option. For example, in Offering 11, the cranium of a child was put together with the mandible of a female adult, forming a unit. The mandible was extremely gracile and fit perfectly. In Offerings 22 and 15, mandibles were also selected to fit the skulls of different individuals. In Offering 141, the priests exchanged the mandibles of two individuals, possibly by mistake (a male and a female). This occurred before the skulls were painted for burial (Aguirre Molina and Robles Cortés 2014; Chávez Balderas et al. 2015).

There are important differences among the effigies deposited in the offerings and the skulls worn by some gods and lords, as depicted in codices and sculptures. It is likely that skulls used as garments of deities and supernatural beings symbolized death, sacrifice, life, and regeneration. We can infer this by analyzing the nature of the gods wearing these elements. As mentioned above, deities bearing these elements were grouped by Boone (1999) as tzitzimime and related deities: Coatlicue, Yolotlicue, Cihuapipiltin, Tlaltecuhtli, and Coyolxauhqui. None of these deities was represented as an effigy skull in the Templo Mayor offerings.

After this complex chain of use and reuse, the skulls representing gods were eventually deposited with the offerings. This interpretation is supported not just by the presence of these iconographic elements but also by their placement on the terrestrial level of the offering along with other representations of the deities. The most convincing iconographic identifications correspond only to Mictlantecuhtli and possibly to Mictecacíhuatl, Cihuacóatl, and Xólotl.

Not surprisingly, skulls used as effigies are connected to death. Mictlantecuhtli rarely carries these ritual objects as part of his garments, probably due to the fact that he is already defleshed and embodies death (folio 15r, Codex Telleriano-Remensis [Quiñones Keber 1995]; folio 12r, Codex Vaticanus B [Anders et al. 1993]). Instead, it is common to see him and his feminine counterpart, Mictecacíhuatl, in the Codices Fejervary-Mayer (folio 18 [Anders et al. 1994]) and Borgia (folios 13, 15, 23 [Jansen et al. 1993]) wearing earplugs made of severed human hands.

The goddess Cihuacóatl is not represented in codices or sculptures bearing skulls as part of her garments. However, she is commonly depicted partially defleshed, with a skeletonized mandible (folio 20, Codex Durán [Durán 1995]; folio 45r, Codex Magliabechiano [Anders et al. 1996]; folio 27r, Codex Tudela [Robertson and Jiménez Moreno 1980]). On page 36 of the Codex Borbonicus (Anders et al. 1991), she appears on top of an altar decorated with skulls with possible lateral perforations. Cihuacóatl was one of the most important goddesses of the Mexica pantheon and undoubtedly was connected with the earth, death, fertility, war, and sacrifice; she was sometimes considered Mictlantecuhtli's wife (Johansson 1998).

The pairing of gods is common in Mesoamerican mythology. In the examples discussed, Mictlantecuhtli was paired with Cihuacóatl and possibly with Mictecacíhuatl, Xólotl, and Quetzalcóatl, the latter represented also with green stone masks. The pairing of the lord of the underworld with Mictecacíhuatl is expected, because they are consorts, sharing some of the same functions such as, for example, welcoming deceased individuals to Mictlan. In the case of Xólotl and Ehécatl-Quetzalcóatl, both deities were considered travelers to the underworld. When night comes to earth, the first god goes to this region accompanying the dead sun, whereas the second god steals the bones from the underworld, creating the new humanity.

The pairing of gods was also important in other regions of Mesoamerica. For example, Chaak Chel and Chaak were paired in Maya mythology in a similar way to Tláloc and Chalchiuhtlicue. According to Gabrielle Vail and Christine Hernández (2012), these deities were associated with the creation of the first humans. Chaak was the god of rain; Chaak Chel provided the earth with both destructive and life-giving water, and was also related to weaving and fertility. According to these authors, evidence of both deities has been found in contexts symbolizing the underworld and related to symbols of fertility, death, and regeneration. Paired female and male deities sometimes exhibit overlapping activities; for example, Mictlantecuhtli and Mictecacíhuatl together received all the funerary goods brought by dead individuals to Mictlan. In other examples, activities are complementary. Such is the case of Tláloc, the god of rain, and Chalchiuhtlicue, the goddess of lakes and streams. The pairing of Mictlantecuhtli and Cihuacóatl can also be considered complementary. On one hand, Mictlantecuhtli is related to natural death, whereas Cihuacóatl has links to sacrificial death and war. Both deities need blood.

The function of these skulls among the offerings can be explained by understanding the archaeological contexts as cosmograms. According to López Luján (1993), these ritual deposits were models of the universe. The sky, earth, sea, and underworld were represented inside these stone boxes. Supernatural beings were represented in these levels in the form of flint knives, figurines, masks, and skulls, among other items; they were reenacting mythical passages and expressing sacred ideals. Effigy skulls deposited were associated with the representations of other gods such as Xiuhtecuhtli, Tláloc, and Ehécatl-Quetzalcóatl.

At the Templo Mayor, the skulls were placed at the bottom of the ritual deposits along with marine organisms and the snout of a sawfish, a telluric symbol symbolizing the earth monster and the watery underworld. In contrast, in offerings buried at the plaza, the skulls were deposited at the higher level. In general, offerings from the plaza are related to the earth, sea, and underworld, possibly because they were buried below the level where the Tlaltecuhtli monolith, the earth, was deposited.

CONCLUSIONS

Decapitation was widespread in Mesoamerica and the Andes. The practice had diverse symbolisms, and the victims themselves embodied different meanings expressed through the postsacrificial treatments and their placement in the ritual deposits. In this sense, a skull can be impersonating a deity, or alluding to an ancestor or a defeated enemy. In the words of Christine Hastorf (chapter 17 of this volume), "with examples of head treatment, head use, and head imagery, we can begin to learn about the range and variation of heads' agency in pre-Columbian societies."

This body part was the most important for ritual purposes in the Sacred Precinct of Tenochtitlan. Regardless of the ceremony or sacrificial technique, the posthumous treatment of the body in most cases involved this anatomical region. While the corpses were discarded and most likely removed from the city, the heads were preserved and reused over time. Similar practices have been documented in the Andes (Verano, chapter 11 of this volume). Data from recent excavations suggests that even manufacture waste and fragmentary skulls were not discarded in Tenochtitlan: these fragments were reused in termination rituals.

As in other cases presented in this volume, the ritual importance of the head can be explained in terms of its symbolism. For the Mexica, this body part reflected personhood; it was equated with the sky and housed the tonalli, the soul related to vitality. Moreover, bones were considered the matter that created life and the recipients of vital forces. Skulls were preserved at the Sacred Precinct as a means of keeping the energy that was released during the ritual sacrifice and, in some cases, allowed the embodiment of the gods through the manufacture of effigies. Skulls were the most powerful, direct, and unequivocal symbol of death.

ACKNOWLEDGMENTS

This project was supported by the Templo Mayor Museum, the Templo Mayor Project, the Foundation for the Advancement of Mesoamerican Studies (grant number 05404), the Lewis and Clark Foundation 2014, and Tulane University. I would like to thank Elizabeth Boone for encouraging this research and for all her comments. Images are courtesy of Editorial Raíces, Proyecto Templo Mayor, and the Museo Nacional de Antropología, with the support of Patricia Ledesma, Enrique Vela, Leonardo López Luján, José Cabezas, Bertina Olmedo, Jesús López, Erika Robles Cortés, Alejandra Aguirre, Israel Elizalde, Michelle de Anda, Boris de Swan, and Marco Antonio Pacheco.

NOTES

1. Although sacrificial victims were supposed to travel to the House of the Sun, no funerals were celebrated for them in Tenochtitlan. They underwent diverse postsacrificial treatments.

2. These burials correspond to "offerings" 3, 10, 14, 34, 37, 39, and 44. Offerings 34–39 contained one individual, while offerings 37–44 held another; that is, each individual was divided into two different receptacles (Chávez Balderas 2007). When these contexts were detected and before excavation, the archaeologists gave them the nomenclature corresponding to offerings. The original nomenclature was preserved, despite the fact that it is clear that they are burials.

3. Evidence from the nonexpansionist period has not been recovered due to the fact that the platform and the plaza corresponding to these periods are buried below later stages.

4. Disarticulation of the cervical region was conducted between C3 and C4 (14 percent), C4 and C5 (27 percent), C5 and C6 (32 percent) and C6 and C7 (27 percent). Disarticulation involving occipital condyles, the first and the second cervical vertebrae, is a difficult process considering the anatomical complexity of this region. In addition, access to this part of the spine is difficult due to the location of the mandible.

5. This practice was illustrated in folio 4r from the Codex Borgia (Jansen et al. 1993). In this image, a head from a decapitated individual (preserving soft tissue) is about to be buried inside a ritual building.

6. Although this feature could also be associated with diagenesis, interestingly it is absent in severed skulls that were buried inside the Templo Mayor offerings soon after their sacrifice.

7. This document is a cognate of the Codex Borgia (Jansen et al. 1993). However, these attributes were only represented in the Codex Vaticanus B (Anders et al. 1993).

8. Sea snail shells (*Oliva* sp.) were depicted as part of the skirts of numerous goddesses, but these elements are also related to males. Consequently, it is not possible to assess which of the skulls might represent the feminine part.

REFERENCES CITED

Aguilera, Carmen

2003 Cihuacóatl: Celestial or Terrestrial. *Latin American Indian Literatures Journal* 1(1):92–108.

Aguirre Molina, Alejandra, and Erika Robles Cortés

2014 Informe de la ofrenda 141. Unpublished report, Proyecto Templo Mayor, Instituto Nacional de Antropología e Historia, Mexico City.

Alvarado Tezozómoc, Fernando de

1944 *Crónica mexicana: escrita hacia el año de 1598.* Notes by Manuel Orozco y Berra. Editorial Leyenda, Mexico City.

Anders, Ferdinand, Maarten E. R. G. N. Jansen, and Gabina Pérez Jiménez (editors)

1994 *Codex Fejérváry-Mayer.* Sociedad Estatal Quinto Centenario, Madrid; Akademische Druck- und Verlagsanstalt, Graz; Fondo de Cultura Económica, Mexico City.

Anders, Ferdinand, Maarten E. R. G. N. Jansen, and Luis Reyes García (editors)

1991 *Códice Borbónico.* Sociedad Estatal Quinto Centenario, Madrid; Akademische Druck- und Verlagsanstalt, Graz; Fondo de Cultura Económica, Mexico City.

1992 *Códice Zouche-Nuttall.* Sociedad Estatal Quinto Centenario, Madrid; Akademische Druck- und Verlagsanstalt, Graz; Fondo de Cultura Económica, Mexico City.

1993 *Códice Vaticanus B, 3773.* Sociedad Estatal Quinto Centenario, Madrid; Akademische Druck- und Verlagsanstalt, Graz; Fondo de Cultura Económica, Mexico City.

1996 *Códice Magliabechiano.* Sociedad Estatal Quinto Centenario, Madrid; Akademische Druck- und Verlagsanstalt, Graz; Fondo de Cultura Económica, Mexico City.

Barrera Huerta, Alan

2014 Isotopía de estroncio aplicado a material óseo humano localizado en ofrendas del Templo Mayor de Tenochtitlan. BA thesis, Escuela Nacional de Antropología e Historia, Mexico.

Becker, Marshall J.

1988 Caches as Burials; Burials as Caches: The Meaning of Ritual Deposits among the Classic Period Lowland Maya. In *Recent Studies in Pre-Columbian Archaeology,* vol. 1, edited by Nicholas J. Saunders and Olivier de Montmollin, pp. 117–39. BAR International Series, 421. British Archaeological Reports, Oxford.

Benavente o Motolinía, Fray Toribio de

1971 *Memoriales o libro de las cosas de la Nueva España y de los naturales de ella.* Universidad Nacional Autónoma de México, Mexico City.

Boone, Elizabeth Hill

1999 The "Coatlicues" at the Templo Mayor. *Ancient Mesoamerica* 10:189–206.

Botella, Miguel, and Inmaculada Alemán

2004 El tzompantli de Zultepec, Tlaxcala. In *Perspectiva tafonómica*, edited by Carmen Pijoan Aguadé, Xabier Lizarraga Cruchaga, and Gerardo Valenzuela, pp. 173–84. Instituto Nacional de Antropología e Historia, Mexico City.

Botella, Miguel, Inmaculada Alemán, and Sylvia Jiménez

2000 *Los huesos humanos: manipulación y alteraciones.* Bellaterra, Barcelona.

Bustos, Diana

2012 Arqueología y genética: estudio biomolecular de material óseo procedente del recinto sagrado de Tenochtitlan. BA thesis, Escuela Nacional de Antropología e Historia, Mexico City.

Chávez Balderas, Ximena

2007 *Los rituales funerarios en el Templo Mayor de Tenochtitlan.* Colección Premios INAH. Instituto Nacional de Antropología e Historia, Mexico City.

2010 Decapitación ritual en el Templo Mayor de Tenochtitlan: estudio tafonómico. In *El sacrificio humano en la tradición religiosa mesoamericana*, edited by Leonardo López Luján and Guilhem Olivier, pp. 317–43. Instituto Nacional de Antropología e Historia; Universidad Nacional Autónoma de México, Mexico City.

2012a Sacrificio humano y tratamientos mortuorios en el Templo Mayor de Tenochtitlan. Master's thesis, Universidad Nacional Autónoma de México, Mexico City.

2012b Análisis de restos óseos: Ofrendas 149, 141, 151 y 111. Unpublished report, Templo Mayor Project, Instituto Nacional de Antropología e Historia, Mexico City.

2014 Sacrifice at the Templo Mayor of Tenochtitlan and Its Role in Regard to Warfare. In *Embattled Bodies, Embattled Places: War in Pre-Columbian Mesoamerica and the Andes*, edited by Andrew K. Scherer and John W. Verano, pp. 171–97. Dumbarton Oaks, Washington, DC.

Chávez Balderas, Ximena, Alejandra Aguirre Molina, Ana Miramontes, and Erika Robles Cortés

2010 Los cuchillos ataviados de la Ofrenda 125. *Arqueología Mexicana* 17(103):70–75.

Chávez Balderas, Ximena, Ángel González López, Norma Valentín, and José María García

2011 Osteoarqueología de campo aplicada al estudio de la fauna: el caso de la Ofrenda 126 del Templo Mayor de Tenochtitlan. *Estudios de Antropología Biológica* 15:117–37.

Chávez Balderas, Ximena, Erika Robles Cortés, Alejandra Aguirre Molina, and Michelle de Anda

2015 Efigies de la muerte: decapitación ritual y modificación de cráneos de la Ofrenda 141 del Templo Mayor de Tenochtitlan. *Estudios de Antropología Biológica* 17:53–75.

Coe, William

1975 Caches and Offertory Practices of the Maya Lowlands. In *Handbook of Middle American Indians*, vol. 2, pp. 463–68. University of Texas Press, Austin.

Durán, Diego

1995 *Historia de las Indias de la Nueva España e islas de tierra firme.* 2 vols. Consejo Nacional para la Cultura y las Artes, Mexico City.

Duverger, Christian

1993 *La flor letal: economía del sacrificio azteca.* Fondo de Cultura Económica, Mexico City.

González López, Ángel

2011 Imágenes sagradas: un estudio iconográfico sobre escultura en piedra del recinto sagrado de Tenochtitlan, Templo Mayor y el antiguo Museo Etnográfico. BA thesis, Escuela Nacional de Antropología e Historia, Mexico City.

Graulich, Michel

2000 Más sobre Coyolxauhqui y las mujeres desnudas de Tlatelolco. *Estudios de Cultura Náhuatl* 31:88–105.

2005 *Le sacrifice humain chez les Aztèques.* Fayard, Paris.

Hernández Pons, Elsa, and Carlos Navarrete

1997 Decapitación y desmembramiento en una ofrenda del centro ceremonial de México Tenochtitlan. In *De hombres y dioses*, edited by Xavier Noguez and Alfredo López Austin, pp. 59–108. Colegio Mexiquense, Zinacantepec; Colegio de Michoacán, Zamora.

Heyden, Doris

1989 Tezcatlipoca en el mundo náhuatl. *Estudios de Cultura Náhuatl* 19:83–93.

Jansen, Maarten E. R. G. N., Luis Reyes García, and Ferdinand Anders (editors)

1993 *Códice Borgia.* Sociedad Estatal Quinto Centenario, Madrid; Akademische Druck- und Verlagsanstalt, Graz; Fondo de Cultura Económica, Mexico City.

Johansson, Patrick

1996 La fecundación del hombre en el Mictlan y el origen de la vida breve. *Estudios de Cultura Náhuatl* 23:69–88.

1998 Tlahtoani y Cihuacóatl: lo diestro solar y lo siniestro lunar en el alto mando mexica. *Estudios de Cultura Náhuatl* 28:39–75.

2006 Mocihuaquetzqueh ¿mujeres divinas o mujeres sini-
estras? *Estudios de Cultura Náhuatl* 37:193–230.

Kanjou, Youssef

2001 El tratamiento postmortem del cráneo en Mesoamérica y Medio Oriente. *Estudios de Antropología
Biológica* 10:473–82.

Klein, Cecelia F.

2000 The Devil and the Skirt: An Iconographic Inquiry into
the Prehispanic Nature of the Tzitzimime. *Ancient
Mesoamerica* 1(1):1–26.

2001 None of the Above: Gender Ambiguity in Nahua
Ideology. In *Gender in Pre-Hispanic America*, edited
by Cecelia F. Klein, pp. 183–254. Dumbarton Oaks,
Washington, DC.

2008 A New Interpretation of the Aztec Statue Called Coatlicue, "Snakes-Her-Skirt." *Ethnohistory* 55:229–50.

Lagunas Rodríguez, Zaíd, and Carlos Serrano Sánchez

1972 Decapitación y desmembramiento corporales en
Teopanzolco, Morelos. In *Religión en Mesoamérica*,
edited by Jaime Litvak and Noemí Castillo Tejero,
pp. 429–34. Sociedad Mexicana de Antropología,
Mexico City.

López Austin, Alfredo

1996 *Cuerpo humano e ideología.* 2 vols. Universidad Nacional Autónoma de México, Mexico City.

López de Gómara, Francisco

1941 *Historia de la conquista de México.* 2 vols. Espasa
Calpe, Madrid.

López Luján, Leonardo

1993 *Las ofrendas del Templo Mayor de Tenochtitlan.* Instituto Nacional de Antropología e Historia, Mexico City.

López Luján, Leonardo, and Vida Mercado

1996 Dos esculturas de Mictlantecuhtli encontradas en el
recinto sagrado de México Tenochtitlan. *Estudios de
Cultura Náhuatl* 26: 41–68.

Mateos Higuera, Salvador

1993 *Los dioses creados: enciclopedia gráfica del México Antiguo.* Secretaría de Hacienda y Crédito Público, Mexico
City.

Matos Moctezuma, Eduardo

1986 *Muerte a filo de obsidiana.* Secretaría de Educación
Pública, Mexico City.

1997 Tlaltecuhtli: señor de la tierra. *Estudios de Cultura
Náhuatl* 27:15–40.

**McEwan, Colin, Andrew Middleton, Caroline Cartwright,
and Rebecca Stacey**

2006 *Turquoise Mosaics from Mexico.* British Museum,
London.

Mendieta, Jerónimo de

2002 *Historia eclesiástica indiana.* 2 vols. Consejo Nacional
para la Cultura y las Artes, Mexico City.

Mendoza, Rubén

2007 The Divine Gourd Tree: Tzompantli Skull Racks,
Decapitation Rituals, and Human Trophies in Ancient
Mesoamerica. In *The Taking and Displaying of Human
Body Parts as Trophies by Amerindians*, edited by
Richard J. Chacon and David H. Dye, pp. 400–443.
Springer, New York.

Mensforth, Robert

2007 Human Trophy Taking in Eastern North America
during the Archaic Period: The Relationship to
Warfare and Social Complexity. In *The Taking and
Displaying of Human Body Parts as Trophies by Am-
erindians*, edited by Richard J. Chacon and David H.
Dye, pp. 222–77. Springer, New York.

Miller, Mary E., and Karl A. Taube

1993 *The Gods and Symbols of Ancient Mexico and the
Maya: An Illustrated Dictionary of Mesoamerican
Religion.* Thames and Hudson, New York.

**Morehart, Christopher T., Abigail Meza Peñaloza, Carlos
Serrano Sánchez, Emily McClung de Tapia, and Emilio
Ibarra Morales**

2012 Human Sacrifice during the Epiclassic Period in the
Northern Basin of Mexico. *Latin American Antiquity*
23(4):426–48.

Moser, Christopher

1972 *Human Decapitation in Ancient Mesoamerica.*
Dumbarton Oaks, Washington, DC.

Muñoz Camargo, Diego

1981 *Descripción de la ciudad y provincia de Tlaxcala de las
Indias del mar océano para el buen gobierno y enno-
blecimiento dellas (1580–1585)* (facsimile). Universidad
Nacional Autónoma de México, Mexico City.

Nagao, Debra

1985 *Mexica Buried Offering: A Historical and Contextual
Analysis.* BAR International Series, 235. British Archaeological Reports, Oxford.

Nájera, Martha Ilia

1987 *El don de la sangre en el equilibrio cósmico: el sacrificio
y el autosacrificio sangriento entre los antiguos Mayas.*
Institutode Investigaciones Filológicas; Centro de

Estudios Mayas, Universidad Nacional Autónoma de México; Mexico City.

Olivier, Guilhem

2004 Tezcatlipoca: burlas y metamorfosis de un dios azteca. Fondo de Cultura Económica, Mexico City.

Olmo, Laura del

1999 *Análisis de la ofrenda 98 del Templo Mayor de Tenochtitlan.* Colección Científica. Instituto Nacional de Antropología e Historia, Mexico City.

Ortiz de Montellano, Bernard

1993 *Medicina, salud y nutrición aztecas.* Siglo Veintiuno, Mexico City.

Pereira, Grégory, and Ximena Chávez Balderas

2006 Restos humanos en el Entierro 6 de la Pirámide de la Luna. In *Sacrificios de consagración en la Pirámide de la Luna,* edited by Saburo Sugiyama and Leonardo López Luján, pp. 53–69. Museo del Templo Mayor, Instituto Nacional de Antropología e Historia, Mexico City; Arizona State University, Tempe.

Pijoan Aguadé, Carmen

1997 *Evidencias de sacrificio humano y canibalismo en restos óseos: el caso del entierro número 14 de Tlatelolco, D.F.* PhD dissertation, Universidad Nacional Autónoma de México, Mexico City.

Pijoan Aguadé, Carmen, Josefina Bautista Martínez, and David Volcanes

2001 Análisis tafonómico de cuatro máscaras-cráneo procedentes del recinto sagrado de México-Tenochtitlan. *Estudios de Antropología Biológica,* 10:503–18.

Pijoan Aguadé, Carmen, and Josefina Mansilla Lory

2010 Los cuerpos de sacrificados: evidencias de rituales. In *El sacrificio humano en la tradición religiosa mesoamericana,* edited by Leonardo López Luján and Guilhem Olivier, pp. 301–16. Instituto Nacional de Antropología e Historia; Universidad Nacional Autónoma de México, Mexico City.

Pijoan Aguadé, Carmen, Alejandro Pastrana, and Consuelo Maquivar

1989 El Tzompantli de Tlaltelolco una evidencia de sacrificio humano. *Estudios de Antropología Biológica* 10:561–83.

Quiñones Keber, Eloise

1995 *Codex Telleriano-Remensis: Ritual, Divination, and History in a Pictorial Aztec Manuscript.* University of Texas Press, Austin.

Robertson, Donald, and Wigberto Jiménez Moreno

1980 *Códice Tudela.* Ediciones de Cultura Hispánica; Instituto de Cooperación Iberoamericana, Madrid.

Román, Juan

1990 *El sacrificio de niños en el Templo Mayor.* Instituto Nacional de Antropología e Historia; GV Editores; Asociación de Amigos del Templo Mayor, Mexico City.

Ruz Lhuillier, Alberto

1989 *Costumbres funerarias de los antiguos mayas.* Fondo de Cultura Económica, Mexico City.

Sahagún, Bernardino de

1997 *Historia general de las cosas de la Nueva España.* Editorial Porrúa, Mexico City.

Seler, Eduard

1903 *Codex Vaticanus 3773 (Codex Vaticanus B).* University of Michigan Library, Ann Arbor.

Sigal, Pete

2010 Imagining Cihuacoatl: Masculine Rituals, Nahua Goddesses and the Texts of the Tlacuilos. *Gender and History* 22(3):538–63.

Sugiyama, Saburo, and Leonardo López Luján (editors)

2006 *Sacrificios de consagración en la Pirámide de la Luna.* Consejo Nacional para la Cultura y las Artes; Instituto Nacional de Antropología e Historia; Museo del Templo Mayor, Mexico City.

Thomas, Louis-Vincent.

1983 *Antropología de la muerte.* Fondo de Cultura Económica, Mexico City.

Tiesler, Vera

2007 Funerary or Nonfunerary? New References in Identifying Ancient Maya Sacrificial and Postsacrificial Behaviors from Human Assemblages. In *New Perspectives on Human Sacrifice and Ritual Body Treatments in Ancient Maya Society,* edited by Vera Tiesler and Andrea Cucina, pp. 14–44. Springer, New York.

Torquemada, Juan de

1977 *Monarquía indiana.* Vol. 4. Edited by Miguel León-Portilla. Universidad Nacional Autónoma de México, Mexico City.

Vail, Gabrielle, and Christine Hernández

2012 Rain and Fertility Rituals in Postclassic Yucatan, Featuring Chaak and Chaak Chel. In *The Ancient Maya of Mexico: Reinterpreting the Past of Northern Maya Lowlands,* edited by Geoffrey Braswell, pp. 285–305. Equinox, Sheffield, England.

Velázquez, Adrián

2000 *El simbolismo de los objetos de concha encontrados en las ofrendas del Templo Mayor de Tenochtitlan.* Instituto Nacional de Antropología e Historia, Mexico City.

Velázquez, Primo Feliciano (editor)

1945 *Leyenda de los Soles.* In *Códice Chimalpopoca,*
pp. 119–64. Universidad Nacional Autónoma de
México, Mexico City.

Wieberg, Danielle, and Daniel Wescott

2008 Estimating the Timing of Long Bone Fractures:
Correlation between the Postmortem Interval, Bone
Moisture Content, and Blunt Force Trauma Fracture
Characteristics. *Journal of Forensic Sciences* 53(5):
1028–34.

Williams, Robert L.

2009 Codex Zouche-Nuttall, Pages 1–41: Narrative Structure, Contents, and Chronologies. PhD dissertation,
University of Texas at Austin.

Xochipiltécatl, Sandra

2004 El tzompantli: arqueología, iconografía, mitos y
simbolismo de un monumento mexica. Master's thesis,
Facultad de Filosofía y Letras, Universidad Nacional
Autónoma de México, Mexico City.

10

Emic Perspectives on Cultural Practices Pertaining to the Head in Mesoamerica

A Commentary and Discussion of the Chapters in Part One

GABRIELLE VAIL

INTRODUCTION

Using a diverse array of data from various time periods and locations throughout Mesoamerica, the authors in part 1 of this volume address a range of questions pertaining to the head. How was it viewed in different regions and at different time periods in relation to an individual's and society's concept of personhood and the self? What types of cranial modifications were practiced, and what did they signify? What types of essences or animating forces were believed to reside in the head, and was modifying the cranium an attempt to seal them?

Other important topics addressed by the authors include what constitutes a true portrait, and what is the relationship between the portrait and the individual portrayed. Also of interest in this respect is the question of how humans can take on the persona of deities, both in life and after death. Issues of identity are another of the central themes of these chapters; the authors discuss how identity is marked in various ways in relation to an individual's head. In addition to modifications to the cranium, they consider hairstyles and treatment of the hair in pictorial representations, the use of face paint, and dental modification.

With the recognition that the body is a cultural construct—a point considered either explicitly or implicitly in each of the chapters—questions concerning how it is molded, including when and by whom, become important features of the discussion. Rites of passage are therefore an important topic considered in these chapters, those occurring both during an individual's lifetime and at the time

of and after his or her death, as are modifications to the skull after death.

I begin my discussion with a brief summary of the individual contributions, emphasizing the data sets chosen for analysis. The chapters focusing on Mesoamerica can be divided along several different axes: (1) regional, with a contrasting emphasis between studies focused on the Maya area and those that examine data from the Basin of Mexico; (2) chronological, including those focused on Classic-period data sets (the majority of the chapters that concern the Maya area, as well as Luis Adrián Alvarado-Viñas and Linda Manzanilla's chapter on Teotihuacan) and those that consider later time periods, in particular the Late Postclassic in both the Maya area and central Mexico; and (3) topical, differentiating between those that focus on how heads were modified during an individual's lifetime and those that discuss postmortem modifications.

In the chapter "What Was Being Sealed?: Cranial Modification and Ritual Binding among the Maya" (chapter 2), William Duncan and Gabrielle Vail discuss the myriad animating essences and forces that have been identified in Classic-period epigraphic contexts, in an attempt to determine which, if any, were the object of containment through cranial modification of infants' heads. Moving beyond the Classic-period data, the authors examine Postclassic and colonial-period sources within this framework, concentrating specifically on childhood rites of passage. This analysis allows them to suggest new interpretations for several of the almanacs in the Madrid Codex and provides a broader context for future discussions of animating essences among Postclassic cultures that relies on data specifically from Yucatán, rather than being filtered through the lens of Postclassic central Mexico due to the influential work of scholars such as Alfredo López Austin (see further discussion below).

In chapter 3, Vera Tiesler and Alfonso Lacadena consider "Head Shapes and Group Identity on the Fringes of the Maya Lowlands." Their discussion focuses on the transmission of a shared cultural identity—a task carried out by women—through various means, including the shaping of infants' heads and spoken language. They find that western lowland Maya populations that likely spoke Western Ch'olan languages exhibit narrow, inclined, and elongated heads, which can be contrasted with those of their Tzeltalan neighbors at Toniná. Similar differences are attested in the southern lowlands, where the morphology of heads differs significantly among Maya speakers and populations from lower Central America. Based on their findings, Tiesler and Lacadena note that "cultural affinities that delineate ethnicity tend to be expressed by shared quotidian practices including but not limited to language, ideology, and group alignment in confrontation with outsiders and foreigners. . . . [A]mong Classic-period Maya lowlanders, head-shaping traditions must have counted among those identity-forging cultural measures in both the private and public spheres." They also claim that there was probably little recognition of affiliations among pre-Hispanic populations that we group together as "the ancient Maya," a point that researchers working in the Maya area would do well to take more fully into account in their analyses.

Chapter 4, by Andrew Scherer, is concerned with "Head Shaping and Tooth Modification among the Classic Maya of the Usumacinta River Kingdoms." Scherer provides a comprehensive discussion of the significance of the head in pre-Hispanic and contemporary Maya cultures, and he demonstrates the importance of the processes of molding and crafting in creating humans. Following this excellent introduction, he analyzes both Early and Late Classic skeletal remains from sites in the Usumacinta region, noting a lower than average percentage of skulls showing cranial modification (when compared to the Maya lowlands overall) in the former period, and a higher than average percentage during the Late Classic period. Like previous studies, he finds, however, that cranial modification occurs among both elite and non-elite populations and among males and females. On this basis, he concludes that the tabular oblique form favored in the western region served not as a means of marking social

affiliation but rather as a reflection of a more general belief found throughout this region in which heads were modified to resemble an ear of maize, in a manner similar to that of the maize deity. Similarly, dental modification was practiced by both elite and non-elite members of society and appears to have been undertaken in most cases to emulate the teeth of the sun god, who had a particularly strong "heat" or life force.

Scherer briefly considers why only certain skulls (and not all of them) were modified, because this was a common practice not only in the Usumacinta region but throughout the Maya area. Although he raises several possibilities, this is a question that requires further and more targeted investigation by bioarchaeologists and archaeologists alike.

The following chapter, by Luis Adrián Alvarado-Viñas and Linda R. Manzanilla, concerns "Cultural Modification of the Head: The Case of Teopancazco in Teotihuacan." Based on extensive excavations, the authors identify the Teopancazco neighborhood of Teotihuacan as the site of specialized craft production, focused specifically on the production of fine garments and headdresses. Examination of the physical remains of 129 individuals found in formal burials revealed seven skulls exhibiting cranial modification from a sample of thirty-eight individuals who were decapitated; five of these displayed tabular erect modification, and the other two had fronto-occipital tabular oblique modification. Each of the seven individuals with cranial modification was nonlocal, leading the authors to suggest that they were members of an elite group of craftspeople who were originally from sites along the corridor to the Gulf Coast and who maintained control over trade routes to their natal communities. Alvarado-Viñas and Manzanilla conclude with the observation that "[i]n a cosmopolitan society, body modification was a privileged tool for the display of ethnic and social differences."

This topic is further examined in chapter 6, "Face Painting among the Classic Maya Elites: An Iconographic Study" by María Luisa Vázquez de Ágredos Pascual, Cristina Vidal Lorenzo, and Patricia Horcajada Campos. The authors compiled and analyzed representations of individuals who exhibit face painting from Classic-period painted contexts, including both polychrome vessels and murals (although the former are more common). The elite individuals portrayed in these contexts were subdivided into specific classifications, including female personages, rulers and courtiers, warriors, ballplayers, and musicians. One finding of particular significance was that some of the elite women had certain designs that linked them to female deities, including the moon goddess. It was also the case that actors performing similar functions seemed to be painted in a similar manner, with the exception of musicians. Particular color choices were examined, with red and earth tones being predominant, but the authors also noted the importance of white and black. Although there is much still to be explained, this pivotal study lays the groundwork for future research on this topic.

In her chapter on "The Importance of Visage, Facial Treatment, and Idiosyncratic Traits in Maya Royal Portraiture during the Reign of K'inich Janaab' Pakal of Palenque, 615–683 CE" (chapter 7), Laura Filloy Nadal considers the nature of portraiture and addresses the question of what qualities, in addition to physical likeness, are required to construct a true portrait. She bases her study on an analysis of several representations of Pakal the Great from Palenque, made both during his lifetime and shortly after his death. She defines a portrait as both body and essence, noting that it shares these characteristics with human personages. Moreover, she follows López Austin (1993:112–39) in his claim that "the resemblance between god and image not only involved a transfer of light substance from the former to the latter; the 'object' charged with this supernatural power was considered to be the god itself." As she notes, studies from the Maya area support this claim as well and are further validated by hieroglyphic evidence.

In chapter 8, Virginia E. Miller addresses a topic that has been the subject of little prior discussion—"The Representation of Hair in the Art of Chichén Itzá." She argues, quite convincingly, that human hair played an important role in Mesoamerica, where it was believed to represent a receptacle for power, to provide protection for the life force that resided in the head, and, through its treatment, to serve as a means of marking gender and social roles. Using representations of human personages in the art from Chichén Itzá (and focusing primarily on murals), she seeks to test the long-standing belief among Mesoamericanists that distinctive head shapes and hairstyles signal ethnic differences. Her findings provide tentative support for this hypothesis in the two distinct—and at times antagonistic—groups represented in Chichén's murals. The possibility that blond hair and superior head flattening are associated with "foreign" (i.e., coastal) populations, and more specifically with merchants engaged in circumpeninsular trade, offers an important hypothesis for further testing.

In the following chapter, Ximena Chávez Balderas considers "Effigies of Death: Representation, Use, and Reuse of Human Skulls at the Templo Mayor of Tenochtitlan." She examines a data set of 108 decapitated victims from the Templo Mayor, which consists of adult males and females as well as subadults and children. She finds that human skulls occurred in temple offerings both as severed heads, which were likely to have been associated with the consecration of the temple, and as god effigies or modified skulls, some of which appear to have been repurposed after having been hung on the *tzompantli* racks, whereas others may have been used originally as architectural decoration or appeared on garments on statues of supernaturals. The latter category occurs most commonly with female deities associated with the earth, fertility, and death; effigy skulls, on the other hand, are most often in the form of Mictlantecuhtli, the god of death. According to Chávez Balderas's interpretation, skulls were incorporated into the Templo Mayor offerings to capture the life force that was released at death: bones, like seeds, were believed to lead to the germination of new life.

These chapters share a number of common themes, in particular concepts of personhood and the self; animating essences; cranial modification and cultural reproduction; rites of passage; issues of identity and ethnicity; and human-deity concurrence. The authors build on a number of seminal studies, including McKeever Furst (1995), Houston et al. (2006), Houston and Stuart (1998), López Austin (1988, 1993), Stuart (1996), and Turner (2007), among others. Their chapters expand on these earlier works, but, perhaps more significantly, they provide empirical data to help test and refine them.

Geographically and temporally, the focus of previous studies has primarily been on concepts of the person and the soul in central Mexico, based on the extensive ethnohistorical documentation available for this region, which relates specifically to Late Postclassic and colonial-period beliefs, and on similar concepts as they relate to Classic-period lowland Maya populations, found primarily in epigraphic contexts but also in iconographic sources from this time period. Little emphasis has been placed on sources from the northern Maya area prior to this volume (see the chapters by Duncan and Vail, and Miller), with the exception of a review of colonial dictionaries (Houston et al. 2006) and Vera Tiesler's extensive compendium in her recent volume on cranial modification (2014). Additionally, little has been written on colonial-period Yucatecan sources that speak to these questions, with the exception of the recent works of Timothy Knowlton (2010, 2015, 2018), some of which still await publication. While the authors in the present volume rely to a large extent on the earlier studies mentioned previously, they also emphasize relevant ethnographic material, as seen especially in the chapters by Duncan and Vail, and Scherer. Another significant innovation of the present volume is the common framework adopted by the authors concerning the role of the head in Mesoamerican cultures, as well as the cultural practices associated with it.

BELIEFS AND CULTURAL PRACTICES CONCERNING THE HEAD IN MESOAMERICAN CULTURES

Ethnohistorical and ethnographic data point to the fact that the head is understood throughout Mesoamerica as the source of perception and is therefore associated with reason and discernment. In this way, it contrasts with the souls or animating essences located in the heart. As Scherer notes in his chapter, Diego de Landa's *Relación de las cosas de Yucatan* (1978) makes it clear that, among the Yucatec Maya, the head, personal development, and fundamental humanness were intimately connected, much as can be seen in ethnohistorical sources from the Nahuatl-speaking region of central Mexico discussed by López Austin (1988).

Evidence of cranial modification can be discerned in the archaeological record over a period of several millennia (Tiesler 2014). Recent studies relate this to an understanding among Mesoamerican cultures that the body—and, by extension, the head—was unformed at birth and was meant to be crafted or molded during a person's lifetime, but especially during childhood and adolescence (Houston 2009; Houston et al. 2006; Scherer 2015). Among the Maya, this molding was like that of crafting objects from clay (Scherer, chapter 4 of this volume). Similarly, for central Mexican cultures, especially during the Postclassic period, children were seen as precious stones and other raw materials that needed to be worked (Joyce 2000).

Much of our understanding of concepts of personhood and animating essences for pre-Hispanic Maya cultures derives from epigraphic records concerning the upper echelon of society. There, we learn that the phrase *u-baah* refers specifically to a person's body (Houston et al. 2006:64); for example, *u-baah k'inich pakal* can be

translated as "it is his body, K'inich Pakal." The phrase can also be used more specifically to refer to an individual's head, and Filloy (chapter 7 of this volume) notes that u-baah refers to "the inherent property of the image as an extension of one's *body-essence*, so that the representation of a person was much more than a mere image." Following Stephen Houston and David Stuart (1998), she argues more specifically that an image contains "the substance and part of the essence and identity of the depicted personage," the two therefore being identified as coessential entities.

Throughout Mesoamerica, the head was the center of a person's identity, and it was the seat of the *tonalli* for central Mexican cultures. The tonalli, claimed by López Austin (1988) to represent one of three body souls, was linked with heat, energy, and vitality. It was said to attach itself to a fetus before birth and had to be protected from harm, as it could abandon the body, causing illness and even death (López Austin 1988). Whether earlier cultures in central Mexico shared in this belief is something that remains to be determined, and the identification of complementary concepts in the Maya area is also still being debated (see the chapters by Duncan and Vail, and Scherer). Perhaps the closest analogues include the Maya concepts of *ik'* (life force, wind, breath) and *k'inich*. Like the tonalli, k'inich is a force linked with energy, heat, and vitality. Both of these forces were believed to reside more strongly in rulers than in other people, and a person's k'inich increased over his or her lifetime (Velásquez García 2011).

Also important to our understanding of Mesoamerican concepts of the body and head is *ich*, the Maya term for "face" or "eye," as Vázquez de Ágredos Pascual et al. remind us in chapter 6. Their discussion of facial painting calls to mind ethnohistorical accounts, such as Landa's mention of covering the body with soot during times of fasting, the ointments women wore on their faces, and the practice of tattooing (Landa 1978:35, 52, 53). Similarly, Landa (1978:33) and other chroniclers describe common hairstyles worn by men and women, although they fail to draw specific connections such as those proposed by later authors (Houston et al. 2006:163–75; Miller, chapter 8 of this volume). The idea that certain types of facial decoration (including painting and tattooing) and hairstyles served to identify those who wore them with deities such as the maize god is a topic that will be considered in greater detail below.

Although difficult, if not impossible, to recognize in

the bioarchaeological record, one of the most important facets of the face was the eyes (also called *ich*). More specifically than the head, one's vision was considered a source of power. The creator deities in the Popol Vuh are identified as being "all seeing"; when they create the first humans, they must dim the humans' sight so that they are not equally powerful. Dimming the eyes (through blinding or blindfolding) is also a means by which deities and other entities having too much power (such as Seven Macaw in the Popol Vuh) are brought down (Vail and Hernández 2013). We are told: "Then the eyes of Seven Macaw were treated. His eyes were plucked, thus completing removing the previous metal from them. . . . Thus the basis for his pride was completely taken away" (Christenson 2007:100). Likewise, the sun's eyes are said to be damaged or torn out during an eclipse, causing this entity to lose its power and the world to plunge into darkness (Vail 2015).

That similar beliefs were also held in pre-Hispanic Mesoamerica can be ascertained from the mutilation of monuments, particularly with respect to the eyes (Houston et al. 2006:170). This demonstrates the coessential nature that Filloy discusses between image and the person portrayed. Duncan and Vail (chapter 2 of this volume) consider the importance of the face—and of the face as representing the whole—in their discussion of the manufacture of wooden deity effigies or masks in the Maya Madrid Codex. Although made of a different material, these masks appear to have a great deal in common with the masks made from the crania of sacrificial victims in central Mexico in that they serve both as offerings for and representations of particular deities (see Chávez Balderas, chapter 9 of this volume). There is much to be gained, I believe, from a more detailed examination of the treatment of the eyes of human figures represented in various media. Figurines may provide a rich source of material on this topic, with the proviso that any studies of this nature must be placed into a precise spatial-temporal context in order to allow the type of fine-grained analysis required.

The use of the *k'uh* glyph, signifying "god" or something having a divine or sacred quality, for a number of the deity effigies in the Madrid Codex is of interest beyond the simple correspondence between image and meaning. Exploration of contemporary Maya beliefs (see Scherer, chapter 4 of this volume) reveals the concept of *ch'ulel* (cognate with *k'uhul*, the adjectival form of *k'uh*) among the Tzeltal Maya of highland Chiapas. The ch'ulel is one

of many possible types of souls that can be found within a single person; it is said to be housed in the heart but to be capable of traveling outside of the body, which may occur when a person is sleeping or inebriated (Pitarch 2010:24–39). How closely this concept relates to that of k'uhul seen in Classic-period inscriptions is a topic that Scherer considers. Unlike the codical examples, Scherer notes that, in the Classic period, k'uhul occurs specifically in contexts relating to royal personages, who are described as the *k'uhul ajaw* ("lord" or "ruler") of a specific "emblem glyph," specifying the name of a particular location or lineage. Whether there is a relationship between k'uhul as used in Classic-period contexts and the concept of ch'uhul among contemporary Tzeltal speakers remains to be determined. Duncan and Vail propose that such a relationship may exist for the Postclassic Maya codices, suggesting that the use of the k'uh glyph to represent deity effigies was not simply a way of specifying their supernatural status but that it also referred to the ch'uhul-like quality of the vital, animate force that inhabited them following their creation.

When referring to humans rather than to supernaturals or humans with divine status, the term *winik* is commonly used. Although the term is usually translated as "man" or "person," Houston et al. (2006:11–12) suggest that it has a broader meaning referring to animate, sentient beings (see the discussion in Scherer, chapter 4 of this volume). Examples occurring in the Maya codices support this interpretation, as winik is used in reference to anthropomorphic beings (such as deer) that appear in scenes in which they are engaged in activities that we normally associate with human actions.

The pre-Hispanic codices from both the Maya area and highland Mexico have proved invaluable to our interpretations of the significance of the head and the many ways in which it was modified (both temporarily and permanently) among pre-Hispanic Mesoamerican populations. The contributions presented by Duncan and Vail (chapter 2) and Chávez Balderas (chapter 9) offer innovative studies along these lines, and it is to be hoped that future research will continue to explore these relatively untapped sources of information. Colonial-era texts and documents in indigenous Mayan languages provide another data set that remains to be more widely examined and applied. This is especially important to counterbalance prior attention on the K'iche' Popol Vuh, which serves as *the* source for many Mayanists, whether addressing highland or lowland cultures, or those from a millennia or more prior to when it was written. Recent studies by Timothy Knowlton of the Books of Chilam Balam (2010) and the Ritual of the Bacabs (2015, 2018) provide a useful overview of how Yucatec Maya people perceived their personhood during the colonial period, a time reflecting the survival of key preconquest conceptions of the body and syncrenistic beliefs and practices.

Many of the concepts expressed by contemporary and colonial Yucatec Maya people, like those discussed previously in relation to the Tzeltal, resonate with the discussions presented in this volume (see especially the chapters by Duncan and Vail, Scherer, and Filloy Nadal). These continuities are exciting to see, and it is clear from the research reported in the previous chapters that a number of general concepts were shared by Mesoamericans across both time and space. What is also evident is the need to examine these concepts in a temporal and spatial framework to avoid conflating them: to perceive the similarities that linked people and cultures in this area and also to discern the differences that made them unique from each other and fostered identities on a more local or regional level. The studies in this innovative volume make an especially good start at achieving this, as does Tiesler's recent monograph on this topic (2014).

METHODOLOGIES AND FINDINGS

Of particular interest to the authors in this volume is the use of a conjunctive methodology to gain an emic understanding of the body, in particular the head (*hool* among Yucatec speakers, or Classic *jol*). Following in the pioneering tradition of recent studies aimed at cultural understandings of cranial modification and related practices (e.g., Duncan 2009; Duncan and Hofling 2011; Lozada 2011; Tiesler 2014; Yépez 2006), the authors use a diverse array of data sets, including physical cranial remains, in conjunction with images painted on polychrome vessels and in murals and codices as well as those portrayed in stone, ethnohistorical sources from both central Mexico and the Maya area, indigenous-language texts, and ethnographic materials, to address questions concerning the meaning of such practices to the people who undertook them. A particular emphasis by many of the authors rests on exploring the ideas presented in 1989 by López Austin, who conceives the body as "both the core and link to the

human cosmos, perceptions, and thoughts. It is both the originating component and the recipient of human action and interaction" (Tiesler 2014:17). It is important to keep in mind, however, that his conclusions rely on his interpretations of data from colonial and Postclassic (codical) sources specifically from central Mexico and that, while they may serve as useful models, they should not be applied to other Mesoamerican cultures or time periods unless there are found to be direct connections between them. The same is likewise true of ethnographic analogy, as several of the volume's authors are careful to point out. Each case study must be examined, ultimately, within its own cultural context, and ethnographic and ethnohistorical sources used with caution to provide models that can then be tested against specific data sets. In the discussion that follows, I further explore the data sets considered by each of the authors to see what they reveal about personhood among the pre-Hispanic inhabitants of Mesoamerica.

Cultural Practices Pertaining to the Heads of Living Individuals

Cultural practices documented in the chapters pertaining to Mesoamerica are varied, but there is both physical and pictorial evidence for artificial shaping of the cranium and modification of the teeth during an individual's lifetime, as well as modification to the skull following an individual's death, which often occurred through sacrificial means. Additionally, ethnohistorical and iconographic sources indicate the importance of other cultural practices involving modifications to the face and head, including using facial paint, wearing certain ornaments and/or adornments (earplugs and occasionally nose plugs), and cutting or dressing the hair in certain styles. Certain of these practices were associated with infancy (i.e., the intentional modification of the cranium), whereas others were associated with adolescence or adulthood (see the chapters by Duncan and Vail, and Scherer).

Studies by Tiesler (2011, 2014) and others indicate that head shaping was a practice that mothers (and/or other female relatives) engaged in with their children, likely initially under the guidance of a midwife. Studies of the crania of both adults and children have shown that the gender of the child was incidental in terms of whether modification was practiced or the type of modification undertaken. Instead, other cultural factors (discussed below) probably accounted for this.

Ethnohistorical sources reveal that, during infancy, gender was not a significant factor in child-rearing practices (Joyce 2000; Tiesler 2014). The fact that midwives are reported as being responsible for instructing the mother in head shaping during the first few days of a child's life is of interest in that these older, postmenopausal women were believed to have special ties to the deity associated with procreation and childbirth, named Ix Chel in Postclassic Yucatán. This raises the question, considered by several of the authors, of the relationship between head shaping and identification with the supernatural world. One especially important connection, as Scherer notes, are similarities between scenes on pottery vessels depicting Maya deities molding human heads and the process by which infants' heads were molded by their human caretakers. The actors in both contexts are understood as artisans and the modification of infants' heads as the first step in creating humans.

For the Usumacinta region, Scherer notes that the form of the cranium was modeled after that of maize, or the maize god, perhaps projecting a visible statement about the origin of the people exhibiting this feature. In her discussion of portraits pertaining to the Palenque ruler Pakal, Filloy Nadal also notes similar cranial modifications associated with his image (and personage), suggesting that his role as ruler merged with that of the maize deity. Miller, on the other hand, notes that approximately 30 percent of the skeletal remains of sacrificial victims in the Sacred Cenote display superior head flattening, a trait that can be linked to cranial modifications practiced by coastal merchant populations, as suggested by research reported by Tiesler (2014). Tiesler has proposed that this form of modification was practiced to foster a resemblance with the form of the merchant deity's head, thereby creating a link between one's occupation and one's patron deity.

There is other evidence to suggest that certain types of modifications were practiced by distinct groups and that they acted as a visual means of distinguishing a particular group from neighboring populations. Tiesler and Lacadena (chapter 3 of this volume) find this to be the case of Maya people inhabiting the western area. An examination of cranial remains and depictions in the artwork at sites such as Palenque distinguish the narrow, inclined, and elongated heads of these populations from those of their neighbors, likely Tzeltalan speakers, at Toniná. To what purpose were these modifications made? Tiesler and Lacadena suggest that the modeled heads are a marker of group identity (and possibly ethnicity) and that there is good evidence for linking them to speakers of the Western Ch'olan languages. Scherer, on the other hand, believes that cranial modifications in the Usumacinta area did not signify a specific group identity so much as a shared underlying ideology.

Venturing outside of the Maya region, Alvarado-Viñas and Manzanilla's study (chapter 5 of this volume) is based on thirteen field seasons of excavations at Teopancazco, one of the neighborhood centers that formed part of Teotihuacan, and the recovery of the bones of 129 individuals. Analysis of the skeletal remains revealed an extremely heterogeneous population, suggesting that this area of the city was inhabited by people from a number of different regions (Manzanilla 2015). Of the individuals excavated, 38 of 129 had been decapitated, and 7 of these exhibited crania with evidence of cultural modification. Of interest to the current study is the authors' finding that most of the individuals who had been decapitated were of nonlocal origin, deriving from the corridor of territory leading toward the Gulf Coast. However, the individuals showing cranial modifications were not from a single lineage or ethnic group; rather, they came from different altitudes and had different genetic signatures.

Interpreting these data remains difficult, although the discovery at both Teopancazco and Chichén Itzá of sacrificed individuals who were clearly nonlocal (as suggested by cranial modifications that set them apart from the local population) raises further questions about both the meaning and the effects of these cultural practices. Although the details remain to be refined, it is clear that group identification and shared ideologies both played a role in the practice of cranial modification.

Other reasons for modifying an infant's cranium have been suggested relating to protecting the infant's soul or animating essence, which remained impermanently fixed until the child was older (Duncan and Hofling 2011; Tiesler 2014). Duncan and Vail consider this possibility in their chapter, noting ceremonies that occur later in a child's life (leading into puberty) that seem to support this idea. The "rebirth" or bathing ceremony described in ethnohistorical sources (referred to by Landa [1978:43–45] as "baptism") is also present in the Maya Madrid Codex. The sprinkling of sacred water on a child's head was apparently meant to strengthen his or her animating force (ik') and possibly heat (k'inich). It likewise appears that these ceremonies may have been intended to dedicate the child to a particular patron or protector deity, much as Markus Eberl (2013) describes taking place in the highland Mexican Borgia and related codices.

Other modifications that can be discerned in the physical record include those made to the teeth. These involved both filing and dental inlays. Scherer reports that in his sample from the Usumacinta region, 62.5 percent of elites (5/8) and 57.2 percent of non-elites (32/56) exhibit some form of dental modification. Like cranial modification, which was also unrelated to status in the Usumacinta area, dental modification was another aspect of the process of molding a Maya person. However, it took place following adolescence, suggesting to Scherer (chapter 4 of this volume) that it marked an important milestone in a person's life and may even have signified the completion of the process of maturing from adolescence to adulthood.

Most commonly, teeth were modified to resemble the ik' symbol, which gave them the appearance of the ik'-shaped teeth of the sun god. As a vibrant source of heat and power, the sun god was a potent symbol for people to emulate. Additionally, the practice of inlaying teeth with rare stones including jade, pyrite, and hematite was also occasionally followed; Scherer found that eight of the thirty-four individuals with modifications to their teeth from the Usumacinta River sample have inlays, most commonly of jade. He notes that jade—like teeth modified in the ik' pattern—has associations with wind and breath (Taube 2005). In combination with the tabular oblique cranial modification practiced in this region, these two types of dental modification serve to symbolize maize as the source of life and the material from which humans are believed to be formed.

Other types of modifications practiced by living people are known to us only through ethnohistorical sources and representations in the iconography, including the use of facial paint and treatment of the hair. From colonial-period sources, we know that the latter played an important role in age-grade rituals and rites of passage, and that treatment of the hair could also be indicative of certain statuses and occupations (see, e.g., Joyce 2000). The wearing of facial and body paint may have had a similar significance, as suggested by sources such as Landa's *Relación de las cosas de Yucatan* (1978:35, 52).

Miller's discussion of hairstyles at Chichén Itzá and in coastal populations (chapter 8 of this volume) adds significantly to our understanding of pre-Hispanic Maya practices and beliefs concerning hair and its treatment, a topic that has received little attention prior to now. Pre-

vious studies (López Austin 1988:221) suggest that hair was perceived to be a source of power and that it served as a means of protecting the life force that resided in the head (the tonalli among Nahuatl speakers). Moreover, it can be linked to human agency in that elaborate, controlled coiffures characterize individuals (most often of the elite class) who are in control of their lives, whereas prisoners and sacrificial victims are typically shown with disheveled hair to indicate their lack of agency (Houston 2001:210–11; Houston et al. 2006:25, 49, 204, 206).

Miller's study focuses on two sets of murals at Chichén that highlight two different ethnic groups—coastal populations and traders/warriors from Chichén Itzá. A particular type of hairstyle seen in Chichén's art, long hair studded with jade beads, may be interpreted as referring to maize as a precious substance (Karl Taube [2005] and others have demonstrated the metaphorical connection between jade and maize), or as highlighting a novel exotic commodity available at Chichén because of the new class of coastal merchants.

Miller also comments on the light-colored or yellow hair that appears in Chichén's murals. She suggests that it may be associated with coastal populations or, more specifically, with sacrificial victims, who are likened to the maize cob that is harvested. In this case, the association would be between its color and that of corn silk.

Miller's study, like that of Alvarado-Viñas and Manzanilla (chapter 5) and Tiesler and Lacadena (chapter 3), focuses on visual cues that are inscribed on human bodies and serve to mark the distinctiveness of one particular group in opposition to their neighbors and those living nearby. These could be permanent (such as cranial and dental modification) or of a more temporary nature. Tattooing, which falls into the former category, remains relatively little explored, but the use of pigments to modify the appearance of the face has received some attention. Both practices must be studied through visual representations, the latter most effectively through painted sources such as codices, polychrome pottery vessels, and murals. The study by Vázquez de Ágredos Pascual et al. (chapter 6) is a welcome contribution to this field of research, especially as it establishes some basic premises that can serve to lay the groundwork for future studies.

Based on an iconographic analysis of Maya pottery vessels, the authors argue that facial painting was employed for various reasons and that each example they survey may have had a different purpose. They show, through their analysis of representations of ballplayers and warriors, that painting the face, in much the same way as wearing clothing and adornments, functioned to differentiate individuals within a group. In the case of warriors, facial paint may also have been employed to hide an individual's features, which the authors attribute to an attempt to dehumanize them and situate them within the framework of an otherworldly experience.

Their analysis also suggests that facial painting may, on certain occasions, have been intended for symbolic purposes. Specifically, they note examples in which painted designs associate individuals with a particular deity. This occurs, for example, in the case of a number of female figures who have designs on their cheeks that resemble those seen with the goddess Ix Chel, or with warriors who have attributes of the Mexican rain deity Tláloc.

The authors consider the symbolism of particular colors, although they note that their study is skewed by the differential preservation of colors on pottery vessels. This is a limitation of their source material, as is the selection of pottery vessels they focus on, which includes a number from unprovenienced contexts, making it difficult to detect regional or temporal variation. Another issue that remains unaddressed includes overpainting on vessels that come from unprovenienced contexts and have entered the art market. The best way to control these factors would be to focus exclusively on provenienced materials, including both pottery vessels and images from murals. The Postclassic codices, although they feature deities rather than human figures, might also provide a useful point of departure.

Other ways in which identity is expressed include transcendent moments (unlike those communicated through permanent modifications such as those to the cranium) in which individuals take on the persona of specific deities. This may occur through dance or masked performances, among other means (see Houston et al. 2006; Looper 2009). These moments may also be captured in artistic representations on various media, in which case they attain permanence. Filloy Nadal (chapter 7 of this volume) discusses this concept in relation to depictions of individuals that can be classified as portraits, a term that refers to an image that moves beyond physical likeness to the subject in that it also contains the subject's essence. In commenting on the various portraits of K'inich Janaab' Pakal, she notes that they are characterized by "their beauty, deformed skull, tonsured forehead, step-cut bangs, elevated forelock, and jade jewels." These attributes served both to uniquely identify the individual portrayed and to highlight his connection with the tonsured maize god, whom Pakal embodied in both his life and his death.

Cultural Practices Pertaining to the Heads of Deceased Individuals

In contrast to the studies previously discussed, the chapter by Chávez Balderas (chapter 9) refers not to modifications made to the head or face of living individuals but rather to those that occurred after death (most commonly through sacrifice). All of the materials she examined, with the exception of one skull, were excavated from contexts within the Templo Mayor dating to Late Postclassic–period Tenochtitlan. They can be classified into two groups—the heads of sacrificial victims, which likely served as dedicatory offerings during the construction of the temple, and a series of modified skulls, some originally associated with skullracks, or tzompantli, and others with basal perforation and the so-called skull masks. This latter group served as effigies of deities, particularly those related to the earth and the underworld, which were deposited in special offerings within the temple.

Chávez Balderas examines the role played by these skulls in Aztec society prior to their deposition in the Templo Mayor offerings. Through an examination of codices, written documents, other skulls recovered from archaeological contexts, and Aztec sculpture, she is able to propose that skulls were worn as costume elements by Aztec priests and were also displayed on the sculptures of certain deities, including those related most closely to death, the earth, war, and regeneration (i.e., the *tzitzimime* and related supernaturals). It is interesting to note, however, that none of these deities is represented in the effigy skulls in the Templo Mayor offerings. Instead, supernaturals in these contexts were portrayed in the form of flint knives (associated with the death god Mictlantecuhtli), figurines, masks, and skulls. Chávez Balderas interprets them as beings that were "reenacting mythical passages and expressing sacred ideals." Effigy skulls were deposited in association with representations of various deities, including the fire god Xiuhtecuhtli, the rain deity Tláloc, and the wind god Ehécatl-Quetzalcóatl.

In considering the victims whose remains were included in the Templo Mayor offerings, Chávez Balderas notes that they included individuals from both sexes and all age classes. All of those analyzed were originally from nonlocal origins but had spent their last years in Tenochtitlan, which she interprets as suggesting that they were more likely slaves than enemies obtained in battle.[1] It is also of interest to learn that the victims were most likely sacrificed by heart extraction or having their throat slit.

DISCUSSION AND
CONCLUDING REMARKS

Chávez Balderas's findings bring to mind discussions of sacrificial victims in other chapters, where we learn that some were marked as being of nonlocal origin through outward physical signs, such as specific forms of cranial modification or depictions of them as having lighter-colored hair than local inhabitants. While the chapters in this section have broadened our understanding of cultural practices in different regions and time periods of Mesoamerica, we are still left with questions that only further research can answer. We have made great strides, however, in our understanding of emic conceptions of personhood and the self, souls and animating essences, and the cohabiting of the realms of the human and divine, and how these relate to the modification practices under discussion. The methodologies adopted by the authors, which pair analysis of physical remains with pictorial representations, epigraphic data sets, and ethnohistorical sources, provide the key to illuminating the emic perspective still further. Additional studies along these lines, broadening the regional and temporal parameters and making use of ever-expanding archaeological, epigraphic, and iconographic data sets, promise to provide an even greater depth of understanding. The contributors are to be commended for bringing to us, like the first humans in the Popol Vuh, a clarity of vision unmatched before now.

NOTE

1.   It is also the case, however, that enemies who were captured for sacrifice were often placed in the service of a temple in honor of a certain deity and that after a period of time they were then sacrificed to that deity.

REFERENCES CITED

Christenson, Allen
2007   *Popol Vuh: The Sacred Book of the Maya.* University of Oklahoma Press, Norman.

Ciudad Real, Antonio de
2001   *Calepino maya de Motul.* Edited by René Acuña. Plaza y Valdes Editores, Mexico City.

Duncan, William N.
2009   Cranial Modification among the Maya: Absence of Evidence or Evidence of Absence? In *Bioarchaeology and Identity in the Americas,* edited by Kelly Knudson and Christopher M. Stojanowski, pp. 177–93. University Press of Florida, Gainesville.

Duncan, William N., and Charles Andrew Hofling
2011   Why the Head? Cranial Modification as Protection and Ensoulment among the Maya. *Ancient Mesoamerica* 22:190–210.

Eberl, Markus
2013   Nourishing Gods: Birth and Personhood in Highland Mexican Codices. *Cambridge Archaeological Journal* 23(3):453–76.

Houston, Stephen
2001   Decorous Bodies and Disordered Passions: Representations of Emotion among the Classic Maya. *World Archaeology* 33(2):206–19.

2009   A Splendid Predicament: Young Men in Classic Maya Society. *Cambridge Archaeological Journal* 19(2):149–78.

Houston, Stephen, and David Stuart
1998   The Ancient Maya Self: Personhood and Portraiture in the Classic Period. *RES: Anthropology and Aesthetics* 33:73–101.

Houston, Stephen, David Stuart, and Karl Taube
2006   *The Memory of Bones: Body, Being, and Experience among the Classic Maya.* University of Texas Press, Austin.

Joyce, Rosemary A.
2000   Girling the Girl and Boying the Boy: The Production of Adulthood in Ancient Mesoamerica. *World Archaeology* 31:473–83.

Knowlton, Timothy
2010   *Maya Creation Myths: Words and Worlds of the Chilam Balam.* University Press of Colorado, Boulder.

2015   Literacy and Healing: Semiotic Ideologies and the Entextualization of Colonial Maya Medical Incantations. *Ethnohistory* 62(3):573–95.

2018   Flames, Icons and Healing: A Colonial Maya Ontology. *Colonial Latin America Review*, in press.

Landa, Diego de

1978   *Yucatan before and after the Conquest*. Translated by William Gates. Dover, New York.

Looper, Matthew

2009   *To Be Like Gods: Dance in Ancient Maya Civilization*. University of Texas Press, Austin.

López Austin, Alfredo

1988   *The Human Body and Ideology: Concepts of the Ancient Nahuas*. 2 vols. Translated by Thelma Ortiz de Montellano and Bernard Ortiz de Montellano. University of Utah Press, Salt Lake City.

1989   *Cuerpo humano e ideología: las concepciones de los antiguos nahuas*. Universidad Nacional Autónoma de México, Mexico City.

1993   *Hombre-dios: religión y política en el mundo nahuatl*. Instituto de Investigaciones Antropológicas, Universidad Nacional Autónoma de México, Mexico City.

Lozada, María Cecilia

2011   Marking Ethnicity through Premortem Cranial Modification among the Pre-Inca Chiribaya, Perú. In *The Bioarchaeology of the Human Head: Decapitation, Decoration, and Deformation*, edited by Michelle Bonogofsky, pp. 228–40. University Press of Florida, Gainesville.

Manzanilla, Linda R.

2015   Cooperation and Tensions in Multiethnic Corporate Societies Using Teotihuacan, Central Mexico, as a Case Study. *Proceedings of the National Academy of Sciences* 112(30):9210–15.

McKeever Furst, Jill Leslie

1995   *The Natural History of the Soul in Ancient Mexico*. Yale University Press, New Haven, Connecticut.

Pitarch, Pedro

2010   *The Jaguar and the Priest: An Ethnography of Tzeltal Souls*. University of Texas Press, Austin.

Scherer, Andrew K.

2015   *Classic Maya Mortuary Landscape: Rituals of Body and Soul*. University of Texas Press, Austin.

Stuart, David

1996   A Consideration of Stelae in Ancient Maya Ritual and Representation. *RES: Anthropology and Aesthetics* 29/30:148–71.

Taube, Karl A.

2005   The Symbolism of Jade in Classic Maya Religion. *Ancient Mesoamerica* 16:23–50.

Tiesler, Vera

2011   Becoming Maya: Infancy and Upbringing through the Lens of Pre-Hispanic Head Shaping. *Childhood in the Past* 4:117–32.

2014   *The Bioarchaeology of Artificial Cranial Modifications: New Approaches to Head Shaping and Its Meanings in Pre-Columbian Mesoamerica and Beyond*. Springer, New York.

Turner, Terence S.

2007   The Social Skin. In *Beyond the Body Proper: Reading the Anthropology of Material Life*, edited by Margaret M. Lock and Judith Farquhar, pp. 83–105. Duke University Press, Durham, North Carolina.

Vail, Gabrielle

2015   Iconography and Metaphorical Expression Pertaining to Eclipses: A Perspective from Postclassic and Colonial Maya Manuscripts. In *Cosmology, Calendars, and Horizon-Based Astronomy in Ancient Mesoamerica*, edited by Anne S. Dowd and Susan Milbrath, pp. 163–96. University Press of Colorado, Boulder.

Vail, Gabrielle, and Christine Hernández

2013   *Re-Creating Primordial Time: Foundation Rituals and Mythology in the Postclassic Maya Codices*. University Press of Colorado, Boulder.

Velásquez García, Erik

2011   Las entidades y las fuerzas anímicas en la cosmovisión maya clásica. In *Los mayas: voces de piedra*, edited by Alejandra Martínez de Velasco Cortina and María Elena Vega Villalobos, pp. 235–54. Editorial Ámbar, Universidad Nacional Autónoma de México, Mexico City.

Villa Rojas, Alfonso

1945   *The Maya of East Central Quintana Roo*. Carnegie Institution of Washington, Washington, DC.

Yépez, Rosaura

2006   *La práctica cultural de modelar la cabeza en dos culturas andinas del Antiguo Perú: Paracas y Chancay; un estudio de los procesos de significación de la cabeza modelada intencionalmente*. PhD dissertation, Universidad Nacional Autónoma de México, Mexico City.

PART TWO

Andes

❧

11

Afterlives of the Decapitated in Ancient Peru

JOHN W. VERANO

One of the most enigmatic aspects of decapitation practices among south coastal Peruvian Paracas and Nasca cultures (900 BC–AD 750) is the near absence of headless bodies in the archaeological record.

—Lisa DeLeonardis, "The Body Context: Interpreting Early Nasca Decapitated Burials"

Isolated human skulls and headless bodies appear sporadically in the archaeological record worldwide (Aufderheide 2009; Bonogofsky 2011; Knüsel and Smith 2013; Talalay 2004). These discoveries often provoke debates about the context and cultural meaning(s) of the intentional separation of head and body. While archaeological evidence suggests that headless bodies received only limited attention (abandonment or prompt burial; in fact, they are rarely found), disembodied heads frequently experience a more complex "afterlife"—one that may involve preparation to preserve the facial features and hair (Orchiston 1970) or modification of the skull, including flaying or defleshing, intentional breakage or sectioning of the cranium, surface decoration, and the attachment of suspensory cords and adornments (Andrushko 2011; Chávez Balderas 2014; Pijoan et al. 1989; Verano et al. 1999). Many historical accounts describe the practice of impaling or suspending severed heads for public display in prominent locations (O'Donnabhain 2011). These severed heads—or portions of heads such as skull bowls—often had an extended

period of use as objects of display and ritual before entering the archaeological record. Elaborate treatments of the head underline its symbolic importance, whether representing a specific person, such as a prominent enemy, or in a more generic form as a member of a particular social group.

DISEMBODIED HEADS IN ANDEAN SOUTH AMERICA

Examples of disembodied heads, both mummified and skeletonized, are known from many ancient cultures of Peru (Cordy-Collins 2001; Proulx 2001; Verano 1995, 2008a) as well as from historical groups in the Andean highlands and tropical rainforest of Peru and Ecuador (Castner 2002; Stirling 1938). The curation of ancestral skulls appears to have been a long tradition in the Andean highlands, which continues into the present (Allen 2002; Arnold and Hastorf 2008), and skulls collected from cemeteries are commonly used in modern times as guardians for homes and property (Mishkin 1946; Allen 2002). The intentional removal of skulls and other bones from tombs in pre-Hispanic times also has been reported from various sites in coastal Peru (Buikstra 1995; Millaire 2002, 2004; Rowe 1995).

Determining the origin, identity, and possible ritual/ political function of isolated skulls continues to be a challenge for archaeologists and biological anthropologists. Attempts have been made to develop theoretical models based on the interpretation (and reinterpretation) of iconography, but these have in many ways added greater complexity to the issue, as these models are difficult to test with archaeological data (Hill 2000; Weismantel 2015). Clearly, not all isolated skulls and mummified heads are the product of interpersonal violence, nor does every isolated skull or headless body represent a "sacrifice," "ritual offering," or "revered ancestor" (Guillén 1992; Lozada et al., chapter 12 of this volume; Verano 1995, 2008a). In order to simplify the discussion here, I will exclude cultural practices such as the removal of dry skulls or other skeletal elements from graves and focus instead on cases that present clear osteological evidence of decapitation of the *living* or the *recently dead*, with a specific focus on the "afterlives" of these decapitated victims.

THE IMPORTANCE OF SEPARATING THE HEAD FROM THE BODY

Decapitation is an act that carries multiple meanings. On its most basic level, it serves as a definitive act of killing, since being headless is incompatible with life. Decapitation is a visually powerful act as well, employed throughout history in the public executions of criminals or war captives (Östenberg 2009). Importantly, separation of the head from the body permanently *dis-integrates* the individual, complicating or denying normative mortuary treatment of the body, a severe form of punishment in and of itself. In all such cases of decapitation, the head is the focus of the event. The body from which it is separated generally receives little attention; it may be discarded in another location and left on the ground to decompose, or it may receive only a perfunctory burial (Buckberry and Hadley 2007). In most cases, the bodies of the decapitated simply disappear from the archaeological record, although other body parts, such as hands or feet, may be collected and curated as well (Alva and Donnan 1993; Donnan and Mackey 1978; Santiago 2011).

In contrast to a headless body, a severed head is both portable and of great visual impact, particularly in the case of recently severed or mummified heads that may display features that allow the recognition of that specific person (Chacon 2007:526; Larson 2014). Unlike decapitated bodies, severed heads may receive elaborate treatment and extended curation. An example from Peru is the mummified head of Atoc, a general whose head was made into a drinking vessel in the early sixteenth century for the Inka ruler Atahualpa, who would drink toasts from it to celebrate his military victories (Hemming 1970:54; Ogburn 2007). In cases such as these, severed heads (willingly or not) have an "afterlife" that transcends that of the body they left behind.

SOUTH AMERICAN TROPHY HEADS

Shrunken human heads were first reported by Spanish explorers in the early sixteenth century, and they continued to be made in the tropical rainforest of Ecuador and Peru until the early twentieth century (Castner 2002; Stirling 1938) (plate 21). Full-size trophy heads (mummified heads that retained the skull) also were prepared by the Mundurucú of Brazil until the early part of the twentieth century (Ihering 1907).

The best-known archaeological examples of human trophy heads are those prepared by the ancient Paracas and Nasca cultures of southern coastal Peru (fig. 11.1). More than one hundred have been excavated from south coast sites since the early twentieth century (Baraybar

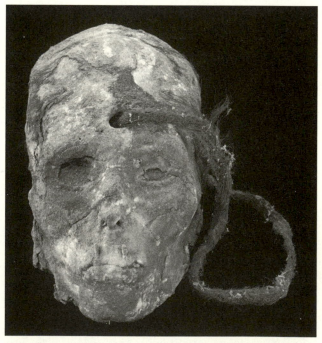

Figure 11.1. A Nasca trophy head, showing pinned lips and a suspensory cord made of the victim's hair emerging from a hole in the frontal bone (AF: 7050) (photo by John Verano, courtesy of the National Museum of Anthropology, Archaeology, and History, Lima).

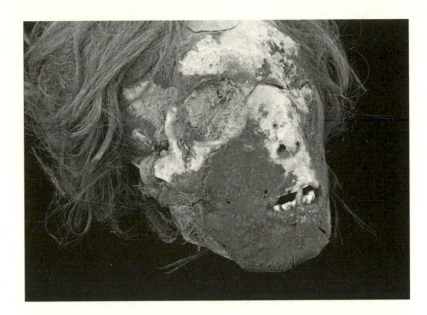

Figure 11.2. A Nasca trophy head, showing stuffing of the eye sockets and attachment of the mandible with cotton textile (AF: 7053) (photo by John Verano, courtesy of the National Museum of Anthropology, Archaeology, and History, Lima).

1987; Browne et al. 1993; Lozada et al., chapter 12 of this volume; Proulx 2001; Silverman and Proulx 2002; Verano 1995; Williams et al. 2001). These heads are easily recognizable by a hole in the frontal bone and breakage to the base or posterior portion of the skull. When well preserved, they retain mummified skin, scalp, and hair, and have a carrying cord that passes through the hole in the forehead and lips that are pinned shut with cactus spines. Their eye sockets and cheeks are often stuffed with cotton textile, apparently to retain a lifelike appearance (fig. 11.2).

Since the earliest reports of Nasca trophy heads by Max Uhle and Julio Tello (Tello 1918; Uhle 1914), there has been debate about the origin of these heads and their ritual significance. While Uhle considered them trophies based on his interpretation of Nasca iconography, Tello believed that these heads were not simply trophies but objects that carried important religious and political symbolism: "La cabeza ha sido ante todo un símbolo religioso; un símbolo de poder; fué el más preciado atributo de los dioses" (Tello 1918:58). Tello noted that, in a sample of eight trophy heads he examined, one was a child and three appeared to be females, and that all eight heads showed cranial deformation in the Nasca style. He concluded on this basis that these were likely not the heads of enemy warriors taken by the Nasca people (Tello 1918).

With a growing number of discoveries of Nasca trophy heads in the late twentieth century, the debate continued over whether these heads should be considered war trophies or not. Based on a collection of eleven heads found Chaviña, Peru, Vera Coelho argued that mummified Nasca heads should be considered ritual offerings rather than

trophies, as they were wrapped in textile, buried with various plant materials, and included the heads of a child and several females in addition to adult males (Coelho 1972; Neira Avendaño and Coelho 1972). More recently, Sonia Guillén proposed the hypothesis that Nasca mummified heads were not war trophies but instead were revered ancestors, based on the argument that the heads had been carefully prepared with particular attention to preserving the facial features (Guillén 1992). This argument, while novel, has little to support it, as there is neither ethnohistorical nor ethnographic evidence from Andean South America that fleshed heads were severed from the recently dead for the purpose of ancestor veneration. In contrast, there is abundant evidence from ethnohistorical sources on the Inka (Ogburn 2007), from numerous iconographic depictions of trophy heads by the Nasca and other pre-Inka societies (Cordy-Collins 1992, 2001; Proulx 2001), and from skeletal remains that documents cases in which the heads of captives and vanquished enemies were severed and modified in various ways (Andrushko 2011; Tung 2012; Verano 2008a). While less common in Nasca art, several examples of ceramic vessels showing decapitated bodies being fed upon by condors have recently been published (Pardo and Fux 2017: 238–39).

Attempts to resolve the revered ancestors or trophies debate continue. A recent attempt to identify the origins of a small sample of Nasca trophy heads using strontium isotopes found that the isotopic signatures fell within the range of a comparative sample of Nasca burials, ruling out distant origins for the heads. However, strontium isotope signatures do not indicate whether or not these heads were acquired in violent encounters. Nor does conflict need to be with long-distance enemies. No archaeologist today would argue that Nasca was an expansive military state that conquered distant polities (Silverman and Proulx 2002). Heads collected in conflicts within and between adjacent south coast valleys would be expected to show similar strontium isotope values. As I have argued elsewhere (Verano 1995, 2007), it is the treatment of Nasca trophy heads, their depiction in Nasca art, their demographic profile (predominantly young adult males), and the archaeological contexts in which they are found that provide the strongest support for their function as trophies. The most parsimonious interpretation is that they were heads taken in armed conflict, and not those of revered ancestors.

WARI TROPHY HEADS

More recent additions to the archaeological record of trophy taking in South America are Wari trophy heads. Previously known only as representations in Tiwanaku and Wari art, the fragmentary remains of more than thirty trophy heads have been excavated from ceremonial structures at the Wari heartland site of Conchopata, as well as at the southern hinterland sites of La Real and Beringa, located in the Majes Valley. The osteological remains of these heads as well as two unprovenienced specimens from the Majes Valley have been analyzed and described in detail by Tiffiny Tung (2008, 2012). Eight examples of trophy heads dating to the Middle Horizon (ca. 600–900 CE) have also been identified by Corina Kellner in her study of the Julio C. Tello skeletal collection from the Las Trancas Valley of the Río Grande de Nasca, southern coastal Peru (Kellner 2006). These new additions to the archaeological record are interesting in several respects. First, the trophy heads from Conchopata were prepared in a manner distinct from that of Nasca heads. The hole for a suspensory cord is located at the vertex of the skull vault rather than in the middle of the frontal bone, as is typical of Nasca trophy heads, and drilled holes are also present on the occipital bone. In some cases, holes were drilled through the ascending rami of the lower jaws, apparently to allow them to be tied to the skulls. Tung notes that the location of the suspensory cord hole in the Conchopata heads would allow them to hang in a horizontal position, like trophy skulls from some North American Indian cultures (Owsley and Jantz 1994; Seeman 1988). Tung's analysis of the Conchopata material revealed examples not only of adults but of at least seven children as well, whose crania were perforated in a similar manner as the adults (Tung and Knudson 2011). Many of the Conchopata trophy heads show evidence of burning, and all were intentionally crushed along with decorated ceramic vessels and placed as offerings in D-shaped and circular ceremonial architecture. No examples are known of burned or crushed Nasca trophy heads, although some have been found buried with simple offerings (Neira Avendaño and Coelho 1972).

In contrast to the Conchopata material, trophy heads from the Majes Valley described by Tung conform to Nasca canons, with suspensory cords through the frontal bone and no drilled perforations through the occipital bone or mandible. Brian Clifton Finucane (2008) has also described fragmentary trophy skulls from the Huarpa-era site of Nawinpukio in the Ayacucho Valley that show a mix of preparation techniques. Middle Horizon trophy heads from the Tello collection show some variations in preparation techniques but are most similar to earlier Nasca heads (Kellner 2006:91–92).

Valerie Andrushko has recently described an intact Wari-era trophy skull from the site of Cotocotuyoc in the Cuzco region, found as an isolated burial feature in a Wari cemetery (Andrushko 2011). It shows unusually elaborate modification, including multiple drill holes with metal tacks on the vault bones (apparently used to fix the scalp or some other object to the skull), a polished bone insert placed in the right parietal bone, and prosthetic teeth replacing ones apparently lost during preparation and handling of the head. This is an example of a head or skull that received unusual attention in its preparation. Although it shares some features with trophy skulls from the Wari homeland, it is distinctive in its complex treatment.

Interestingly, unlike the Nasca case, Wari trophy heads have not been the focus of debates about whether they were trophies or ancestors, although Tiffiny Tung and Kelly Knudson have explored the question by attempting to determine the geographic origins (local or distant) of these heads using strontium isotopes (Knudson and Tung 2007; Tung and Knudson 2011).

In comparing the iconography of trophy taking and the bioarchaeological evidence of such behaviors, chapters in this volume by Deborah Blom and Nicole Couture (chapter 13) and by Sara Becker and Sonia Alconini (chapter 15) note important dissimilarities between the two in the archaeological record of the Lake Titicaca region. They note that while trophy heads held by supernatural beings are depicted in Tiwanaku art, no archaeological evidence has been found anywhere in the Titicaca region of modified human skulls that could be interpreted as "trophy heads," with the possible exception of three partial crania from the Wata Wata site that show extensive perimortem fractures and cut marks suggestive of defleshing or mutilation (described by Becker and Alconini, chapter 15 of this volume). While the three crania do not show evidence of holes made for suspension or other modifications commonly seen in trophy heads, numerous cut marks indicate that they were extensively manipulated. The question remains whether Tiwanaku depictions of severed heads held by deities are purely symbolic representations, or whether heads were indeed severed and modified by the Tiwanaku people. Perhaps, as suggested by Blom and Couture, such evidence simply has not been found archaeologically. While there are ethnographic accounts of the collection and curation of heads in some modern Bolivian communities (described in both Blom and Couture's and Becker and Alconini's contributions in this volume), these practices were observed many centuries after the collapse of Tiwanaku and must be used with caution as potential models for reconstructing Tiwanaku head-collecting practices, particularly in the absence of archaeological evidence.

WHERE HAVE ALL THE BODIES GONE?

In the extensive debates over the function and identity of severed heads in the Andes, one issue that has received relatively little attention is that of the treatment and final disposition of the bodies of decapitation victims (DeLeonardis 2000). One explanation for this is the lack of archaeological evidence of decapitated bodies. More than one hundred Nasca trophy heads are known, and new discoveries continue to be made by archaeologists working on the south coast of Peru (Lozada et al., chapter 12 of this volume; Tung 2012; Verano 1995). What happened to their bodies? Only a few cases of headless Nasca burials have been described in detail. One of these is a case in which a mummified head was removed from a body in a tomb, not taken from a fresh body (Carmichael 1995). The other two are headless burials with associated grave goods. One of these was interpreted as a possible dedicatory burial (DeLeonardis 2000), the other as a sacrificial

offering (Conlee 2007). An alternative interpretation, equally possible in my opinion, is that these latter cases represent burials of the recovered bodies of decapitation victims that were given proper mortuary treatment by relatives. From the archaeological evidence alone, multiple scenarios are possible. What happened to the bodies of other individuals who were decapitated? Presumably these bodies, if buried, entered the archaeological record somewhere, but very few have been found. A dramatic exception is a recent discovery made in a walled compound at the Amato site in the Acarí Valley. In 2006, excavations directed by archaeologist Lidio Valdez recovered a mass burial of more than seventy decapitated bodies (Valdez 2009a, 2009b). A number had remnants of ropes around their ankles, indicating that victims were captured and restrained before being decapitated. The highly variable position of the bodies and the lack of any evidence of respectful burial or funerary offerings suggest perfunctory abandonment of the victims' remains. Where their heads ended up is unknown; they may reside today among collections of trophy heads from other south coast Nasca sites, or perhaps they are buried in some other location. This unique discovery at Amato is important in highlighting the incompleteness of the archaeological record and in suggesting that decapitated bodies await discovery at other sites. The Amato mass burial is also important in providing support for the argument that Nasca mummified heads were taken in violent encounters and not collected from deceased relatives as part of an ancestral cult. It should be noted in this context that headless bodies have not been found at Wari sites either, although they are known from Moche captive sacrifice sites (see below).

DECAPITATION AND PREPARATION OF TROPHY HEADS BY THE MOCHE

The Moche of northern coastal Peru (ca. 100–800 CE) are known to have decapitated war captives, as has been documented archaeologically in several large sacrificial deposits at the Pyramids of Moche (Verano 2001, 2014; Hamilton 2005) (plate 22) and at the site of Dos Cabezas (Cordy-Collins 2001). Modified trophy skulls and skull bowls have also been found discarded in occupational refuse at the Pyramids of Moche (Verano et al. 1999; Verano 2014) (fig. 11.3), and both severed heads and headless skeletons were found in the two large sacrificial deposits at the site. Defleshing cut marks on modified skulls from

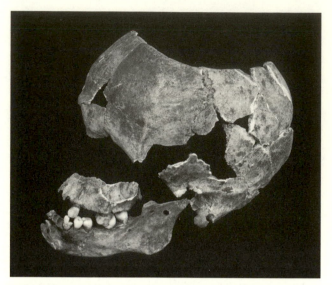

Figure 11.3. Moche trophy skull vessel found discarded in a residential compound at the Pyramids of Moche. It shows perforations for attachment of the mandible, and a section of the skullcap is cut away (photo by John Verano, courtesy of the Huaca de la Luna Archaeological Project).

the Pyramids of Moche indicate that they were prepared from fleshed heads, not from dry skulls collected from burials or other contexts. Their final deposition in sacrificial deposits or as isolated finds in occupational refuse supports the hypothesis that these are trophy skulls, not curated ancestral remains. And, similar to the Nasca and the Wari, Moche artists included trophy heads in scenes depicting warriors and the sacrifice of captives, as well as in scenes with "decapitator" deities who hold sacrificial knives and severed human heads (Cordy-Collins 2001; Uceda, Morales, and Mujica Barreda 2016).

CONTEXTUALIZING SEVERED HEADS

A multidisciplinary approach to severed heads and decapitated bodies is necessary if we hope to properly contextualize these discoveries. Approaches that have been explored to date include determining the biological profile (age and sex) of the decapitated, the ways in which heads were manipulated (as shown by breakage, perforations, and cut marks), and the archaeological context in which heads were found (carefully buried or discarded, located in ceremonial or nonceremonial contexts). The way in which severed heads are depicted in art may provide insight into how they were conceptualized and used,

and ethnohistorical accounts of the Inka making drinking vessels from the mummified heads of prominent enemies provide a comparative reference (Rowe 1946; Ogburn 2007). Finally, some recent studies have employed stable isotope analysis as a means to determine the geographic origin of heads (local or nonlocal dietary signals) (Finucane 2008; Tung and Knudson 2011).

Each of these approaches is helpful in interpreting discoveries of isolated human heads. The biological profile of the victims may indicate the nature and scale of violent conflict, distinguishing between organized warfare (in which the victims are expected to be fighting-age men) and small-scale raiding (in which older adults, women, and children may also be targeted) (Tung 2010; Verano 2014). The retention of articulated cervical vertebrae and cut marks can help distinguish a head freshly severed from a body from a skull taken from a mummified or decomposed body (Klaus 2010; Toyne 2011; Verano 1995). Extensive postmortem modification of the head, such as flaying, defleshing, breaking open the base of or sectioning the skull, and drilling holes for suspensory cords and the attachment of the mandible, are typical features of trophy heads, not of curated ancestral skulls in the Andes (Andrushko 2011; Ogburn 2007; Tung 2008, 2012; Verano 2003, 2008a). The location in which heads are found may provide important contextual information as well. Wari trophy heads have been found intentionally crushed, burned, and buried along with fine ceramic vessels as offerings in ceremonial buildings, while Nasca trophy heads were usually buried in simple pits on hillsides and in various locations at ceremonial centers. Moche modified skulls, in contrast, have been found discarded in residential compounds (Verano 2014; Verano et al. 1999). Of course, the full "life history" of a particular head prior to its final deposition or discard cannot be reconstructed from archaeological evidence alone, although some clues, such as polished and worn bone surfaces from extensive handling and the replacement of lost teeth, may indicate extended use (Andrushko 2011; Verano et al. 1999). Interestingly, while Paracas and Nasca trophy heads have been found as isolated burials in cemeteries (Neira Avendaño and Coelho 1972; Pezzia Assereto 1968), only rarely are they reported as grave offerings in tombs (for a notable exception, see Lozada et al., chapter 12 of this volume). In a study by Patrick Carmichael of the contents of 213 Nasca tombs, only 4 included trophy heads, and in one of them the head appeared to belong to the occupant of the tomb, reunited with his decapitated body (Carmichael 1988:481–83). The rarity of trophy heads or skulls as funerary offerings elsewhere in the Andes suggests that it may have been considered inappropriate (or perhaps even dangerous) to be buried with severed heads or trophy vessels made from one's enemies, although among the Moche, for example, weapons and ceramic representations of captives have been found in high-status tombs of males (Alva and Donnan 1993; Verano 2008b), and in one case in the tomb of a high-status female (Mujica Barreda et al. 2007).

Artistic depictions of supernaturals or armed warriors holding severed heads and knives, or heads shown on poles or suspended by cords, convey a clear message of violent acquisition and intentional display of vanquished enemies (Cordy-Collins 1992, 2001; Proulx 2001; Verano 1995), although these are symbolically charged images that can be interpreted in diverse ways (Verano 2001).

Stable isotope analysis of bone and teeth of trophy heads may be useful for distinguishing locals from those of distinct geographic origins (Knudson and Tung 2007; Tung and Knudson 2011), although this information alone cannot indicate whether a skull was that of an enemy taken in battle or an ancestor brought from another region. Nor can it indicate whether death was natural or by violent means. In these cases, the treatment of heads, the ways in which head taking and display are illustrated in the art of cultures such as the Nasca, Moche, and Wari, and the archaeological context in which these heads are found is of greater diagnostic value, in my opinion, for distinguishing trophies from ancestral skulls.

CONCLUSIONS

Examples of disembodied heads, both mummified and skeletonized, are known from many ancient cultures of Peru. With relatively few exceptions, their bodies have disappeared from the archaeological record, underlining the importance of the head as representing the essence and life force of an individual, whether kin or enemy. Heads intentionally separated from bodies had diverse and often extended afterlives in the pre-Hispanic Andes. While some were defleshed and modified as skull vessels, others were intentionally mummified in order to preserve facial features and hair, making them recognizable after death. The collection, preparation, and use of human heads encompassed a diverse range of activities, including human sacrifice, warfare, and the ritual reinterment of human remains. Ethnographic accounts of the manipulation of skulls in traditional communities in contemporary highland Peru and Bolivia suggest some continuity in indigenous concepts of the symbolic and multivalent nature of human heads, although, as Blom and Couture caution in chapter 13 of this volume, modern ethnographic accounts must not be interpreted uncritically as indicating a homogeneous pan-Andean worldview or as reflecting an unchanging past.

Historical sources on the Inka do provide some insight into the practice of taking and modifying the heads of enemies, although both the iconographic and archaeological record of pre-Inka societies provides much of the physical evidence of trophy taking and display. Despite increasing knowledge of the range of treatments of the head in ancient Peru, debate continues over the symbolic meaning and context of head taking. While theoretical models may provide a means of further exploring the possible meaning of head collection and curation in ancient Andean societies, these models must be supported by well-contextualized archaeological evidence to be convincingly demonstrated.

REFERENCES CITED

Allen, Catherine J.

2002 The Hold Life Has: Coca and Cultural Identity in an Andean Community. 2nd ed. Smithsonian Institution Press, Washington, DC.

Alva, Walter, and Christopher B. Donnan

1993 *Royal Tombs of Sipán.* Fowler Museum of Cultural History, University of California, Los Angeles.

Andrushko, Valerie A.

2011 How the Wari Fashioned Trophy Heads for Display: A Distinctive Modified Cranium from Cuzco, Peru, and Comparison to Trophies from the Capital Region. In *The Bioarchaeology of the Human Head: Decapitation, Decoration, and Deformation*, edited by Michelle Bonogofsky, pp. 262–85. University Press of Florida, Gainesville.

Arnold, Denise Y., and Christine Ann Hastorf

2008 *Heads of State: Icons, Power, and Politics in the Ancient and Modern Andes.* Left Coast Press, Walnut Creek, California.

Aufderheide, Arthur C. (editor)

2009 *Overmodeled Skulls.* Heide Press, Duluth, Minnesota.

Baraybar, José Pablo

1987 Cabezas trofeo Nasca: nuevas evidencias. *Gaceta Arqueológica Andina* 15:6–10.

Bonogofsky, Michelle (editor)

2011 *The Bioarchaeology of the Human Head: Decapitation, Decoration, and Deformation.* University Press of Florida, Gainesville.

Browne, David M., Helaine Silverman, and Rúben García

1993 A Cache of 48 Nasca Trophy Heads from Cerro Carapo, Peru. *Latin American Antiquity* 4:274–94.

Buckberry, Jo L., and Dawn M. Hadley

2007 An Anglo-Saxon Execution Cemetery at Walkington Wold, Yorkshire. *Oxford Journal of Archaeology* 26:309–29.

Buikstra, Jane Ellen.

1995 Tombs for the Living . . . or . . . for the Dead: The Osmore Ancestors. In *Tombs for the Living: Andean Mortuary Practices*, edited by Tom D. Dillehay, pp. 229–55. Dumbarton Oaks, Washington, DC.

Carmichael, Patrick H.

1988 Nasca Mortuary Customs: Death and Ancient Society on the South Coast of Peru. Unpublished PhD dissertation, Department of Anthropology and Archaeology, University of Calgary.

1995 Nasca Burial Patterns: Social Structure and Mortuary Ideology. In *Tombs for the Living: Andean Mortuary Practice*, edited by Tom D. Dillehay, pp. 161–87. Dumbarton Oaks, Washington, DC.

Castner, James Lee

2002 *Shrunken Heads: Tsantsa Trophies and Human Exotica.* Feline Press, Gainesville, Florida.

Chacon, Richard J.

2007 Seeking the Headhunter's Power. In *The Taking and Displaying of Human Body Parts as Trophies by Amerindians*, edited by Richard J. Chacon and David H. Dye, pp. 523–46. Springer, New York.

Chávez Balderas, Ximena

2014 Sacrifice at the Templo Mayor of Tenochtitlan and Its Role in Regard to Warfare. In *Embattled Bodies, Embattled Places: War in Pre-Columbian Mesoamerica and the Andes*, edited by Andrew K. Scherer and John W. Verano, pp. 171–97. Dumbarton Oaks, Washington, DC.

Coelho, Vera Penteado

1972 *Enterramentos de cabeças da cultura Nasca.* Universidade de São Paulo, São Paulo.

Conlee, Christina A.

2007 Decapitation and Rebirth: A Headless Burial from Nasca, Peru. *Current Anthropology* 48:438–45.

Cordy-Collins, Alana

1992 Archaism or Tradition? The Decapitation Theme in Cupisnique and Moche Iconography. *Latin American Antiquity* 3:206–20.

2001 Decapitation in Cupisnique and Early Moche Societies. In *Ritual Sacrifice in Ancient Peru*, edited by Elizabeth Benson and Anita Cook, pp. 21–33. University of Texas Press, Austin.

DeLeonardis, Lisa

2000 The Body Context: Interpreting Early Nasca Decapitated Burials. *Latin American Antiquity* 11:363–86.

Donnan, Christopher B., and Carol J. Mackey

1978 *Ancient Burial Patterns of the Moche Valley, Peru.* University of Texas Press, Austin.

Finucane, Brian Clifton

2008 Trophy Heads from Nawinpukio, Perú: Physical and Chemical Analysis of Huarpaera Modified Human Remains. *American Journal of Physical Anthropology* 135:75–84.

Guillén, Sonia

1992 The Chinchorro Culture: Mummies and Crania in the Reconstruction of Preceramic Coastal Adaptation in the South Central Andes. Unpublished PhD dissertation, Department of Anthropology, University of Michigan.

Hamilton, Laurel S.

2005 Cut Marks as Evidence of Precolumbian Human Sacrifice and Postmortem Bone Modification on the North Coast of Peru. Unpublished PhD dissertation, Department of Anthropology, Tulane University, New Orleans.

Hemming, John

1970 *The Conquest of the Incas.* Harcourt Brace Jovanovich, New York.

Hill, Erica

2000 The Embodied Sacrifice. *Cambridge Archaeological Journal* 10:317–26.

Ihering, Rodolpho von

1907 As cabeças mumificadas pelos indios Mundurucús. *Revista do Museu Paulista* 7:179–201.

Kellner, Corina M.

2006 "Trophy" Heads in Prehistoric Peru: Wari Imperial Influence on Nasca Head-Taking Practices. BAR International Series, 1539. British Archaeological Reports, Oxford.

Klaus, Haagen D.

2010 Bioarchaeology of Human Sacrifice: Violence, Identity, and the Evolution of Ritual Killing at Cerro Cerrillos, Peru. *Antiquity* 84(326):1102–22.

Knudson Kelly, and Tiffiny A. Tung

2007 Using Archaeological Chemistry to Investigate the Geographic Origins of Trophy Heads in the Central Andes. In *Archaeological Chemistry: Analytical Techniques and Archaeological Interpretation*, edited by Michael D. Glascock, Robert J. Speakman, and Rachel Popelka-Filcoff, pp. 91–98. American Chemical Society, Washington, DC.

Knüsel, Christopher, and Martin Smith (editors)

2013 *The Routledge Handbook of the Bioarchaeology of Human Conflict*. Routledge, Abingdon, Oxon, England.

Larson, Frances

2014 *Severed: A History of Heads Lost and Heads Found*. Liveright Publishing, New York.

Lastres, Juan B.

1951 *Historia de la medicina peruana*. Vol. 1, *La medicina incaica*. Imprenta Santa Maria, Lima.

Millaire, Jean-François

2002 *Moche Burial Patterns: An Investigation into Prehispanic Social Structure*. BAR International Series, 1066. British Archaeological Reports, Oxford.

2004 The Manipulation of Human Remains in Moche Society: Delayed Burials, Grave Reopening, and Secondary Offerings of Human Bones on the Peruvian North Coast. *Latin American Antiquity* 15:371–88.

Mishkin, Bernard

1946 The Contemporary Quechua. In *Handbook of South American Indians*. Vol. 2, *The Andean Civilizations*, edited by Julian H. Steward, 411–70. Smithsonian Institution, Bureau of American Ethnology, Washington, DC.

Mujica Barreda, Elías, Eduardo Hirose Maio, and Fundación Augusto N. Wiese

2007 El Brujo: Huaca Cao, centro ceremonial Moche en la Valle de Chicama. Fundación Augusto N. Wiese, Lima.

Neira Avendaño, Máximo, and Vera Penteado Coelho

1972 Enterramientos de cabezas de la cultura Nasca. *Revista do Museu Paulista* 20:109–42.

O'Donnabhain, Barra

2011 The Social Lives of Severed Heads: Skull Collection and Display in Medieval and Early Modern Ireland. In *The Bioarchaeology of the Human Head: Decapitation, Decoration, and Deformation*, edited by Michelle Bonogofsky, pp. 122–38. University Press of Florida, Gainesville.

Ogburn, Dennis E.

2007 Human Trophies in the Late Pre-Hispanic Andes. In *The Taking and Displaying of Human Body Parts as Trophies by Amerindians*, edited by Richard J. Chacon and David H. Dye, pp. 505–22. Springer, New York.

Orchiston, D. Wayne

1970 *Preserved Maori Heads in the Australian Museum, Sydney*. Dominion Museum, Wellington, New Zealand.

Östenberg, Ida

2009 *Staging the World: Spoils, Captives, and Representations in the Roman Triumphal Procession*. Oxford University Press, Oxford.

Owsley, Douglas W., and Richard L. Jantz

1994 *Skeletal Biology in the Great Plains: Migration, Warfare, Health, and Subsistence*. Smithsonian Institution Press, Washington, DC.

Pardo, Cecilia, and Peter Fux (editors)

2017 *Nasca*. Asociación Museo de Arte de Lima; Gráfico Biblos, Lima; Museum Rietberg, Zürich.

Pezzia Assereto, Alejandro

1968 *Ica y el Perú precolombino*. Vol. 1, *Arqueología de la provincia de Ica*. Editora Ojeda, Ica, Peru.

Pijoan Aguadé, Carmen, Alejandro Pastrana, and Consuelo Maquivar

1989 El tzompantli de Tlatelolco una evidencia de sacrificio humano. *Estudios de Antropología Biológica* 4:561–83.

Proulx, Donald A.

2001 Ritual Uses of Trophy Heads in Ancient Nasca Society. In *Ritual Sacrifice in Ancient Peru*, edited by Elizabeth Benson and Anita Cook, pp. 119–36. University of Texas Press, Austin.

Rowe, John H.

1946 Inca Culture at the Time of the Spanish Conquest. In *Handbook of South American Indians*. Vol. 2, *The Andean Civilizations*, edited by Julian H. Steward, pp. 183–330. Smithsonian Institution, Bureau of American Ethnology, Washington, DC.

1995 Behavior and Belief in Ancient Peruvian Mortuary Practice. In *Tombs for the Living: Andean Mortuary Practices*, edited by Tom D. Dillehay, pp. 27–41. Dumbarton Oaks, Washington, DC.

Sallnow, Michael J.

1987 *Pilgrims of the Andes: Regional Cults in Cusco*. Smithsonian Series in Ethnographic Inquiry. Smithsonian Institution Press, Washington, DC.

Santiago, Mark

2011 *The Jar of Severed Hands: Spanish Deportation of Apache Prisoners of War, 1770–1810.* University of Oklahoma Press, Norman.

Seeman, Mark F.

1988 Ohio Hopewell Trophy-Skull Artifacts as Evidence for Competition in Middle Woodland Societies circa 50 BC–AD 350. *American Antiquity* 53:565–77.

Silverman, Helaine, and Donald A. Proulx

2002 *The Nasca.* Peoples of America. Wiley-Blackwell, Oxford.

Stirling, M. W.

1938 *Historical and Ethnographical Material on the Jivaro Indians.* Bulletin 117. Smithsonian Institution, Bureau of American Ethnology, Washington, DC.

Talalay, Lauren E.

2004 Heady Business: Skulls, Heads, and Decapitation in Neolithic Anatolia and Greece. *Journal of Mediterranean Archaeology* 17:139–63.

Tello, Julio C.

1918 El uso de las cabezas humanas artificialmente momificadas y su representación en el antiguo arte peruano. Ernesto R. Villarán, Lima.

Toyne, J. Marla.

2011 Interpretations of Pre-Hispanic Ritual Violence at Tucume, Peru, from Cut Mark Analysis. *Latin American Antiquity* 22:505–23.

Tung, Tiffiny A.

2008 Dismembering Bodies for Display: A Bioarchaeological Study of Trophy Heads from the Wari Site of Conchopata, Peru. *American Journal of Physical Anthropology* 136:294–308.

2010 Childhood Lost: Abductions, Sacrifice, and Trophy Heads of Children in the Wari Empire of the Ancient Andes. *Latin American Antiquity* 21:44–66.

2012 *Violence, Ritual, and the Wari Empire: A Social Bioarchaeology of Imperialism in the Ancient Andes.* University Press of Florida, Gainesville.

Tung, Tiffiny A., and Kelly J. Knudson

2011 Identifying Locals, Migrants, and Captives in the Wari Heartland: A Bioarchaeological and Biogeographical Study of Human Remains from Conchopata, Peru. *Journal of Anthropological Archaeology* 30:247–61.

Uceda, Santiago, Ricardo Morales, and Elías Mujica Barreda

2016 *Huaca de la Luna: templos y dioses Moches = Moche Temples and Gods.* World Monuments Fund Perú; Fundación Backus, Lima.

Uhle, Max

1914 The Nazca Pottery of Ancient Peru. *Proceedings of the Davenport Academy of Sciences* 13:1–46.

Valdez, Lidio M.

2009a Walled Settlements, Buffer Zones, and Human Decapitation in the Acari Valley, Peru. *Journal of Anthropological Research* 65:389–416.

2009b Conflicto y decapitación humana en Amato (valle de Acarí, Perú). *Bulletin de l'Institut Français d'Études Andines* 38:177–204.

Verano, John W.

1995 Where Do They Rest? The Treatment of Human Offerings and Trophies in Ancient Peru. In *Tombs for the Living: Andean Mortuary Practices,* edited by Tom D. Dillehay, pp. 189–227. Dumbarton Oaks, Washington, DC.

2001 War and Death in the Moche World: Osteological Evidence and Visual Discourse. In *Moche Art and Archaeology in Ancient Peru,* edited by Joanne Pillsbury, pp. 111–25. National Gallery of Art, Washington, DC.

2003 Mummified Trophy Heads from Peru: Diagnostic Features and Medicolegal Significance. *Journal of Forensic Sciences* 48:525–30.

2007 Conflict and Conquest in Prehispanic Andean South America: Archaeological and Osteological Evidence. In *Latin American Indigenous Warfare and Ritual Violence,* edited by Richard Chacon and Rubén Mendoza, pp. 105–15. University of Arizona Press, Tucson.

2008a Trophy Head-Taking and Human Sacrifice in Andean South America. In *Handbook of South American Archaeology,* edited by Helaine Silverman and William H. Isbell, pp. 1047–60. Springer, New York.

2008b Communality and Diversity in Moche Human Sacrifice. In *The Art and Archaeology of the Moche: An Ancient Andean Society of the Peruvian North Coast,* edited by Steve Bourget and Kimberly L. Jones, pp. 195–213. University of Texas Press, Austin.

2014 Warfare and Captive Sacrifice in the Moche Culture: The Battle Continues. In *Embattled Bodies, Embattled Places: War in Pre-Columbian Mesoamerica and the Andes,* edited by Andrew Scherer and John W. Verano. Dumbarton Oaks, Washington, DC.

Verano, John W., Santiago Uceda, Claude Chapdelaine, Ricardo Tello, María Isabel Paredes, and Victor Pimentel

1999 Modified Human Skulls from the Urban Sector of the Pyramids of Moche, Northern Peru. *Latin American Antiquity* 10:59–70.

Weismantel, Mary

2015   Many Heads Are Better Than One: Mortuary Practice and Ceramic Art in Moche Society. In *Living with the Dead in the Andes*, edited by Izumi Shimada and James L. Fitzsimmons, pp. 76–100. University of Arizona Press, Tucson.

Williams, Sloan R., Kathleen Forgey, and Elizabeth Klarich

2001   An Osteological Study of Nasca Trophy Heads Collected by A. L. Kroeber during the Marshall Field Expeditions to Peru. *Fieldiana: Anthropology*, n.s., 33:1–132.

12

Head Processing in the La Ramada Tradition of Southern Peru

MARÍA CECILIA LOZADA, ALANNA WARNER-SMITH, REX C. HAYDON,
HANS BARNARD, AUGUSTO CARDONA ROSAS, AND RAPHAEL GREENBERG

INTRODUCTION

The collection and study of trophy heads in the Andes begun with studies by Max Uhle (1901), Julio C. Tello (1918), and Alfred Kroeber (1937) in the first half of the twentieth century. In fact, Uhle coined the term "trophy head" and interpreted these heads as war memorabilia, souvenirs in the form of defeated victims' heads. While "trophy head" is still the term used to describe these heads in the modern literature, it may not encompass the range of cultural practices and attitudes associated with head taking. The removal of the head from the body has been documented extensively among past Andean societies, including the Paracas, Nasca, Wari, Moche, Chimu, Inka, and, more recently, among La Ramada people who inhabited the Vitor Valley of southern Peru about one thousand years ago.

In this chapter, our discussion is centered on the Nasca and Wari cultures, whose trophy heads have been studied from a myriad of different perspectives. Our recent archaeological research suggests that La Ramada people interacted with both Nasca and Wari cultures throughout their history, and, as such, may present a context within which to study the meaning and role of trophy heads. Unlike the majority of the cases discussed in the Andes, these heads have been recovered from collective, semi-intact burials. We provide a description of the archaeological context as well as the demographic and health

patterns of four such heads uncovered over the course of our excavations in 2012. We also present preliminary interpretations, proposing that the heads may have come from males who were engaged in interpersonal violence outside their community. We hypothesize that the heads were removed from the dead bodies at the place of death and transported back to the communities for additional treatment and final burial.

NOMENCLATURE

Western interpretations of the body permeate the literature regarding trophy heads in the Andes. It is within this context that the term "trophy head" is used, based on the theory that they were taken as mementos of war success. This theory does not, however, consider alternative meanings that severed heads may have had in the Andes. Denise Arnold and Christine Hastorf (2008), for example, allude to these shortcomings in their work on the Andean and Amazonian head. They argue that the head, in its many manifestations, is conceptualized in relation to other body parts and is a dynamic symbol of ideology, politics, and ritual. Their work points to a plethora of interpretations of the head in the past and present, and it highlights the complexities and challenges of interpreting these types of cultural practices from the archaeological and bioarchaeological record. Given the extensive ethnographic examples provided by these authors, the term "trophy head" may be misleading or limiting in the sense that the term itself defines a very specific practice and dismisses alternative interpretations associated with the separation of the head from the body. Perhaps more importantly, the term might preclude native understandings of the body. A review of the literature suggests a number of terms that may be worth considering in lieu of "trophy head." These include "severed head," "detached head," "disembodied head," "decapitated head," and "isolated head." It is important, however, to note that these alternatives may also be problematic. For example, "severed head" describes a specific form of manipulating the head. "Disembodied head" ignores the ways in which manipulated heads might be reembodied or transformed into something new, while both "disembodied" and "isolated" head implicitly support the idea of a whole, bound body from which the head was severed.

Thus, researchers must be careful when using the term "trophy head," as it implies specific war practices such as the collection of enemy heads on the battlefield. We choose "isolated head" or, simply, "head" to avoid such connotations. Most importantly, in choosing these terms, we do not mean to assume a Western conception of the body; nor, in choosing "isolated," do we imply that these heads are removed from material and social relations.

NASCA HEADS

The Nasca, who inhabited the southern coast of Peru between 280 BCE and 820 CE, are known not only for their geoglyphs, textiles, and pottery but also for their isolated heads (Proulx 2001; Silverman and Proulx 2002). In 1901, Max Uhle referred to these heads as trophies, positing that they had been collected as war trophies among the Nasca (Uhle 1901). His interpretation was based on accounts of warfare by the Jíbaros from Ecuador, who were known for their skilled preparation of the shrunken heads of their enemies. Known as tsantsas, these reduced heads required significant labor to produce, and their production was embedded in rituals that were meant to ensure the transfer of powers from the victim to the taker of the head (Arriaza et al. 1998).

According to Helaine Silverman (1993), the Peruvian scholar Julio C. Tello was the first archaeologist to collect isolated heads from Nasca-affiliated sites along the central coast of Peru. Contrary to Uhle, Tello (1918) suggested that the manipulation of Nasca heads was not linked to

war but rather that the head was intended to revere ancestors. More than one hundred Nasca heads have been documented since Uhle's and Tello's initial studies (Verano 1995), and debates among scholars have focused on the meaning of such practices and the identity of the heads. John Verano (1995) has suggested that heads represent symbols of defeated enemies based on the fact that the overwhelming majority of the heads belong to males and also on the abundance of Nasca imagery depicting male warriors, males holding severed heads, and males wearing garments such as belts with severed heads attached. Others, following Tello's interpretation, propose that isolated heads were used to honor ancestors based on the significant efforts made to preserve the face (Guillén 1992; Neira Avendaño 1990; Tello 1918).

An alternative scenario is provided by Donald Proulx (2006), who has argued that, among the Nasca, heads were removed in ritual battles between factions of the same ethnic group. Within this context, head removal was not associated with war practices but was done for religious purposes. In such specific contexts, Proulx argues, isolated heads were buried in caches to promote agricultural fertility.

Kelly Knudson and her collaborators have shown that Nasca heads, recovered by Kroeber in 1925 and 1926 and now kept by the Field Museum of Natural History in Chicago, came from the same populations that buried them (Knudson et al. 2009). These results dovetail with the study of ancient DNA conducted by Kathleen Forgey (2011), who used individuals from the same collection together with additional samples recovered from the Pisco Valley to the north and Acarí Valley to the south for comparison. Forgey found that Early Nasca–period heads are derived from Nasca Valley populations. In other words, in this specific case, heads not only came from the same geographic area but also appeared to be linked biologically to Nasca communities that inhabited the Rio Grande drainage. As Forgey states, these heads came from "insiders" and not from members of other societies (2011:299). This research is an important milestone in the study of isolated heads; however, this biological data alone tells us little about the identity of the individuals from whom the heads were obtained.

The meaning behind these practices is further complicated by Christina Conlee's work (2007), which reports that the demographic profiles of the heads change through time. For instance, during the earlier phases of Nasca (1–450 CE), examples of isolated heads included all age groups and both sexes, while later it appears that the practice was primarily confined to adult males. Several interpretations have emerged to explain these demographic patterns. Silverman and Proulx (2002), for example, suggest that with the demise of Cahuachi around 500 CE, male leaders may have engaged in headhunting to enhance their status and power, while Elizabeth Arkush and Tiffiny Tung (2013) argue that the Nasca do not exhibit the archaeological correlates of organized war. Based on the patterns of cranial and postcranial trauma in post-Cahuachi skeletal collections, they suggest that physical violence might have occurred as a result of internal conflict in the later years of this society.

Nasca heads are characterized by the removal of a portion of the occipital and the presence of a perforation in the frontal bone (Verano 1995; Williams et al. 2001). These researchers have identified significant variations within this basic pattern. Some of the more complex preparations included separating the mandible, stuffing the nasal cavities, defleshing, and placing a wig on the scalp. This wide variation in production styles may be related to changes in methodology over time. Alternatively, the lack of standardization in head modification may suggest that the practice was not performed according to established protocols, as is evident among the Wari (Tung 2008). Therefore, among the Nasca, head preparation may have been practiced at the household level rather than performed by specialists who followed regimented patterns.

Despite numerous studies of Nasca isolated heads (Knudson et al. 2009; Verano 1995; Williams et al. 2001), the archaeological record provides only limited contextual information on this practice. A handful of heads have been recovered from single tombs, but the majority of them have been excavated from ceremonial structures and burial pits around these structures (Verano 1995, Williams et al. 2001). In 1989, the largest single cache of heads was discovered in the Nasca region. As reported by John Verano (1995) and David Browne et al. (1993), the collection includes forty-eight skulls, most of which are from males between twenty and forty-five years of age at death, with fronto-occipital cranial modification in a style associated with the Nasca. All individuals came from the same community, as cranial modification in the Andes was used as a sign of group membership (Blom and Couture, chapter 13 of this volume; Lozada and Buikstra 2002). As the cache was disturbed, the precise function of this unique finding remains unknown. Nevertheless, the fact that all skulls exhibited a uniform head form corroborates the hypothesis that head taking occurred within the same community, or at least a group with a shared identity. The extraordinarily diverse contexts within which these heads have been found highlight the various roles and meanings of Nasca heads and suggest that a single explanation for this practice cannot be gleaned from their archaeological context.

The multiple roles bestowed upon these heads appear to be mutually exclusive in terms of interpretation, falling either into a "trophy of war" or "venerated ancestor" dichotomy. It is important, however, to bear in mind that the meaning and roles of isolated heads may have changed during the eight hundred years of Nasca history. Furthermore, it is imminently possible that severed heads may have had multiple, simultaneous uses and meanings; in other words, what is observed in the archaeological record does not necessarily document the full spectrum of activities associated with the procurement, preparation, curation, use, and reuse of these heads. Despite the variation in production and burial location, head taking and curation continued as an essential practice throughout the history of the Nasca, highlighting its importance in their world view.

WARI HEADS

The Wari centralized their power in Huari, near Ayacucho in the highlands of central Peru, around 750 CE and are known as the first expansive empire in the Andes (Schreiber 1992). In contrast to the Nasca heads, the study of the manipulation of heads by the Wari is a relatively recent addition to the Andean archaeological and bioarchaeological literature. Tiffiny Tung (2012) has studied a variety of Wari collections in an effort to reconstruct Wari imperialistic practices from a bioarchaeological perspective. Her study revealed that the Wari engaged in activities such as battles and raids that resulted in a high incidence of cranial trauma. She noted the production of isolated heads from a range of demographic backgrounds that included adults and subadults as well as males and females. Females were considerably less common than males, however. Also, unlike Nasca heads, their production seems to have been tightly regulated. For example, there is uniformity in the location of the hole at the apex of the cranium and similar treatment of the occipital bone (Tung 2008). An analysis of stable strontium isotopes in selected heads demonstrates that not all of them were from the Wari heartland. Individuals apparently from other geographic areas may have been perceived as enemies. Unlike the Nasca heads, Wari heads were recovered from public ritual spaces, including a D-shaped structure (Tung 2008). Isolated heads and displays of body parts by the Wari appear intended to create a culture of fear at a time of imperial expansion (Tung 2012).

From this brief review, it is clear that there were significant differences between Nasca and Wari cultural practices involving heads. For the Nasca, the meaning of isolated heads remains unclear, while the Wari heads may reflect interpersonal violence and power dynamics at a time of expansion outside the Ayacucho basin. Nasca and Wari, the two most widespread cultures present in the area at the time, interacted and influenced each other between 550 and 750 CE, as evident from ceramic forms and settlement patterns (Schreiber and Lancho Rosas 2003). Nevertheless, it is unclear whether such encounters resulted in any detectable convergence in the understanding of the human body, or perceptions of the head and its uses after death.

THE VITOR VALLEY OF SOUTHERN PERU

Recent archaeological work in the Vitor Valley of southern Peru, located approximately forty kilometers southwest and downhill of Arequipa, has offered an opportunity to examine the practice of head manipulation in the the local La Ramada tradition (fig. 12.1). Our initial survey in 2008 identified a wide range of well-preserved sites throughout the valley (Nigra et al. 2017). Among these sites, we recorded seventeen La Ramada cemeteries but no La Ramada habitation sites. In 2012 and 2014, we excavated V-05, a relatively accessible and well-preserved cemetery, in an effort to define the biological and cultural dimensions of La Ramada tradition in the Vitor Valley.

René Santos Ramírez (1980) coined the term "La Ramada" after his excavation and analysis of five burials in the northern Siguas Valley. He places La Ramada tradition in the second part of the Middle Horizon, based on

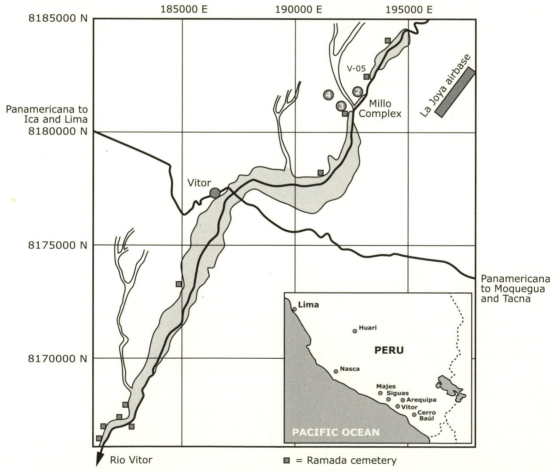

Figure 12.1. The Vitor Valley in southern Peru. Coordinates are projected onto Zone 19K of the WGS84 geode, and each box is 5,000 × 5,000 meters square (figure by Hans Barnard).

TABLE 12.1. OVERVIEW OF THE RESULTS OF RADIOCARBON ANALYSIS OF SAMPLES FROM MILLO 2

SAMPLE	UCI AMS#	MATERIAL	RADIOCARBON AGE (BP)	CALIBRATED DATE (2σ) OX CAL 4.2.3
Millo 2; U5-L12112-SCemN-T4	131675	Vegetal	1625±15	422–530 cal AD (95.4%)
Millo 2; U1-L4169-SC-R1	131679	Camelid hair	1620±15	425–531 cal AD (95.4%)
Millo 2; ULdeT-L12613-SCemN-T18	131661	Charcoal	1600±20	427–550 cal AD (89.9%); 557–573 cal AD (5.5%)
Millo 2; U5-L20291-SCemN-T7	131663	Charcoal	1575±20	442–454 cal AD (2.2%); 463–590 cal AD (93.2%)
Millo 2; 12462	131676	Vegetal	1260±15	770–880 cal AD (95.4%)
Sample 0784	84315	Charcoal	1255±20	730–736 cal AD (1.0%); 771–892 cal AD (94.4%)
Millo 2; ULdeT-L12506-SCemN-T14	131678	Cotton	1250±15	772–882 cal AD (95.4%)
Millo 2; 17385	131677	Vegetal	1245±15	772–885 cal AD (95.4%)
Millo 2; U2-L5339-SC-R8	131660	Charcoal	1240±20	771–889 cal AD (95.4%)
Sample 0804	84318	Charcoal	1240±15	778–891 cal AD (95.4%)
Sample 3037	84313	Charcoal	1235±20	776–896 cal AD (92.2%); 925–937 cal AD (3.2%)
Sample 3043	84316	Charcoal	1235±15	777–895 cal AD (95.4%)
Millo 2; T1-F7-L4151	131662	Charcoal	1220±15	773–819 cal AD (25.9%); 836–897 cal AD (59.2%); 932–958 cal AD (10.3%)
Sample 0756	84317	Charcoal	1210±15	781–792 cal AD (3.5%); 806–904 cal AD (55.7%); 915–966 cal AD (36.2%)
Millo 2; U3-L4373-SC-R5	131659	Charcoal	1205±15	779–812 cal AD (5.8%); 842–905 cal AD (44.4%); 916–969 cal AD (45.1%)
Sample 3038	84314	Charcoal	1200±20	782–789 cal AD (1.6%); 810–847 cal AD (7.9%); 857–978 cal AD (85.9%)
Sample 1047	84320	Charcoal	980±20	1036–1156 cal AD (95.4%)
Sample 1021	84321	Charcoal	957±20	1035–1160 cal AD (95.4%)
Sample 1029	84319	Charcoal	935±20	1047–1083 cal AD (23.8%); 1140–1214 cal AD (71.6%)

three radiocarbon dates around 850 CE (Santos Ramírez 1980). While Santos did not link La Ramada to any known tradition in the Andes, Joerg Haeberli (2001) suggested direct Nasca influence in La Ramada textiles after his study of surface materials from different cemeteries in the area, including the Vitor Valley. In his sequence, Haeberli defines the textile tradition with radiocarbon dates from 144 to 755 CE as Siguas 3. He indicated that textiles from this phase were found in association with the double-spouted lentil-shaped vessels defined by Santos (1980) in La Gamio, La Ramada's cemetery located in the Vitor Valley.

Our excavations also included work at the Millo Complex, a Wari colonial administrative and ceremonial center located in the northern part of the valley and dated to about 850 CE. In Millo 2, we found a significant quantity of La Ramada ceramics within the Wari-style architecture, suggesting that there was close interaction between Wari-associated inhabitants and the local La Ramada culture. In addition, our radiocarbon dates from Millo overlap with those from Santos, further indicating that Wari occupation of the Vitor Valley overlapped with La Ramada, adding to the evidence that some form of interaction occurred between La Ramada people and Wari highlanders (table 12.1). In this respect, La Ramada represents an autochthonous population with both coastal Nasca and highland Wari cultural influences. The radiocarbon dates obtained from V-05 correspond to an early phase of La Ramada occupation in the valley around 550 CE. These dates coincide with those obtained by

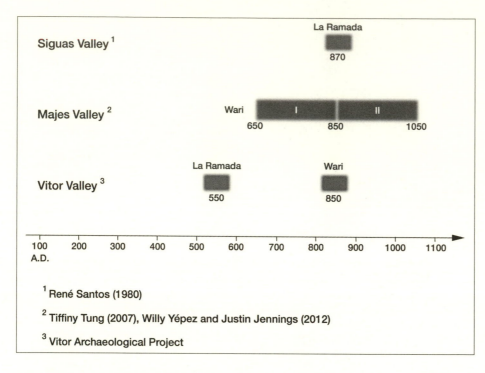

Figure 12.2. La Ramada and Wari radiocarbon dates from the Majes, Siguas, and Vitor Valleys (figure by Anurag Kumar).

Haeberli (2001) and correspond to the Late Nasca period in the Rio Grande region, 440–630 CE. It is during this time that abandonment of the ceremonial and political center of Cahuachi occurs and when much of Nasca head activity took place (Donald Proulx, personal communication, 2015). There is substantial evidence of interaction between La Ramada and the Wari in the Millo complex around 850 CE (fig. 12.2). Based on our study, La Ramada is partly defined by a long-standing mortuary tradition that did not change substantially after the arrival of the Wari in the Vitor Valley. We intend to conduct further excavations in the Vitor region to identify both the nature of La Ramada through its long history and its relationship with the Wari during the Middle Horizon.

CEMETERY V-05

Site V-05 is a cemetery located about two kilometers north of the Wari administrative center, known as Millo 2 (fig. 12.3). Our excavation at V-05 confirmed the presence of La Ramada tradition as defined by Santos and confirms the assessment by Haeberli that there are some Nasca-influenced elements in the textile tradition. Although looting occurred throughout the pre- and postcontact history of the cemetery, many mortuary contexts still contained their original contents such as the typical La Ramada double-spouted lentil-shaped

vessels in situ (fig. 12.4). In fact, human remains were rarely removed, making it possible to reconstruct their life histories and aspects of their mortuary ritual. The predominant burial pattern in this cemetery was a pit shaped like a boot, with the tip oriented west or southwest. There was little variety in the layout and construction of the tombs, apart from some variations in their size and depth. We are not sure if size differences are associated with the status of the deceased or with other aspects of their social persona. The excavated funerary pits exhibited evidence of multiple internments including neonates, subadults, adult males, adult females, and isolated heads. The relationship between the individuals in these group burials is currently under study, with theories ranging from social or biological family groups to community-wide collective burials performed at regimented points in time. Tomb reentry (Lozada et al. 2013) occurred during antiquity and may reflect ongoing interaction between the living and the dead, a practice that may have reinforced collective notions of social or biological identity among all participants (alive or dead) during and after burial.

TRAUMA ASSOCIATED WITH VIOLENCE

Our osteological analysis of the individuals buried in this cemetery revealed at least four adult males and three adult

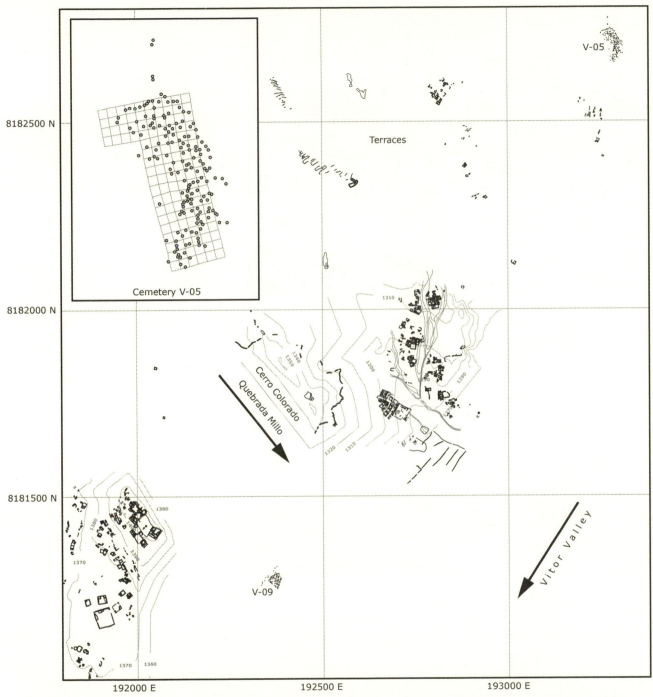

Figure 12.3. The central part of the Millo complex in the Vitor Valley. Coordinates are projected onto Zone 19K of the WGS84 geode, and each box is 500 × 500 meters square. The Wari administrative center, Millo 2, is in the center of the map and the ceremonial site, Millo 3, in the bottom left. Cemetery V-05 is in the upper-right-hand corner. (Our grid consisted of squares measuring roughly 5 × 5 meters; figure by Hans Barnard.)

females who exhibited evidence of trauma possibly associated with interpersonal conflict (table 12.2). For instance, the occupant of tomb 15 showed a depressed fracture caused by blunt force to the left frontal bone. In addition, the left zygomatic bone shows a well-healed fracture, while

a healed lesion in the left temporal bone was produced by a sharp, straight object. Postcranial remains exhibited healed fractures in the anterior and posterior part of the thorax. Similar patterns of cranial and postcranial trauma among the Wari have been attributed to injuries caused

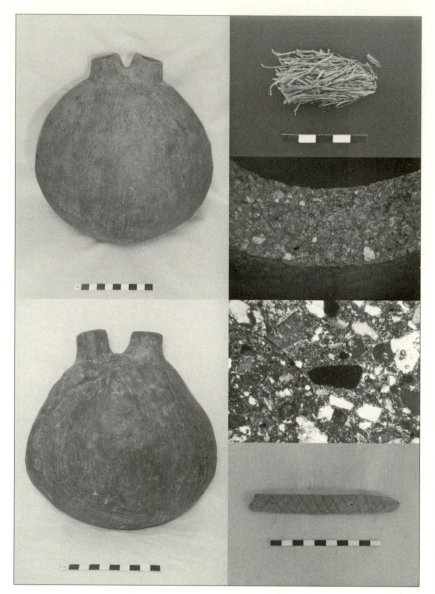

Figure 12.4. Typical La Ramada double-spouted lentil-shaped vessels found in cemetery V-05. Top left: vessel V-05-15-#12491; top right: vegetable bung found inside V-05-15-#12491 on the left; bottom left: vessel V-05-18-#12601; bottom right: pyro-engraved stick found inside V-05-18-#12601 on the left; and center right: macroscopic image of typical La Ramada fabric (V-05-03-#12134) and thin section in cross-polarized light of the typical La Ramada fabric (V-05-13-#12454). The abundant, poorly sorted, angular inclusions were identified as volcanic glass and metal fragments among mostly plagioclase and biotite minerals (photos by Hans Barnard).

TABLE 12.2. OVERVIEW OF THE INDIVIDUALS RECOVERED FROM V-05 DISPLAYING EVIDENCE OF TRAUMA MOST LIKELY ASSOCIATED WITH INTERPERSONAL VIOLENCE

TOMB	ELEMENTS	AGE	SEX	TRAUMA
8	Skeleton; Head only	Adult; Adult	M; M	Healed anterior and posterior thorax trauma; Healed right rib fracture (#8); Healed right clavicle fracture; Multiple healed fractures
14	Skeleton; Skeleton	Adult; Adult	F; F	Healed right rib (#5–7) fractures; Healed left fibula fracture; Healed right rib fracture (#2)
15	Skeleton	18 years	M	Healed right rib fracture (#6); Mid-shaft fracture of left ulna
17	Skeleton	Adult	M	Multiple healed cranial traumas; Healed anterior and posterior thorax trauma; Healed fracture of right radius
18	Skeleton	Adult	F	Healed left rib fracture (#11)

by face-to-face combat (Tung 2008). In our collection, trauma among males was present in both the cranial and postcranial remains, whereas the trauma observed in two female skeletons was limited exclusively to the ribs. These patterns seem to suggest that although interpersonal physical combat was practiced by both sexes, there may have been a gender-specific manner in acts of violence.

HEADS

Our skeletal sample includes four isolated heads that exhibit some Nasca influence in their postmortem treatment, for instance in the location of the frontal perforation and the manipulation of the occipital (Verano 1995; Williams et al. 2001). As can be seen in figures 12.5, 12.6, and 12.7, and plate 23, all specimens have an irregular perforation in the frontal bone. In addition, parts of the occipital and temporal bones have been removed. In two cases, cords protruding from the forehead were found in situ. A cord sample from specimen 12112 yielded a date of 422–530 CE (table 12.1), placing this head at the time of the end of the Nasca culture on the central coast but prior to the emergence of the Wari in the Ayacucho basin.

Detailed examination of these specimens followed standard procedures involving macroscopic human bone analysis (Buikstra and Ubelaker 2004) and CT scans. Three of the four heads were of adult males (table 12.3), while one was younger than twenty years. In the latter case, skeletal sex was indeterminate.

The demographic pattern seen among our sample of isolated heads corresponds to the general Nasca profiles described by Verano (1995) and Tung (2007). Tung's comparative data shows that male adults were the preferred group from which to procure heads, particularly during the Middle Nasca (540–550 CE) and Late Nasca (550–750 CE) periods. In our sample, only one isolated head exhibited healed cranial trauma in multiple locations, which suggests

that this individual engaged in at least one interpersonal combat event. We have not found evidence of acute head trauma that could be interpreted as the cause of death, although this may be due to our relatively small sample. Certainly, postcranial trauma could have been the cause of death in these circumstances and would not be evident in isolated crania.

Altogether, these heads have been recovered from mortuary contexts with multiple individuals. Without DNA analysis, it is impossible to define the biological relationships between the individuals in these contexts. Nevertheless, it appears that the inclusion of isolated heads in such collective burials may be associated with a funerary unit, either biological or social, represented in the mortuary ritual. Below, we provide a summary of these heads and their contexts.

Specimen 12590, Tomb 18

Condition
This specimen is fragmented and exhibits preserved soft tissue. A few patches of the scalp with attached hair were found on the left parietal and the upper-left portion of the occipital bone. While no complete mandible was found, a fragment of the right condyle indicates that the mandible was not detached when processing this head. No evidence of defleshing was detected.

Age
The age range is between twelve and twenty years. The lack of complete fusion of the palatine incisive suture suggests an age at death of less than twenty years, and a socket for a fully developed upper canine indicates that the individual was at least twelve years old.

Sex
Due to the estimated age and fragmentary nature of the head, sex is indeterminate.

TABLE 12.3. OVERVIEW OF THE ISOLATED HEADS RECOVERED FROM V-05 IN 2012

TOMB SAMPLE	AGE	SEX	MANDIBLE	TRAUMA
18; 12590	< 20 years	Indeterminate	Present	No
8; 12385	Adult	Male	Present	Multiple healed fractures
4; 12112	Adult	Male	Present	No
3; 11497	Adult	Male	Absent	No

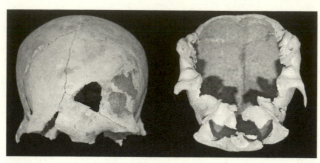

Figure 12.5. Anterior and basilar views of isolated head #12590 (photo by M. C. Lozada).

Perimortem modification

This head exhibits a large perforation located in the frontal bone immediately above the glabella and slightly toward the left orbital margin. The perforation is bell shaped, and cut marks are visible at the base of the bell. The nuchal planum and the basilar portion of the occipital bone have been removed. Three cut marks have been identified on the remainder of the occipital bone (fig. 12.5).

Context

Although the upper part of the tomb was slightly disturbed, the head was found in situ along with the remains of an adult woman (Maass 2014), two infants of approximately thirty-six to forty weeks of age, and an older child between nine and twelve months of age (Cyriac 2014). The head was located in the lower portion of the tomb at the same level as the other individuals, suggesting that all individuals were buried in a single burial episode.

Dates

427–550 CE (table 12.1).

Specimen 12385, Tomb 8

Condition

This specimen is a complete skull that exhibits small patches of soft tissue that still adhere to the bone. No defleshing marks were observed. A vegetal fiber cord protrudes from the frontal perforation. The rope is knotted inside the cranium, perhaps to enable the head to be exhibited or carried. There is evidence of wear in the rope, particularly in the segment that rubbed against the perforation. Within the nasal cavities, small red feathers were found, but this may not be intentional.

Age

Based on a composite scoring system of suture closure, this individual had an age of around forty years at time of death.

Sex

All cranial features including the superior nuchal crest, mastoid process, supra-orbital margin, glabella, mental eminence, and gonial angle were scored as male.

Perimortem modification

The frontal bone shows an irregular perforation of approximately three centimeters above the right orbital rim. The edges are sharp, and there is evidence of cut marks and indentation throughout the margins. The planum and the basilar portions of the occipital bone have also been removed.

Premortem trauma

Unlike the other isolated heads, this specimen shows multiple healed lesions, possibly due to blunt force. One of them is an oval depression (1 × 5 centimeters) located 3 centimeters above the left orbital margin. The second one is a roughly circular depression (2 × 1.5 centimeters) in the posterior part of the right parietal bone, close to the lambdoidal suture. A healed but displaced fracture of the right zygomatic arch was observed and is likely the result of blunt force. From the osteological evidence, it is unknown if these three incidents occurred in a single episode, but it is evident that this individual did not die from these injuries, as there is significant remodeling and bone growth in the affected regions (fig. 12.6).

Context

This specimen was found in a disturbed tomb. An incomplete and partially mummified adult female and an adult male exhibiting healed left rib fractures and evidence of possible ankylosing spondylitis were also present in this tomb.

Specimen 12112, Tomb 4

Condition

This head displays relatively well-preserved soft tissue that includes intricately styled hair with small red feathers placed vertically in the posterior part of the head. A

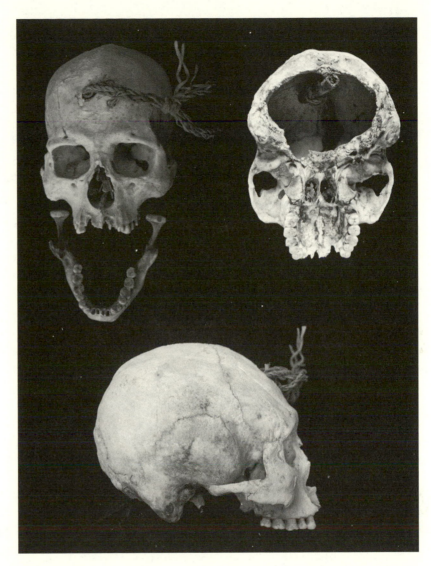

Figure 12.6. Anterior and basilar views of isolated head #12385. Bottom center: lateral view showing healed and displaced fracture of the right zygomatic arch (photo by M. C. Lozada).

vegetal fiber rope protrudes from the perforation of the frontal bone.

Age
All permanent teeth were fully erupted, including all third molars, indicating that this individual was older than twenty-one years at time of death.

Sex
Although covered with soft tissue, all cranial features, including the mandible, are robust, indicating that specimen 12112 was probably from a male individual.

Perimortem modification
This head exhibits an opening in the frontal bone located immediately above the glabella. Portions of the occipital planum and basilar portion were removed (plate 23).

Premortem trauma
None was observed, as determined by the CT scan performed on this specimen.

Context
Although the context was slightly disturbed, the head was found in situ in the lower levels of the tomb and wrapped in an exquisite textile. An individual of fourteen years old was also included in this burial pit.

422–530 CE (table 12.1).

Specimen 11497, Tomb 3

Condition

This specimen does not include the mandible. There is some soft tissue preserved on the scalp and no evidence of defleshing.

Age

All permanent teeth were fully erupted, including all third molars, indicating that this individual was older than twenty years at death. Based on cranial suture closure, this individual was about forty years old at time of death.

Sex

Male, as all morphological features are robust.

Perimortem modification

This specimen shows a large, bell-shaped opening of the frontal bone. The head exhibits the largest perforation of the fontal bone of all four heads discussed here. Portions of the occipital planum and the entire basilar part of the occipital bone are absent; this large aperture extends to include parts of the temporal bones and sphenoid (fig. 12.7).

Context

This head was recovered from a disturbed context. Isolated bones from the pit suggest that the head was buried with a child who was approximately five years old at death and an adult male.

NEW INTERPRETATION

The heads from V-05 are all from mortuary contexts and thus represent an opportunity to study the practices associated with isolated heads. Here, we offer preliminary interpretations related to head preparation and curation, and the possible roles isolated heads played in La Ramada tradition.

These interpretations draw upon previous studies of Nasca and Wari heads while also attempting to move beyond the trophy versus ancestor dichotomy. Most

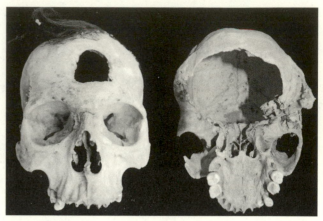

Figure 12.7. Anterior and basilar views of isolated head #11497 (photo by M. C. Lozada).

importantly, in offering these interpretations, we situate our study among other studies of the meanings of the body and, more specifically, the head (Blom and Couture [chapter 13], Hastorf [chapter 17], and Tiesler and Lozada [chapter 1] of this volume).

Head Preparation

At first look, the isolated heads from V-05 share some similarities. None of the heads show any evidence of defleshing. In fact, all of them exhibit patches of scalp with hair, and their mandibles were not removed from the cranium. This suggests that skin and muscle were not purposefully removed. The heads seem to have been removed from the body without damage to the mastoid processes or the gonial angle of the mandible.

A more detailed analysis, however, reveals significant variation in their preparation. As can be seen in figures 12.5, 12.6, and 12.7, and plate 23, the perforation in the frontal bone was not always placed in the same location. In addition, the size and shape of the perforations were not uniform. For example, specimen 12590 shows clean, linear frontal fractures that could only have been created in a recently deceased individual with nondesiccated bone. These fractures appear to be the product of extreme pressure applied when processing this head, suggesting that the individual who processed the head fractured the frontal bone when creating the frontal aperture. It is possible that this procedure was performed by an unskilled or inexperienced individual, or that it was performed hastily.

Variation is again observed among the four heads with respect to the removal of the occipital and temporal bones. A close look at the posterior and basilar parts of the heads shows a lack of standardization and specialization. If specialists had performed these removals, one would expect them to have followed anatomical landmarks such as the mastoid process and the petrous portion of the temporal bone. No drilling perforations were detected, but a combination of cut marks (defined as less than one millimeter) and chop marks (defined as greater than one millimeter) were identified. Cleaner cuts were observed on one side of the basilar portion of the head, which implies that the head was placed in a fixed position, likely on the lap of the person who made them. The lack of uniformity in processing suggests that there was no direct oversight in their production. In this respect, the production of these heads seems to be more reminiscent of the Nasca heads than the Wari heads, which exhibit a certain degree of standardization and may have been the result of a specialized practice.

Head Curation

A detailed examination of specimen 12112 provides additional insight into the curation of isolated heads. This head is the only one that has extensive and well-preserved soft tissue. It is clear that the face was intentionally preserved and perhaps even mummified (plate 23). The nose was stuffed with small sticks, and it appears that the skin was treated or covered with a layer of an unknown material. There is no evidence of skin deterioration. CT scans reveal no signs of trauma or evidence of padding for the cheeks or eyes. This head exhibits an elaborate hairdo. The hair was almost entirely braided beginning at the midline of the scalp. Braids are about thirty centimeters in length, and the hair is not braided along its entire length. The distal ends of two braids protrude into the perforation of the frontal bone. On the posterior part of the head, a clean flap of scalp along the occipital was left in place and used to cover the opening, suggesting that braiding was done after removal of the occipital bone as part of the preparation of the head. The posterior part of the head was adorned with small reddish feathers.

This head was found wrapped in one of the most exquisite textiles recovered from the cemetery (plate 24). The textile measures about three meters long and is notable for its unique and extremely fine decorations, which cannot be linked to either the Nasca or Wari tradition. Traces of textile decomposition are seen in areas where the cloth was in direct contact with the head.

Nearly all of our specimens exhibited traces of scalp and hair, which we interpreted as an intentional consequence of the treatment of these heads. Although the preservation of specimen 12112 stands out within our collection, care was evidently taken to maintain his face. This was suggested by the presence of an unknown substance to preserve the skin and the sticks present in the nasal cavities. This treatment is not without published parallels. Julio Tello (1918) has suggested that the Nasca used the resin of the molle tree (*Schinus molle*) to preserve the skin of such heads. John Verano (1995) and Sonia Guillén (1992) have proposed that some heads were intentionally mummified in order to preserve the person's physiognomy. These preparations would have been undertaken in order to prevent further decomposition after death and removal of the head.

This head may have served a function similar to a portrait, preserving the individual's appearance and perhaps even his personhood. It is clear that great care was taken to preserve facial features and that recognition of individual facial identity was of paramount importance among the people who prepared these heads. Heads of males and particularly male combatants may have been a unique locus of energy and after death a source of vital forces, as the head in the Andes is considered the receptacle of power and vitality (Arnold and Hastorf 2008; Hastorf, chapter 17 of this volume; Proulx 1999; Weismantel 2015). Although these heads were processed in a similar fashion, their recycled identities may suggest that each head contained the essence of the person in life.

HEADS AMONG LA RAMADA

Although the osteological evaluation of the entire collection of isolated heads at La Ramada cemetery, V-05, is ongoing, our preliminary observations suggest that they share some features with the contemporaneous Nasca culture. One important distinction, however, is that the isolated heads found at V-05 were all obtained from burial contexts. We have not uncovered settlement contexts, so we cannot exclude the possibility that isolated skulls were also placed and used in residential or ceremonial contexts. Still, the relative quantity of heads found in burials at V-05 exceeds that found at Nasca cemeteries, indicating that there are some important differences in how heads were perceived and utilized by La Ramada people.

Our findings indicate that some male individuals from La Ramada engaged in interpersonal violence. These activities in life are evident from the cranial and postcranial healed traumas and are similar to those patterns of interpersonal conflict documented for the Nasca (Kellner 2002) and to a lesser degree to the Wari (Tung 2012). Iconography and osteological patterns among the Nasca point to an increase in interpersonal violence after the abandonment of Cahuachi, the capital of the Nasca, around 325 CE. Although La Ramada tradition lacks the rich iconography seen in Nasca ceramic and textile styles, our osteological data supports patterns of violence similar to those of the Nasca in the Vitor Valley, and our radiocarbon dates indicate that this population was contemporaneous with the post-Cahuachi Nasca.

These findings raise several interesting questions. What was the nature of this interpersonal violence, and against whom were people fighting? Does the skeletal evidence suggest ritual battles as proposed by Proulx (2006), or were the battles related to larger geopolitical conflicts? Our four radiocarbon dates from this cemetery, including isolated head 12112, date La Ramada individuals in this cemetery to around 550 AD, before the expansion of Wari into the Vitor Valley. Could evidence of interpersonal violence indicate confrontations with competing groups living in the Vitor Valley or in neighboring valleys such as Siguas and Majes? Because we have only identified La Ramada cemeteries and not their settlements, it is impossible for us to conduct settlement pattern analysis to evaluate evidence of such conflict.

The four heads described in this chapter do not represent a large enough sample to address these issues comprehensively. Still, there are biological and cultural elements that may shed some light on these questions. First, three of the four heads were identified as male. One of the heads exhibits multiple healed lesions, indicating that this adult male was involved in violent activities while alive.

Although the precise function of the heads remains unclear, we propose a new hypothesis that could account for this practice as well as for their inclusion in burial contexts in the Vitor Valley. Instead of representing enemy combatants, we propose that, for La Ramada, the heads were of defeated male fighters who had been killed in combat while away from their community and brought back by survivors for curation and burial. While the removal of the head from the body is congruent with the perception of the head as the locus of the identity of the person, as described in other chapters in this volume (Blom and Couture [chapter 13]; Hastorf [chapter 17]), this practice may also have had practical reasons. The transportation of a dead body from a distant site may have been logistically challenging,

as with European aristocrats who died in warfare far away from their desired burial place (Weiss-Krejci 2005). Among La Ramada, removing the head at the place of death would have been an unusual yet pragmatic procedure. The lack of standardization in their production may reflect the fact that this was done by individuals without the appropriate tools and training to remove heads in a regimented manner. Back in their community, the heads went through careful processing and curation, similar to that demonstrated during the intentional mummification of heads. Standardization thus only occurred after the initial transportation of the heads. Unlike with other individuals, the heads went through multiple stages of processing and were finally buried with other members of the community, highlighting their status in the community.

We propose this interpretation with preliminary data from V-05, while excavation and analysis is still ongoing. This interpretation may also explain the nature of Nasca heads as a whole. Knudson et al. (2009) and Forgey (2011), for example, demonstrated that isolated Nasca heads came from the same geographic area and even from the same biological population. In addition, the massive cache of forty-eight heads in Cerro Carapo show the same type of cranial modification style, reflecting the fact that all individuals were part of the same ethnic group (Browne et al. 1993). Together, it seems reasonable to propose that these heads belonged to the dead bodies of male combatants who had engaged in long-distance warfare, which were collected by their peers, possibly males, from the same ethnic group for appropriate burial. This could also explain the presence of nonmale heads: any instance in which someone died in a situation in which it was impractical to carry the complete body back resulted in the taking of the head only. The variation seen in head treatment and burial location may reflect the circumstances and location of their death.

Our interpretation is supported by the lack of headless burials found in cemetery V-05, a pattern that is also described in the literature on the Nasca. Christina Conlee (2007) and Lisa DeLeonardis (2000) have documented some isolated cases of skeletons without heads, but their limited number does not align with the high proportion of isolated heads that have been documented in the Nasca region (DeLeonardis 2000). This archaeological evidence lends support to the idea that the bodies of male combatants were left at the site of combat and would not be easily identified archaeologically due to decay and dispersal of the remains.

CONCLUSIONS AND FUTURE BIOARCHAEOLOGICAL RESEARCH

Multiple lines of evidences suggest that the Nasca exerted some cultural influence on La Ramada community, which was situated four hundred kilometers away from the capital on the Rio Grande. Specifically, our data shows that La Ramada was not immune to the conflict and violence that became part of Nasca cultural practices during this time. It appears that mostly males were involved in activities that included interpersonal violence, as seen in the cranial and postcranial trauma patterns. The nature of this violence is unknown, and numerous theories have been proposed to explain the practice of preserving heads, including their roles as trophies of combat or as objects of veneration after nonviolent death. We propose an additional theory regarding the possible role of heads in the Vitor Valley that will require further bioarchaeological analysis. Specifically, we propose that males may have left their communities for distant confrontations that would have resulted in casualties. Instead of transporting back complete dead bodies, survivors removed the heads of their slain companions and minimally processed them at the place of death. This practice was premised on the Nasca understanding of the head as the main receptacle of power and identity, and on the impracticality of transporting the dead in their entirety back to their communities from a distant location. The unique status and role of these heads are underscored by the additional stages of processing required to successfully preserve them along with their identifying facial features and hair. Unlike Nasca heads, however, these heads were buried in collective tombs back in their communities, which expresses the powerful nature of the head as a source of energy for the burial group.

This interpretation might help to explain aspects of Nasca heads and Nasca burials observed by DeLeonardis (2000), Conlee (2007), Knudson et al. (2009), and Forgey (2011). We thus propose an interpretation that is not only relevant to V-05 and La Ramada culture but also to the wider region. Perhaps more importantly, we provide an alternative explanation for the presence of isolated heads, which has been the source of much scholarly debate, by avoiding the ancestor-or-enemy question. We intend to continue with our bioarchaeological research in the Vitor Valley, focusing on many of the questions raised here. In particular, a biological distance research study using nonmetric cranial traits is currently underway to assess biological relatedness among the skeletal collection from

V-05. Furthermore, we plan to conduct strontium isotopic analysis in order to pinpoint the geographic origins of these heads and to test this hypothesis among La Ramada people.

ACKNOWLEDGMENTS

The main conclusions in this chapter were previously presented by Augusto Cardona Rosas, María Cecilia Lozada, and Hans Barnard at the fortieth annual Midwest Conference on Andean and Amazonian Archaeology and Ethnohistory at the Field Museum of Natural History in Chicago (February 25–26, 2012); by María Cecilia Lozada, Claire Maass, and Jissy Cyriac at the 113th annual meeting of the American Anthropological Association in Washington, DC (December 3–7, 2014); by Rex C. Haydon, María Cecilia Lozada, Augusto Cardona Rosas, Hans Barnard, and Alanna Warner-Smith at the seventy-ninth meeting of the Society for American Archaeology in Austin, Texas (April 23–27, 2014); and by Michele Smith, María Cecilia Lozada, Alan Coogan, and Juana Lazo at the eighteenth meeting of the Society for American Archaeology in San Francisco (April 15–19, 2015). The field season of 2012 was conducted under Resolución Directorial no. 541-2012-DGPC-VMPCIC/MC, granted to Licenciado Augusto Omar Cardona Rosas (RNA no. CC-9408), and made possible by a research grant to Lozada, Cardona, and Barnard from Dumbarton Oaks and a research grant to Lozada from the National Geographic Society, complemented by a Transdisciplinary Research Grant from the UCLA Vice Chancellor for Research. OmniSTAR of Houston kindly provided free of charge the differential GPS signal used for our survey.

Since the inception of the Vitor Archaeological Project, Ran Boytner, Charles Stanish, Raul Vizcardo, and Willeke Wendrich have offered continuous advice and support. In addition, students who participated in the mortuary excavations (2012) and laboratory season (2013) in Vitor through the Institute for Field Research provided rich discussions of La Ramada mortuary context. We thank Rose Campbell, Jon Clindaniel, Joe Cronin, Emma Hite, Anurag Kumar, Rachel Moy, Marina Perez, Willy Puma, Evan Robinson, and Erika Simborth, who assisted María Lozada and Hans Barnard in the field. Furthermore, thanks are extended to Alan Coogan, Juana Lazo, Michele Smith, and Ron Winters, who studied the textile and artifact collection from the mortuary excavations of V-05. Our friends Cesar and Nelly Nina welcomed us to their home in Vitor and shared their knowledge and passion for this amazing valley. In Chicago, Flavius Beca and Kristie Sanchez provided editorial comments to this manuscript, and Donald Proulx offered insightful advice to our first draft.

REFERENCES CITED

Arkush, Elizabeth, and Tiffiny Tung
2013   Patterns of War in the Andes from the Archaic to the Late Horizon: Insights from Settlement Patterns and Cranial Trauma. *Journal of Archaeological Research* 21:307–69.

Arnold, Denise Y., and Christine A. Hastorf
2008   *Heads of State, Icons, Power, and Politics in the Ancient and Modern Andes.* Left Coast Press, Walnut Creek, California.

Arriaza, Bernardo T., Felipe Cárdenas Arroyo, Ekkehard Kleiss, and John W. Verano
1998   South American Mummies: Culture and Disease. In *Mummies, Disease and Ancient Cultures*, edited by Aidan Cockburn, Eve Cockburn, and Theodore A. Reyman, pp. 190–236. 2nd ed. Cambridge University Press, Cambridge.

Browne, David, Helaine Silverman, and Rúben García
1993   A Cache of 48 Nasca Trophy Heads from Cerro Carapo, Peru. *Latin American Antiquity* 4:274–94.

Buikstra, Jane E., and Douglas H. Ubelaker (editors)
1994   *Standards for Data Collection from Human Skeletal Remains.* Research Series, no. 44. Arkansas Archeological Survey, Fayetteville.

Conlee, Christina A.
2007   Decapitation and Rebirth: A Headless Burial from Nasca, Peru. *Current Anthropology* 48:438–45.

Cyriac, Jissy
2014   The Children of Vitor Valley: A Glimpse into the Social and Biological Conditions of Children in a Pre-Hispanic Ramada Society. BA thesis, Department of Anthropology, University of Chicago.

DeLeonardis, Lisa
2000   The Body Context: Interpreting Early Nasca Decapitated Burials. *Latin American Antiquity* 11:363–86.

Forgey, Kathleen
2011   Nasca Trophy Head Origins and Ancient DNA. In *The Bioarchaeology of the Human Head: Decapitation, Decoration, and Deformation*, edited by Michelle Bonogofsky, pp. 286–306. University Press of Florida, Gainesville.

Guillén, Sonia
1992   The Chinchorro Culture: Mummies and Crania in the Reconstruction of Preceramic Coastal Adaptation in the South Central Andes. Unpublished PhD dissertation, Department of Anthropology, University of Michigan.

Haeberli, Joerg
2001   Tiempo y tradición en Arequipa, Perú, y el surgimiento de la cronología del tema de la deidad central. *Boletín de Arqueología PUCP* 5:89–137.

Kellner, Corina M.
2002   *Coping with Environmental and Social Challenges in Prehistoric Peru: Bioarchaeological Analyses of Nasca Populations.* PhD dissertation, Department of Anthropology, University of California, Santa Barbara.

Knudson, Kelly J., Sloan R. Williams, Rebecca Osborn, Kathleen Forgey, and Patrick Ryan Williams
2009   The Geographic Origins of Nasca Trophy Heads Using Strontium, Oxygen, and Carbon Isotope Data. *Journal of Anthropological Archaeology* 28:244–57.

Kroeber, Alfred L.
1937   *Archaeological Explorations in Peru.* Part 4, *Cañete Valley.* Field Museum of Natural History, Chicago.

Lozada, María Cecilia, and Jane E. Buikstra
2002   *El señorío de Chiribaya en la costa sur del Perú.* Instituto de Estudios Peruanos, Lima.

Lozada, María Cecilia, Augusto Cardona Rosas, and Hans Barnard
2013   Looting: Another Phase in the Social History of a Pre-Hispanic Cemetery in Southern Peru. *Backdirt*: 115–23.

Maass, Claire
2014   Gendering Life and Death: An Osteobiological Profile of Women at a Nasca Influenced Ramadas Cemetery in Southern Peru. BA Thesis, Department of Anthropology, University of Chicago.

Neira Avendaño, Máximo
1990   Arequipa prehispánica. In *Historia general de Arequipa*, edited by Máximo Neira Avendaño et al., pp. 5–234. Fundación M. J. Bustamante de la Fuente, Arequipa.

Nigra, Benjamin T., Augusto Cardona Rosas, María Cecilia Lozada, and Hans Barnard
2017   Reconstructing the Built Environment of the Millo Complex, Vitor Valley, Peru. *Ñawpa Pacha, Journal of Andean Archaeology* 37:39–62.

Proulx, Donald A.
1999   Kopfjagd und rituelle Verwendung von Trophäenköpfen in der Nasca-Kultur. In *Nasca: Geheimnisvolle Zeichen*

im Alten Peru, edited by Judith Rickenbach, pp. 79–87. Museum Rietberg, Zürich.

2001 Ritual Uses of Trophy Heads in Ancient Nasca Society. In *Ritual Sacrifice in Ancient Peru*, edited by Elizabeth P. Benson and Anita G. Cook, pp. 119–36. University of Texas Press, Austin.

2006 Nasca Trophy Heads and Agricultural Fertility. Unpublished manuscript, University of Massachusetts.

Santos Ramírez, René

1980 *Cerámica temprana, estilo La Ramada*. Arqueos Perú, Arequipa.

Schreiber, Katharina J.

1992 *Wari Imperialism in Middle Horizon Peru*. Anthropological Papers of the Museum of Anthropology. University of Michigan Museum, Ann Arbor.

Schreiber, Katharina J., and Josué Lancho Rojas

2003 *Irrigation and Society in the Peruvian Desert: The Puquios of Nasca*. Lexington Books, Lanham, Maryland.

Silverman, Helaine

1993 *Cahuachi in the Ancient Nasca World*. University of Iowa Press, Iowa City.

Silverman, Helaine, and Donald A. Proulx

2002 *The Nasca*. Peoples of America. Wiley-Blackwell, Oxford.

Tello, Julio C.

1918 El uso de las cabezas humanas artificialmente momificadas y su representación en el antiguo arte peruano. *Revista Universitaria* 2:477–533.

Tung, Tiffiny A.

2007 Trauma and Violence in the Wari Empire of the Peruvian Andes: Warfare, Raids, and Ritual Fights. *American Journal of Physical Anthropology* 133: 941–56.

2008 Dismembering Bodies for Display: A Bioarchaeological Study of Trophy Heads from the Wari Site of Conchopata, Peru. *American Journal of Physical Anthropology* 136:294–308.

2012 *Violence, Ritual, and the Wari Empire: A Social Bioarchaeology of Imperialism in the Ancient Andes*. University Press of Florida, Gainesville.

Uhle, Max

1901 Die deformierten Köpfe von peruanischen Mumien und die Uta Krankheit. *Verhandlungen der Berliner Anthropologischen Gesellschaft* 33:404–8.

Verano, John W.

1995 Where Do They Rest? The Treatment of Human Offerings and Trophies in Ancient Peru. In *Tombs for the Living: Andean Mortuary Practices*, edited by Tom D. Dillehay, pp. 189–227. Dumbarton Oaks, Washington, DC.

Weismantel, Mary

2015 Many Heads Are Better than One: Mortuary Practice and Ceramic Art in Moche Society. In *Living with the Dead in the Andes*, edited by Izumi Shimada and James L. Fitzsimmons, pp. 76–100. University of Arizona Press, Tucson.

Weiss-Krejci, Estella

2011 Excarnation, Evisceration, and Exhumation in Medieval and Post-Medieval Europe. In *Interacting with the Dead: Perspectives on Mortuary Archaeology for the New Millennium*, edited by Gordon F. M. Rakita, Jane E. Buikstra, Lane A. Beck, and Sloan R. Williams, pp. 155–72. University Press of Florida, Gainesville.

Williams, Sloan R., Kathleen Forgey, and Elizabeth Klarich

2001 *An Osteological Study of Nasca Trophy Heads Collected by A. L. Kroeber during the Marshall Expeditions to Peru*. Field Museum of Natural History, Chicago.

Yépez, Willie J., and Justin Jennings (editors)

2012 *¿Wari en Arequipa? Análisis de los contextos funerarios de La Real*. Museo Arqueológico José María Morante, Universidad Nacional de San Agustín de Arequipa, Arequipa.

13

From *Wawa* to "Trophy Head"

Meaning, Representation, and Bioarchaeology of Human Heads from Ancient Tiwanaku

DEBORAH E. BLOM AND NICOLE C. COUTURE

INTRODUCTION

In this chapter, iconographic representation, bioarchae-ological evidence, and references from ethnohistorical and ethnographic sources are used to inquire into what human heads can tell us about culturally specific notions of personhood, the body, and social reproduction in the Middle Horizon Tiwanaku polity, which flourished in the south-central Andes from around 500 CE to 1150 CE (fig. 13.1). Tiwanaku sociopolitical integration included state-sponsored feasting and shared art and architectural styles, often centered on Tiwanaku temples located in key communities present throughout Peru, Bolivia, Chile, and Argentina. These communities were built in areas as ecologically diverse as the mid-altitude Moquegua Valley of southern Peru (Goldstein 2005), the eastern lowlands of Cochabamba, Bolivia (Anderson 2009; Higueras-Hare 1996), and the San Pedro de Atacama oases in northern Chile (Costa Junqueira et al. 2004; Torres-Rouff 2008).

The Tiwanaku heartland was located in the southern Lake Titicaca Basin (Janusek 2004; Kolata 1993, 1996; Ponce Sanginés 1972; Stanish 2003). There, expansive irrigation networks, monumental architecture, and a hierarchical settlement pattern included agricultural hamlets and regional centers in the Desaguadero, Katari, and Tiwanaku Valleys. Most prominent of these settlements was the capital city of Tiwanaku.

In Tiwanaku, the importance of heads in the establishment of personhood is evident in the practice of wrapping and molding children's heads, as fetuses and infants (*wawa*) move through a liminal state and are transformed into social persons.

The ontological primacy of the head can also be seen in Tiwanaku art and iconography, where depictions of human figures focus almost exclusively on heads rather than faces or entire bodies. One prominent position that heads played is in the iconographical depiction of "trophy heads" in Tiwanaku artwork. Yet, while heads without bodies are present in Tiwanaku contexts, no evidence of actual trophy heads has been found despite their relatively common occurrence elsewhere in the ancient Andes.

The absence of actual trophy heads invites us to set aside interpretations and debates regarding the trophy head tradition vis-à-vis Tiwanaku state violence, warfare, and conquest, and to consider that the importance of trophy heads—and heads in general—from a cosmological and ontological perspective, as we consider ethnographic and ethnohistorical discussions of trophy heads in some Andean communities, where these heads are wrapped, "contained," and transformed into wawa, which simultaneously refers to "seed" and "offspring." In this chapter, we first step forward in time to discuss what we can glean about childhood age transformations from ethnographic and ethnohistorical sources and how they might be seen on Tiwanaku remains.

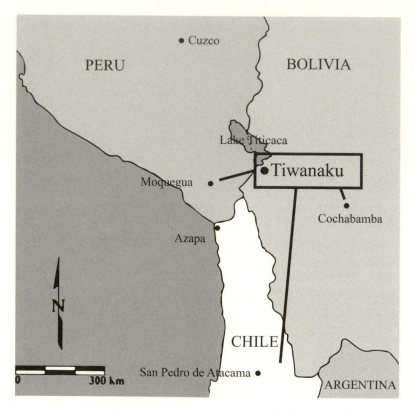

Figure 13.1. Map of the south-central Andes with selected areas of Tiwanaku influence or occupation (image by Deborah E. Blom and Nicole Couture).

TRANSFORMATION: FROM *WAWA* TO PERSON

In many societies in the Andes, fetuses (*sullu*) and babies (*wawa*) are viewed as presocial or wild beings, even slightly dangerous warriors, that are transformed through ritual and everyday practice into social persons (Arnold and Hastorf 2008:52; Canessa 2000a; Graham 1999; Greenway 1998a; Harris 1980:75; Hastorf, chapter 17 of this volume; for additional discussions on social constructs of Andean childhoods and bioarchaeology, see Blom and Knudson 2014; Lozada and Rakita 2013). The transition of fetus to wawa does not take place at birth but during a naming ceremony (Allen 2002; Bolin 2006:27–28; Canessa 2000b:710; Harris 1980). The first haircut (*rutucha*) ends the wawa stage typically at around two years of age, or when a child has grown a full head of hair (Allen 2002:69; Canessa 2000a:134). These rites, importantly, also serve the purpose of developing the social person by providing children (and their parents) with a strong network of fictive kin (*compadrazgo*).

Young children who are in the process of developing possess special qualities, which must be managed by adults. As is common in many societies (including in Mesoamerica), children's spirits grow with them, and their souls are not considered as firmly attached to their bodies as those of adults (Bolin 2006; Inge Bolin, personal communication, 2010; Graham 1999; Greenway 1998a, 1998b; La Barre 1948:122; Morgan 1997:343; Tschopik 1946:552, 1951). Soul loss or loosening can occur readily with frights (*susto*) from falls or even from crossing rivers or changing residence (Tschopik 1946:211–12). As such, Aymara medicine today has well-developed means of preventing and treating susto in children (Blom, personal experience;[1] Greenway 1998a; La Barre 1948:122), as well as preventing hunger, which makes children more vulnerable to threats from physical and supernatural forces (Graham 1997; Leonard 1991). As children age, they become "stronger and less vulnerable to illness than younger children, with a well-integrated life force" (Graham 1997:1703).

If we look to examples of traditional Andean social age categories, Bill Sillar's observation that wawa "spend most [of] their time wrapped up" (1994:50) refers to the notable practice of swaddling and continuously carrying babies and young children in a "manta" or cloth (Arnold and Yapita 2006:104; Baker and Little 1976; Bolin 2006:36; La Barre 1948:126; LeVine 1980; Tronick et al. 1994; Tschopik 1951:163). As well as protecting young children from the cold and injury, carrying children in this way has the benefit of nurturing young children's social formation because mothers keep young children, especially nursing infants, with them in activities such as dancing and attending fiestas as well as during everyday social and economic interactions (Allen 2002:155; Plummer 1966, citing Tschopik's unpublished field notes). Over time, the generic babies move out of their "wild," presocial state and no longer need to be contained. Their social identities are formed, and they become fully human boys and girls.

Swaddling in early childhood is seen as essential in developing well-formed bodies. Lynn Morgan (1997:343), working in the Ecuadoran Andes, recounts that mothers "swaddle their babies . . . to make their legs grow straight."[2] In addition to swaddling, Ecuadoran mothers note that they also "should carefully and frequently mold and shape [their child's] face and nose, its head and shoulders and legs to make them assume the desired shape" (Morgan 1997:343). The belief that it is necessary to shape a child's body as it develops is displayed prominently in the common practice of head molding in the ancient Andes.

CHILDREN'S HEADS: WRAPPING, METAMORPHOSIS, AND TRANSFORMATION

The transformative process of head wrapping was practiced on over 80 percent of Tiwanaku children, with no visible patterns that can be linked to sex, class, or religious status (See Blom 1999 and Blom 2005 for a through discussion of cranial modification practices, as seen ethnohistorically and archaeologically, in the Andes in general and specifically for Tiwanaku). Regional studies of Tiwanaku cranial modification have suggested that the Tiwanaku polity included complementary ethnic or community/regional groups that were largely differentiated by different cranial modification styles (Blom 2005; Hoshower et al. 1995) (fig. 13.2).

In Tiwanaku-affiliated lowland coastal valley sites, fronto-occipital (e.g., tabular oblique) shapes predominated (see also Buikstra 1995; Hoshower et al. 1995; Torres-Rouff 2002, 2003), while annular forms (in which the cross section of the head is more circular) were common in the Lake Katari Valley, which is adjacent to the Tiwanaku Valley in the Titicaca Basin. Individuals interred in the Tiwanaku capital had both modification styles in roughly equal proportion, and some spatial/temporal differentiation has been observed there (Berryman et al. 2009). As described elsewhere in this volume, the association between cranial modification and group identity has strong parallels in other Andean (Mannheim et al. [chapter 14]) and Mesoamerican (Tiesler and Lacadena [chapter 3], Scherer [chapter 4], and Duncan and Vail [chapter 2]) contexts (see also Zabala 2014 for a discussion of the topic in Hispanic America in general).

To date, no clear explanation has a been found for the 20 percent of individuals who have unmodified heads in the Tiwanaku sample. Neither paleopathological studies nor mortuary analyses indicate differential treatment in childhood related to cranial modification, such as neglect or some difference in social identities (Blom et al. 2016). Deborah Blom has suggested that it might be beneficial to not have a head form indicative of a particular group if

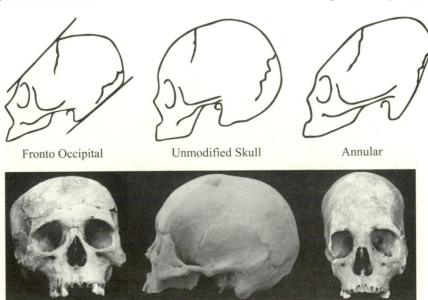

Fronto Occipital   Unmodified Skull   Annular

Figure 13.2. Tiwanaku head modification (images by Deborah E. Blom).

an individual was socially mobile and/or moving between regions, such as we would expect for members of families operating llama caravans (Blom et al. 1998). Incidentally, the only clear victim of repeated abuse found in the Tiwanaku sample was an adult female buried in the lowlands with a strontium isotope signature indicating that she had lived elsewhere as a child; her head form was unmodified (Blom and Knudson 2014). As of now, a clear explanation for why some children's heads were not modified is lacking.

Attaining particular cranial shapes required forethought. Intentional modification of head form was achieved by keeping cranial modifiers made of boards, straps, cords, and/or pads on children's heads for extended periods of time until the age of three to five years (Cieza de León 1984; de la Vega 1966; Diez de San Miguel 1964:244; Torquemada 1995). The cranium was, supposedly, also altered by shaping with the hands (Diez de San Miguel 1964:244).

Adolph Bandelier (1910:175–76) reports that in the Lake Titicaca region, cranial modification was associated with specific headdresses for which children's heads were molded; "the first bonnet was manufactured with many ceremonies and superstitions." Bernabé Cobo (1956) and Ludovico Bertonio (1984), both writing in the seventeenth century, provide a foundation for Bandelier's claims in indicating that Aymara groups shaped their heads to fit their distinctive hats and to promote good health.[3] Thus, cranial modification marked identity as both final form and as technical process, and its motivation included health in addition to beauty and spirituality.

The idea that cranial modification may be necessary for good health is echoed in the work of Duncan and Vail (chapter 2 of this volume) and Duncan and Hofling (2011). Using the rich ethnographic and ethnohistorical records of the Maya, they argue that cranial shape modification was practiced for socialization and embodiment, and specifically for protection against the loss of an animating essence from a "recently ensouled newborn." Metaphorically, sealing up this essence and preventing soul loss is like building a roof on a house. This argument is quite cogent for the Maya, and, since the danger of soul loss for young children is also a common belief throughout the Andes, it provides a potential additional explanation for the practice by the Tiwanaku.

Like the manta that bundles and contains the wawa body described earlier, the bonnet contained and controlled the shape of the child's head, harnessing the wildness of the wawa and creating a social person. While the ethnohistorical and early ethnographic literature seems to argue that heads were shaped to fit the hats, it would be difficult to test archaeologically if heads were being shaped to fit the containers, or the other way around. However, two head shapes seen in the Tiwanaku remains correspond to the two types of Tiwanaku hats found archaeologically (Frame 1990) and depicted on stone architecture, portrait vessels (*huacos retratos*), and ceramic figurines. What other information can be gleaned about the meaning of heads from Tiwanaku material culture?

TIWANAKU HEADS (AND BODIES) IN ART AND ARCHITECTURE

Tiwanaku iconography, as seen on textiles, stone sculptures, engraved bone, and ceramics, is complex and tends to be dominated by abstract geometric motifs. Images of animals (e.g., pumas and condors) are sometimes depicted in profile and as full figures, often in a stylized manner (Alconini 1995; Janusek 2003). Full-bodied depictions of humans and anthropomorphic beings are extremely rare, and anthropomorphic figures in general are also often very stylized (Alconini 1995; Cook 1994; Couture and Sampeck 2003; Janusek 2003).

As such, Tiwanaku representations of people differ in some ways from the artistic conventions of other ancient Andean societies, such as the Nasca and Moche, for which figurative art is more common (Bourget 2006; Donnan 1978; Proulx 2006). Given that many studies of Tiwanaku art and iconography pay a great deal of attention to a small number of well-known stone sculptures of anthropomorphic individuals (Cook 1983, 1994; Isbell and Knobloch 2006, 2009; Kolata 2003; Makowski 2009; Zuidema 2009), the scholarly literature may have generated the impression that depictions of human figures are common.

Some of the best-known examples of Tiwanaku anthropomorphic art are of complete human figures found on stone sculptures (plate 25). For example, the Ponce, Fraile, and Bennett monoliths portray standing, elaborately dressed, elite males (Kolata 2003; Makowski 2009). With the exception of these stone sculptures and rare ceramic figurines such those found on the southern Lake Titicaca island of Pariti (Korpisaari and Pärssinen 2005, 2011) (fig. 13.3), three-dimensional human figures are relatively rare in Tiwanaku contexts, unlike art forms of the Wari or Nasca, for example (Cook 1992, 1994, 1996; Proulx 2006).

Figure 13.3. Ceramic vessels from the Pariti cache (photos courtesy of Antti Korpisaari).

Two-dimensional, whole-bodied anthropomorphic representations are only slightly more common at Tiwanaku. In the monumental Gateway of the Sun, currently housed in the Kalasasaya Temple in the site's central ceremonial district, the main figure is a rayed, anthropomorphic being standing on a miniature stepped pyramid who is sometimes referred to as the "staff god" or "front-faced god" (Conklin 2009; Cook 1994; Isbell and Knobloch 2006; Kolata 2003) (fig. 13.4). Many scholars interpret the central figure as a creator god, perhaps an earlier incarnation of the Inka god Viracocha. The front-faced figure is flanked on either side by a series of "profile attendants"—who have been interpreted by some scholars as elaborately costumed and outfitted elite "warriors." However, rather than elite individuals, these figures also very likely represent supernatural deities or mythical figures.

William Isbell and Patricia Knobloch (2006, 2009) note that the iconography depicted on the Gateway of the Sun is not unique to Tiwanaku but is part of a historically related set of religious figures that was broadly shared across a vast region of the central Andes over the course of nearly two millennia, between approximately 800 BCE and 1000 CE. Some of the pre-Hispanic polities that participated in what they call the "Southern Andean Iconographic Series" (SAIS) include Tiwanaku, Wari, Pucara,

Figure 13.4. Gateway of the Sun, Kalasasaya Temple, with close-up of staff god and attendants (lower image, photo © Jeff Clarke; upper image © Adwo/Adobe Stock).

and communities in the region of San Pedro de Atacama. In her earlier study of this broadly shared iconography, Anita Cook (1994) is careful to point out that there are significant differences in the ways in which specific figures and motifs are depicted between cultures, particularly when it comes to representations of anthropomorphic beings related to the Gateway of the Sun.

With respect to Tiwanaku ceramics, whole-bodied anthropomorphic representations are also rarely seen on *keros*, flared drinking cups. Of the hundreds of ceramic vessels recovered from Tiwanaku that Nicole Couture has studied, very few of the vessels contain anthropomorphic figures that depict the whole body. Generally, only heads are depicted.

The importance of human heads in Tiwanaku art and architecture can be seen most dramatically in the Semi-Subterranean Temple, which was constructed in the center of the capital when Tiwanaku's sphere of interaction was mainly focused on the Titicaca Basin (Janusek 2004; Ponce Sanginés 1990) (fig. 13.5). Thought to be one of the first monumental structures erected at Tiwanaku, the temple has a series of stone carved human heads inset directly into its interior walls. More than two hundred of these "tenon heads" have been documented, and

at the time this structure was excavated, many of them were found still in place.[4] Each one of these is unique, and many are shown wearing headdresses, which may be markers of elevated status or perhaps social/ethnic affiliation. Couture (2002, 2007, 2008) suggests that the tenon heads contained in the temple are effigies, or living icons, of community ancestors from the Titicaca Basin. Yet other architectural elements display heads, such as the two stone, framed heads shown in plate 26.

The inclusion of heads in Tiwanaku architectural elements underscores the importance of the head within the Tiwanaku belief system (Conklin 1991). At Putuni, a palace complex in the core of the Tiwanaku capital, a smaller monolith was found with its head removed (Couture and Sampeck 2003). The decapitation of this monolith probably happened when Putuni and the site were abandoned in the eleventh century. The decapitation of the sculpture follows a practice seen as early as the Late Formative II period (300 CE) at the site of Khonkho Wankane in the neighboring Desaguadero Valley (Ohnstad et al. 2006), as well as in early contexts in the Tiwanaku capital, and underscores the importance of the head as the most significant element of the body of anthropomorphic figures.

While full-bodies figures are rare, the presence of heads

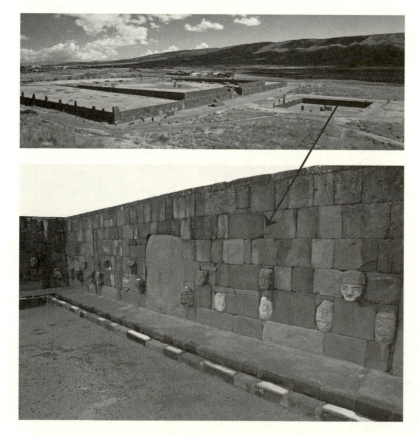

Figure 13.5. Semi-Subterranean Temple with a close-up of a selection of heads (photo © Jeff Clarke).

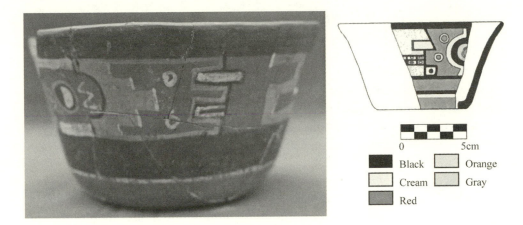

Figure 13.6. Profiles heads on a *tazon* from Putuni (specimen 20846) (images by Nicole C. Couture).

in profile on ceramics are slightly more common. These head profiles, found on fine serving vessels, particularly keros and *tazones* (a type of small bowl), are typically stylized and abstract (fig. 13.6). The profile heads have been interpreted variously as human trophy heads, warriors, sacrificial victims, and ancestors (Janusek 2003:78). One of the most notable aspects of these representations is that they convey the general idea of the head rather than the heads or full faces of specific individuals.

In contrast, portrait vessels, or huacos retratos, realistically portray individuals (fig. 13.7). Couture (2008) argues that these oversize drinking cups represent elites and underscore their role as generous hosts using the commensal politics of feasting as political persuasion. Their dispersal throughout the site further indicates that they were used by the general Tiwanaku population rather than just elites. They also communicate the idea that, in Tiwanaku society, power is embodied in the heads of its rulers, which may contrast with the faceneck jars of the Wari (see Vazquez de Arthur, chapter 16 of this volume), which also convey the image of the generous elite host but with the emphasis on the corpulent, tunic-clad body of the host rather than on the head, which is relatively small. Janusek (2003:79) argues that the huacos retratos depict specific Tiwanaku elite persons, but as of yet we have not identified individual agents, such as those recognized by Patricia Knobloch (2010) for the Wari. Nevertheless, Tiwanaku portrait vessels do have distinguishing facial features such as face paint, tattoos, and facial hair; therefore, future studies in these areas may be fruitful.

In ceramic and other media in which anthropomorphic figures are found, the individuals tend to be male, as indicated by their facial hair and, as Jo Ellen Burkholder (n.d.) has pointed out, robust brow areas and prominent chins. However, fragments of a small female figurine were

found at Putuni (Janusek 2003), and vessels that clearly represents females were recovered by Antti Korpisaari and Martti Pärssinen (2005, 2011) in their excavation of the extraordinary cache of Tiwanaku vessels on the island of Pariti (fig. 13.3).

Included in the Pariti cache is an unusual vessel shaped like a human foot. This departs wildly from other ceramics, in which the only isolated body parts depicted are heads. Interestingly, this foot is decorated with a row of human skulls along its exterior rim. This vessel and its

Figure 13.7. Huacos retratos (portrait vessels). Upper: Mollo Kontu, locus 1055; lower left: Akapana, specimen 14556; lower right: Chij'i Jawira, specimen 33667 (photos by Deborah E. Blom and Nicole C. Couture).

decoration alludes to a long-standing Andean tradition of taking and displaying human body parts, especially heads (Ogburn 2007; Tung 2008; Verano 1995, 2008).

Human-like figures wielding classic trophy heads (see below for a description) are represented iconographically on various media at Tiwanaku, including pyro-engraved bone containers recovered by Martin Giesso at Marca Pata (Janusek 2003), by Janusek (1994) at Akapana East, and by Couture (2003) at the Mollo Kontu mound (fig. 13.8). A similar scene was found on fragments of an incomplete kero from Putuni (Couture and Sampeck 2003), on which an elaborately dressed warrior/*wari wilka* figure (a camelid-like creature with fangs) has a trophy head positioned near his back (perhaps slung on a rope) (fig. 13.8). The figure is shown wielding a *tumi* blade in one hand and wearing an additional tumi as a pectoral. The figure on this vessel is similar to the rows of profile "warriors" depicted on some stone architraves, including the Kantatayita Lintel, on which trophy heads are suspended from their belts or held in their hands (Conklin 1991:283, fig. 3, 284, fig. 5; Cook 1994:fig. 56; Couture and Sampeck 2003:212). Other Tiwanaku stone sculpture depicts feline-human warriors (*chachapumas*) such as the basalt chachapuma recovered near the base of the west stairway of Akapana, a massive temple in the core of the Tiwanaku capital (fig. 13.9). The figure is dressed as a feline and holds a human head in its hands (Kolata 1993).

The stylized and abstract depictions of human heads found on fine drinking and eating vessels (described above) are sometimes also considered "trophy heads." In rejecting the trophy head interpretation, both Burkholder (n.d.) and Couture (2008) point out that a bodiless head does not always mean a trophy head. However, even if we assume that the stylized heads are trophies, all in all, representations of trophy heads are rare for the Tiwanaku. Furthermore, when we do encounter them, they are most commonly in the hands of zoomorphic or supernatural beings rather than human beings. This can perhaps be put into context by turning to the osteological evidence for trophy heads.

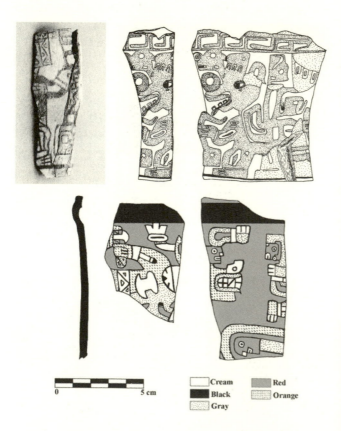

Cream | Red
Black | Orange
Gray

Figure 13.8. Trophy heads on Tiwanaku artifacts. Upper: pyro-engraved bone containers, left, from the Mollo Kontu mound (image by Nicole C. Couture), right, from Akapana East (image courtesy of John W. Janusek); lower: kero sherds from Putuni (images by Nicole C. Couture).

Figure 13.9. Trophy head on a basalt *chachapuma* (photo courtesy of John W. Janusek).

THE OSTEOLOGY OF TROPHY HEADS AND TIWANAKU HEADS

The curation of "trophy heads" was a relatively common practice in many cultures in the ancient Andes, especially where they are frequently represented iconographically such as in Nasca and Wari contexts (Andrushko 2011; Knudson et al. 2009; Ogburn 2007; Proulx 1989; Shimada 1994; Silverman 1993; Tung and Knudson 2008; Tung 2008; Verano 1995). In this volume, Becker and Alconini (chapter 15), Hastorf (chapter 17), Lozada et al. (chapter 12), and Verano (chapter 11) provide a thorough discussion of trophy heads, a term that classically refers to decapitated skulls that have been modified and curated. The modification typically includes breaking out the occipital and running a cord through a hole created in the middle of the frontal bone or at the vertex; the mandible is sometimes also modified. Lozada and colleagues ask us not to assume that "trophy heads" (as they are historically called and commonly discussed in Andean scholarship) solely consist of heads taken from enemies. They suggest that alternative terms be employed in the absence of evidence indicating that we have trophy heads in the true sense of the term. They discuss the benefits and problems of various terms such as "isolated" and "disembodied" heads; we refer the reader to their chapter for this discussion.

The call to not impose Western thoughts on head removal onto other contexts is important for ancient, and even modern, South American societies, since the term "trophy head" does not do justice to the range of ways that heads without bodies are used and given meaning. Some other explanations for the existence of heads without bodies, as discussed in the literature, include sacrifice, ritual offerings, punishment for deviance and other transgressions, ancestor veneration, and even the procurement of heads from cemeteries to serve as protectors or guardians, a practice that we have often observed and that is discussed extensively by Becker and Alconini in this volume (see also Allen 2002; Verano, chapter 11 of this volume). Lozada et al. (in this volume) argue that at La Ramada in Vitor the skulls found in cemeteries may be the heads of fallen warriors brought back to their communities for burial, while Verano (in this volume) argues that evidence from Nasca, Wari, and Inka contexts indicates that trophy heads are just that, the heads of important enemies taken in battle. The work of Verano and Lozada underscores the need for a contextualized approach to interpreting evidence of potential trophy heads.

In the case of Tiwanaku, we see that, in spite of iconographic evidence for their importance, no clear trophy heads have been recovered. We know of no human heads from Tiwanaku contexts that were modified after death, such as those found in Nasca and Wari sites discussed above and recently in the Kallawaya territory of Bolivia (Becker and Alconini 2015, chapter 15 of this volume). Additionally, we have no evidence of decapitation based on analyses of Tiwanaku human remains by Blom in the Titicaca Basin and the Moquegua Valley, and by Christina Torres-Rouff in northern Chile (personal communication, 2014).

Occasionally at Tiwanaku, we do find individual skulls that were deposited without their postcranial skeletons. Individual heads such as these tend to be found with offerings associated with the building or renovation of major monumental structures. The cranium of a young child found at the Mollo Kontu platform mound (Couture 2003) and the concentration of crania uncovered in Akapana contexts (Manzanilla 1992; Manzanilla and Woodard 1990) are excellent examples of this practice. In the Lake Titicaca Basin, the practice of burying heads without bodies has ancient roots and is observed by Christine Hastorf (2003) as early as the Middle Formative (ca. 1000–800 BCE; see also Blom and Bandy 1999).

The lack of trophy heads among the Tiwanaku skeletal remains does not indicate that the Tiwanaku shied away from violence. At Akapana, multiple human sacrifices, usually of young men, are scattered along its exterior terraces, where partial bodies can be found, sometimes splayed atop large deposits of smashed drinking vessels or mixed with camelid remains (Blom and Janusek 2004; Blom et al. 2003; Manzanilla 1992; Manzanilla and Woodard 1990). The mound in the Mollo Kontu sector also contains dedicatory burials, including one with an adult male placed face down with his arms behind his back (Couture 2003). Additionally, Verano (2013) analyzed remains southeast of Kalasasaya that included individuals with evidence of head wounds.

Why, then, do we not see evidence of actual Tiwanaku trophy heads? Perhaps they were kept and passed on from generation to generation and not deposited in the archaeological record, or perhaps preservation is a factor. Trophy heads that have been recovered in other highland Andean sites, such as two ritual structures at Conchopata, a secondary site in the Wari heartland, were burned and smashed before being deposited (Tung 2012; Tung and Knudson 2010). In any case, although we do not see evidence of actual trophy heads at Tiwanaku or associated sites, their representation on ceramic iconography, stone sculpture, and other media certainly indicates their importance in Tiwanaku society.

Generally, discussion on the use of trophy heads focuses on the effectiveness of trophy head taking in striking fear and horror in one's enemies or subjects, and we do not discount the effective role that trophy heads played in statecraft. Like sacrifice, and other forms of ritual violence, the practice is complex and nuanced. For now, rather than focusing on trophy heads as evidence of what Edward Swenson (2003) calls "ritual homicide," we would like to turn the conversation in another, more broadly ontological, direction by considering what we know ethnographically about head taking and curating heads in some areas of the Andes and their relationship with the concept of babies or wawa.

Before moving on, we pause to acknowledge that while ethnographic and ethnohistorical sources can provide valuable perspectives for our work, we recognize the caveats surrounding biases in ethnohistorical data and that ethnography has been criticized as representing rural Andean populations as static and homogeneous ("lo Andino") (e.g., Jamieson 2005; Starn 1991; Weismantel 1991). We hope to avoid the danger of projecting ethnographic analogies uncritically onto the past by grounding our analysis in archaeological data and context.

ETHNOGRAPHIC VIEWS ON TROPHY HEADS, TRANSFORMATION, AND THE CONCEPT OF *WAWA*

Inspired by earlier work on Nasca trophy heads (e.g., Proulx 1989), Denise Arnold and Juan de Dios Yapita (2006) discuss the use of trophy heads historically and ethnographically in the Qaqachaka region of Oruro, Bolivia. Their work and subsequent work by Arnold and Hastorf (2008) draw on the archaeology and ethnography of the Amazon and Andes to paint a picture of the importance of head taking, metamorphosis, and regeneration (see also Hastorf, chapter 17 of this volume). For the people of Ayllu Qaqachaka and others, the actual taking of a head, be that of an enemy, a deceased family member, or an unknown individual recovered from a grave, is only one element of a much longer transformative and regenerative process in which dangerous, powerful objects are

transformed into a regenerative power for those who possess them (see also the discussion of *ñatitas* by Becker and Alconini, chapter 15 of this volume). Arnold and Elvira Espejo Ayca note:

> The objective was to convert the dead enemy trophy head into a living baby or *wawa* of the same group. In these stages of metamorphosis, the energies of the enemy Other was transformed into those necessary to achieve the postwar regenerative harvest of all kinds of "babies" (*wawa*) in the household, the ayllu, and beyond: human, animal and vegetable, even mineral. These transformations are key to understanding the generic use of the term *wawa* in Aymara and Quechua languages. (2009:276–77)

In Aymara and Quechua, *wawa* is a generic term for offspring. It refers not only to human children but also to all kinds of other offspring, including produce from the land, the offspring of animals, and places and objects in the physical landscape that are imbued with animate properties (e.g., shrines, sacred mountains, and stones). In the semantic domain, the concept of wawa includes both the start and the culmination of cycles of growth and regeneration. For example, in the case of livestock (e.g., llamas and alpacas), wawa describes both the fetus and the newborn animal that results from gestation. In the cycle of potato cultivation, wawa refers to the "initial growth of the new plant, tender and unripe, as well as the new tubers that culminate the cycle with the next harvest" (Arnold and Yapita 2006:94). The potato "baby," or wawa, is both seedling and tuber.

In order to appropriate the regenerative powers of the trophy head to produce offspring or seeds, a process of ritual transformation is necessary to *contain* and control the dangerous powers of the head. Symbolically, "containment" can be seen, according to Arnold and Hastorf (2008), in stone borders surrounding fields in which seedlings grow and, drawing on the work of Anne Paul with Paracas textiles, in decorative borders surrounding heads on textiles, in headbands or turbans, and in hat bands. The concept of containment calls to mind Victor Turner's (1967) well-known analysis of the ritual process, in particular the physical seclusion of potentially volatile and dangerous neophytes during the "betwixt and between" liminal phase of *rites de passages*.

CONCLUSION

The processes of transformation described here might be used to frame practices and beliefs about trophy heads as seen in Tiwanaku iconography. We can imagine the containment of heads in architectural elements at Tiwanaku such as the framed heads described above or the hundreds of disembodied stone heads contained in the Semi-Subterranean Temple, which are thought to represent the ancestors of the communities who came to Tiwanaku to take part in rituals at the temple (Couture 2002, 2007). Might we see this structure as symbolic of the capture and containment of these heads? To take this analogy one step further, one can speculate that the walls of the sunken temple are intended to contain the volatile and potentially dangerous energy associated with ritual practices that call for the engagement and/or transformation of ancestral forces.

In Qaqachaka, the most common form of containment is when women create ritual bundles by wrapping captured heads in textiles. In this way, a woman can cause an enemy head to metamorphose into kin or wawa (Arnold and Hastorf 2008:79). This ritual containment of captured heads has parallels in the way that infants, and their heads, were and still are treated in the Andes, including among the Tiwanaku. This ritual containment that transforms trophy heads into kin or wawa can be seen to parallel the way that infants are contained in mantas and the ways that young children's heads are contained in hats or modification devices and transformed. Like human wawa, the trophy heads that are regenerated into wawa of various sorts "spend most of their time wrapped up." Over time, generic babies move out of their wild, presocial, and simultaneously dangerous and vulnerable fetal state into wawa; after that, they no longer need to be contained. Their social identities are formed, and they become fully human boys and girls.

Certainly, any argument that the Tiwanaku people linked the wrapping and transformation of infants' bodies and heads to containment and control of wild, dangerous spirits is speculative. Nevertheless, the power and importance of the practice of both cranial modification and head taking and containment as expressed in art were key elements of the Tiwanaku world view. Supernatural deities and mythical figures, the containment of ancestors, and the representation of elite power are prominent themes of Tiwanaku head imagery. The ways in which children's heads were treated by the Tiwanaku were crucial in the establishment of personhood through cranial modification practices. In addition to being essential for protecting vulnerable children, these practices can be seen as a means of containing wild/presocial young children as they were transformed and reintegrated as fully human subjects who embodied their social group. As we contemplate the primacy of the head as the locus of the embodied person in Tiwanaku culture and Andean society more broadly, we find that an analysis of complementary archaeological and bioarchaeological data sets provides us with a richer insight into culturally specific notions of personhood, the body, and social reproduction.

ACKNOWLEDGMENTS

We would like to thank to the editors of this volume, who also organized the original symposium from which this chapter derived; our many collaborators; and generous funding from several organizations. Our funding sources include the Social Sciences and Humanities Research Council of Canada and the H. John Heinz III Fund (to Nicole Couture and Deborah Blom); the Canadian Foundation for Innovation, the Fonds Québécois de la Recherche sur la Société et la Culture, the Canada Research Chair Program, and the Faculty of Arts Research Fund at McGill University (to Couture); and the University of Vermont's College of Arts and Sciences, the Wenner-Gren Foundation for Anthropological Research, and the National Science Foundation (BCS-1317184) (to Blom). The authors also express their gratitude to the Centro de Investigaciones Arqueológicas, Antropológicas y Administración de Tiwanaku (*CIAAAT*) for providing access to the facilities and collections housed at Tiwanaku. We also offer thanks to the Proyecto Wila Jawira and the numerous other projects and archaeologists who allowed access to collections, images, and field notes to contextualize our data; and to state and local organizations in Bolivia for granting permission to carry out archaeological research at Tiwanaku, including *CIAAAT*, the Unidad de Arqueología y Museos, the Ministerio de Culturas, the community of Wankollo, the municipal government of Tiahuanaco, and the Consejo de Ayllus y Comunidades Originarios de Tiwanaku. Finally, we are profoundly grateful to our friends in the town of Tiwanaku, as well as the many Bolivian and North American students and colleagues who have worked with us, for their generous intellectual, emotional, and logistical support throughout the years.

NOTES

1. We have seen these practices frequently in our own work at Tiwanaku, most prominently when Blom's young son experienced illnesses during our investigations, and our Aymara friends and acquaintances brought ritual specialists in to help.

2. A similar observation about the necessity of swaddling to form proper children's bodies has been made in Mesoamerica, in highland Chiapas, by Patricia Marks Greenfield (2004:29–31) in observing the socialization of girls. There, mothers build on their newborn daughters' upper body stillness and visual attention by swaddling them. This is said to prepare the infant for practices in later life, such as cooking tortillas and, most importantly, weaving with a backstrap loom.

3. In his 1612 Spanish-Aymara dictionary, Bertonio (1984) includes terms and phrases referring to three different head shapes, each produced via a different technique. A number of terms refer to tapered or conical heads (*cabeza ahusada*), but there are a few that refer to round heads (*cabeza redonda*) and flattened heads (*cabeza aplastada*). Apparently, tapered was the most common head shape in the western basin, where Bertonio resided.

4. It should be noted that some of the tenon heads present today were carved and added during the excavation and reconstruction of the temple from 1961 to 1963 (John Janusek, personal communication from Marcelino Quispe, July 2011).

REFERENCES CITED

Alconini, Sonia

1995   *Rito, símbolo e historia en la pirámide de Akapana, Tiwanaku: un análisis de cerámica ceremonial prehispánica.* Editorial Acción, La Paz.

Allen, Catherine J.

2002   *The Hold Life Has: Coca and Cultural Identity in an Andean Community.* 2nd ed. Smithsonian Institution Press, Washington, DC.

Anderson, Karen

2009   Tiwanaku Influence on Local Drinking Patterns in Cochabamba, Bolivia. In *Drink, Power, and Society in the Andes,* edited by Justin Jennings and Brenda J. Bowser, pp. 167–99. University Press of Florida, Gainesville.

Andrushko, Valerie A.

2011   How the Wari Fashioned Trophy Heads for Display: A Distinctive Modified Cranium from Cuzco, Peru and Comparison to Trophies from the Capital Region. In *The Bioarchaeology of the Human Head: Decapitation, Decoration, and Deformation,* edited by Michelle Bonogofsky, pp. 262–85. University Press of Florida, Gainesville.

Arnold, Denise Y., and Elvira Espejo Ayca

2009   A Comparison of War Iconography in the Archaeological Textiles of Paracas-Topará (in Southern Peru) and in the Weavings of Ayllu Qaqachaka (Bolivia) Today. *Textile: The Journal of Cloth and Culture* 7:272–95.

Arnold, Denise Y., and Christine A. Hastorf

2008   *Heads of State: Icons, Power, and Politics in the Ancient and Modern Andes.* Left Coast Press, Walnut Creek, California.

Arnold, Denise Y., and Juan de Dios Yapita

2006   *The Metamorphosis of Heads: Textual Struggles, Education, and Land in the Andes.* University of Pittsburgh Press, Pittsburgh.

Baker, Paul T., and Michael A. Little (editors)

1976   *Man in the Andes: A Multidisciplinary Study of High-Altitude Quechua.* Dowden, Hutchinson, and Ross, Stroudsburg, Pennsylvania.

Bandelier, Adolph F.

1910   *The Islands of Titicaca and Koati.* Hispanic Society of America, New York.

Barth, Fredrik

1969   *Ethnic Groups and Boundaries: The Social Organization of Culture Difference.* Little, Brown, Boston.

Becker, Sara K., and Sonia Alconini

2015   Head Extraction, Interregional Exchange, and Political Strategies of Control at the Site of Wata Wata, Kallawaya Territory, Bolivia, during the Transition between the Late Formative and Tiwanaku Periods (AD 200–800). *Latin American Antiquity* 26:30–48.

Berryman, Carrie A., Kelly J. Knudson, Sara K. Becker, Shannon L. Wilson, and Deborah E. Blom

2009   A Multidisciplinary Approach to Human Skeletal Analysis at Mollo Kontu, Tiwanaku (Bolivia). Paper presented at the seventy-fourth annual meeting of the Society for American Archaeology, Atlanta.

Bertonio, Ludovico

1984 [1612]   *Vocabulario de la lengua Aymara.* Centro de Estudios de la Realidad Económica y Social; Instituto Francés de Estudios Andinos; Museo Nacional de Etnografía y Folklore, Cochabamba, Bolivia.

Blom, Deborah E.

1999   *Tiwanaku Regional Interaction and Social Identity: A Bioarchaeological Approach.* PhD dissertation, Department of Anthropology, University of Chicago.

2005   Embodying Borders: Human Body Modification and

Diversity in Tiwanaku Society. *Journal of Anthropological Archaeology* 24:1–24.

Blom, Deborah E., and Matthew S. Bandy

1999 Human Remains and Mortuary Analysis. In *Early Settlement at Chiripa, Bolivia: Research of the Taraco Archaeological Project*, edited by Christine A. Hastorf, pp. 117–22, 133–36. University of California, Berkeley Archaeological Research Facility, Berkeley.

Blom, Deborah E., Benedikt Hallgrímsson, Linda Keng, María Cecilia Lozada, and Jane E. Buikstra

1998 Tiwanaku "Colonization": Bioarchaeological Implications for Migration in the Moquegua Valley, Peru. *World Archaeology* 30:238–61.

Blom, Deborah E., and John W. Janusek

2004 Making Place: Humans as Dedications in Tiwanaku. *World Archaeology* 36:123–41.

Blom, Deborah E., John W. Janusek, and Jane E. Buikstra

2003 A Re-Evaluation of Human Remains from Tiwanaku. In *Tiwanaku and Its Hinterland: Archaeology and Paleoecology of an Andean Civilization*. Vol. 2, *Urban and Rural Archaeology*, edited by Alan L. Kolata, pp. 435–48. Smithsonian Institution Press, Washington, DC.

Blom, Deborah E., and Kelly J. Knudson

2014 Tracing Tiwanaku Childhoods: A Bioarchaeological Study of Age and Identity in Tiwanaku Society. In *Tracing Childhood: Bioarchaeological Investigations of Early Lives in Antiquity*, edited by Jennifer L. Thompson, Marta P. Alfonso-Durruty, and John J. Crandall, pp. 228–45. University Press of Florida, Gainesville.

Blom, Deborah E., Kelly J. Knudson, John W. Janusek, Sara K. Becker, and Corey M. Bowen

2016 Formation and Transformation of Identities in the Andes: The Constructions of Childhood among the Tiwanaku. Paper presented at the eightieth annual meeting of the Society for American Archaeology, Orlando.

Bolin, Inge

2006 *Growing Up in a Culture of Respect: Child Rearing in Highland Peru*. University of Texas Press, Austin.

Bourget, Steve

2006 *Sex, Death, and Sacrifice in Moche Religion and Visual Arts*. University of Texas Press, Austin.

Bray, Tamara

2000 Imperial Inca Iconography: The Art of Empire in the Andes. *RES: Anthropology and Aesthetics* 38:168–78.

Buikstra, Jane E.

1995 Tombs for the Living . . . or . . . for the Dead: The Osmore Ancestors. In *Tombs for the Living: Andean Mortuary Practices*, edited by Tom D. Dillehay, pp. 229–80. Dumbarton Oaks, Washington, DC.

Burkholder, Jo Ellen

n.d. The Dead at Iwawi; or, Looking for Gender in Just the Right Places. Unpublished manuscript.

Canessa, Andrew

2000a Contexting Hybridity: *Evangelistas* and *Kataristas* in Highland Bolivia. *Journal of Latin American Studies* 32:115–44.

2000b Fear and Loathing on the Kharisiri Trail: Alterity and Identity in the Andes. *Journal of the Royal Anthropological Institute* 6:705–20.

Cieza de León, Pedro de

1984 [1553] *La crónica del Perú, obras completos*. 3 vols. Consejo Superior de Investigaciones Cientificas, Instituto Gonzalo Fernández de Oviedo, Madrid.

Cobo, Bernabé

1956 [1653] *Historia del Nuevo Mundo*. Vol. 2. Biblioteca de Autores Espanoles, 92. Ediciones Atlas, Madrid.

Conklin, William J.

1991 Tuahuanaco and Huari: Architectural Comparisons and Interpretations. In *Huari Administrative Structure: Prehistoric Monumental Architecture and State Government*, edited by William H. Isbell and Gordon F. McEwan, pp. 281–91. Dumbarton Oaks, Washington, DC.

2009 The Iconic Dimension in Tiwanaku Art. In *Tiwanaku: Papers from the 2005 Mayer Center Symposium at the Denver Art Museum*, edited by Margaret Young-Sánchez, pp. 115–32. Denver Art Museum, Denver.

Cook, Anita G.

1983 Aspects of State Ideology in Huari and Tiwanaku Iconography: The Central Deity and the Sacrificer. In *Investigations of the Andean Past: Papers from the First Annual Northeast Conference on Andean Archeology and Ethnohistory*, vol. 1, edited by Daniel Sandweiss, pp. 161–86. Cornell Latin American Studies Program, Ithaca, New York.

1992 The Stone Ancestors: Idioms of Imperial Attire and Rank among Huari Figurines. *Latin American Antiquity* 3:341–64.

1994 *Wari y Tiwanaku: entre el estilo y la imagen*. Pontificia Universidad Católica, Lima.

1996 The Emperor's New Clothes: Symbols of Royalty, Hierarchy, and Identity. *Journal of the Stewart Anthropological Society* 24(1–2):85–120.

Costa Junqueira, María Antonietta, Walter A. Neves, and Mark Hubbe

2004 Influencia de Tiwanaku en la calidad de vida biológica de la población prehistórica de San Pedro de Atacama. *Estudios Atacameños* 27:103–16.

Couture, Nicole C.

2002 *The Construction of Power: Monumental Space and Elite Residence at Tiwanaku.* PhD dissertation, Department of Anthropology, University of Chicago.

2003 Ritual, Monumentalism, and Residence at Mollo Kontu, Tiwanaku. In *Tiwanaku and Its Hinterland: Archaeology and Paleoecology of an Andean Civilization.* Vol. 2, *Urban and Rural Archaeology*, edited by Alan L. Kolata, pp. 202–25. Smithsonian Institution Press, Washington, DC.

2007 The Production and Representation of Status in a Tiwanaku Royal House. In *The Durable House: Architecture, Ancestors, and Origins*, edited by Robin A. Beck Jr., pp. 422–45. Center for Archaeological Investigations, Southern Illinois University, Carbondale.

2008 Talking Heads and the Grateful Dead: Unpacking the Meaning of "Trophy Heads" at Tiwanaku. Paper presented at the seventy-third annual meeting of the Society for American Archaeology, Vancouver, March 26–30.

Couture, Nicole C., and Kathryn E. Sampeck

2003 Putuni: A History of Palace Architecture in Tiwanaku. In *Tiwanaku and Its Hinterland: Archaeology and Paleoecology of an Andean Civilization.* Vol. 2, *Urban and Rural Archaeology*, edited by Alan L. Kolata, pp. 226–63. Smithsonian Institution Press, Washington, DC.

De la Vega, Garcilaso

1966 *Royal Commentaries of the Incas and General History of Peru.* Translated by Harold V. Livermore. University of Texas Press, Austin. First published as *Comentarios reales de los Incas* in 1609.

Diez de San Miguel, Garci

1964 [1567] *Visita hecha a la Provincia de Chucuito por Garci Diez de San Míguel en el año 1567.* Vol. 1. Documentos Regionales para la Etnología y Etnohistoria Andinas. Ediciones de la Casa de La Cultura del Peru, Lima.

Donnan, Christopher B.

1978 *Moche Art of Peru.* Fowler Museum of Cultural History, University of California, Los Angeles.

Duncan, William N., and Charles Andrew Hofling

2011 Why the Head? Cranial Modification as Protection and Ensoulment among the Maya. *Ancient Mesoamerica* 22:199–210.

Frame, Mary

1990 *Andean Four-Cornered Hats: Ancient Volumes.* Metropolitan Museum of Art, New York.

Goldstein, Paul Samuel

2005 *Andean Diaspora: The Tiwanaku Colonies and the Origins of South America Empire.* University Press of Florida, Gainesville.

Graham, Margaret A.

1997 Food Allocation in Rural Peruvian Households: Concepts and Behavior Regarding Children. *Social Science and Medicine* 44(11):1697–709.

1999 Child Nutrition and Seasonal Hunger in an Andean Community. Programa Nacional de Sistemas Agrícolas Andinos, Lima. Working paper, Department of Anthropology, University of North Carolina at Chapel Hill.

Greenfield, Patricia Marks

2004 *Weaving Generations Together: Evolving Creativity in the Maya of Chiapas.* School of American Research Press, Santa Fe.

Greenway, Christine

1998a Hungry Earth and Vengeful Stars: Soul Loss and Identity in the Peruvian Andes. *Social Science and Medicine* 47(8):993–1004.

1998b Objectified Selves: An Analysis of Medicines in Andean Sacrificial Healing. *Medical Anthropology Quarterly* 12(2):147–67.

Harris, Olivia

1980 The Power of Signs: Gender, Culture and the Wild in the Bolivian Andes. In *Nature, Culture and Gender*, edited by Carol MacCormack and Marilyn Strathern, pp. 70–94. Cambridge University Press, Cambridge.

Hastorf, Christine A.

2003 Community with the Ancestors: Ceremonies and Social Memory in the Middle Formative at Chiripa, Bolivia. *Journal of Anthropological Archaeology* 22(4):305–32.

Higueras-Hare, Alvaro

1996 *Prehispanic Settlement and Land Use in Cochabamba, Bolivia.* PhD dissertation, Department of Anthropology, University of Pittsburgh.

Hoshower, Lisa M., Jane E. Buikstra, Paul S. Goldstein, and Ann D. Webster

1995   Artificial Cranial Deformation in the Omo M10 Site: A Tiwanaku Complex from the Moquegua Valley, Peru. *Latin American Antiquity* 6:145–64.

Isbell, Billie Jean

1997   De inmaduro a duro: lo simbólico femenino y los esquemas andinos de género. In *Más allá del silencio: las fronteras de género en los Andes*, edited by Denise Y. Arnold. Biblioteca Andina, La Paz.

Isbell, William Harris, and Patricia J. Knobloch

2006   Missing Links, Imaginary Links: Staff God Imagery in the South Andean Past. In *Andean Archaeology III: North and South*, edited by William Harris Isbell and Helaine Silverman, pp. 307–51. Springer, New York.

2009   SAIS: The Origin, Development, and Dating of Tiahuanaco-Wari Iconography. In *Tiwanaku: Papers from the 2005 Mayer Center Symposium at the Denver Art Museum*, edited by Margaret Young-Sánchez, pp. 165–210. Denver Art Museum, Denver.

Jamieson, Ross W.

2005   Colonialism, Social Archaeology, and *lo Andino*: Historical Archaeology in the Andes. *World Archaeology* 37:352–72.

Janusek, John Wayne

1994   *State and Local Power in a Prehispanic Polity: Changing Patterns of Urban Residence in Tiwanaku and Lukurmata, Bolivia*. PhD dissertation, Department of Anthropology, University of Chicago.

2003   Vessels, Time, and Society: Toward a Chronology of Ceramic Style in the Tiwanaku Heartland. In *Tiwanaku and Its Hinterland: Archaeology and Paleoecology of an Andean Civilization*. Vol. 2, *Urban and Rural Archaeology*, edited by Alan L. Kolata, pp. 30–94. Smithsonian Institution Press, Washington, DC.

2004   *Identity and Power in the Ancient Andes: Tiwanaku Cities through Time*. Routledge, London.

Knobloch, Patricia

2010   La imagen de los Señores de Huari y la recuperación de una identidad antigua. In *Señores de los Imperios del Sol*, edited by Krzysztof Makowski, pp. 196–209. Banco de Crédito, Lima.

Knudson, Kelly J., Sloan R. Williams, Rebecca Osborn, Kathleen Forgey, and Patrick Ryan Williams

2009   The Geographic Origins of Nasca Trophy Heads in the Kroeber Collection Using Strontium, Oxygen, and Carbon Isotope Data. *Journal of Anthropological Archaeology* 28(2):244–57.

Kolata, Alan L.

1993   *Tiwanaku: Portrait of an Andean Civilization*. Blackwell, Cambridge.

1996   *Tiwanaku and Its Hinterland: Archaeology and Paleoecology of an Andean Civilization*. Vol. 1, *Agroecology*. Smithsonian Institution Press, Washington, DC.

2003 (editor)   *Tiwanaku and Its Hinterland: Archaeology and Paleoecology of an Andean Civilization*. Vol. 2, *Urban and Rural Archaeology*. Smithsonian Institution Press, Washington, DC.

Korpisaari, Antti, and Martti Pärssinen

2005 (editors)   *Pariti: isla, misterio y poder; el tesoro cerámico de la cultura Tiwanaku*. República de Bolivia; República de Finlandia; CIMA, La Paz.

2011   *Pariti: The Ceremonial Tiwanaku Pottery of an Island in Lake Titicaca*. Finnish Academy of Science and Letters, Helsinki.

La Barre, Weston

1948   *The Aymara Indians of the Lake Titicaca Plateau, Bolivia*. American Anthropologist Memoirs, no. 68. American Anthropological Association, Menasha, Wisconsin.

Lancy, David F.

2008   *The Anthropology of Childhood: Cherubs, Chattel, Changelings*. Cambridge University Press, Cambridge.

Leonard, William R.

1991   Household-Level Strategies for Protecting Children from Seasonal Food Scarcity. *Social Science and Medicine* 33:1127–33.

LeVine, Robert Alan

1980   A Cross-Cultural Perspective on Parenting. In *Parenting in a Multicultural Society*, edited by Mario D. Fantini and René Cárdenas, pp. 17–26. Longman, New York.

LeVine, Robert Alan, and Rebecca Staples New

2008   *Anthropology and Child Development: A Cross-Cultural Reader*. Blackwell, Malden, Massachusetts.

López Austin, Alfredo

1989   *Cuerpo humano e ideología: las concepciones de los antiguos nahuas*. Universidad Nacional Autónoma de México, Mexico City.

Lozada, María Cecilia, and Gordon F. M. Rakita

2013   Andean Life Transitions and Gender Perceptions in the Past: A Bioarchaeological Approach among the Pre-Inca Chiribaya of Southern Perú. In *The Dead*

Tell Tales: Essays in Honor of Jane E. Buikstra, edited by María Cecilia Lozada and Barra O'Donnabhain, pp. 114–22. Cotsen Institute of Archaeology, University of California, Los Angeles.

Makowski, Krzysztof

2009 Royal Statues, Staff Gods, and the Religious Ideology of the Prehistoric Tiwanaku. In *Tiwanaku: Papers from the 2005 Mayer Center Symposium at the Denver Art Museum*, edited by Margaret Young-Sánchez, pp. 133–64. Denver Art Museum, Denver.

Manzanilla, Linda

1992 *Akapana: una pirámide en el centro del mundo*. Instituto de Investigaciones Antropológicas, Universidad Nacional Autónoma de México, Mexico City.

Manzanilla, Linda, and Eric Woodard

1990 Restos humanos asociados a la pirámide de Akapana (Tiwanaku, Bolivia). *Latin American Antiquity* 1:133–49.

Morgan, Lynn M.

1997 Imagining the Unborn in the Ecuadoran Andes. *Feminist Studies* 23(2):323–50.

Ogburn, Dennis

2007 Human Trophies in the Late Pre-Hispanic Andes: Display, Propaganda, and Reinforcement of Power among the Incas and Other Societies. In *The Taking and Displaying of Human Body Parts as Trophies by Amerindians: Interdisciplinary Contributions to Archaeology*, edited by Richard J. Chacon and David H. Dye, pp. 505–22. Springer, New York.

Ohnstad, Arik, Scott Smith, and John Wayne Janusek

2006 Social and Spatial Disjunction: Landscapes, Politics, and Memory during the Late Formative at Khonkho Wankane, Bolivia. Paper presented at the seventy-first annual meeting of the Society for American Archaeology, San Juan, Puerto Rico.

Orta, Andrew

2000 Syncretic Subjects and Body Politics: Doubleness, Personhood, and Aymara Catechists. *American Ethnologist* 26:864–89.

Platt, Tristan

2002 El feto agresivo: parto, formación de la persona y mito-historia en los Andes. *Estudios Atacameños* 22:127–55.

Plummer, John F.

1966 Another Look at Aymara Personality. *Cross-Cultural Research* 1(2):55–78.

Ponce Sanginés, Carlos

1972 *Tiwanaku: espacio, tiempo y cultura; ensayo de síntesis arqueológica*. Publicación no. 30. Academia Nacional de Ciencias de Bolivia, La Paz.

1990 *Descripcion sumaria del templete semisubterranio de Tiwanaku*. 6th ed. Academia Nacional de Ciencias de Bolivia, La Paz.

Proulx, Donald

1989 Nasca Trophy Heads: Victims of Warfare or Ritual Sacrifice? In *Cultures in Conflict: Current Archaeological Perspectives*. Proceedings of the Twentieth Chacmool Annual Conference, edited by Diane Claire Tkaczuk and Brian C. Vivian, pp. 73–85. Chacmool Archaeological Association, University of Calgary, Calgary.

2006 *A Sourcebook of Nasca Ceramic Iconography: Reading a Culture through Its Art*. University of Iowa Press, Iowa City.

Shimada, Izumi

1994 *Pampa Grande and the Mochica Culture*. University of Texas Press, Austin.

Sillar, Bill

1994 Playing with God: Cultural Perceptions of Children, Play and Miniatures in the Andes. *Archaeological Review from Cambridge* 13(2):47–63.

Silverman, Helaine

1993 *Cahuachi in the Ancient Nasca World*. University of Iowa Press, Iowa City.

Stanish, Charles

2003 *Ancient Titicaca: The Evolution of Complex Society in Southern Peru and Northern Bolivia*. University of California Press, Berkeley.

Starn, Orin

1991 Missing the Revolution: Anthropologists and the War in Peru. *Culture and Anthropology* 6(1):63–91.

Swenson, Edward R.

2003 Cities of Violence: Sacrifice, Power, and Urbanization in the Andes. *Journal of Social Archaeology* 3(2):256–96.

Torquemada, Juan de

1995 [1557–1664] *Monarquía indiana*. 3rd ed. Vol. 2, book 14. Edited by Miguel León-Portilla. Universidad Nacional Autónoma de México, Mexico City.

Torres-Rouff, Christina

2002 Cranial Vault Modification and Ethnicity in Middle Horizon San Pedro de Atacama, Chile. *Current Anthropology* 43(1):163–71.

2003 *Shaping Identity: Cranial Vault Modification in the Pre-Columbian Andes*. PhD dissertation, Department of Anthropology, University of California, Santa Barbara.

2008 The Influence of Tiwanaku on Life in the Chilean

Atacama: Mortuary and Bodily Perspectives. *American Anthropologist* 110(3):325–37.

Tronick, Edward Z., R. Brook Thomas, and Magali Daltabuit

1994 The Quechua Manta Pouch: A Caretaking Practice for Buffering the Peruvian Infant against the Multiple Stressors of High Altitude. *Child Development* 65:1005–13.

Tschopik, Harry, Jr.

1946 The Aymara. In *Handbook of South American Indians.* Vol. 2, *The Andean Civilizations*, edited by Julian H. Steward, pp. 501–73. Smithsonian Institution, Bureau of American Ethnology, Bulletin 143, Washington, DC.

1951 *The Aymara of Chucuito, Peru.* Vol. 1, *Magic.* Anthropological Papers of the American Museum of Natural History, vol. 44, part 2. American Museum of Natural History, New York.

Tung, Tiffiny A.

2008 Dismembering Bodies for Display: A Bioarchaeological Study of Trophy Heads from the Wari Site of Conchopata, Peru. *American Journal of Physical Anthropology* 136:294–308.

2012 *Violence, Ritual, and the Wari Empire.* University Press of Florida, Gainesville.

Tung, Tiffiny A., and Kelly J. Knudson

2008 Social Identities and Geographical Origins of Wari Trophy Heads from Conchopata, Peru. *Current Anthropology* 49(5):915–25.

2010 Childhood Lost: Abductions, Sacrifice, and Trophy Heads of Children in the Wari Empire of the Ancient Andes. *Latin American Antiquity* 21(1):44–66.

Turner, Victor

1967 *The Forest of Symbols: Aspects of Ndembu Ritual.* Cornell University Press, Ithaca, New York.

Verano, John W.

1995 Where Do They Rest? The Treatment of Human Offerings and Trophies in Ancient Peru. In *Tombs for the Living: Andean Mortuary Practices*, edited by Tom D. Dillehay, pp. 189–227. Dumbarton Oaks, Washington, DC.

2008 Trophy Head-Taking and Human Sacrifice in Andean South America. In *Handbook of South American Archaeology*, edited by Helaine Silverman and William H. Isbell, 1047–60. Springer, New York.

2013 Excavation and Analysis of Human Skeletal Remains from a New Dedicatory Offering at Tiwanaku. In *Advances in Titicaca Basin Archaeology-2*, edited by Alexei Vranich and Abigail R. Levine, pp. 167–80. Cotsen Institute of Archaeology, University of California, Los Angeles.

Weismantel, Mary J.

1991 Maize Beer and Andean Social Transformation: Drunken Indians, Bread Babies, and Chosen Women. *Modern Language Notes* 104(4):861–79.

Zabala, Pilar

2014 Source Compilation on Head-Shaping Practices in Hispanic America. In *The Bioarchaeology of Artificial Cranial Modifications: New Approaches to Head Shaping and Its Meanings in Pre-Columbian Mesoamerica and Beyond*, authored by Vera Tiesler, pp. 99–129. Springer, New York.

Zuidema, R. Tom

2009 Tiwanaku, Iconography, and the Calendar. In *Tiwanaku: Papers from the 2005 Mayer Center Symposium at the Denver Art Museum*, edited by Margaret Young-Sánchez, pp. 83–100. Denver Art Museum, Denver.

14

Cranial Modification in the Central Andes

Person, Language, Political Economy

BRUCE MANNHEIM, ALLISON R. DAVIS, AND MATTHEW C. VELASCO

INTRODUCTION

We seek to interpret the practice of cranial vault modification—shaping the form of infant heads developmentally through splinting, binding, or cradle boarding—in the south-central Andes in terms of what we know archaeologically, historically, and ethnographically about the relationships between personhood, place, language, and social differentiation. We track this practice examining two cases from the south-central Andes, one from the Formative period (750 BCE to 300 CE) and one bridging the Inka period through the time of the European invasion (sixteenth century), tracing changes in a childcare practice that became an index connecting personhood to place and language within an "organization of diversity" (Wallace 1961:28). During the Formative period in Cuzco, a single ubiquitous childcare practice produced a variety of nonstandardized head shapes that can neither be categorized by form nor used by archaeologists as proxies for cultural or linguistic difference. In contrast, in Inka and early colonial contexts, varied techniques crafted standardized and distinct head shapes that provide one of the few forms of material evidence for the ways in which cultural and linguistic differentiation played out in everyday settings. Cranial modification, then, is the outcome of social processes differentiated by locality, gender, and age rather than simply a classificatory device.

We work from a case in the colonial period that is well attested historically and archaeologically to the south-central Andean Formative, in order to contextualize cranial vault modification socially. Our objective is to frame what we believe are the central questions that need be asked to understand the practice of cranial modification, questions that are ultimately answerable archaeologically but that are not answerable under the current scatter of data points available comparatively, including bringing the practice of cranial modification into household and settlement-level excavations; mapping distributions systematically across regions (much as R. Alan Covey et al. [2013] have done for pottery types in the Middle Horizon Cuzco); and carrying out archaeogenetic studies with single localized but longitudinal populations. Our emphasis here is distinctly local. Christina Torres-Rouff's pathbreaking systematization (2003) has identified the effects of increased standardization of modification form with the increased organizational complexity of societies. While forms may be increasingly standardized across localities, we approach standardization not in terms of homogeneity of form but as the relative degree to which deliberate modification techniques or related child-rearing practices were used to mold ideal head shapes. Our goal is to understand the process of cranial modification locally and to construct a framework that allows for comparison with other South American societies in local, "bottom-up" contexts, an approach similar to Lisa Hoshower et al.'s study at Omo (1995) but with increased emphasis on daily practices over typology.[1]

Our use of the expressions "person" and "personhood" in a context in which one expects "individuals" and "populations" may be unfamiliar to some readers. "Persons" and "personhood" are constituted relationally and socially, and vary from society to society.[2] In the central Andes, for example, places are persons, social beings, with which humans interact on a quotidian, routine basis (Allen 2002:41; de la Cadena 2015; Dean 2015; Mannheim and Salas Carreño 2015:40–64; Ødegaard 2011; Salas Carreño 2012; Stensrud 2016). Native Andeans attribute the same kinds of motives, desires, and emotions to them as to human persons, and ethnographers have been pressed to invent labels for them: "tirrakuna" (from Quechua "places"), "place persons," and "earth beings," for example. Central Andean personhood is doubly relational: within a specific network of consociates, human and otherwise, coresidential and beyond; and within a relationally structured social ontology (below). This drives our research strategy: to understand Central Andean cranial modification as a socially instituted, semiotic (or cultural) practice that anchored person to place upon an otherwise fluid social landscape where community boundaries were permeable, even as modification itself was indelible.

The first section of this chapter sets cranial modification into broader configurations of personhood, language, and locality in the south-central Andes. We trace these through an ethnohistorical case study from the Colca Valley of Arequipa and then trace the practice to the Formative in the nearby Cuzco region.

WHAT DOES THIS ALL MEAN? NOT ETHNICITY BUT LOCALITY

In his recent book *Par delà nature et culture* (2005; translated as *Beyond Nature and Culture*, 2013), Philippe Descola sketches a typological framework to account systematically for differences in the social ontologies among distinct societies, Native South American and beyond. Particularly important in this regard is his typology of forms of agency, differentiated along two parameters: inherence (or shared inner substance) and physical appearance. Together, these two parameters define four social regimes: naturalism (dominant in Europe since the eighteenth century), animism, totemism, and analogism,

all of which configure relationships between human and other-than-human entities. For example, a social ontology in which humans and some species of animals are treated as having the same inherence—conscious awareness—and different physical appearance (some are jaguars, some humans) would be characterized as "animist." Each of these larger categories themselves encompasses a range of social configurations that similarly lend themselves to typology. The purpose here is not to pigeonhole societies into social ontologies like "naturalist" or "animist" but to establish relational grids that allow us to compare configurations and to show how ethnographic phenomena are configured—to establish relationships of compatibility, incompatibility, and determination among them.[3]

In order to understand the scope and meaning of cranial modification in the central Andes, we need to locate it within a central Andean social ontology—one that characterizes modern rural communities, in which cranial modification is no longer practiced, and that also (by direct historical approach) characterizes their Inka and early colonial ancestors (who did practice cranial modification). We draw inspiration from Descola's framework for two reasons. First, it permits us to provide an orderly and systematic account of the social context. Second, it provides us with parameters with which we can compare the central Andean case with others from Native South America, including Amazonian peoples who continue to practice modification today, to help us better understand what is specific to the cases we are studying. To begin, we need to identify types of social beings or personae, distinguished by types of feeding, by inherence, and by differentiation of appearance. In figure 14.1, we distinguish three critical parameters: (1) shared inner substance; (2) relations of predation (which, apart from relationships between people and places, always involve shared appearance); and (3) ecologically differentiated relations to local places.

Humans share inner substance with localized places (not with "place" in general but with specific "places"). For example, for rural Quechuas, a person who was born in Cuzco is not Qusqumanta, "from Cuzco," but *is* Cuzco, literally made out of the same stuff as Cuzco, expected to return there when she returns to the earth. Both humans and places are social personae related to each other by food sharing. Humans and places also share speech, although this relationship is always mediated, either through ritual specialists (*paqu* and *misayuq*) for humans and places or through bird song for mountains (*apu*). A critical attribute of central Andean place shrines is that they *speak*

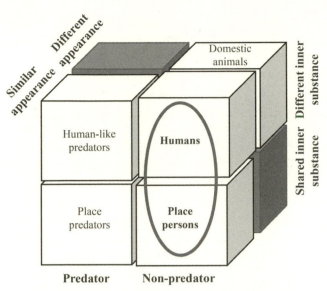

Predator   Non-predator

Figure 14.1. Types of social personae: three primary parameters. Gray cells and hidden cells are empty.

(Curatola Petrocchi 2009); places can speak through mediums, through divinatory ritual, through dreams, and through calls (*waqay*). A minor motif involves the relationships between humans and domestic animals. Humans not only feed and—in ritual—offer libations to domestic animals, but sing to them and receive calls back (Arnold and Yapita 1998b).

Humans share appearance with predators—beings that resemble humans outwardly, that speak, but that consume humans. These are well known in the ethnographic literature (Charlier Zeineddine 2015): *condenados*, who eat human flesh; slaughterers (*ñak'aq*), who consume human fat and sometimes blood; and shape-shifters, such as water spirits (Mannheim 1999) and the foxboy described in Catherine Allen's eponymous book (2011). Humans and place-persons, too, can engage in acts of predation, but with members of the other category: places can swallow humans or capriciously inflict illness on them; humans can mine places, releasing dangerous and capricious beings that can only be appeased through food offerings, including animal—and perhaps human—sacrifice.

An additional parameter that is relevant here is political-economic. The economy of the south-central Andes rested on the circulation of labor—hence, the circulation of people—rather than on the circulation of goods (D'Altroy and Earle 1985:189–92). Cranial modification was an indelible index of individuals to their population—and to their place—of origin.[4]

Late cranial modification took place within the rela-

tionship between human populations and the local places with which they shared substance. Cranial modification marked the human population as belonging to a particular place, especially (as we shall see in the case of the Colca Valley) when two populations were differentiated by distinct ecological relationships to the place. Because the relationship to place was also indexed linguistically, cranial modification also mapped normatively onto linguistic differentiation (also see Tiesler and Lacadena, chapter 3 of this volume).

First Case

The early colonial province of Collaguas (Arequipa) fits this model well. Mannheim discussed it in *The Language of the Inka since the European Invasion* (1991) in the context of a survey of preconquest and early colonial multilingualism in the southern Andes, identifying four basic principles: (1) the identification of linguistic variety with locality; (2) the interdigitation of differentiated linguistic and social groupings, often as a correlate of altitudinal (and so economic) differentiation (a pattern obtained more broadly in the southern Andean region, discussed by Lozada and Buikstra 2005:219); (3) the absence of any mechanism for homogenization of linguistic varieties over space (Rowe 1982); and so, (4) the maintenance of social boundaries as ascriptive rather than as fluid. These features reflect a more general emphasis in the Inka state on social differentiation rather than social homogenization, marked by bundling locality, speech, and dress (Pachacuti Yamqui ca. 1615), indexing local differentiation in a broader, state-organized circulation of labor. These principles played out differently in different localities: (1) the Xaquixguana plain outside Cuzco, which was multilingual into the late sixteenth century; (2) the Río Pampas watershed in Ayacucho, where Inka resettlement practices implanted linguistic differences as indices of ecological differentiation; (3) the region south of Lake Titicaca extending into what is now central Bolivia, where linguistic boundaries mapped economic and occupational hierarchies; (4) the province of Chumbivilcas in Cuzco, linguistically differentiated by ecologically complementary access to productive resources; and lastly, (5) Collaguas, with a similar pattern of differentiation. In all these cases, it is critical that linguistically significant social differences were constituted within a larger organization rather than in terms of temporary, contingent exchange relationships. As individuals, members of one group could not appropriate the social identities or language of the other, creating a larger pattern of stable, interdigitated multilingualism.

Juan de Ulloa Mogollon's late-sixteenth-century account of the province of Collaguas—one of the local reports collated in the *Relaciones geográficas*—describes a system of two ethnic groups entwined in a stable symbiotic relationship. One, the Collaguas, spoke Aymara, although there were some settlements in which another language was spoken, not mutually intelligible with Aymara; the other, the Cavanas, spoke Quechua (although a variety described as "corrupt" by Ulloa, that is, closely related to the variety spoken in Cuzco but distinct from it) (Ulloa 1586:328–29; cf. Doutriaux 2004:73–75; Gelles

1987:9–10; Manrique 1985:30–34; Pease 1977:140; Wernke 2006:179, 2013:chap. 3; Zabala 2014:110–11). According to Ulloa, the Collaguas occupied herding lands in the frigid plateaus and also occupied the poorest agricultural lands in the valleys, but with the Inka expansion they became the nucleus of Inka indirect rule (Wernke 2006). These units in turn were subdivided fractally, first into two ranked local settlements, then again by a ranked moiety division, then—for the lower moieties—into a ranked tripartite division. Steven Wernke (2006) takes this as evidence that the lower moieties were the focus of Inka administrative restructuring but also observes that Inka rule likely ossified the boundaries among ecologically differentiated groups (fig. 14.2).

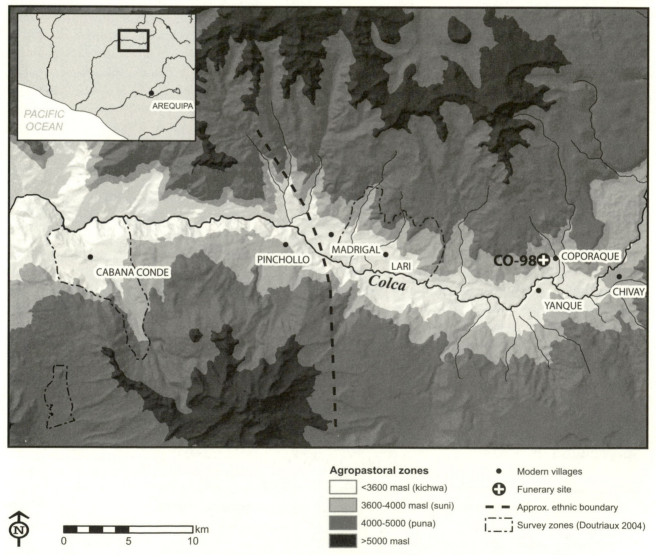

Figure 14.2. The region of the Cavanas and Collaguas. The approximate boundary between the two populations is indicated by a dashed line.

What of cranial modification? Not all localized social differentiation is equal, and within the hierarchy of distinctions, the highest-level distinction, between Collaguas and Cavanas, stands out as the focus of distinctive forms of cranial modification and of bundled differences of language, origin myth, and dress. The higher-altitude Collaguas were associated—by Ulloa—with annular modification (elongated heads), the lower-altitude Cavanas with tabular, "low, bulging heads" (plate 27) (Doutriaux 2004:75).[5]

By Wernke's account, the differentiation between Collaguas and Cavanas predates Inka rule, so it is likely that the modification patterns similarly preexisted the incorporation of the Collagua system into the state. Indeed, new radiocarbon dates from modified crania in the Colca Valley, and their calibrated 2-sigma ranges, fall before the onset of Inka imperialism in the southern Andes, which is traditionally placed around 1450 CE (Velasco 2016:262).

If linguistic differentiation is bundled with ecological differentiation and cranial modification, it is an ascriptive, enduring distinction. Although a number of recent papers have suggested that languages spread over contiguous territory in pre-Columbian times, the bundling of language and cranial modification and the specific (although not extensive) sixteenth-century descriptions of linguistic variability in the region suggest that such models are not viable empirically. Indeed, given that significant social and linguistic boundaries are literally inscribed in the crania, mechanisms of linguistic and cultural spread that rely on imitation are not plausible in the southern Andes more generally. Practices of cranial modification and linguistic differences were leveled later in the colonial period (they were still extant in the 1580s). Among Viceroy Toledo's (1573) Ordenanzas de Charcas (contemporary Bolivia) was an instruction: "Que las indias no apretan las cabezas a las criaturas recien nacidas" (That native women not compress the heads of infants), but many of Toledo's injunctions were ineffectual (e.g., his injunction against the consumption of alcohol), so it is more likely that cranial modification fell into disuse as the social distinctions that supported it were leveled (Stern 1982:59ff.; Mannheim 1991:60). Nevertheless, there continue to be differences today in women's hat styles that mark the Collagua-Cavana distinction (Doutriaux 2004:75).

There is a second, broader issue. Social differentiation inheres in the individual person, not the household or the burial unit. And so, while cranial modification fixed from birth an individual's position in the organization of

diversity, it would have also enabled stable interdigitation with persons who did not share the same inner substance (i.e., indexical relationship to place). Indeed, of the burial units that Miriam Doutriaux reported in her dissertation (2004:185), five sites located in the midvalley district of Lari had elongated crania; one Lari site had a bulging cranium; and three (both midvalley Lari and lower Cabanaconde) were mixed in composition. Some crania were unmodified. And both modification styles were found in both settlement areas (plate 27; fig.14.2). (There is no reason to suppose that any of the groupings that we discussed earlier were endogamous.) A similar pattern of diversity is evident in the Collagua heartland at the site of Yuraq Qaqa (CO-098), the largest complex of aboveground funerary structures in the upper valley, located in the transitional zone (*suni*) between valley-bottom agricultural lands and high-altitude pasturage (fig. 14.2) (Velasco 2014, 2016; Wernke 2013). Nearly forty percent of crania (37 percent, N=137) excavated from six distinct funerary structures do not exhibit intentional modification, undermining a simple correspondence between head shape, place of burial, and ethnicity (Velasco 2016). Moreover, crania modified in the typical Collagua style are not found exclusively in any one chamber. Modified and unmodified individuals were apparently buried alongside one another, suggesting that social boundaries marked by cranial modification were not isomorphic with those emplaced by funerary construction.

If the burial units evidence households of mixed composition, then there are both developmental and interactional meanings associated with cranial modification. Interactionally, what does it mean when a woman with an elongated head walks alongside a group of women with flat heads, with a flat-headed child on her back? Developmentally, what determines whether an infant is selected for modification? Doutriaux's warning that cranial modification is "fluid and elusive" (2004:194) suggests that we need to go beyond a simple taxonomic account in understanding how cranial modification played out in everyday life and across individual life histories (cf. Blom 2005; Blom and Knudson 2014; Blom and Couture, chapter 13 of this volume). Indeed, the territorially discontinuous distribution of cranial modification suggests that Ulloa's dichotomy belies a more complex pattern of interaction on the ground. Were it to in fact index a linguistic dichotomy, it would be the kind of fluid interaction among languages that one finds, for example, between modern-day Machiguenga (Arawakan) and Quechua today in La

Convención, Cuzco (Emlen 2014), in which language shift is bidirectional, many households are composites, and every household has a history of its own.

Second Case

Our second case is from the Cuzco Formative (dating 750 BCE to 300 CE).[6] Although the case is from a site to the north of Cuzco, Yuthu in the present-day district of Maras, rather than from the southwest, both this and the previous case come from a single macro-region. The second case shows a different configuration of features from the first. The two cases are different in scale of population, to be sure. But critically absent in the second case are both a differentiated ecological relationship to place and an indexical relationship between cranial shape and locality.

Compared with the first case, there is little evidence that daily life was organized according to differences in economic status or political influence. Some scholars have suggested that Sahlins-model chiefdoms, with hereditary rank and self-aggrandizing individuals who manipulated power through wealth redistribution, emerged in the Cuzco region for the first time around 500 BCE, centered at large sites with significant ceremonial architecture including the Wimpillay/Muyu Orqo site complex in the Cuzco Valley, Batan Urqo in Lucre, and Ak'awillay in the Anta plain (Bauer 2004; Zapata 1998). Despite this common suggestion, we lack evidence of political institutions that crosscut villages, and pottery styles do not change quickly enough to use surface materials to demonstrate that smaller villages were inhabited at the same time as large villages. Furthermore, typical archaeological indicators of economic inequality, such as variation in quality or elaboration of houses and burials and differential access to prestige goods, have not been found.

Regional settlement patterns suggest that all residents shared the same generalized agropastoral ecological relationship to place. During the Formative period, people relied almost exclusively on domesticated resources including quinoa, potato, corn, llamas, alpacas, and guinea pigs. Allison Davis (2014) identified the agropastoral zones that were easily accessible from Formative-period sites. All sites had easy access to suni zones suitable for almost all agropastoral activities practiced during the Formative period, including dry-season herding of llamas; wet-season herding of alpacas and llamas; farming of quinoa, tubers, beans, and kiwicha on a normal cycle; and farming of tubers on an early cycle. The only significant

portion of the botanical assemblages that could not be produced in this region was maize, and most Formative-period sites had additional access to qhiswa zones where maize could be grown. Very few sites had easy access to the puna. This uniform location in prime and versatile agropastoral land does not suggest differentiated ecological relationships between people and place, at least on a site level (fig. 14.3).

Zooming out, long-distance trade networks carried out by llama caravans were focused on the highlands. Obsidian, probably from Ayacucho or Arequipa, was by far the most common exotic item. Bird or fish bones from the eastern lowlands were very rare, and marine shell was absent. The overwhelming majority of items used for subsistence and ritual were locally available, thus precluding differentiated relationships to distant localities.

Nonstandardized cranial shape in the Formative period does not lend itself to easy typology. At Yuthu (400–100 BCE), the frontal and occipital bones were compressed in an anterior-posterior manner that resulted in the nonuniform expansion of the parietal bones (plate 28). In some cases, the deviation from an unmodified shape was extreme; in others, it was not pronounced. In many cases, the sides were notably asymmetrical, but they were not asymmetrical to the same side across the assemblage. Valerie Andrushko (personal communication) has noted that the same method of cranial modification and a similar variety of outcomes was common throughout the Formative period in Cuzco.

Head shapes would have been noticeable during interactions between adults or older children, thus creating the potential to signal aspects of head-shape understandings and expectations during interactions, but the continuum of shapes would not lend itself to indexing locality. Equally important, there is no archaeological evidence that Formative-period social structure instituted different ecological relationships to place.

DISCUSSION: RECONSTRUCTION OF A SOCIAL LANDSCAPE

Cranial shape results from practices carried out every day by caregivers in a larger context of "good" child-rearing efforts to create whole persons in a particular social and cultural context (Blom and Knudson 2014). Caregiver practices differed between the Collagua case and Formative-period Cuzco. Davis (2011) has argued

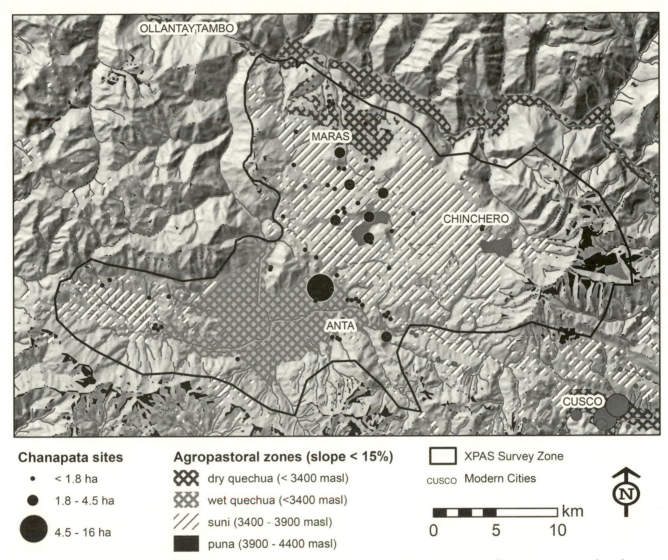

Figure 14.3. Prime agropastoral zones classified according to slope, altitude, and wetness. All Formative-period settlements show preference for locations with easy access to *suni* zones and secondary access to *qhiswa* zones (after Davis 2014).

that in the Formative period, the lack of uniformity probably resulted from a relatively short period of interaction between a caregiver and young child, lasting only as long as the infant was carried. After the child began to walk, the head was left free to develop without binding, allowing the person to develop a unique shape. If head shape was treated as indexing any quality of personhood, the quality must have existed along a continuum, such as being more or less hardworking, honest, or clever. This would be consistent with difference recognized in egalitarian societies that were not organized into multivillage and/or multiecology polities.

In the Collagua case, more standardized practices of

head binding marked individuals as belonging to particular places, a central element of personhood. Although head shapes from Yuraq Qaqa vary with respect to intensity and angle of elongation, relative consistency in the placement of pads and bands on the cranial vault produced a more symmetrical shape that suggests the goal of uniformity, if not always its achievement. More pronounced elongation probably required longer caregiving practice. Cradle boarding may have been used for a short time until the child learned to walk. Binding caps or headdresses could be used for a much longer time, guaranteeing a more uniform result. For example, although not from the same region that we are discussing here, we

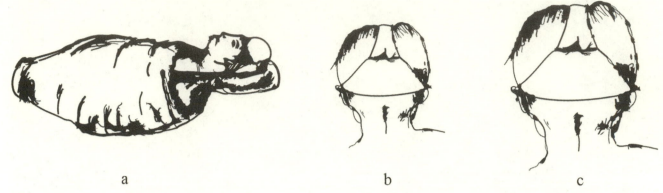

a   b   c

Figure 14.4. Longer modification practice shown producing more standardized shapes. An infant Middle Horizon boy was buried wearing an immobilizing cranial modification device (a) and accompanied by additional hat-like devices of increasing size to be used when walking (b, c) (modified from Allison et al. 1981 by Bekhyon Yim).

know that a Middle Horizon infant boy buried on the coast was wearing a cradle board and was accompanied by three hat-like devices of increasing size to be used when walking (fig. 14.4) (Allison et al. 1981).

In contrast to the Formative case, Collagua caregivers had to decide the position of their children in the organization of diversity of locality. If households were of mixed composition, parents and children did not always share the same inner substance. The higher-altitude Collagua annular modification scheme, similar to (other) Aymara speakers to the south, fits a broader pattern of high-altitude herders. Was the tabular modification pattern used by the lower-altitude populations a reaction to the higher-altitude pattern? And if so, was the tabular technique standardized to the same extent as the annular? Another possibility, not mutually exclusive, is that the tabular form emerged from cradle-boarding practices, which would have initially opposed Cavana head shape as a "zero sign" versus the Collagua annular modification (Jakobson 1939). Ultimately, it will take a detailed multi-sited and diachronic study of how these forms emerged in relation to one another to resolve these questions. Boundary-making mechanisms such as these—which are iconic indices of the populations being bounded—are well attested in linguistic change (Irvine and Gal 2000); we would expect an even better fit when boundary making is literally inscribed on the body (Blom 2005). In short, understanding the practice of cranial modification, then, requires attention that is distinctly local. Contextualizing cranial modification in the south-central Andes requires attention both to the array of features of the social landscape discussed at the beginning of this chapter and to the specific histories of the sites.

ACKNOWLEDGMENTS

Allison Davis's research in Maras was funded by a Fulbright grant. Matthew Velasco's research in the Colca Valley was funded by the Wenner-Gren Foundation for Anthropological Research (grant no. 8542). We are grateful to Miriam Doutriaux and Susan A. Gelman for critical comments.

NOTES

1. See Arnold and Hastorf (2008) for discussion of the circulation of crania in Andean prehistory, contextualized in contemporary Aymara ideas about heads, and Arnold and Yapita (1998a:191–98) and La Riva González (2013:chap. 6) for discussions of beliefs about the head in ontogenic development among Aymaras and Quechuas, respectively. In this volume, Blom and Couture (chapter 13) discuss developmental issues, and the chapters by Becker and Alconini (15), Lozada et al. (12), and Verano (11) provide broad contextualization, with emphasis on the manipulation and circulation, rather than the developmental modification, of heads.

2. We have opted for the widely used Schutzian term "person" (taken from Geertz 1966) but recognize that conceptions of personhood and "individuals" vary as widely among anthropologists as they do culturally. A contrasting approach is to treat individuals as social entities that are composed relationally and are partible ("dividuals"; Strathern 1988:chap. 1), as part of a critique of a more traditional division between "individual" and "society" (see Lebner 2016). There is a substantial body of work disengaging "relationality" from "partibility" in social anthropology (e.g., LiPuma 1998; Sahlins 2013) and in archaeology (e.g., Fowler 2016).

3. This is a classic structuralist research strategy, pioneered

by the Russian linguist Nikolai Trubetzkoy in his study of sound systems, *Grundzüge der Phonologie* (1939), and ported to social anthropology by Claude Lévi-Strauss in his *Les structures élémentaires de la parenté* (1949).

4. Critical, too, in this arrangement is an allocentric rather than egocentric system of orientation and a house-centered rather than descent-centered kinship system, but these are outside the scope of this chapter.

5. Despite similarity in the use of circumferential bindings, the Collagua modification style is distinct from the prototypical annular style, also known as *tipo aimara*, in that it likely involved a combination of pads and bands rather than solely bandages (Weiss 1962). Accordingly, Collagua crania typically exhibit a less-intense elongation and slight bilateral expansion of the parietals, rather than the characteristic conical, "loaf-like" shape of circumferentially modified crania, which tapers posterosuperiorly (Antón 1989:254). Ongoing work by Matthew Velasco is aimed at clarifying this variation, but for the purposes of this chapter, we retain the broad "annular" distinction as commonly employed by physical anthropologists in the Andes. For a comparative account of colonial-era discussions of cranial vault modification in Latin America, see Zabala (2014).

6. These are the radiocarbon dates associated with Chanapata and Chanapata-related pottery (Davis 2011:table B).

REFERENCES CITED

Allen, Catherine J.
2002 *The Hold Life Has*. Smithsonian Institution Press, Washington, DC.
2011 *Foxboy: Intimacy and Aesthetics in Andean Stories*. University of Texas Press, Austin.

Allison, Marvin J., Enrique Gerszten, Juan Munizaga, Calogero Santoro, and Guillermo Focacci
1981 La práctica de la deformación craneana entre los pueblos andinos precolombinos. *Chungará* 7:238–60.

Antón, Susan
1989 Intentional Cranial Vault Deformation and Induced Changes of the Cranial Base and Face. *American Journal of Physical Anthropology* 79:253–67.

Arnold, Denise Y., and Christine A. Hastorf
2008 *Heads of State: Icons, Power, and Politics in the Ancient and Modern Andes*. Left Coast Press, Walnut Creek, California.

Arnold, Denise Y., and Juan de Dios Yapita
1998a *El rincón de las cabezas: luchas textuales, educación y tierras en los Andes*. Facultad de Humanidades, Universidad Mayor de San Andrés, La Paz.

1998b *Río de vellón, río de canto: cantar a los animales, una poética aymara de creación*. Hisbol, La Paz.

Bauer, Brian S.
2004 *Ancient Cuzco: Heartland of the Inca*. University of Texas Press, Austin.

Blom, Deborah E.
2005 Embodying Borders: Human Body Modification and Diversity in Tiwanaku Society. *Journal of Anthropological Archaeology* 24:1–24.

Blom, Deborah E., and Kelly J. Knudson
2014 Tracing Tiwanaku Childhoods: A Bioarchaeological Study of Age and Social Identities in Tiwanaku Society. In *Tracing Childhood: Bioarchaeological Investigations of Early Lives in Antiquity*, edited by Jennifer L. Thompson, Marta P. Alfonso-Durruty, and John J. Crandall, pp. 228–45. University Press of Florida, Gainesville.

Charlier Zeineddine, Laurence
2015 *L'homme-proie: infortunes et prédation dans les Andes boliviennes*. Presses Universitaires de Rennes, Rennes.

Covey, R. Alan, Brian S. Bauer, Véronique Bélisle, and Lia Tsesmeli
2013 Regional Perspectives on Wari State Influence in Cusco, Peru (c. AD 600–1000). *Journal of Anthropological Archaeology* 32:538–52

Curatola Petrocchi, Marco
2009 La función de los oráculos en el Imperio inca. In *Adivinación y oráculos en el mundo andino antiguo*, edited by Marco Curatola Petrocchi and Mariusz S. Ziółkowski, pp. 1–54. Instituto Francés de Estudios Andinos; Pontificia Universidad Católica, Lima.

D'Altroy, Terence N., and Timothy K. Earle
1985 Staple Finance, Wealth Finance, and Storage in the Inka Political Economy. *Current Anthropology* 26:187–206.

Davis, Allison R.
2011 *Yuthu: Community and Ritual in an Early Andean Village*. University of Michigan Museum of Anthropological Archaeology, Ann Arbor.
2014 The Formative Period. In *Regional Archaeology in the Inca Heartland: The Hanan Cuzco Surveys*, edited by R. Alan Covey. University of Michigan Museum of Anthropological Archaeology, Ann Arbor.

Dean, Carolyn
2015 Men Who Would Be Rocks: The Inka *Wank'a*. In *The Archaeology of Wak'as: Explorations of the Sacred in the Pre-Columbian Andes*, edited by Tamara L. Bray, pp. 213–38. University Press of Colorado, Boulder.

De la Cadena, Marisol

2015   *Earth Beings: Ecologies of Practice across Andean Worlds.* Duke University Press, Durham, North Carolina.

Descola, Philippe

2005   *Par delà nature et culture.* Éditions Gallimard, Paris.

2013   *Beyond Nature and Culture.* Translated by Janet Lloyd. University of Chicago Press, Chicago.

Doutriaux, Miriam

2004   Imperial Conquest in a Multiethnic Setting: The Inka Occupation of the Colca Valley. Unpublished PhD dissertation, Department of Anthropology, University of California, Berkeley.

Emlen, Nicholas Q.

2014   Language and Coffee in a Trilingual Andean-Amazonian Frontier Community of Southern Peru. Unpublished PhD dissertation, Department of Anthropology, University of Michigan.

Fowler, Chris

2016   Relational Personhood Revisited. *Cambridge Archaeological Journal* 26:397–412.

Geertz, Clifford

1966   *Person, Time, and Conduct in Bali.* Cultural Report Series, 14. Yale Southeast Asia Program, New Haven, Connecticut.

Gelles, H. Paul

1987   *Los hijos de Hualca Hualca: historia de Cabanaconde.* Centro de Apoyo y Promoción al Desarrollo Agrario, Arequipa.

Hoshower, Lisa M., Jane E. Buikstra, Paul S. Goldstein, and Ann D. Webster

1995   Artificial Cranial Deformation at the Omo M10 site. *Latin American Antiquity* 6:145–64.

Irvine, Judith, and Susan A. Gal

2000   Language Ideology and Linguistic Differentiation. In *Regimes of Language: Ideologies, Polities, and Identities,* edited by Paul Kroskrity, pp. 35–83. School of American Research Press, Santa Fe.

Jakobson, Roman O.

1939   Signe zero. In *Mélanges de linguistique offerts à Charles Bally,* pp. 143–52. Librairie de'Université, Geneva.

La Riva González, Palmira

2013   Au plus près du corps: la construction sociale du corps-personne dans une communauté des Andes du Sud du Pérou. Unpublished PhD dissertation, Department of Social Anthropology, Université de Paris X, Nanterre.

Lebner, Ashley

2016   La redescription de l'anthropologie selon Marilyn Strathern. *L'Homme* 218:117–50.

Lévi-Strauss, Claude

1949   *Les structures élémentaires de la parenté.* Presses Universitaires de France, Paris.

LiPuma, Edward

1998   Modernity and Forms of Personhood in Melanesia. In *Bodies and Persons,* edited by Michael Lambek and Andrew Strathern, pp. 53–79. Cambridge University Press, Cambridge.

Lozada, María Cecilia, and Jane E. Buikstra

2005   Pescadores and Labradores among the Señorío de Chiribaya in Southern Peru. In *Us and Them: Archaeology and Ethnicity in the Andes,* edited by Richard Martin Reycraft, pp. 206–25. Cotsen Institute of Archaeology, University of California, Los Angeles.

Mannheim, Bruce

1991   *The Language of the Inka since the European Invasion.* University of Texas Press, Austin.

1999   Hacia una mitografía andina. In *Tradición oral andina y Amazónica: métodos de análisis e interpretación de textos,* edited by Juan-Carlos Godenzzi, pp. 57–96. Centro de Estudios Regionales Andinos "Bartolomé de las Casas," Cuzco.

Mannheim, Bruce, and Guillermo Salas Carreño

2015   Wak'as: Entifications of the Andean Sacred. In *The Archaeology of Wak'as: Explorations of the Sacred in the Pre-Columbian Andes,* edited by Tamara L. Bray, pp. 46–72. University Press of Colorado, Boulder.

Manrique, Nelson

1985   *Colonialismo y pobreza campesina: caylloma y el Valle del Colca, siglos xvi–xx.* Centro de Estudios y Promoción del Desarrollo, Lima.

Ødegaard, Cecilie Vindal

2011   Sources of Danger and Prosperity in the Peruvian Andes: Mobility in a Powerful Landscape. *Journal of the Royal Anthropological Institute* 17:339–55.

Pachacuti Yamqui, Juan de Santacruz

ca. 1615   *Relación de antigüedades deste reyno del Piru.* Manuscript 3169, 132–69. Biblioteca Nacional, Madrid.

Pease G. Y., Franklin

1977   Collaguas: una etnia del siglo XVI, problemas iniciales. *Collaguas,* vol. 1, 131–68. Pontificia Universidad Católica, Lima.

Rowe, John Howland

1982   Inca Policies and Institutions Relating to the Cultural
        Unification of the Empire. In *The Inca and Aztec
        States*, edited by George I. Collier, Renato Rosaldo,
        and John D. Wirth, pp. 93–118. Academic Press, New
        York.

Sahlins, Marshall D.

2013   *What Kinship Is, and Is Not*. University of Chicago
        Press, Chicago

Salas Carreño, Guillermo

2012   Religious Change and Ideologies of Social Hierarchy
        in the Southern Peruvian Andes. Unpublished PhD
        dissertation, Department of Anthropology, University
        of Michigan.

Stensrud, Astrid B.

2016   Climate Change, Water Practices and Relational
        Worlds in the Andes. *Ethnos* 81:75–98.

Stern, Steve J.

1982   *Peru's Indian Peoples and the Challenge of Spanish
        Conquest: Huamanga to 1640*. University of Wisconsin
        Press, Madison.

Strathern, Marilyn

1988   *The Gender of the Gift: Problems with Women and
        Problems with Society in Melanesia*. University of
        California Press, Berkeley.

Torres-Rouff, Christina

2003   Shaping Identity: Cranial Vault Modification in the
        Pre-Columbian Andes. Unpublished PhD dissertation,
        Department of Anthropology, University of California,
        Santa Barbara.

Trubetzkoy, Nikolai Sergeyevich

1939   *Grundzüge der Phonologie*. Travaux du Cercle Linguis-
        tique de Prague, no. 7. Cercle Linguistique de Prague,
        Prague.

Ulloa Mogollon, Juan de

1586   Relación de la provincia de los Collaguas para la
        descripción de las Yndias que Su Magestad manda
        hacer. In *Relaciones geográficas de Indias* 2:326–33.

Velasco, Matthew C.

2014   Building on the Ancestors: Mortuary Structures and
        Extended Agency in the Late Prehispanic Colca Valley,
        Peru. *Cambridge Archaeological Journal* 24:453–65.

2016   Mortuary Tradition and Social Transformation during
        the Late Intermediate Period (AD 1100–1450): A Bio-
        archaeological Analysis of Above-Ground Burials in
        the Colca Valley, Peru. Unpublished PhD dissertation,
        Department of Anthropology, Vanderbilt University.

Wallace, Anthony F. C.

1961   *Culture and Personality*. Random House, New York.

Weiss, Pedro

1962   Tipología de las deformaciones cefálicas de los antig-
        uos peruanos, según la osteología cultural. *Revista del
        Museo Nacional* 31:15–42.

Wernke, Steven A.

2006   Collagua "Eco-Logistics": Intermediate Elites and
        Hybrid Community Structures in the Colca Valley,
        Peru. In *Intermediate Elites in Pre-Columbian States
        and Empires*, edited by Christina M. Elson and R.
        Alan Covey, pp. 175–210. University of Arizona Press,
        Tucson.

2013   *Negotiated Settlements: Andean Communities and
        Landscapes under Inka and Spanish Colonialism*.
        University Press of Florida, Gainesville.

Zabala, Pilar

2014   Source Compilation on Head-Shaping Practices in
        Hispanic America. In *The Bioarchaeology of Artificial
        Cranial Modifications: New Approaches to Head Shap-
        ing and Its Meanings in Pre-Columbian Mesoamerica
        and Beyond*, authored by Vera Tiesler, pp. 99–128.
        Springer, New York.

Zapata, Julinho

1998   Los cerros sagrados: panorama del período Formativo
        en la cuenca del Vilcanota, Cuzco. *Boletín Arqueología
        PUCP*:307–36.

15

Violence, Power, and Head Extraction in the Kallawaya Region, Bolivia

SARA K. BECKER AND SONIA ALCONINI

INTRODUCTION

The skull, as one of the most important and easily recognized parts of the human skeleton, conveys critical information about the identity, sex, and lifestyle of an individual. Cross-culturally, heads may range in significance from beloved ancestors to vanquished enemies, and these bones can become a potent source of energy and empowerment for the living. In tantric rituals, decorated *thod-pa* skullcaps were used by Tibetan lamas to achieve spiritual enlightenment (Fuentes 2011), whereas Aghori gurus of India use *kapala* skull bowls because they are associated with the life force or *prana* of the deceased person (Bosmia et al. 2013). The Asante of Ghana displayed the skulls and jawbones of enemies on their musical instruments in order to enslave the souls of the defeated (Sheales 2011:156–57). While modern Día de los Muertos rituals use skulls as remembrances of cherished family members, many prehistoric Mesoamerican cultures used skullracks (*tzompantlis*) to instill fear among their enemies (Chávez Balderas, chapter 9 of this volume; López Luján and Olivier 2010).

Whether relatives or adversaries, skulls in the Andes—actual skulls of people who once lived or motifs carved into stone or woven into fabric—can be instantly recognized as human. These heads may be the visual symbols of victory or authority after raiding foreign rivals (e.g., Andrushko 2011; Browne et al. 1993; Finucane 2008; Tung

2014; Tung and Knudson 2008; Verano 2014), or in other circumstances exhibited skulls may be forms of ancestor worship (e.g., Blom and Janusek 2004; Finucane 2008; Hastorf 2003; Lau 2002; Manzanilla and Woodard 1990). Andean heads can also be influential when not on display, buried as part of fertility rituals or contained in chests as objects of power (e.g., Arnold 2005; Arnold and Hastorf 2008). Heads in the Andes, both displayed and concealed, are recognized as potent sources of power in both modern and prehistoric times (e.g., Alconini and Becker 2018; Arnold 2005, 2006; Arnold and Hastorf 2008; Becker and Alconini 2015; Benson and Cook 2001; Forgey and Williams 2005; Proulx 2001; Risør 2013; Salomon 1991; Toyne 2008; Tung 2007, 2008; Verano 1995, 2008).

In this chapter, we continue prior research (Alconini and Becker 2011, 2013, 2018; Becker and Alconini 2015) exploring the significance of three heads buried under a capstone at the Andean site of Wata Wata in the Kallawaya region of Bolivia (fig. 15.1). This find is associated with Tiwanaku culture, dating to a transitional period (200–800 CE) between the Late Formative and Tiwanaku periods in the region. These skulls represent a surprising discovery, as, although detached heads are noted in much of Tiwanaku iconography, there has been a lack of bioarchaeological proof that the motifs represent actual heads taken from individuals (Alconini 1995; Blom and Janusek 2004; Chávez 1992; Clados 2009; Makowski 2009; Isbell and Knobloch 2008; Janusek 2004b, 2008; Kolata 1993b; Oakland 1986;

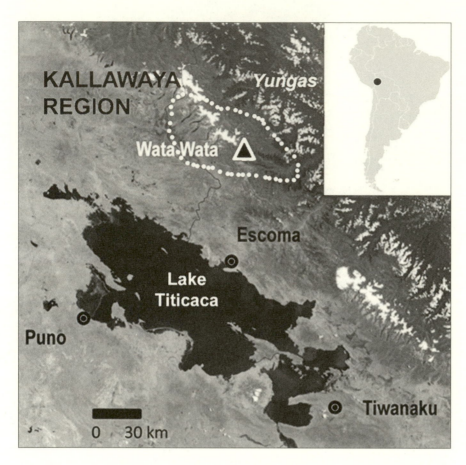

Figure 15.1. Map of the Wata Wata study area.

Smith 2012; Torres 1987, 2001; Young-Sánchez 2004, 2009). In addition, it is unlikely that these people were revered ancestors, as each skull has extensive evidence of intentional violence (i.e., multiple skull fractures, beheading, defleshing, and eye and jaw removal), which would be uncommon in cases of ancestor veneration (Rakita et al. 2005; Sofaer 2006). Instead, drawing on archaeological and bioarchaeological evidence, we hypothesize that these people may be part of some cultural practice in which it was considered necessary to extinguish their lives using extreme levels of violence and to conceal their mouthless skulls in the ground. As such, we discuss the nature of the power the head possesses in the Andes and the different theoretical ways detached skulls hold power. We also describe the archaeology of the Kallawaya area, the history of this locality as home to shamans and herbal healers, and the importance of the Wata Wata site in the regional cultural dynamics. We then explain the skeletal evidence and the uniqueness of this find among other dedicatory offerings and trophy heads in the prehistoric Andes. Finally, we discuss the concept of these heads as symbols of power. We explore ideas that the three detached heads from the

Kallawaya territory were the result of purposeful violence intended to turn the heads into objects of power, or that there was some kind of deviance among these three people that needed to be punished or controlled to limit their influence on others. These heads were then buried at the Wata Wata site possibly as an effort to contain or control the power of these individuals or the strength emanating from their body parts.

THE POWER OF HEADS IN THE CENTRAL ANDES: ANCESTORS, PROTECTORS, TROPHIES, AND DEVIANTS

As noted throughout this volume, heads hold power and embody personhood. In life, they contain and grow knowledge, and promote belonging or difference in everything from hairstyles to head shape. In death, heads serve as remembrance or as a storehouse of vitality a person once held in life. In the Andes, we see that heads without bodies range, first, in how they are treated (e.g., as trophies, disembodied, detached, severed, or isolated) (see

Lozada et al., chapter 12 of this volume), and second, in how visible they are (Arnold 2006; Arnold and Hastorf 2008; Becker and Alconini 2015). They provide "embodied engagement" with the individuals and groups that interact with them, both physically in that they are the skulls of people who once lived and theoretically in the different things they represent depending on usage and perception (Bourdieu 1977; Dornan-Fish 2012; Johnson 1999; Merleau-Ponty 2013). Thus, understanding the context, purpose, and transformations heads are subject to from an emic perspective is important to recognize the power they hold. While we cannot know all of the influences heads hold or held in the past, we can look at the actions people take or have taken to try to discern their influence (Bourdieu 1977; Merleau-Ponty 2013). We can contextually examine the cultural constructions of heads through the intent for which heads were used, their visibility, and the power they hold in specific situations from common perspectives, specifically where heads are considered ancestors, protectors, trophies, or deviants, thus providing a well-measured interpretation of the Wata Wata find.

Ancestors

Worldwide, ancestor veneration involves remembering the roles and influences people had during life. By honoring, revering, and worshiping a deceased relative, favor is shown to the living descendants, group membership can be reaffirmed, and entitlement to lineage-based resources is confirmed (Arnold 2005; Calhoun 1980; Hastorf 2003; Lau 2002; McAnany 1995). When a skull represents an ancestor, heads are well treated; traditionally, the skeletons of people whose bodies achieve postmortem reverence do not show violent treatment (e.g., Finucane 2008; Hastorf 2003; Salomon 1991; Seeman 2007; Sofaer 2006; Verano 1995, 2001, 2008). In addition, heads of ancestors may sometimes be hidden but are often made visible for religious and ritual traditions (Calhoun 1980; Forgey and Williams 2005; Hastorf 2003; Lau 2002; McAnany 1995; Salomon 1991). In some Andean cases, more than just the skull is used in rituals of ancestor veneration, as was noted in the Tiwanaku heartland, where the mostly complete skeletons were well cared for and used in rituals to remember deceased relatives (Blom and Janusek 2004; Manzanilla and Woodard 1990). Thus, the expectation with ancestor heads is a cultural context of caring and visibility at various times during veneration.

Protectors

The worship of deceased ancestors and their bones advocates that the dead have influence on the circumstances of the living. As such, they can move into roles as protectors. However, they need not always be an ancestor to a living person. In the Andes, skulls themselves are important objects to own and utilize (Arnold and Hastorf 2008; Risør 2013; Spedding 2011). According to modern ethnographic accounts of the symbolic nature of Andean skulls, heads protect individuals or promote better livelihood through increased fertility (e.g., Arnold and Hastorf 2008; Proulx 2001, 2006; Risør 2013; Spedding 2011). For example, similar to the Mayan interpretation of the head as seat of the spirit (Houston and Cummins 2004; Scherer, chapter 4 of this volume), native Aymara people believe that the soul or spirit, termed *ajayu*, continues on after death and can be physically linked to the skull (Johnson 2013:156; Risør 2013:67). Traditional fables among the Aymara discuss disembodied heads (known interchangeably as *qati qati*, *layqa qip'i*, or *uma* in different regions of the central Andes) that fall off while a person is sleeping (Schiwy 2009:114–15; Spedding 2011:148–50). For some reason, the head cannot be reattached, and it is powerful enough to take revenge on the person it perceives as preventing its reattachment to the body, or as a step in obtaining justice in certain situations. This traditional view of skulls may be why they are used in hillside ritual offerings. In one example, skulls are buried in an earthen pit, covered with items such as coca leaves, and sealed off with a capstone in the hope that the emanations from them will help rainclouds form (Arnold 2005:119; Arnold and Hastorf 2008:73–77). These hillside skulls can also be part of land reclamation strategies associated with fertility (Arnold and Hastorf 2008). Modern Aymara groups often use chests, ceramic containers, and soil pits to restrain and control the power potentially emanating from crania (Arnold and Hastorf 2008). In fact, human heads, like sprouting plants, are conceived of as a kind of "seed" (Arnold and Hastorf 2008; Blom and Couture, chapter 13 of this volume). These skulls can be interpreted as vital sources of life from which the rest of the human body can be restored or regenerated, again similar to their Mesoamerican counterparts.

In addition to controlling hidden, detached heads as objects of power, skulls, or *ñatitas* (diminutive, turned-up pug noses) have an annual, dedicated festival day on

November 8 in Bolivia (Risør 2013). On Día de las Ñatitas, skulls of both known (i.e., of deceased relatives) and unknown (i.e., received or bought) origin are decorated with items like fresh flowers, fancy hats, and sunglasses and given offerings (e.g., cigarettes, coca leaves, and alcohol). The hope is that this respect will benefit the family that owns the skull in the coming year. The process through which these ñatitas became objects of power and praise may, in part, be rooted in violence. Alison Spedding (2011:156–59) notes that the heads sometimes come from a male who was murdered and decapitated for any number of reasons; his various other body parts are cooked and disposed of. Helene Risør (2013:67) also notes a potential violent origin but expands the idea, suggesting that any violent death would cause a restless spirit. Whatever the cause of death (natural or violent), each ñatita has a name, an origin story, and a mythos associated with the help or protection it has given to living persons who venerate it. Colloquially, stories describe skulls, visible somewhere in the home, that have scared away intruders, or healed the sick when brought to the bedside of a terminally ill patient, or brought economic success after money was placed in their jaws. Ñatitas become family protectors and effective media to attract wealth, particularly for small-scale businesswomen in La Paz. Depending on the sex of the owner, they can also adopt the opposite gender, following the broader principles of duality. In addition, this promise of help or protection is not limited to a single group. Scholars have noted that these ñatitas have been used by thieves and smugglers who seek to avoid detection (Spedding 2011:160–62) as well as by police to help solve local murders (Risør 2013:67).

Trophies

Whether serving as objects of ancestor veneration or as providers of protection, detached heads have been found archaeologically, depicted on Tiwanaku stone sculptures, serving vessels, and textiles (Alconini 1995; Chávez 1992; Janusek 2004a, 2008; Kolata 1993a; Oakland 1986; Young-Sánchez 2004, 2009). For example, objects dangling from the elbows of the portal god carved into stone on the Gate of the Sun in the Tiwanaku capital have been interpreted as isolated heads (Clados 2009; Makowski 2009). However, it is possible that iconographic depictions of detached Tiwanaku heads could also represent violent displays of power. Born from violence, Andean

trophy heads hold power because of their ability to be displayed and recognized as something that was once human. Often taken by the Nasca, Wari, and Moche, the skulls of enemies or captured prisoners were used as war trophies to achieve this affect (Browne et al. 1993; Sutter and Cortez 2005; Tung 2007, 2008; Tung and Knudson 2008, 2010; Verano 1995, 2001, 2003, 2008; 2014; Verano, chapter 11 of this volume). For example, Wari and Nasca trophy heads have drill holes, often on the jaws or upper portion of the skull, so they could be hung or displayed with a cord (Browne et al. 1993; Forgey and Williams 2005; Proulx 2001; Silverman and Proulx 2002; Tung 2008; Verano 2001, 2008). The Moche may have performed similar tactics by modifying the skulls of victims as ritual drinking vessels (Verano et al. 1999). As Valerie Andrushko discusses, "the body part is modified in a way to facilitate public viewing, since trophy-taking requires an audience to maximize its symbolic power" (2011:264). One can imagine the visual impact these displays of dangling heads had on the enemies of the Wari or the captured and soon-to-be victims of the Moche, or watching the victors drink from a human skull.

Within Tiwanaku regions, actual trophy heads are almost nonexistent and evidence of violence is rare compared to other complex societies in Central and South America. One exception is described by Deborah Blom and John Janusek (2004), who point out potential examples of war trophies on the platforms of the Akapana Pyramid in the city of Tiwanaku, where young men were intentionally dismembered and then left exposed, susceptible to carnivores and visible to all local inhabitants. In another exception, John Verano (2013) documented sixteen burials near the Kalasasaya platform mound in Tiwanaku that date to about 700 CE, where all of the individuals were likely part of a single burial episode. Three of the sixteen showed various levels of violence, and in one example it is likely that a child was decapitated. This child's skull also had multiple puncture-like entry wounds that could have been caused by the metal tip of a staff or spear (Verano 2013:173–75). Two of the more complete burials with evidence of violence also showed damage to the crania that occurred at or around the time of death. Verano noted a similarity to the burials described by Blom and Janusek (2004), considering their violent death, but he noted that the Kalasasaya remains lacked cut or chop marks from intentional dismemberment. As such, cases of violence among the

Tiwanaku were not limited to heads, nor have only heads been found as part of any brutal ritual.

Deviants

While not as well-known as the taking of heads as trophies, social deviance as a rationale for decapitation also occurred in the central Andes. Although deviance is culturally defined and contextually shifting, generally speaking, social deviants are those who engage in behaviors, practices, and actions that violate accepted social norms and rules (Durkheim 1978; Macionis and Gerber 2010). As such, they are particularly prominent in periods of social change and unrest. People who were considered deviants were often killed, disfigured, and dismembered. Such marked levels of violence were not only inflicted on individuals who deviated from accepted social norms but also on those considered liminal, dangerous, or uncontrollable. It is no surprise that in the Old World, women were subjected to such practices, particularly those considered witches or druidesses. One of such example was found in a Roman-era cemetery at Lankhills, Winchester, England, that dates to the fourth century CE (Green 1997). Archaeologists have discovered a series of women who were beheaded, their heads purposefully placed between their legs. In addition, a few of these women had their jaws removed. Miranda Green (1997:99) interprets this as an attempt to keep them from casting any spells on the living after their death. The decapitated and jawless interred women may have been seen by the local Celts as backsliding or heretical pagans in a time when Christianity was spreading throughout the region, as well as a victory over powerful women who were considered deviant witches (Catling 2011).

Although scarce, there is also evidence of eye removal as a form of punishment. One documented example involves Greek lawmaker Zaleucus in Locri, Italy, around 600 BCE. After Zaleucus established eye removal as a penalty for adultery, his son was accused of the crime and given this sentence (Heraclides 1971:35; Maximus 2000:65). Those in power decided to waive the deoculation, but Zaleucus, as a man of the law, put out one of his own eyes as well as one of his son's so that the punishment was duly enacted. In part, this punishment may have been prescribed because of ideas concerning the role of eyes in interpersonal connections, such as the amatory gaze, or its opposite, the gaze of the "evil eye" (Franzen 2011:71–72). Traditionally, because people use their eyes to connect to one another both visually and emotionally, eye removal in the classical world may have been used to destroy communities or an individual's participation in the community through the loss of those ties (Franzen 2011:90).

In the New World, ethnographic research reveals the importance placed on shamanistic rituals and healing as well as the possibility of deviant witchcraft in many indigenous cultures. Although such practices varied in scope and nature, their practitioners were often considered beyond social norms and therefore liminal and potentially dangerous. As such, they had the potential to become social deviants. For example, Puebloan peoples of the southwestern United States believe that witchcraft can account for any number of ills such as famine, floods, and undetermined changes in the weather. Witchcraft is also considered hereditary in Puebloan families, and family members of witches can thus fall under suspicion (Walker 1998:267). In this context, J. Andrew Darling (1998:739–40) notes that in the present day, witches can be neutralized by using effigies, which undergo physical "trauma," simulated execution, dismemberment, cutting, simulated defleshing, and burning of various body parts as symbolic acts to hinder the deviant witch. The first European to visit the Zuni pueblo in the southwestern United States, Estevanico (also sometimes called Esteban de Dorantes, Estebanico, and Esteban the Moor), was killed because he was thought to be a witch. To further disempower him, Zuni leaders dismembered Estevanico's body and distributed the parts among themselves (Bandelier 1892:14).

Witchcraft is known among the Aymara, and ethnographers have identified countermeasures the Aymara took to protect individuals from negative spells (Abercrombie 1986; La Barre 1950, 1951; Sebeok 1951). However, early ethnographic accounts note little differentiation between witches, shamans, medicine men, and healers; only their acts are designated as positive or negative, with possible punishment doled out to an originator in the form of individual, karmic retribution (La Barre 1950:40–41). Disembodied heads are also associated with these Aymara healers or shamans, and controlling these skulls adds to a shaman's power. Denise Arnold and Christine Hastorf (2008:66) note that heads, especially those of conquered enemies, can be used by shamans "for both protective and defensive purposes, as well as for more aggressive and belligerent uses."

The heads (i.e., qati qati, layqa qip'i, or uma) also fly and provide a shaman with the ability to survey an area under his or her control, possibly expanding the shaman's authority over new, enemy territory (Arnold and Hastorf 2008).

CULTURAL AND ARCHAEOLOGICAL CONTEXT

The Kallawaya Region

During the Formative era (1500 BCE–500 CE), regions such as Kallawaya, in present-day Apolobamba National Park, Bolivia, were important transition and trading zones. They linked the high-elevation Titicaca basin in the west to the eastern Yunga tropical mountain region and beyond. Exchanges were facilitated by far-reaching llama trading caravans (Bandy 2004; Browman 1984; Chávez 1988; Chávez 1992; Hastorf et al. 2005; Hastorf 2005). Typical goods passing through this region were the kind not easily obtained at high elevations such as corn, coca, colorful plumage from tropical birds, hallucinogens, and hardwoods (Browman 1984; Saignes 1985). In addition, highland "Yayamama-style" Formative-era artifacts and ritual paraphernalia were also found at various sites in these midaltitude regions, suggesting complex interactions between the differing elevations on trade routes.

An archaeological survey of the Kallawaya area (noted by the dotted polygon in figure 15.1) found a total of 1,812 sites dating from before the Formative period (1500 BCE–500 CE) through to the recent Inka era (Alconini 2011, 2016). Of these sites, approximately fifteen dated to the Formative period, and five stand out as regional centers because they were terraced mounds, with excellent visibility of the surrounding landscape, and strategically located along an ancient transportation route (Alconini 2011). These five Formative centers featured monumental architecture materialized in the construction of concentric stone platforms adapted to the natural topography, with public spaces at the summit. Excavations at some of these regional centers, such as Kalla Kallan and Wata Wata, show residential constructions, burial cists, and storage areas on the platforms (Alconini 2011, 2016; Chávez 2009). Both Yunga and Titicaca basin Formative-era ceramics were found at these sites, along with other nonlocal cultural materials (e.g., obsidian and lapis lazuli), suggesting that people from these sites participated in the far-reaching trade networks.

During the Tiwanaku period (500–1100 CE), there were dramatic shifts in the Kallawaya region, including evidence of Tiwanaku-style decorated pottery, the likely adoption of Tiwanaku ritual practices, and possibly even the migration of Tiwanaku peoples into the region (Chávez 2009). As such, there is no significant evidence of a militaristic conquest of local peoples. Rather, it may be that Kallawaya peoples were encouraged to join or participate in the multiethnic Tiwanaku state. Overall in the Kallawaya region during the Tiwanaku period, there was an almost fourfold growth in the number of settlements, a variance in size and function of habitations (i.e., hamlets, villages, and cemeteries), and the development of communities at previously unoccupied higher elevations (above two thousand meters). This evidence points to a consolidation of an agropastoral economy. In addition, the five regional centers located along the main transportation route continued to be used, albeit in different ways than during the Formative. In general, these centers featured an expansion of public spaces on their summits, a change to rectangular-shaped residential architecture, and a restricted distribution of agrarian terraces inferior to spaces at the summit. Such changes were tied to the introduction of decorated and utilitarian Tiwanaku-style pottery (Alconini 2011; Chávez 2009).

The Kallawaya People

Kallawaya's inhabitants are renowned traveling shamans and herbal healers (Bastien 1978; Girault 1969; Meyers 2002; Oblitas Poblete 1978, 1992; Rösing 1995; Saignes 1984) and have been recognized by UNESCO (2008) as a part of the "Intangible Cultural Heritage of Humanity" because of their extensive medicinal knowledge. These healers primarily speak Quechua but also use Machajuyu, a secret language of the Kallawaya that combines Puquina and Quechua features (Aguiló 1991; Saignes 1984). Although their origins are uncertain, we know that by Inka times they had an elevated status due to their knowledge of healing as well as their role as cultural brokers and intermediaries with the eastern Yunga populations dwelling in the jungle (Meyers 2002; Saignes 1984). As a result, they became privileged allies of the Inka and played a central role in the extensive trading routes that crisscrossed the region.

It is also likely that knowledge of curative practices was ongoing through the Tiwanaku period, as there is evidence of religious and healing paraphernalia in a number of funerary caves distributed along Tiwanaku trade routes

(Chávez and Alconini 2016). Although most of the Kallawaya caves were heavily looted, some of the burials were walled in order to protect the remains of single or multiple individuals interred there. One of these was the Callijicho funerary cave from Niño Korin, previously documented by other researchers (Rydén 1957; Wassén 1972). It is located on the cliffs below the Tiwanaku center of Kalla Kallan in Curva, Bolivia. The Callijicho cave contained multiple burials with evidence of trepanation and artificial cranial modification. Grave goods from these burials also showed Tiwanaku-era ritual and medicinal objects consistent with modern Kallawaya herbal healers of the region (Wassén 1972). These included snuff tablets and spoons finely decorated with ritual Tiwanaku iconography, inhalation tubes carved in bone and cane, and a number of textile bags containing medicinal plants (Wassén 1978). In this context, the site of Wata Wata, which was contemporaneous with and of a similar design to Kalla Kallan, is particularly important, considering its history as a Formative-era center that was later co-opted by the Tiwanaku.

The Wata Wata Archaeological Site

The site of Wata Wata, comprising 6.5 hectares, is one of the original five Formative-period regional centers in the Kallawaya region (fig. 15.2). Containing at least five

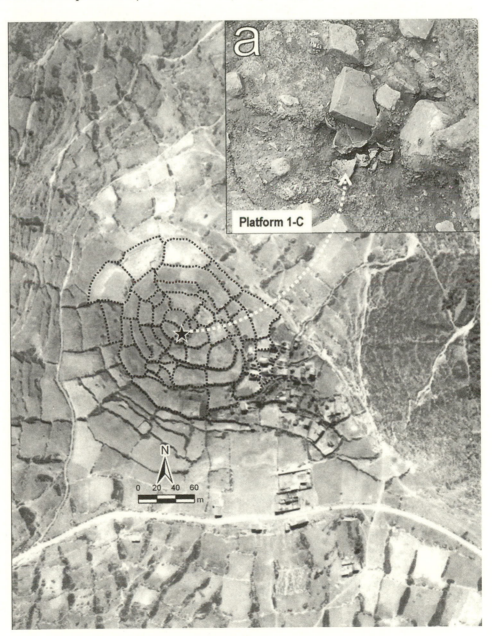

Figure 15.2. The site of Wata Wata. The inset shows the location of the three skulls found in this cache.

concentric platforms, it is located close to one of the main trade routes that penetrate deep into the tropical mountains and has an occupational history spanning from the Formative through the Tiwanaku periods. There were three main building phases: (1) Early Formative through the first half of the Middle Formative (1500–500 BCE); (2) the second half of the Middle Formative and Late Formative 1 (500 BCE–200 CE); and (3) the transition between the Late Formative 2 and Tiwanaku periods (200–800 CE).

During the first phase (1500–500 BCE), the site was a prominent regional center with public spaces on the upper platforms used for large-scale food consumption activities, while lower platforms had circular residential constructions (Alconini 2013; Becker and Alconini 2015). In addition, there were small, semisubterranean, circular stone constructions used for storage or as funerary cists (Alconini 2016). Cultural materials from both the highlands (e.g., clay trumpets, ceramic burners, and burnished pottery with burnt grass, mica, and large quartz grains in the paste) and lowlands (e.g., Yunga-style pottery characterized by the use of ground slate in the paste) were documented at Wata Wata from this time period.

In contrast to the first phase, the scale of residential occupation was limited in the second phase (500 BCE– 200 CE). This is evident in the fact that there were fewer residential structures noted on the lower platforms. Alconini (2016) noted that Wata Wata had become an ancestral shrine, as shown by the increase in the use of burial cists, by the reutilization of sunken storage constructions as funerary chambers, and by the expansion of public food consumption activities on the upper terraces.

By the third phase (200–800 CE), most of the earlier semisubterranean constructions were being reutilized as garbage pits or burial areas. However, in stark contrast with earlier traditions, these new cists held the remains of single, primary inhumations, buried with Tiwanaku paraphernalia. For example, one individual was buried in a flexed position and was entombed with a Tiwanaku-style painted, flaring open bowl, a carved bone spoon with avian motifs similar to those from the Tiwanaku hallucinogenic complex, deer antlers, lapis lazuli beads, and metal scraps (Alconini 2016).

In addition, during the third phase, selected areas of Wata Wata underwent significant architectural renovations, such as at platform 1-C located in the southern apex of the site (noted in figure 15.2). Platform 1-C was a locus of public celebrations, rituals, and food consumption.

During this third phase, the midden and nearby semisubterranean stone constructions at this platform, which had once been used for storage and burial, fell into disuse. A layer of gravel mixed with yellow clay twenty centimeters in thickness was deposited above these constructions as a new floor, covering not only earlier constructions but also previously unoccupied spaces. Associated with this floor was the construction of a set of straight, stone walls. These wall segments run in different directions and were likely part of larger rectangular structures, and their shape shows a departure from earlier, circular constructions. The walls were two courses high and constructed with fieldstones, stone slabs, and partially worked stone blocks. Near the corner of two of the wall segments, a small pit approximately thirty centimeters in diameter and thirty centimeters deep was cut through the floor and the wall foundation. Human skulls were placed in this pit, which was subsequently filled with darker soil and covered with a partially hand-cut stone block (Alconini 2016). This is shown in the insert in figure 15.2. Upon discovery of these bones, the entire cache, including the surrounding soil, was removed to the laboratory for further examination (Becker and Alconini 2015). Overall, our excavation found no evidence of previous habitation below the yellow clay and mixed gravel floor where the three heads were buried. Thus, it is unlikely that they date to either the first or second phase of construction at the Wata Wata site.

DESCRIPTION OF THE WATA WATA SKULLS

The heads found at Wata Wata are from three different adult individuals who underwent extreme violence at or around the time of death (i.e., perimortem). None of the crania show evidence of the trauma that takes place postdecomposition or that is associated with secondary burial, as might be the case with individuals who were buried, disinterred, and then defleshed (e.g., Curry 1999; Simon 2003; Ubelaker 1974) or with ancestor veneration (e.g., Arnold and Hastorf 2008; Fenton 1991; Hastorf 2003; Rakita et al. 2005). In addition, from both site-based and laboratory analysis, all three individuals were interred in the ground at Wata Wata at approximately the same time (Becker and Alconini 2015).

From an inventory of the skull bones present, all three are missing portions of the face, specifically the upper and lower jaw (maxillae and mandibles), all teeth, some

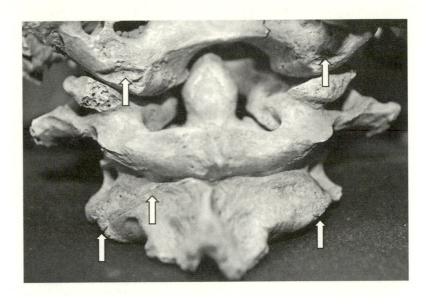

Figure 15.3. Posterior view of cut and chop marks, as noted with arrows, at the articulation of the skull and neck of Individual 1.

fragments of the parietals, and small portions of the posterior and inferior occipital crania. As tooth eruption patterns and dental wear provide helpful bioarchaeological clues to estimating age in skeletal remains (Bass 1981; Buikstra and Ubelaker 1994; White 1991), and these individuals have no jaws or teeth, there was no way to give them a more specific age than "adult." However, their sex can be estimated from the cranial bones present, and they are one male and, possibly, two females.

In terms of the missing facial bones and jaws, all three have damage that is likely from a Le Fort fracture. This type of fracture, commonly noted in modern forensic anthropology, is caused by heavy, blunt force applied to the face (Christensen et al. 2014:352–53; Allsop and Kennett 2002:261–63). This type of trauma, depending on where the force is applied between the mouth and the nose, causes sheering of the facial bones from at least the upper dentition through to some portion of the eye sockets inferior to the nasal bones.

In addition to the Le Fort fractures, all three people had evidence of violent trauma in some combination of chop marks, cut marks, bone scrapes, and depressed skull fractures. Individual 1, one of the possible females, had undergone multiple attempts at being beheaded, as noted by various chop marks into the inferior portion of the skull at the occipital condyles, where the neck articulates with the skull (fig. 15.3), as well as at least ten cut and chop marks on the first and second neck vertebrae (plate 29). This person also has cut marks indicating that the skull was defleshed, including horizontal lines above the eyes that could indicate scalping (fig. 15.4). In addition, scrape marks were noted around the right eye orbit. These indi-

cate that the flesh around the eye, if not the eye itself, was removed (fig. 15.4, inset). This first individual likely also had her jaw removed, as cut marks on the both right and left temporal bones were noted in areas that would have been associated with chewing musculature.

Individual 2 is the only confirmed male in the group. This male has a large fracture associated with blunt force

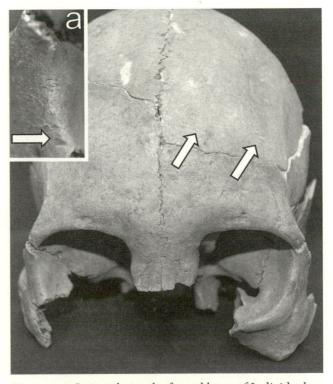

Figure 15.4. Cut marks on the frontal bone of Individual 1, notated with arrows. The inset shows a close-up of cut marks around the eye of this individual.

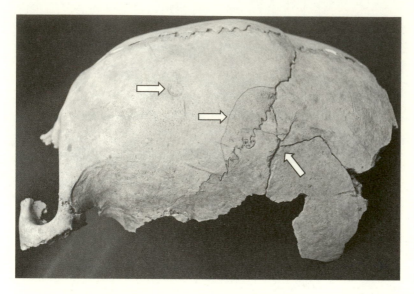

Figure 15.5. Evidence of blunt force trauma on the skull of Individual 2. The top left arrow shows healed trauma, and the bottom and right two arrows show perimortem, high-impact trauma.

trauma on the left side of the head, including radiating and rounded fracture lines that indicate a high-velocity blow or blows at or around the time of his death (fig. 15.5) (Berryman and Gunther 2000; Berryman and Symes 1998). In addition, there are two areas of well-healed trauma, suggesting incidents of interpersonal violence that had a chance to heal. The first injury, on the left frontal bone, is a round circular depression with an adjacent area of

thickened bone (noted in fig. 15.5). The second is likely a broken nose, as the nasal bones are misaligned (fig. 15.6). This second individual also has cut marks around the left eye orbit, likely indicating defleshing around the eye and possible eye removal (fig. 15.6, inset).

Individual 3 (fig. 15.7), another possible female, suffered multiple perimortem injuries, including a small, depressed fracture superior to the fractures on her nose (fig. 15.7, inset). In addition and akin to the other two people, this individual had multiple cut marks around both left and right eye orbits (plate 30), suggesting that the eyes might have been purposefully removed. Multiple cut marks were also noted on both left and right sides of the skull where the mandible articulates with the rest of the skull, as well as the zygomatic and temporal bones near where chewing musculature would have been attached. These marks likely indicate jaw removal at or around the time of death. This person may also have received an additional blow to the head on the right temporal at or around the time of death, as noted by the radiating fracture line similar to the one noted on the second, male individual.

For all three individuals, the sequence of violence is somewhat unclear, except for the second male individual, who had two cases of well-healed trauma. However, we can put some of the injuries into chronological order. The first individual had a few cut marks on the inner table of the bone, which indicates that defleshing took place after portions of the skull were broken. This suggests that the first individual was highly incapacitated or dead while flesh on the scalp was removed. The second and third individuals were likely in the same state—beaten and then defleshed, as cuts were made on top of fracture lines. As for the Le

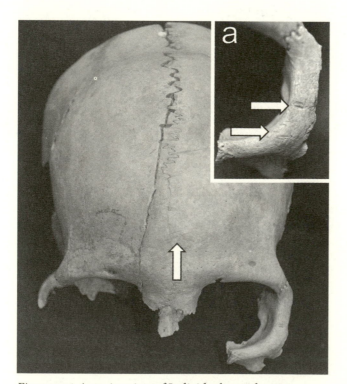

Figure 15.6. Anterior view of Individual 2, with arrows notating cut marks. The inset shows a closer view of the cut marks around the eye orbit.

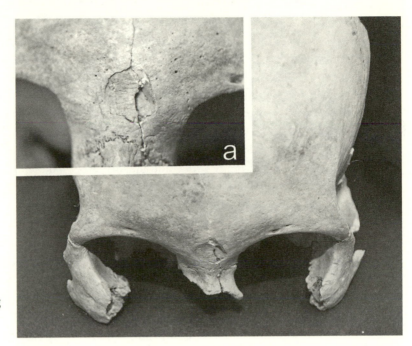

Figure 15.7. Individual 3, with an inset showing a close-up of perimortem trauma superior to the nasal bones.

Fort fractures and the cut marks noted around the areas of chewing musculature, the removal of the upper and lower jaws was likely purposeful, as no bones from these areas or teeth were found. In addition, the skeletal evidence suggests that all three people had their eyes, or at least the flesh around their eyes, removed. It is unclear if they were alive during this process, although the multiple cut and scrape marks differ in variety, depth, and placement on the eye bones of each individual. This could indicate that the victims were alive and struggling while undergoing eye removal, as this activity has been noted elsewhere in the Andes among the Moche as a form of torture (Hamilton 2005), as well as during Inka times as punishment (Guaman Poma de Ayala 2006). However, Andrushko (2011) has described a Wari skull displayed as a trophy head that had similar cut marks around the eyes, likely incurred as part of the defleshing process. Thus, it is not clear whether the cut marks on Wata Wata heads resulted from removing tissue near the eye orbits, or removing the eyes themselves at or around the time of death.

THE POWER OF THE WATA WATA HEADS

Detached heads, noted in Tiwanaku iconography, have been found archaeologically on stone sculptures, serving vessels, and textiles (Alconini 1995; Chávez 1992; Janusek 2004a, 2008; Kolata 1993a; Oakland 1986; Young-Sánchez 2004, 2009). However, prior to these finds, there was very little bioarchaeological evidence of human skull usage in Tiwanaku (Becker and Alconini 2015). In fact, heads detached from bodies in the Tiwanaku heartland were more often associated with dedications or ancestor veneration (Blom and Janusek 2004; Manzanilla and Woodard 1990). As noted in prior research (Alconini and Becker 2018; Becker and Alconini 2015), we do not believe that the Wata Wata skulls were of respected relatives. There is no or almost no evidence of violence inflicted on the bodies of people who are considered ancestors and who are worshipped posthumously (e.g., Finucane 2008; Hastorf 2003; Salomon 1991; Seeman 2007; Sofaer 2006; Verano 1995, 2001, 2008), which is not the case with the three heads examined in this research. In addition, other cases of perimortem violence among the Tiwanaku were not limited to heads, nor have only heads been found as part of any brutal ritual. The Wata Wata find is therefore different from other known types of skeletal violence for this culture, suggesting that harnessing the power of deceased ancestors was not important at the Wata Wata site.

Heads elsewhere in the Andes are often noted for their ability to be displayed and recognized as something that was once human, such as among the Nasca, Wari, and Moche, for whom heads were trophies, or the ñatitas in present-day La Paz, where heads serve as protectors. Comparing the Wata Wata heads to other Andean cases of trophy taking, they share certain patterns of violence, such as perimortem trauma, defleshing, and dismemberment. Nonetheless, the purpose of these heads does not seem to be for display. It is possible that these three Wata Wata skulls represent a one-time trophy display. However, the amount of perimortem modification involved seems like a lot of work to exhibit these skulls on only one occasion. Their internment under a capstone that does not appear to have been repeatedly opened to redisplay the heads is also odd. Additionally, these heads do not match well with other examples of detached skulls in the Andes, because the faces of all three people were broken and dismembered. The removal or disfiguration of most of the face as well as the mouth would seem antithetical to the purpose of a trophy head, whose authority rests at least partly on its recognizability as human. Our exploration of the evidence of the Wata Wata heads and their comparison to other known archaeological and bioarchaeological cases of Andean trophy heads has shown that we must search for alternative explanations, other than only the traditional idea of heads as trophies.

Controlling the power of heads, as seen with the visible ñatitas or hidden cache heads, is a topic that also needs to be addressed with these Wata Wata skulls. While we cannot force modern interpretations onto these prehistoric skulls and we are cautious in our use of ethnographic and ethnohistorical resources, we also cannot discount some of the similarities between this find and heads in the central Andean region. The idea that skulls may be more powerful, lending help via sympathy and empathy to living people, if they have a violent origin could explain some of the trauma inflicted on these three skulls. Extreme violence to individuals was certainly not unknown in the prehistoric Andes, but the trauma noted, including beheading, defleshing, and removal of eyes and jaws without any intention of displaying the skulls, is different from treatments of other known trophy heads. In addition, possibly because these heads were considered powerful items born of violence or because their ability to be restored or regenerated from a "seed" needed to be contained, they were hidden away beneath a capstone at Wata Wata. Such considerations might have been particularly important in the Kallawaya region, traditionally known as the home of powerful traveling shamans, medicine men, and herbal healers. In this context, controlling such powerful individuals might have been an important political strategy to moderate or strip their power.

This strategy of controlling or removing power may have also been applied to deviants—people considered liminal, dangerous, or uncontrollable—especially in times of social or political unrest. Similar to the evidence from

Wata Wata, deviants in other cultures can be subjected to physical violence, including eye and jaw removal (Abercrombie 1986; Catling 2011; Green 1997; Heraclides 1971). Thus, it is possible that the heads from Wata Wata were those of social deviants. This interpretation gains support if one considers that this offering was deposited in a time of political tension and social unrest, during the transition from the Late Formative to the Tiwanaku period. As Tiwanaku expanded into the region to extend its influence, despite the popular religious ideology brought by the newcomers, it is likely that some rejected the encroachment. If the medicinal and shamanistic practices of the local Yunga Kallawaya were already prevalent at this critical juncture, their practitioners might have been considered particularly dangerous and powerful. Although we do not know who the victims (or their decapitators) were, it is clear that the violence was done in a ritualized context. By this time, Wata Wata was an important religious center and part of a growing web of trading corridors that crossed the region. While there are no another cases of comparable violence during this time elsewhere in the prehistoric Andes, it is clear that it occurred during a critical political interface, and in a region that was crucial to the emerging interests of Tiwanaku. Perhaps these individuals were seen as a menace to the emerging social order, or their privileged standing as shamans had become a source of suspicion, or perhaps they were simply the random victims of shifting power balances.

CONCLUSIONS

The evidence presented in this chapter highlights the importance of head taking as a strategy to control the power of important individuals in society, whether these were social deviants, powerful shamans, or rival political leaders. Beyond known cases of decapitation and the use of skulls as trophies, this study has revealed that heads are considered potent sources of power. In the Bolivian Andes, the cache of heads from Wata Wata illustrates a case in which three adult individuals were sacrificed and beheaded during a time of social and political change, associated with the arrival of the Tiwanaku state in the region. Whether these individuals were unwilling victims, members of rebellious factions, or disempowered shamans, the level of violence inflicted on them illustrates the importance of such practices in a context of shifting power balances in the region. This evidence also echoes broader cultural practices in the

Andes in which human heads, whether from a violent or natural death, are considered potent sources of power, as with modern ñatitas. Future research will reveal the genetic profiles of these decapitated victims in Wata Wata, and perhaps even their geographic origins. After further comparative studies in the region, we will also learn whether this was an isolated event or only the first manifestation of ritualized forms of violence exerted by Tiwanaku in its expansion into the eastern tropics.

REFERENCES CITED

Abercrombie, Thomas Alan

1986 *The Politics of Sacrifice: An Aymara Cosmology in Action*. PhD dissertation, Department of Anthropology, University of Chicago, Chicago.

Aguiló, Federico

1991 *Diccionario Kallawaya*. Museo Nacional de Etnografía y Folklore, La Paz.

Alconini, Sonia

1995 *Rito, símbolo e historia en la pirámide de Akapana, Tiwanaku: un análisis de cerámica ceremonial prehispániuca*. Editorial Acción, La Paz.

2011 *Imperial Marginality and Frontier: Kallawayas and Chunchos in the Eastern Inka Borders*. Final project report (2006–2010) submitted to the National Science Foundation, Arlington, Virginia, award no. 0635342.

2013 *Excavations in the Formative Ceremonial Mound of Wata Wata, Kallawaya Region: Assessing Its Nature and Evolution*. Unpublished manuscript, Department of Anthropology, University of Texas at San Antonio.

2016 El Centro de Wata Wata en los valles orientales Kallawaya: género, ritualidad e intercambio en los períodos Formativo y Tiwanaku. In *Otras miradas: presencias femeninas en una historia de larga duración*, edited by Walter Sánchez Canedo and Claudia Rivera Casanovas, pp. 203–16. Instituto de Investigaciones Antropológicas; Museo Arqueológico, Universidad Mayor de San Simón, Cochabamba, Bolivia.

Alconini, Sonia, and Sara K. Becker

2011 Trophy Head Taking among the Tiwanaku: Three Crania from Charazani, Bolivia. Paper presented at the seventy-sixth annual meeting of the Society for American Archaeology, Sacramento.

2013 Remoción craneana, intercambio inter-regional y estrategias políticas de control en el territorio Kallawaya durante la transición del período forma-tivo tardío: Tiwanaku. Paper presented at Encuentro Internacional sobre Recientes Investigaciones: Arqueológicas en Bolivia, Universidad Mayor de San Andrés, La Paz.

2018 Sacrificio, decapitación y remoción ocular: estrategias Tiwanaku de control político y religioso en los valles orientales. In *Tiahuanaco 1903–La Paz 2013: 110 años de colaboraciones arqueológicas francoamericanas*, edited by Instituto Francés de Estudios Andino. Instituto Francés de Estudios Andino, Lima.

Allsop, Douglas, and Kelly Kennett

2002 Skull and Facial Bone Trauma. In *Accidental Injury: Biomechanics and Prevention*, edited by Alan M. Nahum and John W. Melvin, pp. 254–76. Springer, New York.

Andrushko, Valerie A.

2011 How the Wari Fashioned Trophy Heads for Display: A Distinctive Modified Cranium from Cuzco, Peru, and Comparison to Trophies from the Capital Region. In *The Bioarchaeology of the Human Head: Decapitation, Decoration, and Deformation*, edited by Michelle Bonogofsky, pp. 262–85. University Press of Florida, Gainesville.

Arnold, Denise Y.

2005 The Social Life of a Communal Chest: Hybrid Characters and the Imagined Genealogies of Written Documents and Their Woven Ancestors. In *Repensando el pasado, recuperando el futuro: nuevos aportes interdisciplinarios para el estudio de la américa colonial / Remembering the Past, Retrieving the Future: New Interdisciplinary Contributions to the Study of Colonial Latin America*, edited by Verónica Salles-Reese, pp. 92–131. Pontificia Universidad Javeriana, Bogotá.

2006 *The Metamorphosis of Heads: Textual Struggles, Education, and Land in the Andes*. University of Pittsburgh Press, Pittsburgh.

Arnold, Denise Y., and Christine A. Hastorf

2008 *Heads of State: Icons, Power, and Politics in the Ancient and Modern Andes*. Left Coast Press, Walnut Creek, California.

Bandelier, Adolph Francis

1892 *Final Report of Investigations among the Indians of the Southwestern United States, Carried On Mainly in the Years from 1880 to 1885*. Part 1. Papers of the Archaeological Institute of America. Cambridge University, Cambridge.

Bandy, Matthew S.

2004 Trade and Social Power in the Southern Titicaca Basin Formative. In *Foundations of Power in the Prehispanic Andes*, edited by Kevin J. Vaughn, Dennis Ogburn, and Christina A. Conlee, pp. 91–112. Archaeological Papers, no. 14. American Anthropological Association, Arlington, Virginia.

Bass, William M.

1981 *Human Osteology: A Laboratory and Field Manual of the Human Skeleton*. Missouri Archaeological Society, Columbia.

Bastien, Joseph W.

1978 *Mountain of the Condor: Metaphor and Ritual in an Andean Ayllu*. Waveland Press, Prospect Heights, Illinois.

Becker, Sara K., and Sonia Alconini

2015 Head Extraction, Interregional Exchange, and Political Strategies of Control at the Site of Wata Wata, Kallawaya Territory, Bolivia, during the Transition between the Late Formative and Tiwanaku Periods (AD 200–800). *Latin American Antiquity* 26(1):30–48.

Benson, Elizabeth P., and Anita G. Cook (editors)

2001 *Ritual Sacrifice in Ancient Peru*. University of Texas Press, Austin.

Berryman, Hugh E., and Wendy M. Gunther

2000 Keyhole Defect Production in Tubular Bone. *Journal of Forensic Sciences* 45(2):483–87.

Berryman, Hugh E., and Steven A. Symes

1998 Recognizing Gunshot and Blunt Cranial Trauma through Fracture Interpretation. In *Forensic Osteology: Advances in the Identification of Human Remains*, 2nd ed., edited by Kathy Reichs, pp. 333–52. Charles C. Thomas, Springfield, Illinois.

Blom, Deborah E., and John Wayne Janusek

2004 Making Place: Humans as Dedications in Tiwanaku. *World Archaeology* 36(1):123–41.

Bosmia, Anand N., Christoph J. Griessenauer, and R. Shane Tubbs

2013 Use of the Human Calvaria and Skull as Alms Bowls and Drinking Vessels by Aghori Ascetics in Present-Day India. *Child's Nervous System* 29(10):1785–87.

Bourdieu, Pierre

1977 *Outline of a Theory of Practice*. Cambridge University Press, Cambridge.

Browman, David L.

1984 Tiwanaku: Development of Interzonal Trade and Economic Expansion in the Altiplano. In *Social and Economic Organization in the Prehispanic Andes*, edited by David L. Browman, Richard L. Burger, and Mario A. Rivera, pp. 117–42. BAR International Series, 194. British Archaeological Reports, Oxford.

Browne, David M., Helaine Silverman, and Rubén García

1993 A Cache of 48 Nasca Trophy Heads from Cerro Carapo, Peru. *Latin American Antiquity* 4(3):274–94.

Buikstra, Jane E., and Douglas H. Ubelaker (editors)

1994 *Standards for Data Collection from Human Skeletal Remains*. Arkansas Archeological Survey, Fayetteville.

Calhoun, Craig J.

1980 The Authority of Ancestors: A Sociological Reconsideration of Fortes's Tallensi in Response to Fortes's Critics. *Man* 15:304–19.

Catling, Chris

2011 Snacks, Smells, Censorship, and Spells. *World Archaeology* 50(5):65.

Chávez, Juan Carlos

2009 Kalla Kallan, un centro de interacción Yunga-Kallawaya-Tiwanaku en los valles de Charazani-Curva durante el horizonte medio (ca. 500–1150 DC). Thesis, Department of Anthropology and Archaeology, Universidad Mayor de San Andrés, La Paz.

Chávez, Juan Carlos, and Sonia Alconini

2016 Los Yunga-Kallawaya: repensando los procesos de interacción regional en los andes orientales septentrionales. In *Entre la vertiente tropical y los valles: sociedades regionales e interaccion prehispanicas en los Andes centro-sur*, edited by Sonia Alconini. Editorial Plural, La Paz.

Chávez, Karen Mohr

1988 The Significance of Chiripa in Lake Titicaca Basin Developments. *Expedition* 30(3):17–26.

Chávez, Sergio

1992 *The Conventionalized Rules in Pucara Pottery Technology and Iconography Implications for Socio-Political Developments in the Northern Lake Titicaca Basin*. PhD dissertation, Department of Anthropology, University of Michigan.

Christensen, Angi M., Nicholas V. Passalacqua, and Eric J. Bartelink

2014 *Forensic Anthropology: Current Methods and Practice*. Academic Press, San Diego.

Clados, Christiane

2009 New Perspectives on Tiwanaku Iconography. In *Tiwanaku: Papers from the 2005 Mayer Center Symposium at the Denver Art Museum*, edited by Margaret Young-Sánchez, pp. 101–14. Denver Art Museum, Denver.

Curry, Dennis C.

1999 *Feast of the Dead: Aboriginal Ossuaries in Maryland.* Archeological Society of Maryland; Maryland Historical Trust Press, Myersville, Maryland.

Darling, J. Andrew

1998 Mass Inhumation and the Execution of Witches in the American Southwest. *American Anthropologist* 100(3):732–52.

Dornan-Fish, Jennifer

2012 Motive Matters: Intentionality, Embodiment, and the Individual in Archaeology. *Time and Mind* 5(3): 279–98.

Durkheim, Émile

1978 "Introduction to the Sociology of the Family." In *Émile Durkheim on Institutional Analysis*, edited and translated by Mark Traugott. University of Chicago Press, Chicago.

Fenton, James

1991 *The Social Uses of Dead People: Problems and Solutions in the Analysis of Post Mortem Body Processing in the Archaeological Record.* PhD dissertation, Department of Anthropology, Columbia University.

Finucane, Brian Clifton

2008 Trophy Heads from Nawinpukio, Peru: Physical and Chemical Analysis of Huarpa-Era Modified Human Remains. *American Journal of Physical Anthropology* 135:75–84.

Forgey, Kathleen, and Sloan R. Williams

2005 Were Nasca Trophy Heads War Trophies or Revered Ancestors? Insights from the Kroeber Collection. In *Interacting with the Dead: Perspectives on Mortuary Archaeology for the New Millennium*, edited by Gordon F. M. Rakita, Jane E. Buikstra, Lane A. Beck, and Sloan R. Williams, pp. 251–76. University Press of Florida, Gainesville.

Franzen, Christina E.

2011 The Violation of the Eye and the Theft of Vision in Lucan's *Bellum Civile*. *Syllecta Classica* 22:69–93.

Fuentes, Ayesha

2011 Utilizing Terror: On the Adoption and Refinement of Skull Cups in Tibetan Buddhism. Master's thesis, Department of Art and Art History, Tufts University.

Girault, Louis

1969 *Textiles Boliviens: région de Charazani*. Muséum National D'Historie Naturelle, Paris.

Green, Miranda

1997 *The World of Druids*. Thames and Hudson, London.

Guaman Poma de Ayala, Felipe

2006 [1613] *El primer nueva corónica y buen gobierno*. Editorial Siglo Veintiuno, Mexico City.

Hamilton, Laurel S.

2005 Cut Marks as Evidence of Precolumbian Human Sacrifice and Postmortem Bone Modification on the North Coast of Peru. Unpublished PhD dissertation, Department of Anthropology, Tulane University, New Orleans.

Hastorf, Christine A.

2003 Community with the Ancestors: Ceremonies and Social Memory in the Middle Formative at Chiripa, Bolivia. *Journal of Anthropological Archaeology* (22):305–32.

2005 The Upper (Middle and Late) Formative in the Titicaca Region. In *Advances in Titicaca Basin Archaeology–1*, edited by Charles Stanish, Amanda B. Cohen, and Mark S. Aldenderfer, pp. 65–94. Cotsen Institute of Archaeology, University of California, Los Angeles.

Hastorf, Christine A., Matthew Bandy, William T. Whitehead, Lee Steadman, Katherine Moore, José Luis Soria Paz, Andrew P. Roddick, María Bruno, Soledad Fernández, Kathryn Killackey, Amanda L. Logan, Delfor Ulloa Vidaurre, Luis Callisaya, José Capriles Flores, Emily Stovel, Annie Rooth, and Alexander Antonites

2005 *Proyecto arqueológico Taraco: informe de las excavaciones de la temporada del 2004 en los sitios de Kumi Kipa, Sonaji y Chiripa*. Unidad Nacional de Arqueología de Bolivia.

Heraclides Lembus

1971 *Excerpta Politiarum*. Translated by Mervin R. Dilts. Duke University Press, Durham, North Carolina.

Houston, Stephen D., and Tom Cummins

2004 Body, Presence, and Space in Andean and Mesoamerican Rulership. In *Palaces of the Ancient New World*, edited by Susan T. Evans and Joanne Pillsbury, pp. 359–98. Dumbarton Oaks, Washington, DC.

Isbell, William H., and Patricia Knobloch

2008 Missing Links, Imaginary Links: Staff God Imagery in the South Andean Past. In *Andean Archaeology III: North and South*, edited by William H. Isbell and Helaine Silverman, pp. 307–51. Springer, New York.

Janusek, John Wayne

2004a *Identity and Power in the Ancient Andes: Tiwanaku Cities through Time*. Routledge, New York.

2004b Tiwanaku and Its Precursors: Recent Research and Emerging Perspectives. *Journal of Archaeological Research* 12(2):121–83.

2008 *Ancient Tiwanaku*. Case Studies in Early Societies. Cambridge University Press, New York.

Johnson, Brian B.

2013 *The Politics of Affliction: Crisis, the State, and the Coloniality of Maternal Death in Bolivia*. PhD dissertation, Department of Sociomedical Sciences, Columbia University.

Johnson, Mark

1999 Embodied Reason. In *Perspectives on Embodiment: The Intersections of Nature and Culture*, edited by Gail Weiss and Honi Fern Haber, pp. 81–102. Routledge, New York.

Kolata, Alan L.

1993a *The Tiwanaku: Portrait of an Andean Civilization*. Blackwell, Oxford.

1993b Understanding Tiwanaku: Conquest, Colonization, and Clientage in the South Central Andes. In *Latin American Horizons*, edited by Don S. Rice, pp. 193–224. Dumbarton Oaks, Washington, DC.

La Barre, Weston

1950 Aymara Folktales. *International Journal of American Linguistics* 16(1):40–45.

1951 Aymara Biologicals and Other Medicines. *Journal of American Folklore* 64:171–78.

Lau, George F.

2002. Feasting and Ancestor Veneration at Chinchawas, North Highlands of Ancash, Peru. *Latin American Antiquity* 13(3):279–304.

López Luján, Leonardo, and Guilhem Olivier (editors)

2010 *El sacrificio humano en la tradición religiosa mesoamericana*. Instituto Nacional de Antropología e Historia, Mexico City.

Macionis, John J., and Linda M. Gerber

2010 *Sociology*. 7th Canadian ed. Pearson Canada, Toronto.

Makowski, Krzysztof

2009 Royal Statuses, Staff Gods, and the Religious Ideology of the Prehistoric State of Tiwanaku. In *Tiwanaku: Papers from the 2005 Mayer Center Symposium at the Denver Art Museum*, edited by Margaret Young-Sánchez, pp. 133–64. Denver Art Museum, Denver.

Manzanilla, Linda, and Eric Woodard

1990 Restos humanos asociados a la pirámide de Akapana (Tiwanaku, Bolivia). *Latin American Antiquity* 1(2):133–49.

Maximus, Valerius

2000 *Memorable Doings and Sayings*. 2 vols. Translated by D. R. Shackleton Bailey. Harvard University Press, Cambridge, Massachusetts.

McAnany, Patricia

1995 *Living with the Ancestors: Kinship and Kingship in Ancient Maya Society*. University of Texas Press, Austin.

Merleau-Ponty, Maurice

2013 *Phenomenology of Perception*. Translated by Donald Landes. Routledge, New York.

Meyers, Rodica

2002 *Cuando el sol caminaba por la tierra: orígenes de la intermediación Kallawaya*. Plural Editores, La Paz.

Oakland, Amy S.

1986 Tiahuanaco Tapestry Tunics and Mantles from San Pedro de Atacama, Chile. In *Junius B. Bird Conference on Andean Textiles*, edited by Ann Pollard Rowe, pp. 101–21. Textile Museum, Washington, DC.

Oblitas Poblete, Enrique

1978 *Cultura Callawaya*. Ediciones Populares Camarlinghi, La Paz.

1992 *Plantas medicinales en Bolivia: farmacopea Callawaya*. Editorial Los Amigos del Libro, Cochabamba, Bolivia.

Proulx, Donald A.

2001 Ritual Uses of Trophy Heads in Ancient Nasca Society. In *Ritual Sacrifice in Ancient Peru*, edited by Elizabeth P. Benson and Anita G. Cook, pp. 119–36. University of Texas Press, Austin.

2006 *A Sourcebook of Nasca Ceramic Iconography: Reading a Culture through Its Art*. University of Iowa Press, Iowa City.

Rakita, Gordon F. M., Jane E. Buikstra, Lane A. Beck, and Sloan R. Williams (editors)

2005 *Interacting with the Dead: Perspectives on Mortuary Archaeology for the New Millennium*. University Press of Florida, Gainesville.

Risør, Helene

2013 "Captured with Their Hands in the Dough": Insecurity, Safety-Seeking and Securitization in El Alto, Bolivia. In *Times of Security: Ethnographies of Fear, Protest and the Future*, edited by Martin Holbraad and Morten Axel Pedersen, pp. 57–79. Routledge, New York.

Rösing, Ina

1995 *La mesa blanca Callawaya: contribución al análisis, observaciones intraculturales y transculturales*. Editorial Los Amigos del Libro, Cochabamba, Bolivia.

Rydén, Stig

1957 *Andean Excavations 1: The Tiahuanaco Area East of Lake Titicaca*. Series no. 6. Ethnographical Museum of Sweden, Stockholm.

Saignes, Thierry

1984 Quienes son los Callahuayas: nota sobre un enigma histórico. In *Espacio y tiempo en el mundo Callahuaya*, edited by Teresa Gisbert. Instituto de Estudios Bolivianos, Facultad de Humanidades, Universidad Mayor de San Andrés, La Paz.

1985 *Los Andes orientales: historia de un olvido*. Instituto Francés de Estudios Andinos; Centro de Estudios de la Realidad Económica y Social, Cochabamba, Bolivia.

Salomon, Frank

1991 "The Beautiful Grandparents": Andean Ancestor Shrines and Mortuary Ritual as Seen through Colonial Records. In *Tombs for the Living: Andean Mortuary Practices*, edited by Tom D. Dillehay, pp. 315–53. Dumbarton Oaks, Washington, DC.

Schiwy, Freya

2009 *Indianizing Film: Decolonization, the Andes, and the Question of Technology*. Rutgers University Press, New Brunswick, New Jersey.

Sebeok, Thomas A.

1951 Materials for an Aymara Dictionary. *Journal de la Société des Américanistes* 40(1):89–151.

Seeman, Mark F.

2007 Predatory War and Hopewell Trophies. In *The Taking and Displaying of Human Body Parts as Trophies by Amerindians*, edited by Richard J. Chacon and David H. Dye, pp. 167–89. Springer, New York.

Sheales, Fiona

2011 Sights/Sites of Spectacle: Anglo/Asante Appropriations, Diplomacy and Displays of Power, 1816–1820. Sainsbury Research Unit for the Arts of Africa, Oceania and the Americas, University of East Anglia, Norwich, England.

Silverman, Helaine, and Donald A. Proulx

2002 *The Nasca*. Blackwell, Malden, Massachusetts.

Simon, Sara K.

2003 The Effect of Chiefdom Formation on the Health of Aboriginal Populations in the Chesapeake Bay Area of Maryland and Virginia. Master's thesis, Department of Anthropology, California State University, Los Angeles.

Smith, Scott

2012 Generative Landscapes: The Step Mountain Motif in Tiwanaku Iconography. *Ancient America* 12:1–70.

Sofaer, Joanna R.

2006 *The Body as Material Culture: A Theoretical Osteoarchaeology*. Cambridge University Press, Cambridge.

Spedding, Alison

2011 *Sueños, kharisiris y curanderos: dinámicas sociales de las creencias en los andes contemporáneos*. Editorial Mama Huaco, La Paz.

Sutter, Richard C., and Rosa J. Cortez

2005 The Nature of Moche Human Sacrifice. *Current Anthropology* 46(4):521–49.

Torres, Constantino Manuel

1987 *The Iconography of South American Snuff Trays and Related Paraphernalia*. Göteborgs Etnografiska Museum, Gothenburg.

2001 Iconografía Tiwanaku en la paraphernalia inhalatoria de los Andes centro-sur. In *Huari y Tiwanaku: modelos vs. evidencias, segunda parte*, edited by Peter Kaulicke and William H. Isbell. *Boletínde Arqueología PUCP* 5:427–54.

Toyne, J. Marla

2008 *Offering Their Hearts and Heads: A Bioarchaeological Analysis of Ancient Human Sacrifice on the Northern Coast of Peru*. PhD dissertation, Department of Anthropology, Tulane University, New Orleans.

Tung, Tiffiny A.

2007 From Corporeality to Sanctity: Transforming Bodies into Trophy Heads in the Pre-Hispanic Andes. In *The Taking and Displaying of Human Body Parts as Trophies by Amerindians*, edited by Richard J. Chacon and David H. Dye, pp. 481–504. Springer, New York.

2008 Dismembering Bodies for Display: A Bioarchaeological Study of Trophy Heads from the Wari Site of Conchopata, Peru. *American Journal of Physical Anthropology* 136:294–308.

2014 Making Warriors, Making War: Violence and Militarism in the Wari Empire. In *Embattled Bodies, Embattled Places: War in Pre-Columbian Mesoamerica and the Andes*, edited by Andrew K. Scherer and John W. Verano, pp. 227–56. Dumbarton Oaks, Washington, DC.

Tung, Tiffiny A., and Kelly J. Knudson

2008 Social Identities and Geographical Origins of Wari Trophy Heads from Conchopata, Peru. *Current Anthropology* 49:915–25.

2010 Childhood Lost: Abductions, Sacrifice, and Trophy Heads of Children in the Wari Empire of the Ancient Andes. *Latin American Antiquity* 21(1):44–66.

Ubelaker, Douglas H.

1974 *Reconstruction of Demographic Profiles from Ossuary Skeletal Samples: A Case Study from the Tidewater*

Potomac. Smithsonian Contributions to Anthropology, no. 18. Smithsonian Institution Press, Washington, DC.

United Nations Educational, Scientific and Cultural Organization

2008   Third Session of the Intergovernmental Committee. Andean Cosmovision of the Kallawaya, electronic document, https://ich.unesco.org/en/RL/andean-cosmovision -of-the-kallawaya-00048, accessed August 15, 2015.

Verano, John W.

1995   Where Do They Rest? The Treatment of Human Offerings and Trophies in Ancient Peru. In *Tombs for the Living: Andean Mortuary Practices*, edited by Tom D. Dillehay, pp. 189–227. Dumbarton Oaks, Washington, DC.

2001   The Physical Evidence of Human Sacrifice in Ancient Peru. In *Ritual Sacrifice in Ancient Peru*, edited by Elizabeth P. Benson and Anita G. Cook, pp. 165–84. University of Texas Press, Austin.

2003   Mummified Trophy Heads from Peru: Diagnostic Features and Medicolegal Significance. *Journal of Forensic Sciences* 48:525–30.

2008   Trophy Head-Taking and Human Sacrifice in Andean South America. In *Handbook of South American Archaeology*, edited by Helaine Silverman and William H. Isbell, pp. 1047–60. Springer, New York.

2013   Excavation and Analysis of Human Skeletal Remains from a New Dedicatory Offering at Tiwanaku. In *Advances in Titicaca Basin Archaeology–2*, edited by Alexei Vranich and Abigail R. Levine, pp. 167–82. Cotsen Institute of Archaeology, University of California, Los Angeles.

2014   Warfare and Captive Sacrifice in the Moche Culture: The Battle Continues. In *Embattled Bodies, Embattled Places: War in Pre-Columbian Mesoamerica and the Andes*, edited by Andrew K. Scherer and John W. Verano, pp. 283–310. Dumbarton Oaks, Washington, DC.

Verano, John W., Santiago Uceda, Claude Chapdelaine, Ricardo Tello, María Isabel Paredes, and Victor Pimentel

1999   Modified Human Skulls from the Urban Sector of the Pyramids of Moche, Northern Peru. *Latin American Antiquity* 10:59–70.

Walker, William H.

1998   Where Are the Witches of Prehistory? *Journal of Archaeological Method and Theory* 5(3):245–308.

Wassén, S. Henry

1972   *A Medicine-Man's Implements and Plants in a Tiahuanacoid Tomb in Highland Bolivia*. Göteborgs Etnografiska Museum, Gothenburg.

1978   Instrumentos y plantas de un curandero indio en una tumba de la zona Kallawaya. In *Cultura Callawaya*, edited by Enrique Oblitas Poblete, pp. 521–56. Camarlinghi, La Paz.

White, Tim D.

1991   *Human Osteology*. Academic Press, San Diego.

Young-Sánchez, Margaret

2004   *Tiwanaku: Ancestors of the Inca*. University of Nebraska Press, Lincoln.

2009   (editor)   *Tiwanaku: Papers from the 2005 Mayer Center Symposium at the Denver Art Museum*. Denver Art Museum, Denver.

16

Semiotic Portraits

Expressions of Communal Identity in Wari Faceneck Vessels

ANDREA VAZQUEZ DE ARTHUR

INTRODUCTION

The long-lasting tradition of trophy head taking in South America is a powerful testament to the significance of heads for ancient and modern Andean societies. However, heads can function in a number of ways, as very different kinds of objects. In *Heads of State*, Denise Arnold and Christine Hastorf discuss how the transformation that a trophy head undergoes during the curation process marks a critical turning point for the meaning and purpose of the head. Based on Arnold's ethnographic fieldwork in modern Qaqachaka, a trophy head, acquired by a male warrior in battle when he eliminates his enemy, is later transformed by his wife through rituals involving wrapping the head in textiles, pouring libations, and burning incense, until the enemy head eventually transitions into a benign symbol of regeneration (Arnold and Hastorf 2008). The trophy head and the curated head are thus regarded as two very different kinds of things, despite being physically the same object. In a sense, the curated head becomes an image or reproduction of the original trophy head, complete with a new range of power and potential that the trophy head did not have. In its new role as an image, a curated head may now operate within, and contribute to, a greater system of visual language about heads and human imagery. As images, curated heads can be compared with various other types of anthropomorphic objects and images, from the fake heads placed atop mummy bundles, to the stylized images of heads woven onto textiles, to ceramic head jars and cups used for toasting an enemy's demise. Ancient Andean visual culture is rife with anthropomorphic imagery, yet how this imagery works and what it expresses is often far from simple. Semiotically, how precisely does the image of a human—of a head, a face, or an entire human body—signify a sense of personhood? Moreover, when does an image of a human signify a *specific* person, as in the case of a portrait?

So far, a tendency to focus on more naturalistic representations, such as Moche head vessels, has caused discussions of Andean portraiture to fixate on the desire to express individual identity. And while less naturalistic renderings of human faces admittedly do seem less expressive of individuality, identity as an aspect of personhood need not be rooted in the experience of the individual. Thus, nonmimetic images may also function as portraits in the sense that they express identity, even while they may not privilege or be driven by individuality.

The Wari civilization of the Middle Horizon (600–1000 CE) provides an alternative case study for investigating images of human heads and faces that act as representations of identity. Wari imagery is notoriously non-narrative, preferring instead to communicate through standing figures and sometimes even isolated body parts, with human heads and faces being an especially prominent category of representation. In the absence of narrative context, however, many of these images have been overlooked in discussions of ancient Andean portraiture. How might such enigmatic images serve as devices of communication and expression?

The faceneck vessel as one particular category of human imagery may provide a unique window into Wari representations of identity that appear to actively resist the strategies of naturalism and mimesis. In approaching such seemingly static images, the questions we ask of these objects must be different from those asked of images that more readily exploit conventions of naturalism. Before asking *who* these images represent—a warrior, a ruler, a prisoner—I prefer to focus on *how* they represent, and on *how* they make meaning. This study considers primarily pairs and groups of faceneck vessels as instances of multiplicity that may provide special insight over singular objects. Not only does a focus on multiple images draw attention to the numerous and varied ways that Wari artists made use of repetition, but moreover, examples of faceneck vessels made in pairs and groups depict a way of identifying oneself that is outside or beyond the individual experience, and instead these works function as signifiers for community.

PORTRAITURE IN THE ANCIENT ANDES

Discussions regarding Andean portraiture have tended to gravitate toward Moche head vessels, sometimes referred to as portrait heads, while other instances of human imagery, like faceneck vessels, have received less attention (fig. 16.1). It is plain to see why: Moche head vessels are compelling for their vivid naturalism. The delicately hooded eyelids, softly modeled lips, and asymmetric

features lend these images an uncanny sense of realism. And while these lifelike images would indeed be at home among, for example, the portrait busts of ancient Rome, the brief turn toward such high degrees of naturalism—limited temporally to Moche Phases III and IV and geographically to the Chicama, Moche, and Virú Valleys—calls for a consideration of how naturalism fits into the broader domain of visual culture in the Andes. In some ways, the visual culture of the Moche stands apart from that of most other ancient Andean societies. As Esther Pasztory has observed, the imagery found across the large and varied body of Moche art is often filled with action, imbuing the scenes with a strong sense of narrative, and there is more attention to the natural world and the story of humanity (Pasztory 1998). Nevertheless, Christopher Donnan's thematic approach to the interpretation of Moche imagery has shown that many seemingly straightforward images—an owl, a boat, a hand gesture—can in fact function as abbreviations for more complex themes or narratives and thus operate within a greater system of symbolic imagery (Donnan 1978). In essence, Moche visual culture was not limited to the production of images that functioned according to a basic, one-to-one signifier/signified mode of representation, but, rather, images participated in a complex system of visual language (Jackson 2008).

In his study of Moche ceramic head vessels, Donnan posits that these highly naturalistic images are examples of "true portraiture," which he defines as "showing the anatomical features of a person with such accuracy that the individual could be recognized without reliance on accompanying symbols or texts" (2004:3). Donnan's treatment of the subject rests on the idea that the images are

Figure 16.1. Comparison of a Moche head vessel with a Wari faceneck vessel. (a) Stirrup-spouted portrait vessel of a man, Moche, ca. 200–500 CE. Yale University Art Gallery, 1956.27.7 (photo by Andrea Vazquez de Arthur). (b) Jar with human face and double-headed serpents, Wari, ca. 600–800 CE. Dallas Museum of Art, Otis and Velma Davis Dozier Fund, 1997.120. Ceramic, 33.65 × 26.67 × 22.86 cm (image courtesy of Dallas Museum of Art).

meant to be mimetic representations of real individuals, and further, that the identities of these real individuals are the same identities being represented in the ceramic image. Moreover, this interpretation demonstrates a commitment to the idea that physical characteristics, such as scars and facial hair, are more important expressions of identity than accessories indicative of rank or social status such as headgear, ornamentation, and face paint. The latter point is made explicit by Donnan's interpretation of groups of identical faces depicted with variations in headgear, face paint, and accessories as representing multiple portraits of a single individual who is shown dressed and adorned in various ways (2004:93–111). But is the identity *of the image* defined more by the features of the person or by the emblems of the adornments? While the faces of these vessels may in fact have been modeled on actual individuals, the stance that, as images, the variations are meant to represent a single individual rests on the notion that Moche portraiture privileged anatomical mimesis over other modes of visual communication. Given the complexity of Moche visual culture, I believe that there is considerable potential for head vessels to have functioned as something other than mimetic portraits. If, in fact, it is the adornments that carry the burden of representing identity, the degree of naturalism of the human face that wears those adornments becomes less significant to the image's function as a communicative device. In short, there is a place for portraiture in the absence of naturalism.

As an alternative to Donnan's view of portraiture, Richard Brilliant locates the definition of portraiture in the critical link between the image and the identity of the real individual referenced by the image, with less emphasis on how that link is shown. He states: "The very fact of the portrait's allusion to an individual human being, actually existing outside the work, defines the function of the artwork in the world and constitutes the cause of its coming into being" (1991:8). In essence, a portrait is a representation of a real individual: a person with a name. Beyond that, the manner in which that person's identity is represented is up to the conventions of portraiture for that society, and ultimately in the hands of the artist.

Within the European artistic tradition, this critical relationship between image and subject is most often achieved through mimesis, relying on formal resemblance to immediately call to mind the identity of the subject in the portrait. Outside the European artistic tradition, however, portraiture is frequently achieved without mimesis, relying instead on other conventions for expressing

identity. Consider, for instance, the portraits of Gudea, governor of Lagash during the third millennium BCE. As Irene Winter has argued, Gudea's physical characteristics are better understood as "signature traits" that act iconographically to illustrate certain ideals of rulership, rather than as the description of his likeness. His broad chest signifies his vitality, his large ears communicate that he is wise and attentive, and his muscular arm depicts him as a strong ruler (Winter 2009). Following ancient Near Eastern conventions of kingly portraiture, portraits of Gudea participate in a visual language that communicates the expectations and ideals of rulership (Bahrani 2003).

In the absence of any of Gudea's skeletal remains, Winter regards all of his features as iconographic rather than physical. Laura Filloy Nadal's compelling argument regarding the portraits of K'inich Janaab' Pakal is similar to Winter's, only Filloy Nadal is able to match some of Pakal's traits to his remains, confirming that at least part of his image is rooted in mimesis (Filloy Nadal, chapter 7 of this volume). Drawing from a selection of known portraits of Pakal, Filloy Nadal terms the combined physical and iconographic signifiers Pakal's "idiosyncratic traits" and uses them to identify a number of unnamed portraits. Her approach speaks to the function of portraiture as a reflection of certain aspects of an individual's identity, yet portraits can be just as effective in their ability to construct that identity as well. The images of Gudea and K'inich Janaab' Pakal are undoubtedly portraits because they represent named individuals, regardless of whether the images are symbolic, realistic, or a combination of both. More importantly, their images are more than mere copies of an individual's likeness, also serving to construct the identity of that individual as a great ruler.

Considering the weight placed on "naming names," so to speak, in Brilliant's definition of a portrait, the study of Andean portraiture is deeply hindered by the fact that ancient Andean civilizations never developed a written language. Unlike the labeled images of Gudea and K'inich Janaab' Pakal, no inscriptions exist to link Andean images of humans to specific individuals. This begs the question, are nonliterate societies capable of producing portraits? Surely the definition of portraiture cannot rely so heavily on an outsider's ability to identify the image, and in fact there is evidence to suggest that ancient Andean societies did indeed practice portraiture, insofar as they produced objects and images meant to function as representations of actual people.

For instance, Maarten van de Guchte writes about a

category of Inka sculptures called *huauques*, a Quechua term meaning "brothers" or brother-statues (van de Guchte 1996). These statues were usually made of stone or gold and functioned as direct representations of the Inka, although they likely bore no natural resemblance to his image. According to sixteenth- and seventeenth-century sources, some are described as having human traits, while others had either animal traits or no identifiable shape at all. Nevertheless, they are consistently associated with specific rulers, and both Pedro Sarmiento de Gamboa (*Historia Indica*, 1572) and Bernabé Cobo (*Historia del Nuevo Mundo*, 1653) provide lists of brother-statues with their corresponding rulers (van de Guchte 1996:258–60, table 1). These examples of nonmimetic effigies that represent specific Inka rulers go a step further as reproductions in that they could even be consulted in the absence of the Inka himself. As representations that were specific to individual, historical Inka rulers, these effigies can be described as portraits according to Brilliant's definition, yet without their interpretation by colonial sources they would likely never have been recognized as such by modern viewers. Thus, studying portraiture in the ancient Andes requires us to reconsider the ways in which an image or object might come to reference a person's identity. The highly stylized, even generic appearance of Wari faceneck vessels poses an intriguing opportunity to study portraiture in a broader sense. By letting go of the need to name the individual in the portrait, to see or recognize the individual person in the material image, the approach outlined below instead considers portraiture as the expression of identity itself.

THE WARI

During the Middle Horizon, the Wari civilization expanded its sphere of influence outward from the capital city of Wari, located in the central highlands of Peru near the present-day city of Ayacucho, ultimately reaching all the way to the Pacific coastline as far south as Moquegua and as far north as the region around Cajamarca. Although the precise nature and extent of Wari influence and control is contested among Wari archaeologists and scholars (Jennings 2010), some agree that the wide distribution of Wari settlements and the infiltration of Wari-style prestigious goods throughout the Andes makes a strong case for the Wari being something more powerful than a singular state and perhaps behaving more like an expansive empire (Bergh 2012; Isbell 2008; Schreiber 1992). Most of the development and expansion of the Wari civilization occurred around 600–1000 CE, during Epochs 1 and 2 of the Middle Horizon according to Dorothy Menzel's chronology (Menzel 1964; Giersz and Pardo 2014).

During this time, Wari artists developed a distinct brand of iconography, drawing in part on the previous artistic traditions of Nasca and Pucara, eventually producing substantial measures of skillfully crafted textiles and ceramics in addition to works of other media. Yet despite the beauty of the works and the complexity of their facture, more than a few people have observed that the range of subject matter explored by these artists is relatively limited (Makowski 2014; Pasztory 1998; Sawyer 1963; Stone-Miller and McEwan 1990–1991). Certain themes such as the staff deity complex and face-fret motifs appear again and again with remarkable consistency. Even so, Alan Sawyer's decisive article "Tiahuanaco Tapestry Design" reveals the astonishing manner in which Wari artists manipulated and experimented with these themes, indicating that Wari societies nevertheless had a very sophisticated relationship with images (Sawyer 1963). Sawyer's analysis of a Wari tapestry-woven tunic from the Museo Nacional de Arqueología, Antropología e Historia del Perú in Lima (RT-1650) examines how Wari weavers derived a uniquely abstract image from a highly conventional motif. This tapestry is an example of how virtuosity and innovation can exist within a highly regulated system of coded imagery. In *To Weave for the Sun*, Rebecca Stone comments on the significance of the approach Wari weavers took to manipulating traditional motifs:

> It is interesting to reflect that the creation of increasingly illegible versions was *not* the result of increasing misunderstanding of the image, since the various figure parts and their interrelationships are not garbled. . . . Rather, the various changes made to the stock elements of the staff bearer and other motifs demonstrate a deeper, wholly artistic understanding of the image's underlying structure. (Stone-Miller 1992:35–36)

When considered alongside the coded nature of the iconography itself—with its rules for which figures can appear in what poses, holding which kinds of objects and under what circumstances—the manipulation of this iconography does not necessarily act in contradiction to its meaning but rather becomes a method for conceptually enhancing the expression of the image as a whole. Besides abstraction, another method that is frequently used in the production of Wari images is systematic repetition. On tapestry tunics, figures are continuously flipped and repeated seemingly without end, and repetition occurs in ceramics as well. Iconographic designs are frequently repeated on a single ceramic vessel, while in other cases the object itself is what is repeated or duplicated. Here, I focus on the systematic repetition of human imagery in Wari ceramics, specifically in multiples of faceneck vessels. I ask how such treatments of the human image might be considered a type of Wari portraiture that rejects mimesis in favor of a more semiotic approach to the visual expression of identity.

THE FACENECK VESSEL

Turning now to the faceneck vessel, these objects characterize a particular category of human image that is prolific throughout the span of Wari influence. While there is certainly a substantial degree of variability across Wari faceneck vessels in terms of iconographic style, craftsmanship, and size, they are at the same time very consistent in overall proportion and form, allowing the faceneck to stand apart as a distinct category of vessel. By and large, they are more alike than different, and although they are related by their anthropomorphism to trophy heads and head vessels, facenecks are fundamentally different objects in that they have bodies as well as heads. Frequently, Wari faceneck vessels carry just enough detail to communicate that the body of the vessel acts as the body for the face on the vessel's neck. The vessel body may be painted with only scant references to a tunic or pectoral collar below the chin, or it may depict a full costume or even a complete set of arms and legs. Often, the faces are rendered as complete heads with precisely defined hairstyles or headdresses. A deep sense of humanity or personhood is present in the most elaborate faceneck vessels, but through consistency of form across the category of the faceneck this sense of personhood carries through to even the simplest of facenecks—those without corporeal decoration and that may instead rely on nothing more than a pair of eyes and a protruding nose to communicate their humanity. The ones that do depict more complete human figures and display carefully detailed garments and hairstyles overwhelmingly appear to be male, raising questions about the connection between faceneck vessels and gender identity.

Alternatively, because many of the simpler vessels lack the potential to express any gender at all, namely those with unadorned heads and bodies, it is possible that gender difference was simply less important than the other kinds of identities that faceneck vessels were intended to express. Part of the problem with gender identity lies in the fact that there are few confirmed representations of women in Wari visual culture, and the markers of female gender remain largely unexplored, clouding our sense of the feminine, the masculine, and the gender neutral.

Compared to the highly sexualized imagery of the Moche, which favored graphic representations of male and female genitalia, Wari imagery appears austerely asexual. One of the few instances of Wari visual culture in which the expression of gender difference is made relatively overt is on a collection of oversize urns excavated from the coastal site of Pacheco in the Nasca drainage, some of which currently reside in the collection of the Museo Nacional de Arqueología, Antropología e Historia del Perú in Lima. These ceremonial urns are elaborately painted inside and out with representations of the frontal staff deity, a prominent figure throughout Wari visual culture. The insides of the vessels show four staff deities, which Menzel suggests are meant to represent both male and female variations of the staff deity according to differences in their garments and accessories (Menzel 1964:26). The male variants wear sleeved tunics tied around the waist with a belt tipped with bird heads. The other pair of figures wear tunics decorated with two types of plants, corn and perhaps some type of flower, and wear a cape or mantle draped over the shoulders. The distinction between male and female gender may still appear rather subtle here, but the variation in garments appears to reference gender difference. In colonial depictions of Inka women, including the illustrations of Felipe Guaman Poma de Ayala, elite women are typically seen wearing a large mantle over their shoulders, usually affixed with one or more *tupu* pins (Guaman Poma de Ayala 2009). The tupu is an adornment typically associated with female dress, and it can be worn with the ornamental disk facing either up or down (Ann Rowe, personal communication, 2016).

A rare instance of what looks to be a clear representation of a *human* female figure in Wari ceramics is a Pachacamac-style figurine of a well-dressed woman from the collection of the American Museum of Natural History in New York (41.2/8596). Her femininity is signaled by the long length of her garment and the three tupus pinned at each shoulder. Of note is her lack of any head covering and her precisely shaped hairstyle that covers her ears and is parted in the middle. As Virginia Miller notes in her research on Maya hairstyles, the distinctive ways that hair is cut and styled is an effective indicator of gender and other social identities (Miller, chapter 8 of this volume). The long garment with horizontal rather than vertical banding, as well as the prominent central hair part and lack of headdress, are also seen in the female figures of a vessel from the coastal site of Maymi in the Pisco Valley (Anders 1990:fig. 12b). From these few pieces, a pattern of Wari female markers begins to surface.

In 1899–1900, the German archaeologist Max Uhle excavated in the Supe district of Peru, where he unearthed many ancient tombs containing grave goods. Among his findings from a grave possibly in Las Selinas de Huacho was a ceramic faceneck vessel, which he described as a "red vase representing a seated man holding cup" (Phoebe A. Hearst Museum of Anthropology). Yet, given the figure's centrally parted hairstyle that covers the ears and the pair of tupus at each shoulder, the piece emerges as an expression of female identity (fig. 16.2). Her pectoral ornament and the double lines painted on her cheeks are similar to those of the female figurine above, and the gentle curvature of the vessel body mimics that of both the standing figurine and the three figures on the vessel from Maymi. When seen from the side, her loose hair and the pectoral ornament appear to be tucked beneath an implied mantle, from which her arms emerge below. Evidently, Wari artists did produce female faceneck vessels, and thus they cannot be considered a solely male-gendered category of

object. Furthermore, even the occasional female faceneck vessel opens the door for facenecks of indeterminate gender to be either male or female, or perhaps gender was not always the most critical factor of one's identity.

Moving beyond matters of gender difference, this study now turns to another identity binary: the individual versus the group, or the difference between "I" and "we." Through an analysis of pairs and groups of faceneck vessels that considers their multiplicity as a semiotic device, I hope to show how these objects are capable of expressing a sense of communal identity.

PAIRS OF FACENECK VESSELS

In the Andes, instances of paired objects and images become fast indicators of dualism, the philosophical framework that permeates Andean political and social organization. However, materialized duality can be an expression of difference, or it can convey a sense of sameness—two ontologically diverse concepts. The Tello Obelisk from Chavín de Huantar is an early example of duality articulated through the pairing of male and female iconography. Centuries later, the sumptuous peanut necklace from the Moche tomb of the Lord of Sipán exhibits a similar impression of duality through the pairing of ten gold and ten silver beads (Alva and Donnan 1993). In both instances, two opposite but complementary elements—male/female, gold/silver—are brought together to make one visual statement. Another frequent example of duality in Andean material culture are pairs of matching *keros*—a

Figure 16.2. Female faceneck vessel excavated by Max Uhle from Supe district. Phoebe A. Hearst Museum of Anthropology, University of California, Berkeley, 4-7659. Ceramic, 26 cm tall × 46 cm circumference (photos by Andrea Vazquez de Arthur).

type of ceremonial drinking cup distinguished formally by having a narrow base with straight walls that widen from the bottom to the top, often flaring gracefully at the rim. Many identical pairs of keros are known from the Inka Empire, but a remarkable pair of keros comes from the Wari site of Castillo de Huarmey on the north coast. The ceramic cups are decorated with a scene of battling warriors shown in relief (Giersz and Pardo 2014:figs. 80a, 80b, 80c). The image, achieved via mold-stamping and accented with painted details, is the same on both cups. On each cup, two pairs of warriors are shown as if facing off in battle. Although each warrior is individualized by the weapon in his grasp, a strong sense of duality is expressed through the nested duplication of like elements: two pairs of two warriors, depicted on two identical keros. Such pairs of matching keros were likely used for ritual drinking or toasting, perhaps between two leaders of different communities sealing a pact. In this kind of ritual context, the sameness of the cups performs the bond between the participants.

There are several known instances of pairs of faceneck vessels from all areas of the Wari Empire. Some of these are identical duplicates, while others are better described as matching sets of nonidentical pieces. An example of the first type is a pair of twin faceneck vessels in the collection of the Museo Nacional de Arqueología, Antropología, e Historia del Perú in Lima (plate 31). The personages depicted on these pieces are identical in every detail. Both figures are bearded, with three vertical yellow streaks painted beneath the eyes and another down the center of the nose, and each wears a four-stranded necklace. The figures may be bareheaded, as the solid black

section at the top of each spout cascades seamlessly down the back of the vessel, taking the form of an uninterrupted shock of long black hair. Given that facial hair is infrequently represented on Wari faceneck vessels, the notable mustache and goatee on this pair of facenecks stands out as a predominant indicator of their sameness. Do these vessels represent one person, or two individuals? What can be drawn from the doubling of such a distinguishing feature like facial hair? While it would not be impossible for this pair of facenecks to represent actual twin brothers, this interpretation rests on the assumption that faceneck vessels are meant to be mimetic representations of individual people. Were this the case, one would expect that faceneck vessels would often portray the distinguishing physical characteristics of their real-life counterparts. On the contrary, what this pair of facenecks shares most with other pairs of facenecks is their sameness to each other — the repetition of imagery across two vessels — a sameness likewise shared with the pair of warrior keros described above.

Consider another pair of identical faceneck vessels that were, like the keros, also found at the Middle Horizon Epoch 2 site of Castillo de Huarmey and that are notable for their matching costumes (fig. 16.3). Like the bearded facenecks described above, these vessels are highly anthropomorphic vessels that depict figures "in the round" insofar as they have a front and back. Each figure of this pair is shown wearing a black headpiece with white diamonds and a netted tunic belted at the waist, with a bold, black-and-red interlocking pattern below the belt. Milosz Giersz and Patrycja Przadka Giersz interpret this elaborate garment as perhaps a tie-dyed tunic

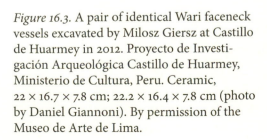

Figure 16.3. A pair of identical Wari faceneck vessels excavated by Milosz Giersz at Castillo de Huarmey in 2012. Proyecto de Investigación Arqueológica Castillo de Huarmey, Ministerio de Cultura, Peru. Ceramic, 22 × 16.7 × 7.8 cm; 22.2 × 16.4 × 7.8 cm (photo by Daniel Giannoni). By permission of the Museo de Arte de Lima.

covered in metal plaques that have been sewn onto the tunic above the belt (Giersz and Pardo 2014:140). In addition, the figures wear large ear ornaments and bands around their wrists and ankles, and a dramatic mane of long hair divided into multiple sections spreads out across the reverse of each vessel (Giersz and Pardo 2014:fig. 86a). In contrast to the bearded facenecks, the faces of this pair are generic, no different than the standard Wari type, and can easily be interpreted as representing two completely different people who are dressed in the same way. Although the figures hold no weapons, Giersz and Przadka Giersz identify them as warriors, viewing their matching garments as military uniforms (2014:140). This identification alludes to the representation of two distinct individuals who identify under the same office or profession.

A comparison between the pair of bearded faceneck vessels and the pair of faceneck vessels wearing matching garments that privileges mimetic representation might lead one to conclude that the bearded twins share a physical likeness while the garment twins may instead share an occupational likeness. However, this interpretation discounts the fact that the bearded twins also don matching necklaces and face paint, and the garment twins possess not only matching clothing but matching hairstyles as well. Rather than privilege one kind of shared trait over another, I propose that what both pairs of facenecks convey most powerfully is the repetition of like features. Through the strategy of duplication, they ultimately communicate a message of duality wherein two of something become one of something. In other words, the inherent sense of doubling given in each case by the presence of two identical figures ultimately gives way to the being of one pair.

Gary Urton, in his study of what he describes as "a Quechua ontology of numbers," investigates the language of numbers and numeric expressions used by modern Quechua speakers as a means of gaining access to deeply rooted Andean notions about the meaning of numbers. He stresses how important it is to understand the meaning of numbers when working with a society so preoccupied with numerics that, with the *khipu*, it developed a complex system of numerical notation but never invented any kind of phonetic script. While scholars are divided over the question of whether the people of the Wari Empire spoke a variant of Quechua or Aymara, many linguistic concepts overlap between Quechua and Aymara, even though they are distinct languages (Heggarty and Beresford-Jones 2012).

Urton's inquiry into the nature of odd and even numbers reveals that, in the Quechua language, even numbers are conceived as complete pairs while uneven numbers are seen as "one member of a natural or potential *pair*" (Urton 1997:61). The terminology for odd and even is therefore particularly relevant to gaining insight into the practice of doubling and pairing in ancient Andean imagery. What meaning might a pair of images or objects carry when viewed within the framework of an Andean ontology of numbers? As Urton has observed, the Quechua language has several terms that describe there being two of something, demonstrating the complexity and the importance of pairing in the Andean worldview. According to Urton, *ujnintin* means two, as in "one thing that is divided into two parts," a term not to be confused with *iskaynintin*, which also means two, but specifically "two things that are separate, each of which is a complete unit" and thus *not* a pair. Meanwhile, *ch'ullantin* denotes "the two together that make a pair" or "a pair of similar persons or things" (Urton 1997:table 2.5). This term accurately describes the two pairs of facenecks vessels described above—the bearded twins and the garment twins. But yet another term that may add even more color to the meaning expressed by these two pairs of faceneck vessels is *khalluntin*, meaning "the one together with its mate/pair" (Urton 1997:table 2.5). Subtly different from ch'ullantin, a term that seems to describe the act of two beings becoming one pair, khalluntin seems to push the meaning of a pair toward a state of being in which one is incomplete without its other. For clarity, Urton gives as an example of khalluntin two halves of a textile that have been sewn together to create a single garment, such as a tunic or *unku* (Urton 1997:table 2.5). In addition to the idea of completeness embedded in the term khalluntin, there is the added notion that the meaning carried by a khalluntin pair breaks down when the two halves of the pair are separated; one half of an unku is no longer an unku. Likewise, if one of a pair of twin facenecks is viewed by itself, removed from the context of its other, its ontological state changes. It becomes stripped of its identity as being half of a pair, and it fails to signify duality.

In other cases of paired vessels in which the specimens are not identical, the expression of duality is not one of doubling but of complementarity. This concept of pairing is described in Quechua as *yanantin*, meaning "two opposite but complementary things intimately bound together" (Urton 1997:63). In the case of another pair of faceneck vessels from Castillo de Huarmey, the figures at first

Figure 16.4. A pair of Wari faceneck vessels excavated by Milosz Giersz at Castillo de Huarmey in 2012. Proyecto de Investigación Arqueológica Castillo de Huarmey, Ministerio de Cultura, Peru. Ceramic, 26 × 14.5 × 10.2 cm; 25.9 × 14.6 × 9.8 cm (photo by Daniel Giannoni). By permission of the Museo de Arte de Lima.

glance seem completely identical, but on closer inspection they differ in one very meaningful detail. Each figure holds a *Spondylus* shell in his left hand, but one holds his palm facing inward, with the shell pressed to his chest, while the other holds his palm facing outward, as if pushing the shell away (fig. 16.4). Together, the gestures seem to express the concept of reciprocity—the complementary actions of giving and receiving. For ancient Andean civilizations, it was the codependency between communities and their economy of reciprocity that engendered the paradigm of dualism that persists throughout Andean material culture. This idea of reciprocity is expressed by the Quechua word *ayni*, a term perhaps best understood through the Spanish expression *hoy por ti, mañana por mí*, or "today for you, tomorrow for me." Ayni succinctly communicates the idea of mutual obligation intrinsic to the reciprocity of gift giving and receiving. In this way, ayni describes the cooperation between families on a local scale, and on a larger scale it extends to the practice of feasting—a form of gift giving—as a political strategy for imperial expansion. By hosting lavish feasts for the elite members of other societies, the Wari gained their allegiance along with access to desired lands and resources. This included the necessary labor to grow more crops, build more settlements, and produce more sumptuary goods for elite consumption, ultimately allowing the Wari Empire to expand well beyond its highland origins. In a sense, this pair of faceneck vessels is not simply a depiction of individual figures, but rather figural representation is acting in the service of signifying the greater idea of reciprocity.

The way in which these two vessels function semiotically as a pair is made even more clear through the term *khalluntin*, but in contrast to this term as applied to the previous pairs of identical facenecks, here we see the term fully realized. Not only is each vessel "together with its mate," but here the two vessels, with their complementary actions, depend on each other to make meaning. Like half an unku that ceases to function as an unku, either of these vessels alone cannot communicate the idea of reciprocity and therefore cannot function properly as a sign. In the exhibition catalog *Castillo de Huarmey: el mausoleo imperial Wari*, Krzysztof Makowski notes that, compared to the Moche, Wari figurative imagery is lacking in action and narrative, instead tending toward isolated figures; Makowski further states that "the limitations in figuration specific to textile decorations were never overcome" (2014: 198). Perhaps this fascinating pair of faceneck vessels provides a key to how Wari artists used figural representation as a semiotic device, rather than a mimetic one, to communicate complex ideas. The two vessels work in tandem to express reciprocity, effectively performing their meaning through bodily gesture.

What the *Spondylus* faceneck vessels share with the bearded twins and the garment twins, beyond the strategy of repetition, is the pairing of bodies, specifically human bodies, to make a statement. The anthropomorphism of the vessels alludes powerfully to a sense of identity, but in the place of individual identity we are instead faced with the identity of the pair. Having seen the pair together, the individual vessel, separated from its mate, appears mute and incomplete. The nature of these images as expressions of identity therefore depends on their coupling, wherein the bond between two individuals supersedes the significance of either one alone.

GROUPS OF FACENECK VESSELS

The notion that the individual is supplanted by the multiple is perhaps more evident in groups of coordinating faceneck vessels. At least four instances of groups of faceneck vessels are known from archaeological excavations. Two come from offerings of ritually smashed pottery: one from the highland site of Conchopata (Cook 1984–1985; Isbell 1984–1985) and one from Pacheco on the south coast (Menzel 1964), both from Middle Horizon Epoch 1 (600–850 CE). A third offering from the south coast site of Corral Redondo from Middle Horizon Epoch 2 (850–1000 CE) consists of several oversize faceneck vessels that were found to contain dozens of feathered panels (Linares Málaga 1990; King 2012). Finally, a group of six black faceneck vessels was found in a tomb at Castillo de Huarmey on the north coast, which also dates to Middle Horizon Epoch 2 (Giersz and Pardo 2014). The fact that these four cases are widely dispersed across the geographic region under Wari influence, and date from all periods during which the Wari civilization was active, speaks to the pan-Wari significance of pottery groups, particularly of the faceneck variety.

Conchopata

Conchopata is an important site located in the Wari heartland, very close to the capital city of Wari. The pottery smash at Conchopata was excavated in 1977 as part of a salvage excavation in a joint effort by the Huari Urban Prehistory Project directed by William Isbell and the Huari Project of the Instituto Nacional de Cultura directed by Abelardo Sandoval. From twenty-two to twenty-five oversize faceneck vessels had been shattered in antiquity and buried together as an offering. The sherds were found buried in an oval-shaped pit slightly more than two meters below the surface. Just north of this offering, archaeologists found a burial with five individuals, probably all young females (Cook 1984–1985). The offering of shattered faceneck vessels dates from Middle Horizon Epoch 1B (700–850 CE), and the iconography on the vessel bodies is thought to confirm an innovative turn toward centralized hierarchy in Wari religious ideology that occurred earlier at

the same location of Conchopata during Middle Horizon Epoch 1A (600–700 CE) (Isbell 1984–1985).

Originally standing roughly four feet high, the stature of these vessels is extraordinary, as is the iconography painted on them (fig. 16.5). Nearly all the vessels feature the staff deity complex around their barrel-shaped bodies. In the center, a large deity stands atop a stepped platform, facing forward and holding a staff in each outstretched arm. The stylization of this staff deity (also called the front face deity) bears close resemblance to the iconography on the Gate of the Sun and other stone monuments at Tiwanaku, although the Tiwanaku monuments may date to a later period of the Middle Horizon (Isbell 1984–1985). The staff deity is flanked on either side by two rows of smaller, winged profile attendants, who alternately face toward or away from the staff deity. Above this very powerful scene, a rather naturalistically modeled face is sculpted into the neck of each vessel, with hooded eyelids, a plump face, a carefully shaped nose, and full lips. The overall effect is of a human figure wearing a tunic that depicts supernatural iconography. Across the twenty-two to twenty-five facenecks, there are four variants of facial types: one type has no facial hair or additional facial markings beyond the

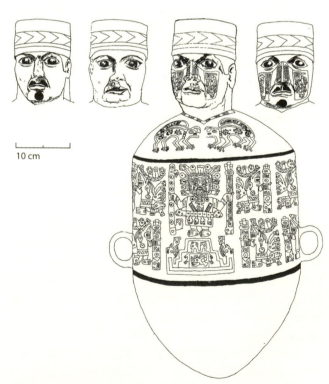

Figure 16.5. Wari faceneck vessels excavated at Conchopata in 1977 (drawing by Anita Cook). By permission of Anita Cook.

painting of the eyes, one type has a moustache and small beard on the tip of the chin but no other facial decorations, one type has no facial hair but has decorations painted on the cheeks and nose, and, lastly, one type has a moustache and small beard and the same decorations on the cheeks and nose (Cook 1984–1985:55). Anita Cook hypothesizes that the four distinct variants have to do with a hierarchical ranking system, perhaps related to age, based on the theory that a plain face represents youthfulness while facial hair is meant to represent maturity (1984–1985:61). Again, this theory slips toward a mimetic interpretation, whereas Wari artistic production—including this group of facenecks—seems to operate in a more systematic manner. Instead, the four variants may be viewed as operating within a binary system that works according to the presence or absence of two possible attributes: facial hair and painted decorations. These two types of attributes perform the four possible combinations, or perhaps four possible identities. As a group, the variations potentially hold more meaning in the context of each other than any one can hold on its own.

Several factors single out this group of faceneck vessels from other Wari ceramic works. First, they are the largest Wari faceneck vessels known. Second, the style of the iconography is very unusual. While the staff deity complex remains paramount for Wari ideology and artistic expression throughout the Middle Horizon, and the staff deity and profile attendants are depicted again and again in both textiles and ceramics, nowhere else are they rendered in such a stylized manner as they are on this group of faceneck vessels. Third, the variation between faces within an otherwise related group is unparalleled. In addition to the four types of faces discussed above, Cook describes each face as "distinctly different" in a way that diverges from the standardization of the staff deity complex depicted on the vessel bodies, as if striving for individuality (1984–1985: 60). Yet it is not clear that such irregularity from one face to the next was the desired effect. Other examples of faceneck groups do not exhibit this sense of individuality in facial features, and in fact the face tends to be the most generic feature of the faceneck vessel as a whole. The desire for facial conformity is further enhanced by the use of ceramic molds, which were used at the same site of Conchopata (fig. 16.6), although the degree of difference from face to face indicates that they were not used on the faceneck vessels from this particular cache (Pozzi-Escot B., 1991). Perhaps the sense of individuality that arises from such naturalistic modeling

Figure 16.6. Ceramic mold of a face, excavated at Conchopata. Universidad Nacional de San Cristóbal de Huamanga, Ayacucho (photo by Andrea Vazquez de Arthur).

was, like the unusually stylized figures of this particular instance of the staff deity complex, ultimately viewed as undesirable within the Wari artistic tradition.

Pacheco

The Robles Moqo–style pottery smash from Pacheco also dates from Middle Horizon Epoch 1B, but it may postdate the Conchopata offering, and in fact Richard MacNeish dates the Robles Moqo–style later than Menzel does (MacNeish 1981). Excavated by Julio C. Tello in 1927, the Pacheco pottery smash is the largest known Wari offering deposit and consists of some three tons of potsherds from a variety of vessel forms, one of which is the faceneck form. Tello never published his notes from the excavation, so little is known about the context of the offering, only that the shattering of large quantities of ceremonial vessels and burying them together as found at this offering deposit is very similar in practice to the offering at Conchopata. The faceneck vessels from this offering are some of the most anthropomorphic facenecks of the Middle Horizon (plate 32). Evocative of small men, they are remarkably naturalistic with delicately modeled hands and feet, and elegantly dressed in finely made tunics and fancy hats. At least two or three variants exist. The most recognized variant wears a tie-dyed tunic and has its face painted in a manner that seems to reference the tie-dye technique. The face is divided bilaterally, as are several examples of Wari tie-dyed tunics. The proper right side is divided into a few large color fields, while the proper left side is painted with a more densely compacted geometric pattern of interlocking frets. This particular facial pattern appears on other Wari images, and a corresponding character has been named "Agent 100" by Patricia Knobloch (2002). A second variant wears a tightly striped tunic, has a few markings painted across the face, and wears the pelt of a spotted feline as part of an elaborate headdress. A possible third variant also wears a striped tunic, but the stripes are wider, as if depicting a lesser-quality tunic, and the figure wears no face paint and appears to lack the feline-pelt headdress. This study will focus only on the first variant, as many copies of this model were found in the Pacheco offering. Most of these vessels are housed in the collection of the Museo Nacional de Arqueología, Antropología e Historia del Perú in Lima, but other vessels and fragments of the same variant are held at other museums. Added to the fact that the pottery from this offering at Pacheco was all found shattered and has undergone much reconstruction, it is difficult to ascertain exactly how many of this particular variant of faceneck vessel originally existed.

While many Wari faceneck vessels feature some facial markings, most often on the cheeks, face paint that covers the entire face is unusual and acts less like decoration and more like a mask. Masks are historically used to conceal a person's identity, allowing the wearer to project an alternative identity. Moreover, face paint that covers the entire face is an effective technique for transforming several identities into one. Even a solid color of face paint, as long as it covers the entire face, will obscure any differences of facial structure from one person to the next, enhancing the effect of resemblance. Take, for instance, the popular performance troupe Blue Man Group as a modern example of this strategy, wherein three men who do not particularly look alike become indistinguishable beneath a layer of blue paint. Thus, the complexity of the pattern on the Pacheco faceneck vessels, and the fact that it covers the entire face, overwhelms the identity of its wearer, effectively acting more like a mask compared to more typical Wari facial markings that are confined to the cheeks. When this effect is multiplied across several bodies, the identities of the individuals all but vanish, displaced by the presence of the pattern and whatever meaning it evokes. In short, individual personhood is supplanted by the collective.

Corral Redondo

This sense of sameness is carried through in the offering deposit of several large faceneck vessels found at Corral

Redondo. This site is located near the village of La Victoria, where the Ocoña Valley meets the Churunga Valley on the south coast of Peru. The site was excavated in 1943 after local people in the area struck through a hollow in the ground and discovered an ancient feathered textile (King 2012). Further excavations by local people resulted in the unearthing of seven or eight oversize faceneck vessels, each measuring approximately three feet in height, as well as a burial mound containing mummies, which were subsequently burned by the local excavators. Unlike the offering deposits from Conchopata and Pacheco, the faceneck vessels were found intact, and each was filled with several feathered panels. The direct association of the vessels with the mummies of the burial mound further distinguishes this offering from those at Conchopata and Pacheco, although the context of the mummies and their precise relationship to the offerings of ceramics and feathered panels remain unknown. Heidi King's research into the published reports of this archaeological discovery reveals a discrepancy regarding the precise number of faceneck vessels that were found. Out of three different reports, two say that eight faceneck vessels were found, while one report mentions only seven but specifies that all seven measured about one meter tall by two meters in circumference (King 2012). One explanation for this discrepancy may be that there were indeed eight faceneck vessels found buried at the site, but one vessel was considerably smaller than the others (Heidi King, personal communication, 2015).

Even if only the seven faceneck vessels of the same size are considered to compose a group, the vessels are far from identical to each other; rather, each is vibrantly painted with a different image across its body (fig. 16.7). Materially, the current of sameness that runs through this group is most fully expressed in their identical faces, whose features vary stylistically from the other faceneck vessels discussed thus far. The large, staring, wide-set eyes that sit beneath a pronounced brow, the sharply pointed nose, the tight-lipped mouth, the overall blocky shape of the head with a chin that sits directly atop the vessel body evoke the heft of a heavyset man, adorned by pointed ears that project like wings from each side of the head. These features are painstakingly standardized in every variant from this group, giving the figures an almost familial resemblance. The strategy for creating a sense of cohesion among the vessels is therefore the opposite of that of the earlier Conchopata group. Rather than differing faces on matching bodies, here the design on the bodies is what

Figure 16.7. Wari faceneck vessel excavated at Corral Redondo in 1943. Museo Nacional de Arqueología, Antropología e Historia del Perú, Lima, C-64874. Ceramic, 83.5 × 86 cm (photo by Andrea Vazquez de Arthur).

varies, while the faces maintain a uniform likeness. In fact, because the faces are so similar, the designs on the bodies can exhibit a considerable degree of freedom without hindering the sense of unity across the group.

Castillo de Huarmey

The effect of uniformity achieved by the faceneck group from Corral Redondo is typical of Wari faceneck vessels in general and is furthermore consistent with the pattern across Wari artistic productions in all media in that a certain degree of standardization seems to have been desirable. With the exception of the Conchopata group, which is an anomaly in more ways than one, the effect achieved by producing a highly standardized face was apparently successful enough to repeat on faceneck vessels throughout the realm of Wari influence. This effect is in full display among the final group of faceneck vessels I discuss here, a set of six medium-sized, satin black vessels, all smiling together in unison (Giersz and Pardo 2014:fig. 51). Compared to some other faceneck vessels, these works may

appear plain. They have smooth, globular bodies with no handles or protrusions. Unpainted, they are devoid of any design elements, and their press-molded faces give them an air of redundancy. These vessels were found buried in pairs, along a row of ten carefully constructed miniature "tombs" in the royal mausoleum of Castillo de Huarmey. In addition to the six faceneck vessels, four somewhat larger, nonanthropomorphic vessels were also found buried in the same row of tombs. Specifically, this row of mini-tombs lies just beyond, but in close proximity to, the main burial chamber, where the bodies of fifty-four elite women were found interred. The vessels' tombs are shallow and lie just below the surface of the burial chamber's cap of trapezoidal adobe bricks. It is interesting to note that, buried at approximately the same level as the vessels, in a layer of fill below the topmost layer of rubble but above the layer of elite funeral bundles, archaeologists found the bodies of six teenagers presumed to be sacrificial offerings (Giersz 2014). Like the group from Corral Redondo and Pacheco, these facenecks appear to discard all sense of individuality in favor of adopting a group identity, and yet their carefully separated tombs allude to the significance of their number, articulated through the separateness of their bodies. The precise meaning of the number six in the context of this royal burial is not easy, and perhaps impossible, to discern. What is worth noting is the potential for quantities to be themselves carriers of meaning, much like the way in which the pairing of objects can evoke complex notions about relationships and reciprocity.

The notion of group identity is an important one in the Andes, whereby a person's community, or ayllu, can hold sway over his or her ritual, economic, and cosmological realm. Ayllu is another Quechua term, a language that explicitly underscores the importance of community and group identity through the suffix -*ntin*. When added to the end of a word, -*ntin* expresses the concept of "together as one," as in the name for the Inka Empire, Tawantinsuyu. The Inka conceived of their empire as consisting of four regions, or *suyus*—Cuntisuyu, Kollasuyu, Chinchaysuyu, and Antisuyu—and the term "Tawantinsuyu" means not just a conglomerate of four regions but specifically four regions bound together as one. Essentially, when the four suyus are brought together with the suffix -*ntin*, they relinquish their independence and become one kingdom, even while their boundaries, or bodies, remain intact. The concept of "together as one" seems integral to the faceneck groups of Pacheco, Corral Redondo, and Castillo de Huarmey, and even to some extent in the case

VAZQUEZ DE ARTHUR

of Conchopata, although these facenecks seem to subtly resist the sense of unity by simultaneously projecting a sense of individual personhood. Perhaps this group only became fully united once the vessels were smashed and buried together, their fragments intermingling for eternity like an impossible jigsaw puzzle. In the decades since their discovery in 1977, archaeologists and conservators are still struggling to reassemble their discrete bodies.

CONCLUSION

In writing about the relief sculpture at the Assyrian palace of Nimrud, Zainab Bahrani has lamented the fact that the repetition of images in Assyrian visual culture is too often overlooked, or even criticized for being uncreative (Bahrani 2014). Ancient Andean visual culture is likewise teeming with instances of repetition, notably in collections of Wari faceneck vessels. Unfortunately, looting and otherwise incomplete excavation and collection practices likely occludes many more instances of faceneck vessels that were produced as multiples, but recent excavation projects like the Castillo de Huarmey Archaeological Research Project, directed by Milosz Giersz, suggest that faceneck vessels, among other types of ceramics, were commonly produced in sets (Giersz and Pardo 2014).

As images, Wari faceneck vessels have the potential to serve as portraits in that they express ideas about identity, particularly in their dress and adornments (Cook 1992; Knobloch 2002). Moreover, faceneck vessels created in pairs and groups carry the potential for depicting a sense of identity beyond or contrary to individuality, instead expressing identity as the experience of belonging. It may be that the number of members within a set remains highly relevant, while the difference between members gets washed away by conformity. They may be viewed not so much as portraits of individual people who relate to each other but as portraits of the very nature of the relationship itself. This perspective brings a new layer of signification to these objects. Made up of discrete bodies but identifying as one, these portraits of pairs and groups signify communal identity; yet, through the very separateness of their bodies, however generic, each vessel inherently alludes to an existing referent, living or dead. Hence, the garment twins, with their detailed references to specific articles of attire, may at once represent extant members of an elite or privileged class while also express-

ing the experience of brotherhood through their likeness to each other. Likewise, the *Spondylus* vessels together communicate the concept of reciprocity, but embedded in that concept are the agents—the giver and the receiver—who make reciprocity possible on the ground. Thus, the choice to use human figures to convey broader concepts holds the potential to communicate in more than one way.

The communal identity expressed in groups of faceneck vessels becomes ever stronger the more the individuality of each vessel is suppressed. The effect is perhaps most powerful in the Pacheco group, wherein the discrepancies between the vessels' faces disappear amid a sea of geometric patterning. It is least powerful in the Conchopata group, in which clearly marked differences in the faces between members of the group have the effect of overshadowing the similarity of their tunics. In the greater context of Wari visual culture, and faceneck vessels in particular, the Conchopata vessels come across as perhaps a failed experiment, as though a conflict between the desire for conformity and the need to communicate difference was unable to be resolved with the artistic strategies used, and so this approach was never repeated. Nearly every other faceneck vessel produced by artists working within the Wari field of influence apparently preferred to keep the features of the face as generic as possible, at times using molds to better achieve this goal. It is as though something about the power of the human image needed to be controlled in order for the faceneck vessels to function properly as signifiers.

Wari faceneck vessels, with their standardized features and inactive poses, demand that the viewer see more than simply a human reflection. As images with the potential to communicate semiotically, their resistance to naturalism, and to mimesis, ceases to be a hindrance to their expressiveness. Naturalism and mimesis are freeform methods of depiction, but as much as these methods flourish in illusionistic traditions of visual culture, they are poorly suited for the coded visual language of the Wari civilization. The human form maintains a place of value and importance, but it must operate within the greater system of Wari imagery and iconography to communicate effectively.

REFERENCES CITED

Alva, Walter, and Christopher B. Donnan

1993 *Royal Tombs of Sipán*. Fowler Museum of Cultural History, University of California, Los Angeles.

Anders, Martha B.

1990 Maymi: un sitio del Horizonte Medio en el Valle de Pisco. *Gaceta Arqueológica Andina* 5(17):27–39.

Arnold, Denise Y., and Christine A. Hastorf

2008 *Heads of State: Icons, Power, and Politics in the Ancient and Modern Andes*. Left Coast Press, Walnut Creek, California.

Bahrani, Zainab

2003 *The Graven Image: Representation in Babylonia and Assyria*. University of Pennsylvania Press, Philadelphia.

2014 *The Infinite Image: Art, Time and the Aesthetic Dimension in Antiquity*. Reaktion Books, London.

Bergh, Susan E. (editor)

2012 *Wari: Lords of the Ancient Andes*. Cleveland Museum of Art, Cleveland.

Brilliant, Richard

1991 *Portraiture*. Harvard University Press, Cambridge, Massachusetts.

Cook, Anita G.

1984–1985 Middle Horizon Ceramic Offerings from Conchopata. *Ñawpa Pacha* 22–23:49–90.

1992 The Stone Ancestors: Idioms of Imperial Attire and Rank among Huari Figurines. *Latin American Antiquity* 3(4):341–64.

2012 The Coming of the Staff Deity. In *Wari: Lords of the Ancient Andes*, edited by Susan E. Bergh, pp. 103–21. Cleveland Museum of Art, Cleveland.

Donnan, Christopher B.

1978 *Moche Art of Peru: Pre-Columbian Symbolic Communication*. Fowler Museum of Cultural History, University of California, Los Angeles.

2004 *Moche Portraits from Ancient Peru*. University of Texas Press, Austin.

Filloy Nadal, Laura

2018 The Importance of Visage, Facial Treatment, and Idiosyncratic Traits in Maya Royal Portraiture during the Reign of K'inich Janaab' Pakal of Palenque, 615–683 CE. In *Social Skins of the Head: Body Beliefs and Ritual in Ancient Moseamerica and the Andes*, edited by Vera Tiesler and María Cecilia Lozada, pp. 109–27. University of New Mexico Press, Albuquerque.

Giersz, Milosz

2014 El Hallazgo del mausoleo imperial. In *Castillo de Huarmey: el mausoleo imperial Wari*, edited by Milosz Giersz and Cecilia Pardo, pp. 69–99. Asociación Museo de Arte de Lima, Lima.

Giersz, Milosz, and Cecilia Pardo (editors)

2014 *Castillo de Huarmey: el mausoleo imperial Wari*. Asociación Museo de Arte de Lima, Lima.

Guaman Poma de Ayala, Felipe

2009 *The First New Chronicle and Good Government: On the History of the World and the Incas up to 1615*. Translated and edited by Roland Hamilton. University of Texas Press, Austin.

Heggarty, Paul, and David Beresford-Jones (editors)

2012 *Archaeology and Language in the Andes: A Cross-Disciplinary Exploration of Prehistory*. Oxford University Press, New York.

Isbell, William H.

1984–1985 Conchopata, Ideological Innovator in Middle Horizon 1A. *Ñawpa Pacha* 22–23:91–126.

2008 Wari and Tiwanaku: International Identities in the Central Andean Middle Horizon. In *Handbook of South American Archaeology*, edited by Helaine Silverman and William H. Isbell, pp. 731–59. Springer, New York.

Jackson, Margaret A.

2008 *Moche Art and Visual Culture in Ancient Peru*. University of New Mexico Press, Albuquerque.

Jennings, Justin (editor)

2010 *Beyond Wari Walls: Regional Perspectives on Middle Horizon Peru*. University of New Mexico Press, Albuquerque.

King, Heidi

2012 Featherwork. In *Wari: Lords of the Ancient Andes*, edited by Susan E. Bergh, pp. 207–15. Cleveland Museum of Art, Cleveland.

Knobloch, Patricia.

2002 Who Was Who in the Middle Horizon Andean Prehistory? San Diego State University, electronic document, http://whowaswhowari.sdsu.edu/, accessed September 8, 2017.

2012 Archives in Clay: The Styles and Stories of Wari Ceramic Artists. In *Wari: Lords of the Ancient Andes*, edited by Susan E. Bergh, pp. 122–44. Cleveland Museum of Art, Cleveland.

Linares Málaga, Eloy

1990   *Pre-Historia de Arequipa Marzo, 1990–1991.* Consejo
        Nacional de Ciencia, Tecnología e Innovación Tec-
        nológica; Universidad Nacional de San Agustín,
        Arequipa.

MacNeish, Richard S.

1981   Synthesis and Conclusions. In *Prehistory of the Aya-
        cucho Basin, Peru.* Vol. 2, *Excavations and Chronology,*
        edited by Richard S. MacNeish et al., pp. 199–257.
        University of Michigan Press, Ann Arbor.

Makowski, Krzysztof

2014   Élites imperiales y símbolos de poder. In *Castillo de
        Huarmey: el mausoleo imperial Wari,* edited by Milosz
        Giersz and Cecilia Pardo, pp. 189–209. Asociación
        Museo de Arte de Lima, Lima.

Menzel, Dorothy

1964   Style and Time in the Middle Horizon. *Ñawpa Pacha*
        2:1–106.

Miller, Virginia E.

2018   The Representation of Hair in the Art of Chichén Itzá.
        In *Social Skins of the Head: Body Beliefs and Ritual in
        Ancient Mesoamerica and the Andes,* edited by Vera
        Tiesler and María Cecilia Lozada, 129–40 University of
        New Mexico Press, Albuquerque.

Pasztory, Esther

1998   *Pre-Columbian Art.* Cambridge University Press,
        Cambridge.

Phoebe A. Hearst Museum of Anthropology

Phoebe A Hearst Museum of Anthropology, University of
        California, Berkeley, electronic document, https://
        webapps.cspace.berkeley.edu/pahma/search/
        search/?musno=4-7659&displayType=full&maxresults
        =50&start=1, accessed May 15, 2016.

Pozzi-Escot B., Denise

1991   Conchopata: A Community of Potters. In *Huari
        Administrative Structures: Prehistoric Monumental
        Architecture and State Government,* edited by
        William H. Isbell and Gordon F. McEwan, pp. 81–92.
        Dumbarton Oaks, Washington, DC.

Sawyer, Alan R.

1963   Tiahuanaco Tapestry Design. *Textile Museum Journal*
        1(2):27–38.

Schreiber, Katharina J.

1992   *Wari Imperialism in Middle Horizon Peru.* Museum of
        Anthropology, University of Michigan, Ann Arbor.

Stone-Miller, Rebecca

1992   Creative Abstractions: Middle Horizon Textiles in the
        Museum of Fine Arts, Boston. In *To Weave for the Sun:
        Andean Textiles in the Museum of Fine Arts, Boston,*
        edited by Rebecca Stone-Miller, pp. 35–42. Museum of
        Fine Arts, Boston.

Stone-Miller, Rebecca, and Gordon F. McEwan

1990–1991 The Representation of the Wari State in Stone
        and Thread: A Comparison of Architecture and
        Tapestry Tunics. *RES: Anthropology and Aesthetics*
        19–20:53–80.

Urton, Gary

1997   *The Social Life of Numbers: A Quechua Ontology of
        Numbers and Philosophy of Arithmetic.* University of
        Texas Press, Austin.

Van de Guchte, Maarten

1996   Sculpture and the Concept of the Double among
        the Inca Kings. *RES: Anthropology and Aesthetics*
        29–30:256–68.

Winter, Irene

2009   What/When Is a Portrait? Royal Images of the Ancient
        Near East. *Proceedings of the American Philosophical
        Society* 153(3):254–70.

17

Using Their Heads

The Lives of Crania in the Andes

CHRISTINE A. HASTORF

The preceding chapters share the important theme of the body within a Native American framework by emphasizing the cranium and its extrasomatic power. Each of these chapters illustrates how heads have been clearly materialized in past societies, through imagery but also through the actual material use and reuse of heads. Gathered from painted or woven images, burials, and carvings, these heads demonstrate a substantial amount of diversity in their use, as shown in this volume. With examples of head treatment, head use, and head imagery, we can begin to learn about the range and variation of heads' agency in pre-Columbian societies.

The cranium and its imagery epitomized the identity of a person and personhood. Evident from the diversity of image replication on ceramic vessels and textiles, heads served as a spiritual locus of the indigenous universe—a locus for the concentrated powers in things that cycle energy. The head has played a prominent role in Native American physical embodiment studies as well, for it was engaged in a diverse set of tasks, destined to protect, to give life energy, to represent, to emulate sacred forces, and to recycle identity within the Native world. Well beyond death, heads and their material vestiges continued to be powerful loci for exploring social integration, social distinction, social meanings, ancestor veneration, sacrifice, power, and control, activating a system of ideas about nature and the individual in society (Arnold and Hastorf 2008; Turner 2012:490). We now know that heads, or

stand-ins for heads, are not just religious items and not just cultural identity features; they also have political, economic, and spiritual force.

Among the contributors to this volume, Sara Becker and Sonia Alconini (chapter 15) and John Verano (chapter 11) compare and contrast how heads were acquired, treated, and curated, allowing us to learn the history and recycling of head use, that is, the range of powers they might have carried in their postmortem lives. From these chapters, we learn of some of the possible meanings of heads in these different societies; from curated trophy or enemy heads to captured heads that allowed for the retention of power, to recycling life force through the heads' participation in ceremonies and actions, to purposefully dispatched captured heads, making a show of conquering power, to ancestral heads retaining the family's energy, to the heads of locals brought home for reburial after being killed in battle.

Most of the Andean chapters in this volume focus on the Early Intermediate to the Middle Horizon time frame, approximately 200–1100 CE. Over this time span, the use of heads is common throughout central and south-central Andean groups, clearly demonstrating how heads became empowering material during the time after populations had settled on the landscape. While each Andean chapter engages with at least one past use of Andean crania, providing a wide range of examples, overall, these archaeologist cases could benefit from more contextual data. Such data will allow us to better understand the diversity and power of crania in these settings. In the Andes, there are many possibilities for power channeling of each cranium encountered. These possibilities open us to potential cultural meanings of these clearly potent materials in these past societies. Head imagery can directly link to living persons, with the portraits of people on vessels or through the masks and costumes worn and embroidered on textiles, but crania clearly have active afterlives in these societies, as Verano makes clear in his overview chapter on the broad engagement with heads across the South American continent. This idea is further elaborated in the chapters by Deborah Blom and Nicole Couture (chapter 13), and Bruce Mannheim et al. (chapter 14), in which heads cite and embody group identity. Blom and Couture clearly inform us about how modified crania were signaling group identity at the same time as they were reflecting transformation and potency in the Middle Horizon Tiwanaku sphere, through reuse, curation, containment, and wrapping, keeping the soul and its essence protected for later use, like a seed. At that time, heads were important in civic ceremonial locations but also in rural ones, where heads helped crop fertility. Mannheim and his colleagues also focus on what modified children's crania inform us about past group identities in two regions, the Colca Valley and the Cuzco region. In both of these areas, the scholars set out to discuss identity dynamics through nonstandard head modification in these earlier Formative settings. Their discussion is framed by Philippe Descola's ontological work on human and nonhuman relations within society. Although they do not substantially engage with this model, Mannheim and colleagues do at least highlight the animism/agency that crania carry, especially once they have been altered by human work, by modification and curation. This human commitment to material things creates energies beyond the individual, as described beautifully by Catherine Allen (1988) with the concept of *sami*. Therefore, collected or captured crania gain potential power or the vitalism of *camay* through the curation and care that living women bestow on them, as discussed below. Transformation, wrapping, and containment keep souls and identities protected, enclosing their potential. This holds the promise of future kin creation and the next generation of human offspring, plants, and animals.

Sara Becker and Sonia Alconini's chapter presents a powerful example of this theme of head engagement in the Andes, that of head taking and the harnessing of or at least redirecting of their power by sequestering them, altering them, and then "storing" them in hidden/protected locations. The male and possible female heads in the Kallawaya region of Bolivia were clearly not treated like most corpses. They were not ancestors nor trophy heads, but held different roles in death if not in life. This Kallawaya data suggests that these adults had been considered extra powerful or dangerous people, as their heads were treated differently from others in death. The three (and probably more) had to be altered so their souls could not return or participate in future activities in Kallawaya. They were powerful and dangerous, and, like Alison Spedding's modern Andean examples (2011), they had to be murdered in order to redirect or capture their power. Removing eyes and cutting off jaws stops their sight and speech. They were either too powerful in their own group, or they were foreign and therefore dangerous. Denise Arnold (2005) finds modern-day behavioral patterns that are similar to these archaeological and historical practices of keeping heads and other objects in niches, housing sacrificial offerings safely to control their power. "Sacred" pits, located on the sides of the important "guardian" mountains of contemporary Andean communities, contain the bones of sacrifice, which hold potencies that are not for the everyday.

This complex of ideas and associated cultural and political actions concerns appropriating the masculine powers of taking powerful heads and converting them, whether by ritual means or through the containment facilitated by death, into more beneficial regenerative energy for one's own group (Arnold and Yapita 2006:107–9, 274–76). This theory emphasizes how the creative and aesthetic appropriation of outside forces (the enemy spirit of a taken head) is made useful by revivifying something dead and transforming its potential into one of *regeneration*, that which drives through time the generation of new beings, and their interchange between groups. It is a theory that traces a warrior-weaver, male-female aesthetic, in which destruction gives rise to construction, as an Andean variant of the theory of "ontological depredation" put forward by Eduardo Viveiros de Castro and others in a lowland Amazonian setting (1992).

While these heads might not link to all the deposited heads in the Americas, two important activities linked to these three heads are metamorphosis and regeneration. Heads participated in helping dangerous situations or objects transform into potent objects of power. One begins with a head and ends with a *wawa* offspring, a child or a potato baby seedling. Older people in Qaqachaka remember how a particular goal of interethnic warfare was the capture on the part of a married man of an enemy trophy head. This married man (head giver) would then surrender the head to his wife (head taker), who was charged with wrapping it in a finely woven black cloth, frequently decorated with woven skull designs, with the aim of transforming the spirit embodied in the head into a child of her own group (Arnold and Espejo Ayca 2004:351, 356). This same black mourning cloth is used with special "medicines" in a kind of witchcraft that defends the ayllu boundaries at politically tense moments, sometimes with the aim of killing the enemy. After use, the wrapped heads are kept in the household. The cloth used is always of raw, undyed wool. This act of wrapping is considered to be a specifically female activity in and of itself, the female gendered creative counterpart to male warfare, as it entails rebirthing the enemy spirit (or perhaps an animal) into the family domain (Arnold and Yapita 2006). In this female complex of wrapping and unwrapping in Qaqachaka and its accompanying rituals, libations making, and incense burning, as in the tsantsa rituals of the Shuar/Jívaro described by Anne Christine Taylor (1996) and Philippe Descola (1996), an enemy head is gradually converted into a head of one's own group, with local honor and power. This ritual activity concerns the "metamorphosis of heads," which Denise Arnold and Juan de Dios Yapita discuss at length in their book of that title (2006), and which John Verano and María Cecilia Lozada et al. discuss in their chapters of this volume (11 and 12, respectively), demonstrating how widespread these concepts were in South America.

Within the range of afterlives of heads, one potent afterlife comes from taking heads home to curate. Late Formative and Tiwanaku-period stone *chachapumas* (people with feline face masks) hold curated heads in their hands, illustrating how curated heads were used in ceremonies during the period 200–1000 CE. These female wrapping rituals are common and occur in multiple domains today as they did in the past. When the women of Qaqachaka sing to their llamas today, they say that their songs act as placental-like wrappings, which serve to rebirth the creatures (wawas), born in the hills but then brought into the domestic house space (Arnold and Yapita 2000:166). In the Andes, llamas are not viewed as "domesticated" animals but as animals reared in this house space, as are children. The way that people wrapped their dead in the early Chinchorro burials of the Atacama Desert, and in the Paracas peninsula *fardo* mummy bundles, might have been perceived as seed-like, in anticipation of rebirth, as Pierre Duviols implies for the mummies of the ayllus of

central Peru (called *mallki*), well into the colonial period (1971:380–83). The later highland data, discussed here, has lost the wrapping evidence due to taphonomic impacts, but surely each of these encountered crania was initially wrapped when it was placed in the ground.

More specifically, the capture of an enemy head, and the following female ritual actions concerned with its transformation, metamorphosis, and regeneration through care by wrapping, libation making, and the offering of incense, are thought to help provide for the family in question over a three-year period (Arnold and Yapita 2000). This sequence of curation practices capitalizes on the spiritual powers present in the captured head, which will radiate a generalized power capable of producing a series of generic "babies"—kin creation under the head taker's (wife's) control (impacting human, animal, and vegetable babies). In this sense, the generative spirit of the seed-like head is transferable, with the power to proliferate offspring for its new keeper, the new people, animals, and plants, as Blom and Couture discuss. Cranial modification is therefore an extension of this three-year period of transformation once a baby is born, as the young child is continually being incorporated into the community through the gradual cranial deformation, this transformation completed by wrapping the cranium.

Throughout the three-year period after the capture of a head, male strength derived from having captured it and perhaps from having imbibed the spirit thought to reside in the gray matter within the cranium, which seems to be transferred implicitly to the belly of the wife. This is represented, too, in the ambiguity in Andean languages for the term "belly" (Quechua *wijsa*, Aymara *puraka*), applied to both the digestive (stomach) and reproductive (womb) tracts, whereby a warrior who has eaten brain matter could pass on the spirit contained therein, through sexual activity, to his spouse, who then gives birth to a child; thus, the taken head is converted into manifold babies (Arnold and Hastorf 2008:50). The recycling of political power and life-force energy therefore participates in kin creation by augmenting new growth and offspring with each new cranium brought into the community.

These ideas have much in common with the process of metamorphosis that Beth Conklin describes in the case of the lowland Wari of western Brazil (1993, 1995). There, a head-taking male would consume ample, sweet maize beer that his wife had produced, to become fat and "pregnant." Through sexual activity, he would then pass on the captured spirit of the enemy head he had taken to his wife's belly, from whence it is reborn into their own group.

The possibility that a head taken in warfare later undergoes a parallel and female-gendered series of transformations in its conversion into the new babies of a household is supported by a variety of ideas. For example, a great deal of ethnographic literature in the Andes and other parts of the Americas would suggest that childbirth for women is comparable to warfare for men. Historical sources suggest that the birth of new offspring was documented by the state, both under the Aztec and the Inka, as a part of the tributary obligations of groups under their dominion. In the Andes, both birth and tributary cycles are measured in six-month cycles. This would suggest that the family and immediate group cycles of death and regeneration, derived from head taking and baby birthing, became integrated at some stage into wider state patterns of tribute and recompense in which the state served as the ultimate head taker from groups under its dominion. This evidence further suggests that, in pre-Hispanic societies, childbirth labor provided by women and warrior activities done by men were both potential sources of tribute to the state. Later colonial practices seem to have reinterpreted this form of tributation in more material terms, with taxation in goods rather than in productive labor, but for the Inka it was clearly in labor and therefore in individuals to complete labor. It is very likely that this individual work relationship to the state power apparatus originated in the Tiwanaku polity.

The ambiguous status of a new baby, as partly a descendant of a taken enemy head, is confirmed in many cultural practices in the region in the present day. For example, in many regional childbirth practices, there is the implicit idea that a new baby is considered a foreigner in the group and that birth giving is infused with a particular sense of danger for the mother, deriving from the enemy nature of the fetus. Tristan Platt (2001) suggests that the baby is perceived to be an enemy to his or her own mother! These reflections are affirmed by the still pervasive cultural idea in the Andes that new babies are warriors who must not be mollycoddled with instant breastfeeding or instant attention to their demands, as they must be become strong and defend their selves and the honor of their kinfolk. In this context, the practices of child-rearing are directed toward domesticating this enemy spirit, in order to incorporate the child fully into one's own ancestral group. This again links directly to wrapping the head as part of this transformation and control of this potential enemy.

There is much iconographic evidence to support this process of metamorphosis and transference in archaeological material. For example, many ceramics from Paracas and Nasca illustrate head images in the genital area of corpulent women. In a publication on Nasca iconography, Donald Proulx (2006:129) suggests that these kinds of female figures are associated with fecundity, engaging with heads but also with plants, rayed faces, and serpents. The alimentary aspect of this configuration of ideas is made material in the frequent images of heads resting on the long tongues of stylized beings like sprouting plants. This more mythical concept links to another major theme covered in this book, heads as mythic images of power, linked to fertility, moon, sun, heavens, and other living powers.

Archaeological evidence of similar ideas concerning energy capture and control is seen in the woven containment of captured heads to appropriate the spiritual energies therein and redirect them toward a more beneficial regenerative growth, as found in some pre-Columbian woven examples. For example, Anne Paul (2000) calls attention to the use of images of twisted and interlaced threads, associated with trophy heads, in the iconography of various sacred sectors within the Early Horizon complex of Chavín de Huántar, on ceramics, stone, and cloth. The twisted hair of the front-faced deity of the Raimondi Stone is an obvious example. Paul asks if these same images on textiles might have had a sacred power that would impart spirituality to the images and objects in which they appear. More specifically, she suspects that these twisted images might have provided the very mechanism of border containment, like the wrapping of the spirit thought to dwell in the head, which would then allow the appropriation of its energy later for particular purposes. In her essay, Paul asks whether this ancient, visual expression might refer to a preoccupation with tapping the same kind of head-derived energy or power as that contained by modern-day textile (and agricultural) borders. If so, then for Paul this woven iconography in the Chavín style would seem to be concerned with trapping this spirit within the confines of the sacred precincts in order to appropriate its power to impart spirituality to certain objects or places. Such a protective border is also seen in the contemporaneous Titicaca basin Formative stone carvings, where heads, animals, and watery beings all are enclosed (fig. 17.1).

Today, the construction of the person in the highlands, related to the construction of personhood in general, is associated with the way that spiritual power, particularly of males, is centered in the head. This ramifies into a series of gendered differences in the construction of political

Figure 17.1. Middle Formative stone plaque from Chiripa, Bolivia (drawing by the Taraco Archaeological Project).

and spiritual status throughout a person's life. The head, whether wrapped early on in life or not (transforming its shape), is the site of human spirituality and sensibility, the spirit, *ajayu* in Aymara. Heads are also the names given to community authorities, deriving their power from certain deities associated with heads located in *uywiris* across the landscape (Astvaldsson 2000; *uywiri* in Aymara, *waka* in Quechua). These masculine deities are often called "stone grandfathers" and can reside in carved mobile stones, which are also called *conopas* or *illas*. These leaders have the power to speak using language that commands civil obedience, and they also have power over natural forces that helps fertilize or effect in some way the female earth, plants, animals, and fish. Their associates, the portable stone uywiris, are usually wrapped in cloth and carried by the leaders to ceremonies.

Head curation in the highlands is both physical and metaphorical, even if crania are not always encountered archaeologically. This is illustrated in this book; Blom and Couture (chapter 13) note that, at Tiwanaku, 80 percent of human bodies that have been encountered had their heads manipulated (bound). Binding helps retain and

gain the soul and spirit (of the enemy), if we assume that we can link this set of ideas about heads at least to the Middle Horizon. In the archaeological record, there is evidence that some heads receive elaborate work both pre- and postmortem. Valerie Andrushko (2011) provides an excellent example of a postmortem Wari-phase (Middle Horizon) cranium that was elaborately decorated with inlays found in the Cuzco region, much like the Maya elite whom María Luisa Vázquez de Ágredos Pascual and colleagues discuss in their detailed argument about face painting and meaning (chapter 6 of this volume).

Both whole-body and killed-head stones and weavings (not only heads but also the imagery of heads) further suggest how that spirit power was embedded in the head. In Andean imagery, heads are often expressed as being much larger than natural in proportion to their owners' bodies; recall the Raimondi Stone from Chavín de Huántar, where the head spans almost half of the stone image, and the main figure of the Gateway of the Sun at Middle Horizon Tiwanaku, where the head is almost equal in size to the body.

At Wari, on the other hand, the "body" jar ceramics have huge bodies and small heads (the neck of the jar). It is this body that provides the gift of drink at ceremonies, but it always needs a head to be able to do so. A thirty-head cache has been uncovered at Middle Horizon Conchopata, but unlike the Nasca heads discovered at Cerro Carapo in the Nasca basin, which were intact (Browne 1993), these were crushed and burned with carrying holes in different locations. These brief head examples presented here and elsewhere throughout this volume tell a story of diverse and rich head adornment and curation in many Native American settings.

We can take away several points from the ethnographic, historical, and archaeological evidence for heads being transformative and generative through their many after-lives discussed in this book. There is no reason to think that all of the possibilities for using heads could not have been active in every one of the societies mentioned here. While it might not be easy to identify specific meanings of the head in any one group's past due to incomplete evidence in the archaeological record, all the chapters share one important point—the power and life force of the material head in any of its manifestations existed in their cultural contexts. From what we learn in these archaeological chapters, Andean groups held to an animistic worldview, where things, places, and people embody a life force; where things are animated with energy, having agency within their lived spheres, which is especially manifested throughout the use

cycle of a human head, even up to the present-day *ñatitas*
and stone uywiris/wak'as in the highlands.

REFERENCES CITED

Allen, Catherine

1988   *The Hold Life Has: Coca and Cultural Identity in an
       Andean Community.* Smithsonian Institution Press,
       Washington DC.

Andrushko, Valerie A.

2011   How the Wari Fashioned Trophy Heads for Display: A
       Distinctive Modified Cranium from Cuzco, Peru, and
       Comparison to Trophies from the Capital Region. In *The
       Bioarchaeology of the Human Head: Decapitation, Deco-
       ration, and Deformation*, edited by Michelle Bonogofsky,
       pp. 262–85. University Press of Florida, Gainesville.

Arnold, Denise Y.

2005   The Social Life of a Communal Chest: Hybrid Charac-
       ters and the Imagined Genealogies of Written Docu-
       ments and Their Woven Ancestors. In *Remembering
       the Past, Retrieving the Future*, edited by Verónica
       Salles-Reese, pp. 92–131. Pontificia Universidad Javeri-
       ana, Bogotá.

Arnold, Denise Y., and Elvira Espejo Ayca

2004   La cabezas de la periferia, del centro y del mundo
       interior: una comparisión de la iconografía belica
       en los textiles arqueológicos de Paracas-Topará y del
       ayllu Qaqachaka (Bolivia) contenporánea. In *Tejiendo
       sueños en el Conon Sur: textiles andinos; pasado,
       presente, futuro*, pp. 348–64. Editorial Victoria Solanilla
       Demestre, Universitat Autònoma de Barcelona, Barce-
       lona.

Arnold, Denise Y., and Christine A. Hastorf

2008   *Heads of State: Icons, Power, and Politics in the Ancient
       and Modern Andes.* Left Coast Press, Walnut Creek,
       California.

Arnold, Denise Y., and Juan de Dios Yapita

2000   *El rincón de las cabezas: luchas textuales, educación
       y tierras en los Andes.* Facultad de Humanidades y
       Ciencias de la Educación, Universidad Mayor de San
       Andrés, La Paz.

2006   *The Metamorphosis of Heads, Textual Struggles, Educa-
       tion, and Land in the Andes.* University of Pittsburgh
       Press, Pittsburgh.

Astvaldsson, Astvaldur

2000   *Jesús de Machaqa: la marka rebelde.* Vol. 4, *Las voces de
       los wak'a: fuentes principales del poder político Aymara.*
       Centro de Investigación y Promoción del Camp-
       esinado, La Paz.

Browne, David M., Helaine Silverman, and Rúben García

1993   A Cache of 48 Nasca Trophy Heads from Cerro Car-
       apo, Peru. *Latin American Antiquity* 4:274–94.

Conklin, Beth A.

1993   Hunting Ancestor: Death and Alliance in Warí
       Cannibalism. *Latin American Anthropological Review*
       5(2):65–70.

1995   "Thus Are Our Bodies, Thus Was Our Custom": Mor-
       tuary Cannibalism in an Amazonian Society. *American
       Ethnologist* 22:75–101.

Descola, Philippe

1996   *In the Society of Nature: A Native Ecology in Amazonia.*
       Cambridge University Press, Cambridge.

Duviols, Pierre

1971   *La lutte contre les religions autochtones dans les Pérou
       colonial.* Instituto Francés de Estudios Andinos, Lima.

Paul, Anne

2000   Protective Perimeters: The Symbolism of Borders in
       Paracas Textiles. *RES: Anthropology and Aesthetics*
       38:44–68.

Platt, Tristan

2001   El feto agresivo: parto, formación de la persona y nito-
       historia en los Andes. *Anuario de Estudios Americanos*
       57(2):633–78.

Proulx, Donald

2006   *A Sourcebook of Nasca Iconography.* University of Iowa
       Press, Iowa City.

Spedding, Alison

2011   *Sueños, kharisiris y curanderos: dinámicas sociales de
       las creencias en los Andes contemporáneos.* Editorial
       Mama Huaco, La Paz.

Taylor, Anne Christine

1996   The Soul's Body and Its States: An Amazonian Per-
       spective on the Nature of Being Human. *Journal of the
       Royal Anthropological Institute* 2(2):201–15.

Turner, Terence S.

2012   The Social Skin. *HAU: Journal of Ethnographic Theory*
       2(2):486–504.

Viveiros de Castro, Eduardo

1992   *From the Enemy's Point of View: Humanity and Divinity
       in an Amazonian Society.* Translated by Catherine V.
       Howard. University of Chicago Press, Chicago.

Contributors

Sonia Alconini, PhD, is an associate professor at the University of Texas at San Antonio. She has worked for more than thirty years in the Andean region, where she has studied various pre-Columbian cultures and archaeological regions of the highlands, intermediate valleys, and the tropical East. Many of her studies focus on the eastern Inka border and the way these border spaces generated complex forms of interaction between the Inkas and various eastern tropical polities. She has published and edited more than six books, in addition to a series of articles in peer-reviewed journals.

Luis Adrián Alvarado-Viñas, MA, works as a physical anthropologist, specializing in osteology, for the Instituto Nacional de Antropología e Historia in Mexico City.

Hans Barnard, PhD, is an associate adjunct professor at the Department of Near Eastern Languages and Cultures and associate researcher at the Cotsen Institute of Archaeology at the University of California, Los Angeles. As an archaeological surveyor, photographer, and ceramic analyst he has worked on sites in Armenia, Chile, Egypt, Ethiopia, Iceland, Panama, Peru, Sudan, Syria, Tunisia, and Yemen. He is affiliated with the Institute for Field Research and the Museo Egizio (Turin). With Willeke Wendrich, he has published *The Archaeology of Mobility: Old World and New World Nomadism* (2008), and with Kim Duistermaat, *The History of the Peoples of the Eastern Desert* (2012).

Sara K. Becker, PhD, is a faculty member in the Department of Anthropology at the University of California, Riverside. Her research interests and publications focus on the pre-contact health of North and South American indigenous groups and traditional labor practices among the modern Aymara of highland Bolivia. Her primary interests include the modeling and reconstruction of prehistoric labor among the Tiwanaku culture (500–1100 CE) of Bolivia and Peru, one of the earliest state-level societies to develop in the altiplano of the Lake Titicaca basin. She is

the author of multiple articles published in peer-reviewed journals and edited books.

Deborah E. Blom, PhD, is an associate professor and chair of the Department of Anthropology at the University of Vermont. She is a bioarchaeologist whose work addresses intersecting social identities, body modification, migration and colonization, mortuary practices, and health over multiple attitudinal zones in early south central Andean states. Her recent National Science Foundation–funded study investigates cultural constructions of Andean childhoods in ancient Tiwanaku society (500–1100 CE).

Augusto Cardona Rosas, MA, is a Peruvian archaeologist who has directed the Centro de Investigaciones Arqueológicas de Arequipa since 1997. In addition, he conducted the Proyecto de Inventario Arqueológico del Valle de Arequipa, which involved the evaluation of archaeological sites in the southern Peruvian province of Arequipa. Currently, he works for the Ministerio de Cultura in the Proyecto Qhapaq Ñan, and, in this capacity, Cardona identifies and evaluates portions of the Inka road system in Quebrada de la Vaca. He is the author of multiple articles, and his well-known book *Arqueología de Arequipa* is a critical synthesis of work from this part of Peru.

Ximena Chávez Balderas, PhD candidate, has worked on funerary practices and the treatment of human remains at the Templo Mayor Project, specifically the meanings, forms, and pathways of cremation rituals among the Aztecs. She is currently finishing her dissertation at Tulane University in New Orleans.

Nicole C. Couture, PhD, is an associate professor with the Department of Anthropology at McGill University. Her research focuses on the production and representation of social memory, identity, and affiliation in complex urban settings. Through her investigation of residential neighborhoods at the site of Tiwanaku, Bolivia, she addresses the ways in which different forms of individual and community identity are expressed in mortuary practices, residential space, and ceremonial architecture.

Allison R. Davis, PhD, is the author of *Yuthu: Community and Ritual in an Early Andean Village* (2011). Her specialties include early village societies (particularly of the Andean Formative), complex societies, the emergence of social inequality, mortuary archaeology, and landscape archaeology.

William Duncan, PhD, is a bioarchaeologist and has published profusely on body practices among the Postclassic Itzá and in Zapotecan Oaxaca, focusing on culturally sensitive interpretations of the mortuary record and Native cosmology.

Laura Filloy Nadal, PhD, is a professional restorer at the Museo Nacional de Antropología in Mexico City, where she specializes in the material insignia of ancient Maya aristocracy. She holds an MA and a PhD in archaeology from Paris-Sorbonne University and has received additional training in anthropology and museography. Her recent published work has focused on Maya funerary masks and dynasticism.

Raphael Greenberg, PhD, is an associate professor of archaeology at Tel Aviv University. His primary research interests include Bronze Age urbanization, migration and cultural transmission, and the role of archaeology in contemporary society.

Christine A. Hastorf, PhD, professor of anthropology, University of California, Berkeley, focuses her research on social life, political change, agricultural production, plant use, foodways, and methodologies to better understand the past. Her coauthored book *Heads of State: Icons, Power, and Politics in the Ancient and Modern Andes* (with Denise Arnold) has been an important contribution in interpreting the role of the head in the prehistoric cultures of the Andes.

Rex Haydon, PhD, professor of orthopedic surgery at the University of Chicago, focuses some of his research on the evaluation of trauma in archaeological skeletal samples. Prior to medical training, he completed his PhD in anthropology at the University of Chicago in 1993, focusing on the analysis of ancient DNA in the Chiribaya of southern Peru. For the past twenty years, he has worked with María Cecilia Lozada to interpret pathologic conditions involving ancient human remains, focusing on the broader meaning of these conditions and using them to address questions regarding population health, social conditions, and sociocultural responses to disease.

Patricia Horcajada Campos, PhD, works at the Department of Art History at Universitat de València (Spain), where she specializes in pre-Columbian art, with special focus on ancient Maya iconography. She is member of La Blanca Project and the project Arqueometría del Color en el Area Maya. She is the author of several scientific conference papers and articles published in Spain, France, Mexico, and the United States.

Alfonso Lacadena (1964–2018), PhD, was one of the leading Mesoamerican epigraphers worldwide. His interests lay in Maya and Aztec writing systems and comparative grammar research in ancient languages. In 2011, he received the Proskouriakoff Award from Harvard University.

María Cecilia Lozada, PhD, is a research associate in the Department of Anthropology at the University of Chicago. Her multidisciplinary approach integrates human osteology, archaeology, and ethnographic methods in an effort to reconstruct the lifestyles of past Andean societies. Lozada has been the principal investigator for the Tarapacá Archaeological Project (Chile) and is currently leading the Vitor Archaeological Project (Peru). Her publications include *El Señorío de Chiribaya en la Costa Sur del Perú* (2002), and edited volumes such as *The Dead Tell Tales: Essays in Honor of Jane E. Buikstra* (2013) and *Archaeological Human Remains: Global Perspectives* (2014), both coedited with Barra O'Donnabhain.

Bruce Mannheim, PhD, professor of anthropology at the University of Michigan, is a leading linguistic anthropologist specializing in Quechua, the language of the Inka and now the most widespread Native American language family. He is author of *The Language of the Inka since the European Invasion* (1991) and numerous articles on Andean languages, cultures, and history, spanning several academic disciplines. He currently collaborates with archaeologists in an effort to promote cross-disciplinary approaches to the Andean past.

Linda Manzanilla, PhD, counts as one of the leading authorities in Mesoamerican and world archaeology. She is an associate member of the National Academy of Sciences, based in Washington, DC, and a member of the Colegio Nacional de Ciencias in Mexico City. She has dedicated the past three decades of her academic career to research of the pre-Columbian capital of Teotihuacan and the origin of state formations in different parts of the world.

Virginia Miller, PhD, is a recently retired faculty member of the Department of Art History at the University of Illinois at Chicago. Her research focuses on a range of topics in Maya art and architecture, particularly the iconographic traditions of northern Yucatán during the Terminal Classic, including Chichén Itzá.

Andrew Scherer, PhD, is a bioarchaeologist currently working as an assistant professor at Brown University in Providence, Rhode Island. Scherer has a prolific track record of published research on Maya skeletal remains including body modifications and the use of human remains in mortuary rites and acts of veneration. Most of his contributions integrate data from bioarchaeology, archaeology, and epigraphy.

Vera Tiesler, PhD, serves as a research professor at the Universidad Autónoma de Yucatán in Mexico, where she coordinates its Laboratory of Bioarchaeology and Histology. Her research is interdisciplinary and aims to illuminate the human side of the past, with special focus on Mesoamerican populations. Recent published work includes the books *Natives, Europeans, and Africans in Colonial Campeche* and *The Bioarchaeology of Artificial Cranial Modifications*.

Gabrielle Vail, PhD, works at the New College of Florida in Sarasota and has dedicated her prolific professional career to the study of Postclassic iconography, hieroglyphic texts, and codices to contribute to the understanding of rituals, religion, and world views of Mesoamericans, specifically Maya groups.

María Luisa Vázquez de Ágredos Pascual, PhD, obtained her MS in geography and history from Universitat de València (Spain) and PhD in history of art from Universitat Politècnica de València (Spain). She also completed a master's in history of religions at the Instituto de Ciencias de las Religiones at Universidad Complutense de Madrid. She is a professor of art history at Universitat de València. Her research focuses on the archaeometrical study of Maya mural painting, and more recently on the physical-chemical analysis of body paint and perfume used in ancient Mesoamerica.

Andrea Vazquez de Arthur, PhD candidate, addresses the art history and museography of the Wari Empire of ancient Peru (600–1000 CE) in her work. She is currently concluding her doctoral dissertation at Columbia University in New York, titled "Portraits, Pots, or Power Objects? On the Imagery and Ontology of Wari Faceneck Jars."

Matthew C. Velasco, PhD, is an assistant professor in the Department of Anthropology at Cornell University in Ithaca, New York. He specializes in the bioarchaeological analysis of skeletal and mummified human remains from highland Peru. His current research explores the effects of ethnogenesis on social inequality and political consolidation during the Andean Late Intermediate Period (1100–1450 CE). Velasco's broader theoretical interests include embodiment, the social construction of space and landscape, and the politics of death and burial. His work on late pre-Hispanic mortuary practices has been published in *Cambridge Archaeological Journal* (2014).

John Verano, PhD, is a professor at Tulane University in New Orleans and has recently been appointed senior fellow at the Dumbarton Oaks Research Library (Harvard University). He specializes in human skeletal biology, paleopathology, bioarchaeology, and forensic anthropology in Andean South America. He has authored many publications on these topics and directs a number of field projects in Peru.

Cristina Vidal Lorenzo, PhD, obtained her doctorate in archaeology from Universidad Complutense de Madrid. She is a professor of art history at Universidad de Valencia and the director of La Blanca Project in Petén, Guatemala. Her research focuses on Maya art, archaeology, and architecture. She is the recipient of several research grants and served as the principal investigator of International I+D+I Projects.

Alanna Warner-Smith is a doctoral student in the Department of Anthropology at Syracuse University in Syracuse, New York. She is a National Science Foundation Graduate Research Fellow. She has worked in Turkey, Peru, Barbados, the Bahamas, and Guatemala. Her dissertation research focuses on nineteenth-century immigration.

Index

❦